CHAPTERS IN
WESTERN
CIVILIZATION

℘

VOLUME II

CHAPTERS IN

Western Civilization

SELECTED AND EDITED BY THE
CONTEMPORARY CIVILIZATION STAFF OF
COLUMBIA COLLEGE, COLUMBIA UNIVERSITY

Volume II SECOND EDITION

NEW YORK: MORNINGSIDE HEIGHTS

COLUMBIA UNIVERSITY PRESS

PREFACE TO THE FIRST EDITION

HIS VOLUME contains nine chapters on various phases of Western society since the French Revolution. Though it may be used independently of the volume which precedes it, its aim is similar: to help the student understand what has gone into the making of present-day institutions and ideas.

In the Columbia College "C.C." course these readings serve as background for the second volume of the source book *Introduction to Contemporary Civilization in the West*. They are, however, self-sufficient, and can be used for a variety of purposes, either with or without source materials.

Of the nine "chapters" in this volume, four are articles specially written by men either now or formerly associated with Columbia University. One of these articles has been prepared for the present volume; the other three, originally prepared for the Contemporary Civilization Manual which the present project supersedes, have been revised by their authors or by the editors. The remaining five chapters have been selected from various publications.

We wish to thank the publishers mentioned in the table of acknowledgments for their kind permission to use material appearing under their imprint.

Editorial Committee

JOSEPH L. BLAU
JUSTUS BUCHLER, *Chairman*
GEORGE T. MATTHEWS

June, 1948

PREFACE TO THE SECOND EDITION

T HIS NEW EDITION of the second volume of "Chapters" has been expanded to nearly twice its original length, so that its chapter headings now correspond with those of the second volume of its companion source book, *Introduction to Contemporary Civilization in the West.* In addition to the publishers mentioned in the table of acknowledgments and the persons whose aid and advice have been indicated in Volume One, the Committee wishes to thank Merritt H. Moore for his kind permission to reprint the selections from George H. Mead.

Editorial Committee

JOSEPH L. BLAU
RALPH H. BOWEN
PETER J. GAY
SIDNEY GELBER
GEORGE T. MATTHEWS
RICHARD M. MORSE, *Chairman*
STEPHEN W. ROUSSEAS

Columbia University
September, 1953

CONTENTS

CHAPTERS IN
WESTERN
CIVILIZATION

❧

VOLUME II

Chapter I

THE ROMANTIC OUTLOOK AND
ITS EXPRESSIONS

꒰

REACTION AGAINST THE AGE OF REASON

THE INITIAL steps in the transformation of the eighteenth-century world into that in which men live to-day were marked by a strong current of reaction against the scientific methods and ideals of the Age of Reason. Toward the close of the century there developed in Europe a number of tendencies representing in part a reaction against the ideas of the Newtonian world, in part a recrudescence of forces that had remained present in Western civilization since the Renaissance. These tendencies, loosely grouped together as romanticism, emphasized the emotional rather than the rational side of human nature, a richly diversified development of individuals and groups rather than a mathematical uniformity, and, most significant of all, the genesis and growth of things rather than their mechanical ordering. The first half of the next century was marked by conflicting conceptions, the struggle of the old society against the revolutionary ideals, the middle class notions against the rising forces of an industrial civilization, of romanticism against the steady advance of scientific knowledge. Out of these cross-currents there gradually was effected a fusion between the eighteenth-century ideals and the newer tendencies, an intellectual atmosphere favorable to the acceptance of the great nineteenth-century idea of Evolution. Supported by the rapid economic and social changes, and confirmed by the vast new body of experimental science, this idea of growth and development was broadened to include and color all man's interests; while at the same time scientific investigation pushed on until it could claim to have sketched out the broad outlines of a wholly naturalistic explanation of the entire realm of human experience. The resulting changes and readjustments in philosophic, religious, and social thought and ideals, diverse and often conflicting as they were, have probably exceeded in importance and extent those necessary to transform the world of Saint Thomas and Dante into the universe of Newton and Locke. To these changes we must now address ourselves.

This chapter is from *The Making of the Modern Mind* (pp. 395–425, revised ed.; Boston, Houghton Mifflin Co., 1940), by John Herman Randall, Jr.

It was inevitable that the Age of Reason should provoke men to a reaction. A comparison of the eighteenth- with the thirteenth-century synthesis cannot fail to-day to reveal that, however great the scientific formulation of the former, and however wide its extent and scope, it was a far less adequate vehicle for the expression of all the manifold tendencies and interests of human nature. Not only does the point of view of Dante seem far closer to the experience of the average man, and far easier for him to grasp and assimilate—science and a scientific temper of mind are at best rare and difficult things, to be acquired by much labor and exertion, and perhaps above the attainment of a considerable body of men—but an exclusive emphasis on reason and intelligence certainly fails to take account of much that is both eternal and valuable in human experience. It was no accident that the scientific age of the Enlightenment produced little than can rank with the world's greatest art and poetry. The palaces and gardens of Versailles, the artificial fêtes of Watteau, the heroic couplets of Pope, the sparkling comedy of Molière, and the wit of Voltaire—these were the natural fruits of the Newtonian world, and great as they are they include but a small part of the experiences that have been expressed in the highest works of art. In spite of its many and just claims, the Age of Reason to-day is in disrepute; and it is in disrepute, not because its beliefs were not true, not because they were not sound, but because the ideal of life it offered men was thin and flat and meager. Man may be a rational animal, but his animality is more deeply rooted than his rationality; he cannot live by truth alone. In the nineteenth century most men were either not rational enough, or too rational, to accept the rationalism of the Enlightenment. They either went backwards, for example, to a frank supernaturalism founded on faith, or they went on to a naturalism that could see the greatness and the values of the religious traditions without falling into the pit of too naïve a literal-mindedness. . . .

It is idle to debate the question whether the movement of romanticism was a step "backward" or "forward." That it was to be expected, is clear; that it meant the overshadowing of some things of priceless importance is also as clear as that it brought into the world a new and needed emphasis upon sides of man's variegated personality that in theory at least had been neglected. It may perhaps be said of the eighteenth century ideal of a life from which all that is not rational and useful is excluded, what Rousseau said of pure democracy, that it is fit only for a society of gods; and men are not gods, nor would they wish to be. If we to-day find that science has pursued its path unmindful of whether its sacred fires purify or destroy the good life, and that men's strivings after better things are rarely illumined by the light of exact knowledge, much of that divorce must be attributed to romanticism. If we moderns can fairly claim that our aspirations rest on a sounder basis than did those of Thomas and Dante, and that we have tempered science with saving wisdom better than did the Age of Enlightenment, that too must be attributed to the more or less happy union we have managed to effect between Reason and Romanticism. For better or worse, the nineteenth and twentieth centuries are blest with a rich heritage from the romantic revolt; nor does it seem that that heritage can ever permanently disappear from human experience.

EMPHASIS ON THE LESS RATIONAL SIDE OF HUMAN NATURE

Fundamentally, that tendency or attitude to which we have given the name of Romanticism was a reaction against a too narrow construing of human experience in terms of reason alone. It was an emphasis on the less rational side of human nature, on everything that differentiates man from the coldly calculating thinking machine; and correspondingly a revolt against viewing the world as nothing but a vast mechanical order. It was the voicing of the conviction that life is broader than intelligence, and that the world is more than what physics can find in it. It was the appeal from science alone to the whole breadth and expanse of man's experience; its creed, if so formless a persuasion can be said to have a creed, has been admirably summed up by him who is perhaps the foremost [recent] romanticist, Bergson: "We cannot sacrifice experience to the requirements of any system." Experience, in its infinite richness and color and warmth and complexity, is something greater than any intelligible formulation of it; it is primary, and all science, all art, all religion, is but a selection from a whole that must inevitably slip through whatever human net is set to catch it. In this sense, even our science, in breaking from the narrow and fixed forms of eighteenth-century mechanics and mathematics, and becoming frankly inquiring and experimental, has felt the romantic influence; while our knowledge of nature and human nature has been vastly heightened and deepened, and under its spur has almost added a whole new dimension. The virtues of the romantic attitude are its open-mindedness, its receptivity to whatever of truth and whatever of value any experience may reveal; as William James put it, although the past has uniformly taught us that all crows are black, still we should continue to look for the white crow. Its besetting vice is that it may lead men to disregard all standards of truth and value, to refuse to make any of the distinctions that are essential to an ordered life; like the drunken man, who accepts all things as of equal worth, the romanticist often fails to criticize his experience, and in the mere joy of living remains oblivious to the greater joys of living well.

Goethe, the great poet of romanticism, can serve as the best illustration of its strength and of its weakness. His indefatigable energies drove him into almost every path of life and every field of human endeavor; and in each he accomplished a few perfect bits and much that is of value. Yet aside from a few lyrics which, the crystallization of passing emotions, need no larger setting, he never produced, in poetry, in science, in philosophy, a perfect whole; superb in individual passages as is his *Faust,* it is not a finished work of art. Goethe himself, his mind, his genius, his life, remains far greater than anything he wrote. Though he aspired after the stars, he never really saw them; he never rose far enough above the level of human experience to criticize it, to discern clearly what is and what is not of worth. Hence while he throbs with the very pulse of life, in its infinite fullness, he never reaches the heights from which the Greeks and Dante and Shakespeare saw it as a whole with a definite meaning for man; he never found any other justification for life save life itself.

As Santayana puts it:

Goethe gives us what is most fundamental—the turbid flux of sense, the cry of the heart, the first tentative notions of art and science, which magic or shrewdness might hit upon. . . . In fact, the great merit of the romantic attitude is that it puts us back at the beginning of our experience. It disintegrates convention, which is often cumbrous and confused, and restores us to ourselves, to immediate perception and primordial will. That, as it would seem, is the true and inevitable starting-point. . . . It follows, however, that one who has no philosophy but this has no wisdom; he can say nothing that is worth carrying away; everything in him is attitude and nothing achievement. . . . Here is profundity, inwardness, honesty, waywardness; here are the most touching accents of nature, and the most various assortment of curious lore and grotesque fancies. . . . How, indeed, should we draw the sum of an infinite experience that is without conditions to determine it, and without goals in which it terminates? Evidently all a poet of pure experience can do is to represent some snatches of it, more or less prolonged; and the more prolonged the experience represented is the more it will be a collection of snatches, and the less the last part of it will have to do with the beginning. . . . To be miscellaneous, to be indefinite, to be unfinished, is essential to the romantic life. May we not say that it is essential to all life in its immediacy; and that only in reference to what is not life—to objects, ideals, and unanimities that cannot be experienced but may only be conceived— can life become rational and truly progressive? Herein we see the radical and in- alienable excellence of romanticism; its sincerity, freedom, richness, and infinity. Herein, too, we may see its limitations, in that it cannot fix or trust any of its ideals, and blindly believes the universe to be as wayward as itself, so that nature and art are always slipping through its fingers. It is obstinately empirical, and will never learn anything from experience.

THE NATURAL NO LONGER EQUIVALENT
TO THE REASONABLE

From this general attitude of romanticism there follow a number of more definite tendencies. In emphasizing the less rational side of human nature, the early romanticists accepted the eighteenth-century ideal of the Natural, but they gave to it a new interpretation. This is very clear in Rousseau, who is sometimes regarded as the fountainhead of the later movement, but whose importance seems rather to consist in his popular expression of tendencies that had already been germinating for some time. Rousseau went as far as any of the rationalists in deifying the "natural man"; but his conception of what is natural in human nature was derived, not from the Newtonian order of nature, but rather from his own personal experience. For him the natural man is not the rational thinker, judging everything by its usefulness to himself and his fellows, but rather the man of passion and feeling. Intelligence and reason, he believed, are largely the products of social environment, an environment that seizes upon the plastic nature of the child and distorts it by pressing it into a traditional mould that must remain alien to it. "Everything is good as it comes from the hands of the author of nature; but everything degenerates in the hands of man." "The whole sum of human wisdom consists in servile prejudices; our customs are nothing more than subjection, worry, and restraint. Civilized man is born, lives, and dies in a state of slavery; at his birth, he is sewn up in swaddling clothes, at his death, he is nailed in a coffin; so long as he preserves the human form he is fettered by different institutions." "We must choose between making a man and a citizen; for we cannot make both at once." Yet since man must live with his fellows, he must live his life in accordance with law; but if he is to remain free, if he is to retain in society the good tendencies which are his by nature, he must be governed and directed by the laws of his own nature. The whole aim of education should be thus to preserve the natural man, and ensure that the habits he forms are not the artificial ones of custom and tradition and reason, but rather those in which his nature will flower of itself. Rousseau's elaborate scheme of education, recounted in the *Émile,* is to preserve the child from any formal teaching by other human beings. It is primarily negative, consisting, "not in teaching the principles of virtue or truth, but in guarding the heart against vice and the mind against error." If this endeavor is successful, the real education of the child will come from the free development of his own nature, his own powers, his own natural inclinations. "All instruments have been tried but one, the only one which can succeed—well-regulated liberty." "The only habit which the child should be allowed to form is to contract no habit whatever."

What this means, of course, is that the instinctive judgments, primitive emotions, natural instincts, and first impressions are more trustworthy as a basis for action than all the reflection, the caution, the experience that comes from association with others. "Morality and religion are not matters of reasoned thinking, but of natural feeling. Man's worth depends not on his intelligence, but on his moral nature, which consists essentially of feeling; the good will alone has absolute value." That is to say, the sentiments are the important element in our mental life, and it is not through the development of the intelligence that man becomes perfect, but through the development of feeling; for the ideal man is he that is filled with sympathy for his fellows and is "inspired by religious feeling, gratitude, and reverence."

It is this conception of human nature as essentially feeling that forms the basis for all Rousseau's theories. He feels that the tenets of Deism are true, and therefore while he agrees in the doctrines of his religion with the rationalists, he founds them, not on reasoned demonstrations, but on the religious feelings that he finds natural to the human breast. Similarly, though he uses the machinery of the orthodox political thinking of his day, his fundamental conviction of the equal worth of all individuals is likewise founded upon what he felt in his heart to be true. And in his *Confessions* he sought to lay bare his soul, proclaiming that at last he would show the world a real man—a picture which certainly contains little of the rational.

Even before Rousseau the first efforts of novelists had succeeded in displaying the subordinate part played by reason in the average life. The French romances and the meandering portrayals of the female heart with which Richardson gained great popularity led to a large number of sentimental outpourings, of which Mackenzie's *Man of Feeling,* who floods every page with copious tears at the slightest provocation, is perhaps the most extreme example. On the other hand, writers of clearer vision, like Fielding and Smollett, in portraying "real men," had presented even more cogent reasons for doubting the complete adequacy of the popular psychology that saw the only motive of human nature as rational self-interest.

TRADITION FOUND TRULY NATURAL

Rousseau's emphasis on the original feelings and passions of mankind was revolutionary in intent: he wanted to transform social institutions until they conformed to these needs of human nature. But it is just as easy, if one takes —

feeling rather than reason as a criterion of truth, to feel that the accustomed and the traditional is natural to man, and that radical proposals for alteration are unnatural and even inhuman. On the whole, since the great French Revolution was so largely the outcome of eighteenth-century rationalism, the romanticists tended to align themselves on the side of the conservative opposition; and since feelings could easily change, romantic poets like Coleridge and Wordsworth passed rapidly from an initial enthusiasm to revulsion and repudiation when their hearts were hardened by the reign of terror and the Napoleonic attacks. Moreover, it is much easier for traditional beliefs in politics or religion to defend themselves by their "instinctive appeal to the human heart" than to elaborate a rational apology; and hence traditionalists in every field found in Rousseau's method, though not in his conclusions, a golden opportunity. That rationalism led consistently to criticism and reform, while romanticism was at the disposal of every sentiment, only reinforces what has been already said as to the lack of any standard in the latter attitude.

The conservative side of romanticism was clearly foreshadowed by a man who himself could hardly be claimed for the movement, Hume. In breaking down by his appeal to experience not only the rational defense of the religious tradition, but just as well the rational method itself in science, he showed with great force that human nature is largely a matter of habit and custom. What seems reasonable and axiomatic is really the effect of education and existent institutions. It was natural that this skepticism as to the power of reason should have led Hume to fall back upon custom and habit as the only foundation of beliefs; the genuine skeptic, who sees no certain truth anywhere, can hardly share the enthusiasm of the doctrinaire revolutionary, who has no experience but only reason to support him. After all, if we can find no secure truth in religion and politics, we had best adhere to the established church and the established government; it at least has the advantage of being established. Hence skeptical souls, from Montaigne to Lord Balfour, have often been convinced Tories and traditionalists; they see no reason for believing that anything else would be better. When to this distrust of reason is added the positive feelings for familiar institutions endeared by long association, it is easy to see how romanticism became the bulwark of beliefs that had seemed to crumble before the onslaughts of rational criticism.

EMPHASIS ON FAITH—AS A SUPPORT TO RELIGION

If the eighteenth century saw the rise of determined opposition to trust in reason, it saw also the positive counterpart of reliance upon faith. Naturally this complete denial of rationalism appeared first in the interests of religion, since it was in religion that reason first revealed its destructive conclusions. As the century wore on, far-sighted religious leaders who understood the complete skepticism and the dogmatic atheism in which the Enlightenment was bound to end, and to whom the religious traditions of mankind were nevertheless important and dear, rejected completely the specious support which rationalism had seemed to offer to the fundamental doctrines of Christianity, and, following the advice of Bayle and Hume alike, turned to the impregnable foundation of faith. In mysticism, in the inner experience of the soul, they sought the surest bulwarks against disbelief and what seemed to them its attendant moral laxity. This movement of "pietism" first appeared on a large scale in Germany, as a reaction, not against the radical rationalism of the Deists and their successors, but against the equally barren and formal orthodox rationalism of seventeenth-century Lutheran scholasticism. Its influence was felt in England by Welsey, who made it the basis of the great evangelical revival against all degrees of rationalism. Finally the appeal to the inner experience was itself rationalized and systematically formulated by Kant, into whose thought the pietistic tradition entered as a powerful factor.

In Germany the theological and political controversies that culminated in the Thirty Years' War had accentuated the tendency to emphasize doctrinal orthodoxy and correct belief at the expense of the religious and moral life. The abstract Protestant scholasticism that had come to be the essential thing in both the Reformed and the Lutheran churches left many with the sense of a great lack. The man who raised the standard of revolt was a Lutheran pastor, Spener, who in a popular book published in 1675, *Pia Desideria,*[1] called men to emphasize the "religion of the heart," a personal religion flowering in a purer moral life, rather than the formal and ecclesiastical religion then prevalent. Spener did not attack any part of the orthodox system, but he did claim that parts of it were much more important than the rest; and he wished to bring into special prominence those which had a direct effect upon the personal religious life, particularly the doctrines of salvation. The value of a belief for him was in its practical bearing. He emphasized the doctrine of regeneration, and insisted that the all-important thing was the transformation of character through vital union with Christ. Only where the life is actually changed, and the spirit of Christ's love controls one's conduct, has a person any right to think that he has been born again and is among the saved. Not some external sacramental system administered by a church, but the inward experience of

[1] [*Devout Yearnings.*]

conversion and faith, is the kernel of the Christian life. Purity, piety, holiness of life—that is, moral character—these are the essentials.

Since our entire Christianity consists in the inner or new man, and its soul is faith, and the effects of faith are the fruits of life, I regard it as of the greatest importance that sermons should be wholly directed to this end. On the one hand they should exhibit God's rich benefits, as they affect the inner man, in such a way that faith is advanced and the inner man forwarded in it. On the other hand they should not merely incite to external acts of virtue and restrain from external acts of vice, as the moral philosophy of the heathen does, but should lay the foundation in the heart. They should show that all is pure hypocrisy, which does not come from the heart, and so accustom the people to cultivate love to God and to their neighbors and to act from it as a motive.

Spener's followers emphasized Biblical study for practical and devotional purposes, depreciation of scholastic theology and its controversies, the feelings and will at the expense of the intellect, love for mystical and devotional literature, the necessity of personal faith and growth in Christian perfection, and the formation of *collegia pietatis* or lay groups for prayer and character-building. They stood for a reaction to some of the medieval tendencies, particularly in the need and means of salvation, and in the turning from the common worldliness of the average Christian to an asceticism fostered by group activity in the world rather than monastic withdrawal from it. But in its emphasis on these groups of laymen, and its hostility to ecclesiasticism, sacramentarianism, sacerdotalism, and in fact all dependence on the organized ministrations of the church, it was as profoundly individualistic and disintegrating in its way as rationalism itself. It substituted a new orthodoxy for the older correctness of doctrine; what it refused to tolerate was the impious life.

Most of the German pietists remained within the Lutheran fold, where they soon became the dominant party and founded a large number of institutions for the care of the poor, of orphans, for the education of the young, and for the promotion of missions to the heathen. But the most thoroughgoing pietists were the Moravian Brethren, founded by Count Zinzendorf, who formed separate communities exemplifying the pure Christian life, and dispatched earnest and self-sacrificing missionaries to all parts of the world, from Greenland to Ceylon. Many of these Moravian groups settled in the congenial Quaker atmosphere of Pennsylvania, where, as the "Pennsylvania Dutch," they have exerted great influence on the religious life of America.

The same reaction against formal rationalism and moral laxity was led in England by John Wesley. Here, however, the movement was a revolt, not against scholasticism, but rather against Deism, skepticism, and religious indifference within the Church of England. Wesley was converted to the "religion of the heart" by a small group of Moravians in London, in 1738; and for fifty years he and his brother Charles and his friend Whitefield conducted evangelical revivals throughout England and America. In England as in Germany the bulk of the evangelicals remained within the State Church, where they formed the so-called "Low Church" party; but the more thorough-going also broke away to found the Methodist Church. Wesley found fertile soil for his message among the growing factory population of the North, which not even the rationalistic humanitarians had thought worth bothering about. It is not too much to say that until the factory legislation that began in the 1830's, the Wesleyan evangelicals were the only men who did much to relieve the suffering and to further the education of the working classes.

In opposition to the humanistic and rationalistic notion of the dignity and worth of human nature, Wesley insisted on the older doctrine of original sin and the Fall. "The fall of man is the very foundation of revealed religion. If this be taken away, the Christian system is subverted, nor will it deserve so honorable an appellation as that of a cunningly devised fable." Hence the divine power of grace, through faith in Jesus Christ, is essential to the leading of a moral and Christian life. The rationalistic theory that revelation merely makes clearer the knowledge of man's duty, seemed utterly inadequate; man needs not only knowledge, put power to act in accordance with it. Hence Wesley emphasized the whole traditional doctrine of Christ's redemption and atonement, and attacked the very conception of natural religion. He who trusts to his own virtue, who lives honestly and uprightly and purely, but does not depend for salvation upon Christ alone, is the most dangerous of men. There is hope for the most abandoned sinner; he may be brought to a sense of his corruption and helplessness, and of his need of divine grace. But the righteous man who prides himself upon his own rectitude and moral strength, is lost. The religious man will not, like the rationalist, do his duty recognizing it as God's will, but will do it as the result of a vivid religious experience and an ever-present consciousness of the divine power and goodness.

Every good gift is from God, and is given to man by the Holy Ghost. By nature there is in us no good thing. And there can be none; but so far as it is wrought in us by that good Spirit. Have we any true knowledge of what is good? This is not the result of our natural understanding. The natural man discerneth not the things of the Spirit of God; so that we can never discern them until God reveals them unto us by His Spirit.

Thus reason is impotent, and the only true knowledge comes by a special spiritual organ, Faith.

Faith is that divine evidence whereby the spiritual man discerneth God and the things of God. It is with respect to the spiritual world what sense is to the natural. It is the spiritual sensation of every soul that is born of God. . . . Till you have these internal senses, till the eyes of your understanding are opened, you can have no proper apprehension of divine things, no just idea of them. Nor consequently can you either judge truly or reason justly concerning them; seeing your reason has no ground whereon to stand, no materials to work upon.

Faith and faith alone is sufficient; all rational argument either for or against religious truth falls away.

Thus the whole appeal to faith in the interests of the religious tradition resulted in a new orthodoxy, evangelicalism. It was this orthodoxy, and not the older Calvinism, that was spread in England and America through the great religious revivals of the beginning of the nineteenth century; and it is this evangelical orthodoxy, very different from the medieval doctrine and from the Reformation doctrines alike, that is strong to-day as "Fundamentalism." Its main features are primarily the result of the reaction against the eighteenth-century rationalism. What has been its general effect?

It put an end to the barren rationalism of the eighteenth century; it substituted immediate experience for reasoned demonstration, direct knowledge for indirect, in the religious sphere, and so circumvented the skeptics whom the apologists were impotent to overcome; it brought the feelings once more into repute, and aided the nineteenth century reaction against the narrow intellectualism of the eighteenth; it gave a new meaning and an independent value to religion; it promoted individualism and emancipation from the bondage of ecclesiasticism; and, above all, it vitalized and revived religion throughout the length and breadth of the land. On the other hand, it brought back much of the old system, including many of its most obnoxious features which rationalism had relegated to oblivion, as it was supposed, for ever. It turned its face deliberately toward the past instead of toward the future in its interpretation of man and his need. It sharpened the issue between Christianity and the modern age, and promoted the notion that the faith of the fathers had no message for their children. Becoming identified in the minds of many with Christianity itself, its narrowness and medievalism, its emotionalism and lack of intellectuality, its crass supernaturalism and Biblical literalism, its want of sympathy with art and science and secular culture in general, turned them permanently against religion. In spite of the great work accomplished by evangelicalism, the result in many quarters was disaster. (A. C. McGiffert).

FAITH AS A SUPPORT TO REVOLUTIONARY TENDENCIES

But while the new appeal to faith as against reason found expression in these great popular revivals of doctrines drawn from the older religious tradition, it was just as strongly a radical force as well. The feelings, the passions, and the intuitions of the natural man, when made the ultimate source of all knowledge and aspiration, led as easily to principles and attitudes that were genuinely subversive of the whole established order. If a Spener and a Wesley appealed to intuition and faith to support the old, a Rousseau could with equal facility use them to confirm a burning zeal for a new order. And when the spirit of romanticism had finally captured a large part of the intellectual classes, the orthodox realized with amazement that faith was an even more wild and wayward thing upon which to found an established system than dangerous reason itself. The inner experience of men by no means agreed in leading to the conclusions of Paul or Wesley, but gave birth rather to a host of strange and new religions and philosophies the like of which had never been on land or sea. At the height of the romantic period it almost seemed that every man's intuitions were a law unto himself, and even single individuals, as they ran the gamut of human life from youth to age, poured forth in inexhaustible profusion a kaleidoscopic gallery of new visions of the world and man, lovely and beautiful as the iridescent bubble, and as thin and impermanent. It is not for nothing that the Catholic Church has always preferred rationalism to the uncontrollable experience of the individual, tempered ever with an insistence upon authoritatively given premises; and has elevated her Thomases above her mystics, suspicious of even Augustine himself, the root of all heresies. When the really great apologies for the past were provoked by the French Revolution, Burke and De Maistre rejected alike the rationalism of a Bentham and the intuition of a Rousseau, and turned to the pure authority and appeal of a time-honored tradition.

The possible revolutionary implications of faith had already been made plain in the seventeenth century, when the Quakers George Fox and Barclay disregarded all customs and traditions in response to the clear vision of the "inner light." The Quakers, while remaining true to the Christian tradition —alone of all sects, they claim—in the name of their private experience of the voice of God stood up against kings and prelates as even the Calvinists never did. And both the German pietists and the English evangelicals, while they started as movements within the state churches, flowered in the independent organizations of the Moravian Brothers and the Methodist Church. When feeling and intuition made its appearance in the political and social field as well, it was until the Revolution nearly always on the side of the middle-class revolt against the old régime. For however much romanticists and rationalists might differ, they agreed in one thing: they were convinced individualists. Hence both equally served as the intellectual expression of the aspirations of the individualistic commercial classes. Rousseau and Bentham and Locke had one thing in common: they demanded freedom from governmental restrictions. The romantic attitude came in to reinforce the rationalistic critique of tradition, and to add fire to the clear light of reason; and if the rationalists were not always reasonable, neither were the romanticists always irrational. So long as there was a common inspiration, hatred of the old system, and a common interest, the demands of the middle classes, they could well coöperate.

In every land romanticism at first added fuel to the flames kindled by the rationalists. In France, Rousseau; in Germany, the revolutionary poets of the so-called "Storm and Stress," the Goethe of *Goetz von Berlichingen* (1771), and the Schiller of *The Robbers* (1781), *Fiesco,* and *Kabale und Liebe* (*Plot and Passion*) (1784); in England, the Coleridge of the first part of the *Ode to France,* the Wordsworth of the *French Revolution,* and the more consistently revolutionary Shelley of *Queen Mab, Hellas,* and *Prometheus Unbound,* to say nothing of Byron; and in America the later Transcendental individualists Emerson and Thoreau—all sang songs of Promethean revolt under the inspiration of the radical social changes of the end of the century. The poets put into lyrical rhapsodies the emotions they felt for the principles developed by the rational scientists. . . .

EMPHASIS ON THE INDIVIDUAL PERSONALITY
AND ITS EXPRESSION

. . . As against the eighteenth-century disregard of everything not universal in human nature, the romanticists emphasized individuality and personality above all things. Their whole ideal for man was, not the spread of rational knowledge and science, but rather the fullest development of the unique potentialities of every man. We have seen how Rousseau built his educational program about such an ideal; it was eagerly adapted by the Germans Basedow, Pestalozzi, and Froebel, and introduced to the United States by Horace Mann. By the German poets and thinkers Goethe, Fichte, and Schlegel, by Coleridge and Carlyle in England, by Emerson in America, the whole aim of culture and of life was proclaimed to be the development of the freedom, individuality, and self-expression of the individual. "Be yourself; cultivate your personality; gain the largest possible acquaintance with all the rich heritage of the best that has been thought and said in the past; above all strive for the richest and most varied experiences with your fellowman; only thus can you develop into a truly noble personality." By some poets and artists this was interpreted as meaning, "If necessary break all the laws of God and man in order to express yourself"; but on the whole this disregard of law and convention and complete trust in the insight and instincts of the individual justified itself in rich and noble and intensely fascinating lives. Though none of the real leaders went so far as to counsel disregard of others, and most saw in devotion and service to the welfare and the similar development of other personalities a most important means of self-development, it is indisputable that the markedly individualistic emphasis of the romanticists provided a powerful stimulus and a respectable justification for the economic individualism that was building the factory system and modern capitalism. A Goethe or an Emerson, in counseling self-reliance, may not have had the remotest idea of producing the self-made business man and "captain of industry"—the phrase comes from the hero-worshiping Carlyle—but the influence has trickled down by devious channels until even to-day our magazines are full of appeals to "Cultivate your personality—make $50,000 a year"—a horrible travesty upon the romantic ideal.

Here again the best example of the richness, the humanity, the strength, and the weakness of the romantic attitude is to be found in Goethe, who managed to include in his titanic output every divergent tendency of the movement. His adaptation of the old Faust legend is one long passionate yearning for the richness and the fullness of life. Into it he wrought his youthful passion and aspiration, and his mature wisdom, the distillation of his own varied experience. Faust, the weary student, has learned the vanity of all sciences; his years of toil have brought him nothing but barren learning. He turns in disgust to magic, in the hope that there, in the Macrocosm, the totality of all wisdom, he may find himself face to face with truth. He does; but he finds also, as the romanticists felt in rejecting eighteenth-century science, that not even perfect science, perfect truth, will suffice; it is life, not the picture of life, for which he yearns. Experience, the totality of human experience and life—that alone will satisfy him. But when he conjures up the Earth-Spirit and sees the monstrous vision of all life spread before him, he cringes; not at one leap, not the whole of life, is given to any mortal to enjoy. Such general experience bursts the bounds of any personality; Faust must content himself with a long and painful acquisition of those experiences which he can assimilate. So he summons Mephistopheles, the spirit of that growth and development which must involve the destruction of the old with the assumption of the new—of experience, in a word, in the only form that it can come to man. The latter confirms Faust in his belief that

> Gray and ashen, my friend, is every science,
> And only the golden tree of life is green.

Faust longs for life, in its pains and joys, its pleasures and sorrows; and that Mephistopheles can give him, growth and development through living. So the two go out into the world to live through the various events that can come to man, festivity, love, crime, remorse, power and wealth, beauty, the glory of the past and its recreation in the present, artistic activity. Finally, in laboring ruthlessly for what he takes to be the good of others, Faust finds satisfaction; and in that moment his life is done and his lesson learned. But there is, there can be, no real end; growth may be cut down, but it can never stop, for him who is truly saved. In whatever heavens there be Faust will go on using the angels to develop his personality and tasting of the joys and sins of the Celestial City.

> This is wisdom's final word:
> Worthy alone is he of life and freedom
> Who conquers them anew each day.

He who strives, strays, yet in that striving and straying finds his salvation. And the angels, carrying Faust's soul to its new scenes of endeavor, sing:

> Whose ceaseless striving never tires,
> We have the power to save him.

NATURE INTERPRETED IN PERSONAL TERMS

But the romanticists did not stop with making personality the key to human life; they read its striving and growth into nature also, and behind the screen of mechanistic physics they saw the real world as at bottom a process of realizing ideals. In many ways they sought to interpret the universe in personal terms, feeling that will and aspiration, the deepest things in human experience, must be akin to the fundamental forces of nature. This faith-built doctrine is called idealism; its cardinal tenet is that the experiences of the heart and soul are safer guides, when once we seek to penetrate further than our science can go, than the reason that can find only a mechanistic order. Since faith is such an individual thing, and since what is deepest in the human soul can hardly admit of objective determination, the idealists naturally differed among themselves as to what in the heart of man must be taken as the true key to the riddle of reality in the world. For Kant, the feeling of moral obligation was fundamental, and he saw the world beyond the reach of science as essentially a universal moral order. For his follower Fichte, not duty so much as the ceaseless striving after perfection stirred his soul; and hence for him the world was a great moral struggle of the forces of good against the powers of evil, in which the great Will of which individual men are but the members sets up obstacles that in overcoming them it may rise to ever higher levels. The poets saw the world as an activity of the creative imagination, the religiously minded saw it as a God calling unto men, the romantic scientists, as a superhuman reason unfolding itself in time and space. For Fichte, who gloried in the good fight, it was a Will that must ride on to victory; for Schopenhauer, who felt the sad futility of human aspiration, never resting, never satisfied, ever seeking that which it lacks, it was a dumb and aimless Will whose uneasy groping can bring only pain and sorrow and sadness. These far-flung imaginative visions of what life can mean to those who live it, will stand as undying monuments to those who conceived them; they can hardly be judged by the standards of rational and literal truth which their creators scornfully rejected. Whatever may be thought of them as literal descriptions of what nature is really like, it will remain true that they are sublime poetic insights into the possibilities of human experience. When Fichte proclaimed that the world, when looked upon as the scene of man's moral duties, does become for him such a place, he was speaking the truth; as he was when he said that the kind of world a man lives in, that is, what seems to him of worth and value, is determined by what kind of a man he is. There is a most important sense in which it is true that the reformer lives in a world of moral struggle, the poet in a world of poetic beauty, and the scientist in a world of scientific truth. The only error of romanticism would consist in believing that these self-made worlds are factually true in a scientific sense; as interpretations of human experience in terms of its significance they are true beyond question.

Romantic idealism, in a word, is poetry, not science, and it is the poets who give its best expression. To them the world is instinct with a spirit that answers to the call of man; nature is no dead machine, but a living force in whom we dwell and move and have our being. In communion with nature they find with Wordsworth the true wisdom, which is still a very human wisdom. Not in science, but in the poet's vision, lies truth.

> One impulse from a vernal wood
> May teach you more of man,
> Of moral evil and of good,
> Than all the sages can.
> Sweet is the lore which Nature brings;
> Our meddling intellect
> Mis-shapes the beauteous forms of things:
> — We murder to dissect.

To one thus open to the universe in every sense, it is truly divine.

> For I have learned
> To look on nature, not as in the hour
> Of thoughtless youth; but hearing oftentimes
> The still, sad music of humanity,

Nor harsh nor grating, though of ample power
To chasten and subdue. And I have felt
A presence that disturbs me with the joy
Of elevated thoughts; a sense sublime
Of something far more deeply interfused
Whose dwelling is the light of setting suns,
And the round ocean and the living air,
And the blue sky, and in the mind of man:
A motion and a spirit, that impels
All thinking things, all objects of all thought,
And rolls through all things.

Whatever their differences in interpretation, the romanticists all agreed in feeling behind phenomena some great will or force or super-personal personality to which the name God might not inappropriately be applied, and toward which the religious feelings might be directed. But for them God was a very different being from the God of the eighteenth-century rationalists. For the latter, he was the creator, the watch-maker, absolutely apart from his universe, with whose works man might become familiar but with whom in himself it was impossible to hold any communion. This external deity completely disappeared for the romanticists and idealists: the world was no machine, it was alive, and God was not its creator so much as its soul, its life. Of this universal life of God all things were a part, but man more particularly was its highest expression. This theory of the so-called "immanence" or indwelling of God approaches pantheism, from which it differs chiefly in interpreting the life of the universe through the soul of man rather than through the observed course of nature; and hence it was natural that Spinoza, who had similarly identified God and Nature, should attain wide popularity among the romanticists. The task of reinterpreting his scientific religion, of translating it from Cartesian science into romantic poetry, was accomplished by Herder in his *Dialogues on God* (1787). From this little book flowed an increasing stream of faith in the immanence theory; the universe is divine, and to be open to its every influence, to live in closest harmony with it and develop in response to its development, is to know God and feel one's self a part of his spirit. It was on such a basis that, under the leadership of Schleiermacher, men rehabilitated and transformed the religious faith that the Age of Reason had seemed to make impossible for an intelligent man. In a word, romanticism *is* religion. [Schleiermacher says:]

The reflection of the pious man is only the immediate consciousness of the general existence of all that is finite in the infinite, of all that is temporal in the eternal and through the eternal. To seek and find this in all that lives and moves, in all becoming and all change, in all doing and suffering, and even in immediate feeling to have and know life itself only as this existence—this is religion. And so religion is life in the endless nature of the whole, in one and all, in God; having and possessing all in God and God in all. . . . The usual conception of God as a single being outside of the world and behind the world, is not the beginning and end of religion, but only a way of expressing it that is seldom entirely pure and never adequate.

THE ROMANTIC SCIENCE OF THE INDIVIDUAL

The more intellectualistic of the romanticists carried their emphasis on individuality not only into the interpretation of human life and of nature as a whole; they tried to develop a new kind of science within the very realm which Kant had left for the undisputed sway of physics. Returning in some ways to the Aristotelian and medieval conceptions of the object of knowledge, they insisted that even science, to be adequate, must try to describe the individual in terms of its relations to the larger wholes of which it is a part, and not merely seek the general laws of the behavior of a multitude of individual things. Hegel, the most rationalistic of all the romanticists, if indeed he can be properly said to belong to that school in any strict sense, made this conception of knowledge exceedingly popular. For him, really to understand and explain any thing or event in the world meant to set it off from every other thing in the universe, and to show its particular place in the great totality of things. Not connection with some preceding cause, but connection with the whole of the great world process, gives true understanding. Philosophy, the highest wisdom, seeks thus to interpret phenomena in terms of their significance, their purpose in the whole, their value in serving the great all-embracing ideal of the universe. To comprehend all there is to know about any object whatever, a watch, for instance, we must really understand the whole of nature, mechanics and time and motion, and the whole of human society and its life throughout history, in which time and time-keeping play so important a part. Nothing exists in and by itself, but only as a part of a total world of interrelated individuals into which it must be set and from which it must be distinguished. This conception is familiar enough from the lines of Tennyson,

> Flower in the crannied wall,
> I pluck you out of the crannies,
> I hold you here, root and all, in my hand,
> Little flower—but *if* I could understand
> What you are, root and all, and all in all,
> I should know what God and man is.

In one form or another this conception of a science of the individual has entered widely into the aim of knowledge, along with the Newtonian science of causal relationships.

INTEREST IN HUMAN HISTORY AND TRADITION

This tendency is closely allied to a still further attitude which, of all romanticism, most powerfully influenced the nineteenth century. If knowledge means fitting things into a larger whole, if nature is alive and growing, if the feelings that attach men to larger groups and to the past are more fundamental than reason, then human history and human traditions take on a new and vital significance. To understand any belief, any ideal, any custom, any institution, we must examine its gradual growth from primitive beginnings to its present form. The character of an individual and the civilization of a nation are the result of a long development; they are to be judged and evaluated only in the light of a thorough knowledge of their past. And if man's life is such a slow growth, the universe to which it is the surest key must also be a process of evolution. Time and history are of fundamental importance. Viewed in such a light, the eighteenth-century science of human nature was utterly transformed. Every one of the conceptions that had sprung from Locke and Newton gave way to a quite different set; the genetic and historical method supplanted the analytical and mechanical, first in human affairs, and then in every branch of natural science, and from being the very model of science mathematics found itself reduced to an almost incomprehensible anomaly. The test of any institution or idea was no longer its reasonableness and its utility, but its origin and its history. From being the useful, the rational became the traditional. *"Die Weltgeschichte ist das Weltgericht,"* sang Schiller: history is the final court of appeal. Hegel, who founded his whole philosophy on this assumption, summed it up in the dogma, "What is rational is real, and what is real is rational," interpreting both as the great cosmic process of universal evolution.

The romantic conception of growth and expansion and development as the fundamental thing in human experience, and therefore in the universe at large, naturally coalesced with the rationalistic conception of progress, as typified by Condorcet in France and Lessing in Germany. Together they led to an emphasis on the ceaseless change of human institutions, on the value of each stage and on the necessity of further alteration. Crude attacks on the old and bitter hostility to the new were both deprecated; history revealed the steady march of mankind toward some far-off divine event. Every nation, every religion, every institution, every group, was essentially the embodiment of some ideal unfolding itself according to its own laws through time. The task of the wise man is to study the past to discover those laws of development, and then play his part in the further unfolding. Philosophies of history, purporting to reveal just such ideals and their laws of growth, were very popular. Herder, in his *Philosophy of History for the Education of Mankind* (1774), and his *Ideas for the History of Man* (1784), set the fashion that was most systematically elaborated by Hegel.

For Hegel, the all-important thing in man is the growth of his spirit, the process of thinking that involves a continual revision and abandonment of the old. Hence the world itself, the whole of existence, is at bottom just such a process of thinking. Not reason, in the sense of some static organ for picturing the world, not logic in the sense of some system of fixed laws, but dialectic, the very process of thinking, is the supreme reality in man and nature. Being, the world, the totality of all things, the absolute—this is in essence a great process of Becoming. To exist means to be always growing, always rejecting some of the old and combining it in new forms. Every institution is the march through time of the Absolute Spirit realizing itself. For the world, as for Goethe's Faust, life is continual striving after some never-attained goal; its meaning and significance lie in the striving itself, and hence, while to cease growing is to die, in reality every stage of the infinite attainment is valuable and good in its own place. For Hegel, as for Leibniz and Pope, whatever is is right; but this only means that everything that exists is a necessary moment in the advance to something further. It is for man to examine every institution, discover the particular ideal it embodies, and carry it forward in accordance with the necessary laws of its growth. To rebel at anything is the height of folly and unwisdom, but to attempt to stop the march of progress and evolution, to find satisfaction in the present stage, is, as in *Faust,* death.

Universal history is the exhibition of Spirit in the process of working out the knowledge of that which it is potentially. And as the germ bears in itself the whole nature of the tree, and the taste and form of its fruits, so do the first traces of Spirit virtually contain the whole of that history. . . . The history of the world is none other than the progress of the consciousness of Freedom. . . . The destiny of the spiritual world and *the final cause of the world at large,* we allege to be the *consciousness* of its own freedom on the part of Spirit, and *ipso facto* the *reality* of that freedom. . . . That the history of the world, with all the changing scenes which its annals present is this process of development and the realization of Spirit—this is the only true *theodicy,* the justification of God in history. Only this insight can reconcile Spirit with the history of the world—viz., that what has happened, and is happening every day, is not only not "without God," but is essentially his Work.

Valuable as was this emphasis on the continuity of tradition, so far as it gave a more adequate knowledge of the forces actually at work in society, it is easy to see how in the hands of conservatives shocked by the spirit of the Enlightenment enforced by revolutionary assemblies it could become a potent instrument of reaction. To this use was it put in Germany by the patriotic "historical school" that, starting from jurisprudence, sought to carry into all social action a new *laisser-faire*—a Hands Off! that was directed to the preservation of old forms and institutions. Law and society cannot be rationally guided; they must grow of themselves. Savigny became the official theorist of this new traditionalist application of the romantic doctrine of development. "All law," he insisted, "comes into being in the manner which prevalent, but not quite exact, idiom designates as the *law of custom;* that is, it is first produced by custom and popular faith, then through jurisprudence; *everywhere, that is, through internal, silently working forces, not through the arbitrariness of a lawgiver."*

If this is true, each age does not act arbitrarily and in an egoistic independence, but is entirely held to the past by common and indissoluble bonds. Each epoch then ought to admit certain previous elements, which are necessary and at the same time voluntary; necessary in the sense that they do not depend on the will and arbitrariness of the present; voluntary in the sense that they are not imposed by an outside will (such as that of the master in regard to his slaves) but that they are given by the very nature of the nation considered as a whole which subsists and maintains itself in the midst of its successive developments. The nation of to-day is only a member of this perpetual nation. It wills and acts in this body, and with this body, so that it can be said that whatever is imposed by the body is at the same time freely accomplished by the member.

On the whole this romantic faith in traditional growth was a conservative and anti-revolutionary force, especially in Germany; but its fundamental ideas of continuity and change brought with them a point of view that was destined to transform the face of thought. For these were to be the categories of the new evolutionary science; and from romanticism was received the greatest stimulus to a study of man and the world in terms of their genetic development. This is the inestimable debt science owes to irrationalism.

The romantic reaction which began with the invasion of 1794 was the revolt of outraged history. The nation fortified itself against the new ideas by calling up the old, and made the ages of faith and of imagination a defense from the age of reason. Whereas the pagan Renaissance was the artifical resurrection of a world long buried, the romantic Renaissance revived the natural order and restored the broken links

from end to end. It inculcated sympathy with what is past, unlovable, indefensible,—
especially with the age of twilight and scenes favorable to the faculties which the
calculators despised. The romantic writers relieved present need with all the abound-
ing treasure of other times, subjecting thereby the will and the conscience of the
living to the will and conscience of the dead. Their lasting influence was out of
proportion to their immediate performance. They were weak because they wanted
strictness and accuracy, and never perceived that the Revolution was itself historic,
having roots that could be profitably traced far back in the ages. But they were
strong by the recovery of lost knowledge, and by making it possible to understand,
to appreciate, and even to admire things which the judgment of rationalism condemned in the mass of worthless and indiscriminate error. They trifled for a time
with fancy, but they doubled the horizon of Europe. They admitted India to an
equality with Greece, medieval Rome with classical; and the thoughts they set in
motion produced Creuzer's *Comparative Mythology* and Bopp's *Conjugations,*
Grimm's enthusiasm for the liberty and belief of Odin's worshipers, and Otfried
Müller's zeal for the factor of race. (Lord Acton).

To live is to grow, to assimilate more and more of the riches of the world,
to project upon the background of the setting of human life more and more
of the infinite possibilities resident in human nature, and in so doing, to become more and more aware of the infinite ties binding all men to each other
and to the great forces of the universe of which they are the noblest manifestation—in a word, to live is to bend all one's energies toward the creation of a
higher, better, and richer world, to realize God himself in the universe. This
was the sum of the wisdom and the aspiration of the romanticists. No wonder
that Wordsworth could write,

> Bliss was it in that dawn to be alive,
> But to be young was very heaven!

Chapter II

COUNTERREVOLUTION AND REACTION

❦

THE SETTLEMENT OF 1815

WHATEVER may have been the theories of government current at the time, the practical control of the political world in 1814 and 1815 was in the hands of the monarchs and their advisers, especially those of England, Austria, Russia, and Prussia. But the sudden collapse of the Napoleonic empire in 1814 found these allied powers with only partially-laid plans for the reconstruction of Europe. All efforts had so long been turned to fighting "the Usurper" that almost no attention had been given to the questions that would arise after his overthrow. The confusion of aims would have been even greater had not Castlereagh, the British foreign minister, succeeded in drawing together the four great powers in the Treaty of Chaumont (March, 1814). This treaty restated certain decisions already arrived at—the establishment of a confederated Germany, the division of Italy into independent states, the restoration of Spain to the Bourbons, the independence of Switzerland, and the enlargement of Holland—and provided further that the alliance now formed should continue for twenty years after the war had ceased, and that the powers should make a final settlement in a future peace congress. Besides uniting the great powers—England, Austria, Russia, and Prussia—for the final struggle with Napoleon and laying down some of the bases of a final peace, the Treaty of Chaumont became the corner stone of the European Alliance which was to determine the balance of power for several decades.

The general provisions of the Treaty of Chaumont were confirmed in the first Treaty of Paris in May, 1814, by which the four great powers, together with Spain, Portugal, and Sweden, made a formal peace with France, and restored, with slight modifications, the French frontiers of 1792. Finally, the powers arranged for the holding of a congress in Vienna to round out a general peace settlement.[1] Before the meeting of this congress the only points on which

---

This chapter is from *Reaction and Revolution, 1814–1832* (pp. 63–94; New York, Harper and Bros., 1934), by Frederick B. Artz.

[1] This congress was not, strictly speaking, to be a peace congress, because peace had already been made by the *first* Treaty of Paris, in which the issues between France and the Allies had been settled. The state of war had ceased both in fact and in law, and France could now claim representa-

the four principal allied powers agreed were that they themselves should settle all important matters, that neither France nor the smaller states should do more than to acquiesce in their final decisions, and that the congress itself should only give a formal ratification to agreements previously made. The treaty carefully avoided the thorny subject of the final disposition of Saxony and Poland. At the time no one seems to have realized how deep were the differences among these allies, and through what a series of bickerings, recriminations, and threats the negotiations were to proceed. During the summer of 1814 conferences among the allied statesmen were held in Paris and London, but little progress was made.

The gathering in Vienna in the autumn of 1814 brought together six monarchs, the Emperors of Austria and of Russia, the Kings of Prussia, Bavaria, Württemberg, and Denmark, and representatives from all the minor states of Europe, together with a host of miscellaneous hangers-on and fortune-seekers.[2] The real work of the Congress was done by Castlereagh (whose place was taken in February, 1815, by the Duke of Wellington), Metternich, Alexander I, and Hardenberg, and to a less extent by Talleyrand after he had wormed his way into the councils of the others. Metternich had the constant aid of his secretary, Gentz, while Hardenberg usually acted for Frederick William III. Alexander preferred to keep matters in his own hands, though he constantly received advice from his large staff, from Stein on German affairs, from Czartoryski on those of Poland, from Capodistrias on the Balkans, and on many other matters from the Corsican, Pozzo di Borgo, from the German Nesselrode, and his old tutor, the Swiss Laharpe.

Some important decisions were formulated in committees appointed from time to time for some special investigation, such as those on Switzerland, Italy, the slave trade, the German Confederation, diplomatic precedence, international rivers, and statistics of population. The ministers of the great powers met nearly every morning for an informal conference in Metternich's apartments. From time to time the three sovereigns of Austria, Russia, and Prussia met to review the matters that had been previously discussed by their ministers. Besides these meetings, innumerable private conferences were going on at all hours. The representatives of the smaller states were consulted only at such times and on such terms as suited the representatives of the great

---

tion with the other powers as a regular member of the European states-system. Herein the situation differed from that of 1919.

[2] No appreciable difference would have been made in the final settlement if a large majority of these representatives had failed to appear. They gave the congress a picturesque setting and they seem to have enjoyed greatly the endless round of balls and entertainments furnished by the almost bankrupt Austrian government and by the nobility.

powers. The Austrian government maintained an elaborate spy system. Letters were opened, wastebaskets were searched by servants in the government's pay, and people in all ranks of society were used to collect bits of information. Some of the other governments maintained secret agents in Vienna. The net result of all this spying is hard to estimate, though its final influence seems to have been slight.

If any statesman took the leading rôle in the negotiations, it was Castlereagh. He usually provided the plan of action and then calmly set about procuring its acceptance. His consistent aim was, as he said later, "not to collect trophies, but to bring back the world to peaceful habits." He represented a government that, for economic reasons, was anxious to have Europe return to peaceful conditions as soon as possible. England was then, as she was after the World War, more heavily burdened with debts than any other state, her public finance was in disorder, her warehouses were bursting with manufactured goods waiting for the reopening of continental markets, and her people were suffering from great economic distress. . . .

The important decisions were all made by the four great powers, to which group Talleyrand was admitted in January, 1815. The attention of the whole of Europe was, in the meantime, focused on Vienna. Every group and every interest from Spain to Russia thought it saw opening before it the opportunity to realize its hopes. Liberals and nationalists, political and religious reactionaries, and all the rulers from the pope to the most petty German princeling, seem to have deluded themselves into believing that the congress would reconstruct society according to their hearts' desires.

Certain matters had been decided by earlier treaties; others were still to be settled—above all, the final disposition of Saxony and Poland. The long negotiations over this knotty problem nearly brought the powers to war. Alexander kept his troops in Poland because, in spite of earlier promises, he was determined to hold the country and to carry through his program of reconstituting old Poland as a Russian dependency. In this plan he had secured the backing of the King of Prussia, who had agreed to relinquish the Prussian part of Poland if Alexander would work for the annexation of Saxony to Prussia. Both Metternich and Castlereagh opposed the plan, principally because they felt that the aggrandizement of Russia and the advance of the Muscovite frontier to the west would upset the balance of power in Europe. International adjustments could best be guaranteed by strengthening the central part of the continent against France on the one hand and against Russia on the other. Here, finally, the intervention of Talleyrand and the mediation of Castlereagh, who continued his efforts to keep peace among the peacemakers, was to bring a compromise. In January, 1815, Castlereagh, Talleyrand, and Metternich signed a secret treaty of alliance which bound their governments to furnish contingents for a common army in the case of a Russian or a Prussian attack. This new alignment forced both Russia and Prussia to withdraw from their former positions. The diplomats then proceeded to strike a balance. Prussia got about two-fifths of Saxony, and Russia was allowed to reconstitute part of the old Polish state as the new kingdom of Poland.

The rest of the agreements took several months of further negotiations. On the ninth of June, a Final Act, a kind of codification of the work of the congress, was signed by nearly all the powers both great and small. Holland received the Austrian Netherlands and Luxemburg; Genoa and part of Savoy went to the Kingdom of Sardinia, and Prussia was given lands along the lower Rhine—all with the idea of erecting a series of strong bulwarks which would prevent an attack by France on the peace of Europe. This establishment of Prussia on the Rhine, which ultimately made her the national champion of Germany against France, proved to be the most important territorial change made by the congress. In Germany Prussia received Swedish Pomerania in addition to part of Westphalia, two-fifths of Saxony, and territories in the Rhineland; Hanover was enlarged, and the other states were carved up to suit the wishes of Austria and Prussia. A loose German Confederation of thirty-nine states, the *Deutscher Bund,* was created under the presidency of Austria. In Italy, besides the enlargement of the Kingdom of Sardinia, the Bourbons were restored to Naples, though only after the congress broke up, just as shortly before they had been restored to France and Spain. The Papal States were returned to the pope; Lombardy and Venetia went to Austria to compensate her for the loss of the former Austrian Netherlands, which she did not want anyway; and in northern and central Italy three small duchies, Tuscany, Parma, and Modena, were placed under Austrian princes. Thus, in both Germany and Italy Austria held the dominant influence. Switzerland was guaranteed her independence and neutrality, an arrangement which proved the most durable achievement of the congress. Norway was taken from Denmark and joined to Sweden, which in turn gave Finland to Russia. By the terms of the first Treaty of Paris England received Cape Colony, Heligoland, Malta, Ceylon, Mauritius, and islands in the West Indies. Later she received a protectorate over the Ionian Islands. At Vienna she secured from the powers agreements for opening certain rivers to navigation and for abolishing the slave trade; termination of the traffic in slaves was an uncompromising demand of the British Evangelicals and Non-conformist groups who, through their fanatical zeal and their insistence that most of the peace negotiations be subordinated to this reform, not only greatly endangered the acceptance of their own program but seriously interfered with Castlereagh's efforts at Vienna.

Such was the most important international settlement between that of 1648 at Westphalia and that of 1919 at Paris. It was the fashion of the liberal historians of the nineteenth century to denounce the decisions of the Congress of Vienna. Since 1919, however, it has become clear that the diplomats called together at the close of a general European war are so bound by earlier agreements and by the exigencies of the moment that they cannot build a New Jerusalem. They are fortunate if they are able even to reconstruct an old order. In 1815 neither the statesmen nor the peoples of Europe had any thorough understanding of the vague principles of nationality and democracy. Moreover, there was, at the time of the Vienna Congress, a widespread distrust of these revolutionary ideas. It is as incredible that the statesmen of 1815 should have made them the basis of a reconstructed Europe as that the delegates at the conference of 1919 should have revamped Europe in accordance with the precepts of communism. After the overthrow of Napoleon the diplomatists quite naturally resorted to the familiar ideas of the balance of power and to the notions of legitimacy, and tried to fuse them into some sort of compromise that would guarantee Europe a period of peace. Whatever may be said against them, they were, most of them, reasonable, fair-minded, and well-intentioned. These qualities were most strikingly revealed in their treatment of France and in the general absence of rancor in their decisions. Patriotic Frenchmen sometimes claim that it was as hard for France to lose territories like Belgium, which had been occupied for twenty years, as it was for Germany to give up large slices of territory in 1919, but the disinterested outsider can hardly accept the comparison. The fact is that reasonable Frenchmen were generally satisfied with the first Treaty of Paris, and that even after the imposition of the harsher terms of the second treaty Europe enjoyed nearly a half-century of peace on the basis of the Vienna settlements.

While the Congress was still in session, Napoleon had escaped from Elba, and on March 1, 1815, had landed on the south coast of France. Without firing a shot or shedding a drop of blood, he had marched northward, and within twenty days had reëstablished himself on the French throne. He began at once to negotiate with the allied powers but they would have nothing to do with him. The plenipotentiaries of England, Russia, Prussia, Austria, and some of the smaller powers proclaimed him an outlaw and pledged themselves "not to lay down their arms until Napoleon is rendered wholly incapable of again disturbing the peace." The allied armies were hastily reassembled. Early in June, 1815, Napoleon pushed north into Belgium to defeat the English army under Wellington before Blücher and the Prussians arrived. Though at first successful at Ligny on June 16, 1815, his plan failed and he was over-whelmed two days later at Waterloo. Driven back to Paris, he abdicated on June 22, fled to the coast, and delivered himself into the hands of the English.

The entrance of the allied forces into Paris brought the plenipotentiaries together again. After prolonged and often embittered negotiations, they signed, on the twentieth of November, the second Treaty of Paris. France was obliged to restore most of the works of art taken by Napoleon, to agree to pay a heavy indemnity, and to support an allied army of occupation until it had been paid. Her boundaries were reduced to the limits of 1790, and it was due only to the moderating counsels of Castlereagh, Wellington, and Alexander that she was not compelled to cede Alsace-Lorraine and lands along the northern frontier. On the same day another agreement was signed by the four great powers which bound them in a Quadruple Alliance to maintain by armed force the arrangements of Chaumont, Vienna, and Paris for twenty years, both in regard to the territorial boundaries and to the exclusion of Bonaparte and his dynasty from the throne of France. An attempt of Alexander to embody in this treaty a provision that would oblige the signatories to intervene in France to maintain Louis XVIII and the Charter of 1814 was rejected by Castlereagh. His contention, which remained fundamental in his point of view until his death in 1822, was that England could not guarantee any more than the general settlement of boundaries. She would not intervene in the internal affairs of any state except in one case—the possibility of a Bonaparte returning to power in France. The treaty called also for periodic meetings of representatives of the four powers, "for the purpose of consulting upon their common interest and for the consideration of the measures most salutary for the maintenance of the peace of Europe." The ascendancy of the great powers in general European affairs was herein for the first time clearly set forth, and along with this the principle of a European concert and the idea of diplomacy by congresses and conferences.

Two months before this Tsar Alexander had presented the various European monarchs with a draft of the Holy Alliance. This curious document, in which Baader and Mme. de Krüdener had a hand, stated that the rulers of Europe would in future regulate their acts in both domestic and foreign affairs according to the benign principles and precepts of the Christian religion. Castlereagh referred to the document as a "piece of sublime mysticism and nonsense," and most of the other statesmen were equally contemptuous. It is only fair to say, however, that the so-called Holy Alliance was for Alexander only a makeshift, a mere fragment of a much larger scheme for the reconstruction of Europe in accordance with advanced principles. The tsar had made an effort to gain a hearing for his plans at Vienna, but the practically-minded statesmen of the powers regarded him as either a dangerous Jacobin or a clever schemer with ulterior motives. So Alexander never got beyond the acceptance of the preface of his program. . . .

The Alliance had no direct influence on affairs, for "charity" and "love" are not capable of being stated in diplomatic terms. The powers of the Quadruple Alliance pursued a conservative and repressive policy in the years following the peace, so that the contrast between high-sounding principles and actual practice quite naturally produced in the minds of the peoples of Europe the suspicion that their rulers were hypocritically leagued against them. In the popular mind, the Holy Alliance remained for a half-century confused with the Quadruple Alliance.

The representatives of the powers, having sent Napoleon to St. Helena, having redrawn the map of Europe, and having provided the machinery for perpetuating their territorial settlement, returned to their own capitals to occupy themselves with the domestic situation.

THE REACTION IN ENGLAND

In the overthrow of Napoleon the British navy and British subsidies had played a major rôle, but the celebrations over Waterloo had hardly passed before it became evident that victory in a modern war is little more profitable than defeat. The high prices obtained for foodstuffs during the wars suddenly collapsed and the English countryside, which not so long before had been famed as the land of roast beef and plum pudding, was now peopled by wretches—as Cobbett describes them—"in ragged smock-frocks with unshaven faces, with a shirt not washed for a month and with their toes peeping out of their shoes." The misery of the agricultural classes was increased by the bad harvests of 1815 and 1816. Within a few years half the population in many parishes was on the poor-rates. In the factory towns thousands were thrown out of work, and even for the employers, with markets fluctuating and uncertain, the struggle for survival was desperate. Banks and commercial companies went to the wall by the hundreds. At the same time taxes were very heavy because the state was burdened by a larger debt than ever before incurred by any nation. As a result of this maladjustment thousands in the towns and on the land were on the verge of utter destitution and the whole country was filled with discontent.

Unusual statesmanship was needed to meet these difficulties, but the government was directed by men who, though they had carried the country to final victory in the long struggle with France, had nothing in their training which fitted them to handle the widespread distress and discontent. In their view the successful conclusion of the wars had invested the whole existing social and political system with a halo of sanctity. They looked upon those who advocated any measure of reform as dangerous firebrands. In contrast with the governments of most of the continental states, that of England was without an adequate police force. The ministers, falling into clumsy methods of military repression, depended for information not on competent detectives but on the tales of private spies and on agents provocateurs. The larger towns were, for the most part, still dominated by little oligarchies, seldom public-spirited and often corrupt, while the country districts, and those that were country one year and town the next, were under the rule of squires whose idea of governing was merely to enforce the old laws in the old ways.

Like the civil administration, Parliament was in the hands of a closed caste which was at the time directed by the Tory party. The long danger of French invasion had enlisted on its behalf all the patriotic sentiment exploited by the Whigs in the days of Louis XV. George III had strengthened this Tory reaction by a policy of granting large numbers of peerages. As a result, the official Whig leaders had gone politically to sleep in their country seats, and their party had almost ceased to exist. After 1815 it suffered not only from numerical weakness, but also from internal disunion. The Grenvillite group seceded in 1818 and in 1822 joined the opposition. The few outspoken radicals in the party, like Admiral Cochrane and Sir Francis Burdett, indulged in such extravagant language that they only dragged the whole party into further disrepute. But for the energy of one Whig member, Henry Brougham, the opposition in Parliament would, for a time, almost have disappeared. The Whigs, however, even if they had been in power, might have shown as little understanding of conditions as did the Tories, for in the unreformed Parliament, where both parties represented only the upper classes, neither side showed any fundamental disagreement with, or even any great dislike for, the other. Knowing that some day the turn of the political wheel would put them into office the "outs" usually guarded themselves in their attacks on abuses which sooner or later might benefit them. Until 1822 the most conservative wing of the Tory party dominated Parliament. The leading figures in the Cabinet, Liverpool, the prime minister, Castlereagh, the secretary for foreign affairs, and Eldon, the lord chancellor, had no program after 1815 except that of repressing all internal dissent. At the same time they implored the country to enjoy "the blessings of peace and order." This Tory domination was made possible not only by the success of the party in concluding the wars, but also by the great wave of popular discontent which swept through the lower classes of the nation and frightened the aristocracy and the bourgeoisie into accepting this policy of repression.

As neither the Tories nor the Whigs showed any understanding of the social misery that was growing in the land, the agitation for reform fell into the hands of groups of radicals outside Parliament. These radicals had no common organization or program, though nearly all of them shared the idea that the road to improvement lay through a reform of Parliament. Before 1820 neither Bentham nor Owen, who had little interest in political reform, had found much of a following. Far more influential were individuals like Cobbett and groups like the Hampden Clubs. These organizations had been founded by Major Cartwright before the end of the wars. Their membership, though small, was widely distributed through the larger towns. Their program centered chiefly on the need of reforming the House of Commons where, as Cartwright had said, one found nothing but "idle schoolboys, insignificant coxcombs, toad-eaters, gamblers, public plunderers and hirelings." After 1816 the dues of these societies were reduced to one penny a week, and their program was broadened by the inclusion of a demand for universal manhood suffrage. The local organizers of these radical groups, which resembled the secret liberal societies in many continental countries, borrowed the tactics used by the Methodists. There was the same plan of local organization with trifling dues, the same open-air meetings conducted in a highly emotional atmosphere, and a similar paid service of itinerant preachers. During the years 1816 to 1819 most of the public gatherings that so outraged the authorities were organized by members of these societies.

Even more influential in arousing public opinion were a number of freelance reformers, first among whom stood Cobbett, the greatest of all English popular journalists. Cobbett's close first-hand knowledge of actual conditions among all layers of the population and his deep sincerity gave point to his violent invective. In 1816 he began to get out an edition of his *Political Register* for two pence, and so for the first time in history put a newspaper within reach of the lower classes. Farmer and mill-hand, in cottage and tenement, read in its columns of the unfairness of the law courts, of the game laws, and of the electoral system, of the abuses of taxation, and of the millions of pounds poured out by the state to the holders of sinecures; the last-named abuses were the chief causes of popular discontent in the period. Cobbett advised his readers, however, to stop using violence and urged them to join the Hampden Clubs and to work peaceably for the reform of Parliament. Although his economics were often wild and his insight limited, of all the authors of the movement that finally aroused the Whigs to action and later brought about the Reform Bill of 1832, he was the most powerful. Henry Hunt and Thistlewood stand out beside him as the two best known agitators among the popular leaders of discontent. Hunt was a forceful mob-orator; Thistlewood, the chief figure in the Cato Street Conspiracy of 1820, was a violent demagogue.

By 1816 the full force of unemployment and high prices began to be felt. An epidemic of violence and bread-rioting in the towns, of strikes in the mining districts, and of incendiarism in the country broke out all over England. The radicals tried to give this discontent a political program by holding public meetings. The indifference of the Tory ministry to the distress, combined with an unwillingness to differentiate between reasonable demands for parliamentary reform and mere mob-violence, was first shown at the time of a series of outdoor assemblies held at Spa Fields, near London, in the autumn of 1816. In one of these meetings Hunt, in a fiery speech, denounced the system which taxed bread, beer, clothing, and the other common necessities of life and which used the proceeds to pension "the fathers, brothers, mothers, sisters, cousins, and bastards of the borough-mongers." Everything passed off peaceably, except for the looting of a few bakeshops in the evening. In December a second large meeting was addressed, before Hunt's arrival, by Spence, one of the most violent of all the radical agitators. A small group of men, after hearing the speech, rushed off, seized a gunsmith's shop, killed its proprietor, and paraded noisily through Cheapside. The outbreak was given wide publicity in the papers, and was used by the ministry to frighten the upper and middle classes.

These meetings and an attempt on the regent's life led to the appointment of secret parliamentary committees in 1817 to examine, not the causes of discontent, but the activities of the reform societies. The committees in their alarmist reports alleged that a traitorous conspiracy was under way, that it was proposed to seize the Bank of England and the Tower of London, to arouse the army to mutiny, and to effect a general Jacobin revolution. The evidence had been furnished chiefly by a disreputable informer named Castle whom the government was using also as an agent provocateur. As a result of its investigation, Parliament forbade all public meetings, suppressed all societies not licensed by government officials, and suspended the Habeas Corpus Act (until March 1, 1818). The country was swept with an hysterical fear; one magistrate refused to sanction a mineralogical society on the pretext that the study of such a subject led to atheism. The courts tried a number of rioters and supposed conspirators and instituted suits against offending newspapers which, in some cases, resulted in heavy sentences and, in others, in dramatic acquittals. Public meetings ceased for a time and discontent was driven underground. Cobbett went to America, whence he began to write home of the glories of a republic with no established church or titles. . . .

The newspapers and the periodical press, however, continued to present a grave problem to the ministry. Great periodicals, like the Whig *Edinburgh Review,* and most of the sixteen London dailies, as well as the principal provincial papers, had such large incomes from advertising that they were beyond being bought by the government. The *Times,* an independent paper, the Whig *Morning Chronicle,* and even the Tory *Morning Post* were given to plain speaking, though they always seemed pale in comparison with Cobbett's *Political Register.* The press remained the only effective outlet for criticism of the existing régime. Many editors and newspaper owners were haled into court for jury trial, but the state's case often failed because the prosecution labeled all criticism as treason. Since the penalty for treason was usually death, juries refused to convict. During all the discussion of discontent great stress had been laid by the government on the irreligious character of the radical propaganda and in 1818 Parliament presented its solution of this problem by granting a million pounds to build more churches.

The repressive legislation of 1817, combined with the improvement in trade conditions and an abundant harvest, brought a lull in the agitation for reform. Nevertheless the election of 1818 returned thirty more Whigs to Parliament. This indicated that the governing classes were by no means as unanimous in their support of repression as the ministry imagined. A moderate opposition was growing both within the Tory ranks and among the Whigs. It was still very timid and its chief efforts were directed not toward the delicate problem of parliamentary reform but toward such questions as the reform of public finance and of criminal law. . . .

Another economic flurry in 1819 brought on a wave of unemployment and a revival of radical agitation. The ministry still continued its old policy of carrying on from day to day, repressing all opposition outside Parliament and piously hoping for things to get better of themselves. The economic depression of 1819 proved to be far less severe than that of 1815–1817, but the political crisis became more acute. During a series of strikes among the cotton workers in northern England, which continued for several months, a number of agitators began to organize groups of the dissatisfied, and to hold public meetings. Their language was often violent but their program called only for repeal of the Corn Laws and reform of parliamentary representation. On these points the manufacturers and the workers were in agreement, though the millowners, fearing violence, still played into the hands of the Tory ministry.

Some of the radical agitators formed a plan to hold mass meetings in the larger cities of the North and the Midlands at which unofficial representatives to Parliament were to be elected. An outdoor gathering, held at Birmingham in July, 1818, and attended by about 25,000, elected Sir Charles Wolseley "legislative attorney and representative" of the city. The government thereupon issued orders that no more such meetings should be held. But at Manchester the radicals had already decided to follow the example of Birmingham, and a public meeting had been called for the sixteenth of August. A number of the men who were to take part in it underwent some preliminary drill, in order that they might move on to the field with military regularity. Banners with various inscriptions were prepared to decorate the processions. The authorities, however, had been vigilant; troops had been moved to Manchester and special constables had been enrolled. The entire country was in a ferment of expectation.

On the appointed day about 60,000 men, women, and children had gathered in St. Peter's Fields when Henry Hunt rode up in a carriage. He mounted the speaker's stand; the vast multitude became silent. But he had hardly begun his address when a squadron of cavalry suddenly started to force its way toward the platform. The vast throng fell into a wild panic and began to rush away. In ten minutes the field was cleared; the ground was left strewn with the wounded, and with hats, shoes, walking sticks, and torn banners. Eleven people had been killed, and several hundred hurt. A howl of anger and disgust arose throughout the length and breadth of England. To make matters worse the regent and Lord Sidmouth, the home secretary, without waiting to make inquiries, sent their congratulations to the local authorities. For this victory of the government over their fellow citizens the radicals at once coined the name, the Battle of Peterloo. The memory of it long endured. . . .

In spite of protests from the Common Council of London and other highly placed bodies, the ministry was again able to play upon the fear of the upper classes. In November Parliament discussed and passed the Six Acts, the most repressive laws Great Britain had known for generations. In the long debates memories of the French Revolution cropped up repeatedly. Was the government, asked the ministers, to imitate the weakness of Louis XVI and his government and go along idly while the throne and the altar perished as they had in France? The Ultras in France and the reactionary statesmen in Germany, Spain, and Italy were all, at the time, using the same language. Of the Six Acts, the first forbade the practice of military exercises by unauthorized persons; the second provided for the speedy trial and drastic punishment of all offenders against public order; the third empowered the magistrates to issue warrants for the search of arms in private houses; the next authorized the seizure of seditious or blasphemous libels and the punishment of their authors; the fifth restricted public meetings to those called by government officials and prohibited all gatherings held to examine complaints against church and state; and the last subjected all publications below a certain size to the heavy stamp duty already levied on newspapers. All, except the third and fifth, were designed to be permanent. Wellington wrote of the Six Acts to Pozzo di Borgo, November 25, 1819, "Our example will render some good in France as well as in Germany, and we must hope that the whole world will escape the universal revolution which seems to menace us all."

Lord Grey and Lord Holland denounced the Six Acts in Parliament, the latter declaring that the laws already on the statute books were sufficient to prevent disorder, and that the new powers now given to the state were liable to serious abuse. Above all, he insisted that public meetings are "a vent, comparatively innocuous, of that discontent which if suppressed might seek refuge in conspiracies." Gradually the opposition was being forced to take a stand. A Whig motion in the House of Commons calling for an inquiry into the Peterloo affair secured a hundred fifty votes. The majority, however, still backed the ministry. It was little wonder that by 1819 thousands of Englishmen were deeply convinced that the governing classes were in league against their welfare.

THE RETURN TO BOURBON RULE IN FRANCE AND SPAIN

If an old and establishment government like that of England found peace as beset with difficulties as war, it is little wonder that the new régime in France faced still more perplexing problems. Lack of experience in handling a parliamentary government and the rancorous hatreds created by the revolution made continuity of policy nearly impossible. Indeed, the revolution had created such a fundamental cleavage in French society that until 1870 it proved impossible for any régime to maintain itself longer than two decades. The Restoration in France was inevitably an age of extremes. Ultramontanes and atheists, absolutists and democrats, men who had joined the camp of the émigrés at Coblenz and men who had sat in the Convention met in the

Chambers and in society. Many of them seemed more ready to begin the revolution all over again than to try to live in peace.

The sudden collapse of the Empire in 1814 found both the French and the allies still undecided as to who should succeed Napoleon. A small Bourbon faction in France was making spasmodic attempts to communicate with allied headquarters where, however, decision was for a long time delayed because of conflicting views. In the meantime Bordeaux declared for the old royal family. Largely on the insistence of Castlereagh and Talleyrand the allies finally agreed to accept the Comte de Provence as Louis XVIII. Soon, under the inspiration of the ever-ready Talleyrand, the Senate, the Municipal Council of Paris, and other official groups voted for the return of the Bourbons as the best guarantee of peace. In the midst of the general distress and discouragement in France, the allies sent Napoleon to Elba and Louis returned from England.

At once everyone began to wonder what the new king would do. The French people showed little enthusiasm for these forgotten Bourbons, whose very names the press of the Empire had been forbidden to mention. Before the new monarch arrived, his brother, the Comte d'Artois, and a group of returning émigrés were trying to get control of the situation. Fully realizing the danger of their counter-revolutionary designs and desiring to curb their ardor, as well as to satisfy the tsar, Louis XVIII issued a proclamation shortly after landing in France. In it he promised not to disturb anyone for his opinions, and agreed to grant a constitution. This charter, he promised, would assure the payment of the public debt, freedom of the press and of religion, equality before the law, and would guarantee full property rights to those who had purchased national lands during the revolution. This Déclaration de Saint-Ouen seems to have had a reassuring effect on everyone, except the circle of the Comte d'Artois.

The new monarch entered Paris in May, 1814, and took up his residence at the Tuileries, where the servants busied themselves sewing the royal coat of arms on the carpets and chairs over the tops of the Napoleonic eagles. After a few days of deliberation the Constitutional Charter was drawn up by a committee of former ministers, senators, and deputies of the Empire. The document, which, according to the secretary, was thrown together like the text of a comic opera, embodied the promises made in the Déclaration de Saint-Ouen. It guaranteed the land settlement of the revolution, and the continuance of Napoleon's autocratic system of local administration, his codes, his Legion of Honor, and his educational system. For the central government it established a parliamentary order similar to that of England, a régime which, as time showed, fitted ill with the highly centralized and authoritarian administrative system of the empire. The monarch was to share the direction of the government with a Chamber of Peers nominated by himself, and with a Chamber of Deputies elected for five years on a very restricted franchise. The document was vague and contradictory on important points, above all on the matters of ministerial responsibility, control of the press, the method of holding elections, and the right of the king to issue ordinances. The preamble, quite in the spirit of the Ancien Régime, announced that the Charter was the monarch's gift to France, while the document itself was dated "in the nineteenth year of our reign." Only usage and experience could reveal what the Charter would mean. The mass of the population was apathetic toward these changes. The French, like the other peoples of Europe, seemed to be willing to accept anything that would assure a return of peace.

During the first Restoration (1814–15) the only active and organized party in France was that of the ultra-royalists, commonly known as the Ultras, headed by the Comte d'Artois. He established himself in the Pavillon de Marsan in the Tuileries, and his circle at once became a kind of invisible government. Artois prided himself on being surrounded by men who had never served any of the revolutionary governments and who, out of devotion to their monarch, had stayed out of France or had lived in seclusion for a quarter of a century. The Ultras wished to turn over the whole Napoleonic administrative machine to men of ardent royalist connections (the two Napoleonic institutions they approved of were the police and the prefects), to return to the émigrés all property that had not been sold, to indemnify the others, to subject the press to a severe censorship, and to abolish the Napoleonic Université de France.

In 1814 and 1815, Ultra agents went about the provinces securing support for their program from the municipal councils. The exaggerated statements made by these extremists and by some of the higher clergy, especially their extravagant threats that the government might take back the clerical and noble lands sold during the revolution, aroused the peasants and brought serious discredit on the new régime even before it was under way. Other ill-timed acts on the part of the government itself aggravated the situation. To save money the army was greatly reduced, and many Napoleonic officers were put on half-pay. These disgruntled soldiers were soon scattered all over France, sowing hatred against the Bourbons. In Paris the allied agents, the Duke of Wellington and Pozzo di Borgo, were meddling in French affairs. Louis XVIII and the new order seemed nowhere to find friends.

When Napoleon returned from Elba in March, 1815, he was accepted by the army as preferable to the Bourbons. In nearly every town, as he moved northward toward Paris, he was greeted with tales of the popular dread of a restoration of the Ancien Régime, and with bitter denunciations of the priests. Louis XVIII fled to Lille and then to Ghent and Napoleon easily re-established himself. But he soon discovered that he could not hope to remain in power unless his government were liberalized. He was under the ban so far as the allied powers were concerned and in France he faced the hatred of the clergy and of many of the nobility and the apathy and fear of the middle classes. He could only hope to hold his position by again rousing the old revolutionary ardor of the masses. Forced to act quickly he called in Benjamin Constant to prepare, in imitation of the Bourbon Charter, an "Additional Act to the Constitutions of the Empire." The document, the sixth constitution France had known since 1789, provided for a responsible ministry, jury trial, and freedom of the press. This makeshift was presented to the French people through a plebiscite in which only a million and a half bothered to vote. France was evidently weary of constitutions, and uncertain, too, of the desirability of this latest régime. Napoleon's destiny, however, did not depend on what the French thought of him for he was soon overwhelmingly defeated by the allied powers and forced to abdicate.

Louis XVIII returned in July, 1815, to a situation of great complexity and uncertainty, but at once he showed his renewed determination to maintain a régime that would "heal the wounds of the revolution." His enemies, especially the Bonapartists, made fun of this gouty old gentleman who had arrived "in the baggage of the allies." But Louis proved to have unexpected judgment and courage. Rich in the patience acquired in weary years of exile, he showed a surprising willingness to make concessions and even to use men like Talleyrand and Fouché whom he personally despised. Yet despite all his efforts a White Terror broke out in the provinces. Because of the ease with which Napoleon had returned to power, the Ultras were able to convince many people that a great plot was on foot to overthrow the newly established government.

The whole country was in a state of hysteria. At Orleans, a mob burned a large portrait of Napoleon in one of the principal squares, and then took bayonets and smashed a bust of him. A group of infuriated royalists at Carcassonne butchered a live eagle caught in the mountains. Mobs in the Vendée and in the south of France murdered men who had been prominent in the revolution, and the local authorities did not venture to intervene. Not content with butchering their victims, the royalists went further and insulted the corpses. Marshal Brune, a brave Napoleonic officer, was struck down at

Avignon; at his burial the coffin was broken open and his body tossed about and cast into the Rhone. The king, in order to mollify the Ultras, ordered the trial of a number of the officers who in 1815 had gone over to Napoleon. Apparently he hoped that some of the more prominent ones would escape. When an industrious prefect captured Ney in the provinces, Louis exclaimed, "This is a piece of stupidity that will cost us dearly." Brought back to Paris, Ney was tried by the Chamber of Peers, declared guilty of treason and shot. A number of other Napoleonic officials were imprisoned and executed by the government.

In the midst of this wave of royalist reaction, the first elections for the new Chamber of Deputies were held. The nobility and the upper middle class, the only groups which had the right to vote, were so anxious for peace that they returned a majority of Ultras. In a moment of amiable enthusiasm Louis XVIII called it the *Chambre Introuvable*.[3] The first result of the election was the resignation of the provisional Talleyrand-Fouché ministry and the formation of a cabinet of moderate Royalists under the Duc de Richelieu (1815–18). Included in it were the Duc Decazes, a personal favorite of Louis XVIII, and a group of men who backed the monarch's program of trying to steer a middle course between reaction and revolution.

The new ministry soon found itself blocked by the Ultra majority in the Chamber of Deputies. The Ultras hated Louis XVIII, whom they dubbed the "crowned Jacobin" and "King Voltaire." They set about embarrassing him and his ministers in every way possible. The more intransigent Ultras proposed to abolish the Université de France and demanded an immediate restitution of the *biens nationaux*.[4] They did succeed in abolishing divorce, in banishing a number of men prominent in the imperial régime, in muzzling the press (few sessions of the Chambers during the Restoration passed without some changes in the press-laws and the electoral system), and finally in passing a law setting up special courts to try persons suspected of treason. These *Cours Prévôtales* soon became notorious for their high-handed methods, which seriously interfered with the king's policy of conciliation. Suspected persons were arrested and held for weeks without trial; semi-military methods of procedure were used, and fines and terms of imprisonment were imposed in wholesale fashion. Some of the worst judicial abuses took place in Grenoble, where an outbreak in the garrison was brutally put down.

All over the country business was disorganized as a result of the sudden end of the wars, but the declaration of Baron Louis, the minister of finance,

[3] [The *Undetectable Chamber*.]
[4] [*National lands*.]

that the new government would recognize the debts of the Empire, held out
the hope of better conditions. But during the years 1816 and 1817 the economic
situation was very bad, both in the towns and in the country districts. The
harvests were as meager in France as elsewhere in Europe. The food required
by the 150,000 men in the allied army of occupation forced up prices in the
eastern departments even above those in the rest of France. In some districts
the population was starving. In the midst of this growing distress and uncertainty, the behavior of the Chamber only aggravated the situation. On the
advice of the allied powers, who feared that its Ultra policy might provoke
a revolution, Louis XVIII dissolved it by royal decree in September, 1816.

The next four years, from 1816 to 1820, were, from the political angle, the
calmest of the Restoration. New elections returned a Chamber of Deputies
of a more conciliatory stripe, and in both chambers the king and Richelieu
had the backing of a majority of moderate royalists. What were to become
the great political parties of modern France were just beginning to gather
their forces, though as yet no regular party organizations had come into
existence. At the extreme right of both houses sat the Ultras, while at the extreme left were a number of determined liberals. Both these groups disliked
the Charter and would have been glad to modify or abolish it, but the Ultra
opposition was, before 1820, the more effective. Its members employed nearly
any means to discredit the king and the ministry. In the sessions of the
Chambre Introuvable they had defended the Charter against the king, insisting that its terms required the monarch to choose his ministers from the
leading parliamentary group (the Ultras). Then, hoping that the peasants
would show a greater enthusiasm for their program than did the upper middle class, the Ultras in 1816 demanded a wide extension of the suffrage. The
Liberals jeered at these champions of divine right who were now mouthing
the phrases of British Whiggism. As one wit put it, the Ultras were "entering
into the spirit of the Charter as the Greeks entered the Trojan horse." After
1816 the Ultras of the Right and the Liberals of the Left on occasion joined
hands to embarrass the Center and the ministry, for, as the Ultra journal, the
Drapeau Blanc,[5] said, "Better a Jacobin than a Ministerialist!"

The combination of the Ultra Right and the Liberal Left was not yet strong
enough to prevent coöperation between the king, the ministry and the Center.
In 1817 the ministry carried through the Chambers a new electoral law extending the vote to 88,000 (out of a population of thirty millions), and a law
providing for a renewal each year of a fifth of the membership of the lower
house. It also carried through a reorganization of the army along more demo-

cratic lines, and, by paying off the indemnity to the Allies, obtained the liberation of the occupied territory. The arrangement for the payment of the indemnity of seven hundred million francs and the reception of France into the Quintuple Alliance at the Congress of Aix-la-Chapelle were largely the work of Richelieu. The Ultras pushed their plan to discredit him even to the point of urging the allied powers to continue the military occupation of France. This action, together with a disagreement with the king on electoral policy, led Richelieu to resign in 1818; Louis XVIII then reformed the ministry under Dessoles and his favorite, Decazes. A more liberal press law was passed in 1819, and the new electoral law brought into the Chamber of Deputies a number of more outspoken Liberals, like the Abbé Grégoire, some of whose sayings, as "Kings are in the moral order what monsters are in the physical," had made his name widely known throughout France.

The sessions of the Chambers in 1818 and 1819 grew steadily more acrimonious. Embittered Ultras, like La Bourdonnaye, and Liberal firebrands, like Manuel and Foy, rose on the slightest pretext to refight the battles of the revolution. Even Constant, who believed in the Restoration compromise, was now veering to the Left. At no time in modern France have fundamental principles of government been so thoroughly debated as in these legislative sessions of the Restoration. The deeper implications of the debates were most effectively embodied in the lofty discourses of the moderate royalist, Royer-Collard. Through all the discussions ran a conflict as to whether the social, educational, and administrative settlement of the revolution should be continued and broadened, or narrowed, or even destroyed. The debates in the lower house were printed in the official *Moniteur* and commented on in the ultra-royalist *Quotidienne* [6] and *Drapeau Blanc,* in the more moderate *Journal des Débats,* and in the liberal *Constitutionnel,* which for a time had the largest circulation of any newspaper in Europe. Although newspapers were relatively expensive, the reading public in shop, café, and at the fireside followed the parliamentary war with lively interest. This world of newspapers and politics offered, comparatively speaking, a new experience for the French people who now, for the first time, were making an extended experiment in representative government. In this lies the great importance of the Restoration in the political history of modern France. By 1819 the return of prosperity and the conciliatory attitude of the king were gradually winning the trading classes and the peasants to the support of the new régime.

While Louis XVIII was showing such remarkable shrewdness in reëstablishing the Bourbon monarchy in France, his cousin, Ferdinand VII, was rapidly

[6] [*Daily.*]

driving Spain toward revolution. The Spanish monarch reëntered his kingdom in March, 1814. The enthusiasm of the mass of the Spanish people who
had been fighting for years for his return greeted him at the frontier: everywhere he was acclaimed as the "well-beloved" and the "long wished-for."
This soon convinced him that, during the long struggle with Napoleon, he
had become the living symbol of a national ideal, and that now he could have
a free hand in settling his accounts with the handful of liberals. In 1814 it
would not have been possible to convince the masses that he had fawned on
his jailer, Napoleon, and that he had even congratulated Joseph Bonaparte
on his accession to the throne of Spain. On the tenth of May, soon after he
reached Madrid, prominent liberals in the city were arrested, and hurried off
to prison amidst the jeers of a mob that yelled, "Long live the absolute king,
long live the Inquisition, down with the Freemasons!" The next morning
the city was placarded with a royal proclamation dissolving the Cortes and
announcing, "Not only do I refuse to swear to observe the Constitution [of
1812], or to recognize any decrees of the Cortes, but I declare Constitution
and decrees alike null and void, today and forever."

Ferdinand then proceeded to reëstablish the Inquisition, to return the ecclesiastical and feudal property that had changed hands since 1808, and to
restore the seigniorial rights and jurisdictions of the nobles in twenty-five
thousand villages in Spain. For this he received the enthusiastic support of
most of the aristocracy and the clergy. Foreign books and newspapers were
seized at the frontiers, while in Spain itself the government permitted the
publication of only two newspapers. An English traveler in Spain said of these
newspapers, and much the same could have been said of the press in the Austrian Empire and in the Italian states, that they contained nothing but reports
of the weather and "accounts of miracles wrought by different Virgins, lives
of holy friars and sainted nuns, romances of marvelous conversions, libels
against Jews, heretics, and Freemasons, and histories of apparitions."

In making all these changes, Ferdinand was not only restoring the pre-
revolutionary power of the monarchy, the nobility, and the church; he was
going back to an even older system of governing that nullified all the reforms
of the eighteenth century. After 1814 he ruled partly through a group of ministers and partly through a court camarilla, one member of which had formerly
been a water-carrier and another a porter. He played one group against another; he allowed no one to remain for long either in the ministry or in the
palace clique, and dismissal was usually accompanied by exile or imprisonment. Between 1820 and 1830 he had thirty ministers. The Duke of Wellington protested against these policies, and Louis XVIII, in refusing the proffered

help of a Spanish regiment after Napoleon's escape from Elba, showed his disgust with Ferdinand's behavior.

This scandalous régime, which the young American scholar, George Ticknor, characterized as a "confusion of abuses," did nothing to relieve the economic distress of the exhausted and poverty-stricken people which had fought so bravely against the French invaders. All the public services were neglected, commerce and industry were ruined, the treasury was bankrupt, and the army and navy went unpaid and underfed. Seville, Cadiz, and the other commercial cities were full of merchants ruined by the long wars and by the revolt of the Spanish colonies in the New World. As a result, the upper middle class grew increasingly restless, and the liberal party which had framed the Constitution of 1812, though it represented only a small minority of the population, began to reorganize its forces and to conspire against the government. Discontent spread in the army, whose officers had been brought into contact with French liberal ideas during the wars, and in the larger ports, where the economic depression was worst. The rapid growth of secret societies and the increase in membership of the Masonic lodges, as well as a series of small outbreaks between 1815 and 1817, showed that the restored monarchy was resting on the weakest of foundations.

THE HAPSBURG DOMINATION IN MIDDLE EUROPE: THE AUSTRIAN EMPIRE AND THE GERMANIC CONFEDERATION

From the Baltic to Sicily the destinies of Middle Europe were in the control of the Hapsburgs. Throughout all these lands the fall of Napoleon had been welcomed with enthusiasm; on the return of peace the mass of the population in every state settled back into acceptance of the existing order. To them the governments did not seem despotic; they had no sense of oppression, such as the British and to some extent the French people would have felt had they been living under Hapsburg rule. The censorship of the press and the arrest of a few students or conspirators passed unnoticed among the rank and file. But among small groups of students and army officers, among members of the lesser nobility and the commercial classes there was dissatisfaction and conspiracy.

Although the discontented elements differed in their projects of reform, all were agreed in their hatred of Metternich. Through the next decades they developed such a portrait of him as a tyrant and even a monster that it has now become difficult to estimate him with any degree of fairness. . . . Metternich's whole policy was centered in his devotion to the imperial house he served, and that out of its needs he elaborated a general European program of conservatism. In the delicately balanced Hapsburg system, the German, Italian, Slav, and Magyar lands were all geared into the central dynastic wheel in such a way that the introduction of democratic institutions or the recognition of national entities anywhere could easily upset the Hapsburg machine everywhere. The task of holding together such a federated empire, made up of half the races and religions of Europe, presented problems of administration practically unknown in London or Paris. Metternich was by aptitude and training a diplomat rather than an administrator, and after 1815 he was inclined to rely too exclusively on diplomacy for the support of the existing system. Whatever one may think of him, however, he was not a mere fanatic of order; indeed, this eighteenth-century gentleman, who to the end of his life loved to read Voltaire, was not a fanatic of anything. His failure, in the long run, lay in the fact that he could think of no way of preserving what was except by preserving it as it was.

The internal condition of the Austrian Empire, which lay at the center of the Hapsburg domains, had been little affected by the Napoleonic wars; the population accepted the government's censorship and its paternal rule. The provinces of Austria, as well as the outlying sections of the empire inhabited by Czechs, Slovaks, Magyars, Rumanians, and Croats, had local diets which were constituted in the medieval fashion of estates. They met rarely and for brief sessions; that of Hungary had no meeting from 1812 to 1825. They possessed no real power. Throughout the empire there was practically no middle class, only nobles and peasants. The strongest parts of the government machine were the police and the army. The administration carefully distributed the latter; Hungarian regiments garrisoned Lombardy and Venetia, German soldiers were sent to Bohemia, and Croats defended Hungary. The central administration at Vienna, in striking contrast to that at Berlin, was not coördinated. There was no regularly organized ministry; each department went its own way or rusted in its groove. Metternich tried to improve this administrative chaos, but failed to make way against old privileges and vested interests.

In the German world outside Austria the princes drifted back into an eighteenth-century way of living. Heine effectively characterized the little German despotisms of the time: "When I was at the top of the St. Gotthard Pass, I heard Germany snoring. . . . She slept peacefully under the protection of her thirty-six monarchs. In those days, crowns sat firmly on the princes' heads, and at night they just drew their night caps over them, while the people slept peacefully at their feet." The thirty-nine German states, following the arrangements made at Vienna, were now united into a federated *Bund* under the presidency of Austria, though only a part of the Austrian Empire and a section of Prussia were included. In the Assembly of the Confederation the King of England was represented for Hanover, the King of Denmark for Holstein, and the King of Holland for Luxemburg. The loosely organized *Bund,* together with the great personal prestige enjoyed by Metternich, especially in Berlin, enabled the Hapsburgs to dominate the Germanies more effectively than at any time since the Thirty Years' War. In 1816 the representatives of the princes met for the first time in a Diet at Frankfort. It soon became evident that this aristocratic body, directed from Vienna and helpless without a real executive, an army, or a system of local administration, was not the unifying and democratic assembly of which German patriots had dreamed during the War of Liberation. Small groups of liberals and nationalists were not slow in starting agitation against the whole arrangement. Decade by decade their clamor increased. In 1847 Prince Hohenlohe called the Diet "the bed in which Germany has slumbered for thirty years." Earlier Görres had said that the *Bund* gave the German people "an unlimited right of expectation."

Within the various German states the promises of constitutions, made in the heart of the last conflict with Napoleon and embodied in Article XIII of the Federal Act, were only in part fulfilled. The Grand Duke of Saxe-Weimar was the first to grant a written constitution, and between 1818 and 1820 the rulers of Bavaria, Württemberg, Baden, and Hesse-Darmstadt took similar action. This was done in part to show their defiance of Austria and in part to get more enthusiastic support from the new districts added to their states by the Congress of Vienna. These constitutions, like the French Charter, were all royal grants; none recognized the sovereignty of the people. The suffrage was limited to a small group of wealthy landowners, and the administrative bureaucracy, as in France, often interfered in the elections.

All over the German world the liberals were waiting to see what Prussia would do. In May, 1815, Frederick William III had promised his people a constitution, but month after month passed and no such document was forthcoming. Behind the scenes in the royal court at Berlin a bitter quarrel was raging between Hardenberg, who had originally urged the monarch to grant a constitution, and an absolutist group led by Prince Wittgenstein, the agent of Metternich. Finally, in 1817, the Prussian monarch announced the creation of a Council of State, and it became evident that the project of a constitution had, for the time being, been abandoned. No action was taken toward the establishment of a central parliamentary order until 1823. Great was the disappointment of the German liberals and nationalists who, having hoped that

Prussia would take the lead, now looked to the south and central German states, rather than to Austria or Prussia, as the home of liberty and progress.

But Prussia was compensated for her loss of prestige in other ways. The Council of State, made up of princes of the royal house, heads of the army, departmental chiefs, and nobles from the various provinces, brought the scattered districts of Prussia under one central administration. With the help of a university-trained bureaucracy, which was just coming into use, the government in some measure redeemed a reactionary policy by developing the best administrative efficiency in Europe. Modern Prussia has been made not by legislators, but by the honest and capable administration of bureaucrats and soldiers. Public finance, the army, the educational system and, after 1818, the tariff régime were greatly improved. Between 1815 and 1866 the extension and improvement of the civil and military administration of Prussia did far more for German unification than did any other force.

A cartoon of the time of the War of Liberation showed the German people dragging their frightened princes out from under the table, setting them on their feet, and urging them to fight the usurper. Now the liberals complained that, although it was the German people who had defeated Napoleon, it was only these same cowardly princes who were profiting by the peace settlement. The universities became the chief centers of this discontent. Students returning from the wars in 1815 began to organize societies, *Burschenschaften,* to improve student morality, to break down the older types of local patriotism, and to stir the youth of the land with nationalist ideals. The leaders of the movement corresponded with each other and created a loose central organization for these societies, which by 1816 had members in sixteen German universities.

The most active of these student groups was at Jena, where the indulgence of the Grand Duke of Saxe-Weimar allowed the members to discuss and to publish freely, and to parade with their picturesque "Teutonic costumes" and their black, red and gold banners, the colors of a volunteer corps of the War of 1813. The Jena society in 1817 arranged a gathering of all the *Burschenschaften* at the Wartburg Castle, to celebrate the fourth anniversary of the Battle of Leipzig and the tercentenary of Luther's *Theses.* On October 17 about four hundred students from twelve universities assembled. Luther's "Ein' feste Burg" [7] was sung, speeches were made by professors from Jena and by a number of students, Luther and Blücher were praised, and the students were urged, in very general terms, to dedicate their lives to the "holy cause of union and freedom." In the evening one group formed a torchlight procession and marched to a hilltop opposite the castle. There, about a great bonfire, more

---

[7] ["A Mighty Fortress (is our God)"; one of Luther's most famous and popular hymns.]

speeches were made and several books, among them Kotzebue's *German History* . . . and the *Code Napoléon,* together with a corporal's cane, a wig and other symbols of tyranny were thrown into the flames. It was all a rather juvenile escapade, but the effect produced on the German world was great, for it was the first public protest against the settlement of 1815.

The *Burschenschaft* at the University of Giessen contained a small group of republicans led by Karl Follen, a brilliant student of law. He preached a mystical doctrine of republicanism and tyrannicide and even talked of assembling a mob on the battlefield of Leipzig and proclaiming a republic. In March, 1819, Karl Sand, a young and mentally unbalanced theological student and a follower of Follen, murdered the dramatist, Kotzebue, an agent of Alexander I of Russia. Shortly afterward a student in Nassau made an attack on the head of the government there. During his trial, Sand maintained that he had had no accomplices and that he had carried through his deed unaided. In spite of all efforts of the prosecution, no evidences of a general plot could be discovered. Sand was condemned to death. . . .

Metternich made capital of all this, and used the occasion to tighten his grip on the German states, especially on Prussia. . . . After the murder of Kotzebue, he called together representatives of the nine principal German states. They met at Carlsbad in August, 1819. While the British Parliament was considering the Six Acts, the German diplomats drew up a series of decrees. These were presented to the Diet at Frankfort on September 20 and this body, which had dragged out discussion of the Federal Act for more than four years, now ratified Metternich's Carlsbad Decrees in less than four hours. The decrees provided that the *Burschenschaften* and the gymnastic societies established by Jahn be dissolved, and that inspectors for each university and censors for the press be appointed, both of which provisions strengthened the power of the secret police. At a conference of representatives of some of the German princes held at Vienna in 1820 a so-called Final Act was agreed upon. The resistance of the governments of Bavaria and Württemberg to the growing power of Metternich made it impossible to force them to withdraw their constitutions. Nevertheless, Metternich now obtained from all the governments an agreement limiting the subjects which might be discussed in the Chambers. All the delegates recognized the right of the federal organs to intervene in any state where the legislature dared to assert its supremacy over the monarch.

The conference at Carlsbad in 1819 had created a Federal Commission at Mainz to study the discontent in the Germanies and to keep the governments informed. This commission continued to function for nearly eight years, and, though it was never able to discover any organized plot, it instituted proceedings against 161 individuals of whom forty-four were acquitted. Metternich was convinced that the secret societies all over Europe, and especially those in Germany and Italy, had an effective central organization in each country as well as an international bureau. Neither assumption has ever been proved. A few radicals, above all an Italian exile, Buonarroti, who lived in Geneva, dreamed of such an international liberal organization. They corresponded and conspired to further the idea, but without any important results.

At the conferences called at Austria's behest between 1817 and 1820, Metternich succeeded in frightening the tsar, the King of Prussia, and the monarchs of most of the German states. After 1819 the persecution of liberals increased. In Prussia, Jahn was imprisoned, Arndt lost his position at the University of Bon, and Görres fled to Strasbourg. Spies were sent to hear the sermons of Schleiermacher, Stein was watched by the police, and Börne was forced to flee from Hesse-Darmstadt. By 1820 it was clear to German liberals that both Austria and Prussia, the two states which could force through a program of German unification, were hostile to liberty. The great hopes raised by the War of Liberation were not to be realized easily.

THE HAPSBURG DOMINATION IN MIDDLE EUROPE:
THE ITALIAN STATES

Much the same situation existed in Italy as among the German states. There was a similar apathy and indifference on the part of the masses and the same disappointment and restlessness in higher circles of the population. But discontent was more widespread than in Germany. Italy had suffered less and gained more from the changes made by the French Revolution than either Spain or Germany. For nearly two decades the Italians had had excellent codes of law, a fair system of taxation, a better economic situation, and more religious and intellectual toleration than they had known for centuries. At the same time, the populace had been surprised to see how easily the temporal power of the pope could be abolished and their monarchs driven into exile. Everywhere old physical, economic, and intellectual barriers had been thrown down and the Italians had begun to be aware of a common nationality.

The last years of the Empire, with the theft of art works, the Continental Blockade, the heavy taxes, and the conscription, had made Napoleon's imperial rule as hated in Italy as it was elsewhere. Hence his overthrow was widely acclaimed. When it became evident, however, that Austria would use all her powers to restore the Ancien Régime, Italian liberals at once protested. The peace settlement was made at Vienna without any consideration whatever for

Italian hopes. It doomed Italy to remain, until 1860, the mere "geographical expression" of Metternich. Over the whole peninsula lay the shadow of Hapsburg domination. Austria's influence in Italian affairs had grown steadily through the eighteenth century, and the settlement of 1815 simply completed the process. Austria ensured her control by her dynastic connections with the reigning Italian families, by a treaty with Naples and another with Tuscany, and by the use of the secret police of all the Italian states who were obliged to report to the Austrian authorities. As the system worked out, the secret police of the various states, coöperating with that of Austria, functioned as a sort of Hapsburg administrative system from one end of the peninsula to the other. This political police aroused a profound abhorrence among the Italians. The irritation created was precisely of the kind which the patriots could most effectively use. The dark machinations of the political spy could be set off most effectively against the life of the shining young patriot-hero who was caught in the subtle toils of the police and was delivered over to a martyr's fate of prison, exile, or death.

In the individual states, the governments set up by the returning rulers combined the worst features of the old order and of the French rule, the obscurantism of the former, and the political police and the foreign control of the latter. Some French institutions were abolished; those that remained lost their effectiveness because of the policies of the restored rulers. In the south, including three-eighths of the peninsula, was the Kingdom of the Two Sicilies. The monarch, Ferdinand I, an ignorant reactionary like his nephew, the King of Spain, was bound by a secret treaty with Austria not to introduce liberal reforms. At Metternich's bidding he abolished the Constitution which, in 1812, the British had helped introduce in Sicily, and which Ferdinand had promised to observe. He restored many of the monastic lands, invited in the Jesuits, and reconstituted the Holy Office. His chief minister, Canosa, summed up the royal theory of government when he remarked that "the first servant of the crown should be the executioner." The police, though unable to curb the worst brigandage in western Europe, committed such atrocities on liberals that the representatives of England and Russia protested. The lower elements of the population were miserably poor and sunk in superstition, laziness, and filth. They remained strongly royalist and clerical and after 1815 were frequently used by the government against the middle class liberals.

In the Papal States conditions were not much better. Consalvi, who had served the papacy so well at Vienna, tried to introduce reforms in local administration, but he could make no headway against the Zelanti, the reactionary party at the papal court. So he turned his efforts to furthering the

European interests of the Holy See. All the innovations introduced by the French, from law courts to vaccination, were abolished, priests filled all the public offices, and "the images of the Madonna again began to roll their eyes." Brigandage was nearly as bad as in the Kingdom of the Two Sicilies. The police spent much time in hunting down "a class called thinkers." At times there were in Rome, besides many political prisoners, as many as three thousand suspects confined to their houses between sundown and sunrise. The general administration of the Papal States was so wretched that in 1821 the powers issued a common note of complaint against the abuses. Characterizing the situation with much foresight, the Piedmontese ambassador wrote, "It is only reasonable to suppose that, if the present state of things continues in Rome, some fundamental crisis will take place. The most probable outcome is that the great city will become merely an ecclesiastical capital, retaining only the shadow of imperial power."

In the rest of the Italian states a fairly honest administration was combined with political tyranny and repression. The ablest monarch among the rulers of the four duchies, Modena, Parma, Tuscany, and Lucca, was Francis IV of Modena. He was a treacherous and ambitious man, who was regarded by the liberals as a sort of Cesare Borgia. After his restoration he spent his best energies intriguing to gain more power in the peninsula. Although he was generous in his treatment of the poor, he feared and persecuted the middle class. In Tuscany, the Hapsburg Archduke Ferdinand III and his chief minister, Fossombroni—whose dicutm was "Tomorrow, tomorrow—dinner will spoil, the state will wait"—returned to the political methods of eighteenth-century despotism. The government gave shelter to refugees from the Romagna and Naples; it permitted the publication after 1820 of the *Antologia,* a liberal literary review; and allowed the Florentines to send help to the Greek insurgents. Florence was the only Italian city where the dramas of Alfieri and Niccolini could be played. Still, the archduke's government irritated the people by maintaining an elaborate system of spies, and amused them when, on the discovery of Giotto's portrait of Dante beneath the whitewash on the walls of the Bargello, it had the colors altered lest they suggest the revolutionary tricolor. Commerce and manufacture flourished under a laissez-faire régime, and the easy-going Tuscans seem to have been reasonably contented.

In the Kingdom of Piedmont Victor Emmanuel I and his staff returned to Turin wearing powdered wigs, and the monarch soon instituted a general clearing-out of much that the French had introduced. As in Lombardy and Tuscany, the Jesuits were excluded, and the secular clergy were controlled by the state. In a certain old-fashioned honesty and efficiency of administration, and in the attention paid to the army, the Kingdom of Piedmont resembled Prussia. Yet the young Cavour, living in Turin, a "city half-barracks and half-cloister," found his native land "an intellectual hell." Economically the country prospered, profiting especially from the annexation in 1815 of the great port of Genoa.

The richest and the best administered section in all Italy was the Lombard-Venetian Kingdom, a territory which conferred on its possessor the strategic keys to the peninsula, the four great fortresses of Mantua, Verona, Peschiera, and Legnago, known as the Quadrilateral. In spite of some traces of local self-government, the two provinces were ruled directly from Vienna. The Austrian government built excellent roads and bridges and introduced the best system of state education that existed anywhere in Italy. These advantages, however, could not hide the fact that the Hapsburg rule, in matters of policing, taxation, and tariff policy treated the provinces like conquered territories. The censorship was so severe that even the works of Dante had to be expurgated. Metternich reminded the inhabitants that "the Lombards must forget that they are Italians." Milan had the most cultivated aristocracy and the most prosperous middle class in Italy. In these circles the rule of Austria became very unpopular. . . . From Sicily to the Alps Italy, like Germany, was ultimately ruled from the Hofburg in Vienna.

As the whole life of the Italian people had been more deeply affected by the changes of the French Revolution than that of the Germans or Spaniards, it was natural that after 1815 the hatred of reaction should be more widespread. This dissatisfaction took different forms, each of which in turn contributed to the freeing of Italy. Among the intellectuals in the north the nationalist propaganda of a group of literary men began to take root. During the revolution Alfieri, the father of modern Italian patriotic literature, had used his dramas to denounce all forms of arbitrary government and had preached the ideal of a free and united Italy. Although he died in 1803, his influence increased, and many a Carbonaro knew by heart long passages from his tragedies. In the next decades a series of novels and plays and poems by Foscolo, Berchet, Pellico, Manzoni, Niccolini, Giordani, and Leopardi emphasized the value of literature as a means of arousing a new spirit of national unity among the Italian people. . . . The movement took deep hold of the rising generation; Mazzini, Cavour, and Garibaldi all found Foscolo's novels the most inspiring reading of their youth. Few of these literary men were members of the Carbonari, though Pellico joined the sect and took part in the conspiracy that produced the Revolution of 1821. He and several others suffered exile or imprisonment. Their ideas of the glories of Italian culture and their hope for a brighter national future spread in the universities. The results were seen after 1820 when the universities began to furnish to the nationalist movement its thinkers and writers.

The only organized opposition to the existing order, before 1831, took the form of secret societies. During the Napoleonic period groups which resembled the *Tugendbund* [8] in Germany had been organized against "the Usurper." These organizations, like the liberal associations in Spain, and after 1821 in France, were often recruited in part from the membership of the Freemasonic lodges. Originally the lodges had been favorable to Napoleon, who had used them to stabilize his régime. But in the later days of the Empire they had turned against him. From the Freemasons the liberal secret societies borrowed their complicated system of organization, their ritual of initiation, and certain signs and passwords. The lodges and the secret societies, after 1815, usually maintained friendly relations, though most of the conspiring was done in the secret political associations. The earliest of these was the Carbonari of Naples, founded before 1810. Gradually similar groups were formed in the other states, the Federati in Piedmont, the Guelfi in Bologna, the Adelphi in Lombardy. Before the downfall of Napoleon these societies had been strongly clerical and opposed to the French régime, but after 1815 they became liberal and nationalist in purpose. Thousands flocked into these organizations. There were between fifty and a hundred thousand members in the Kingdom of the Two Sicilies alone in 1820. This large membership included some criminals and adventurers, but the majority was made up of doctors, lawyers, students, overtaxed small proprietors, civil and military officers who had served under the Napoleonic régime, and some of the lower clergy.

These groups corresponded with each other, though they had no central organization, as the governments believed. Beyond a hatred of Austria and of tyranny in general, they had no common program. In Sicily the secret societies wanted the expulsion of the Neapolitans; on the mainland the Neapolitan groups plotted for the establishment of a constitutional régime; in the Papal States the conspirators hoped for a government by laymen; and in Piedmont they wished to introduce a constitution. Some were liberal monarchists; others were republicans. As Mazzini pointed out later, their great weakness lay in their failure to think and plan in terms of the whole peninsula. Despite their poor organization and the lack of a common program the secret societies were able in 1820 to start a revolution in Naples and in 1821 in Piedmont. By that time discontent was wide and deep, and, as time was to show, neither police vigilance, nor the galley, nor the gallows was able to stamp it out. Persecution only fanned and scattered the smoldering flame.

[8] [*League of Virtue;* a secret society of German students, 1808–16.]

Chapter III

THE INDUSTRIALIZATION OF SOCIETY

🙠

O N THE DAY when the nineteenth century began its weird and glorious
history, the United States was a nation of almost four million people
and France was a political threat for all Europe. Within less than
ten years after that day, the United States controlled the lion's share of one of
the world's richest continents, while France under her soldier emperor had
virtually converted Europe into a single political unit. Yet in spite of these
remarkable events, it is neither to the United States nor to France that one
must turn in order to find the vital forces which were molding the modern
economic world. Once again, the economic laboratory was England, and
once again the experiments were fraught with importance for the entire world.

The major cause for England's economic progress by 1700 had proved to
be the efficiency of her business organizations; the secret of her still greater
progress by 1800 can be attributed to the combination of these organizations
with improved industrial technology. Revolutionary methods in the metallurgical industries, revolutionary machinery in textile manufacturing, together with the use of water and steam power, produced a wholly different
apparatus of production. Meantime agriculture underwent a complementary
development. Commercial changes in the sixteenth and seventeenth centuries
had hastened the growth of population. The resulting pressure on food supply
set in motion a new tendency toward land enclosure, a process which rapidly
gathered momentum in the last four decades of the eighteenth century and
changed rural England from a nation of open fields to one of enclosed separate
farms. The physical changes involved in this enclosure movement were more
visible but far less important than the social alterations which accompanied the
rearrangement of the land. In the course of seventy-five years, the small landowners practically disappeared, while the places of these sturdy yeomen were
taken by wage-earning agricultural laborers hired by business or gentlemen
farmers who administered large and often huge estates. Boldly defying tradi-

This chapter is from *Some Origins of the Modern Economic World* (pp. 63–94; New York,
The Macmillan Co., 1935) by E. A. J. Johnson.

tion, a few of these capitalist farmers experimented with new crops, new techniques, and new machinery. Their example slowly convinced others, so that the nineteenth century brought in to British agriculture a new era which relied upon a co-operation of science and capitalism.

These same elements were combined by a new race of industrial leaders who revolutionized the technology of the textile and metal industries. By harnessing fire and water through the use of machinery, they produced a system of production which involved heavy investments in fixed form. At the same time, the new scheme required concentration of laborers in large workshops. Like the "putting-out system," this new mode of industrial organization employed the wage system, but it added a new discipline of factory hours and the supervision of foremen and superintendents. The new technology and the new discipline geared up production to unprecedented speed; for the fallible skill of the artisan there was substituted the automatic regularity of the machine. Regularity and mechanical precision became indeed the chief productive virtues of the new industrial process; a new, impersonal kind of skill was thereby born which made possible the mass production of the modern world.

Hand in hand with agricultural and industrial metamorphosis went a more remarkable commercial expansion than the world had ever seen. Tireless textile machinery fed out millions of bolts of cloth for merchants to sell. To America, Asia, Europe, and Africa flowed inexpensive cottons: light comfortable cloth which rapidly replaced coarse, homespun flax or woolen textiles, and catered to the wants of very ordinary people. To remote parts of the world went also English hardware, cutlery, and other manufactures which new methods had cheapened. England saw visions promising that she would become the "workshop of the world" whose products would be sold in every important foreign market.

By 1800, England in her economic organization was therefore far ahead of other nations. In agriculture she had definitely abandoned medieval organization; in industry, her factory system and machine methods had shown their technical advantages; in commerce, her world had grown larger both territorially and numerically. Meantime the organization of all departments of English economic life had not only grown more capitalistic but in industry the form of capitalism had undergone significant change. Because of the far-reaching importance of these inter-related developments in agriculture, industry, and commerce, each segment of England's economic structure in 1800 must be analyzed separately.

During the hundred years from 1700 to 1800, England's population had grown by almost three millions. This rapid natural increase could be fed because English agriculture became far more efficient in the eighteenth century than ever before. Large quantities of capital were invested in drainage, in soil improvement and in better livestock. The expensive medieval system of fallowing ground was gradually abandoned; indeed it could be abandoned because superior ways of enriching the soil were discovered experimentally. New agricultural methods were definitely hastened also by land enclosure. By itself, enclosure did not make land more productive; it did, however, create a legal framework within which new experiments could be conducted, and it thereby released the initiative and enterprise which characterized the eighteenth century.

The condemned and lamented enclosure movement of Elizabethan and Jacobean days had practically spent itself by the end of the first quarter of the seventeenth century. Quantitatively, this early tendency toward agricultural reorganization had not been extremely important; moreover the majority of fields enclosed had been carved out of demesne or common waste land. Except for the continued exchange of strips and the resulting accumulation of compact bundles, arable fields had remained practically undisturbed. The government, moreover, definitely disapproved the earlier enclosure movement. Eager to achieve stability in a changing economic world, the Tudors staunchly resisted any and all forces which threatened to produce violent change; consequently, commissioners of enclosure were appointed (first under Edward VI) to investigate complaints about the conversion of arable fields into sheepwalks. By the eighteenth century, all this was changed. Parliament was now dominated by landlords whose economic interests were untowardly affected by the disparity between rising prices and fixed rents. Their circumstances demanded means for increasing the revenues derived from the soil, and with the approval of Parliament they set about to enclosure the time-sanctioned open fields and pastures.

The process of enclosure within a specific village began by a petition addressed to Parliament by the leading landowners requesting the passage of a Bill of Enclosure. Although the petition required the assent of the owners of four-fifths of the land, enough concentration of ownership already existed in many areas to make only a few signatures necessary. In theory, Parliament was next required to investigate the probable effect of enclosure upon the rights of all members of the particular agricultural community in which enclosure was proposed. Actually, the small landholders found it too expensive to present their objections, and it seems clear that in hundreds of instances the interests of landowning minorities were disregarded cavalierly. When enclosure had been authorized, the lands of the village community were surveyed, parcelled out, and fenced at the recipient's cost. Loss of common pasture right or common waste privileges were theoretically compensated by individual areas of land now held in severalty. But in practice, the entire process of reorganization fell into the hands of the lords, the large commoners, and the local rector. In the interests of this group, the whole structure of land-holding was recast; in their interest, the traditional common privileges of thousands of small farmers were abruptly and ruthlessly cancelled.

The importance of the eighteenth-century enclosures can be appreciated both from the extent and the rapidity of the process. From 1702 to 1797, Parliament passed 1,776 enclosure acts which authorized the creation of fenced fields out of 3,142,374 acres which had hitherto lain common.[1] The small landholder, as Mantoux has so accurately said, "could but look on helplessly while these changes took place. . . . He could not prevent the commissioners reserving the best lands for richer men. He was constrained to accept the lot assigned for him, even though he might not consider it an equivalent of his former property." Before enclosure, the small farmers' activities in arable and pasture farming had been spatially distinct; on their lands, in the open fields they raised their grain, while on the common pastures, they grazed their animals. After enclosure, the small farmers had but single plots of land for both arable and pasture uses. Except for differences in the soil, the poorer yeomen were not untowardly affected in the amounts of arable land; in pasture, however, they were infinitely poorer. If a small landowner's rateable share of a partitioned common pasture proved to be one acre, private ownership of this additional acre was by no means equivalent to a former privilege of pasturing, for example, several sheep, a cow, and a flock of geese on the commons. Left poorer by enclosure, the small farmers did not long survive and their exodus from the agricultural villages constituted a veritable social revolution in the closing years of the eighteenth century and the beginning of the nineteenth.

[1] The gathering momentum may be seen from the increase in enclosure during the course of the century:

	No. of Acts	Acres Involved
1702–1714	2	1,439
1714–1727	16	17,960
1727–1760	226	318,778
1760–1797	1,532	2,804,197

The new status of the cotters was even more precarious than that of the small yeomen. Although cotters had previously possessed no legal right to common land whatever, they had used the commons. Deprived of these extra-legal privileges, they were actually pauperized by enclosure. As long as the woolen industry flourished, some of the impoverished cotters could find employment; parallel developments in industry, however, rapidly weakened the old domestic cloth industry. Caught between the upper millstone of land enclosure and the lower millstone of rural industrial decay, the cotters and small landholders had usually but three alternatives: to leave their ancestral homes, to find employment as agricultural wage earners, or to become dependent on local poor relief.

Thus by undermining the economic security of small landholders and cotters, the eighteenth-century English enclosure movement precipitated two much decried results: depopulation of the countryside [2] and concentration of landowning. After a few years of bitter struggle, many small landowners were glad enough to sell their small fenced plots to their prosperous neighbors. A stream of small yeomen and cotters tore up their long established roots and trekked away from the ancient villages to seek their fortunes in the rising industrial towns or abroad. Mobility, which could be achieved in the medieval world only by flight or by payment of *chevage,* was now an indirect consequence of Parliamentary action. Unforseen and unintended, the development of capitalistic agriculture helped to produce that strong tendency toward personal mobility which was to become characteristic of the modern economic world!

Although the redistribution of the land involved untold hardship, the effect upon agricultural efficiency was salutary. Technical progress had been practically impossible in the open fields and common pastures. Methods of crop rotation had necessarily been uniform, inhibiting experiment, while systematic stock-breeding was out of the question. Mongrel cattle roamed over the close-cropped common pastures, lean, scrawny, half-starved creatures weighing less than half as much as modern cattle. Enclosure provided every farmer, intelligent enough to experiment, with his own laboratory, wherein he could embark on new crop rotations, and wherein he could develop his livestock by systematic breeding. Not very many eighteenth-century farmers availed themselves of these opportunities. The crust of custom had indeed been broken by the enclosure movement, but many a year was yet to pass before the hard understructure of customary agricultural methods could be

[2] Goldsmith's "Deserted Village" voiced the concern of many Englishmen over depopulation of the countryside.

dissipated and destroyed by the example of a few pioneers of scientific agriculture.

Yet one must not underestimate the influence of these pioneers. In spite of criticism, adverse fortune, and unpopularity, they continued their experiments. Converts to new methods at first were few, but they did increase, and gradually knowledge of the new techniques spread. Science became more and more the handmaiden of the farmer, a union slowly becoming characteristic. Out of this union were to come innumerable blessings in the form of better crops; larger, fatter, and more nutritive animals; together with a progressive reduction of the proportion of total labor supply devoted to farming. Modern agriculture can properly be said to have originated in England during the eighteenth century. A few remarks about some of the persons responsible for these far-reaching innovations are therefore appropriate.

The most effective popularizer of new methods of cultivation and crop rotation was indisputably Jethro Tull. He combined in rare degree theoretical knowledge and practical realism. His writings were based on years of careful research and painstaking experiment. Deep ploughing, persistent cultivation, and continuous rotation, he regarded as the three recipes for abundant harvests. Old-fashioned farmers held the new methods in contempt but fortunately Tull found a devoted disciple in Charles, second Viscount Townshend who retired from political life in 1730 and devoted himself to agriculture. Following Tull's advice, he experimented with clover and turnips, drilling in his seed rather than sowing it broadcast, and devised a standard four-crop rotation. By these methods Townshend converted his previously barren, sandy, wastes into rich productive land; increased his rents, and prospered. Meantime another agricultural pioneer had achieved scientific results in stock-breeding fully as important as those of Jethro Tull in arable farming. Robert Bakewell, the popularizer of scientific stock-breeding was a yeoman farmer; as a consequence, his new methods were more quickly adopted than those of Tull and Townshend. By careful inbreeding, Bakewell developed compact, small-boned sheep, which were easy to fatten and which could therefore be quickly prepared for market. . . . Bakewell's sheep possessed high value not merely in wool but also as butcher meat. Systematic breeding and close attention to feeding made it possible for Bakewell to produce wholly new types of cattle as well. His great success, however, was with sheep, although in all departments of stock-breeding he had shown the way. Other breeders followed his example with amazing results. Whereas the average weight of cattle at Smithfield market was only 370 pounds in 1710, after the new experiments of Bakewell and his followers were adopted, the average rose to 800 pounds in 1795. Yet although Tull, Townshend, and Bakewell had laid the groundwork for better arable and pasture farming, the diffusion of these and other new methods can largely be attributed to Arthur Young. In his voluminous writings, Young assembled a great fund of information about agricultural methods, systems of land tenure, condition of roads, and kindred subjects. A militant crusader for better farming, Young travelled extensively, observing agricultural practices, and lecturing to thousands of farmers on the advantages of enclosure and systematic farming. The government recognized the importance of his educational work by choosing him as secretary for the Board of Agriculture when that organization was created in 1793.

By the beginning of the nineteenth century, many of the principles upon which modern agriculture is based were already established in England. Agricultural pioneers had revealed the advantages of enclosed fields, of scientific experiment, and of investment of capital in land improvement. Farming had been changed from the servile occupation of medieval times; it was now a calling appropriate to nobility or king.[3] Indeed farming became fashionable with rather peculiar benefits inasmuch as the fashion brought into agriculture persons of ability and wealth, persons able to understand the importance of science, and financially competent to assume the risks of experiment. As a consequence, capital was invested in better breeding stock, in better implements, in subsurface drainage, and in fertilizers. Meantime chemistry had emerged as a most useful science, and as early as 1757, Francis Home had pointed out the importance of chemistry in agriculture. By the turn of the century, the Board of Agriculture had appointed, as its Professor of Chemistry, Humphry Davy, who for a decade lectured on agricultural chemistry.

England had therefore provided a laboratory wherein these important experiments in agriculture were conducted. A small but extremely influential group of educated farmers had emerged, who transformed farming from a tradition-hampered occupation to a capitalistic-scientific business. Financial costs of experiment confined the new ways of agriculture to persons with means. The new methods came therefore to be associated with capitalist farmers whose interests in agriculture were primarily pecuniary. At their hands, as Lord Ernle has said, "farms ceased to be self-sufficing industries, and became factories of beef and mutton." Yet making money in agriculture depended very largely upon creating more and better farm products and, as

[3] George III had a model farm at Windsor and took great pride in his nickname, "farmer George."

a result, the agricultural pioneers by their capitalist inspiration gave impetus
to that feverish quest for new ways of increasing agricultural productivity
which has finally created an awkward dilemma for the modern world.

The dramatic changes in agriculture, which the eighteenth century had
witnessed, were paralleled by even more far-reaching transformations in English commerce and industry. Markets widened with unprecedented rapidity,
and the very increase in demand generated boldness of business policy. Meantime a great burst of invention revolutionized the technology of the textile
and the metallurgical industries. The combined result was an epoch-making
change which historians since 1837 have called the "Industrial Revolution."
Actually, the forces which had slowly been developing were now rapidly
producing effect; the so-called "revolution" was really the fruition of a long
series of preparatory changes. Capitalist reorganization of agriculture provided one of the most important domestic events of a preparatory nature. At
the same time, commercial development opened up larger outlets for English
manufactured products, as well as sources of new imports. Increased demand
soon brought pressure on the apparatus of production, and a set of most remarkable technical changes occurred as a result.

The growth of England's foreign trade during the eighteenth century may
be roughly measured by the increase in the tons of shipping leaving English
ports. Fully six times the tonnage cleared the customs in 1800 as in 1700. Although the joint-stock companies and the regulated companies had opened up
world markets, they were unable to keep these areas completely monopolized.
Harrassed on the sea by privateers, and hampered at home by jealous competitors able to enlist Parliamentary aid, the exclusive trading companies lost
their commercial advantages. London, which had been the center of seventeenth-century foreign trade, encountered increasing competition from ports
in the west and the north of England. India, America, and Africa became
lucrative areas of foreign trade, and the latter two continents proved especially
profitable areas of exploitation for the merchants of Bristol and Liverpool. The
East India Company still continued to be the greatest single company dealing
with that vast area which Lord Clive conquered, bringing from this densely
populated land spices, silks, and cotton textiles. Meantime, England's expansion into the Caribbean had created a large market for slaves, while commercial privileges obtained by the Treaty of Utrecht gave England a still
larger market for negroes. Sugar, grain, lumber, and tobacco made up the

major commodities which the British colonies in America yielded. These specified articles of trade from India, Africa, or America were either imports or re-exports. With what were they purchased? The answer to this question reveals the wide variety of industrial occupations already flourishing in England. Woolens and worsteds, hardware, coal, earthenware, pewter, brass; these were England's chief exports; but to this list must be added a host of unimpressive commodities, ranging from buttons to snuff-boxes. With such prosaic goods, English merchants purchased the rare textiles of the Orient, the strong black slaves of Africa (for re-export), and the raw materials of America.

The ancient woolen and worsted industry found the new trend of English trade distinctly disadvantageous. Tropical and subtropical areas provided no market for woolens. At the same time, the imported Indian silks and calicos proved far more comfortable than English woolens. As a result, the domestic demand for woolens declined, causing the clothiers to make bitter war on the India Company. For a time Parliament could not decide whether to favor the importers or the wool manufacturers, but although the India Company was strongly entrenched, the complaints of the woolen industry could not be disregarded. The beginnings of a policy of protection for England's ancient industry may be discerned from such hesitant legislation as that of 1665 which required that every person who died in England be buried in a woolen shroud, or from that of 1697 requiring judges, students, and professors to wear woolen gowns. The woolen manufacturers, however, demanded something more than these cumbersome gestures; they pressed for vigorous legislation and succeeded in obtaining a prohibition against Indian fabrics in 1700, and in 1721 the passage of a law which forbade the wearing of printed or painted calicos.

Although the Calico Act was expressly intended to protect the English woolen and silk industry against the competition of cotton textiles, there are, as Professor Usher has said, "few instances in history of so great a discrepancy between expectations and results." In spite of the threat of a £20 fine which hung over the head of every wearer of calico, and in spite of the £5 reward offered to informers, the wearing of cotton cloth apparently could not be curbed. As a concession to popular demand for lighter textiles, the Manchester Act of 1735 legalized the wearing of cloth made from an admixture of cotton and linen. Actually Parliament in attempting to succor the woolen industry had succeeded in protecting England's feeble domestic cotton industry from East Indian competition. Growing slowly but soundly, the English cotton industry practically doubled during the first half of the eighteenth century.

Not until 1774 was the Calico Act repealed. Almost immediately after came more new inventions which made the English cotton industry not merely as efficient as that of the Orient but more! Thus commerce had provided wage-earning consumers with textiles more attractive than woolens. An effort to protect the English wool manufacturers against the competition of Oriental cloth actually helped to build up England's domestic cotton industry. This unintended protection created an industry which was in turn compelled to resort to the use of machinery in order to compete with cheap Oriental cotton textiles in world markets. Finally, by the use of machinery, such an advantage was gained that England became the foremost cotton manufacturing nation in the entire world. The history of the English cotton industry is therefore an episode of great importance. It clearly revealed to the modern world (as did also the iron industry) the importance of machinery in industrial production.

To refer to the eighteenth century in England as an "age of invention" is accurate enough if one does not imply by that phrase any singular or mysterious manifestation of mental activity. Modern biology and psychology have revealed that inventive capacity is widely distributed while the history of science has clearly demonstrated that a single invention is not an isolated occurrence but in reality the synthesis of a previous set of unintegrated innovations and discoveries. Yet the actual exercise of latent inventive capacity is forcefully stimulated by environmental conditions; only in this sense is "necessity the mother of invention." Educational forces and economic circumstances in eighteenth-century England co-operated in inducing a wholly unprecedented exercise of hitherto unused inventive capacity, and succeeded in producing a very remarkable set of mechanical and chemical inventions. But far more important than the single episode of new invention was the heritage which was passed on to the modern economic world. The educational forces have been carefully preserved, making invention a normal and regularly expected event of our generation. Professor Whitehead once said that the greatest invention was really the "invention of invention!" Substantially this is what eighteenth-century England accomplished.

Textile machinery began in the woolen industry but found its first real area of usefulness in cotton manufacturing. Two questions immediately arise. Why did machinery emerge in an industry so highly organized as woolen manufacturing under the putting-out system? Why did it proceed faster and farther in a new industry rather than an old? The answer to the first question centers around certain obvious shortcomings of the clothiers' productive organization and around increasing insistence on quality cloth by cloth-buyers. The answer to the second illustrates clearly the amount of control which dispersed cloth-workers actually possessed over the woolen and worsted industry. By terrorism they delayed the use of machinery in the woolen industry.

So successful had the facilities for marketing English cloth become by the first quarter of the eighteenth century that the network of clothier organized cloth-workers could scarcely keep pace. Relative scarcity of weavers, together with an insistent demand for wider cloth, provided the occasion which called forth the inventive power of John Kay. A combination of a skilled weaver and a good mechanic, Kay had a total experience large enough to appreciate the limitations of the traditional looms. Cloths over thirty inches wide required two weavers to pass the shuttle back and forth. By combining simple mechanical principles, long familiar, Kay made it possible for one person to weave wide cloth. His "fly shuttle" was equipped with wheels and was shot back and forth over a traverse raceway by the alternate impact of suspended hammers. The invention proved doubly important: its use increased the speed of weaving at the same time that it reduced the man-power needed, and its extended use made yarn relatively scarce so that spinning came to be the bottle-neck which now definitely obstructed the expansion of the textile industry.

Although experiments with spinning machinery had been made before the middle of the eighteenth century, no successful machine was produced. Meantime the extended use of the fly shuttle had, by 1760, thrown the textile industry out of balance. This widely appreciated situation proved to be the environmental basis for another manifestation of inventive capacity. The first practical spinning machine which resulted may be said to be similar to the fly shuttle in one respect—it was a mechanical, hand-operated device. The inventor, James Hargreaves, a weaver and carpenter, realized, as did every other weaver, that relative scarcity of yarn was an important cause for weavers' unemployment. He found a practical solution for a problem which many mechanics and millwrights were trying to solve. His spinning "jenny," a multiple spinning wheel operating several spindles and provided with a mechanical carriage for drawing the threads, involved no change in the organization of the spinning industry. No special workshops were needed; neither was the cost of a machine prohibitive for well-circumstanced spinners.

The fly shuttle and the spinning jenny were therefore complementary, one improving the quality and increasing the output of cloth, the other accomplishing like results in spinning. But mechanical spinning made slow headway in the woolen industry. Spinners, who had experienced a little wave of prosperity after the introduction of the fly shuttle, bitterly opposed the new machines and there began a long period of industrial terrorism and sabotage which persisted for almost a half century. The woolen industry was England's "ancient trade," its very antiquity had rendered its personnel resistant to change. As a consequence, it was in the cotton industry, unhampered by tradition and circumstantially protected, that the new machines found an area of real usefulness.

Correlative with technical innovations in weaving and spinning came necessarily a tremendous interest on the part of the public. Meantime, throughout the eighteenth century, scientific inquiry had increased rapidly. Scientific bodies like the Royal Society had collected, in its *Philosophical Transactions,* all kinds of ingenious proposals for practical application of mechanical principles, while organizations like the Society of Arts offered prizes for a successful spinning machine. Popular interest and scientific information therefore combined to create a most hospitable atmosphere for the work of inventors. Unlike Kay and Hargreaves, both of whom were engaged in cloth-making, the next outstanding figure in the history of textile machinery was a rank outsider. Barber and wig-maker though he was by trade, Richard Arkwright not only patented a remarkable spinning machine, but established factories in which his machinery was used, and accumulated a huge fortune as a successful cotton manufacturer. Arkwright may therefore be regarded as the founder of the factory system since it was he, more than anyone else, who had the entrepreneurial boldness to break definitely with the great body of traditional practices which previously governed the organization of the textile trades. It was he who combined vigorous managerial ability with scientific technology and helped lay the foundations for a type of industrial production which has become characteristic in the modern economic world.

Arkwright's "water frame," although not original with him,[4] was based on the principle which underlies the method most commonly employed in modern spinning: twisting by means of grooved rollers and drawing by proportionately faster rotation of a series of rollers. This principle had been discovered as early as 1738 by Lewis Paul and John Wyatt and had apparently been used by Thomas Highs[5] in 1767, the same year that Hargreaves patented the jenny. The appearance of Arkwright's machine nevertheless marks a turning point in the textile industry. Whereas the fly shuttle and the spinning jenny were more complex machines than any previously employed, they were still hand-

[4] After two lawsuits against alleged infringers of his patent (one lost, the other won) Arkwright's competitors in turn brought suit against him for fraudulently patenting Thomas Highs' invention. A jury found Arkwright guilty in 1785, and the Crown accordingly cancelled his patent.

[5] Who apparently accomplished something quite frequent in the history of invention: a rediscovery of a device previously invented.

operated tools, designed to be used in the old scheme of organization. Arkwright's machine required power [6] as well as relatively heavy investments in fixed form. Yet large and permanent investment as a requisite for industrial production was not a new thing; ocean shipping, mining, and iron-making had for a long time required large investment. But the combination of machinery, power, permanent investment, and regimentation of industrial laborers, was substantially new. In this sense, the factory system, involving a divorce of ownership of tools [7] from artisanship, can with propriety be dated from the establishment of Arkwright's water-power cotton mill in 1771. From that time, industrial capital rather than trading capital pushes forward as a significant element in industrial production.

Arkwright's amazing business career cannot here be described. One or two episodes, however, are so important that a few words of explanation are necessary. Roller spinning produced precision twisting and drawing, yielding finer thread. This technical advantage made it possible to weave fine, pure cotton cloth by means of the water frame. Arkwright's competitors, unable to make use of the new invention because of his patent rights, protested to Parliament that production of pure cotton cloth violated the Manchester Act which, it will be recalled, had only legalized cloth produced from an admixture of linen and cotton. Undaunted, Arkwright appealed to Parliament, pointed out the national importance of developing the cotton industry, and, singlehanded, persuaded Parliament in 1774 to repeal the legislation which obstructed his business. The next year this erstwhile barber obtained another patent which covered a series of integrated textile machinery including devices for carding, roving,[8] and for feeding raw cotton into the carding machines. These inventions,[9] together with the water frame, converted cotton manufacture into a machine system of interdependent parts, driven by water-power, a system which embraced the entire process except weaving. Hence the manufacture of thread was now technically in advance, and once again weaving became the bottle-neck of clothmaking.

Technical apparatus, however, does not by itself constitute a factory system, but Arkwright's genius soon provided the missing ingredients. He was a born captain of industry. If he lacked capital, he was able to obtain it from

---

[6] First operated by horse power; after 1771 by water, hence the name "water frame."

[7] Arkwright's first water-power mill cost some £12,000, a sum obviously too large for any cloth-worker or for any group of artisans to provide.

[8] The process of forming carded cotton into coarse ropes preparatory to the making of threads by twisting and drawing these "rovings."

[9] Subsequently proven to be the inventions respectively of Daniel Bourne, Thomas Highs, and John Lees.

partners whom he persuaded to relinquish managerial duties.[10] Nor did he
find difficulty in attracting laborers, employing as many as six hundred in a
single mill at Manchester in 1780. Skillfully combining large quantities of
capital and large aggregates of labor, he rose to a position of industrial preeminence and was knighted. Although his cotton industry expanded rapidly
from one factory to several, this remarkable business man retained control and
exercised supervision over all. With money-making his primary goal, he did
not hesitate to employ every method calculated to attain his end; if chicanery
or even dishonesty seemed necessary, he did not disdain to employ either; if
laws barred his path, he lobbied for legislative revision, and his phenomenal
success marked him as a person to be imitated; as a consequence, Richard
Arkwright became, for better or for worse, the model for thousands of business men both in his own and in subsequent generations. A new world of
machinery and world markets had emerged, providing ample exercise for the
energy, the business acumen, and even the ruthlessness of a new race of business men. The rapid emergence of a great number of gifted entrepreneurs in
the eighteenth century is, in fact, another chapter in the history of invention.
Occupational mobility, which had been hastened by the decay of the craft
gilds and by agricultural reorganization,[11] released countless persons of genuine ability from conventional restraints, and the resulting atmosphere of business freedom elicited from each powers of conducting business enterprise
hitherto unperceived and unknown! The art of factory administration may
indeed be considered one of the most important inventions that the eighteenth
century produced.

For this new race of business men really put the interlinked textile inventions to practical tests, and by that very process indicated the next technical
problem to be solved. Thus it was not merely the water frame that made yarn
abundant and spinners scarce; it was also Arkwright's business ability which
adapted business organization and thereby released the productive power of
roller spinning. By converting spinning into a factory process, appropriate machinery for mechanical weaving became the imperative next step, and the solution for this problem was found by an English clergyman. Although Edmund
Cartwright patented a crude power loom in 1785, years were required to make
the machine a commercial success and to overcome opposition. Weavers, who

---

[10] This method of capital accumulation for new textile ventures became typical and remained so
until such large amounts of capital were needed that the joint-stock company, which had proved
its usefulness in commerce, was introduced.

[11] Many former yeomen became successful industrialists during the last quarter of the eighteenth
century; Mantoux has aptly said that these displaced farmers "provided building maerials, so to
speak, for the construction of a new class."

had prospered from the increased production of yarn, bitterly opposed the new invention and destroyed the huge weaving factory which Cartwright and some Manchester spinners had erected in 1789. Moreover, the clergyman inventor proved to be a poor business man; more practical ability than his was required to adapt the power loom to factory use. By the turn of the century, however, power weaving had succeeded both at Glasgow and Manchester, although almost another half century passed before the new method really superseded the traditional hand loom weaving.

Other minds meantime had progressively improved the several processes of cloth-making. Samuel Crompton, son of a Lancashire yeoman, succeeded in building a spinning machine (1779) which combined the best features of both Hargreave's jenny and the water frame, a compound machine which by use of rollers made possible precision twisting, while at the same time by employing a movable carriage, produced exceedingly strong, fine thread. This machine completed the technical triumph of English machine spinners over East Indian hand spinners. No longer did the English spinners need to fear any competition. Cheapness and quality, the mainspring of modern machine production, had been achieved. Printing of cloth by means of the calico cylinder carried the technical advance still farther, while improved knowledge of chemistry made it possible to adapt the bleaching trades to a scientific process. The whole scheme of textile manufacture was now revolutionized, and in the wake of technical advance came a resulting conquest of world markets.

It should be noted, however, that it was cotton manufacture rather than England's ancient woolen industry which became the real area of technical change. Until 1800, the woolen industry "remained essentially provincial and local." Some introduction of machinery occurred to be sure, but it met with bitter resistance on the part of skilled craftsmen who saw in the new methods a monstrous competitive force which threatened them with ruin. This artisan protest, widespread and for a time thoroughly effective, was at once a manifestation of surviving craft-gild principles and a forewarning of a new type of resistance against insecurity which crystallized during the nineteenth century in trade union philosophy. Thus fear of exploitation and of unemployment produced riots and destruction of machinery in the eighteenth century, while the same fear of insecurity produced jurisdictional disputes, restriction of output, and sabotage in the next. Either form of resistance is symptomatic of a fundamental change in capitalist organization of industry which the "Industrial Revolution" had caused.

Indeed, this alteration in capitalist structure is probably one of the most important consequences of the adoption of scientific technology. Complex machines, integrated manufacturing processes, and the use of power required concentration of production in factories where supervision could be provided constantly. Machines, buildings, and equipment for generating water or steam power, in turn, required large investments in fixed form. As contrasted with the investment of the seventeenth-century clothier, which was primarily tied up in inventories of semi-finished goods, the factory owners of 1800 were compelled to sink huge sums in permanent equipment. Profits depended upon successful and constant utilization of this mass of capital. Proper administration of this new form of industrial capital presented a thoroughly difficult problem, one which has, in fact, grown more and more difficult to cope with as the amount of permanent investment has progressively increased. Much of the sordidness of English factory life in the first half of the nineteenth century can be attributed to the inexperience of factory owners in dealing with this quite modern problem of heavy "sunk" costs, of profitably utilizing equipment which can give off its usefulness only over long periods of time. The early English factory owners saw no other solution than to employ their machinery as continuously as possible. Drawing their labor supply from persons already habituated to long hours of labor they were able to compel their workers to submit to fourteen or even sixteen hours of labor under the close supervision of factory officials. Moreover, the machines themselves were taskmasters, setting an invariable pace which the wearied hands of factory workers were compelled to follow. The new discipline mercilessly dictated what each operator must do, almost reducing laborers to automatons in an impersonal rhythm of industrial regularity. Karl Marx caught the imagination of all critics of modern production when he designated labor under the factory system as "wage-slavery." So it was and so it is: a servitude fully as exacting as any type of slavery, but with this difference, that wages presumably supply the reward which induces persons to accept voluntarily the monotony, the irksomeness, and the restraint which modern industrial discipline involves.

Mass production, an indispensable element of the modern world, was first successfully achieved, therefore, in the English cotton industry as a consequence of the combination of scientific technology with the vigor of the capitalist proprietorship. Contemporaneous with these experiments in cloth-making, fully as important innovations were introduced in the metallurgical trades; fully as important, because they completely revolutionized the metal trades, thereby making possible an abundance of iron and steel for structural purposes, for the vehicles of transportation and for constructing the new machinery for the mass-production factories. The cotton industry may be said to have provided an object lesson which demonstrated beyond peradventure the importance of elaborate power-driven machines; the development of the iron and steel industry made machinery itself possible.

"Iron especially in the form of steel," it has cogently been said, "provides the structural basis of industrial civilization." It forms this structural basis, because of strength, malleability, abundance, and relative cheapness. All of these qualities were profoundly influenced by new methods of smelting, forging, and fabricating iron, discovered in the eighteenth century. The use of iron, or of steel for that matter, was nothing new; ancient [12] and medieval[13] societies employed these materials for tools and weapons, and the sixteenth century had witnessed new uses for iron especially in the manufacture of cannon. Since a long chain of technical improvements in iron-making can be traced which reach back centuries behind the Industrial Revolution, why should eighteenth-century England be singled out as an especially important episode in the history of iron and steel? The answer is simple: English ironmasters discovered a new fuel for smelting iron ore, thereby removing the chief obstacle to the production of cheap pig-iron; they also were able to avail themselves of new chemical processes and of steam power, thereby producing superior qualities of iron and steel. Thus, by making better and cheaper iron and steel, the ironmasters of England laid the structural foundations for a type of civilization wholly different from the one into which they were themselves born.

Until the eighteenth century, iron ore was smelted in England, as elsewhere, by means of charcoal. But over centuries, charcoal production had decimated English forests, and with growing scarcity of fuel, costs had risen in the iron industry. Faced with sharp competition from Sweden and Germany, the English iron mining and smelting industry declined so seriously during the seventeenth century that the handwriting was on the wall; unless a new fuel could be found, England would become almost entirely dependent upon foreign sources of pig-iron. This situation was particularly aggravating in view of the patent fact that Great Britain possessed both an abundance of iron ore and of coal. The problem was therefore strictly technical.

For a century, repeated efforts had been made to find a solution with no real success. Then came, sometime between 1709 and 1719, a great discovery by

[12] Military needs of the Roman Empire, for example, had led to great development in the technique of forging and tempering.

[13] Belgium was probably the leading medieval iron producing area, although Arabia, Spain, Sweden, and Germany were also contributing considerable amounts.

Abraham Darby, who, by coking the coal, and by using powerful bellows, succeeded in smelting iron by means of coal. As in the case of the textile machinery, lack of balance between interdependent segments of an industry had apparently hastened the process of invention. Expansion of markets had greatly stimulated those industries which used pig-iron as raw materials; their increased demand called forth more intense effort on the part of English iron smelters to solve a problem which had long baffled them. Production of cheap pig-iron, however, was only a beginning; there still remained the task of converting pig-iron into malleable iron cheaply and efficiently. Experiments begun in 1762 by John Roebuck and by Thomas and George Cranage in 1766, were carried to completion by Peter Onions, in 1783, and by Henry Cort, in 1784. Cort's "puddling process" of purifying iron, together with his use of rolling mills, completely altered the iron industry. Meantime steel-making underwent corresponding improvement; by smelting prepared iron at high temperatures in sealed crucibles and by the use of charcoal and ground glass, Benjamin Huntsman was able to produce steel of excellent quality. All these metallurgical processes, discovered by practical men, represented chemical innovations which proved eminently useful although they were quite imperfectly understood. Indeed this very obscurity exerted a profound influence upon pure science, which sought complete explanation and, as a result, soon became a useful ally of the practical world of industry.

The chemical discoveries made by Darby, Onions, Cort, and Huntsman, could not by themselves, however, have revolutionized the iron and steel industry. A series of mechanical inventions also contributed abundantly to metallurgical progress. Conversion of pig-iron into malleable by means of coal required more powerful blowing machinery and this gap was filled by a water-power blowing machine invented by John Smeaton in 1760. Nine years later, James Watt succeeded in building a workable steam engine. With Matthew Boulton as his partner, Watt next embarked upon the commercial manufacture of stationary steam engines. As a result, power of definite and predictable amount became available for blowing, hammering, and rolling. Chemical and mechanical inventions could thereafter be integrated into a complete technology, making possible the manufacture of iron and steel by factory methods.

Cheap and efficient iron found an important new market in factory machinery. Iron equipment replaced the early wooden textile machinery, a process made possible largely by Henry Maudsley's improved metal lathe which facilitated the construction of mechanically precise, power-driven machines. John Wilkinson, meantime, had constructed a metal boring machine which made the drilling of accurate pump and engine cylinders possible, an invention which played no small part in making the steam engine a practical success, and consequently an indispensable aid to the metal and textile industries.

The economic effects of the new metallurgical processes may be seen quite easily from the statistics of output. Whereas England produced only 68,000 tons of pig-iron in 1788, in 1806 she produced 250,400 tons. Foreign iron was no longer imported, did not in fact need to be imported since England now produced nearly half of the total world supply. Not only did pig-iron production provide ample raw materials for subsequent stages of metal manufacturing but its accelerated rate of production actually threw the iron industry out of equilibrium and thereby hastened the process of complementary invention. John Wilkinson, by perfecting the manufacture of cast iron, astonished his contemporaries by making huge castings for iron bridges, while by the use of close set rollers he produced sheet-iron plates out of which he constructed the first iron canal boat. Wilkinson was among the few persons who seemed to sense the potential importance of iron and steel; he predicted that iron would ultimately play a dominant part in industrial civilization. Boldly experimenting, he found a host of new uses for iron, constructing iron chairs, iron pipes, iron vats for breweries, iron bridge girders, iron ship plates, and finally, for himself, an iron coffin!

It is perhaps inaccurate to classify all the foregoing innovations in the textile and metal industries as "scientific." Almost all of the important inventions were conceived by practical men, who had precious little knowledge either of mechanics or of chemistry. A large portion of scientific knowledge, however, is always derived from practical experience, while pure science constantly finds an important area of usefulness in explaining accurately why certain empirically discovered techniques are successful. In eighteenth-century England, this task of examination, explanation, and improvement was promptly attacked by men with scientific training, and in the history of the steam engine is found an illustrative example of the practical benefits which can arise from scientific revision. For James Watt invented the steam engine, not by originating the idea of such a contrivance, but by applying a well known physical phenomenon (the capacity of steam to expand) to an existing machine (Newcomen's atmospheric pumping engine). Yet this work of "critical revision" proved to be of salutary importance; it really introduced a new era, in which science became the indispensable servant of modern capitalism.

Two quite different steam pumps, one patented, in 1698, by Thomas Savery, the other, in 1705, by Newcomen, represented the progress which had been made in the application of steam power fifty years before Watt's work began. Both devices were useful and workable, especially Newcomen's engine which was extensively employed for pumping mines, filling water-wheel reservoirs, and for operating city water-works. Technically, Savery's engine was closer to the modern steam engine than Newcomen's, since it forced water, which had risen into a partial vacuum by atmospheric pressure, upward by employing the expansive power of steam. Newcomen's engine, on the other hand, merely made use of the vacuum created by condensing steam. Alternate infusion and condensation of steam in a cylinder fitted with a piston which was connected with a counterpoised beam, provided up and down motion. Yet this clumsy fire engine, although very wasteful of energy in the alternate heating and cooling process, was a thoroughly practical device which satisfied all but the critical. To this category of critical thinkers, James Watt belonged. His scientific training did not allow him to regard a machine which relied upon the alternate heating and cooling of a steam cylinder as satisfactory, and in 1761 he commenced a series of laboratory experiments on steam pressure. Out of these experiments came Watt's basic contribution: the idea of a separate condensing chamber. At the same time, he concluded that Savery had followed a sound plan by employing the expansive power of steam. By readopting this idea, and by making use of a condenser, Watt transformed Newcomen's atmospheric engine into a steam engine. Later he devised a method for converting steam power into rotary motion and with this invention his improved steam pump became capable of generating motive power for an infinite number of uses.

Watt's place in technical history ought not, however, to be measured solely by his invention of the condenser or by his conversion of mechanical pulsation into rotary motion. By systematically investigating the scientific facts which physicists had discovered concerning heat and steam pressure, and by applying underlying principles to an empirically developed machine, James Watt, more than any other person, deserves to be honored as the founder of truly scientific industrial technology. He bridged the gap between pure science and empirical discovery at exactly the place where connection would provide greatest immediate practical benefit. Moreover, by his subsequent partnership with one of the outstanding business men of all England, he was able to introduce steam engines into all kinds of industrial uses. Substantially, Watt was therefore instrumental in weaving together the empirical discoveries of his predecessors with theoretical physics, and at the same time able to prove the worth of this synthesis in a capitalist world.

Nor did it take long for industrial capitalism to realize the importance of the steam engine. Watt's shrewd partner, Matthew Boulton, knew exactly how to appeal to the mine owners who provided the first market for the new machines. Instead of selling engines for a fixed price, the firm of Boulton and Watt required their customers to remunerate them for the cost of building and installing a steam engine and to pay a royalty of one-third the saving in coal consumption which the new engine (as contrasted with a Newcomen engine of the same power) actually provided. Thus technical superiority became both the selling argument and the basis of reward. Although this direct appeal to the money-making motive (which is germane to capitalism) led to frequent disharmony between the engine manufacturers and the engine users, it perforce led to a rapid adoption of steam power in mining operations. Meantime, in 1781, Watt had perfected his device for converting the power generated by steam into rotary motion. The province of the steam engine now immediately enlarged, first in metal working (blowing, hammering, and rolling) next in flour mills, stone-crushers, and sugar-cane mills, while in 1785, steam power was first applied in a spinning factory. By 1800, steam was everywhere replacing water-power with extremely important results. No longer did factories need to be located near rapidly flowing streams; [14] the location of industry came now to be determined by nearness of raw materials in some cases, nearness to markets in others, or availability of labor in still other cases. Steam power had created a new form of industrial mobility destined to be of great importance. For it was steam power more than any other single factor which permitted the concentration of industry in cities and thus facilitated that strong trend toward urbanization and industrial compactness which has become both a blessing and a curse in the modern economic world!

Centuries of scientific inquiry had yielded a body of scientific principles which were available for industrial utilization. The elementary mechanical and chemical applications of science which have been sketched in the preceding pages were only a prelude to the extensive employment of scientific facts in industry which could now be undertaken. The initial steps had been taken under the pressure of peculiar economic circumstances which confronted England in the eighteenth century. From the time of Watt, capitalism formed an indissoluble partnership with physical science, and out of this union has come the complex technology of the modern world. But this alliance has roots which are primarily economic, although it has had consequences which are not merely economic but sociological and political.

The appeal of the new technology to the business men of the eighteenth

[14] The early cotton factories were of necessity located where water-power was available, in country villages rather than cities.

century was strictly pecuniary. Machine spinning lowered costs at the same time that it produced finer, stronger, and better thread; smelting of iron by coke similarly reduced the price of pig-iron, while the manufacture of malleable iron by the puddling process likewise made manufactured iron not only cheaper but better. The steam engine was adopted for a similar reason: it reduced the cost of producing energy while at the same time it permitted factories to be located where all other costs of production would be least. Scientific technology revealed its potential ability to further the making of business profits, and for this reason and this alone was it adopted as an integral part of modern capitalism.

The eagerness with which business men sought the advantages of the new cost-reducing technology revealed itself both in a quest for patent privileges and in an effort of the unprivileged to evade patent rights. The seventeenth-century war between the exclusive trading companies and the interlopers was re-enacted in a new setting. Arkwright made a fortune by patenting a machine which he did not invent while, contrariwise, a petition was circulated by steam engine users to persuade Parliament to cancel Watt's patent. Inventors armed with patents often found their privileges of small value since unscrupulous competitors unblushingly copied their machines. More and more, business men divided into two categories: those who made money because they had technological advantages arising from legal privileges, and those who were prevented from making money because of the existence of these legal privileges. Clearly the latter were in the majority and the logical consequence was a rising opposition of business men against the engrossing of technical advantage.

Nor did this single form of monopoly exhaust the category of privileges which the new race of business men condemned. There was money to be made in industry and in commerce providing no restraints of a political nature were imposed. Freedom to hire whomsoever they wished, freedom to make whatever they thought advisable, freedom to sell wherever they pleased, became the tripartite demand of the captains of industry. The corporative spirit of the medieval business men was dead and buried; a feverish era of ruthless competition became the order of the age.

And one basic reason for this aggressive tendency in business enterprise was really sociological. No longer did the maker of goods need to be passive. If only costs could be lowered, the very process would create a new demand. An uprooted peasantry, freed from the restraint of custom by virtue of agrarian reorganization, and with want scales made flexible by the rapid demolition of the old village communities, provided one fertile area for the creation of this new variety of proletariat demand. Moreover the spread of the wage system had made each wage earner the sole judge of how his own wants should be satisfied. Skillful appeal by cheapness or by chicanery might divert a portion of thousands of these wage incomes to the advantage of particular manufacturers. Tempting buyers has always been an important element in business success but clearly when there are more buyers and when an increasing proportion are ignorant or ill informed, this field of endeavor necessarily becomes more important. Moreover, the domestic market represented merely one market for the manufacturers of textiles, hardware, clothing, pottery, or jewelry. English mercantile agencies had by 1800 spread throughout the entire world. Every handicraft village became a potential market for the factory-made articles which scientific technology made possible; everywhere in the entire world demand could be created if only cheapness and attractiveness could be combined. In this vast world market, which transcended distance and social stratification, lay potential profits unpredictably large, and English business men seem to have promptly realized this combination of economic fact and sociological peculiarity quite clearly. One by one, other nations came to appreciate the importance of an artificially created demand. When this occurred, political significance is subjoined to technological consideration, and presently the economic imperialism of the modern world becomes an aggravating phenomenon.

Chapter IV

THE DOMINION AND TRIALS OF ECONOMIC LIBERALISM

❧

1. CLASSICAL ECONOMICS AND ITS CRITICS

ECONOMIC LIBERALISM AND THE IDEALIZATION OF CAPITALISTIC INDIVIDUALISM

EVERY IMPORTANT socio-economic system, if it has any duration, produces a compatible body of ideals designed to defend and justify it. Institutions and practices that are the accidental or fortuitous product of historical circumstances come to be invested with a sort of divine wisdom and perfection. This was true, among other forms of society, of the patriarchal empires and of the feudal system. It was not less true of the later capitalistic order that gradually gained dominance between the fifteenth century and the twentieth.

But the social results of the new industrialism were not all happy. . . . It was not long before there arose sharp criticisms of capitalistic methods and philosophy. In this chapter we shall be concerned chiefly with (1) the rise of the apology for capitalism in the form of Economic Liberalism, and (2) the attack upon this attitude from many angles of dissent.

In order that we may appreciate fully the nature and implications of the apologies for capitalism, it is desirable to have a clear conception of the character of capitalistic ideals as they had evolved by the close of the first Industrial Revolution. The ideals of competitive capitalism have been forcefully summarized by Stuart Chase in what he calls "the bible of free competition":

Buy in the cheapest and sell in the dearest market, that profit may be at a maximum. Charge all that the traffic will bear.

Tolerate no monopolies. Let supply and demand work unfettered. Prices for goods can thus never remain long too high. When Company A starts making an

---

This chapter consists of material by two different authors. Section 1 is from *The History of Western Civilization* (Vol. II, pp. 378–89; New York, Harcourt, Brace & Co., 1935), by Harry Elmer Barnes, with the collaboration of Henry David. Section 2 is from *The Commerce of Nations* (pp. 173–84, 195–99, 240–42; New York, W. W. Norton & Co., 1950), by J. B. Condliffe.

unreasonable profit, Company B will promptly come charging into the field, increase the supply of goods, and so force the price down to fairer levels.

Let every capitalist strive to outdo every other capitalist, in order that the weak may fall and the strong survive, and so keep the most vigorous and the most efficient at the top. Every man for himself, and the devil take the hindmost. Encourage individualism.

Let profit be the motive for every industrial action. Prayerfully followed, profit is the perfect guide.

Specialize and standardize the tasks of labor.

Tolerate no interference from labor, work it as hard as possible, and pay it not more than a survival wage.

Use all the resources of the Government and of its armed forces to find and hold foreign markets, but tolerate no government interference in internal matters.

The first great body of doctrine that extolled the new capitalistic order is known as Economic Liberalism. It is also identified with the economic doctrine of laissez-faire and the political theory of individualism.

This type of theory cannot be properly appraised unless the historical circumstances surrounding its origin and diffusion are taken into consideration. It began before the Industrial Revolution as an attack upon the archaic legislative restrictions that had grown up as a part of the mercantile commercial and colonial system. In so far as it helped to clear away these obstructions to economic freedom, it contributed to the coming of modern industrial society. After the Industrial Revolution had arrived, however, its later adherents utilized the laissez-faire concepts to defend the new capitalistic order and to prevent, so far as possible, the abolition, through remedial legislation, of the grave social evils it created.

The founders of Economic Liberalism were the group of French writers in the middle of the eighteenth century to whom we have earlier referred as the Physiocrats, so named from the work of one of their adherents, Dupont de Nemours, entitled *Physiocracy, or the Natural Constitution of That Form of Government Most Advantageous to the Human Race* (1767). They derived their basic doctrine from the English Deists and the French *philosophes,* to the effect that social, political, and economic phenomena are governed by the same natural laws that Newton and his associates believed they had proved to rule the physical universe. They were convinced that the perfection of all human social institutions could best be realized by letting them freely conform to this natural order, a condition which they believed would most certainly be brought about under a régime of unlimited competition. If man refrained from legislation and any attempt to control economic processes by artificial means, then God and His natural order would have full sway. One reason for human unhappiness and prevailing misery, so they said, was the operation of a large number of archaic and restrictive laws which, being statutory and unnatural, were holding back the free dominion of natural law in the affairs of men.

Accordingly, the Physiocrats vigorously advocated the immediate and total abolition of all restrictive legislation and the introduction of an era of laissez-faire individualism. The only desirable functions of the state were the protection of life and property, the erection of public buildings and other public works, and the promotion of education, so that man might grasp more surely the principles of natural law. Extensive social legislation was regarded as dangerous, since it would surely impede the operation of those beneficent natural principles upon which these advocates placed their chief reliance. The Physiocrats contributed views of less significance through their interpretation of social progress in terms of the net product of agriculture and their scheme of a reform in public finance, which centered about the notion of a single tax on land. The moving genius among the Physiocrats was François Quesnay (1694–1774), who was ably seconded by Gournay, Mirabeau, Dupont de Nemours, Mercier de la Rivière, Baudeau, and Le Trosne.

The general notions of the Physiocrats concerning individualism and the inactivity of the state received the support of the distinguished French economist and statesman Turgot (1727–81), and intrigued the first great systematic writer on political economy, the Scotch philosopher Adam Smith (1723–90).[1] The chief significance of Adam Smith for the history of social reform is that he embodied the laissez-faire thesis in a notable work, *An Inquiry into the Nature and Causes of the Wealth of Nations* (1776). This received so wide a circulation and attracted so extensive a following for Smith's doctrines that the eminent historian Buckle, nearly a century later, regarded this book as the most influential and beneficial one ever written. In spite of his general acceptance of the Physiocratic position as to the proper functions of the state, Smith abandoned to a considerable degree their excessive laudation of agriculture, and emphasized the prime value, to a state, of commerce and manufacturing industry. Especially did he revive the Platonic doctrine of the importance of the division of labor and specialization in increasing and improving productivity. His emphasis upon the part played by labor in production paved the way for the later views of Ricardo and the Socialists with respect to the "labor theory of value." His advocacy of free trade on the ground of the ad-

---

[1] [It is important to remember that Smith had formulated his views before he became acquainted with Physiocratic ideas. When he came to know the doctrines of the Physiocrats, he accepted them as reinforcing his own position.]

vantages of an international division of labor was one of the most forceful arguments ever advanced for commercial freedom.

Smith died before the Industrial Revolution had fully developed even in England, and there is good evidence for holding that he did not even foresee the complete course of this transformation, much less stand out as a conscious apologist of the new capitalist class. But his doctrines were of a sort that fitted in admirably with the policy of noninterference. This the capitalist manufacturers desired to have prevail, in order that they, if not their employees, might enjoy the alleged "blessings of the perfect freedom of contract." Smith's notions were therefore expanded and exploited by the middle class and sympathetic economists to provide an authoritative theoretical opposition to social legislation designed to advance the interests of the industrial proletariat.

The most extensive development of the concepts of Adam Smith naturally took place in England, where he had written and where that commercialism which was most congenial to his views was the furthest advanced, but he was honored by reverent disciples in every important European state and in the United States. His most distinguished English disciples were Thomas Robert Malthus (1766–1834); David Ricardo (1772–1823); James Mill (1773–1836); John Ramsay McCulloch (1789–1864), and Nassau William Senior (1790–1864). The one thing that, in particular, distinguished the doctrines of Smith from those of his disciples was the greater social pessimism of the latter, a difference that may be explained in part by the sweeping changes in the economic and social environment in the interval that had elapsed since Smith's death.

While the chief importance of these writers consists in their elaboration of the supposed virtues of the competitive order, each contributed some special interpretation of some originality and significance. Malthus held that remedial legislation is not only harmful, as interfering with the natural order of things, but is also useless so far as any hope of improving the poorer classes is concerned. He maintained that even though the distribution of wealth should be equalized, no permanent good could result. Since population tends to increase more rapidly than the means of subsistence, the normal disparity between population and the available means of support would ultimately be restored and with this would come a return of poverty and misery. The proletariat creates its own misery through an excessive birth rate, and the only hope of enduring relief lies in the restriction of the birth rate through the postponement of marriage.

Ricardo paid particular attention to the subject of the distribution of wealth. Mainly from the Physiocratic notion that the wages of agricultural laborers tend toward the minimum of subsistence and from Malthus's doctrine of population, he derived his famous "subsistence theory of wages." According to this dogma, wages tend towards a level that allows the laboring class to exist and perpetuate itself without either increase or decrease. If wages are increased the population grows accordingly. Hence the folly of legislation designed to enlarge the income of the proletariat, for the resulting increase of population would absorb the monetary gain and prevent any diminution of poverty and misery. Moreover, higher wages would lower profits, curtail industrial initiative, increase unemployment, and very soon increase poverty and misery. Further, Ricardo attacked the landlords by maintaining that rent tends to absorb an ever greater share of the social income, and that the interests of the landlords are opposed to those of all other economic classes. Finally, he laid the basis for the Marxian theory of value by holding that, within certain definite limitations, value is determined by the amount of labor involved in the production of goods—a doctrine vigorously attacked by many later economists.

James Mill brought into Economic Liberalism the Utilitarian philosophy of Bentham regarding the maximum good for the largest number. This ideal Mill and his associates believed to be attainable only through the operation of the principles of Economic Liberalism. Mill's clearly written treatise did much to popularize the theories of Ricardo, who was a prolix and involved writer. Of all this group of writers, Mill had the most naïve and limitless confidence in the benevolence of the middle-class manufacturers and merchants. McCulloch was the chief systematizer of the principles of Economic Liberalism, and, somewhat illogically, was the most sympathetic member of the group towards the laboring classes, being a supporter of Place and Hume in their attempt to legalize trade-unionism. He is particularly known for his elaboration of the "wages-fund" doctrine, which held that only a specific sum could be diverted into wages without wrecking the whole industrial process. This is the reverse of a notion popular today to the effect that unless enough money is put into wages to produce mass purchasing power the whole capitalistic system will inevitably fold up.

Senior represented the final and most extreme stage of Economic Liberalism through his attempt to perfect economics as a purely abstract and objective science—a science of wealth and not of welfare—and by his ardent opposition to even the mildest form of legislation beneficial to the laboring classes. He warned against legislation to shorten the hours of labor, contending that profits are made only in the last hours of the day. Hence, to shorten the working-hours would end profits, discourage the industrialists, and lead to the closing of the factories and mines. Senior was dubbed by his critics "Last Hour" Senior.

In the writings of John Stuart Mill (1806–73) we detect a break with the most cherished traditions of Economic Liberalism. Mill held that only the processes of production were subject to the control of natural law and hence not to be disturbed by human legislation. This view, justifying social control of the distributive process, opened the way for extensive legislation regulating wages, interest, rent, and profits.

While most of these writers took little active part in politics, their ideal of "perfect competition for the employers and subjection for the workers" was eagerly adopted by Richard Cobden, John Bright, and other members of the Manchester School, and by the new Liberal party. Such notions were very useful in the campaign to reduce the power and privileges of the landed aristocracy and to enforce and perpetuate the servile and helpless status of the laborers. Further, their notions were widely popularized, and their general views were as much the order of polite conversation in British parlors as Rousseau's notions of the state of nature had been in the French salons of half a century before. The bourgeois entrepreneur had replaced the noble savage of the previous century as the recipient of idealized admiration.

In France, the doctrines of this later version of Economic Liberalism were espoused by a number of economists, the most notable of whom were Jean Baptiste Say (1767–1832) and Frédéric Bastiat (1801–50). Say's position was very similar to that of Senior. He maintained that political economy is purely a descriptive science and not in any way a practical art. The economist should simply study and formulate economic laws and should never usurp the functions of the statesman. Reversing the position of the Physiocrats, he laid special stress upon the social contributions of manufacturing. Say was the most enthusiastic of all the eulogists of the new era of mechanical industry. He was the French bourgeois economist of the period in much the same way as Guizot was the statesman of this group. Bastiat revived the optimism of Adam Smith and, as an ardent admirer of Cobden, devoted his attention chiefly to an advocacy of free trade. The function of the state, he held, was solely to maintain "order, security and justice." So enthusiastic were Say and Bastiat over the supposed beneficial activities of the new manufacturing and commercial classes that some less scientific followers denied that poverty or misery even existed.

In Germany, Economic Liberalism was defended by Johann Heinrich von Thünen (1783–1850) and Karl Heinrich Rau (1792–1870), while in America Henry C. Carey (1793–1879) first introduced the classical political economy, though he differed from Smith's English disciples by reviving the optimism of Smith and attacking the pessimism of Malthus. Moreover, he advocated national protectionism in contrast to the free-trade doctrines of most others of the liberal school.

Though it will be evident that Economic Liberalism was as distinctly a capitalistic movement as Socialism has been a proletarian agitation—that, as Cliffe Leslie expressed it, "they created a science for wealth rather than a science of wealth"—nevertheless, their efforts accomplished much that was good. Before state activity to solve the problems created by the Industrial Revolution could begin in an effective manner, it was necessary that the antique rubbish of mercantilism should be cleared away. This was the great contribution of the Economic Liberals and their political adherents, even though they offset much of the value of their destructive efforts by their opposition to progressive legislation. It should also be pointed out in passing that the Economic Liberals were aided (1) by the contemporary philosophy of Romanticism, with its denial of the possibility of artificially accelerating the rate of political progress; and (2) by the political individualism that had been set forth by Wilhelm von Humboldt, was later taken up by John Stuart Mill in his earlier days, and was eulogized by Herbert Spencer.

In England, the more notable practical effects of Economic Liberalism were: (1) The growth of free trade, associated with the work of Huskisson, Cobden, Bright, Peel, and Gladstone; (2) the abolition of such archaic political restrictions as the Test and Corporation acts, which had restricted the political rights of Dissenters; (3) the increase of the political powers of the middle class in the central and local government by the Reform Bills of 1832 and 1835; (4) the abolition of slavery in the colonies through the efforts of Wilberforce and Buxton; (5) the repeal of the savage criminal code as a result of the work of Romilly, Mackintosh, Buxton, and Peel; (6) the development of a policy of preventive treatment in the handling of the problem of poor relief, which was evident in the notable Poor Law of 1834; and (7) the first concessions to a more liberal policy of imperial government through the leadership of Lord Durham, Edward Gibbon Wakefield, and others.[2]

In France, serfdom and the guild monopolies were abolished before the close of the eighteenth century; Guizot directed the Orleanist régime solely in the interests of the capitalists; and Bastiat's doctrines were able to win Napoleon III for free trade.

In Prussia, Stein and Hardenberg secured legislation looking towards the complete abolition of serfdom and of guild monopolies, and the development of municipal self-government. Following 1819 a more liberal economic and

---

[2] In these reforms the Economic Liberals were, of course, aided by the Philosophical Radicals and the Utilitarians.

commercial policy was embodied in the famous *Zollverein*,[3] the work of Maassen, Bülow, Eichhorn, and Von Motz. Most of the other German states followed Prussia in this liberalizing policy, and some, like Baden, quite outdistanced it in this respect.

It will be apparent, however, that none of this legislation materially benefited the new proletariat. Indeed, some of the legislation of this period was specifically designed to paralyze the efforts of the laborers for self-improvement, and the agitators for the abolition of Negro slavery in the colonies passed by unnoticed the industrial slavery that existed at home among their own white countrymen.

During the closing period of the popularity of Economic Liberalism this individualistic doctrine gained support from another source, namely, the evolutionary hypothesis as interpreted by Herbert Spencer (1820–1903). The Deists and the Physiocrats had derived their notions from the hypothesis that the physical universe is presided over by a lawgiving and law-abiding Providence. Spencer invoked the new agnostic naturalism in support of individualism. He held that social evolution, like biological evolution, is a natural and spontaneous process with which man should not interfere. Human well-being can best be insured by letting evolution take its course. If man tries to intervene and hasten the process, disaster is likely to result. Cosmic evolution was thus assigned the place that had been given to God in the Deistic scheme adopted by the early Economic Liberals. To the latter, human legislation was an affront to God. To Spencerians, it was a defiance of the all-pervading evolutionary process. As late as 1905 the Supreme Court of the United States based an important decision on Herbert Spencer's *Social Statics,* and in 1912 the conservatives brought out a new edition of the book in the effort to defeat Theodore Roosevelt and his Progressive party.

ENGLISH PHILOSOPHICAL RADICALISM AND UTILITARIANISM

Utilitarianism, a term used by Jeremy Bentham and given wide currency by John Stuart Mill, is the designation usually applied to the school of writers headed by Bentham (1748–1832) and including, among others, James Mill, George Grote, John Austin, Alexander Bain, and John Stuart Mill. They represented primarily the spirit and tenets of Economic Liberalism as applied in political theory. Their work constituted about the only significant contribution of England to this field between the time of Burke and that of Spencer. Essen-

---

[3] [*Customs Union* (1819–67); a movement, under the leadership of Prussia, to establish a uniform tariff for the Germanies. By 1867 all non-Austrian German states were members of the union.]

tially, they were a further development of that Philosophical Radicalism in England which grew out of English sympathy with the French Revolution, and was represented by William Godwin, Thomas Paine, William Cobbett, Francis Place, and a group of literary figures, including Shelley, Byron, and Wordsworth. This group of early Philosophical Radicals stood in direct opposition to the satisfaction that Blackstone and Burke expressed over the alleged perfection of British institutions. They maintained the necessity of sweeping changes to eliminate ancient superstitions, archaic laws, outgrown institutions, and brutal practices.

In his earlier years Bentham might have been logically classed with this earlier group, for his first notable work—*A Fragment on Government* (1776) —was a violent attack upon the complacency of Blackstone. But he gradually developed a broad and constructive philosophy of reform and thus remolded radicalism into Utilitarianism. His doctrines were based upon the hedonistic psychology, which aimed to increase human happiness,[4] and upon the ethical slogan of "the greatest happiness for the greatest number"—a principle earlier enunciated but not greatly developed by Hutcheson, Beccaria, and Priestley. Institutions were to be judged according to their contributions to the attainment of this "greatest happiness." Bentham's practical program of reform, however, indicated that, like the Economic Liberals, he regarded unrestricted competition and enlightened self-interest as the chief avenues through which his Utilitarian program could be realized. He was especially emphatic about the sanctity of contracts. Bentham's chief concern, in short, was with the abolition of archaic and restrictive legislation, but he did urge some positive reforms, such as education of the masses, the extension of savings, institutions, public-health legislation, a new poor law, and prison reform. Bentham and his immediate followers might seem to have regarded the "greatest good for the greatest number" as best attainable through conferring "the greatest amount of goods upon the business classes." Yet his principles, if honestly and logically interpreted, were excellently suited to justify a large amount of positive remedial legislation in behalf of the proletariat.

In this way, indeed, the Utilitarian premises later became an important force supporting constructive social legislation. In fact, this evolution of Utilitarianism into social reform is evident even within the circle of its own adherents. John Stuart Mill eventually emerged from an exponent of marked individualism into a vigorous supporter of social legislation in the interest of the laboring classes and a not unappreciative student of distinctly Socialistic proposals.

Probably the most important achievements of this group in the way of di-

---

[4] Anticipated by Machiavelli, Hobbes, Hume, and Helvétius.

rectly aiding the lower classes were the work of Francis Place and Joseph Hume in securing the temporary legalization of trade-unionism, the Poor Law of 1834, and some indirect benefits from liberal political reforms and health legislation. They also made important contributions towards securing the abolition of outworn practices and obstructive legislation, an achievement that we described above in dealing with the practical results of Economic Liberalism.

THE RISE OF OPPOSITION TO ECONOMIC LIBERALISM

There were a number of theoretical weaknesses in Economic Liberalism, which quickly attracted the opposition of political economists. While Smith had actually assumed to be more concerned with the wealth of a "nation" than that of a social class, it is nevertheless true that his followers seemed more agitated over the wealth of the new business class than over the problem of increasing the prosperity of the entire nation. This brought down upon Economic Liberalism the criticism of economists who presented a national or social theory of wealth.

These latter writers maintained that the increase of the wealth of particular individuals or classes is no safe criterion in estimating the value to the state or society of an economic, social, or political policy. This was the point of view especially of the Englishman Lord Lauderdale (1759–1839) and the Scotch-Canadian John Rae (1786–1873). Lauderdale, in his *Inquiry into the Nature and Origin of Public Wealth* (1804), differentiated clearly between public wealth and private riches, and held that the latter were usually gained at the expense of the former. He showed how public wealth depends upon abundance and private riches upon scarcity—a vital fact not comprehended as yet by many statesmen of our own era. This led him to distinguish public from private interest and to justify legislation designed to protect the former. By appealing to authorities from Aristotle to his own day, as well as by logical analysis, Rae, in his *New Principles of Political Economy* (1834), proved to his own satisfaction that remedial state activity was more in harmony with the principles of nature and society than laissez-faire and pure competition. He thus undermined the very foundations of Economic Liberalism.

The position of the Economic Liberals generally, and of Senior and Say in particular, that the economist must restrict his science to purely abstract and descriptive discipline and must rigidly refrain from advocating any positive policy of statesmanship or social reform, was vigorously attacked by Jean Charles Léonard (Simonde) de Sismondi (1773–1842), an itinerant but versatile Swiss scholar. He was the most distinguished and effective exponent in his age of the notion that economics must assume responsibility for promoting general prosperity and social reform, a point of view since urged with vigor by such economists as Schmoller, Gide, Webb, Hobson, Hamilton, Douglas, and others. He saw clearly that economics should be intimately concerned with the problems of practical statesmanship and applied sociology, and more than any other writer of his time he foreshadowed modern social or "welfare" economics. Moreover, his actual program of reform embraced most of what is now included in trade-unionism, factory legislation, and social insurance. In taking this attitude he stood almost alone in his age, but his doctrines were later accorded respect, as economics swung back more to the social point of view.

The Economic Liberals were, as we have seen, internationalists and exponents of free trade. This position was attacked by the early nationalistic economists, Adam Heinrich Müller (1779–1829), Friedrich List (1789–1846), and Henry C. Carey. They defended the policy of a protective tariff to give national self-sufficiency and prosperity. The nation, rather than individuals, classes, or human society as a whole, received their special solicitude. They were not, however, inflexibly dogmatic in this position. List, in particular, held that after the Industrial Revolution had become thoroughly established in a country, free trade might be beneficial. To aid "infant industries" in the first stages of industrial development a protective tariff was, however, in his opinion indispensable. List was far more liberal and flexible in his ideas than contemporary protectionists.

The Economic Liberals erred in the direction of too great an abstraction and absolutism in economic doctrines. They generalized too much from contemporary conditions and were confident of the universal and eternal applicability of their economic laws and theories. They were also careless of facts that ran counter to their theories. Indeed, when Ricardo was once reproached because his doctrines did not tally with certain facts, he retorted that it was so much the worse for the facts. These defects were corrected in theory at least by the early representatives of the so-called Historical school of economics, chiefly Richard Jones (1790–1885) in England and Bruno Hildebrand (1812–78), Wilhelm Roscher (1817–94) and Karl Knies (1821–98) in Germany. The predominance of the Germans in this group has led to the practical identification of the Historical school with German economists. These writers ridiculed the element of absolutism in the classical economic doctrines. They maintained that no type of economic theory could be true except for the age from which the facts or premises were drawn. Therefore, economic theories must change with historical alterations in the economic constitution of societies. There can be neither invariable economic laws nor valid economic theories that ignore the dynamic element of economic change. Their emphasis on the necessary relation between fact and theory also suggested careful statistical studies of actual social and economic conditions. The latter frequently and logically led to advocacy of remedial legislation.

It has been shown that Economic Liberalism was primarily an economic philosophy and a political program designed in the interest of the capitalists, who, in English politics, belonged for the most part to the Whig or Liberal party. It was but natural, therefore, that it would be assailed by the one powerful party whose economic and political interests were diametrically opposed to those of the business elements, that is, by the landed proprietors who made up the bulk of the Tory or Conservative party.

The Tories had a number of reasons for disliking the capitalists. In the first place, there was the social aversion of the aristocrats for what they regarded as the rich parvenu eager to break into their ranks. Then they feared that the new industrialism might destroy forever the "Merrie England" in which the landlords were supreme. Again, they entertained a jealousy of the growing political strength of the middle class, especially after the latter had forced through the Reform Bill of 1832 giving more power to the industrial cities. Finally, the economic interests of the two classes were fundamentally opposed; the Tories desired a continuation of the Corn Laws to keep the price of grain high, while the business class wished for their abolition to secure cheap wheat and therefore, according to the current economic reasoning, cheap labor.

The Tories were extremely fortunate in finding a point of attack upon the capitalists that enabled them to cloak their political and economic rivalry under the mantle of humanitarian sentiments and to entertain a reasonable hope of increasing their political following among the proletariat. The strategic line of attack decided upon by the Tories was factory legislation. This would reduce the prosperity of the manufacturers by compelling them to grant higher wages, shorter hours, and the introduction of better physical conditions and appliances in their factories. Possibly, too much has been made of this point of Tory self-interest by recent writers who have followed Arnold Toynbee in emphasizing the political and economic selfishness that motivated the landlord factory-reformers. Some of the leaders in this movement, especially Lord Shaftesbury, were governed by real humanitarian impulses, but it can at least be said that they were especially fortunate in finding a type of humanitarianism that harmonized particularly well with their economic and political interests. They showed little solicitude for the abuses that they themselves perpetuated among the rural workers.

The leaders in the earlier stages of this "Tory social reform" were Anthony Ashley Cooper, seventh Earl of Shaftesbury (1801–85), Michael Thomas Sadler (1780–1835), Richard Oastler (1789–1861), and John Fielden (1784–1849), a public-spirited manufacturer. They secured the appointment of the parliamentary investigating commissions whose reports have furnished the present generation with most of their sources of information concerning the conditions among the laboring classes in England during the first half of the nineteenth century, and they obtained much remedial legislation designed to alleviate or eliminate these evils of early industrialism.

It is impossible in the space available to describe in detail the contents of this legislation, but its general character can be indicated. The factory acts of 1802, 1819, 1831, 1833, 1844, 1847, 1850, and several minor laws of the sixties secured the ten-hour day for the laboring classes in practically all factories. They also provided real factory inspection, safety appliances, better sanitary conditions, and a general discouragement of child labor. Women and children were excluded from mines, and better hours and safety devices were provided for in mines by acts of 1842, 1855, and 1872. The distressing evils in the employment of juvenile chimney sweeps were eliminated by laws of 1834 and 1840. Particularly the result of the efforts of Shaftesbury were the important Factory Act of 1833 and the famous Ten-Hour Bill of 1847.

Political jealousy and economic rivalry between the upper classes and the middle classes were thus able to achieve for the betterment of the proletariat much more than the latter and their sympathizers were able to obtain for themselves. While Shaftesbury may have been motivated mainly by genuine humanitarian impulses in his campaign for social reform, it is doubtful if the same can be said for the continuator of his policy, Benjamin Disraeli (1804–81). That he thoroughly understood the oppression of the peasantry and the industrial proletariat no reader of his *Sybil* can doubt. Yet little evidence exists that he was touched by any real personal sympathy for the oppressed, and much leads one to the conclusion that his concessions to the lower classes were founded upon purely partisan motives and personal ambitions. In part, he continued Shaftesbury's social legislation, but his appeal for the support of the proletariat was primarily political. By the Reform Act of 1867 he extended the suffrage to the more prosperous portion of the urban laboring class.

This type of social reform again appeared in England during the Conservative-Unionist régime of the nineties, when it was particularly associated with the name of Joseph Chamberlain. This benevolent paternalism, born of political rivalry, was confined in its earlier stages chiefly to England, for there alone had the new business class attained sufficient proportions to attract the organized opposition of the landed interests. It appeared at a later time in other European states, most notably in the Bismarckian social-insurance and labor legislation.

2. THE CLASSICAL THEORY OF INTERNATIONAL TRADE

ASSUMPTIONS AND CONTENT

The theory of international trade first outlined by Ricardo and later systematized by John Stuart Mill was based upon three major, and a number of minor, assumptions. What the classical economists constructed was an abstract model. They defined international trade, for the purpose of their analysis, as the exchange of goods which took place in the conditions which they assumed to represent the fundamental, irreducible skeleton of essential trading relationships. Such a model could never be and was not intended to be realistic. Its purpose was to discard the unessential detail which complicates and obscures the working of fundamental principles. The conclusions drawn from analysis of such an abstract model must always be modified before they can be safely applied to actual conditions in the world of reality. The usefulness of the model depends upon the skill of the theorists in choosing assumptions and definitions which correspond with the essential realities of the trading world.

The three major assumptions of classical theory were: (1) that within a country labor and capital moved freely and without friction; (2) that between countries they did not move at all; and (3) that the supply of money consisted of gold or gold substitutes which necessarily were adjusted automatically to trading needs.

It should be emphasized that the classical economists were trying to discover the fundamental and permanent relationships of cause and effect in trading across national boundaries. Therefore they confined their analysis to the long-run conditions that would be established when temporary dislocations of production and employment had been resolved. They did not concern themselves with these short-run temporary dislocations, since they believed that in a competitive system the labor and capital displaced by imports would find alternative employment. This is the meaning of their first major assumption—that within a country labor and capital moved freely and without friction. As early as 1819, however, Mathew Carey was impressed by the fact that the flood of imports into the United States, with the expansion of British production and trade at the close of the Napoleonic Wars, had caused widespread unemployment among American craftsmen.

He therefore attacked this first assumption of the classical theory with great vigor. Where, he asked, were these craftsmen to find alternative employment? The reply of the classical economists was that they were concerned with the long run, and that in the long run the displaced craftsmen would be absorbed into other industries in which the United States had a comparative advantage in production costs. In their view, the appearance of temporary unemployment was a complicating detail which did not invalidate the logical conclusions of their theory. These conclusions were unassailable, granted the assumptions upon which the theory rested. Carey's view was that, theory or no theory, the unemployment was real. Hence, he argued, the assumptions were so unrealistic as to make the theory useless and misleading.

In regard to the second assumption, John Stuart Mill made it clear that he was aware that the assumptions of the classical theory did not correspond with reality. He recognized that there was a growing tendency for both labor and capital to move more freely between countries, so that in practice the distinction between domestic and international trade was not as sharp as it was assumed to be in the model set up for analysis. For the purpose of this analysis, he defined international trade as the exchange of goods between areas among which labor and capital could not be transferred. This definition led him to remark that certain kinds of international trade which did not conform to his definition should be discussed as if they were species of domestic trade. Thus he considered the trade between England and the West Indies as being similar to the trade between town and country, rather than to international trade as he defined it. Obviously this almost casual exclusion of certain categories of international trade from the model being analyzed limited the validity of the conclusions drawn from the analysis. A great and growing part of the international trade of the latter nineteenth century was of the kind which Mill excluded by his definition from consideration in the classical analysis. The fact is that the precision of the classical doctrines was achieved only by defining international trade in a way which was highly limited and artificial, even in Ricardo's own time. The model constructed for analysis was admirably fitted to throw light upon the questions which the classical economists were concerned to study. These were the fundamental principles of international trade in the conditions assumed. But those conditions excluded much of the developing trade even of their time.

Since by definition the classical theory arbitrarily excluded the transference of capital and labor between nations, it was, in terms commonly though not very appropriately used, a static rather than a dynamic theory. It was confined to a consideration of the long-run consequences of trade between two communities at a given moment, given the resources available to each community at that moment. It did not attempt to deal with the development of trade over a period of time. It is true that John Stuart Mill admitted as an exception the validity of the argument for protection in appropriate circumstances to growing industries—the infant-industry argument—but this formed no part of the classical doctrine. The infant-industry argument had been common in mercantilist literature; but the Ricardian theory excluded it from consideration by defining international trade in such a way as to exclude the possibility that capital and labor might be attracted to a developing country of abundant resources. Thus the classical theory was a snapshot rather than a movie—an explanation of why and how international trade is carried on at a particular moment of time rather than an explanation of economic development over a period of time.

The third major assumption was that the money used as a standard of value consisted of coins, or notes redeemable in coin or bullion, and that the coins circulated at their value as bullion. This money was assumed to be convertible into gold or silver bars and to be freely exchangeable either as coin or as bullion between countries. Its value was fixed at its bullion value, and the rate of exchange between two currencies was easily calculated by comparing the intrinsic value of the precious metal in their coins. In these conditions, the supply of the precious metals would automatically adjust itself to the needs of trade in each country. . . . All the elaborate mercantilist devices for increasing the national supplies of treasure were self-defeating. . . .

What is important for our purpose is the fact that the theories of the classical school are valid only upon the basis of the three major assumptions stated above. The main theorems that were built upon these assumptions constituted a complete system of thought answering the three major groups of questions set forth at the beginning of this chapter. The first theorem, known as the theory of comparative costs, explains the conditions in which trade will arise. The second theorem, known as the price specie-flow theory, explains how payments are made between national currency systems. A corollary of this theorem explains how, in the process of making payments, the precious metals are distributed among countries in accordance with trading needs. The third theorem, to which Mill gave the name of the theory of international values, is now known as the theory of reciprocal demand. It explains how the terms of trade are arrived at, and how the gains from trade are divided between nations. Together, these three theorems constituted a closed and rigorous system. It was the first and until quite recently the most useful, indeed the only, complete and rigorous theory available to explain the workings of international trade. . . .

THE TERRITORIAL DIVISION OF LABOR

A trader, alert for profit, will buy wherever he can do so cheaply. If he buys outside his own country for sale within it, or buys at home to sell abroad, he must calculate many extra costs—transport, taxes, the cost of transferring payment, and usually a great deal of paper work in meeting tax and statistical requirements at the frontiers. In new or poorly organized trades, he must often take a risk on the quality of the product or on its acceptance by consumers. The difference in price between the home and foreign market must usually be considerable if he is to face all these expensive complications in trading across national frontiers.

In course of time, however, international trade tends to become canalized—and to some extent standardized. The quality of the product and the sources of supply become known; trading connections are organized; the consumers' demand can be estimated; transport, duty, and other costs are known; and the paper work can be reduced to routine. Goods can then move from country to country along established routes whenever a somewhat narrow price differential makes such movement profitable.

Whether the trade is new and somewhat hazardous or well-established and moving as the result of close profit calculations based on long experience, it is this price differential which causes it to move. Apart from exceptional cases where the market is miscalculated, no trader ever goes to the trouble of buying in a foreign market goods he can buy more cheaply at home. He buys abroad because the price of a commodity is cheaper there in the simple and absolute sense.

The classical economists were practical men. They knew how trade was carried on. Ricardo, for example, stated clearly that trade arose as a result of absolute price differences. After all he was a successful stock-exchange broker, perfectly familiar with practical business methods, and not likely to invent a theory which would seem nonsensical to his business associates. But unlike the majority of them, he was concerned to probe into the reasons why cloth could be bought cheaply in England and sold in Portugal at a profit. The conclusion to which he came was this. If traders were left alone to pursue their own profit by buying in the cheapest and selling in the dearest market, the result of their activities in the long run would be that each country would come to specialize on producing and exporting those commodities in which its comparative advantage, as measured in labor cost, was greatest.

This theory, or law of comparative cost or of comparative advantage, is now associated with Ricardo's name, though Robert Torrens was perhaps the first to state it. Ricardo himself did not use this exact phraseology. His followers regarded it as his greatest contribution to economic science, and the case for free trade came to be postulated upon it. It is of some importance, therefore, to get a clear understanding of what this theory of comparative cost purported to prove.

Earlier economists, notably Adam Smith, had made a strong case for free trade by demonstrating the advantages of specialization, or of what Torrens in a happy phrase later called the territorial division of labor. But they had been content to argue their case for free trade on the broad ground of the advantages of specialization. It is relatively easy to demonstrate the simple truth that it pays to specialize. Individual experience can be drawn upon to show that any person can maximize his productivity by concentrating upon those things which yield the best return for his time. . . .

Many of the earlier mercantilist writers had noted the advantages of specialization, but, as Adam Smith did, they based their discussion upon such natural advantages as climate and geographical situation. Unlike Ricardo, they did not assume that enterprise, labor, and capital were confined within national boundaries. Indeed, Adam Smith pointed out that merchants were not necessarily citizens of any particular country and commented upon the lack of patriotic sentiment in business. It is true that he wrote before the advent of factories dependent on steam power. But he was very emphatic that "a very trifling disgust will make him (the merchant) remove his capital, and together with it all the industry which it supports, from one country to another."

The conclusion that goods would be produced in the countries where their real costs of production were lowest, and that labor and capital would be attracted to those countries where production costs were low, was unpalatable to those who like Ricardo were concerned to make a case for free trade. In order to make this case on laissez-faire grounds, it was necessary to meet the protectionist argument that under free trade industries might move to countries where natural resources were abundant and labor costs cheap. Such movement clearly took place within national boundaries, but the Ricardians assumed that labor, capital and enterprise were immobile internationally. International trade was defined as taking place between areas where such transfers were impossible. Upon the basis of this definition, the Ricardians developed the law of comparative cost. The international distribution of productive resources was taken as fixed. . . .

The law of comparative cost is best stated by using Ricardo's own arithmetical illustration. He assumed that England could produce a quantity of cloth with the labor of 100 men for a year, and a quantity of wine with the labor of 120 men for a year. In Portugal the same quantities of cloth could be produced by the labor of 90 men and of wine by the labor of 80 men. Both cloth and wine, therefore, could be produced more cheaply (in terms of real cost measured in labor time) in Portugal. Upon the reasoning of earlier economists, there would be a tendency for the production of both to increase in Portugal. Ricardo, however, assuming that capital and labor could not move from England to Portugal, demonstrated that both countries would gain if England concentrated on cloth and Portugal on wine. If each country was of the same size, enough cloth for both could be produced in England by the labor of 200 men, leaving the labor of 20 men to be used for other purposes. In Portugal enough wine for both countries could be produced by the labor of 160 men, leaving the labor of 10 men free. Assuming the complete mobility of labor and capital within each country, it followed that this freed labor would be quickly absorbed in other employment. Each country would then be better off by concentrating on the kind of production in which it had the greatest comparative advantage. . . .

It is not necessary to abandon the case for territorial specialization, or the theory of comparative cost, simply because it can be shown that even in Ricardo's day the factors of production were not entirely immobile between countries. The modern explanation of international trade runs in terms of the most profitable combination of the factors of production in different countries. Thus where labor is abundant and capital is scarce, there is likely to be a comparative advantage in producing goods with a high proportion of labor cost. Where technical and organizing skills are lacking, the export of simple raw materials is more likely than that of highly manufactured commodities. And where capital is abundant and organization is at a high level, there will tend to be a comparative advantage in concentrating upon complex manufactures. . . .

Even a relative immobility of the factors of production—greater difficulty in transferring resources between countries than within a country—is sufficient to warrant the formulation of a theory of comparative advantage. As long as there is a relative immobility of the factors of production, it is clear that, in the absence of government restrictions, trade will continue because it brings mutual benefits. If labor and capital cannot move, the goods they produce will be exchanged. In many important respects the recent strengthening of nationalism has made this assumption of immobility more realistic than it was in the nineteenth century. Men and equipment are now less free to move between countries. . . .

THE GAINS FROM TRADE

. . . [Another] group of questions to be considered in a theory of international trade is concerned with the nature of the gains from trade, and with their division among the trading nations. The classical economists took a broad view of these questions. They were not much concerned with national advantages. They propounded the theory of reciprocal demand to explain the division of the gains from trade. But they were much more interested in the volume of trade to be shared than they were in determining precisely how its gains were divided. The reason for this was their belief that each nation would get the share to which it was entitled by the competitive efficiency of its industries.

The mercantilist writers, however, had been much concerned with national wealth and power. Adam Smith, their severest contemporary critic, did not attack this preoccupation. What he was concerned to demonstrate was that—provided adequate precautions were taken against sudden overwhelming attack—the wealth of a community was best promoted by allowing individual merchants to trade freely for their own profit. It might sometimes be necessary in exceptional situations to sacrifice wealth in order to maintain national power. Such an exceptional situation, he believed, was the necessity for maintaining the Navigation Acts in order to build up naval strength.

On the assumption that a nation maintained the defenses necessary to ward off sudden attack, he always returned to his contention that a nation would grow strong by becoming rich. Subsequent experience has borne out his wisdom. During the nineteenth century England grew rich and powerful as her trade expanded. Even in the preceding centuries her natural defenses had enabled her to develop a freer economy than any of her continental rivals. That freedom gave her a long start in developing the new industrial methods that assured her leadership in the Industrial Revolution.

Throughout the nineteenth century Britain's strong power position cost her little. Secure from land attack, she was able to avoid the heavy burdens of universal military service. A small professional army (incredibly small in retrospect), backed by naval power, sufficed to garrison a great empire. The navy dominated the narrow seas around the British Isles and policed the trade routes of the world. In a crisis, therefore, Britain was sure of having time to mobilize all her power. In doing so, she could draw upon the resources of the whole trading world except that part closed off by a continental enemy. . . .

When the [Napoleonic] wars were . . . ended in 1815, most of the economists and the overwhelming majority of the business community displayed consistent critical opposition to almost all increases in government expenditures, including those for military and naval purposes. Reduction of taxes to a minimum, abolition of all interference with private enterprise, and the elimination of discriminatory preferences for national shipping and for colonial trade, were among their cardinal doctrines.

England grew rapidly in wealth, power, and prestige. The growth of the United States was even more rapid. Despite some friction, there was a strong sentiment in both countries that any difficulties between them could and should be settled without resort to war. This sentiment grew and widened until those who worked for free trade came to identify their cause with the cause of peace. They came to believe that universal free trade would promote peaceful prosperity among all nations. The belief that free competitive trade would bring peace with prosperity may have been naïve, but at least it demonstrates the completeness with which the free traders had dissociated themselves from the mercantilist preoccupation with economic warfare as a means of achieving national power.

The classical economists likewise displayed little interest in employment, which had also been a preoccupation of the mercantilists. They discarded the fear of imports, the fear that an adverse balance of payments would result in a loss of gold, reduce the monetary circulation, lower prices, and so cause periodic industrial depression and social distress. This was in part because they were concerned with the analysis of long-term equilibrium, and therefore brushed aside the incidental consequences of short-term departures from that equilibrium as irrelevant and unimportant. However, their attitude was largely based upon a robust belief in the virtues of competition.

In discussing the division of the gains from trade it is necessary first to stress these broad conceptions of the classical economists. Their complete rejection of mercantilist philosophy, and their adoption of completely opposite attitudes explain their indifference to specific calculations of the exact or even approximate division of the gains from trade. What they were interested in was the most efficient use of the productive resources of the world leading to an expanding world trade. In this trade, they were confident, each country would get its share according to its efficiency. . . .

Impelled by such beliefs and confident of their own competitive power, the merchants who led the free-trade movement in the second quarter of the nineteenth century pushed vigorously ahead with their campaign for unilateral economic disarmament. They were not unaware that it was necessary to reduce tariffs all over the world, but they were determined to begin this reduction at home. Their attack was first and foremost on monopoly and privilege in England. Whether other nations had the good sense to follow their example or not, they were resolved to take away the protection which the tariff on wheat gave to the landowners and thus to cripple the political power of the aristocracy. Therefore they had little interest in using the tariff as a bargaining weapon in trading deals with other nations. Nor were they interested in narrow calculations to discover which of two trading countries had the better of any particular bargain or of trade in general. The enormous expansion of trade which they confidently and rightly prophesied would give opportunities to all. How much of the benefit would accrue to their own country they were content to let rest upon its efficiency and enterprise. . . .

THE DISSENTERS

In recent years it has been recognized that many contemporaries of Ricardo refused to accept either the validity of his theoretical analysis or the conclusions of practical policy which he derived from it. J. M. Keynes has emphasized the independence of Malthus and has credited him with recognizing many of the facts upon which Keynes's own theories were built in recent years. But Malthus did not stand alone in this respect. Of the dissenters whose theories are important for the study of international trade the first group to be noticed are those who, in new countries or in countries of backward economic development, disputed the free-trade doctrines on economic grounds. Primarily these writers relied on the infant-industry argument as the core of a theory of economic development. The *locus classicus* of their argument is to be found in Alexander Hamilton's *Report on the Subject of Manufactures,* presented to the House of Representatives in December, 1791. Though not immediately recognized at its full importance, this report came to be regarded as authoritative when the first American tariff campaigns were vigorously organized at the close of the Napoleonic Wars. . . .

The second group to be considered is the colonial reformers. The guiding spirit of these was Edward Gibbon Wakefield. Their monument is the association of self-governing nations in the British Commonwealth. Its political importance in our world needs no emphasis, but its economic importance is also

considerable. Current ideas of regional economic organization are clearly foreshadowed in the colonial theories worked out by this group of colonial reformers.

The third group of dissenters were those responsible for the steady growth
of socialist doctrine from the earliest decades of the nineteenth century. . . .
In this body of dissent, whether expressed in the evolutionary sentiments of
utopian socialism or in the revolutionary accents of Marxism, are to be found
the ideas of technical efficiency, of planned economies for full employment,
and of distributive justice, which are today among the most important elements in all discussions of national policies affecting international relations.

The challenge to free trade on political grounds constituted a fourth body
of dissent from the classical economic doctrines. This challenge proved to
be crucial. The revival of protectionist ideas in Europe—notably in Germany
—sprang from political even more than from economic causes. Friedrich List
was the prophet of economic nationalism and his arguments fell on fertile
ground as the integration of the German states into a great new empire in
the heart of Europe disturbed the balance of power. The rise of Germany was
the most portentous development of the latter half of the century, but nationalism was not confined to Germany. Trade can surmount tariff barriers. But
it cannot cope with the suspicions and uncertainties created by economic warfare waged as a supplement to diplomacy based on armaments.

The contributions of these dissenting groups to economic thought have
been obscured by the acclaim given to the classical economists whose theories
had been carried into practice in the free-trade experiment which seemed
to be the foundation of England's predominant commercial and financial
position in the nineteenth century. The influence of the classical economists
was further increased because their theories provided a logical, analytical
framework on which later economists could build. The heresies were never
wholly forgotten. Throughout the nineteenth century they were repeated
from time to time. But they could not win intellectual recognition as long as
the policies advocated by the orthodox school seemed to be vindicated in practice. In our own time, however, when regional blocs are developing, when full
employment and national economic development are accepted slogans, and
when economic strategy can be neglected only at the risk of national survival,
a more attentive hearing may perhaps be given to these voices from the past.

Chapter V

SOCIAL CRITICISM AND PROGRAMS
OF REFORM

℘

1. SOCIAL CRITICS OF THE EARLY NINETEENTH CENTURY

EARLY CHRISTIAN SOCIALISM

THE NEW CAPITALISM and industrialism and the doctrines of its theoretical apologists among the Economic Liberals were frequently identified with the philosophy of materialism. This naturally led to opposition from the churchmen and the faithful of all types. While programs of social reform hostile to Economic Liberalism were put forward by Catholics, High Churchmen, Broad Churchmen, and Dissenters, one unifying purpose runs through all of their work, namely, the desire to socialize Christianity and thereby to capture social reform for the Church. They thus hoped to secure for religious institutions the gratitude and support of the numerous members of the proletariat.

The origins of modern Christian Socialism may be traced to the work entitled *The New Christianity* (1825) by the French sociologist Henri de Saint-Simon. In this work the contrast between the social doctrines of Christ and the traditionalism and ritualism of the historical Church was clearly drawn, and a striking appeal was made for the socialization of religion.

In the field of Social Catholicism there were a number of interesting developments, particularly in France under the Bourbon restoration and the Orleanist monarchy. The movement began, as we have seen, as a revival of emotionalism, obscurantism, and political reaction in the doctrines of Chateaubriand, De Bonald, and De Maistre (1753–1821). But the growth of democracy affected Church as well as State in France, and several exponents of the reli-

---

This chapter consists of material by two different authors. Section 1 is from *The History of Western Civilization* (Vol. II, pp. 389–402; New York, Harcourt, Brace & Co., 1935), by Harry Elmer Barnes, with the collaboration of Henry David. Section 2, designed especially for the present volume, has been revised from its form in the first edition and is by Charles Frankel.

gious revival clearly understood that if they were to make any headway they
would need to liberalize the Catholic standpoint. This was partially achieved
by Antoine Frédéric Ozanam (1813–53), who founded the Society of St.
Vincent de Paul and linked up Neo-Catholicism with practical philanthropy;
by Alphonse de Lamartine (1790–1869), who attempted to connect the Catholic movement with the growth of republican sentiment in France; by Robert
de Lamennais (1782–1854), who tried unsuccessfully to harmonize Catholicism with the principles of the French Revolution and political democracy;
and by Philippe Joseph Buchez (1796–1865), who shared the historical viewpoint of the German school of economists, tried to prove the spirit of Christianity to be revolutionary, anticipated the "Guild Socialism" of Bishop von
Ketteler and Franz Hitze, and advocated a scheme of coöperative production
and distribution.

The Protestant members of this first important group of Christian social
reformers are those who have usually been specifically designated as Christian
Socialists, but this title could with equal accuracy be extended to the Catholic
reformers just named.

The leaders in the Protestant aspects of this movement were chiefly Anglican
clergymen of the Broad Church party, though there was considerable support
accorded by the Unitarians and the Methodists. The most prominent members
of the Christian Socialist group in England were John Frederick Denison
Maurice (1805–72), Charles Kingsley (1819–75), and Thomas Hughes (1822–
96). Others of influence who adhered to their general point of view were John
M. F. Ludlow (1821–1911) and John Lalor (1814–56).

Maurice, usually regarded as the founder of the movement in England, was
especially interested in the education of the laboring class. Kingsley analyzed
the social problems of his day in powerful sermons and such telling books as
Alton Locke, Yeast, and *The Water-Babies.* Like Buchez, he urged the formation of workingmen's organizations and the institution of coöperative associations.

Probably the most enduring contribution of English Christian Socialism to
social reform was the impulse that it gave to the organization of coöperative
and profit-sharing societies, of which one, based on the work of Owen—the
famous Rochdale Pioneers—has endured to the present day. The coöperative
movement spread rapidly on the Continent and has developed particularly
in Denmark and Belgium. The English Christian Socialists actually imported
their ideas on workers' associations and coöperation mainly from Buchez's
work in France, since Owen's work in England was at the time associated
with anti-Christian notions. The other important result of Christian Socialism

in this first stage was the aid it gave to the cause of the education of the proletariat and to arousing the interest of the Anglican Church in social reform.

The impulse to social reform within the Anglican Church originated by
the Christian Socialists attracted even members of the High Church party, and
the leaders of that emotional reaction, the Oxford Movement, such as Hurrell
Froude, Newman, Keble, and Pusey, lent their support to the development
of trade-unionism and the betterment of housing-conditions among the poor.
Finally, even the dissenting sects, particularly the Quakers and the newer
evangelical organizations, took a very significant part in agitating for remedial
legislation for the poorer classes. This social impulse in Christianity spread
even to the United States, where much interest was shown by W. E. Channing
and the New England Unitarians and Transcendentalists.

THE ESTHETIC REVOLT AGAINST MATERIALISM AND MISERY

The Industrial Revolution has produced nearly all the material comforts of
modern life and has created many new forms of art and beauty as well. Nevertheless, at least in its first stages, the new industrialism, with its dismal factories, clouds of smoke, and filthy tenements, was extremely ugly and repulsive
to the esthetic temperament and humanitarian impulses alike. Therefore, the
new order of things and its supporters among the Economic Liberals were
vigorously attacked by those who were the representatives of the literary and
artistic standards of the age.

This so-called esthetic revolt against the new industrial order was of a rather
varied sort, ranging all the way from the purely cultural protest of such men
as Matthew Arnold to the conversion of leading literary figures such as George
Sand and William Morris to overt Socialistic programs. While most of the
leading figures in art and literature during the second third of the nineteenth
century were repulsed by the new industrial developments, a few can be singled
out as the leaders in the esthetic protest. Among these were Robert Southey
(1774-1843), Thomas Carlyle (1795-1881), Samuel Coleridge (1772-1834),
Charles Dickens (1812-70), Charles Reade (1814-84), John Ruskin (1819-
1900), Matthew Arnold (1822-88), William Morris (1834-96), Ralph Waldo
Emerson (1803-82), George Sand (1804-76) and Leo Tolstoy (1828-1910). Of
this group the most important were Dickens, Carlyle, Ruskin, George Sand,
Tolstoy, and Arnold.

Dickens was probably the ablest and most effective critic among the literary
figures who protested against the evils of the Industrial Revolution, as well as
those which had come down from an earlier era—the criminal law and prisons,
for example. He saw about him the miserable factory towns, the unspeakable

conditions in the mines, the long hours of labor, insufficient wages, and the ruthless oppression of women and children. His whole personality was revolted by these products of laissez-faire and the new capitalism. His reaction is mirrored in a classic passage from *Martin Chuzzlewit:*

Bethink yourselves . . . that there are scores of thousands breathing now, and breathing thick with painful toil, who . . . have never lived at all, nor had a chance of life. Go ye . . . Teachers of content and honest pride, into the mine, the mill, the forge, the squalid depths of deepest ignorance, and uttermost abyss of man's neglect, and say can any hopeful plant spring up in air so foul that it extinguishes the soul's bright torch as fast as it is kindled!

Dickens not only attacked the industrialists, but also the usurers who fattened upon the unfortunates in the England of his day. He also wrote effectively in behalf of the campaign for better housing and sanitation in the new industrial cities.

Carlyle is significant chiefly as a devastating critic of the materialism and the economic abstractions of the classical school. He had little or no constructive program of reform beyond a willingness to wait for some unique genius to appear with a ready-made solution. Ruskin was as bitter as Carlyle in his criticism of the new industrial society and its ideals, but he offered a program for the solution of existing problems through his advocacy of the restoration of the dignity of labor, the institution of a régime of industrial coöperation, state education, government workshops, and state insurance for the working classes. A part of his program bordered on the Guild Socialism of a slightly later period, but he put education above all other types of relief for the situation. A trace of the temptation to a utopian flight from reality appeared in his "Gild of St. George."

George Sand, of a slightly earlier period, imbibed freely the utopian and revolutionary Socialism of the forties in France, and by her writings did much to popularize these notions, in particular the doctrines of Pierre Leroux. Tolstoy's reform program was somewhat retrogressive and irrational, though less so for a writer with the agrarian background of Russia than for one writing in the midst of Western industrialism. He advocated a complete abandonment of the new industrialism, a return to an agrarian age, and the organization of the agrarian economy according to the principles of the Russian *mir,*[1] with its communistic and coöperative practices considerably expanded. Arnold, an admirer of the authoritarian and positive Prussian state,

[1] [Russian form of village community compounded of heads of families who elected elders to represent the village in relation to the government. The *mir* decided when to plow, plant, reap, etc. for the village. It held title to the land the usufruct of which was enjoyed by the peasants working it.]

laid the literary basis for the introduction of the Hegelian theory of the state into England.

While one can appreciate the real and valid motives for this revolt of the esthetic temperament against the repulsive features of modern industrial society, this group offered little in the way of workable constructive reforms. Few, except those who went over to Socialism, had any real reform program. Only an impractical person could accept the proposal of some of them that society should revert to a pre-Industrial Revolution economy in which kings lived with fewer personal comforts than the average workingman of today. Further, even those who, like Ruskin, had some program to offer, were scarcely in line with modern industrial democracy, but desired the establishment of some sort of authoritative and benevolent paternalism.

In spite of all this, the esthetic protest was a real contribution to the reform cause. It effectively insisted that an increase in material gain was no complete justification of a new order of civilization, and maintained that modern industrialism must make a place for the assertion of the ideal and the esthetic. . . .

UTOPIAN SOCIALISM AND THE RECONSTRUCTION OF THE SOCIAL AND ECONOMIC ENVIRONMENT

Those extremely daring schemes of social reform which are conventionally known as "utopian" appear most frequently after some great transition that brings with it an abnormal degree of misery. The Industrial Revolution, the greatest of all such transitions, and probably the most productive of accompanying misery, naturally brought forth an unprecedented number of utopian plans for the solution of existing social problems, but all of these programs were more realistic and practical than the somewhat fanciful utopias of the sixteenth and seventeenth centuries which we analyzed in an earlier chapter.

In the most fundamental sense Utopian Socialism of the first half of the nineteenth century was a revolt against the semifatalism of Economic Liberalism. The latter had represented society as the product of natural laws and forces, had accused the proletariat of being the authors of their own miseries, and had sharply denied the possibility of improving conditions artificially through constructive human legislation. Utopian Socialism denounced these assumptions of Romanticism, individualism, and Economic Liberalism, and revived the notions of the French Revolution to the effect that human intelligence and ingenuity are fully equal to the task of forging a new social and economic order. It held that human nature is primarily the product of the social environment and that, accordingly, the solution of contemporary

evils is to be found in the creation of a better set of social institutions and
practices. They maintained that man can, by rational thought, determine his
own social system and social relations. Some, like Fourier, even claimed that
man may by well-conceived legislation anticipate the normal course of social
evolution and devise short cuts to the ideal goal.

The pioneer in the utopian literature of this period is conventionally assumed to be Count Henri de Saint-Simon. But . . . he can be quite as
truly regarded as the formulator of the chief theses of Comtian sociology or
as a forerunner of Christian Socialism. The other utopias would have developed out of the surrounding conditions and ideas had Saint-Simon never
written. Saint-Simon's most important contribution to social science and
ultimately to social reform was his contention that the social problems created
by the Industrial Revolution were so serious that a distinct science of social
reconstruction must be evolved to deal with them. Comte attempted to
systematize this new social science—Sociology—of which Saint-Simon had
seen the need.

The disciples of Saint-Simon further developed his diverse notions. En-
fantin and Bazard emphasized the communistic principles to be found in that
primitive Christianity which Saint-Simon so much admired. Leroux defended the notion of the social and moral equality of mankind and stressed
the essential solidarity of society and the community of interests of all social
classes.

The foremost of the French utopians was François Charles Marie Fourier
(1772–1835). He was one of the most thorough believers in the possibility of
reforming mankind through the creation of an ideal social environment. This
he believed would be found in an "apartment-house utopia"—a coöperative
community or *phalange* of some 1,800 individuals in which each would work
at a congenial occupation. He hoped ultimately to see human society reconstituted as a world-federation of these phalansteries, the capital of which was
to be located at Constantinople. Fourier did not envisage a society that would
wholly abolish all private property or attempt to equalize all classes and individuals. He worked out what he believed to be a proper fractional distribution of the social income between labor, capital, and management. While he
did not profoundly affect France, no other member of the utopian group attracted so large and sympathetic a following in America. Many Fourierian
groups were established in the United States, the most famous of which was
Brook Farm, founded and conducted by some of the most noted members of
the "Brahman caste" of New England literary lights. The other notable

French utopian reformer was Etienne Cabet (1788–1856), whose followers established an experimental community first in Texas and later in Nauvoo, Illinois.

The leading English Utopian Socialist was Robert Owen (1771–1858), who came into the field of utopian theorizing fresh from a practical demonstration of the possibility of establishing an ideal industrial community. At his cotton mills in New Lanark he had organized an advanced industrial community, which, at the opening of the nineteenth century, possessed many of the features that characterize the most progressive industrial organizations of the present day. It was unique at that time. While Owen gave his support to almost every type of constructive philanthropy that was current in his day, he is known especially for his agitation in behalf of factory legislation and trade-unionism, his vigorous advocacy of industrial coöperation, and his concrete plan for ideal industrial communities. The latter did not differ markedly from that of Fourier, though the individual groups were to be slightly smaller. Although his plan was adopted in several places in the United States, most notably at New Harmony, Indiana, these trials resulted in little practical success. The enduring mark that Owen left on social reform consists chiefly in his support of many plans for aiding the solution of existing evils and in his emphasis upon the peculiar virtues inhering in coöperation. More recent echoes of the utopian movement have been William Morris's *News from Nowhere,* Edward Bellamy's *Looking Backward,* and several utopian novels by H. G. Wells.

Significant as were the notions of Utopian Socialism in emphasizing the ability of society consciously and artificially to solve its own problems, this type of Socialism could scarcely lead directly into Marxian Socialism. It was too impractical and, from the standpoint of the Marxians, it was not sufficiently democratic. The utopians did not set forth plans designed to aid the proletariat alone, but aimed at a reconstruction of all society. In a very real sense they were as much the forerunners of modern French "Solidarism" as of Marxian Socialism. Between Utopian and Marxian Socialism there intervened the stage of "Transitional Socialism" through which Socialism was made a revolutionary and proletarian movement.

While the great majority of the Utopian Socialists were concerned chiefly with the reformation of the new industrial society, there was one writer, the learned British physician Charles Hall (about 1740–1820), who anticipated Henry George and contended that the main cause of the evils of the age was private property in land and the concentration of land in great estates. In his

Effects of Civilization, published in 1805, Hall argued for the nationalization of land as the remedy for the abuses and oppression of his age. Dr. Beer has thus summarized his doctrines:

> The division of land into large dominions, and the inequality consequent upon that division, gave to the rich an absolute power over the non-possessors, whom they use for the purpose of increasing the stock of wealth. Private property in land led to manufactures, trade, and commerce, by which the poor are made poorer still, and the small possessors are deprived of the little they possess and thrown into poverty.
>
> The division of the land being thus the original cause of the evil, the reform of society must evidently start by removing the cause. The land, therefore, should be nationalized and settled with small farmers. The land should be restored to the nation, and the nation to the land. Agriculture should be the main occupation of all. Of the sciences and arts only those should be preserved and promoted that are necessary for the prosperity of agricultural pursuits.

Hall was not, however, unaware of the evils of industrialism and early capitalism. He clearly formulated the labor theory of value, the notion of surplus value, and the doctrine of the class struggle. He held that labor creates values but receives only wages. The difference between values and wages constitutes the basis of the private wealth of the industrialists and landlords. This private wealth is taken away from labor because of the weakness of the latter. Hall also laid stress upon the fact that the rich profit from the wars that the poor have to fight.

TRANSITIONAL OR REVOLUTIONARY SOCIALISM

The most important figures in the so-called Transitional Socialism were the "Ricardian Socialists," William Thompson (1785–1833), John Gray (died about 1850), Thomas Hodgskin (1787–1869), and John Francis Bray (about 1840); the Frenchmen Louis Blanc (1813–82) and Pierre Joseph Proudhon (1809–65); and the Germans Wilhelm Weitling (1808–70) and Ferdinand Lassalle (1825–64). Proudhon, however, played a more prominent part in founding modern Anarchism, and Lassalle is equally important as an advocate of State Socialism.

So far as his practical reform program is concerned, Thompson was a disciple of Robert Owen, but his *Inquiry into the Principles of the Distribution of Wealth Most Conducive to Human Happiness* (1824) contained a very clear statement of the famous Marxian conception of the doctrine of "surplus value." He maintained that labor produces all value and should get the whole product, but under capitalistic society it is cheated out of a great part of its just income. Gray criticized the bourgeois society of his day, accepted the labor theory of value, and advocated state intervention. Hodgskin turned the theory of the natural order against the Economic Liberals by attempting to show that capitalism was an artificial and not a natural product. Bray elaborated the economic interpretation of history as well as the labor theory of value.

Louis Blanc was one of the first to insist that the only effective help that the proletariat can expect must come from their own efforts. They themselves must make effective their most basic right—the right to labor. He believed that the laboring classes would have to triumph through an economic revolution, either peaceful or violent. His post-Revolutionary program consisted in "social workshops," which practically meant state support and control of industry according to a democratic plan of organization. In the French Revolution of 1848 his plan was ostensibly tried out, but since it was operated by his enemies, who only desired to discredit it, the scheme proved a hopeless failure. Certain phases of Blanc's doctrine roughly resemble the later programs of Syndicalism and Guild Socialism.

Proudhon made an especially bitter attack upon the institution of private property, or rather upon the abuses of private property that then existed. But he was equally critical of the doctrine of Communism. He proposed to base the income of everyone solely upon the amount of labor performed, the unit value of which was to be equal and uniform among all members of society. Following the Revolution of 1848, he attempted to secure the establishment of a national banking system founded upon this labor scrip, but he failed utterly in this. Standing at the opposite pole from Say and Bastiat in his attitude towards modern capitalism, he is chiefly significant for his effective onslaught upon the abuses of the bourgeois régime.

Weitling, a Magdeburg tailor who later came to the United States, anticipated Marx by a comprehensive and trenchant review of the evils that modern capitalism had brought to the workingmen and by an eloquent appeal to the proletariat, urging them to rise in their own behalf and overthrow their capitalistic oppressors. His program was a curious combination of proposals similar to certain notions of Fourier, Saint-Simon, and Proudhon—Fourier's conception of "attractive industry," Saint-Simon's notion of expert direction of society, and Proudhon's proposal for an exchange bank based on labor scrip.

Lassalle made important historical, legal, and philosophical attacks on capitalism and private property, stressed the fact that the laborers can only escape from bondage through political activity, and assumed a leading part in urging and guiding the formation of the first significant labor party in Germany. His concrete plan for reform called for state workshops much like those proposed by Louis Blanc, but this phase of his doctrines and activity had little subsequent influence. Transitional Socialism thus in many obvious ways prepared Europe for Marxian Socialism.

EARLY PHILOSOPHICAL ANARCHISM

It might be thought that the Economic Liberals had achieved the most perfect apotheosis of the individual, but another contemporary school exceeded them in this respect, namely, the early Philosophical Anarchists. The Economic Liberals at least proposed to retain the state to preserve life and protect property, but the Anarchists advocated the total abolition of the state and all coercive juristic institutions.

The first of this group was William Godwin (1756-1836), whose *Enquiry concerning Political Justice* (1793) was the most enthusiastic elaboration of the extreme Rationalistic notions of the French Revolution by an English social philosopher. He held that all evils in society result from the detrimental effect of repressive human institutions. He proposed that all collective and coercive organizations larger than the parish should be abolished; that the unequal distribution of wealth should be done away with; that the institution of marriage should be wiped out; and that mankind should be free from everything save the moral censure of their associates, thereby being made ready for their ultimate perfection through the influence of reason.

Proudhon inveighed mightily against the bourgeois state, which he regarded solely as an institution for exploitation and oppression. His ideal society was to be founded upon that combination which may readily be created in abstraction, but has never yet been realized as a practical condition, namely, "the union of order and anarchy." He believed that if the obligations of contract could be enforced, society would function perfectly. But he scarcely comprehended that until human institutions have reached a higher state of perfection there can be no assured enforcement of contractual obligations without the authority of the law behind them. In the United States, Josiah Warren (1799-1874), earlier an enthusiastic follower of Robert Owen, developed doctrines somewhat similar to those of Proudhon but quite independent of Proudhon's influence. His more important works were *True Civilization* (1846) and *Equitable Commerce* (1852).

While Godwin, Proudhon, and Warren rejected the utility of the state, they stressed the importance of society—of the concept of humanity. It was left for Max Stirner (1805-56) in his *The Ego and His Own* (1844) to exalt the individual above even humanity and society, to assert that the individual constitutes the only true reality, to maintain that the only limitation upon the rights of the individual is his failure to obtain what he desires, and to contend that "the only right is might."

Though these early Anarchists were guilty of many excesses of statement and offered no well-reasoned substitute for the state that they proposed to destroy, they did perform a real service by insisting that the state, at least as long as it is undemocratized, may be unjustly oppressive and a legitimate object of suspicion on the part of those excluded from participation in it.

THE POLITICAL REVOLUTIONS OF 1848

We have already noticed how in the winter and spring of 1848, the masses throughout central, southern, and western Europe, led on by the bourgeoisie themselves in many areas, rose in the attempt to secure for themselves freedom from oppression through participation in political activity. In the German states freedom from political autocracy was desired; in the Hapsburg realms and in Italy not only political liberty but also freedom from the social and economic burdens of feudalism was aimed at; in France the political participation of the masses and the overthrow of the oppression of the bourgeoisie were the goal; and in England the Chartists hoped to achieve economic betterment and that participation in the world of politics which had been denied to the mass of Englishmen in the Reform Bill of 1832. For various reasons, primarily the fatal divisions of the revolutionists through national, party, or economic rivalry, the movements failed in every country, although the abolition of serfdom in the Hapsburg possessions was a permanent achievement. The failure of these political revolts of the masses turned many into economic channels of attack upon the forces of privilege and helped on the growth of revolutionary and Marxian Socialism.

THE RISE OF HUMANITARIANISM

Associated with the rise of science, mechanical industry, and the new capitalism were not only various social and economic doctrines defending or criticizing capitalism, but many types of humanitarian reforms designed to increase the well-being of mankind.

In the middle of the eighteenth century, political oppression and arbitrary government were still common. A citizen might be imprisoned or executed in arbitrary fashion in most places outside England and the lesser asylums of freedom. Criminals were treated with atrocious brutality. In many states religious intolerance persisted, torture and imprisonment still being common in the handling of religious dissent. Dissenters were generally excluded from important political offices. The relief of the poor was imperfect and inadequate. In many places they were left to starve or shift for themselves. In others the responsibility was still that of the Church. Where public authorities had taken it up the organization was usually unscientific and inequitable. Human slavery among whites had been pretty much abandoned, but Negroes were still enslaved by the whites in colonies and in the Southern states of the United States. The Catholics had for centuries been interested in the salvation of peoples overseas, but the Protestants had done little missionary work before the end of the eighteenth century.

The evolution of political liberalism was partially achieved in the English revolutions of 1649 and 1689, the American Revolution, the French Revolution of 1789, the European revolutions of 1830 and 1848, and the Russian Revolution of 1905. These important political uprisings seriously curbed political autocracy, usually put the middle class into the saddle, established the right of revolution, and gained at least the semblance of equality for all before the law.

We shall now consider a series of important reforms which sought to reduce human misery and increase the happiness of man. The background for this movement lay in the rise of Deism. . . . The humanitarian movement spread to the Quakers and the Evangelical groups. The antislavery crusade was led by the Evangelicals, who also took a prominent part in urging factory and mine reforms in the nineteenth century. They and the Quakers also worked for educational reform, as well as for improvement of prison conditions.

One of the worst survivals of barbarism in Europe in the eighteenth century lay in criminal law. Men were still subjected to torture during the process of trial in many countries. Sentences were severe and punishments extremely brutal. The death sentence was often imposed for such a trivial offense as petty theft. Corporal punishment, including branding and mutilation, was still common. Debtors were commonly imprisoned. Prisons were reserved chiefly for debtors and those accused of crime prior to trial. These prisons were mostly filthy, uncomfortable, and brutally administered.

The barbarous criminal law was attacked by Voltaire and Montesquieu in the middle of the eighteenth century. The latter's *Persian Letters* especially satirized the European criminal law of this period. But the most influential reformer in the field of criminal law was the Italian nobleman Cesare di Beccaria (1738–94). His *Essay on Crimes and Punishments* (1764) was probably the most effective book written in the whole history of criminal-law reform. He argued that the prevention of crime is more important than punishment; that torture should be abolished; that punishment should be used to deter men from committing crimes rather than to inflict social revenge on an individual; that imprisonment should be substituted for corporal punishment; and that capital punishment should be abandoned. Indeed, with the exception of the recent application of psychology and psychiatry to crime, Beccaria suggested most of the essentials of criminological progress that have been achieved in the century and a half since his work was published.

Beccaria's ideas deeply influenced the reform of the criminal codes of the American states after 1776, the new criminal code of Revolutionary France, and the reform of the British criminal code by Bentham, Romilly, Buxton, Mackintosh, and Peel in the first half of the nineteenth century. In 1800 there were about two hundred capital offenses in the British criminal code. By 1861 they had been reduced to three: treason, murder, and piracy. Torture was gradually abolished in European criminal procedure and fair and humane trials were provided for accused persons. Imprisonment for debt was slowly outlawed. It did not disappear even in the United States until the Jacksonian period, when it was submerged by the rising tide of democratic enthusiasm.

The reform of the criminal law was paralleled by the increased use of imprisonment as the usual method of punishment and by an improvement in the character of the prisons. We have already pointed out that down to the middle of the eighteenth century corporal punishment and fines were the chief devices employed in the punishment of criminals. Jails and prisons were used mainly for accused persons and debtors. But the American Quakers were repelled by the copious shedding of blood and the other barbarities connected with corporal punishment. Therefore, just as soon as Pennsylvania obtained its independence in 1776 it was ordered that imprisonment at hard labor should be instituted in the place of corporal punishment. Soon the Pennsylvania system of prison discipline, based on continuous solitary confinement, became world-famous. But a competing type—the Auburn system—soon appeared. This provided for solitary confinement at night and for association in prison shops during the day. These two systems struggled for supremacy during the nineteenth century. The Auburn system won most favor in the United States, the Pennsylvania system in Europe. In either case, it meant the abandonment of brutal whippings, the lopping-off of ears, branding, and other usual brutalities of the preprison era. In England the work of the American Quakers and other reformers like Louis Dwight was paralleled by the prison-reform efforts of John Howard (1726-91) and Elizabeth Fry (1780-1845). The main progress in prison administration in the last century has consisted in the triumph of the notion that prisons are places for the reformation of convicts rather than for the mere punishment of criminals. Special institutions have been established for women, children, insane criminals, feebleminded criminals, and the like, thus insuring more specialized and competent treatment of each type.

Religious intolerance was widely prevalent in the eighteenth century. Catholics, dissenting Protestants, and Jews were usually excluded from public office and often subjected to prolonged imprisonment. In England, for example, the Corporation Act of 1661 disqualified all but Anglicans from municipal government, and the Test Act of 1673 excluded orthodox Roman Catholics from both civil and military service. An act of 1678 also denied them membership in either house of Parliament. In some other countries religious persecution was far worse. After the Revocation of the Edict of Nantes in France the French Protestants were frequently butchered in droves. Jews were uniformly badly treated and almost always excluded from office.

Religious toleration first gained headway in Holland and Switzerland. In 1689 England passed the Toleration Act, which forbade the imprisonment of dissenting Protestants solely because of their religious views. The Test and Corporation Acts were repealed in 1828. The next year the Catholic Emancipation Act was passed, admitting Catholics to most of the important public offices in England. The Jews had to wait until 1858 for the passage of laws admitting them to Parliament. In France religious toleration was very generally secured during the Revolution, following 1789, and the progress of the French Revolutionary principles in other states furthered religious toleration. The American Constitution of 1789 guaranteed religious freedom, and the several states soon abandoned their religious tests for suffrage. Rather barbarous treatment of Jews has continued down into the present century, but tolerance and decency in regard to religion, with some persistent and notorious lapses, have gradually won headway. . . .

In the gradual establishment of scientific public relief of the poor England took the lead. The marked increase of pauperism following the rise of sheep-farming in the fifteenth and sixteenth centuries made ecclesiastical relief of the poor inadequate. Between 1563 and 1601 a series of laws were passed providing for public support of paupers, but the administration of the law was left in the hands of local authorities. The system persisted with few changes down to 1795, when the so-called Berkshire method was established. According to this, relief was to be administered on the basis of the size of the family and inadequate wages were to be supplemented out of the poor-relief funds. This invited pauperism, illegitimacy, and the demoralization of the relief system. Reform finally came in the great Poor Law of 1834, which was an embodiment of the principles of Jeremy Bentham. It was based on the idea of the prevention of pauperism as well as the relief of the worthy poor. It forbade giving relief in homes except to the aged and the sick. It required others to enter a workhouse to get aid. It provided for a logical and economical unification of local areas in administering relief. Since that time the administration of poor relief has been better organized on a national basis in England.

The British precedents in poor relief were rather generally adopted in the United States, modified by the so-called Indiana system. Even more scientific have been some of the Continental schemes, especially in the cities. The most famous is the Hamburg-Elberfeld system, which insures careful inspection of needs along with maximum economy in the administration of relief. These earlier and more crude methods of administering relief have been supplemented in our own day by elaborate social-insurance codes designed to make direct relief less necessary. . . .

More humane treatment of the insane was brought about during this era. In 1750 it was still generally the rule to keep the insane chained up in brutal fashion in jails and poorhouses. A French physician, Philippe Pinel (1745–1826), was the first to take a civilized attitude towards these unfortunates. As superintendent of a French institution for the insane, he ordered the chains stricken off the inmates. He showed that it was safe and effective to deal with most of the insane without fastening them with chains. The most influential figure in establishing hospitals for the insane was an American woman, Dorothea Lynde Dix (1802–87), perhaps the foremost American humanitarian of the first half of the nineteenth century. She carried on an extensive and successful campaign in behalf of the building of hospitals for the insane and the transfer of these unfortunates from poorhouses, jails, and prisons.

Another phase of the humanitarian movement was the attack on Negro slavery. An English clergyman, William Wilberforce, secured the passage of an act by the British Parliament abolishing the slave trade in 1807. But the reformers were further determined to end slavery in the British Empire. The Quakers, led by Thomas F. Buxton, took the lead in this, but they were aided by other clerical groups. Finally, in 1833 Parliament passed a bill abolishing slavery in the British Empire after August 1, 1834. It required a great Civil War to abolish slavery in the United States, and it persisted in fact if not in law in many tropical colonies until well into the present century.

Missionary enterprise cannot be omitted from this brief summary of early humanitarianism. The Catholics had been interested in saving the souls of the heathen ever since the Apostolic age, but the Protestants did not enter deeply into such activity until the eighteenth century. The Society for the

Propagation of the Gospel in Foreign Parts (Anglican) was established in 1701. A large number of Protestant societies devoted to foreign missions were formed in the last decade of the eighteenth century. While these societies were theoretically devoted to saving souls, they also did much to introduce European ways of life among the backward peoples. . . .

Finally, we may refer briefly to the rise of popular education. Free public instruction first arose on a large scale in Prussia in the latter part of the eighteenth century. Here the benevolent despots saw the value of an educated public. The French revolutionists, influenced by Rousseau, also favored public instruction. In England the first public aid to education was authorized by an act of 1833. During the nineteenth century, British support of education mainly took the form of state aid to private schools. But in 1918 a national public education system was set up. Public education in the United States received its first great impetus from the wave of democratic optimism that came to a crest in the age of Andrew Jackson. Democracy was a powerful factor in promoting interest in public education. The democrats believed that all men were equal in native capacity and that equal opportunities in education would insure actual equality in life and achievement. . . .

2. EARLY MARXISM

During the 1830s and '40s the concepts of the "Utopian Socialists" became a target of merciless criticism by another group of able thinkers committed to fundamental social change. Of these early "Communists" two were outstanding: Karl Marx, a brilliant doctor of philosophy from the University of Berlin, and Friedrich Engels, a German businessman residing in England.

Marx, who combined idealistic striving with a keenly analytical mind, was too nonconformist to secure an academic appointment. He turned to journalism and at the age of twenty-four became the editor of a radical paper which was soon suppressed. In 1843, shortly after his marriage to Jenny von Westphalen, of noble family, the young couple went to Paris where Marx became the editor of the *Franco-German Year Books*. The aim of these books, he declared, was "the fearless criticism of all existing institutions" and not the formulation of a new dogma. Only one number of the *Year Books* appeared, but it contained an article by Engels which condemned capitalist economy as unjust. In the autumn of 1844 Marx, with the collaboration of Engels, published *The Holy Family*. This contains the germs of the so-called materialistic conception of history and of the theory of the class struggle, which were to become two of the basic principles of the Marx-Engels theory. The next year

(1845), at the instigation of the Prussian government, Marx was forced to leave Paris for Brussels. Upon the outbreak of the revolutionary movement of 1848 he returned to his native land, only to be promptly expelled as a socialist agitator. He fled to London where, in poverty, he spent the rest of his life studying, writing, and meeting with other opponents of capitalism. It was here that he prepared his monumental work, *Das Kapital* (*Capital*), which, like Rousseau's *Social Contract* and Darwin's *Origin of Species,* was to exert an influence out of all proportion to the number of its readers.

While in Brussels Marx became a member of a radical organization called the League of Communists or, as it was first known, the League of the Just. Engels attended the first congress of this League, held in London in the summer of 1847. The second congress, which met in December of the same year, commissioned Marx and Engels to prepare a new program. The result was the famous *Communist Manifesto.*

"Marxism" or "dialectical materialism" can be conveniently divided into three main parts: (1) the general laws or principles of "dialectics"; (2) the materialist or economic interpretation of history; (3) the economic analysis of capitalism, based on the concept of "surplus value." Marx himself believed that his economic theories did not absolutely require the general framework of dialectical materialism for support, and his theory of history can also be argued on independent grounds. Nevertheless, there is in Marx's writings, and in Engels', a general unity of language and approach; and the subsequent history of socialism, and particularly revolutionary socialism, has tended to emphasize the inclusive, systematic aspects of Marxism even more than did the systematic-minded Marx himself.

The "dialectical" side of "dialectical materialism" goes back to Hegel's attack upon Aristotelian logic, and to his attempt to produce a logic which, so he alleged, would be able to deal more adequately with the phenomena of historical and natural change and evolution. The specific "laws of the dialectic" are too technical for discussion here, although it is worth remarking that the formulation of them either by Hegel or Engels has left the overwhelming majority of philosophers—at any rate, in countries where philosophy is relatively free from political dictation—profoundly unconvinced. In the hands of Marx and Engels, the emphasis on the "dialectical" structure of nature seems to have had two principal purposes: (1) to exhibit the ubiquity of change and evolution, and the historical character of human thinking, and (2) to show the tight connection between theory and practice. Philosophers, Marx felt, have thought they were merely interpreting the world; but, in fact, their theories have been intimately involved in preserving, or occasionally in changing, a specific set of social institutions at a particular moment in history; and the real function of philosophy, he was convinced, was not merely to comment on the world, but to provide ideas which would help to change it.

The "materialist" aspect of "dialectical materialism" was in large part a reaction against Hegel's idealism and the conservative philosophies which it nurtured. The general "materialism" of Marxism was a way of arguing for the general applicability of scientific methods to social affairs and human relations, and it was a way of arguing against ecclesiastical morality, clericalism in politics, and philosophical attempts to buttress existing social orders by showing that they served "eternal" ideals or illustrated a cosmic plan with which man could not rightly or safely interfere. The "materialism" of Marxism itself shows many of the features of the nonmaterialist philosophies which it attacked; and while Marx, in his best moments, was a responsible scholar and a historian of surpassing scope and powers of observation, not all his work is an undiluted exemplification of scientific methods. From the point of view of the scientific study of history or economics, much of it is marred by hasty generalization from insufficient evidence, and by an excessive preoccupation with practical political objectives. There is, besides, less warrant than Marx thought for his sanguine belief that developments in science give logical support to philosophic materialism. Nevertheless, Marx's "materialism" was one of the great efforts in the nineteenth century to stabilize and shape a program for empirical social inquiry, and especially for applying the important idea of evolution to the study of social institutions.

The most important feature of Marx's materialism was the economic interpretation of history, and its corollary, the idea of the class struggle. Marx wrote:

In the social production which men carry on they enter into definite relations . . . [which] constitute the economic structure of society—the real foundation on which rise legal and political superstructures and to which correspond definite forms of social consciousness. The modes of production in material life determine the general character of the social, political, and spiritual processes of life.

This theory has frequently been misinterpreted as a theory about human motivations. In fact, however, it is an *institutional* theory and not a theory about individual psychology. It does not assert that conscious economic motives are necessarily primary in human behavior. What it does assert is that human decisions are made within a context of habits and alternatives which are determined by social conditions, and that economic problems are so ubiquitous and pressing that economic institutions naturally exercise a predominant influence on human affairs. Marx's hopes with respect to socialism, indeed, were that socialism would make economic problems less pressing, and so would release human beings from excessive bondage to economic institutions.

To the extent that Marx argued that economic institutions are "ultimate" in the interpretation of history, he went farther than the logic of the case would permit, since it is doubtful that any single element in the historical process can be regarded as "ultimate" in all cases. Furthermore, it is not always clear whether, when Marx spoke of "the economic foundation" of society, he meant technology or property relations or both. On the whole, he seems to have meant that changes in technology produce "contradictions" which necessitate changes in the institutions of property and which are "reflected" in political, intellectual, and cultural spheres as well. But if this is what he meant, it would seem that he should have recognized something else, such as scientific inquiry, as a decisive historical factor, since such independent inquiry is among the essential conditions of technological invention. Nevertheless, despite its many weaknesses, Marx's economic interpretation of history provided a needed corrective to prevailing modes of historical interpretation, and there are today very few historians or students of politics who do not give economic factors a very important place in their analysis and explanation of social events.

Marx's theory of class struggle held that all past economies were "class" economies and that the struggle between economic classes was the fundamental process determining the shape and occurrence of other events. He believed, however, that technological conditions were now such that, if the industrial proletariat took control of society, and all persons were transformed into producers, society would be emancipated "from all exploitation, oppression, class-distinction and class struggles," and the historical warfare between economic classes would finally come to an end. It was to this end that Marx propagandized for working-class solidarity as the indispensable prelude to the overthrow of capitalism.

Marx's theory of class struggle dramatized what had been the frequently overlooked fact that property is itself a form of power over human beings and is, therefore, not exempt on *a priori* grounds from the sort of moral consideration or political control which is ordinarily invoked in other areas where men exercise power over men. Further, his theory called attention to one of the most portentous sociological phenomena of the nineteenth century—the emergence of the industrial working-class. Nevertheless, Marx's theory of classes, and the economic interpretation of history which is consequent upon it, is extremely oversimplified. It defines classes with respect to relationship to the property system and source of income, and it pays relatively little attention to other factors, such as type of occupation or the difference between salary and wages, which are of considerable importance. It does not take account of other forms of "class struggle" which are not wholly economic in nature, such as those between and within bureaucracies, or between civilian and military groups, or between governors and governed, to which liberal political theory has traditionally drawn attention. Furthermore, although Marx remarked that socialism might be attained by peaceful means in countries with a strong parliamentary tradition, his general emphasis on economic factors and the warlike structure of society led to a systematic depreciation of the possibilities of legislative reform, and, in a quite practical way, to an underestimate of the amount of co-operation between classes which is also a feature of any going social system.

Even more important, Marx not only exaggerated the struggle between classes, but he overestimated the conditions making for harmony and solidarity within a single class. His two-class image of the social order provided him with a symmetrical interpretation of history that was extremely useful for propagandistic purposes, but it led to the systematic neglect of other important social classes, most particularly the peasantry. This mistake has plagued Marxists ever since. And in general, Marx's theory of social classes, together with his confidence in the future, is probably responsible for the single most important flaw in Marxism—the failure to say anything specific about socialism itself, how it will work, and how it will eliminate the exploitation and class struggle which have been the great source of human misery in the past. Because Marx felt that class struggle was exclusively a phenomenon of property systems, he apparently assumed that a change in the property system was sufficient to eliminate it; because he held a simplified theory of social classes, he held a too simplified theory of social change; and because he reposed such confidence in the over-all direction of historical change, he rarely considered in any systematic way alternative programs for dealing with social problems, and so never got down to cases in his specific arguments on behalf of socialism.

The economic basis of the Marxian system and the central theme of *Capital* is the theory of surplus value. This theory, resting on the "labor theory of value" developed by Locke and the classical economists, and formulated by Marx, can be summarized as follows:

The common *social substance* of all commodities *is labor.* . . . A commodity has a *value* because it is a *crystallization of social labor.* The *greatness* of its value or its relative value depends upon the greater or less amount of that social substance (labor) contained in it; that is to say, on the relative mass of labor necessary for its production. The *relative values of commodities* are, therefore, determined by the *respective quantities or amounts of labor, worked up, realized, fixed in them*. (Marx, *Value, Price, Profit*, 1865.)

Profit, said Marx, constitutes the difference between what the laborer gets in the form of wages and what he produces. And this difference is "surplus value." Under the capitalist system, Marx held, labor is exploited by the capitalist, for the latter robs the worker of part of the benefit of his toil, and in doing so also lays the foundation of economic instability and depression. Very few economists today, including most of those who are critical of capitalism, give much credence to the theory of surplus value as an instrument for explaining economic phenomena. Nevertheless, it apparently served Marx as a useful guide, and helped him and later Marxists to call attention, as had few previous economists, to such problems as cyclical unemployment and depression, the tendency towards monopoly and the concentration of capital, and the development of economic imperialism.

Chapter VI

POLITICAL LIBERALISM IN A CLIMATE OF NATIONALISM: *I*

℘

1. FROM METTERNICH TO BISMARCK

NINETEENTH CENTURY Europe is dominated politically by two great Germans, Metternich and Bismarck. Between them comes the strange interlude of Napoleon III, who vainly endeavored to strike a compromise between revolution and the counter-revolution, and to prevent the leadership of Europe from being transferred from France to Germany. The two Germans present striking points both of similarity and contrast. Both were defenders of conservatism against revolution, both were champions of the authoritarian principle against Liberalism, both set up monarchy and aristocracy against the leveling propensities of the democrats. But while Metternich was a man of the Catholic South, Bismarck was a man of the Protestant North, while the former relied on the ancient imperial tradition of the Habsburgs, the latter substituted the brand new kingship of the Hohenzollerns. Metternich hated nationalism as much as he hated Liberalism, for both were fatal to the survival of the Austrian monarchy. Bismarck cleverly exploited nationalist sentiment in the interests of Prussian absolutism and drove Austria out of Germany. The fundamental difference between them is that Metternich failed while Bismarck succeeded. The Austrian Chancellor fought blindly against the tendencies of the age: the German Chancellor showed greater genius by forcing those very tendencies to serve his purpose. Liberalism triumphed over Metternich but succumbed to Bismarck.

Metternich was the less fortunate in that he was fated to deal with a young and vigorous revolutionary movement embodying political ideals whose

---

This chapter consists of material by three different authors. Section 1 is from *The Age of Revolution* (pp. 134–57; New York, Roy Publishers, 1949), by J. J. Saunders. Section 2 is from *History of Europe in the Nineteenth Century* (7th ed., pp. 261–317; Bari, Laterza & Sons, 1948), by Benedetto Croce, translated especially for this volume by A. C. Danto. Section 3, designed especially for the present volume, was written for its first edition by William O. Shanahan.

weaknesses had not yet been fully revealed in practice. He was forced to defend a venerable and antiquated régime, upon which the dust of ages lay thick, against ardent spirits intoxicated by the new gospel of popular freedom, the rights of man, and national self-determination. It was not surprising that it proved a losing battle. For several years after 1815 he was able indeed to drive the revolutionary agitation underground by turning the Tsar Alexander's Holy Alliance into a kind of League of Autocracies, pledged to suppress Liberalism whenever it might appear above the surface. The dangerous outbreaks of 1820 were with some difficulty put down, but the Greek revolt from 1821 onwards, which Russia supported and which Metternich wished to treat merely as another revolutionary rising to be crushed by common action of the Powers, destroyed for a time the unity of the absolutist front. This division in their enemies' camp was the opportunity of the Liberals, who in 1830 won a series of startling victories. The Bourbons lost the throne of France and were replaced by the bourgeois monarchy of Louis Philippe; Belgium revolted against Holland, the Italians rose against Austria and the Poles against Russia. These last two insurrections tied the hands of Metternich and the Tsar, and prevented them from intervening against the revolutionaries in the West. The independence of Belgium and of Greece, the granting of constitutions in several of the smaller German States, and the successful Anglo-French intervention in favor of Liberalism in Spain and Portugal, were so many blows struck at Metternich's system. The West was obviously lost to autocracy and legitimism, Central Europe was wavering, the dreaded revolution was moving steadily eastwards. The Polish rising at least had been crushed with pitiless severity, but the fact that a Great Power like France, the old center of revolution, had gone over to Liberalism and that since the Reform Bill of 1832 the middle classes were in power in England, boded ill for the future.

Shaken by these defeats, the Chancellor could only concentrate on saving Austria's position in Germany and Italy, where unfortunately it was her fate to come into direct conflict with the rapidly growing demand for national unity and constitutional liberty. In no other countries, except for the land of its origin, had the French Revolution produced such an electrical effect. Politically disunited since the early Middle Ages, intimately connected with the representative institutions of medieval supranationalism—the Papacy and the Holy Roman Empire—Germany and Italy had long been curiously amorphous entities, parceled out into petty principalities at the mercy of stronger centralized Powers. The Emperors, ambitious of dominating the fair lands south of the Alps, neglected their German kingdom and allowed the local princes to attain virtual independence. The Popes, fearing lest a powerful dynasty in the peninsula should threaten their liberty as spiritual heads of Christendom, worked to keep Italy divided. In the days of the Emperor Maximilian and Ulrich von Hutten, of Machiavelli and the Medici, there seemed a chance that Germany and Italy might follow the example of France, Spain, and England and acquire a unified government. But the Reformation and the Thirty Years' War disrupted the German body politic still further, while the military weakness and mutual jealousies of the Italian States allowed first Spain and then Austria to establish an overlordship that passed almost unchallenged until the nineteenth century.

Even in the last years of the Enlightenment slight stirrings of national consciousness became evident in both countries. Herder in Germany had put forth the doctrine of the *Volkseele,* the collective soul of a people; the Romantics turned youthful minds towards the old forgotten past of the Niebelungenlied and the Minnesinger and even of Woden and Thor, and Italian audiences in the 1770's and 1780's applauded fanatically the poetic dramas of Alfieri (1749–1803), where "tyrants" were held up to execration and the glories of a "free government" were eloquently extolled. The Revolution, with its attacks on feudalism and clericalism, was warmly welcomed in Upper Italy and in the Rhineland, where the middle classes were strongest. The Republican armies and Napoleon after them swept away the old confusing mosaic of principalities with their petty princes and comic-opera little courts, abolished feudal law and introduced the civil code, administrative unity, and economic freedom—reforms heartily approved by the bourgeoisie, denounced by the nobility and clergy, and viewed with indifference by the peasantry, who formed the bulk of the nation. The Napoleonic kingdom of Italy and the Confederation of the Rhine were but pale shadows of the mighty unified nations that were to arise in the mid-nineteenth century. German nationalism really dates from the fall of Prussia in 1806, which stung the people into a desperate revolt against the French conquerors, and found its prophet in Fichte (1762–1814), whose famous *Addresses to the German Nation,* delivered in Berlin in the dark days of 1807–08, though little heeded at the time, mark the opening of a new era. . . .

The German War of Liberation of 1813 and the revolt of the Italians against Napoleon's rule encouraged the hopes of the Liberals. Great was the disillusion when at the general settlement of 1815 it was found that Prussia did not intend to grant the constitution that had been promised, that Austria was still to be permitted a predominating share in German affairs, and that Italy was to be disintegrated afresh by restoration of all the old kingdoms, duchies, and principalities that the Revolution had swept away. Agitation against the

Holy Alliance and its decrees sprang up among the middle classes in the cities, who felt themselves cheated of the benefits the Revolution had conferred. These men—lawyers, teachers, university students, business men—were to be the most fervent champions of Liberal constitutionalism. Where they were numerous and influential, as in the North Italian towns and the great cities in the Rhineland, Liberalism held sway; where they were weak, as in South Italy and East Prussia, the feudal and conservative elements were able to put up a strong resistance to innovating ideas.

Austria's position was stronger in Germany than in Italy. In the latter country she was hated as an alien power: in the former she could be attacked only on the grounds of her hostility to popular government and national unity. How the Germanic Confederation and the Italian principalities were to be turned into national States was a perplexing problem: between 1815 and 1870 most people thought a federal system the only solution. After all, federalism appeared to work well both in small countries like Switzerland and large countries like the United States. A centralized government would mean that one State must be given supreme authority over all the rest. Such a solution was ruled out in the case of Germany because neither Austria nor Prussia would abdicate in favor of the other, and in the case of Italy because of the delicate question of the Papacy. Thus the federal plan in various forms was advocated in Italy by men like Mazzini and Gioberti, and was actually put in practice in Germany by Bismarck himself as late as 1867.

Metternich's position became more critical after 1830. Continual agitation, fomented chiefly by Mazzini, went on in Italy; Austrian rule in Lombardy and Venetia, though neither corrupt nor inefficient, grew increasingly unpopular, while the Magyars in Hungary and the Czechs in Bohemia stirred uneasily. In Germany Prussia was quietly consolidating the territory she had gained in 1815; the reforms which Stein and Hardenberg had inaugurated after the disaster of 1806 were maintained and slowly extended, though a constitution was still refused, and in 1834 Metternich was disconcerted by the news that Prussia had concluded a Zollverein or customs-union with most of the other German States from which Austria had been excluded. Prussia's widely scattered territories made the abolition of internal customs barriers a *sine qua non* of her economic development; the smaller States which lay in her way had to be persuaded to admit Prussian goods free of duty, and this internal free trade system was speedily adopted over the greater part of non-Austrian Germany. It was a blow to Austria's prestige, yet Metternich could do little. The Emperor Francis died in 1835, but his successor Ferdinand was eccentric almost to the point of insanity, and the Chancellor's task was rendered heavier. In 1840 the accession of a romantic idealist to the throne of Prussia in the person of Frederick William IV aroused the high hopes of all Liberal Young Germany—hopes that were partly realized by the attempt of the new king to evolve a parliamentary constitution out of the old provincial diets. In 1846 there occurred what Metternich had thought an impossibility: the election of a Liberal Pope. This was the beginning of the end. The reforms of Pius IX revived the latent nationalism of Italy in its most violent form; the agitation in Hungary assumed formidable proportions, and worst of all, there were rumblings in Vienna itself. In his last days of power Metternich found himself in strange alliance with Guizot, the "conservative-liberal" minister of Louis Philippe, who was maintaining the bourgeois Orleans monarchy against the attacks of socialists and extreme democrats, and in more congenial agreement with the Tsar Nicholas. The Republic of Cracow, the center of Polish agitation against Austria and Russia, was suppressed in 1846. It was Metternich's last victory.

The Orleans monarchy fell in 1848. It had throughout rested on a narrow class basis and was dependent on the votes of the upper bourgeoisie. The old aristocracy, Bourbonist almost to a man, sulked in isolation, the Catholics could not forgive its anticlericalism, the Bonapartists derided its feeble foreign policy and declared that only an Imperial restoration could re-establish France's prestige abroad, the Republicans declared they had been cheated in 1830, and the socialists denounced the greed and corruption of its wealthy supporters and its callous indifference to the sufferings of the wage earning proletariat. Opposed by many and supported by few, Louis Philippe's somewhat inglorious régime was overthrown almost without resistance and a Republican-Socialist government set up in its stead. The fall of the Orleans monarchy sent a mighty wave of revolution rolling across Europe. It was in February that Louis Philippe and Guizot fled from France: in April Metternich joined them in exile in England.

His fall marked the end of a forty years' struggle to maintain the integrity of the absolutist system. The rising tide of democracy had submerged him at last, yet the cause he defended was not wholly lost, for the old régime possessed more vitality than had been suspected. The revolutionaries, though noisy and violent in the cities, had little following in the country, were ill organized and badly-led (except in Hungary), and reckoned without the still powerful forces of tradition and loyalty. The socialistic movement in France was ruthlessly crushed by the propertied classes, and before the year was out Louis Napoleon as President of the Republic was wielding a power

as great as that exercised by Louis Philippe. The desperate efforts of the
Italians, under the rather unwilling leadership of Charles Albert, to shake off
the Habsburg rule were foiled by Radetsky's well organized armies. Czech
dreams of an independent Bohemia were shattered by Windischgrätz's cannon
at Prague. The Southern Slavs, infuriated at the contempt with which they
were treated by the German and Hungarian Liberals, assisted the Imperial government to suppress the revolt in Vienna. The Prussian democrats misman-
aged the situation so badly that the King was able to rid himself of them and
establish a safe conservative constitution. The Frankfurt Parliament, which
was to draw up a constitution for the whole of Germany, split up into quarreling groups and parties—Republicans and Monarchists, Particularists and
Nationalists, Federalists and Centralists—and only when it was too late did
they compose their differences and offer the crown of a United German
Empire to Frederick William of Prussia. But by this time Austria was recovering herself, the revolutionary agitation was dying down, the loyalty of
the army had been tested, and Schwarzenberg, who had succeeded to Metternich's position, announced that Austria would never consent to be excluded
even in part from a united German State. In face of Austrian disapproval
Prussia dared not consent to assume the leadership. Frederick William refused the proffered crown.

Austrian Liberalism fell between two stools: loyalty to German nationalism
and loyalty to the general principle of national self-determination. It wished
to maintain the integrity of the Habsburg realm, and so lost any chance of
winning over the Czechs and Italians who desired full autonomy. It could
not rid itself of the German feeling that the Slavs were an inferior race and
therefore not entitled to the same rights as the more "advanced" national
groups. When it became clear to the Viennese revolutionaries that they were
not strong enough to win through without assistance, they allied themselves
with the Hungarian rebels under Kossuth and so lost the sympathy of the
Croats and Slovenes whom the Hungarians had persecuted. Windischgrätz's
victorious army from Prague was able to recapture Vienna and re-establish
the Imperial authority in the German provinces. But Hungary defied all
efforts to subdue her, until Russia offered help to Austria and the Tsar's Cos-
sacks finally broke the resistance of the Magyars. Victorious at home, Schwarzenberg was also able to reassert Austria's supremacy in Germany by forcing
Prussia to withdraw her forces from the State of Hesse, which she had occupied under pretext of putting down disorders there. This "humiliation of
Prussia," acknowledged by the agreement of Olmütz in 1850, was followed

by Schwarzenberg's successful demand for the restoration of the old Germanic Confederation. The clock had been put right back. The position of 1815 seemed to have been restored.

The European outlook in 1850 might have depressed the stoutest democrat. The popular risings had everywhere failed. Germany and Italy were as far as ever from unity, and the Austrian supremacy had been re-established over both countries. Mazzini's Roman Republic had been destroyed by the French themselves. Louis Napoleon was about to abolish the very Republic to whose headship he had been elected. The Austro-Russian suppression of the Hungarian Revolution recalled the palmist days of the Holy Alliance. Trials, imprisonments, shootings, floggings, press prosecutions went on as in 1820 and 1830. The yoke of absolutism had again been riveted on Europe.

There was, however, from the Liberal point of view some slight ground for hope. The upheavals in the Habsburg dominions had at least succeeded in destroying serfdom and partially freeing the peasants from the grip of the great landed proprietors in Hungary, Bohemia, and the German provinces. Even Schwarzenberg made no attempt to go back entirely on the agrarian reforms carried through by the revolutionaries during their short tenure of power. At least one Italian state—the kingdom of Sardinia—had preserved the parliamentary constitution which had been set up in the mad days of 1848, and so in radical eyes assumed the character of an oasis of democracy in the desert of absolutism. As regards France, it soon became clear that the Second Empire, resting as it did on popular plebiscites, could not altogether ignore the strong Liberal sentiment in the country: it kept up some form of parliamentary government, never became an unqualified autocracy, and soon made an attempt to strike a compromise with Liberalism. In 1852–53 two events happened which gave heart to the Liberals. The first was the death of Schwarzenberg, who, had he lived, might have prevented Bismarck transferring the supremacy of Germany from Austria to Prussia, and the second was the outbreak of the Crimean War.

The Crimean War should have been primarily an Anglo-Russian affair. The occupation of the Danubian provinces of Moldavia and Wallachia by the Tsar, following a hint that Russia was contemplating anew her favorite scheme of partitioning the "sick man's" territories, was sufficient to rouse the bellicosity of an England tired of forty years' peace and already delighted with Palmerston's successful bullying of foreigners from Greeks to Chinese. The advance of Russia beyond the Danube had been viewed with uneasiness by England since the days of Catherine the Great, for the British government preferred the trade routes of the Levant to remain in the possession of the feeble Turkish power rather than to fall into the strong grasps of the Tsardom. England found her anti-Russian policy warmly supported by Napoleon III, whose attitude was dedicated, not by trivial disputes between Greeks and Catholics over the custody of the Holy Places, but by the desire to strengthen the Empire by a successful war, to set aside the peace treaties of 1815, and to revenge himself on Russia for his uncle's defeat at the hands of Alexander I in 1812. The disgrace of Moscow was to be wiped out in the Crimea. So England and France made war on Russia, and after the most desperate efforts took Sebastopol and broke her naval power in the Black Sea. The Crimean may have been one of the most unnecessary wars in history, but it had momentous consequences.

First, it gravely damaged the prestige of Russia which had stood high since her defeat of Napoleon forty years before, and proved to an astonished world that the colossus had feet of clay. Secondly, it aroused the jubilation of the Liberals all over Europe, for Russia under Nicholas I had been regarded as the very incarnation of absolutism and the sworn enemy of popular freedom, so the defeat of the Power which only a few years before had intervened decisively to crush Hungarian Liberalism was welcomed as a blow to the reactionary forces that might prove fatal. Thirdly, it undermined the faith of large sections of the Russian people in their government and led to demands for drastic reforms. The disasters of 1855 prepared the way for the emancipation of the serfs in 1861 and encouraged the growth of a revolutionary movement which fought the Tsardom for half a century and finally ruined it. Nihilism and its later development Bolshevism were born on the bloodstained fields of Inkerman and Balaclava. Fourthly, it re-established the position of France, whose lustre had grown dim during the prosaic reign of Louis Philippe, and at the Congress of Paris in 1856 Napoleon might well feel that he had done much to efface the bitter memories of 1812–15. Fifthly, it wrecked the friendship between Russia and Austria, since the Tsar naturally expected some help from the Habsburgs in gratitude for his action in 1849, whereas Austria, fearful of the extension of Russian influence in the Balkans, was inclined to support France and England. The result was that when Austria's turn came, in 1859 and 1866, she had to fight her battles alone. Sixthly, it gave a new lease of life to the decadent Ottoman Empire and postponed for twenty years the emancipation of the Christian races of the Balkan peninsula. Finally, Cavour's action in sending a Sardinian contingent to fight with the allies in the Crimea ensured for his country a seat at the peace conference, enabled him to bring the Italian question before the Powers of Europe, and induced the French Emperor to promise his assistance in driving the Austrians out of Italy.

Unquestionably, Napoleon III in 1856 was the most important man in Europe. Few characters in history have been more variously estimated in their own lifetime than he. Derided at first as a futile adventurer, he came to be feared after the *coup d'état* as a dangerous and subtle schemer, and finally after he led France to disaster in 1870 was half-forgotten and despised as an incompetent failure. His contemporaries seem to have been made unable to decide whether he was a fool or a knave. Palmerston thought him shrewd and cunning: Bismarck found it easy to bluff him. His reputation has suffered from the fact that his career closed in utter ruin and that after Sedan nobody cared to attempt a defence of the Emperor and his régime. There can be no doubt that he lacked entirely the clear intelligence, cool judgment and quick decision of his illustrious uncle. Probably there was no more simplicity than subtlety in him, especially in his later years when disease had dulled his faculties. The secretiveness and reserve, which led many to regard him as a Machiavellian intriguer and to talk of his "sly look" and his "fish-like eyes," was perhaps a legacy of his Carbonaro days when he had belonged to revolutionary societies and led a fugitive life in the underworld of great cities dreaming of how he could restore the Napoleonic empire. The charge of insincerity brought against him can hardly be sustained. The socialistic ideas he expressed in his early pamphlets were not mere claptrap: he did genuinely wish to improve the lot of the poor, and he gave the French workmen privileges they had never before possessed. He honestly believed in Italian nationalism when few other people in France did, and he did his best to help the Italians achieve their unity. He sympathized sincerely with the Poles but he was not in a position to assist them. He did ardently desire the peace of Europe and made vain efforts to solve international problems by round table conferences. He really thought that his government was the most satisfactory that could have been devised for France, that it "closed the era of revolutions by satisfying the legitimate needs of the people" by the reconciliation of order with liberty. But though full of good intentions, his vacillations and bad judgment exasperated friend and foe alike and drove one party after another into opposition. Moreover, the fact that he had forcibly overthrown the régime he had sworn to uphold gave his Republican enemies every chance to denounce him as a perjured usurper.

Ten years of success were followed by ten years of failure and 1859 is the dividing line. It was in that year that Cavour's persuasive eloquence and

Orsini's bomb induced him to take up the cause of Italian liberation, for which he had fought in his youth. Cavour, the cleverest statesman Italy had produced since Alberoni, had read aright the lesson of 1848: the Italians were not strong enough to drive the Austrians out of their country unaided. The assistance of one of the Great Powers was needed. Much sympathy for Italy existed in England, but apart from some indirect naval help, little was to be expected from that quarter. France alone remained, and even Napoleon would consent only at a price. Nice and Savoy, mainly French-speaking provinces which had been temporarily annexed to France during the revolutionary and Napoleonic eras, were to be ceded permanently, then Napoleon would act and clear the Austrians out "from the Alps to the Adriatic." Such was the program agreed upon by Cavour and the Emperor at the secret meeting at Plombières.

The program was only partially carried out. Cavour cunningly provoked Austria (who had lately been pursuing a more liberal policy in Lombardy and Venetia) into a war in which she appeared the aggressor; France joined forces with Sardinia, and after a fierce struggle Austria was ousted from Lombardy. So far all was well: Austria was fighting alone, since Russia was savagely indignant at the cold neutrality her former friend had displayed during the Crimean War and was not sorry to see the Habsburgs in trouble. But it soon became clear that German national feeling would not be unmoved by the defeat and humiliation of what was after all a Germanic Power, and a threat of Prussian mobilization on the Rhine alarmed Paris. Nor was France unanimous in its approval of Napoleon's policy. The Liberals and democrats might applaud, but many Frenchmen asked why they should help to create a strong State next door to them, while the Catholics protested that the victory of the Italian Revolution (which the Siccardi laws of 1855 had shown would be strongly anti-clerical) would endanger the Papacy and destroy the Temporal Powers. So instead of advancing into Venetia, Napoleon entered into secret negotiations with Austria and signed an armistice by which it was agreed that Lombardy alone should be given up. Cavour was furious at what he regarded as Napoleon's "treachery," but he was compelled to bow to the inevitable. In any case, the war had given a tremendous impetus to the revolutionary movement, and Austria was no longer in a position to save the anti-Liberal Italian princes. The dukes of Parma, Modena, and Tuscany were driven from their dominions; Garibaldi's red shirts landed in Sicily with the connivance of the British Fleet, and crossing over to Naples, destroyed the effete Bourbon monarchy; Cavour, fearing the impetuous adventurer would proclaim a republic, violated the neutrality of the Papal

States in face of the protests of Europe by sending Sardinian troops across Central Italy to join forces with Garibaldi's volunteers in the south, and by 1861 only Venetia (under Austrian rule) and Rome (under Papal rule supported by the French) remained un-incorporated into the new kingdom of Italy, of which Victor Emmanuel of Sardinia was proclaimed king a few months before Cavour's death.

The Italian Revolution, to which the spectacular victories of Garibaldi imparted a romantic hue, was hailed with enthusiasm by the Liberals. Never perhaps did their cause seem brighter than in the early 1860's. The triumph of representative government, of popular rights, of free trade, of political equality, of religious toleration, of humanitarianism, of the principles of 1789, was evidently at hand. The system of Metternich was dead. The Holy Alliance was no more. Italy was practically free. Parliaments were coming into being in countries which had hitherto remained utterly impervious to democratic ideas. Slavery had been finally abandoned by all the nations of Europe: the infamous traffic in negroes was at an end. The American Civil War ended in victory for the Abolitionist North. Cobden's free-trade treaty with Napoleon III in 1860 brought down the tariff walls not only in France but in most other European countries. In Russia, hitherto the very citadel of reactionary despotism, a reforming Tsar was on the throne, and the emancipation of the serfs in 1861 evinced the genuineness of his Liberalism. In France the "Liberal Empire" of 1860 had succeeded the scarcely disguised absolutism of Napoleon III's first years. In England the aristocratic Whiggism of Palmerston gave place to the more radical Liberalism of Gladstone, and the second Reform Act in 1867 gave the vote to the working classes. When, in 1864, Pope Pius IX protested against the anti-Christian features of the new bourgeois democratic age in the famous "Syllabus of Errors" and anathematized the proposition "that it was the duty of the Roman pontiff to come to terms with progress, liberalism and modern civilization," it was widely believed that the Papacy had signed its own death-warrant. Liberalism had come to stay. Few realized then that actually it had passed its zenith and that the man was at hand who was to challenge its supremacy and send it on the road to decline. In 1862 Otto von Bismarck became Minister President of Prussia.

The great statesman who, in a few short years, was to make a Prussianized Germany the most powerful military empire in the world, came from a part of Europe where an old-fashioned feudal agrarian economy survived intact, untouched by the urban industrialism of capitalist magnates and the democratic propaganda of Liberal politicians. His family had for centuries been landowners of the English squire type in Brandenburg and East Prussia:

they belonged to the class known as Junkers, descendants of medieval German knights and barons who had carried the culture of their home country into the backward Slav regions and reduced the native population to the status of serfs. They lived like patriarchs on their vast estates, dispensing paternal justice to their numerous dependants, conscious of the social and military eminence of their class, scornful of the innovations of money grubbing burgesses and the egalitarian notions of democratic reformers who pretended that the peasant was as good as his lord! Were they not the truest Germans, the defenders of Germanic culture against the barbarous hordes of Slavdom? In this semi-feudal, aristocratic, stiffly conservative atmosphere Bismarck grew to manhood. In his youth he was a swashbuckling country squire with a long succession of duels and drinking-bouts and love affairs to his credit, a lover of the open life, riding for miles a day over forest and heath and shooting game on the marshy flats of the Baltic coast. He hated the close, confined air of towns and quarreled with his mother because she preferred the fashionable society of the capital to the companionship of the boorish and uncultured gentry of East Prussia. In early manhood he was converted to a pietistic sort of Christianity, and though his religious convictions may never have been deep, he probably retained to the end the Old Testament idea of the God of battles fighting on his side. Intended for a diplomtic career, he had already held several minor posts when, in 1847, he was elected to the Prussian Landtag or Diet, which Frederick William had called as the first stage towards the granting of a constitution, where he distinguished himself by the ability with which he defended the traditional monarchy against the radicals. He viewed the revolutions of 1848 with abhorrence, but they taught him some useful lessons: the alacrity with which the masses will follow an able leader, the supreme importance of the army, and the futility of parliamentary debates in the face of really grave crises. But for the loyalty of the army to the dynasty, the Habsburg empire would have collapsed in 1848. If a great popular leader had arisen in Prussia, the revolution would have won in Germany. If Prussia had possessed a powerful army, she would not have suffered the crushing humiliation at the hands of Austria at Olmütz in 1850. Already Bismarck was convinced that Germany must be unified, not along liberal, but along conservative lines, that Prussia must be the leader of the new German State, that Austria must be excluded and that as she could be ejected only by force, her rival must be strong enough to overcome her before any outside Power had the chance to intervene. During the 1850's, when he held diplomatic posts at Paris and St. Petersburg, he worked carefully to prepare the ground. The situation was none too favorable. The defeat of Russia in the Crimean War revived the Liberal agitation everywhere, and an attenuated form of parliamentary government was set up in Prussia, to Bismarck's disgust. He tried to take advantage of Austria's defeat in the war of 1859 to secure the revocation of the Convention of Olmütz, but German sentiment was strongly pro-Austrian and nothing could be done. However, Prussia's army was being thoroughly reorganized by Roon, and King William, who came to the throne in 1861, was a safe conservative, unlike his erratic and unstable predecessor, a competent soldier and a firm believer in military preparedness.

The refusal of the Prussian Diet, where the Liberals had a majority, to sanction Roon's army reforms created a deadlock between Crown and Legislature, and the King, who was meditating abdication, at last called on Bismarck to solve it. Thus began in 1862 the great career that was to startle Europe. In his first speech to Parliament the new Minister threw down the gauntlet to the Liberal opposition. "The unification of Germany," he cried in a famous sentence, "cannot be achieved by speeches and the votes of majorities, but by blood and iron." A new and harsh note, ominous for the future! With high-handed efficiency he circumvented the Diet, secured the support of the Upper House and forced the reforms through in defiance of the Lower. The process of breaking parliaments had begun!

Events now moved with amazing rapidity. The army was soon ready: a pretext must be found for a war with Austria, still smarting under the defeats of 1859. But beforehand the friendly neutrality of the rest of Europe must be secured. The Polish rebellion of 1863 gave Bismarck his chance of winning the gratitude of Russia, which he did by checking all attempts on the part of France to mediate on behalf of the Poles. The Tsar received more support from Prussia than from Austria—a fact which helps to explain his attitude in 1866. The Liberals, who sympathized with the Poles, were bitterly critical, but Bismarck knew that in any case the resurrection of an independent Poland would encourage the "German" Poles in Posen to rise. The complicated affair of the Schleswig-Holstein duchies, which, though members of the Germanic Confederation, were ruled by the King of Denmark, enabled him to enlist German patriotic sentiment on his side, to try out the new Prussian army, and to provide an occasion for quarreling with Austria. When the Danes attempted to incorporate the duchies in their kingdom, Bismarck persuaded Austria to join him in forcibly expelling them, since Vienna was afraid it would lose the leadership of Germany if it refused to intervene in a affair which had strongly roused nationalist feeling. The Austro-Prussian forces made short work of the Danish opposition, and the duchies were divided between the two Powers. Opportunity for creating friction existed in abundance, relations between Austria and Prussia grew increasingly strained, and in 1866 the fight for the supremacy broke out.

The War of 1866 was Bismarck's masterpiece. A more favorable moment could scarcely have been chosen. Russia's friendship had been assured through his attitude towards the Polish rebellion. Italy had joined forces with Prussia on being promised Venetia in the event of victory. The greater part of France's army was absent in Mexico, where Napoleon was trying to create a Latin Empire to counteract the influence of the United States, and so the French government was unable to make its full weight felt in Europe. French opinion was anxiously watching events in Germany, but Napoleon believed there was no real danger: Austria and Prussia were well matched, the struggle between them would be long and mutually exhausting, and the country as a whole would be weakened for a long time to come. Moreover, had not Bismarck hinted at "compensation" for France on the left bank of the Rhine and in Luxemburg, and possibly even in Belgium? Many Germans themselves were bewildered and indignant at Prussia's proceedings: they felt she was forcing on a civil war among the German peoples, and nearly all the smaller states from Bavaria and Saxony downwards sided with Austria. Yet the war was over in seven weeks. The great military machine perfected by Roon and Von Moltke moved with clockwork precision: the railways were used to the full to shift about enormous masses of men: Austria's German allies were scattered like chaff, the Prussian forces entered Bohemia, and on the field of Königgrätz the work of Frederick the Great was completed and the leadership of the German nation transferred at long last from Vienna to Berlin. The speed at which the campaign was fought astonished Europe and thoroughly alarmed the French, who viewed with terror the rise of a mighty military empire across the Rhine. Intoxicated by success, King William and the army chiefs proposed a triumphal entry into Vienna and the annexation of a large part of Austrian territory. But Bismarck would have none of it. Austria had been beaten, but she must not be crushed and humiliated: her neutrality might one day be useful to Prussia, it were better therefore to treat her leniently. She lost no territory save Venetia, which Bismarck, true to his promise, handed over to a grateful Italy, but was compelled to assent to the dissolution of the old German Bund of 1815 and the creation of a new North German Confederation under Prussian aegis. Some of the smaller States like Hanover and Hesse-Cassel were punished for supporting Austria by outright annexation to Prussia: the Catholic kingdoms south of the river Main were left to themselves. Austria was excluded entirely from German affairs, and was thus forced to seek compensation in the Balkans (which brought her into conflict with Russia and led ultimately to the cataclysm of 1914), and to counteract the growing agitation among the Slav races of her empire by raising Hungary to an equal partnership with herself. The war of 1866 created in 1867 the Dual Monarchy of Austria-Hungary.

The unification of non-Austrian Germany was not complete. The Southern States viewed aggressive Prussia with fear and dislike. Only in one way could they be brought within the new Reich that Bismarck was planning: by joining with Prussia in a nationalist war against a foreign aggressor. That war could be fought only against France, and if successful would wipe out for ever the memories of 1806. This is not to say that Bismarck deliberately planned the war of 1870. France herself hurried on the catastrophe, believing that she was strong enough to deal with Prussia before the latter got really dangerous. Bismarck knew that France would be a stiffer proposition than Austria, and he was fearful of foreign intervention if the war lasted too long. All he could do was to sow distrust and suspicion of Napoleon in the minds of Europe; thus at the critical moment in 1870 he revealed to England Napoleon's negotiations concerning Luxemburg and Belgium and so destroyed for a time English sympathy for France. The German statesman's efforts to keep France isolated were wonderfully successful. With Russia he was still on friendly terms, and in any case the Tsar was not likely to help a country which had defeated him in the Crimea and had expressed open sympathy with the rebels in Poland. Austria could hardly be supposed to harbor cordial feelings towards the Power which had driven her out of Lombardy in 1859. England under the pacific rule of Gladstone would certainly stay neutral, especially after the revelations of Napoleon's designs in the Low Countries. Italy was in a painful dilemma: France had helped her in 1859, Prussia had helped her in 1866; should she choose sides or keep out of the struggle? Finally, she remembered that the French were still occupying Rome and that Napoleon's defeat would enable her to seize the papal city and complete the Risorgimento. No help came to France from the Italians.

The pretext for the war when it came was the Hohenzollern candidature in Spain. It cannot be denied that the French put themselves in the wrong by their arrogant and overbearing attitude and that though they entered the war "with a light heart" as one of their Ministers said, they were almost entirely unprepared. Bismarck had got them where he wanted them. The "editing" of the Ems telegram, for which he has been severely criticised, was undoubtedly a piece of sharp practice, but the French were already determined on war and it is doubtful if it made much difference. The war itself repeated the triumphs of 1866, though the French put up a far stiffer resistance than the

Austrians, and not until Paris had fallen six months after the opening of hostilities did the exhausted nation accept the onerous terms proposed to it. Bismarck had attained his goal: all Germany had been united in this fight against the national enemy, and it was the king of Bavaria who acclaimed the Prussian sovereign German Emperor in Louis XIV's palace at Versailles. Yet the Treaty of Frankfurt (1871) was a bad mistake. Moderation had been shown to Austria, but none was shown to France, who was stripped of two provinces and saddled with a crushing indemnity. It is difficult to assess Bismarck's responsibility for these harsh terms. We are told that the military chiefs, who felt they had been cheated in 1866, forced his hand and extorted the annexation of Alsace-Lorraine as a guarantee against future French attack and were supported in their demand by the South German States who remembered Louis XIV's devastations of the Palatinate and insisted on a strong frontier. The Chancellor may also have felt that the two provinces (which indeed were largely German speaking) would be a pledge of German unity, since they had been won by the combined efforts of the north and the south. It is true that in 1870 the populations of France and Germany were about equal and that no one could have foreseen that within the next forty years the latter would completely outstrip the former and so make it certain that France would never again be in a position to challenge the German power single-handed. It is also true that the humiliations inflicted by Napoleon on Prussia in 1806 were quite as bad as those inflicted by Bismarck on France. Yet Bismarck could have afforded to be generous, and his failure to be so created in France the bitter desire for "la revanche" and so led to the war of 1914 and to the "Carthaginian peace" of 1919, when Germany was treated as France had been in 1870.

1870 was undoubtedly one of the great turning points in European history. The overthrow of France ended the hegemony she had exercised over Western Europe for nearly three centuries and shifted the center of gravity to the great Teutonic people placed between the Latin and the Slav. The danger point was no longer Paris but Berlin. The process of unification and the military triumphs that had completed it seemed to change the character of the German people. . . . [They] became imbued with the Prussian spirit, whose origin is to be sought back in the days of the Great Elector, and the "barrack-square" mentality, the disciplinary efficiency and the proud self-assertiveness, spread throughout the entire nation. The rest of the Continent, uneasy at the sudden emergence of an enormously powerful military empire in their very midst, feverishly sought security from possible attack by arming to the limit of their capacity. Huge fleets and armies, the size of which would have staggered the conquerors of antiquity, consumed more and more of the national revenues and spelt ruin to the rosy hopes of universal peace which had been widespread only a few years before.

Finally, the rise of the new German Empire was the beginning of the end of Liberalism, which had defeated Metternich but was itself beaten by Bismarck. As late as 1860 it was possible to believe that the Liberal creed was destined in a short time to become universal: before the century was out it was clear that the era of individual liberty, humanitarian pacifism, free trade and "the rights of man," was passing away to be succeeded by an age of aggressive nationalism, State-worship, militarism, racial exclusiveness, and despotism supported by the masses. "The Parliament of Man, the Federation of the World" receded rapidly into the background. Bismarck fought with amazing success the ideas the French Revolution had let loose over Europe. He captured nationalism for the conservative cause. He utilized the democratic device of universal suffrage to strengthen the position of the governing class. He paid lip-service to parliamentary government, but the Reichstag was nothing and the Chancellor and the Emperor everything. He abolished free trade, and the prosperity of Germany advanced by leaps and bounds. He even tried to "kill by kindness" a new enemy far more dangerous than the old—Socialism—and nearly succeeded. The dismay of the Liberals is well expressed by the Italian philosopher Croce, one of their last survivors:

The Liberals were distressed by doubts of their own faith, because they no longer beheld before them one of those old régimes in which authority—poorly supported by allies of clerical and aristocratic cliques, deserted by men of intellect and culture, incapable of progress, reactionary and backward—revealed so that all might read its inferiority in the historical struggle. Instead they saw a State that had rejected popular government, based itself on authority, taken its rulers only from above, and was obtaining such triumphs as no other State in Europe had the ability or the audacity to challenge: a State perfect in its mechanism and in its administrative work and a people that was the best taught and the richest in knowledge and learning of all the peoples of the world and before whom there was unfolding as well a vast field of activity in economic production and commerce.

The Counter-Revolution had at last found a leader.

2. THE AGE OF PEACE AND DISQUIET

In the period that followed 1870 Europe witnessed neither a resurrection of the old absolute monarchies nor an outburst of new Caesarisms. Such things were rarely projected and rarely attempted, and the few storm clouds that seemed to threaten were dispersed, leaving behind them a calm sky, clearer than before.

France, which common opinion, supported by the evidence of the past eighty years of French history, judged to be the country of violent incidents and incapable of a stable life of liberty, now established and consolidated her war-born republic with firm resolution and great prudence. Those eighty years of history, during which she had suffered the most varied and opposed regimes, each vainly seeking the point of balance, did not lead France to the final destruction which many feared and for which many of her enemies hoped. Instead, she gained the experience that at last set her on the right course, which she took as though driven by the force of events—in itself a sign that the course was correct. The conservative Third Republic, which Thiers (authorized by a long personal experience) liked to call "The Republic without Republicans"—meaning that it lacked the 1848-variety of republican who had led the Second Republic to ruin—initially displayed every aspect of being merely makeshift and provisory, but turned out to be surprisingly durable and not to be displaced by any other form of government. In its early days it had to suppress the insurrectionary *Commune* of Paris, a convulsive movement of armed men, defeated but unresigned to defeat—a movement wherein absurd federalistic ideas rose again to the surface, while tendencies toward a social republic stirred beneath. At the same time France had to avoid the restoration of monarchy which would have brought her, once again, to an intolerable condition of instability. She might still have retaken this once-traveled road had she not been saved from the danger through the help of the Count of Chambord, the legitimist pretender, who stubbornly demanded the white Bourbon banner as the condition for his return to the throne he claimed to have inherited. This served to make clear what restoration implied and pointed up the widening abyss which divided the present from the past.

But the Republic had a further danger to overcome, the danger of becoming too rigidly conservative, paralyzed through fear of so-called "radicals" and the lingering after-images of 1793, 1848, and 1871. France might thus have gone constitutionalist rather than parliamentary, with the almost monarchical authority granted her president and with the actual power in the hands of the military and the clergy. It was this that MacMahon, time and again during his presidency, attempted to establish with the various cabinets which he summoned and commanded, until finally he himself yielded to the inevitable and resigned in 1879. Many individuals who had looked to MacMahon in the hope of a *coup d'état* were left disillusioned, and Grévy, the new president, declared himself to be "sincerely obedient to the great parliamentary rule" in his first message to the nation. Indeed, to show that there was no longer anything to fear from radicalism or revolution, he had the parliamentary body transferred from Versailles to Paris.

Twice again the danger of, or desire for, a reactionary *coup d'état* re-emerged in France, and each time it was frustrated. The first time this happened was between 1886 and 1889, with the wildly acclaimed General Boulanger, a popular hero and dear to the masses. From his success the masses hoped to gain not merely "revenge" against Germany, but also that vast vague redemption, which the masses always expect, from all evils, political and otherwise. But even from the uncertainty of his movements and his schemes, it could have been seen that Boulanger was more or less consciously (and more often impelled by others than by himself) tending toward something not unlike what the Second Empire had been. Although he achieved a clamoring electoral success in 1888, and although he was elected the following January in Paris, the statesmen of France showed him nothing but scorn and disdain, dubbing him "The Vaudeville General" or "A Napoleon without the Italian campaign." He personally lacked the resoluteness to march with his fanatics against the seat of government, and finally, after having been tried and condemned, he was obliged to flee to Belgium, where he ignominiously took his own life. The second incident took place ten years later, at the time of the case of Captain Dreyfus and the protracted dispute over the justness or unjustness of his sentence—a dispute which, though it appeared to be a moral-juridical conflict, was in effect a renewed attack upon, and defense of, republican institutions. For the ranks of the anti-Dreyfusards and the anti-Semites were enlarged, and their political party was strengthened, by the former adherents of Boulanger together with reactionaries, royalists, and great numbers of priests, monks, and all manner of clericalists who thought that by supporting the military they could turn it against the government. But these were stoutly opposed by a united republican and socialist force; and when Dreyfus was at last set free, when his innocence was established and legally recognized, the wave of reaction was broken. The liberal order emerged from the struggle not merely intact but reinvigorated and militant as well. This was apparent from the work to which the victors subsequently turned their hands—work which was not so much revenge for the past as it was wise precaution for the future.

In rival Germany, meanwhile, the abolition of restriction of liberty was pondered by Bismarck. Creator of the German Empire, Bismarck did not consider as definitive the constitution that he had given the nation, together with a national parliament and universal suffrage. These were political expedients to which he had resorted, but they were not at all in harmony with his own ideals which remained, as always, those of absolute monarchy conjoined with his own omnipotence as chancellor; and with every obstacle, impasse, or annoyance that he encountered with parliament, his thoughts ran to the extreme possibility of a *coup d'état* as the only immediate remedy. This attitude of his may be seen in his letters, especially in those written between 1878 and 1882, in which he speaks of the Germans as ruining the "Nüremburg toy" which had been given them, because they were inept at handling it. He writes that he foresees a time when Schwarzenberg's statement, once uttered at Olmütz *à propos* the Austrian constitution, a statement which asserted that "it is an institution which has not proven sound," would have to be asserted of the German constitution as well. And he is forever insisting that the only solid and substantial thing in all of Germany is the German prince; that it is up to the German princes to decide whether it is not better to put an end to all this, and to return to the ancient federal Diet, preserving the Military and Customs Union, but abolishing parliament from their midst. In the last years of his chancellorship Bismarck placed all his hopes on the young prince who was later to become William II. Unlike his father, Prince Frederick, the young man showed himself to be intolerant of parliamentary rule, like "a true soldier of the old guard," a "man of iron," just what Germany needed. But when the young man, the symbol of all Bismarck's ideals and aspirations, ascended the throne, and when Bismarck, again in 1890, irritated with a parliament which he felt to be insufficiently docile, informed the new emperor of his schemes, he was not heeded. Bismarck's notion was, first, to present to Parliament demands for increased military funds as well as for a harsher anti-socialist law; then, upon parliament's easily predictable refusal, it could be dissolved two or three times, the socialists could be deprived of electoral rights by decree, the secret ballot could be abolished, and if necessary cannon could be turned to as a last resort. But the sovereign was at that time seeking the favor of the people and the parliament; and so, after thirty uninterrupted years of governing, Bismarck fell at last from power. He had neither a party nor a current of popular opinion to support him: his scheme was thus the air castle of a solitary man—a man capable of great things in war and diplomacy, but unable to interpret the demands of men's souls, which vary with the times. But when in his retirement he heard the words and observed the deeds and gestures of the second William, Bismarck's judgment and doctrine shifted. He began repeatedly to assert that the way to salvation lay in "strengthening the effectiveness of parliament"; that parliament must necessarily "criticize, check, admonish and, in certain cases, guide the government";

and that in the past he may have at times proceeded in a somewhat "dicta-torial manner," by too stringently repressing national representation. These tardy reflections showed both what his robust mind had lacked and how he, the founder of states, was ill-equipped to be the educator of peoples. And especially was this the case with his own people, for whom, in this respect, he was if anything their miseducator. For if he did not in fact succeed in carrying through his *coup* against universal suffrage, he nonetheless succeeded in ar-resting Germany at the constitutionalist phase and thus prevented her from passing over into the parliamentary one.

In the early years of his ministry the liberal party had stood its ground and resisted his oppression; but after the war of 1869 it consented to support his foreign police for nationalist ends, hoping thereby to receive reciprocal do-mestic concessions on his part. This support, given him by the national-liberals, who constituted the strongest faction in parliament, continued after 1870 to be animated by the same hope. This enabled Bismarck to put through his seven-year military-service bill as well as his financial reforms and permitted him to combat the Catholic Center. . . . But when Bismarck turned to pro-tective tariffs, and when, for this as well as for the repression of socialism, he sought the support of the conservatives and wooed the Catholics, his former allies were no longer of any use to him. They merely stood in his way, and he would not listen to the conditions that they specified as the price he would have to pay for their further collaboration. These conditions would have meant that liberals, both of the right and the left (the "progressives"), would have entered the Prussian ministry, and Bismarck was firmly resolved to take no step which would lead to a ministry composed of parties. This would at any rate have been impossible, for the old Prussia had not been assimilated into a liberalized Germany: on the contrary, a more or less liberal Germany had become the mere adjunct of Prussia. And Prussia retained intact the character which had been hers ever since the post-1848 reaction, the character of a monarchy which had granted but a few constitutional concessions to a parliament chosen in accordance with a strict class system. This relationship was just the reverse of that which obtained in Italy, where a liberal Piedmont annexed to herself an Italy which turned liberal and fused with her. Prussia remained the foundation of the German Empire always; and even in 1898 Chancellor von Höhenlohe, one of Bismarck's successors, remarked in his diary that, when seated amongst the "Prussian Excellencies," he could clearly distinguish between the liberalism of the south and the feudalism of the north. . . .

The alienation of the liberals from Bismarck, after the passage of special anti-socialist legislation, signalized the disintegration of the liberal party, which henceforth sundered into factions while the number of its deputies substantially declined. Nor did it compensate for its lack of numerical strength in the country by a more vigorous, profound, or firm liberal faith. Many of the liberals were in fact not liberals in the political sense at all, but liberals in the economic sense, free-traders, who expressed the economic requirements of the Germany of that time. Others, some of whom were amongst its more prominent representatives, continued to assert the primacy of the State, and thought of liberty as a set of rights, which the State might concede or recognize. This faction excoriated parliamentarism as the great evil, and would limit its prerogatives to administrative criticism and opposition. As modest as the activity of the German parliament had been, Treitzchke, one of the pre-1870 liberals who became increasingly Bismarckian, feared that it might nevertheless have committed the sin of "excess parliamentarism!" . . .

Amongst other peoples the parliamentary system had either been established long since, as in England, or it had been introduced along with other liberal institutions, or it came gradually and in practice to replace some constitution which had originally been more monarchical in nature. . . . European society was generally leaning in a democratic direction, as the phrase went. It might have been more to the point to say that she was emerging from the guardianship of restricted ruling cliques, from the tutelage of a liberal aristocracy which had guided her through revolutions and into new state structures, and that Europe was now forming a political class all her own, more mobile and more varied, to suit the great variety and mobility of interests and demands, all of which must be evaluated and reconciled.

A sign and instrument of this continuous progression was the gradual extension of franchise which, in nearly all the countries of Europe, culminated in universal suffrage. This, which in a prior time had been instituted by conservatives or reactionaries and adopted for conservative and reactionary ends, now served the countertendencies of movement and progress. France had received it as a legacy of the Second Empire. Italy, after the reform of 1882, which quadrupled or quintupled the number of electors, received it finally in 1912. Belgium, which still had the property system, adopted it towards the end of 1892; and even though a plurality had to be obtained, the number of voters was multiplied tenfold. Austria had already expanded her suffrage in 1896, and made it universal eleven years later, hoping thereby to reduce the battles and assuage the passions of the democracy and the working classes, as well as of her many national groups and their unruly conflicts. And thus it went in the majority of other European states, including those of

Germany (Baden in 1904, Bavaria and Würtemburg in 1906); but it did not happen so in Prussia. When the reform of 1893 had secured and assured the preponderance of conservatives and centrists, Prussia condescended to rearrange her constituencies somewhat, and to increase, by about ten, the number of deputies. In Switzerland the constitution was revised several times until, finally, experiments were made in direct government by the people, in terms of initiative and referendum and of sanctions. England, after the reform of 1885, augmented by two and a half millions her electoral body; but the major element in her progress toward popular government was the predominance and power which she gave the House of Commons over the House of Lords. . . . For the House of Lords was deprived of the right to reject financial legislation; and it could not reject and send back to the House of Commons any piece of legislation which it had once before rejected—so long as such legislation should be approved of by the House of Commons in three sessions in the course of two years.

Moreover, salaries and security came to be introduced for the representatives of the people in almost every country, a thing made necessary by the transformation that was taking place in the political class, which heretofore had been drawn, for the most part, from the landowners and members of the upper bourgeoisie. The various monarchies that had survived in most of the countries with parliamentary regimes took on a very modest character now, for the primary political initiative no longer came from their quarters. But they were surrounded with respect, for they stood above the strife of parties, performing a mediating and moderating function, and they were the custodians of the common statutory liberties. William II blustered onto this tranquil scene of European monarchy; the pomp with which he delighted to embellish his power and his person was novel in this period and created at first a mixed impression, compounded of wonder and doubt, which gave way finally to astonishment at a spectacle which took on the air of a side show. . . . But in the end, after repeated wild gestures and wild words from William, the German parliament and people themselves underwent a belated revulsion; and William was made to promise more carefully to observe the laws of silence and reserve—the royal prerogatives of modern times.

Since the form of liberal government, now intrinsic to European society, came also to be regarded as the sign and *sine qua non* of civilization, it was a natural desire to see it everywhere imposed. . . . But surely, the mere institutional and juridical form, though it has its importance, does not suffice to measure the degree of a people's liberty, nor does it guarantee the real existence of that liberty. Nor does the suffrage, more or less extended or even universal, tell us anything of the breadth and depth of liberalism. Indeed, in certain cases there is a higher degree of liberal feeling, outlook, and action in a country with restricted franchise than in a country where it is broadest. For, as we have said, universal suffrage is often a cherished instrument of the enemies of liberty, of feudalists, clerics, kings, demagogues and opportunists. England, for example, had a suffrage narrower than that of either France or Italy or even Germany; and the voter there had to satisfy, amongst other things, the condition of owning his own home or of earning a certain stipulated income as represented by the amount of rent he paid. Still, the life of liberty in England was not inferior to that in Italy and France, and without doubt it was superior to that in Germany. Spain, on the other hand, had enlarged her suffrage enormously; nonetheless her politics were in fact conducted by the king and buttressed by the army and the clergy. So the alternating government of the Canovas and the Sagastas, the moderates and the progressives, made little genuine difference: parliament in that country had neither authority nor vigor, and was taken up, for the most part, with academic oratory. In Austria the parliamentary altercations were related, not to any intensity of political activity, but to hates and jealousies between the various national groups of the empire. But these conflicts were overruled by what was known as the "Austrian spirit" of the court nobility and functionaries, and for long periods the government was really absolutist, whatever parliamentary masquerade it affected. In Hungary the Magyars dominated in a manner more often absolute than not, restricting the rights of assembly and free speech, restricting or corrupting the press, placing royal commissars in the cities, and so forth. And when in 1913 the electoral system was reformed, provision was made that the power should not leave the hands of the Magyar minority. . . .

Singular in this respect was the condition of the German people. Perhaps the best educated, the most disciplined and industrious group in Europe, the German people profited from the new unity and power to which their nation had ascended, by giving rise to a stupendous development in commerce and industry, science and technology, knowledge and culture of every variety and sort. And yet, though they were able to produce an honest and capable administrative and bureaucratic class from their midst, as well as a valiant military class disciplined along the lines of the Prussian tradition, the Germans were incapable, somehow, of producing a properly political class. The lack of "political sense" was more than once recognized by the Germans themselves, who wondered at this odd deficiency when all else was so excellent. In their historical writings they glorified the "hard men of blood" who had, according to them, given Germany her temper. Such histories contributed to the so-called *Sedanlächeln*—the "Sedan smile"—which was cultivated on the lips of the German Philistine, and which expressed a sense of superiority over other peoples and a special contempt for the Latin races, decadent or decaying, and for their puny parliamentary squabbles. The contempt extended even to England, which was said to be the land of "pseudo-Germanism," a nation not of warriors but of shopkeepers. Disquisitions on theories of the state abounded in their literature, in contrast with the frugality of such writings by the English and the poverty of such writings by the Americans, who, as Lord Bryce remarked, had no use for theories on the subject and were content to use tradition and law as the basis for their constitutional concepts. Bismarck had little esteem for the professors and mocked them freely, reminding them with irony that "politics is not an exact science, as milords the professors seem to think." But Bismarck himself, surely, had done little to create a political class: for such a class to have emerged, some preparation would have been required in parliamentary debate, party fights, alternations in government, and a lively intercourse between the people and its representatives. In a subsequent inquiry Max Weber was able to show that the national conscience, which Bismarck had imposed upon the German people because of his own high civic sense, permitted politics to be run altogether from above, while a faithful and sedulous bureaucracy executed the thought and will of the chancellor, be he great or small, and of the emperor, be he foolish or wise. And so isolated was that little band of politicians, who had gone through the experience of 1848 and the more recent one of the post-1860 Prussian parliament, that as their ranks were gradually diminished by retirement and death, none came to replace them. Thus a new group of statesmen grew up, a group whose collective portrait has been left us in the memoirs of von Bülow, the third successor to Bismarck. Von Bülow was himself typical of the new group in his peculiar unawareness of what constitutes the function of one who controls a people's destiny and of what responsibilities he owes both to his fellow men and to history. The only parties that were able in any way to preserve their political physiognomy were, as it turned out, those which Bismarck persecuted and which he would like to have extirpated—the Catholic Center and the socialists. The former had its faith and the latter its ideals, and they neither obeyed the government's beck and call nor relapsed, in parliament, into mere representatives of agriculture or of this or that branch of industry.

Bismarck scented a possible danger that the German Catholics were in fact the survivors of the Austrian anti-Prussian party in Germany, and it has sometimes been thought that he persecuted them for this reason. His persecution has been connected, too, with the fact that they could create, or cause to be created, an embarrassing situation for him, because of their ties with the clergy of Posen and with the Guelph or Hanoverian party, and with the fact that they obeyed the international power of the papacy. This obedience, greater even than that of the French legitimists, led them to put pressure on the new empire to bring about some military intervention calculated to restore temporal power to Rome. But perhaps none of these reasons, singly or collectively, explains the form which Bismarck's persecution of them assumed, unless we somehow take into account his anger (an evil counselor in any case) and also the intoxication which accompanies absolute power—an intoxication which blinds one to the limitations imposed on power by the very nature of things. . . . Bismarck let descend a storm of laws and provisions against the Catholic Church, but the faithful herded together about their clergy and their bishops, who permitted themselves to be hounded and deposed rather than give way. So the Catholic associations actually grew, and the Catholic press gained new life and wide circulation; while in Rome the Pope protested, inveighed, and condemned. Indeed, Bismarck himself came gradually to recognize that he had taken a blind alley, and as sober reflection took the place of impulse and anger within him, the causes for his earlier alarm at Austrophiles, Hanoverians, Poles, and Papists diminished, and he found that he now had need of the Catholic Center. For he required that the Catholics augment the German conservative movement so that he could carry through his planned alienation of the liberal-nationalist party which had served him thus far. And he who had declared that he would never go to Canossa, went to Canossa: in 1880 Bismarck opened negotiations with the papal nuncio; in 1882 he recalled almost all the deposed bishops and reinstated them; and he relaxed the laws he had proclaimed. . . . He declared later that the question of principle remained unresolved nevertheless, that the "ancient quarrel between prince and priest has not reached a final conclusion in Germany"; and indeed, it was only in terms of the ancient polarity between royal and ecclesiastical power that he was able to conceive it. But he did allow the German professors to embellish it with a name, *Kulturkampf,* the "fight for civilization"—a name which the Catholics sarcastically translated as "the fight against civilization." And the Catholics were not altogether wrong, for to fight conscience with violence is not civilization. Nor was there, in fact, any need to conduct a special and harsh crusade for civilization in Germany—a country of many religions where scarcely a third of the population was Catholic, where culture was in flower, and where the authority of criticism and science was great.

A more genuine *Kulturkampf* was then being waged in the Catholic countries themselves, a fight which had begun a century or so earlier when their absolute monarchs had freed them from the chains of theocratic bondage. The battle was now being conducted by liberal governments who were aware —as the old monarchies could never have been aware—of the true nature of the conflict and who sought to replace a culture with a culture, a doctrine with a doctrine, or, as we may say here, a religion with a religion. . . . The process, which we call secularization, could have been observed in Italy at that time. She, in her recent capacity of a unified and liberal state, had wrested the temporal power from the Papacy, which was no longer defended by the better Catholic elements and which, because of the behavior of the papal government, had come to be the object of universal execration. Italy was now carrying toward perfection those reforms left imperfect by the old monarchies or those which they had hesitated to perfect: abolition of the ecclesiastical tribunal and other clerical privileges, suppression of monasteries and convents and confiscation of ecclesiastical property, exclusion of theological instruction from the universities, and so forth. What it amounted to was a modernization of education and culture. . . .

France had a longer task to perform and a greater effort to exert. For the clerics had long been complete masters during the Second Empire; and they, in the early days of the Third Republic, believing a legitimist restoration to be in the offing, acted as though the times of Charles X had returned once more. Celebrating with an orgy of pilgrimages and processions, they protested in favor of the Pope and against the secularistic legislation of Italy and demanded a war to return Rome to him. This was tolerated and even favored by MacMahon, as when DeBroglie sought to suppress anticlericalist and antitemporalist demonstrations and stigmatized civic funerals as "scenes of impiety." Many obstacles to the consolation of a parliamentary republic came from the clericals, who encouraged a *coup d'état* from MacMahon, who at that time had the advice and counsel of Monsignor Dupanloup on religious and ecclesiastical matters. Thus the attempt to establish the parliamentary republic went hand in hand with the fight against clericalism, and once again in 1875 Gambetta uttered the battle cry that had echoed ten years earlier, "Clericalism—there is the enemy!" while the radicals demanded separation of church and state. Then, in 1877 the parliament issued a special mandatory order against ultramontane demonstrations, and there followed in 1879 decrees for the dissolution and dispersion of the Jesuits and unauthorized congregations. Elementary education which, ever since the Falloux Law had remained in the hands of monks and friars, was secularized in 1881 and made compulsory and free, and at the same time provision was made for the secular instruction of girls. In 1882 the schools were declared to be religiously "neutral." "Neutrality" was no doubt a myth (as Simon pointed out), but it was at least an opportune myth for the new religion of critical inquiry that was replacing the old religion of revelation and miracles. In 1886 it was prescribed that all teachers must be laymen. . . .

But the real catastrophe for clericalism was precipitated by the attack upon the Republic by the Catholics in the Dreyfus *affaire* and by the behavior of the Roman Curia at that time. The clerical rage that seethed behind a mask of patriotism and high nationalism was revealed to the republicans at last, so that soon after the defeat of the anti-Dreyfusards, the Assumptionist congregation was dissolved along with its newspaper, *La Croix,* which during the battle had been one of the most outspokenly impudent journals. Soon afterwards a law was passed against those congregations which, amongst other things, divided Frenchmen against Frenchmen—congregations which, because of their educational methods, set the parochially educated youth and the publicly educated youth against one another, weakening thus the moral unity of the French nation. . . . The law became increasingly severe as it passed through parliament, and it was severely applied; and a few years later, when dissension with the Holy See grew more acute, France broke off diplomatic relationships with the Papacy, and the step was finally taken to separate church and state. This was in 1905: the Concordat of 1815 was repudiated; the state was declared to be nonsectarian; and all citizens were recognized as having equal freedom of conscience and worship. Further, any state or municipal subsidies that had been extended to particular cults were withdrawn; ecclesiastical property was distributed to local charitable institutions; and the ecclesiastical buildings, together with the parish houses and the dwellings of the bishops, were left to be used by any duly constituted cultural association. The French Catholics, and finally even the Church of Rome herself, became resigned to the inevitable reaction that their own acts had provoked and made feasible. In the years that followed they succeeded only in setting up certain associations, not like those which the state established, but "canonico-legal" ones, and even these were more consonant with the liberal conception of separation. . . .

Modern civilization now had a clear course before it and a central task to perform, the task, namely, of mustering its own strength for dedicated combat with the old faith. The danger of a Catholic reaction, along the lines of the counterreformation, was hardly probable, since all the real conditions for the emergence of such a movement were lacking. Nor, indeed, was there a Spain, as there had been in the sixteenth century, able to support a reactionary movement with arms and state power (though to add an amusing anecdote, the last king of Spain, Alphonso XIII, moved by mindfulness of the past when he was in Rome, offered his sword to the Pope in defense of Holy Cause). Even the conception which many then formed, concerning the internationally effective power of the Pope, must be held to have been exaggerated; for there were too many ties binding the Catholics of various countries to their governments and to the active parties which operated in their states. It is clear, for example, that the Catholics of Germany primarily defended their own cause against Bismarck, and not that of the distant Pope. And though the Italian Catholics did at times, and in certain places, obey the order to abstain from voting, it was in general the case that—when laziness or indifference did not overcome them—they voted for the deputies who best represented their interests and who best had gained their amity and admiration. The Catholics of France, when Leo XIII counseled them to co-operate with the Republic, did not act concertedly and obeyed him but poorly; and the Irish Catholics did not heed the Pope's admonitions to them nor his plea for moderation when their national protest came to be accompanied by acts of terror. When the Catholic clergy supported the Czech against the German element in Austria, the Germans of that country replied with a loud *Los von Rom,* "Secede from Rome!" and quit the Catholic Church by the thousands. The major strength of the Church lay in the indefeasibility and immutability of her dogma and discipline. This gave her at once the advantages and disadvantages of an utterly immobile creature: a mobile creature may stumble from time to time—but it can at least go forward.

There were some attempts at reform within the bosom itself of the Church. The movement of the so-called "Old Catholics" in Germany will do as an example, for it was at once typical and relatively the most important of them all. This movement did not recognize the new doctrine of papal infallibility. The "Old Catholics" proposed to return to the church of the seventh century and to abolish sacerdotal celibacy and other similar things, but the movement lost impetus and, like anything of a hybrid nature, soon succumbed. At the turn of the century, under the influence of lay philosophy and historiography, there arose an impetuous movement amongst the more cultured Catholics which was known as "modernism," a contradictory notion, which, while shunning Protestantism, sought to open Catholicism to historical criticism and at the same time to preserve the tradition and unity of the Church, together with pontifical authority and dogmatic forms. From her old and well-equipped entrenchments, the Church defended herself resolutely and with valor against modernism, condemning the movement in 1907 in the encyclical *Pascendi,* rooting it out and casting it to the flames. Of course, the victory cost her the loss of a substantial number of the most learned and distinguished minds she possessed, but this was far less grave than would have been the loss of her *raison d'être,* which would inevitably have occurred had she conceded or compromised in any way.

Just as in his fight against the Catholics, Bismarck failed in his even more violent tussle with the German socialists—which again shows the inefficacy of authoritarian methods and the ineptitude of Bismarck's policy when it was exercised in fields other than those in which foreign nations compete. The socialist propaganda which was increasingly disseminated amongst the German laboring classes, the large number of socialist newspapers, the growing number of votes obtained by socialist candidates (in 1877 they received close to half a million)—all this alarmed Bismarck and provoked his natural inclinations to resort to policelike or military tactics. After failing to persuade parliament to put teeth into several articles of the penal code, Bismarck decided to make political profit of two attempts which had been made on the life of the Emperor in 1878. Exaggerating the importance of these attempts and distorting their political significance, Bismarck dissolved parliament, called for new elections in October, 1878, and then forced through a special law which had previously been rejected, prohibiting any societies, meetings, and publications of a socialist or communist character. Also the power was given him to prevent certain individuals, who were considered agitators, from living in certain centers; to close public houses, book shops, and other places socialists were likely to gather; and to declare a state of siege wherever the peace seemed to be menaced. Notwithstanding the dismay which these prohibitions and their accompanying sanctions initially engendered, and despite the fears, apostasies, and the cowardly denunciations which took place, the socialist ranks remained intact. They transferred their presses to Switzerland, and their leaders went abroad. And though the socialist vote fell to 300,000 in 1881, it already passed the half-million mark in 1884, and in 1887 it soared to nearly 800,000. The special law, which originally was to have been valid for a year and a half, was prolonged to twelve; and Bismarck, who had no intention of modifying his methods, had no choices other than to make it still stricter and more severe or to attempt a *coup d'état* and thence to deprive the socialists of the right to vote. This latter desperate alternative, which he finally took, provided, as we have seen, the occasion for his fall from power; so that it may be said that it was socialist activity that drove him at last from the political arena. He had not barred the road, but had instead made it smooth for them; and from now on their representation in the German parliament was steadily on the increase. By 1912, they had become the strongest faction there, with a hundred and ten deputies. Indeed, thanks to the electorate of Berlin, several socialists even penetrated the sacrosanct, semifeudal Prussian chamber!

Bismarck, who usually understood and practiced only negative and repressive methods and had neither faith nor ability in the positive methods of liberty, actually adopted social legislation, a genuinely positive technique, for combatting socialism. This legislation was intended to destroy the foundation and impulse of socialism by satisfying the legitimate needs of the working class. And so he created the fund for sick workers in 1883, insurance against work-incurred accidents in 1884, and old-age and disability insurance in 1889. These laws gave the stimulus to social legislation throughout Europe; but, from another point of view, they constituted simply a more vital resumption of a movement begun fifty years earlier in England, not to cite even earlier examples (since such laws were not unknown even to the old absolute monarchies). But useful as they were, the conservative-authoritarian spirit behind the laws was not likely to inspire anything but mistrust on the part of the workingman. Besides, it was felt by them that these provisions were really due to socialist activity *per se.* . . .

In a real and practical sense, it was surely Ferdinand Lassalle who gave the impetus and direction to the German labor movement between 1862 and 1864. He at that time founded the General Workers' Union and simultaneously demanded universal suffrage and the secret ballot, both necessary to the progress of the workingman. The suffrage was obtained later through Bismarck, who granted it for his own ends, much as Louis Napoleon had done in France. But, as it turned out, the workingmen used it for *their* own ends and against Bismarck himself, and it was no longer possible to deprive them of it. Karl Marx, too, played a part in the movement by raising a banner around which rallied another workingman's association in Germany. Marx was able to effect this, first, by means of the International Working Mens' Association (the First International), founded in 1864 in London and enduring through many vicissitudes for nearly a decade, and, secondly, by means of the doctrines which he introduced and which, for the sake of compromise, he tempered in the beginning with such concepts as liberty and justice, which he actually despised as prejudices. These two associations, the Marxian and the Lassallian, after a long period of antagonism and many attempts by each to usurp the place of the other, were led by necessity finally to unite in 1875 at the Congress at Gotha. There they made mutual concessions on the doctrinal level by combining the ideas both of Lassalle and of

Marx; but they also gave life to a compact workingman's party which began to send representatives to the imperial parliament: two in 1871, nine in 1874, twelve in 1877. It was this growing number of socialist deputies, as well as the increasing number of votes given to socialist candidates, that provoked Bismarck's reaction. After the repelling of this reaction, in the course of which it gained the social legislation, socialism achieved a further moral victory. For the new Emperor (though he was later to change his tune) began by flattering the workingman's class and claims, and he solemnly affirmed, with the world as his witness, not only the graveness and urgency of the social question, but also the necessity of confronting it with fervor and solving it "with a warm heart and a cool head." This would be, he declared, "the second great task of Germany after the Reformation," and he forthwith summoned an international conference on labor problems in Berlin.

By now, the insurrections of the laboring classes, such as the Parisian street battles of June of '48, were but a distant memory. And the *Commune* of 1871 had not, really, opened a new era in which the conquest of the bourgoisie and the dictatorship of the proletariat over them was to be achieved, although Marx liked, for the sake of propaganda, so to transfigure it and although it was so pictured by the fearful imagination of the rich, the timid, and the gentle. The older socialisms had neither impelling force as examples nor actual value as doctrines, and so they receded into the pantheon and golden legend of the party and were venerated as "precursors"; while men like Owen, Fourier, and Saint-Simon still bore the label, fixed on them by Marx, of "Utopian Socialists." The new socialist reality was in fact the reality of electoral assemblies and parliamentary representation, although the consequences of these institutions were still slowly unfolding, and their ultimate implications could as yet not be discerned. . . .

Minor impediments and entanglements inhibited the merger of socialism and liberalism in France. The Marxian dialectical interpretation of history, the conception which regarded the structure and superstructure of the world of ideals as a mere cover up for underlying economic interests, the demand that the party remain totally uncontaminated by the concepts and sentiments of other parties (all reprobate because all "bourgeois"), the necessity to push bourgeois production and civilization to their extreme limits in order to bring them to destruction and thus convert them into their opposites— all these notions, and more, were congenial to the Germans, who are a very theoretically minded people, fond of complicated ideas. But they made little appeal to the French. The revolutionary tradition of French socialism took its tone from Blanqui's insurrectionism, an idea which proposed to reform society through rational legislation—once control of the seat of government had been seized. But the military executions and the deportations which followed the *Commune,* together with the state of siege which was protracted for several years; the subsequent disintegration of the *Internationale;* the memory of defeats, suffered in the course of the century by the working-classes—these had robbed the insurrectionary tradition of all hope and drive.

When the Republic was firmly established and when the state of siege was lifted at last, amnesties were granted to the survivors of the *Commune,* and the problems of the workingman could once again be taken up. The radicals and the extreme left-wing republicans had, already, included in their political programs a special part called "The Social Program." This proposed to bring about legal recognition of the trade unions (*syndicats*), legal restriction of the working day, and worker's insurance; and also to introduce a graduated income tax, nationalization of mines and railroads, elected rather than appointed judges, and so forth—a program much like the so-called "Minimum Program" of Germany. Thus the socialists found allies amongst the radicals and republicans who would co-operate just so long as the socialists did not insist upon a future communist society and other similar Marxist notions. And so, in 1882, another workman's party was formed alongside the already existing Marxist workingman's party of Guesde and Laforgue. The new party came to be the more important of the two, consisting of socialists who were soon known as "possibilists," because they proposed only to demand those reforms which were in practical terms *possible* at any given time. Co-operation in parliament, and eventually in government as well, was implicit in such a program; and when Juarès, elected deputy in 1895, drew up a blueprint for a parliamentary socialist party, he did so with the agreement of the radicals. At the time of the Boulanger episode, Guesde, then the leader of the Marxist group, declared in a style characteristic of his school that the conflict was between bourgeois parties and was thus a matter of indifference to the proletariat. But the new socialists took a very active part indeed in the political conflicts of their time and, in unison with the republicans, took the liberal-secular side in the Dreyfus affair, against clericals, militarists, and reactionaries. After this crisis, in 1899, the socialist Millerand joined the cabinet of Waldeck-Rousseau as minister of industry and commerce. This event subverted the calculations of the Marxian scholastics and was roundly condemned at the Dresden Congress, after which, and (as they said) so as not to break the unity of the party, other assemblies in France joined in the denunciation—even some assemblies and groups who would have applauded the event as having been necessary for the defense of a threatened republic, and as a token of the growing political maturity of the socialist party. All this produced, finally, a split; the French socialist party (the Marxians) separated from the parliamentary socialists and the "independents." In the elections of 1902, when there was a conflict over the religious policy, the parliamentary socialists allied with the republican extreme left to harvest a clamorous victory; in 1906 Briand left the socialists to participate in the Sarrien cabinet, and another socialist, Viviani, became minister of labor the following year.

The influence of Marxism in England was negligible, although it was in that country that Marx elaborated his doctrines and from which he directed the First International. . . . On the other hand, the theories of Henry George, concerning the nationalization of land, excited a high and ardent interest, which was but natural in a country where one third of the land was in aristocratic hands and was kept, in great part, as pasture, park, hunting reserve, and playground. The attempt was never made in England either to suppress or persecute socialism nor were great efforts or troubles required in order to bring it into rapport with liberalism. For from the beginning, the problems of labor were, so to speak, spontaneously built into the framework of British society and politics: liberal and conservative alike were concerned with them, and so there was little occasion for specific socialist activity. The socialism of the Fabians, as their name itself suggests, was liberal in spirit: eschewing sudden and violent uprisings, the Fabians advised society in any way that was compatible with what they felt was the natural development of society—a development which was proceeding from an uninhibited freedom of competition toward a social organization of production. Equally reformist and non-Marxian was the independent Labor Party, formed in 1893; while the trade unions themselves attended to what was practical, necessary, and feasible. Bernstein, who had lived in London for a time, drew from what he witnessed in England the example and stimulus for his revision of Marxism and of social democracy in Germany. He wrote, in 1899,

No responsible socialist any longer dreams of an imminent victory of socialism through catastrophic means nor through a sudden conquest of parliament by a revolutionary proletariat. On the contrary, the work is being more and more transferred to municipalities and other autonomous centers of administration; and the habit of despising this has been lost, while here and there important relationships with the corporate movement are being established. . . .

Generally throughout Europe there was now a widespread good will and a disposition to propose, promote, and accept social legislation—not any longer and not exclusively for conservative purposes, but because it was seriously felt to be morally right. The Bismarckian laws for old-age, illness, and accident insurance were adopted, in the course of time, by other states; and other health laws, at various times and of various sorts, were introduced in Germany and elsewhere. These were followed by still other laws, governing the equality of employer and employee obligation, prohibiting night work for women and children and restricting it for male workers, determining the length of the work week and providing obligatory rest periods, and reducing the working day. Around 1890 the demand arose that the working day be limited to eight hours, and at any rate the number sank below the fourteen-hour level which had formerly been customary in many factories. In England, at the time of Disraeli, the work week was restricted to fifty-six hours; and in France, by 1894, the working day was limited to ten hours. Other laws were passed regulating home labor, workers' housing, and the preference which was to be given to labor co-operatives in the hiring of hands for public works, and so on. Trade unions, syndicates, labor confederations, and professional unions received legal recognition, while labor councils and special committees were instituted by the various ministries until, finally, there were even ministries of labor. . . .

The increasing power of industry and wealth ascended in a grand crescendo during this period in Europe, and especially after 1890. The technological discoveries of that time, together with their technical application; the variety of production; the expansion of markets and the ever more rapid modes of transportation are things well known. . . . As symbolizing the entire rhythm, we might consider the population of Europe, which at the beginning of the century had been 180,000,000 and which had now increased to 450,000,000—not to reckon in the millions who went to the Americas and other new lands: the United States had herself grown from 5,000,000 in 1800 to 77,000,000 in 1900. Indeed, whatever statistics we examine, we discover numbers which at once recall such facts to our minds and are symbols of these facts as well. In Belgium, for example, in 1850 industry employed a capital of three hundred millions and in 1913 seven billions; and her great port of Antwerp handled in 1840 a traffic of 240,000 tons which rose, by 1914, to 14,000,000. The world production of anthracite went from 130,000,000 tons in 1860 to 650,-000,000 tons in the last years of the century.

Colonial expansion, too, was a rapid and accelerating trend, and markedly so after 1880 when, in emulation of England who was then extending, consolidating, and administering her empire, a hunger to possess colonies seized nearly all the states of Europe. France brought her empire from less than 725,000 square miles to twelve times that number, with 50,000,000 inhabitants.

Germany, who had no colonies before 1884, soon was third in rank with accessions in Africa, Oceania, and certain ports in the Far East. Italy occupied Eritrea, and later Tripolitania; Belgium, through the labors of Leopold II, obtained colonies in the Congo; and Spain, though she lost Cuba and the Philippines, the remnants of her old colonial dominion, clung still to the coast of Morocco. Russia, meanwhile, continued to expand into Asia; and the United States, after 1896, had her imperialism. The feelings which led to these enterprises were compounded of many elements: of presumed economic advantages, in part real and in part imaginary; of power and political prestige; and of a nationalistic fervor which would have the language, customs, and culture of the home country exported to all parts of the world. "France," declared the colonialist Ferry in 1885, "wishes not merely to be a free country, but a great one as well, extending, wherever she can, her customs, language, arms, flag, and genius." Finally, colonialism was a product of a greater love for humanity and for universal civilization. England gave her empire a liberal character, permitting those parts of it which possessed a certain level of civilization—the dominions of Canada, Australia, New Zealand, and South Africa—to have liberal and democratic institutions. These dominions had their own laws and governments, independent commercial relationships, their own army (and some even desired their own navy); but they remained united with the mother country in a spontaneous fashion, by reason of mutual convenience and interest, a common language and tradition, and consonant ideals. Economy was truly global: Europe was nourished with grain from the world's four corners; for her own production of it did not suffice, she having given her soil over to other crops and different uses.

An over-all prosperity went hand in hand with the production of wealth, even if, in some places and amongst certain strata of the world's population, misery and want went undiminished. Indeed, misery and want were rendered sometimes more intolerable by the very proximity of prosperity, and poverty was at times intensified by the very rapidity of economic transformation. Everywhere could be observed a shift in the proportion between urban and rural populations: the centralization and growth of an industrial population and the formation of a numerous class of technicians and factory workers was inversely accompanied by a diminution, and almost a disappearance, of craftsmen and petty entrepreneurs. Education was on the rise in every class; more reading was being done in more languages; and the newspapers, thanks to telegraph and telephone, presented every day, and almost every hour, a picture of life the world over. Sometimes it happened that a debate, a polemic, or a question which arose in one country would excite mens' minds in every country: so it was with the Dreyfus affair.

This era, so filled with activity and enjoying a peace never before known to Europe, has nonetheless come to be known as a "prosaic age"—a judgment that has persisted in the books of its historians. And it has also been judged a "skeptical and dissatisfied age"—a judgment that seems strange and perverse unless we locate the era in relationship to the spiritual crisis begun in 1848 and reaching a crest in 1870. The practical activity, which had led to the liberal order and the benefits to be drawn therefrom, was no longer conjoined with a high and genuine understanding of this activity—with an understanding capable of appreciating its deeper meaning and inestimable worth. Hence true religious and moral impulses were weakened; and weakened, too, was the capacity to probe the fundamental concepts and, through criticism, to reanimate them. And the inner life of conscience, where suffering, sorrow, and anguish can be regathered, purified, and converted into forces of consolation and creativity, was itself subdued and mortified.

In the late years of the eighteenth and the early years of the nineteenth century, Germany had become the philosophical Athens of the modern age; and once again, after two thousand years, humanity was offered a feast of reason as original as it was bountiful. Although some believed that she, through her rise to high national and political power, would bring her thought to a new and grand fruition, the quality of it declined instead. Germany grew mentally impoverished and lost the function she had exercised as the energizing knower who fertilized the minds and thoughts of all peoples. The labors of her scientists went assiduously on, and their erudition was great, but there were no flashes of genius, and the patrimony of her classical age was allowed to lie inert, forgotten or despised. In the country of Kant and Hegel, the fields of thought were narrowed: one might observe there neocritics, psychologists, physiological psychologists, and other worthy individuals, full of high intentions and down-to-earthness, but with neither vigor nor courage. Elsewhere men like Spencer and Arigò met with huge success, and a hollow positivism and evolutionism stultified mens' minds. Even when liberty itself was theorized about or defended, the defense and the theories were empirical and superficial. . . .

If, then, the activity of the era seems prosaic and narrow, this is not because it was so in fact; for in fact the impulse of the preceding historical era was made magnificently actual. Instead, it is because the intellects who considered this development were prosaic and narrow, because a narrow and prosaic imagination set it in a poor light, because a narrow prosaic spirit, instead of embracing it and lending it warmth, ignored it or despised it. Here was a dangerous lack of thoughts and ideals, which might have persisted for some time without doing great harm, were it not that this void had almost the attractiveness of false ideals. This could have been seen already in the literature of low romanticism and decadentism; and false ideals were arising everywhere now, contaminating all political thought. In philosophy a certain reawakening was taking place which made the mean positivism and crude naturalism of the time seem intolerable; but philosophy showed only a partial indication that she was returning to her grander tradition, and for the most part lost herself in mysticism, pragmatism, and other irrationalisms. Nonetheless, the false ideals in political life, irrationalism in the life of reason, as well as enfeeblement of conscience and the inner life, might have been vanquished by criticism and education. Or they might have worn themselves out like everything of little vigor and no intrinsic worth, giving rise to their opposites and to better things. But to the mental and spiritual dangers was added another danger, altogether and effectively practical, which was born of Europe's international relations. And this new danger, giving substance to such dispositions of the spirit, nourished them, excited them, and precipitated them, finally, into action.

3. POLITICAL LIBERALISM: ITS BASES, POLITICS, AND FORMULATIONS

THE BASES OF LIBERALISM

For the nineteenth century no political doctrine was of such decisive importance as that of liberalism. In it was to be found an expression of the ideals of the age that emerged from the British constitutional experience of the eighteenth century and from the French Enlightenment. These powerful influences molded a political doctrine that eventually displaced those forms of absolutism that survived the French Revolution. In the liberal forms and policies of government the way was prepared for democratic citizenship in states dedicated to freeing individuals, each for his own "pursuit of happiness."

Liberalism as a philosophic principle rests on the doctrine that human actions, to be moral, must be voluntary, and to be voluntary must be an act of choice or conscious consent. In the free and unhampered action of the individual, liberalism sees the goal of social organization. As an attitude, liberalism consequently is opposed to all authority coming from above, and trusts enlightened self-interest for the maintenance of the public good. In its defense of liberty, liberalism differs from conservatism in that liberalism as a program is unwilling to regard existing privileges as liberties. Although liberalism is not theoretically committed to individualism, the liberalism of 1815–50 tended to emphasize freedom of individuals from government and to limit the conception of freedom to the possession of rights, rather than to the creation of opportunities.

Liberalism as a creed was, then, a principle of individualism and of liberty. In individualism, liberalism saw not only an infinite spiritual value but a positive principle of political organization; the free individual was conceived as the atom of the modern political state. Liberation of man's energy and initiative is the first principle of social action and reconstruction. Hence liberty becomes of paramount importance for the realization of the individual's capacities. The liberty with which liberalism is concerned has its source in freedom of contract rather than corporative or class privileges. Translating the liberty associated with human personality into political principles became, therefore, the first task of liberalism as an historical movement.

Liberalism remained without form and without influence in the history of Europe until it became clear that political liberty was necessary for maintaining that freedom and individualism to which the humanists of the Renaissance had given non-political expression. Hence control of the government and the achievement of guarantees within the state became the immediate goal of the persons and parties which became known as liberal. Realization of their program of controlled government and guaranteed individual liberties did not come on the Continent until the nineteenth century; indeed, the first half of that era was marked by political struggles to achieve that end. By the middle of the nineteenth century liberal ideas were sufficiently impressed upon European life to insure the characteristic form of constitutional-parliamentary politics among the western states. Constitutional liberalism put an end to the power of the feudal aristocracies and absolute rulers.

Apart from those more remote conditions of the growth of liberal thought, which have been traced in an earlier section, there were two great traditions on which liberalism nourished itself. These were the Lockean and French rationalist definitions of liberty, the product of the secular natural-rights philosophy of the eighteenth century, and, secondly, the practice of British government, particularly after the formulation of the Bill of Rights of 1689. In the first, the natural-rights theory of government maintained that political and public liberties stemmed from inherent individual rights. And by making the individual and his rights the end of government, the liberals used a theoretical lever against the absolute states based on classes and interests. Moreover, the natural-rights theory of liberty brought to an end the earlier forms of contractualism that had been used by some earlier rationalists to justify absolutism.

A logical expression of the French rationalist definitions of liberty based on natural law appeared in the *Declaration of the Rights of Man* (1789), one of the classic statements of liberalism that the eighteenth century produced. Here in the preamble and the first four articles was a vigorous and able summation of the liberal thought of the age:

The representatives of the French people, organized in the National Assembly, considering that ignorance, forgetfulness or contempt of the rights of man are the sole causes of the public miseries and of the corruption of governments, have resolved to set forth in a solemn declaration the natural, inalienable, and sacred rights of man, in order that this declaration, being ever present to all the members of the social body, may unceasingly remind them of their rights and their duties; in order that the acts of the legislative power and those of the executive power may be each moment compared with the aim of every political institution and thereby may be more respected; and in order that the demands of citizens, grounded henceforth upon simple and incontestable principles, may always take the direction of maintaining the constitution and the welfare of all.

In consequence, the National Assembly recognizes and declares, in the presence and under the auspices of the Supreme Being, the following rights of man and of the citizen.

1. Men are born free and remain free and equal in rights. Social distinctions can be based only upon public utility.

2. The aim of every political association is the preservation of the natural and imprescriptible rights of man. These rights are liberty, property, security, and resistance to oppression.

3. The source of all sovereignty is essentially in the nation; no body, no individual can exercise authority that does not proceed from it in plain terms.

4. Liberty consists in the power to do anything that does not injure others; accordingly, the exercise of the natural rights of each man has for its only limits those that secure to the other members of society the enjoyment of these same rights. These limits can be determined only by law.

The other great tradition of liberalism in the eighteenth century, namely the practice of British government, produced a literary monument not less enduring in Sir William Blackstone's *Commentaries on the Law of England* (1765–69). Although his systematic treatment of the British Constitution gave rise to the impression that the law was rational and impeccable in form, and though Blackstone was consistently loyal to the law, the *Commentaries* became a bible of liberalism. Here was set forth in concise order the system of laws that defended property, protected the individual, and limited the executive—in short, an entire panoply of practical and liberal achievements. In the doctrine of parliamentary sovereignty, which Blackstone explicitly defended, liberals of the coming age found hope and profitable example. And to Blackstone might be attributed some of the zeal for a careful legal definition of government, part of the faith in the transplanted machinery of English government which a later generation of continental liberals exhibited.

Beyond the theoretical description of the English Constitution there was the great example of the successful operation of the British government. In what was essentially an aristocratic republic, the landed-gentry and mercantile classes had become the guardian of the public liberties. Sometimes their zeal was extended beyond guardianship to glorification of the laws, as in the case of Edmund Burke, whose writings revealed the conservative nature of Whig liberalism. Continuous adding of practical liberties, interplay of parties, defense of the laws against the sovereign, the amassing of all these in a never-ending history constituted, according to Burke, the nature of British law. This traditional constitutionalism, confronted after 1789 with the antitraditional and rationalist principles of the French revolutionaries, produced a compromise form of nationalistic constitutionalism, which served as the justification of the political power of the middle classes.

In England the growth of the industrial middle classes in the eighteenth century had presented the Constitution with a problem of assimilation that did not take political form until the Reform Bill of 1832. That the bourgeois class should be content with participation in the Constitution and its liberties rather than desirous of a revolution was a testimony to the apt guardianship of the Constitution in the hands of the British aristocracy. In France, on the other hand, the middle classes discarded the national tradition of government in favor of rationalist theories, and advocated political progress at the expense of tradition. Eventually this influence came to predominate, even in Britain, and with this achievement the coöperation of the two great traditions of liberalism was assured.

In addition to these major traditions there came the impetus toward liberalism given by the success of the American Revolution and the Constitution of the United States, with its elaborate separation of powers, checks and balances, bill of rights, and other typical features of liberal politics.

THE POLITICS OF LIBERALISM

Though the interaction of the British and Continental middle classes immediately after 1815 was in large measure responsible for the unitary development of liberalism, the bourgeoisie had not then become the single defender of the doctrine, nor were the industrial middle classes on the Continent as yet numerous enough to give substantial support to liberalism. In

England the industrial and commercial classes shared with the aristocracy the ideal of loyalty to the political liberties of Englishmen, and the aspirations of both English parties after 1832 gave no evidence of desire among these classes to share their liberties with the lower classes. On the Continent, the slow growth of the industrial middle classes left the championship of liberalism to the "middle class of the land" or lesser gentry and to the commercial interests. To assert that liberalism was a political ideal solely of the middle classes would be an oversimplification; for in the Austrian Empire the aristocracy contributed notably to its support, and in Hungary the gentry was the basis of the lively parliamentary life that flourished before 1848. In Bohemia the traditional and national aristocracy, out of opposition to domination by Vienna and the Habsburgs, cherished the ideal of constitutions and individual liberties. Liberalism could hardly be said to have permeated Russia, but its principal adherents there were enlightened nobles and the military classes. In Italy, liberalism was the ideological property not only of the middle classes but of the aristocratic members of the ruling house of Savoy, Cardinal Gizzi, and, until 1848, of Cardinal Mastai, who became Pope Pius IX. Irrespective of their individual class origins the intellectuals were the liberal leaders and it was among professional groups and in the universities that liberalism had its headquarters.

Whatever the basis of its class support, the doctrine of political liberalism represented an agitation for specific legal guarantees of personal freedom through the development of constitutionalism. Even the age of legitimism which followed the Congress of Vienna was in this respect a modest step forward toward truly liberal institutions, for in the two great governmental documents of this era, the French *Charte* [1] (1814), and the *Bundesakte* [2] (1815) of the German Confederation, the ideal of written constitutions and limited government was conceded. Though both these governments rested on a contractual rather than a natural-rights conception of legal rights, and were essentially aristocratic in tone, the parliamentary life that they provided trained a new generation of liberals in party procedure and political debate.

Conceiving national political life in constitutional terms on the basis of a natural-rights philosophy of liberties became, therefore, the primary aim of the liberals. In practice this meant both in England and on the Continent a rigorous opposition to the crown and an application of Montesquieu's *garantisme*,[3] a system designed to secure the individual against encroachment by

[1] *Charter.*
[2] *Federal Act* or constitution.
[3] *Structure of guarantees.*

the state. That these ideals should be enshrined in a written fundamental law was a natural outcome, for only in a government with an explicit definition of precisely limited powers could free-functioning individuals thrive. Hence in the constitution liberals sought guarantees of free economic and political life, freedom of the press, of association, and of conscience, protection for property, a broadened suffrage, and a bill of rights to insure personal liberty.

These aspirations did not necessarily imply a lack of faith in monarchical institutions. In fact, a limited monarchy rather than a republic was the liberal fashion. Here and there in Europe liberal thought opposed monarchies, as in the republican ideas of Mazzini, but another Italian liberal, Vincenzo Gioberti, was able to utilize Catholic and papal principles of state organization. Through all the vicissitudes of French politics before 1848 the middle-class liberals were loyal to the idea of a monarchy, while in Britain there was not the slightest public hint of republican agitation. It was notable that the movement for Italian liberation was captured by a liberal-minded ruler of Piedmont, whose *Statuto* [4] of 1848 became the cornerstone of Italian liberal politics, and that in 1849 liberals of the Frankfort Parliament were willing to make Frederick William IV of Prussia a constitutional monarch in Germany.

In addition to the principles of constitutionalism and monarchism, the doctrine of federalism was implicit in most nineteenth-century liberal theory. It appears strikingly in the thought of Benjamin Constant, whose writings were decisive for the evolution of liberalism in France, where he consistently championed the independence of local authorities against the central government. Federalism was further brought home to the French by the writings of De Tocqueville about the theory and practice of democracy in America. And in Germany there was little disagreement among liberals that the problem of unification would have to be solved along federal rather than unitary or centralized lines. That the federal solution triumphed even when German unification was in conservative hands was a tribute to the power and reality of the idea. Besides the application of federalism in national political organization, liberalism looked with favor on this principle for the solution of international problems. This legacy of liberalism has survived to the twentieth century, but in the nineteenth century its only practical application was found in the federal organization of the British Empire.

EVOLUTION OF LIBERAL THOUGHT

It was in Britain that liberalism achieved most complete expression, and continental observers made the facetious assertion that England exported the

[4] *Constitution.*

doctrine along with steam engines. Certainly no other European nation could boast a liberal tradition like the British Constitution with its salient features of a limited monarch, a supreme legislative body, a cabinet system, and the rule of law, and none of the appurtenances of the absolute state, such as secret police or bureaucracy. The marvelous adaptive facilities of this order contributed far more to the popularity of liberalism than the experience and theory of the Continental states. Aided by Jeremy Bentham's vigorous use of utilitarianism as a basis for legal reform, English liberalism rapidly outgrew laissez-faire optimism and the dogmas of natural rights, and attained its fullest formulation in the works of John Stuart Mill, who put it on the philosophical foundation of empiricism and utilitarianism. But his writings appeared at the very period when liberalism was beginning to allow the state positive functions, and when the exceptions to the rule of "the less government the better" were so numerous that the practical application of his system of individual liberty began to disintegrate. So it was that even in Victorian England a new generation of liberals began to conceive the state of liberty in terms of the "progress of the nation" and to assign to government more than the police functions of Spencer's "anarchy-plus-a-constable" theory.

In much the same order the evolution of liberal thought may be traced in France where the early liberals had tried to restrain the state with legal formulae, but a later generation—the writers of the age of Napoleon III—began to emphasize the liberal state's positive duties. In Constant, Lamennais, and De Tocqueville, French liberal thought found its main exposition. Constant, the father of the French liberal party and the most consistent political philosopher of his time, found in the principle of state limitation, which asserted that any gain by the state was a loss to the citizens, the main precept of political action. De Tocqueville, whose *De la démocratie en Amérique*[5] (1835–40) was more than a description of American government, strongly emphasized the need for safeguards of liberty even in a democratic constitution.

A powerful but temporary support for French liberalism was brought into play by Lamennais, who sought to attach intellectual Catholics to the liberal fold. His thesis that the Church could flourish only in a free society led him to champion such liberal doctrines as the separation of church and state, freedom of the press, and freedom of conscience. These ideas were elaborated and presented with remarkable clarity in the journal *Avenir*[6] (1830–31), which he and his associates, Montalembert and Lacordaire, issued. But their thesis that

[5] *Democracy in America.*
[6] *The Future.*

the Catholic Church ought to establish itself by spiritual force in a free society met little support in Papal circles, and the encyclical *Mirari vos* (1832) stifled the movement. Although the influence of the group was short-lived, their ideals were perpetuated, partly in the works of Lamartine who shared Lamennais's views, and more pointedly in the common demand of the anticlerical liberals of Spain and Italy for the separation of church and state.

The Italian tradition of liberalism adhered in the main to the rationalist basis of French thought, but there were remarkable variations in the application of the principles. This division of aim among the Italian leaders partially explains the failure of the revolts in 1848. With Daniel Manin favoring a federal republic, Mazzini a unitary republic, and Gioberti a federal monarchy, the cause of Italian liberalism was seriously impeded by internal conflicts. Briefly, from 1846 to 1848, the Papacy under Pius IX had lent its aid to the liberal cause, following the doctrine of Gioberti that the national movement ought to identify itself with tradition and establish a federal union under the headship of the Pope. Excesses associated with Mazzini's Roman Republic drove the Pope from liberal ranks, however. After the fiasco of 1848, Italian liberalism was saved only by the example of Cavour and the loyalty of Victor Emmanuel to the constitution of Piedmont. Around this document, which was modeled on the revised French *Charte* of 1830, Italian liberals formed an imposing party for a liberal constitutional monarchy.

In Germany, where the significant ruling dynasties tended to remain aloof from liberal ideals, the cause of liberalism was forced into the arenas of the smaller states whose monarchs had granted constitutions under the provisions of the *Bundesakte* of 1815. But there were important conditions of German life, such as the remarkable self-sufficiency of local government, which lent support to the liberal movement. The fact that the attempts to settle the problem of German government proceeded constitutionally and with reference to governmental limitations created a political atmosphere advantageous to liberalism. In the main, however, it is true that the idea of liberalism was approached in Germany with greater philosophical thoroughness than political insight. Although German liberalism tended to retain an academic flavor, there were examples of political training in active parliamentary life. Such was the case in Baden, where Karl von Rotteck and Karl Theodor Welcker received their political experience. Their literary work powerfully influenced the acceptance of the doctrine of liberalism in Germany, for in the *Staatslexikon* [7] which they issued from 1834 to 1848 German liberals found a systematic exposition of liberal political theory. With the French revolution of

[7] *Dictionary of the State.*

1830 profound changes in the form of the German governments occurred, and though the brief impulse of liberalism came quickly to an end, the experience prompted liberals to communicate more with one another and with foreign exponents of their ideas. Through the numerous liberal conventions which were held after 1839 the idea gained support that such a device might be able to unify Germany along liberal and constitutional lines.

The great opportunity of the German liberals came in 1848, the year of revolutions, and although the Frankfort Parliament produced a constitution on the model of that of the United States, all hope of success vanished when Frederick William IV spurned the crown that was offered him. After 1848 liberalism waned as the impulse behind the movement for German unification, but in the politics of the states in the south and west of Germany it remained an important force. But as a factor in the German national political life, liberalism had to yield before the bureaucratic tradition of Prussia and the philosophical triumph of the ideals of the organic state.

The discouraging setback to liberalism on the Continent in 1848 did not affect the Belgians, whose constitution of 1831 survived to play an important role in the history of the nation. This remarkable document, product of the debates in England on the Reform Bill and the alterations in the French *Charte* of 1830, was unique in its recognition of the full sovereignty of the people. No other constitution of the era of political conflict before 1848 made the government, including the ruling monarch, so completely an instrumentality of the popular will.

The Belgian constitution may be cited as a clear example of liberal achievement in the era before 1848. For the ensuing period, liberalism, faced with problems associated with extensive industrialization and heightened nationalism, had to modify considerably its trust in enlightened self-interest from which had followed its atomistic concept of human society and the negative role assigned to the state.

Chapter VII

POLITICAL LIBERALISM IN A CLIMATE
OF NATIONALISM: *II*

❧

1. THE WORKINGS OF NATIONALISM

BASES OF NATIONALISM

THE HISTORICAL ERA which followed the French Revolution was sharply distinguished from all others by the prominence of nationalism in the political life of the European peoples. This new historic force was fundamental in the revolutionary turmoil and political revision that characterized the next half century. In short, the keynote of the political history of this period might be said to be the reworking of the traditional forms of European politics into nationalist and liberal terms. Nationalism was not invariably associated with liberalism in this period, but its significance was certainly derived from the revolutionary impulse that the union implied.

There had always been a manifestation of nationality in Europe, that is, a loyalty to an ethnic or linguistic group whether it had achieved political independence or not. But whatever the causes or reasons for this feeling of historic or cultural or racial comradeship among peoples, it had never in earlier times called forth an extreme devotion. Similarly patriotism, or love of one's native land, has existed among all human beings since the beginnings of agriculture. A typical example of how these ancient forces interacted before the French Revolution may be found in the case of the Austrian army, which, although composed of exceedingly diverse nationalities, was said by military experts of the age to be the most patriotic in Europe. The sentiments of nationality and of patriotism were compatible but remained independent of each other. But nationalism as a vital social force arose only when these two principles of

---

This chapter consists of material by three different authors. Section 1, designed especially for the present volume, was written for its first edition by William O. Shanahan. Section 2 is from *Imperial Russia, 1801–1917* (pp. 3–16, 28–79; New York, Henry Holt & Co., 1932), by Michael Karpovich. Section 3 is from *The Coming of the First World War* (pp. 42–62; London, Longmans, Green & Co., 1949), by Nicholas Mansergh.

loyalty were fused and focused, with doubled emotional force, on specific political ambitions. Its power after 1815 derived from the fact that increasing numbers of Europeans subordinated their other loyalties to this new cause. How this came about necessitates a recapitulation of some of the most influential events in modern European history.

The differences among peoples had been sharpened by such events as the Reformation and the rise of national monarchies. For example, in England, where nationalism first appeared, the combination of Protestantism, a constitutional monarchy, and geographic isolation combined to produce a nationalist feeling while the sentiment still slumbered on the Continent. Similarly the doctrine of Mercantilism, by increasing the authority of the state in economic life, and by making clear that economic rivalry was conducted along national lines, encouraged nationalism. The Industrial Revolution and the wealth it produced gave added confidence to Englishmen in their own institutions. By differentiating the basis of their economic life from that of the Continental peoples, as well as by promoting a higher standard of living, at least for the upper classes, British industry and commerce became British traits. These developments were manifested less on the Continent, where provincial and dynastic loyalties tended to prevail until the age of the French Revolution.

For purposes of generalization, the spread of nationalism among the Continental peoples after 1815 may be attributed to five factors operative in the eighteenth century and in the age following the French Revolution: (1) the crumbling of the cosmopolitan and Catholic traditions of Europe under the rationalist attack of the Enlightenment; (2) the principles and precepts of the French revolutionaries; (3) the military struggles against Napoleon; (4) the movement of Romanticism; and (5) the rise of an intelligentsia, centered in academies and universities, concerned with an appraisal of human society and history.

While the philosophers of the Enlightenment may have been citizens of the world, the emphasis of their thought helped indirectly to bring forth the age of nationalism. Most significant of all, the rationalist attack on traditional Christianity broke down the community of religious faith. When the religious faith and creeds were abandoned as unreasonable, the need was felt by the intellectuals, who were to become the principal supporters of nationalism, to seek another creed. This they found in loyalty to the nation. With the great vogue of classicism in the eighteenth century, the example of ancient Greek and Roman patriotism was familiar to the educated classes. While it is true that few of the philosophers were ardent nationalists, they paved the way for the civic enthusiasms of Rousseau and the Revolutionists. To this end the great discovery of the eighteenth century—the concept of society—served nobly. As the antithesis to the notion of individuality, the idea of society was instrumental in preparing intellectuals to attribute a prior and independent standing to the idea of nationality.

These intellectual contributions were without historic significance until the French Revolution. Not only was the secular state strengthened at the cost of the church, but the concept of citizenship, which had been irrelevant under absolutism, called forth an extreme devotion to and sacred regard for the national political order. Love of country, intolerance of political or national differences, and an elaborate ritual of patriotism expressed in song, speech, costume, and banner characterized the Jacobin phase of the Revolution. They were the first to take official cognizance of language as the basis of nationality and, through a scheme of national education and insistence upon the French language, sought to unify the nation in this respect. Democratic government became at this time a corollary of nationalism, for it was obvious that it could be most effective within a linguistically and culturally homogeneous group. But the proper emotional ingredient of these Jacobin achievements was supplied by their introduction of national conscription. In the new armies composed of citizens, devotion to nationality and patriotism for France became blended into a higher degree of secular fanaticism than had ever characterized any European army. This fanaticism for the French revolutionary principles and for the cultural-linguistic-historic unity that was France comprised true nationalism.

Other European peoples caught this new fever in the wars that the French Revolution called forth. Particularly in the struggle against Napoleon, the peoples of Europe discovered their unique linguistic and historic unity. In the bitterness and the rebellions brought forth by French domination, a devotion to the principle of nationality was born. In Austria, England, Spain, and Prussia, the opposition to the French endured the longest and aroused the most hostility. Through the popular armies which these powers created to fight Napoleon, the ideal of supreme devotion to the political state based on nationality was implanted in the masses. It was not without significance for the future of nationalism that the final campaigns of the revolutionary wars, particularly in 1813–15, were waged not by hired mercenaries, characteristic of the age of absolutism, but by forces drawn from every sector of the population and fired by a common allegiance to the nation.

The feeling of nationalism which the French Revolution had aroused was not allowed to die in the period after 1815. Metternich could work indefatigably for the perpetuation of dynastic and provincial traditions, but the intellectual spirit of the time played into the hands of the nationalists. For nationalism had found a powerful ally in Romanticism. The emotionalism that was at the bottom of the Romantic movement was a kindred impulse to nationalism. Romanticism as a literary phenomenon was exhibited in the concern of scholars and littérateurs with national history, folklore, and the common people. History conceived in vigorous national terms was a prime discovery of Romanticism, and in the glorified tales of the past a powerful incentive for nationalism was unleashed. In the identification of the spirit of a people with its history, culture, and language, Romanticism helped to define the social group called the nationality.

Closely associated with the Romantic movement, but not in every case inseparable from it, was the rise of an intellectual class which, consciously or unconsciously, acted as a propaganda agent for the cause of nationalism. By and large these individuals were connected with universities; indeed, the founding of the University of Berlin in 1809 might well be accounted as a landmark in the history of nationalism. Certainly the shift in the emphasis from theology to political economy, natural science, and history, which one can find in the content of studies in German universities after 1815, portended a change that was to implant nationalist principles in the minds of succeeding generations of graduates. Since most university graduates entered the professions and government service, active proponents of nationalism assumed important offices in society. But it was the devotion of professors and teachers to philology, law, history, and literature, which developed a lore of national folkways and spread the idea of nationalism among the educated classes.

THE POLITICS OF NATIONALISM

This combination of forces was decisive for nineteenth-century history. Like liberalism, the doctrine of nationalism found its main outlet in politics, and the aim of the nationalists might be stated simply as the achievement of an independent political state based on nationality. The first and most obvious mark of nationality was language, and the cult of the national speech and national literature reached remarkable heights. The Pan-Slav Congress, meeting in Prague in 1848, found the Czechs extolling their literature as a mirror of the national spirit. The character of a people, as well as all those persistent virtues which were assumed to qualify it for independent political life, was taken to be revealed in the speech and national literature. The folk character of a people was assumed to be immutable and to have arisen from its special conditions of life, its historic conflicts, basic occupations, and race. It was also assumed that the divisions of men along lines of nationality exhibited virtues transcending those possessed by individuals. Herder, a German cultural nationalist, made a typical analysis:

As a mineral water derives its component parts, its operative powers, and its flavor from the soil through which it flows, so the ancient character of peoples arose from the family features, the climate, the way of life and education, the early actions and employments that were peculiar to them. The manners of the fathers took deep root and became the internal prototype of the race. . . . The more secluded they lived, nay frequently the more they were oppressed the more their character was confirmed.

Closely related to the national character was the philosophical notion of a national spirit or *Volksgeist*. Savigny, a German jurist, found it to be an expression of a people's political life, but in most cases it was asserted as an argument for the achievement of a national and liberal political order. Although the idea of national genius had been recognized by Montesquieu, the *Volksgeist* was a philosophical abstraction of German writers who used it to explain the "oneness" of a people. It was less emotional than the semi-popular analyses of national character and therefore had a greater appeal among the intellectuals.

Religion was not without significance as a mark of nationality. For the Irish and the Poles, Catholicism became an integral part of the consciousness of nationality, and an all important one because the religion of the oppressors was not Catholic. Among nations which enjoyed political independence, the national religion was extolled as a mark of divine approval, as a manifestation of the national character, or as the guardian of the traditional virtues of the land. In the religious impulses and the piety of the people, theorists discerned a true manifestation of the national life. National Protestant churches lent themselves more readily to the cause of nationalism, but the international character of the Catholic Church did not seem to prevent nationalities from insisting that Catholicism was one of their distinctive traits. Gioberti, for example, regarded Catholicism as the spiritual aspect of the "moral primacy of the Italian people." For the Balkan peoples the Greek Orthodox faith became a mark of national unity, setting off the Slavs from the Turks and the western Europeans.

Many other factors added to the feeling of nationality. Nation-wide occupations such as farming, fishing, or ranching were said to express the national soul. The typical national terrain, mountainous or flat, added to the unity that a people felt, while their native costumes, songs, dances, or architecture added to the sense of uniformity and similarity that they experienced. But no single element transcended the importance of language for nationality, since it was not only the most obvious mark, but the most uncompromising line of political cleavage. Nationalities struggling to achieve political unification sought to make their political frontiers coincide with their linguistic boundaries. In the efforts of linguistic groups to achieve freedom nationalism became the partner of liberalism.

Both doctrines manifested themselves as programs of action in the realm of politics, and it was not entirely unnatural that the intention of the liberals was nationalist and vice versa. The supporters of both doctrines were recruited from the intellectual classes, and in the minds of these persons liberalism and nationalism were complementary as well as consistent principles for the re-organization of European political institutions. While a certain number of conservatives were nationalists, practically all the liberals were. Other forms of nationalism, humanitarian or conservative, virtually disappeared from European public life between 1815 and 1850. The importance of the intellectuals as nationalist leaders can hardly be overestimated. The doctrines of both liberalism and nationalism were publicized by the same agencies, the universities, schools, the press, and the national literatures, and the appeal, while not exclusively intellectual, was received, nevertheless, with greater enthusiasm and acclaim among the educated.

The ready acceptance of liberalism and nationalism among these classes owed much to Jeremy Bentham's formulation. Liberal nationalism as a special form of the cult of nationality had arisen in England and was propagated there in the writings of the father of the utilitarian school. After 1815 the interaction of Continental and English liberalism, as well as the political settlement effected without reference to nationalism by the Congress of Vienna, assured the spread of the doctrine among educated Europeans. Bentham, though a cosmopolite in the best eighteenth-century sense, found much to glorify in English speech, liberties, and ideas. Nationality he clearly recognized as a product of race, climate, and religion, and he was among the first to insist that nationality and government ought to coincide.

Bentham's influence was mirrored in the ideas of the national revolutionaries who fought Napoleon; it spread rapidly on the Continent after 1815. Baron vom Stein, whose personality and leadership were in the main responsible for the reorganization of the Prussian state before 1813, expounded the liberal nationalist ideas of the English school. Stein's plan for a united Germany under a constitutional and liberal government failed, but his example was important for the later generation of German liberal nationalists. In Spain the English influence was strong and the constitution of 1812 represented a combination of liberal and national ideas. Though the political atmosphere was discouraging after 1815 for the free political life of nationalities, and liberalism was submerged under a wave of restored monarchs, the literate classes kept up an unceasing agitation and a constant opposition to the system of Metternich. The inevitable outcome was the series of revolutions that marked European political and social history from 1815 to 1848.

Because of the failure to achieve a nationalist state without violence, liberals themselves were forced to abandon their hope for peaceful change. Liberal nationalists were for the most part strongly pacifist. They had reacted against the bloodshed and the wars of the French Revolution and were determined to exploit the means of peaceful change to bring about a liberal and national order in Europe. Once the right of self-determination had been exercised, the nations of Europe, they hoped, would coöperate with one another, and through material and intellectual competition a new order of peace and prosperity would be ushered in. This aspect of liberal nationalism was best expressed by Mazzini, who hoped to make Europe a coöperative society organized on a national basis.

But the liberal nationalists erred in assuming that optimism, ideals, and wishful thinking would cause the monarchs, aristocrats, and adherents of the old regime to abdicate political power. Subject peoples in the Russian, Austrian, and Turkish empires were not freed upon petition. Increasingly the existing liberal national states found that if other states were to be created upon their principles, diplomacy or military intervention had to be forthcoming. Within the empires composed of many nationalities, political freedom could be won only at the cost of armed insurrection and years of deadly fighting. To list the wars of national unification that occurred between 1815 and 1870 would show that bloodshed had become the normal cost of attaining national political life. Even Switzerland, traditional haven of peace, was torn in 1847 by the War of the *Sonderbund* [1] which forced liberal constitutions on the seven conservative cantons.

Several generations of violent warfare served to transform the nature of nationalism. Even liberal nationalism was profoundly modified by the years of war and revolution which saw the consolidation of its political program. From its alliance with liberalism, nationalism swerved to join forces with more dogmatic and intolerant creeds of nation worship. From this union developed the race doctrines and mystic cults of the nation that belong to later history. For the future nothing was more important for nationalism

---

[1] *Separatist League* of the seven Catholic cantons (1845–47) whose military defeat by the majority of federalist and liberal cantons was a pre-condition of the modern Swiss constitution.

than the idea that a people must resort to arms to defend its national political—
system. This idea took form in the institution of conscription, which placed
the burden of fighting upon every citizen and made the cause of war sacrosanct. For the future of Europe the triumph of the nationalist form of state in
the nineteenth century had its fruition in an intensified rivalry among nations
and a resort to war on a scale which dwarfed the conflicts of any preceding
age.

2. IMPERIAL RUSSIA

In the cultural life of Russia, chaos and confusion prevailed throughout a
considerable part of the eighteenth century. The old civilization of Muscovite
Russia, which had begun to lose its unity and strength in the course of the
seventeenth century, had received its death blow at the hands of the reforming Tsar. But a certain period of time had to pass before it could be replaced
by another equally complete system of beliefs and ideas. Through the pro-
verbial "window," an opening which Peter had cut in the wall that separated
Russia from west-European culture, various foreign influences—German,
Swedish, Dutch, French and English—began to pour into the country in an
ever-increasing stream. The first results of this impact could not be otherwise than bewildering. Among the small group of educated Russians many
lost their mental balance. The result was either a slavish imitation of foreign
patterns carried to extremes or else an extraordinary mixture of new ideas and
old habits. With few exceptions there was neither stability nor originality in
the intellectual and moral make-up of the men of the period. Quite obviously,
all that had been so eagerly and so rapidly borrowed from abroad had to be
digested and assimilated before a truly national civilization could be erected
on new foundations. At first even the necessary means of expression were
badly lacking. Until the second half of the eighteenth century Russia possessed no adequate publishing facilities, no press, not even a properly developed literary language. Not until Catherine's reign were tangible results obtained in all these directions and the ground prepared for creative achievements.

THE EMPIRE IN THE NINETEENTH CENTURY

In the beginning of the nineteenth century we find the period of preparation completed and the Empire an accomplished and firmly established fact.
Even at that time it was by far the largest state in Europe. It had spread all
over the east-European plain from the Baltic and the Arctic Ocean in the

north to the Black Sea and the Caspian in the south; in Asia it possessed the whole of Siberia. Further expansion during the nineteenth century made the territory of the Empire equal to one-sixth of the surface of the globe. These new acquisitions were Finland, the central region of Poland (in addition to the border provinces annexed by Russia in the course of the three Partitions), Bessarabia, Transcaucasia, Transcaspian and Central Asiatic territories, and the Amur and Maritime provinces in the Far East. Impressive as those gains were, they were less significant than the acquisitions of the preceding period. Nor was it necessary for Russia, in this new phase of her imperial expansion, to make the same strenuous efforts and to endure the same sacrifices as before.

With the advent of the nineteenth century Russia for the first time in her history felt secure. Her old rival Poland was for the time being completely eliminated. Sweden had apparently resigned herself to the loss of her Baltic supremacy. Russia's relations with Turkey had undergone a profound change, Russia no longer being on the defensive, but, on the contrary, developing an aggressive near-Eastern policy of her own. As far as Russia's Asiatic frontier was concerned, the conquest of the Caucasus and of Central Asia was achieved in a series of colonial wars which were scarcely felt in the center of the Empire. Finally, in the Far East, Russia did not meet with any strong antagonists up to the beginning of the present century and thus was able to extend her territory in that region practically without fighting. From the beginning of the nineteenth century on, Russia's position among European nations was no longer questioned. She was generally recognized as one of the great European powers and she began to play an active, at times even a decisive, part in European affairs.

The territorial and ethnographic composition of the Empire was highly complex. Its nucleus was the old Tsardom of Moscow—the center, the north and the southeast of the European Russian plain, which had been gradually settled in the course of the preceding centuries by the Great Russian branch of the Russian people. Since the time of the Polish partitions the Russian sovereigns had also possessed all the lands that had been settled by the Little Russians (Ukrainians) in the Southwest and the White Russians in the West. Other acquisitions brought within the boundaries of the Empire territories with certain non-Russian groups: Finns, Baltic Germans, Latvians, Esthonians, Lithuanians, Poles, Moldavians, Georgians, Armenians, Tartars, and many other Asiatic tribes.

The Empire, however, was more homogeneous than many persons believe. Not only did the Great Russians represent the largest ethnographic group, but they formed a solid block in all the central regions of the Empire. And if we add to the Great Russians the Ukrainians and the White Russians, the numerical preponderance of the Russian stock over the non-Russian nationalities becomes even more decisive. Both the Ukrainian and the White Russian national movements belong to a much later period. In the first half of the nineteenth century the problem of dealing with these groups was not particularly difficult. The same would be generally true of the more backward border provinces of the Empire where, as in the Caucasus, in the Transcaspian territories and in Central Asia, the imperial administration, with all its mistakes and deficiencies, was undoubtedly a civilizing force.

An infinitely more difficult problem was presented by the western provinces of the Empire. Here the imperial government had to deal with populations in many respects on a higher level of civilization than the Russians and with a tradition of independent or semi-independent existence behind them. Of these the Poles and the Finns were, of course, the outstanding examples. For some time both Poland and Finland retained a special status within the Empire. The Russian government recognized their privileges until the latter came into an acute conflict with the growing centralizing tendencies of the imperial administration; then they were either curtailed or abolished. Here the imperial régime was a failure. To the end of its existence it was not able to establish a permanent *modus vivendi* that would be satisfactory to both sides.

Another difficulty faced by the imperial administration was that of the enormous distances that separated one part of the Empire from another. This difficulty was felt very acutely throughout the first half of the nineteenth century when the ways of communication remained but feebly developed. The first paved highway between St. Petersburg and Moscow was completed in 1830 and thirty years later Russia still had only a little over five thousand miles of such roads. The first railroad was built in 1838 and during the next few decades railroad building progressed rather slowly: in 1867 all the railroad lines in Russia formed less than three and a half thousand miles. It is hardly necessary to point out that this state of affairs was a tremendous obstacle to the smooth and efficient functioning of the imperial machinery. When Alexander I died in Taganrog, in November, 1825, it took one week for the news of his death to reach St. Petersburg. One can easily imagine the situation when less important matters were involved. The more remote provinces of the Empire were, of course, particularly affected. Because of this lack of adequate means of communication Siberia, for instance, remained throughout the nineteenth century a thinly populated colony. It was not until the construction of the Trans-Siberian railroad, in the early years of the twentieth century, that this vast region became an integral part of the Empire.

LEGACY OF THE PAST: AUTOCRACY, NOBILITY, SERFDOM

The government of the Empire in the early nineteenth century was an absolute monarchy, not subject to any constitutional limitations and not limited in practice by any rival institutions or strongly entrenched social groups. Born simultaneously with the formation of a national state in Russia, the autocracy owed its continued existence and the gradual growth of its power to the exigencies of national defense and imperial expansion. Since the days of Peter the Great it had lost its earlier semireligious and patriarchal character, but it did not abdicate any of its powers. If anything, it became even stronger than it had been before. The old feudal aristocracy had passed away, the traditional council (Duma) of the boyars had been abolished, the National Assembly (*Zemski Sobor*) had disappeared, and the Church had lost its independence; the autocracy alone remained.

In the course of the eighteenth century the Russian autocracy became thoroughly westernized. It was now a Grand Monarchy of the same type which had arisen in western Europe during the first centuries of the modern period. It stood in particularly close relationship to the German monarchies of the Hapsburgs and the Hohenzollerns. Its psychology was practically the same as that in Berlin and in Vienna. Its ideal was a "regulated state"—an essentially western conception—and it liked to attribute to itself a civilizing mission within the boundaries of the Empire.

Nor was this an altogether empty claim. It was an autocrat who in the early part of the eighteenth century carried through a sweeping cultural reform and laid the foundations on which modern Russian civilization gradually arose. And after Peter the Russian autocracy, irrespective of the personal qualities of its representatives, continued on many occasions to take the lead in the cultural development of the country. Catherine II is, of course, an outstanding example. Whatever one may think of the defects of her policies, one must admit that her patronage of arts and letters, her interest in education, her measures to promote social welfare, give her the right to be considered an "enlightened despot." Alexander I tried to exemplify enlightened despotism of this type when he ascended the throne in 1801.

The Russian Empire of the early nineteenth century inherited from the preceding period not only its form of government, but also its social organization. At the top of the social ladder stood the first estate in the country, the nobility. By this time there were very few noble families left which could trace their origin back to the old feudal aristocracy of medieval Russia. The new nobility was of a more recent origin. It gradually grew out of that class of "military service men" which the autocracy had created in the course of the sixteenth and seventeenth centuries for the purposes of national defense and imperial administration. During the reign of Peter the Great the nobles still were merely "royal servants," obliged to serve the government to the utmost of their capacity. In the course of the eighteenth century, however, they succeeded in gradually getting rid of this obligation while retaining, and even greatly increasing, their privileges. During the reign of Catherine II they became a privileged order, enjoying special economic and social rights which were no longer conditioned upon service and which were embodied in a charter granted to them by the sovereign (1785). The nobles were freed from both personal taxation and compulsory military service and they were also exempt from corporal punishment. They had the exclusive right of owning serfs and, up to 1801, they even enjoyed a monopoly of land-ownership. By the same charter of 1785 they received a corporate organization with the right to hold assemblies for the discussion and management of their affairs. They were also permitted to elect their own officers (marshals of the nobility) in each province and district.

Important as these privileges were, they were not meant to free the nobles from governmental control. Nor were they based on a constitutional foundation. The charter that had been given to the nobles by an autocratic sovereign could be taken away from them by another autocrat (it actually was abolished by Paul I only to be restored later by Alexander I). Thus the nobles' privileges by no means constituted a limitation of autocracy: they were social and economic, not political. If under Catherine II the nobles played an all-important part in the government, this was due to the peculiar conditions of the time —the necessity for a sovereign who had but a doubtful legal claim to the throne to base her power on the support of the nobility. Neither Paul, nor Alexander I, nor Nicholas I felt entirely dependent on this support and no one of them can be truly called a "nobleman's tsar."

And yet, with all these reservations, it still must be admitted that, because of its social importance, the nobility certainly exercised great influence in state affairs. Economically it was by far the strongest group in Russia so long as landownership remained the chief source of wealth in the country. The nobles alone constituted "society" in the limited sense of the word, shining at the imperial court and dominating the social life both in the urban centers and in the country districts. Well into the nineteenth century the nobility and the educated class remained almost synonymous terms. It was from their ranks that most of the officers in the army and officials in the civil administration were recruited. In the provinces they were supreme up to the second half of the nineteenth century. Not only did they possess patrimonial jurisdiction over the serf population of their estates, but as a rule they also held all the important offices of local administration.

The basis for the economic and social predominance of the nobility was serfdom, another institution that was a legacy of the past. Together with autocracy and the new nobility serfdom developed in that period of Russian history when a national state was being formed under the leadership of Moscow. Its appearance was due partly to economic causes which tended to increase the material dependence of the peasants upon the landlords. But this economic process was greatly strengthened and accelerated by a governmental policy which had both financial and military aims in view. The peasants were by far the largest group of taxpayers in the country and they alone were able to furnish the labor which was necessary for cultivating the lands of the "military service men." To insure the collection of taxes and the cultivation of lands the government wanted to check the migrating tendencies of the Russian peasants, to make them stay where they were, in other words to attach them to the soil. By the middle of the seventeenth century the process of enserfment had been completed. It remained for the eighteenth century to extend serfdom territorially and to make its bonds stronger.

By the beginning of the nineteenth century the authority of the landlords over their serfs became in fact all-embracing and almost unlimited. The landlord had the right to dispose of the person of his serfs: to sell them, to mortgage them, to give them away as a gift. He also had the right to exploit his serfs' labor without compensation. Some of them he would retain in his household as domestic servants, while the majority would be employed as laborers on his land. Or he might substitute for this *corvée* a monetary contribution—a kind of quit-rent—paid to him by the serfs out of their earnings. Moreover, the landlord exercised police authority over his serfs and he was their sole judge in all but grave criminal cases. The government, however, did not abdicate entirely in the landlord's favor. His was the duty to provide food for his serfs in the periods of bad harvest and famine. A legal limit was set to the exploitation of serfs' labor: as far as the *corvée* was concerned, three days a week was officially proclaimed to be the maximum (1797), although in a great many cases the landlords disregarded the government's legislation. Finally, the landlords were prohibited by law from maltreating their serfs. But again, as in the case of excessive exploitation, the law was far from being always enforced and many offenders undoubtedly remained unpunished.

Between the nobility at the top and the peasantry at the bottom of the social ladder stood the middle classes of the Russian society—various categories of city inhabitants and the clergy. Neither in numbers [2] nor in influence were these groups particularly important. The relative weakness of the middle classes remained one of the outstanding features of Russian social organization up to the very end of the imperial régime; it was, of course, even more pronounced at the beginning of the nineteenth century. Urban life was still but feebly developed, and no strong and influential bourgeoisie of the west-European type existed. Under the law the higher catgories of the merchants enjoyed some of the privileges that belonged to the nobility: like the nobles they were exempt from personal taxation, compulsory military service, and corporal punishment. Nevertheless, their social status remained an inferior one. As a class, they had no voice in matters of government. They did not play an important part in the cultural life of the country and they did not belong to "society." They remained a group apart, almost a caste, the young men rarely marrying outside of their own class and, as a rule, inheriting from their fathers both their social status and their occupation.

The same would be true of the clergy. Although they benefited from similar exemptions, it is impossible to see in them a privileged order. With the exception of a small number of the higher clergy, the social position of the group was a humble one, while the life of the parish priests in country districts did not differ to any noticeable degree from that of the peasants.

NEW TENDENCIES—POLITICAL IDEAS AND ECONOMIC DEVELOPMENT

Russian history is rich in contradictions. The one that was brought about by Russia's westernization is perhaps particularly striking. In opening the way to west-European influences the Russian autocracy was guided chiefly by considerations of a practical nature: it wanted first of all to strengthen national defense and to improve the machinery of government. But by pursuing this course it inevitably fostered the development of new tendencies which ultimately were bound to undermine its foundations. Thus, in a way, the autocracy was working for its own destruction.

To confine the process of westernization to the borrowing of west-European technique, while preserving intact Russia's cultural isolation, was practically impossible. Western technique and western ways of living were inevitably

---

[2] At the end of the eighteenth century the peasants constituted 94.5 per cent of the population, the city inhabitants less than 3.5 per cent, the nobility a little over 1 per cent and the clergy 1 per cent. Of the whole peasantry, 55 per cent were serfs belonging to private landlords while the rest were crown serfs or free peasants.

followed by western ideas. And among these were ideas of constitutional government, civil equality and personal liberty. Under Catherine II the government itself sponsored for a while the spread in Russia of the French philosophy of "Enlightenment"; the writings of Montesquieu, Voltaire, Diderot and other Encyclopedists received the sovereign's stamp of approval. It is true that Catherine succeeded in combining an intense admiration for the principles of French philosophy with an equally strong conviction that autocracy was the only possible form of government in Russia. It is also true that her original enthusiasm for liberal ideas cooled down considerably after the outbreak of the French Revolution and, by the end of her life, almost completely disappeared. But not all of her subjects were ready to draw conclusions from the precepts of their French teachers similar to those drawn by the Empress, nor were they willing to stop when she wanted them to go no further. In the second half of the eighteenth century "Voltairianism" became quite an important feature in the intellectual life of the small group of educated Russians.

Another powerful influence was that of Free Masonry with its ideas of universal brotherhood and its emphasis upon civic duty. With many persons it was nothing but a pose or a passing intellectual fashion; but there was also a minority of sincere and serious-minded men for whom the new ideas had a vital and permanent significance. Already in Catherine's time we see the formation in Russia of a liberal public opinion and the beginnings of political opposition. It is not without justification that Novikov and his group of Moscow Masons, on the one hand, and Radishchev with his famous book, "A Journey from St. Petersburg to Moscow" (1790), on the other, are considered as precursors of the Russian *intelligentsia* of a later day.

All three bases of the traditional social and political order were made subject to attack and criticism. To the principle of autocracy was opposed the ideal of constitutional government. The predominance of the nobility was disputed in the name of civil equality; serfdom was attacked as an intolerable social injustice. So far the opposition was confined merely to a small group of educated men and it took the form of a literary crusade rather than that of organized political activity. But even in this form it was significant as the beginning of a movement which grew uninterruptedly, increasing in strength and in volume until it resulted in an open conflict between the government and the liberal section of public opinion. In the eyes of these men autocracy had ceased to be an historical necessity. With imperial expansion completed in its main outlines and with security from foreign attack more or less guaranteed, there seemed to be no longer any justification for a permanent dictatorship. And with the development of national culture the civilizing mission of autocracy began to be questioned as well. The educated Russians became of age and began to resent governmental tutelage. Before long they would demand for themselves a share in the management of national affairs.

While intellectual progress was leading men to challenge the wisdom and validity of the existing social and political order, important changes were gradually taking place in the economic life of the country. Ultimately these changes were bound to undermine serfdom and with it the social predominance of the landowning nobility. Many decades still separated Russia from the period when she was to feel the full strength of the Industrial Revolution with its inevitable and far-reaching consequences. But even in the beginning of the nineteenth century one can clearly discern some new phenomena which were preparing the ground for this Revolution. Accumulation of capital inside of the country and the increasing participation of Russia in international trade led to a more rapid growth of industry and commerce. Under the influence of this development agriculture, although still based on serfdom, began to change its character. The landlords were becoming more and more interested in producing for the market. This was particularly true in the fertile South where agricultural production, thanks to Russia's rapidly increasing exports of grain, was greatly stimulated. In the North, where the land was not so fertile, the landlords displayed a constantly growing desire to turn from agriculture to other fields of economic activity. Here they would employ the labor of their serfs in the factories built on their estates, or else derive their income chiefly, if not exclusively, from their serfs' earnings.

Both in the South and in the North the economic system based on serfdom was trying not without some success to adapt itself to new conditions. But as time went on, it became more and more obvious that in the long run serfdom was incompatible both with industrial progress and the growth of capitalistic agriculture. The productivity of serf labor was low and it could not be substantially raised. Scarcity of free labor was a serious obstacle to the further development of industry. A conflict between serfdom and the vital needs of the nascent Russian capitalism was becoming inevitable.

CIVILIZATION AND PUBLIC OPINION

. . . During the thirty years of Nicholas I's reign [1825–55] autocracy remained supreme and nobody dared to come out in the open to challenge its formidable power. But if there was no political action, there was plenty of thinking, which became increasingly intense as a result of the impossibility of applying theories to life. Alexander Herzen, himself a contemporary, has called this period "an amazing time of outward slavery and inner liberation." At first, however, the thoughts of the generation that followed the Decembrists were not directed towards politics. They passed through a period of enthusiastic interest in abstract philosophical principles as expounded by the German idealistic philosophy of the time. From Schelling through Fichte to Hegel—such was the way that was followed by the outstanding representatives of "Young Russia" until the majority of them became for a while "desperate Hegelians." But there was something in the very intensity of their philosophical studies which indicated from the outset that all these theories meant for them much more than mere intellectual speculation. It was in the debating "circles" of the period, centered chiefly around the University of Moscow, that there were formed some of the most characteristic features of the later Russian *intelligentsia:* its idealism and also its impracticability, its emphasis upon theory and its unwillingness to compromise, its interest in ethical problems and its desire to serve humanity. It was also in the course of these discussions that young noblemen of progressive tendencies first joined hands with those representatives of the lower classes who began to find their way into educated society. In the days to come these new elements were destined to give the *intelligentsia* a group-consciousness of its own and to contribute to the triumph in its ranks of more radical tendencies. Of the earlier members of this group Belinski, the first Russian literary critic of note, was by far the most remarkable. By turning literary criticism into a vehicle for carefully veiled political and social propaganda he was able to exercise a powerful influence upon the youth of his generation, thus defeating to a considerable extent the vigorous efforts of the censor.

In the forties of the nineteenth century we see the formation in Russia of strong currents of thought, already somewhat political in nature. It was in those years that the battle was raging between the Westerners and the Slavophils. The main theme of discussion was the meaning of Russian history and the future course of Russia's destiny. For the Westerners the difference between Russia and western Europe was one of degree only. Because of the unfavorable circumstances of her historical development Russia was behind the western nations in her political and social institutions as well as in her civilization. Fundamentally, however, she was passing through the same phases of historical evolution, and her task was to advance with redoubled energy along the road of westernization and to catch up with the more advanced nations of the western world. Westernism became, therefore, a cardinal tenet with all the groups of educated Russians who desired for their country a constitutional government. In their philosophy the Westerners, as a rule, were Rationalists, and their attitude towards religion was either hostile or indifferent. For the

Slavophils, on the other hand, the difference between Russia and the western world was one of kind, not of degree. Russian history had been radically different from that of western Europe, and her civilization was based on entirely different principles. It was the difference between the Romano-Germanic world, on the one hand, and the Slavonic world, on the other (hence the name of the Slavophils). For the Slavophils Russia's original civilization, in which her Greek-Orthodox religion played an all-important part, was a cherished possession that should be by all means preserved intact. Instead of following the lead of western nations, threatened with inevitable decay, Russia was to say a new word in human history. More particularly, the evils of western industrialism could and should be avoided. In her peasant commune Russia had a highly valuable institution on the basis of which a better economic system, and one that would satisfy the demands of social justice, could be eventually erected. Neither was there a place in Russia for the west-European parliamentary constitutionalism. The peculiar Russian type of government was a benevolent autocracy assisted by an advisory popular body such as the National Assembly (*Zemski Sobor*) of the seventeenth century.

At first glance the Slavophil doctrine looked like a replica of the officially sponsored formula which read "Orthodoxy, Autocracy, Nationalism." This is why the Slavophils have been so often accused of reactionary tendencies. However, this is a serious mistake. The Slavophil doctrine, as expressed by its early exponents, was permeated with a broadly liberal spirit. The autocracy they were thinking about was not like that of Nicholas I, with its suppression of public opinion and glorification of bureaucratic control. It was a patriarchal and in a way even a democratic monarchy, serving the cause of social justice and based upon freely-given popular support. Similarly, the Slavophil's conception of Orthodoxy was that of a free and independent Church which would occupy a leading place in the country's spiritual life because of its inherent strength and not because of governmental protection. And finally, what they wanted was a spontaneous and untrammeled development of Russian nationality and not a rigid formula of official nationalism forced upon the country from above.

Here then was a common ground on which the Westerners and the Slavophils could meet. Both schools were in favor of public control over the bureaucracy, both were asking for personal liberty, and, above all, both insisted on the abolition of serfdom.

Another important phenomenon in the history of Russian political ideas of the period was the birth of Russian socialism. Its origin was also west-European, but in this case the predominant influence was French, not German. The writings of Saint-Simon and Fourier served as the starting point for the development of the Russian socialist doctrine. As yet this doctrine was of a purely theoretical nature and it was confined to a few intellectuals; nevertheless, it was in this very circle of literary men that theories were worked out which a few decades later became a source of inspiration for revolutionary activity. In their general outlook these early Russian socialists, of whom Alexander Herzen was the most outstanding representative, occupied a peculiar position midway between the Westerners and the Slavophils. They shared with the Westerners a critical attitude towards Russia's past and present as well as a preference for rationalistic philosophy, but they stood closer to the Slavophils in their distrust of west-European parliamentary democracy, in their belief that it was Russia's mission to bring a new message to the world, and also in their idealization of the present commune, which seemed to them the nucleus of a better social order. It is hardly necessary to add that the socialists were even more strongly opposed to the existing political régime than either the Westerners or the Slavophils.

THE REFORMS OF ALEXANDER II

The reign of Alexander II (1855–81) is a landmark in Russian history; during this period there occurred a series of far-reaching reforms which profoundly changed the life of the country. Alexander II was not a reformer by nature. But he was intelligent enough to be able to read the signs of the times, and courageous enough, at least during the early part of his reign, to subordinate his personal feelings to considerations of state. Some of his reforms suffered at the outset from compromise with vested interests; others were distorted as a result of the reaction which set in during Alexander's own lifetime. Because of these facts the "Great Reforms" have sometimes been harshly criticized and their wisdom has been questioned in the light of subsequent developments. The proper historical approach, however, is to judge them on the basis of a comparison with the old order of things which they were designed to modify. They stand this test, and the customary division of nineteenth-century Russian history into pre-reform and post-reform periods seems to be fully justified.

By far the most important event of the reign of Alexander II was the abolition of serfdom (1861). Such an act could hardly be postponed any longer. Economic development and pressure of public opinion were steadily undermining the foundations of serfdom while the restlessness of the serfs made the government fear another general peasant uprising. Like his predecessors, Alexander II began by trying to persuade the landlords to take the initiative;

accordingly he pointed out to them that it was "better to abolish serfdom from above than to wait till it begins to abolish itself from below." When, however, he saw that this initiative was slow in manifesting itself and that the majority of the Russian nobles were still clinging to the rights which they enjoyed under serfdom, he decided to take matters into his own hands. It was the government which forced upon the unwilling nobility an open discussion of the reform, and it was the government which declared in the early stages of this discussion that the emancipation must be accompanied by a land settlement for the liberated serfs. The reform was actually carried through by the autocratic sovereign, in coöperation with a few enlightened bureaucrats and the liberal section of public opinion, against strong opposition on the part of the majority of the nobles. For three years a fierce struggle went on over the terms of the proposed settlement; if the final results were not entirely satisfactory to the peasants they still were immeasurably more advantageous to their interests than if the whole matter had been left in the hands of the landlords.

The legal aspect of the reform, the abolition of human bondage, stands out as its most conspicuous and, at the same time, its most beneficial feature. The very fact that over 40 millions of human beings were liberated goes far to justify the description of the Emancipation as "perhaps the greatest single legislative act in the world's history." However, the economic side of the reform is obviously open to criticism. Generally speaking, the peasants retained in their hands that part of the land which they had been permitted as serfs to use for their own maintenance. The landlords were compensated for the loss of this property by the state, but the peasants had to repay the sum to the Treasury in annual installments spread over a period of forty-nine years. Conditions varied with different localities and different groups of the peasantry, but in most cases the land allotments were too small, and the redemption payments proved to be too heavy a burden for the peasants. Even so the reform involved a forcible alienation of a very substantial part of the landlords' property, and in Russia the terms of the land settlement consequent upon the Emancipation were considerably more generous than they had been in west-European countries. One feature of this settlement, however, was rather unfortunate. As a rule the land was not given outright to individual peasants but was transferred to the village communes whose members were to receive equal allotments along with the right of periodical redistribution. In pursuing this course the sponsors of the reform were guided partly by interests of fiscal policy (the commune was made responsible for the payment of its individual members' taxes and redemption installments), and partly by a desire to prevent loss of land by the peasants and the formation of a rural proletariat. Subsequent developments showed, however, that the commune was not able to perform successfully the functions expected of it, while at the same time it became an obstacle to agricultural progress.

The Emancipation was highly significant not only in itself but also as a starting point for a number of other important reforms. With the abolition of serfdom the patrimonial jurisdiction and police authority which the landlords had exercised over their serfs disappeared automatically, and at the same time a blow was dealt to the prestige of the nobility in the country districts. A thorough reorganization of local government, up to this time entirely in the hands of the nobles, became imperative. In 1864 the so-called Zemstvo institutions were established in Russia. Three groups participated in the elections to the District Zemstvo Assembly: the private landowners, the peasant communes, and certain categories of the urban population. The District Zemstvo elected a permanent governing board and sent representatives to the Provincial Zemstvo, which in turn elected its own governing board. Both in the districts and in the provinces the Zemstvos concerned themselves with problems of public welfare, while general administrative functions and the exercise of police authority remained in the hands of crown officials. The Zemstvos in order to carry on their work were permitted to levy taxes for local needs. Their membership was elected on the basis of an unequal franchise, with the landowning nobility still occupying the most prominent place. Nevertheless, when compared with the situation before the reform this system was a decided step forward. The principle of self-government was openly recognized and an opportunity was given to various social classes to coöperate in improving local conditions. That this opportunity was not neglected is shown by the fact that during the period of their existence the Zemstvos performed a highly valuable work which greatly contributed to the economic and cultural progress of rural Russia.

Scarcely less important than these changes in local government was the reform of the law courts (1864). To appreciate its significance one has to take into account the conditions which existed in the first half of the nineteenth century. The old courts were among the worst features of pre-reform Russia. Based on class distinctions, the administration of justice was in the hands of ill-paid, badly-trained and frequently corrupt magistrates who were subservient to the authorities and to the wealthier classes. The hearings were secret and there were no lawyers to protect the interests of the defendant. The procedure was slow and costly in the extreme. The reform of 1864 proclaimed the principle of "laws equally just to all" and did away with class distinctions. The courts were made independent of the administration, the judges became irremovable and were properly remunerated. Trials were made public, the jury was introduced, and the Bar was established. The whole procedure, from the lowest courts to the highest, was thoroughly reorganized. From that time on Russia possessed a judicial system which could compare favorably with those of other civilized countries.

The last reform of major importance was the reorganization of the army (1874). Up to that time the whole burden of military conscription had rested on the lower classes of the population, who had to serve in the army for a very long period of time and under extremely harsh and exacting conditions. The reform of 1874 established universal military service. The term of actual service was reduced from twenty-five to six years, and its conditions were improved to a very considerable extent. Treatment of soldiers became immeasurably more humane, the whole system of training was reorganized, and special attention began to be paid to the problem of general education in the ranks. Like the new courts, the new army was a symbol of Russia's modernization.

RUSSIA AFTER THE REFORMS

It is not difficult to see that all the major reforms of Alexander II tended in one direction, the breaking down of legal barriers which the old order had erected between the various classes. The abolition of serfdom did away with the fundamental distinction between those who were and those who were not personally free. In the Zemstvo assemblies the liberated serfs sat side by side with their former masters and were looked upon, at least theoretically, as equals of the representatives of other classes. The new courts introduced the ideal of "laws equally just to all" and as a rule adhered to this ideal in practice. And finally, the reorganized Russian army was based on the democratic principle of compulsory military service on the part of every citizen. It must be said, however, that even after the Emancipation the peasants did not become full-fledged citizens. As members of the village commune they could not dispose of their property and their freedom of movement was somewhat limited. For minor offenses they were tried by special courts on the basis of special laws. And the poll-tax, which they still had to pay and from which other classes were exempt, was a mark of their social inferiority. But even with these limitations, the general effect of the reforms was to bring Russia many steps nearer civil equality.

The same leveling process was at work in the field of economic and social relations. As a result of the Emancipation the nobility lost not only a considerable part of their land, but also their free supply of labor. Hindered by lack of initiative, of special training and of capital, many of the former serf-owners failed to adjust themselves to new conditions. There were many cases of downright bankruptcy, and still more numerous were the occasions when the owners of the estates preferred to sell their land rather than to struggle against adverse circumstances. The transfer of land from the nobles to the non-noble owners remained one of the outstanding phenomena in the economic life of Russia up to the end of the imperial régime. Together with the nobility's land ownership, the social hegemony of the nobles within the country was gradually passing away.

What was lost by the nobles was gained by other social classes. It was only after the Emancipation that there began in Russia that advance of the middle classes which had been going on in western Europe for centuries. The accelerated development of industry, to which more attention will be paid in another section, resulted in the growth of a bourgeoisie; wealth other than in land began to serve as a foundation for high social position. Growth of trade made the merchant class more numerous and more important and there was a noticeable effort on the part of many merchants to rise above their former social and cultural standards. The reforms, moreover, opened new fields of activity which did not exist before. Work in the Zemstvos and in the new courts, even in some of the governmental departments, began to attract many public-spirited men who under the old order would have shunned governmental service and condemned themselves to inactivity. Economic progress called for an increasing number of technical specialists; the growing demand for popular education and a general intellectual awakening were responsible for a notable increase in the numbers of teachers, writers, and journalists. For the first time in Russian history the doctor, the lawyer, the university professor, the engineer, were coming to the forefront as important and influential members of society. One may say that a new class, that of the professional men, made its appearance in Russia.

By all these changes the Russian *intelligentsia* [3] which had been formed in the preceding period was greatly affected. Confined in the beginning to the progressive members of the nobility, the ranks of the *intelligentsia* were now rapidly increased by professional men and representatives of the middle classes in general. No longer were the enlightened noblemen the standard-bearers of education and progress. Their place was being taken by the middle class intellectuals, who as a rule were less refined in their culture and more radical in their social and political views. It was only with the appearance of the mid-

---

[3] The word *"intelligentsia"* is used in this study in a limited sense, to designate the politically-minded part of the educated class in opposition to the government.

dle-class element that the *intelligentsia* acquired a definite group-consciousness and became the backbone of the political opposition.

In no other field was the advance of the middle classes so pronounced as in that of education. The reforms played the part of a powerful stimulant to the intellectual life of the country; there was a widespread and incessantly growing demand for knowledge on the part of practically all groups of the population. Throughout the second half of the nineteenth century one can observe a steady progress both with regard to the universities and the secondary schools; moreover, it was in this period that, thanks to the active participation of the Zemstvos, a real start was made in the field of primary education. The number of schools not only increased, but the distribution of students between the various social classes also underwent a significant change. In this field as in others the nobility was gradually losing its former predominance; by the end of the period students of noble origin represented but a minority both in the universities and the secondary schools. As for governmental policy, it remained, as before, self-contradictory, fluctuating between a fairly liberal stand at one time and a decidedly reactionary one at another. But no artificial obstacles could effectively block the cultural progress of the middle classes and, to a lesser extent, even that of the peasantry. The development which was taking place in the schools was but a reflection of the general trend of social evolution within the country. Beginning with the period of the reforms a democratic society was growing in Russia under an autocratic government.

THE REVOLUTIONARY MOVEMENT UNDER ALEXANDER II

It may seem at first puzzling that the reforms of Alexander II, far-reaching as they were, failed to satisfy the progressive groups of Russian society and that the first two decades after the Emancipation saw the growth in Russia of a political opposition which was far more outspoken and determined than it ever had been before. To say that this opposition was entirely provoked by governmental reaction would be hardly correct: the first revolutionary proclamations, calling for a bitter struggle against the government, appeared as early as 1861–62, when the reform movement was still at its height; the first attempt against the emperor's life took place in 1866, only five years after the Emancipation. The revival of the political opposition should be ascribed rather to that general atmosphere of change and renovation which the Great Reforms brought into Russian life. As in the early days of Alexander I, the reformist policies of the government again played the part of a powerful stimulus for the development of advanced political and social ideas among the educated classes of the Russian people and, as before, progressive public opinion moved ahead of the government. To the reforms that had been granted the opposition answered with a demand for more reforms.

For the liberals [4] the abolition of serfdom and the introduction of local self-government was but a prelude to what they called "the crowning of the building," the establishment in Russia of a system of national representation. Some of the constitutional projects of the period emanated from the nobility who desired political gains as compensation for their economic losses under the Emancipation settlement. Other projects were of a more unselfish origin and were dictated by a theoretical predilection for constitutional government. The radicals went much further than the liberals. What they wanted was not to substitute a parliamentary régime for autocracy, but to bring about a complete destruction of the old social order.

From the outset the revolutionary movement of the sixties and the seventies was completely dominated by the socialists. It was during these decades that Russian socialism acquired both a definite doctrine and a fighting organization. Both in theory and in practice it differed considerably from the west-European socialism of the same period. It was based not on the teachings of Karl Marx but on the ideas of Russian writers such as Herzen and Chernyshevski. It shared the Slavophils' belief in the peculiarities of Russia's historical development and it looked upon the Russian peasant, living in his village commune, as a socialist by instinct and tradition, whose mission it was to save Russia from capitalism and to bring her directly into the communist era. Partly because of this theory and partly because of the fact that Russian capitalism still was in the first stages of development, the early Russian socialists, with few exceptions, were much more interested in the peasantry than in the industrial workers. Their socialism, in other words, had an agrarian character. Another fundamental feature that distinguished the majority of Russian socialists of the period was their complete distrust of parliamentary democracy, which in their eyes had no value whatsoever even as an intermediary stage of development. What they wanted was a more or less immediate social revolution and not a gradual approach to socialism by the long way of evolution.

At first, however, there was no unanimity of views as to the proper means to bring about the revolution. Some admitted the necessity of a preliminary

---

[4] The words "liberalism" and "liberal" are used in this study in their European sense, namely, to designate the party of moderate and peaceful reform as distinguished from the revolutionary socialists.

period of propaganda to educate and organize the peasantry, while others were confident of their ability to stir up a general peasant uprising without much preparation. Both methods were tried by those who "went to the people," but neither proved to be a success. The propagandists were not understood by the peasants and at the same time were easily detected by the police, while the revolutionary appeals of the more impatient among the Populists failed to provoke a general insurrection. It was then that the idea of a direct attack upon the government, led by an organized minority, took hold of the minds of the majority of Russian radicals. At the time when west-European socialism was beginning to ally itself with mass movement, as expressed either in trade-unions or in political labor parties, the Russian socialists saw themselves forced to choose the narrow and perilous path of revolutionary conspiracy.

The prevalence of this tendency among the radical groups of the *intelligentsia* was due in no small measure to the policy of the government. The liberal ardor of Alexander's early years was all but spent in the strenuous effort to carry through the abolition of serfdom. This and other reforms met with a tremendous opposition on the part of those reactionaries who never become reconciled to the new order of things. Throughout the reign of Alexander II they continued to struggle with the more liberal elements for predominance in governmental councils, with the easily influenced emperor vacillating between the two mutually exclusive policies. The enemies of the reforms skillfully used every opportunity to strengthen their position with the sovereign. Events like the Polish insurrection of 1863 and the first attempt upon Alexander's life in 1866 were interpreted as indicating the danger of concessions and the necessity of a sterner policy. With the growth of the revolutionary movement these arguments acquired a more telling effect: in order to combat radicalism it was deemed necessary to curtail the reforms that had been granted. Censorship was again strengthened and freedom of teaching limited. Press cases and political offenses were exempt from trial by jury. Side by side with the regular court procedure there was gradually set up an elaborate system of exceptional jurisdiction under which offenders were dealt with either by military tribunals or by means of mere administrative orders. The Zemstvos were subject to strict governmental supervision and their activities were constantly interfered with by local authorities. Above all, a firm resistance was offered to any suggestions favoring the limitation of autocracy and the extension of the principle of self-government to the management of national affairs.

The reaction was not able to nullify the effects of the reforms and to restore the old order of things, but it greatly impeded Russia's progress, and, by generating bitterness and distrust, made extremely difficult a peaceful solution of the country's outstanding problems. One of the worst features of this policy was its failure to discriminate between the radical aspirations of the revolutionaries and the more moderate demands of the constitutionalists. With a few notable exceptions the rulers of Russia were unable to appreciate the wisdom of a policy that would combat revolution by reform. An attempt of this kind was made in the last years of Alexander's reign by his Minister of the Interior Loris-Melikov, a wise and able statesman, who, while fully determined to stamp out revolutionary activities, was nevertheless prepared to satisfy some of the desires of the progressive groups of Russian society. He finally succeeded in persuading the emperor to approve his project (sometimes erroneously referred to as a "constitution") of inviting representatives of public bodies to coöperate with the government in working out a program of further reforms. His attempt was frustrated by the assassination of Alexander II by the revolutionaries in March, 1881.

This tragic event was the outcome of the desperate struggle which a small band of determined revolutionaries waged against the government during the last years of Alexander's reign. In 1879 the revolutionaries became organized under the name of the "Will of the People." It was a highly centralized and secret body, with terrorism as its chief weapon. Assassination of several prominent officials was followed by a series of daring attempts upon the life of the emperor. Although the efforts of the terrorists were finally crowned with success, the whole movement must be considered as politically futile. It is significant only because it reveals the character and mutual relations of the main forces involved in the struggle. On the one hand we see the uncompromising and stubborn autocracy, on the other equally uncompromising and stubborn revolutionaries. Caught between the two fires were the advocates of a middle course, the Russian liberals who, while the radicals were throwing bombs to which the government answered by executions, confined themselves to voicing their demands and offering counsels of moderation. The tragedy of the constitutional movement in Russia lay in the fact that it represented middle class liberalism without a sufficiently active and numerous middle class from which to recruit its strength. Deprived of an adequate social base of its own, it could not ally itself wholeheartedly with either of the two extremes and so was doomed to fail in its efforts to bring about a peaceful regeneration of the country.

POLITICAL REACTION UNDER ALEXANDER III

Alexander III (1881–94) was profoundly influenced by the circumstances of his accession. A staunch conservative, he had consistently sided with the reactionaries against the liberals while still heir to the throne. The assassination of his father confirmed him in this attitude. Here was a direct attack on the sovereign power, led by forces of destruction, which had to be repulsed and suppressed without mercy. It was under the influence of this tragic event that Alexander III decided to discard the Loris-Melikov project, already approved by his father but unpublished. A manifesto of the new emperor announced to the Russian people his firm intention to "strengthen and guard the autocracy from any possible encroachments." After a brief period of hesitation and uncertainty, during which some of the reforming tendencies of the previous reign were still permitted to exist, the government of Alexander III finally started upon the road of complete political reaction. This reactionary course was pursued until the end of the reign and was bequeathed by Alexander III to his son and successor, Nicholas II.

To a very considerable extent this policy was shaped and inspired by a man whose very name became a symbol of reaction, Constantin Pobedonostsev. A former professor of civil law in the University of Moscow, Pobedonostsev had been Alexander's tutor since the latter's early youth and had gained an undisputed ascendancy over the mind of his royal pupil. As Procurator of the Holy Synod he was now one of the most influential members of the government and he remained in this position throughout the reign of Alexander III and the early part of that of Nicholas II. Pobedonostsev was more than a mere reactionary statesman; he was a philosopher of reaction. In ringing terms he denounced parliamentary democracy, freedom of the press, separation of church and state, and even universal education as great fallacies of modern times working for the destruction of all that was vigorous and healthy in a nation. From these unmitigated evils he wanted to save Russia at any cost. Under his influence the old formula "Orthodoxy, Autocracy, Nationalism" was revived and given new strength in its practical applications. Not only was the revolutionary movement stamped out for the time being, but even moderate liberals were sternly rebuked and silenced. Censorship was again strengthened and freedom of teaching was further curtailed. The laws concerning local self-government were revised and the Zemstvos became subject to much stricter governmental supervision. Simultaneously, the representation of the nobility in the Zemstvo assemblies was considerably increased at the expense of other classes. The nobility once more became a favorite with the crown. The idea was that the nobles represented the natural mainstay of autocracy and as such should be helped to regain their predominant position. Among other things the nobles were called upon to assist the government in exercising paternalistic control over the peasantry. In 1889 the office of "land captain" was created. These "land captains" were local officials appointed by the government from among the landowning nobility to exercise administrative power and even to a certain extent judicial authority over the peasants in the country districts.

The support of orthodoxy was expressed in a policy of persecution of religious dissenters, the so-called "old believers" and the sectarians.[5] Some of these were practically denied any legal status and were accordingly driven underground. The position of the Roman Catholics and the Lutherans (the most numerous of the Protestant denominations in Russia), however, was considerably better. They were legally recognized as religious bodies, having their separate church organizations and owning property. But even they were discriminated against. To try to convert a Greek Orthodox into a Roman Catholic or a Lutheran was a crime punishable under the law, while it was equally a crime to try to prevent a Roman Catholic or a Lutheran from becoming a Greek Orthodox. In cases of mixed marriages children automatically became Greek Orthodox irrespective of their parents' wishes.

The policy of the government in support of the domination of the Greek Orthodox Church found a counterpart in its attitude towards the national minorities. Here the slogan was "Russia for the true Russians." Those of the supposedly pure Great Russian origin had to be given preference over the White Russians and the Ukrainians, not to speak of the representatives of alien races. In the border provinces "Russification" became the order of the day. Efforts were made to force the non-Russian inhabitants of these regions to give up their own national traditions and to recognize the superiority of Russian culture. This policy was pursued with particular stubbornness with regard to Poland which had lost, after the suppression of the insurrection of 1863, the last remnants of its former autonomy. Even the German barons of the Baltic provinces, who for generations had been loyal subjects of the Russian monarchy, now were also discriminated against, although in a somewhat milder fashion. The chief sufferers of all, however, were the Jews. Since the beginning of the nineteenth century the majority of them had been kept

---

[5] The "old believers" were a group that split off from the Greek Orthodox Church in the latter part of the seventeenth century. They differed from the official church in questions of ritual only. On the other hand, the sectarians, such as the Dukhobors and the Molokans, followed religious doctrines that were fundamentally different from those of the Greek Orthodox Church.

within a certain restricted area known as the "Jewish pale." Under Alexander III the boundaries of the "pale" were narrowed and the prohibition against living outside the "pale" was strictly enforced. The civil rights of the Jews were subject to many obnoxious restrictions and only a limited number of Jewish youths were permitted to enter the schools and the universities.

From the historical point of view the reactionary policy of Alexander III represented a hopeless anachronism. It was an attempt to restore a past that was dead beyond any possibility of resurrection. To base the governmental policy on an alliance between autocracy and nobility was to ignore the whole trend of Russia's social evolution since the Emancipation. With the abolition of serfdom the very basis of the nobility's power and influence was irreparably destroyed. Neither economically, nor socially, nor intellectually were the nobles any longer in a position to dominate the country to the exclusion of other classes. No less unfortunate than this alliance with the nobility was the tendency to replace the broad conception of the Empire as a political structure sheltering many races and nationalities by a rigid formula of exclusive nationalism, reposing on a narrow ethnical basis. This was a decided step backward if compared with the more cosmopolitan outlook of the imperial government in the days of Catherine II or in the early part of the nineteenth century. It was a symptom of a mortal disease: the Russian autocracy was doomed to speedy decay, and while approaching the end it was losing its imperial consciousness.

THE INDUSTRIAL REVOLUTION

It has already been shown that early in the nineteenth century capitalistic tendencies became clearly discernible in the economic life of Russia. Yet so long as Russia's national economy remained dominated by serfdom, these tendencies could not develop to the utmost of their possibilities. In this respect, too, the Emancipation was the turning point. After a certain period of inevitable confusion, during which the economic life of the country tried to adjust itself to new conditions, there began that process of accelerated industrial progress along capitalistic lines which might be designated as the coming into Russia of the Industrial Revolution. The period saw the rapid development of those technical means without which no real capitalistic advance was possible. Extensive railroad building was one of the outstanding features of Russian life in the latter part of the nineteenth century. At first concessions for the construction of railroad lines were granted by the government to private companies. As a rule, however, these proved to be rather inefficient and their activities were accompanied by all kinds of questionable financial transactions.

With characteristic paternalism the government soon decided to take matters into its own hands. A number of private railroads were purchased by the Treasury and new lines were built and operated directly by the government. State railroads finally became the predominant type in Russia, while those private lines that were permitted to exist were subject to a rather strict governmental control. By the end of the nineteenth century Russia was adding to her railway mileage more rapidly than any other country in Europe. If the development of her railroad system still lagged behind the needs of the country, this was due partly to the fact that she had started extensive railroad building rather late and, even more, to the enormous size of her territory.

Another problem of great importance was that of credit facilities. Prior to the reform period Russia had practically no credit system worthy of the name. It was only after the Emancipation that modern banking began to develop in the country. Here, of course, private initiative had to play the most important part. But even in this field the participation of the government was far more active than in the capitalist countries of western Europe. Besides the State Bank of the usual type the Russian government established some special credit institutions of its own. Finally, one of the chief concerns of the government during the decades in question was the improvement of the monetary situation. Since the Crimean War Russia had been living under a most unsatisfactory régime of depreciated paper currency. From 1862 on a number of fairly able ministers of finance attempted to establish the gold standard by gradually increasing the Treasury's reserve. But it was not until 1897 that this attempt proved successful. The effect of this monetary reform upon Russia's economic progress hardly needs to be emphasized. Not only did it create conditions of stability for commercial operations within the country, but by putting Russian currency on a basis of parity with those of other countries it also made possible a very considerable influx of foreign capital into Russia in the form of loans and investments.

Closely connected with railroad building and financial reforms was the rapid industrial development of the country. Striking progress was achieved in the metallurgical industry, greatly stimulated by the discovery of vast deposits of coal and iron in South Russia. Another branch of industry which, towards the end of the century, showed remarkable progress was the manufacture of textiles, particularly in Central Russia. Trade grew with industry and there was a significant increase in the number of joint-stock companies, a comparatively recent phenomenon in Russian economic life.

No other single man among the Russian statesmen of the period was so closely connected with the industrial revolution as was Witte, Minister of

Finance from 1892 to 1903. If Pobedonostsev was a symbol of political reaction, Witte's name stood for economic progress. Far from being a liberal, he was a splendid opportunist, a business man in politics, and a "modern" in his general outlook and methods. Devoid of any personal charm and not always able to inspire confidence in those around him, he must be given credit for the magnitude of his schemes and the technical skill he displayed in their execution. It was Witte who finally carried through the monetary reform in spite of strong opposition and it was he again who for some time actually directed railroad building in Russia, being largely responsible among other things for the construction of the great Trans-Siberian railroad in 1892–1904. A firm believer in industrialization and with an ideal of an economically self-dependent Russia before his eyes, Witte spared no effort to support the development of Russian industry by a policy of tariff protection, governmental guarantees, and subsidies. . . .

THE LIBERATION MOVEMENT AND THE RUSSO-JAPANESE WAR

During the reign of Alexander III political discontent and social unrest were largely kept underground. But the accession of Nicholas II (1894–1917) opened a new period in the history of the Russian revolutionary movement. The new sovereign, whose fate it was to become the last of the Romanovs, assumed his duties with an intention "to maintain the principle of autocracy as firmly and unswervingly as it was by his lamented father." The reactionary policy of Alexander III was followed in practically every direction; in some respects it was even intensified. Thus, for instance, the first serious attempt was made to violate the autonomy of Finland, which up to that time had managed to preserve its privileges more or less unmolested. The Zemstvo representatives who, upon the accession of the new emperor, dared to express in a most loyal manner their hope for a more liberal policy, were sternly rebuked for these "senseless dreams" of theirs. Pobedonostsev's influence remained supreme and other staunch reactionaries continued to occupy the most important posts in the administration. Very soon, however, it became clear that the government was no longer able to prevent the outbursts of political discontent by mere repression and that forces of opposition were growing within the country over which the autocracy was gradually losing its control. From the late nineties the opposition began to assume a more widespread and at the same time an increasingly radical character, until it culminated in 1905 in an open and partially victorious conflict with the government.

This "liberation movement," as it is known in Russian historiography, differed substantially from the earlier phase of the revolutionary development.

Due to the general democratization of Russian society that had been going on since the reforms of Alexander II, and also as a result of the Industrial Revolution, the opposition now acquired a much wider social basis than it had ever possessed before. It was also much better organized and it worked out a more definite program. One of the fateful events of the period was the appearance in Russia of Marxian socialism, with its emphasis on the revolutionary mission of the industrial proletariat and the primary importance of the class struggle. In the growing class of factory workers, dissatisfied with labor conditions, the Russian followers of Karl Marx found a fertile soil for their propaganda. In 1898 there was organized a Russian Social-Democratic party (S.D.'s in abbreviation) which several years later split into two factions, one headed by Plekhanov and the other by Lenin. The former, called the Mensheviks, expected the forthcoming Russian revolution to be of a "bourgeois" character, which would bring about the establishment in Russia of a political democracy as a preliminary step on the way to socialism. The latter, the Bolsheviks, insisted on the necessity of proceeding directly from the overthrow of autocracy to the complete realization of the socialist ideal. Another socialist party which was organized about the same time and which took the name of Socialist Revolutionaries (S.R.'s in abbreviation) revived the agrarian tradition of the Populists by concentrating its attention on the peasantry. With its slogan "All land to the working people" it found a ready response on the part of the peasants suffering from "land hunger." In their tactics the S.R.'s also followed the example of the earlier Russian revolutionaries by choosing terrorism as one of their chief weapons, with the result that a series of assassinations of unpopular officials took place. While both the S.D.'s and the S.R.'s were able to win a considerable popular following, the leadership remained in the hands of the intellectuals: active members were still chiefly recruited from the enthusiastic youth of the educated class. One of the most characteristic features of the Russian revolutionary movement was the great part played in it by university students. Again and again the normal academic life of the universities was interrupted by students' political strikes and demonstrations.

Paralleling the growth of socialist parties was the development of a liberal movement aiming at the establishment in Russia of a representative government and a constitutional régime. From the beginning Russian liberalism found refuge in the Zemstvo assemblies. The government tried hard to keep the Zemstvos within the narrow limits of non-political local activities but, in spite of this, the progressive elements among the Zemstvo workers were inevitably becoming more and more involved in national politics. In the absence of any parliamentary institutions the Zemstvos played the part of a school of self-government. By the end of the nineteenth century, however, liberalism was able to find many recruits among the professional groups which had been steadily growing since the Emancipation. It was the combination of these two elements—the Zemstvo workers and the members of liberal professions—which brought about the formation in 1903 of the so-called "Union of Liberation." Guided by such men as Struve and Miliukov, both of them outstanding scholars and writers, and counting in its ranks some of the finest intellects in the country, the "Union of Liberation" assumed for a while a leading part in the opposition movement to which it gave its name. It served also eventually as a nucleus for the Constitutional Democratic party, popularly known as the Cadets. . . .

THE REVOLUTION OF 1905

The revolution of 1905 did not result in the destruction of the old social order desired by the radicals, nor did it bring about a complete realization of the more moderate demands of the constitutionalists. Yet its effects were far-reaching enough to permit us to consider it as beginning a new period in Russian history. In no less degree than the reforms of Alexander II, it modified the whole life of the nation and opened the way to new and significant developments.

During the first period of the revolution the Russian autocracy had to face a formidable coalition of all the forces of opposition within the country. For the time being the liberal constitutionalists and the radical socialists were acting in common. Late in 1904, after the assassination of the Minister of the Interior Plehve, the government first relaxed its policy of suppression; the Zemstvo conferences became instrumental in formulating the immediate demands of the opposition: convocation of a representative assembly and the grant to the Russian people of civil liberties guaranteed by a constitution. The Zemstvo program was immediately taken up by various professional groups at a series of political banquets held all over Russia during the winter of 1904–05. A number of professional unions, organized for obviously political purposes, were finally merged into an impressive Union of Unions, headed by Miliukov, the recognized leader of the constitutionalists. While this organization of liberal forces was going on in the open, the socialists intensified their underground activities. The Social Revolutionaries were responsible for several dramatic assassinations of prominent reactionary officials and, at the same time, applied themselves to the task of stirring up rebellion among the discontented peasants of the rural districts. The Social Democrats, on the other hand, concentrated their attention on the industrial workers of the cities whom they tried to win over to their revolutionary program. Their task was greatly facilitated by the events of January 9, 1905, when a procession of St. Petersburg workers, headed for the imperial residence to present their grievances to the Tsar, was fired upon by the troops, and many workers killed or wounded. The effect of "Bloody Sunday" was to intensify the radicalism of the working masses and, during the spring and summer of 1905, all the industrial regions of Russia saw a veritable epidemic of strikes, which almost completely disorganized production. Simultaneously, spurred by revolutionary propaganda, the "land-hungry" peasants rose in many provinces of European Russia, burning and looting the neighboring estates and occasionally murdering the landlords.

Another important factor in the situation was the revolutionary movement among the national minorities of the border regions. Bitterly resenting the policy of enforced "Russification" which had been applied to them by the government during the previous decades, the Poles, the Jews, and the inhabitants of the Baltic provinces and of Transcaucasia, all joined hands with the Russian revolutionaries for a struggle against the common enemy. It must be said, however, that as yet this was not a separatist movement. In most cases the demands of the national minorities did not go beyond a program of equal rights and local autonomy. What they wanted was not to secede from the Empire, but to see it reorganized on a democratic and federalist basis.

Faced with this formidable array of hostile forces, the government found itself in an extremely difficult position. Engaged in a disastrously unsuccessful war, materially disorganized, and morally isolated, it tried for a while to save the situation with minor concessions. It was forced to admit defeat, however, when confronted, in October, 1905, by an unusually effective general strike, which for a few days almost paralyzed the whole life of the country. In this emergency Nicholas II turned for advice to Witte. With characteristic realism this experienced statesman offered his sovereign one of two alternatives: either to establish a military dictatorship or else, if this was not feasible, to grant the people a constitution. With the bulk of the army still in the Far East and the spirit of the immediately available troops rather uncertain (there were isolated revolutionary outbreaks both in the army and in the navy), the emperor reluctantly chose the latter of these suggestions.

A manifesto of October 17, 1905, granted the Russian people civil liberties and a representative legislative assembly, based on a democratic franchise. . . .

It was in this atmosphere of mutual distrust and hostility that the State Duma, as the Russian representative assembly was called, had to begin its activities. Elected on the basis of a fairly democratic franchise, the first two

Dumas (1906 and 1907) had a brief and troublous existence. Both were entirely controlled by the opposition and both were unwilling to coöperate with the government which, in its turn, found their demands far too radical and utterly unacceptable. The inevitable result in each case was the dissolution of the Duma after a very short session. In June, 1907, the government finally decided to effect a drastic revision of the franchise by means of an imperial decree. This amounted virtually to a *coup d'état* as the Fundamental Laws, published in 1906, stipulated the consent of the Duma for any change in the electoral law. The procedure served its purpose, however, and the Third Duma, elected in 1907, had a safe governmental majority. If the stormy career of the first two Dumas can be viewed as an epilogue to the revolution of 1905, with the Third Duma begins the history of the Russian constitutional experiment.

THE DUMA AND THE GOVERNMENT

The political order established in Russia after the revolution of 1905 has often been described as "sham-constitutionalism," and the Duma has been disparaged as a mere "smoke-screen for autocracy" or a "convenient tool in the hands of the government." For the prevalence of this idea the representatives of the Russian opposition must be held largely responsible. In the heat of their struggle for a real parliamentary government it was natural for them to emphasize and even to exaggerate the many limitations from which the work of the Duma had to suffer. To a historian, however, the period appears in a somewhat different light. Even if there was no parliament in Russia, there certainly was a constitutional régime. And although the tsar retained his historical title of autocrat, this was rather a mere verbal concession to the centuries-old tradition and a glaring anachronism. In reality his power was no longer absolute because it was limited by the Fundamental Laws, which provided for the obligatory concurrence of the Duma in legislation. Strictly speaking, the Russian autocracy ceased to exist with the publication of the manifesto of October 17, 1905.

Of course, it must be admitted that the Duma, as finally established, was not a real parliament in the modern European sense of the word. To begin with, it did not represent the whole people, being based on a limited and unequal franchise which favored the large landowners and the city bourgeoisie to the detriment of the lower classes. National minorities also were discriminated against as compared with the purely Russian element of the population. Equally important were the limitations imposed upon the powers of the Duma. Under the Fundamental Laws, which could be changed only upon the initiative of the crown, the emperor enjoyed the exclusive right of directing foreign policy and the complete control of the executive. The ministers were responsible to him only and all the appointments both in the army and in the civil service were made in his name and required no further confirmation. Parts of the budget were declared to be "iron-clad," that is exempt from examination by the Duma. Article 87 of the Fundamental Laws reserved for the government the right to promulgate emergency legislation, in the intervals between the Duma sessions, by means of imperial decrees. This proved to be a convenient device to pass those measures which would meet with strong opposition. Although such laws had to be subsequently submitted to the Duma for ratification the latter, confronted in each case with an accomplished fact, usually found its freedom of action greatly hindered. Finally, to create one more check upon the activities of the Duma, the old bureaucratic Council of State was transformed into an upper chamber and its consent was made requisite for the passage of bills into laws. As only one half of its membership was elected, and that from public bodies representative of the upper groups of Russian society, while the other half was appointed by the crown, the Council of State could be counted upon to offer effective resistance should the Duma display an undesirable zeal for reform.

Yet one cannot discard the Duma as a negligible factor in Russian political life after 1907. Of great importance was the very fact that the principle of self-government now was extended to the field of national administration, from which heretofore it had been so consistently excluded. Moreover, in spite of all the above-mentioned limitations, the Duma still was able to exercise a real influence upon the conduct of national affairs. Although, as we have seen, it was not an adequate representation of the Russian people, it nevertheless could voice the demands of independent public elements and from its tribune governmental policies could be subjected by the opposition to an outspoken criticism not subject to censorship and receiving the widest publicity possible. Nor was the Duma entirely powerless in its relations with the executive. It still retained the right to examine and vote upon the greater part of the budget, and consequently every minister who desired to pass his estimates through the Duma was somewhat bound to seek its good will. The other weapon in the hands of the legislative chamber was its right of interpellation, that is, of asking explanations from the heads of the executive departments. And although, even in case of a unanimous censure, nothing happened to the minister in question so long as he retained the confidence of his sovereign, the Russian bureaucrats did not remain entirely insensitive to the attitude of popular representatives. As a matter of fact, under the influence of the Duma many departments of the central government became notably modernized and liberalized.

Finally, during the few years of its peaceful existence the Duma was able to pass various legislative measures constituting in their entirety quite a creditable positive achievement. A scheme of universal education was introduced and appropriations were voted for a corresponding annual increase in the number of primary schools throughout the Empire. Measures were taken to endow the peasants with full civil rights, putting them on a basis of equality with other classes; the office of "land captain" was abolished and the jurisdiction of the justices of the peace was extended to country districts. The Zemstvo institutions were established in nine additional provinces, important labor legislation was passed, and a very substantial improvement was achieved in the field of national defense. To sum up, the Duma succeeded "in making itself an indispensable factor in the national life of Russia and in retaining, in spite of all the obstacles in its way, the vital essence inherent in the very principle of popular representation" (Miliukov).

The relations between the Duma and the government remained not very satisfactory even after the drastic change in the electoral law which assured the preponderance of moderate elements in the legislative chamber. The sponsor of this measure, Peter Stolypin, Prime Minister during 1906–11, hardly could be called a consistent constitutionalist, in the strict sense of the word, as he seldom hesitated to apply extra-constitutional methods whenever he thought it necessary. It must be admitted, however, that he sincerely valued the coöperation of the Duma in legislative activity and had no thought of going back to the old autocratic ways of governing Russia. . . . In 1911 he was assassinated by an agent of the secret political police who at the same time was a member of a revolutionary organization. Only a few months before Stolypin had himself defended in the Duma the use as *agents-provocateurs* of such double-dealing persons, seeing in it a necessary weapon in the government's war on the revolutionaries.

After Stolypin's death the governmental policy towards the Duma became more inconsistent and vacillating. To the end of the imperial régime there was no unified cabinet in Russia, each minister being directly responsible to the emperor, with the Prime Minister occupying a position of merely honorary chairmanship. The result was that while some of the members of the government were more or less liberally inclined and desired to coöperate with the Duma, others were undisguised reactionaries and did not hesitate to display their hostility toward popular representation. With the emperor ill-suited to the rôle of constitutional monarch and not always willing to play the part

at all, the reactionaries were able at times to get the upper hand in governmental councils and to place some irritating obstacles in the way of the legislative assembly. It was as a result of this policy that the moderate wing of the
Duma gradually began to shift its position to the left until the way was
prepared for a political understanding between the Cadets, on the one hand,
and the Octobrists and even some of the Nationalists, on the other. The alignment of Duma parties on the eve of the World War foreshadowed a new conflict between the constitutional opposition and the forces of reaction entrenched
in the government. And of the two the opposition had a much better chance
of success because it was supported by the general trend of Russia's social and
intellectual evolution.

3. NATIONAL POWERS IN IMPERIALIST RIVALRY

An age which has lost its faith is ill-fitted to pass judgment upon the age
of Imperialist expansion. The sordid lure of easy wealth, the struggle for
power, the lust for domination are motive forces well understood to-day, but
the faith, the idealism, the passionate zeal to bring justice and civilization to
the darkest corners of Africa, whose wretched inhabitants were the victims
of Arab slavers, of pest and disease, are things of which little is now understood. Yet those easy phrases about the "Scramble for Africa" suggest only
one part of the story, that part that does so little credit to the continent which
claimed to be in the vanguard of civilization. The other is to be found in the
lives of the missionaries, the early administrators and most memorably in
the heroic journeys of the great explorers. In the pages of Livingstone's private
Journal there is scarcely a page which does not betray his unshakeable belief
that, wherever he went, he was watched and guided by his Maker. "You
know," he wrote to a friend after the discovery of the Shiré Highlands, "how
I have been led on from one step to another by the over-ruling Providence of
the great Parent, as I believe, in order to achieve a great good for Africa."
In the Chancelleries of Europe a constant preoccupation with the struggle for
power left men little time or inclination to think of achieving "a great good
for Africa," so it is as well for the reputation of European peoples in the dark
continent that so many of the explorers were so profoundly concerned with
the welfare of the native races. The imprint of their work rests indelibly upon
the African continent to-day.

The opening up of Africa was the work not of governments but of individuals possessed of great courage and remarkable powers of endurance. There
is something very revealing in that description by a companion, of Living-

stone "tramping along with the steady, heavy tread which kept one in mind that he had walked across Africa." But where individuals had pioneered, governments soon intervened, and it is only with the motives that prompted their intervention that we are concerned. The political and economic importance of Africa was popularly overestimated. In Western Europe it was commonly believed that the acquisition of colonies was the high road to rapid economic development. Many writers, principally, though not only, German, failed, as Mr. A. J. P. Taylor has written,

to grasp the truth about the British Empire—that it had come into being as the result of British commercial enterprise and industrial success; and they asserted the reverse, that the prosperity and wealth of Great Britain were due to the existence of her Empire. The German campaign for colonies rested on the simple dogma— give Germany colonies and the Germans will then be as prosperous as the English.

Such popular beliefs may have influenced the minds even of autocratic governments, but they were not the directing force in overseas colonial expansion. The rulers of Europe thought primarily in terms of political not economic advantage and it was on the struggle for power in Europe that their eyes were always fixed. Expansion overseas was for the Continental States, not an end, but a means to an end.

Bismarck was a late and always a sceptical convert to "colonialism." His indifference was a source of strength. In the colonial field he could play the hand that best suited his purpose in Europe. For it was on the European scene that his eye was always riveted. And not his alone. . . . But the balance of forces in Europe left France after 1870 with the alternatives of enlarging her Empire overseas or a policy of resignation. Alsace-Lorraine could only be a question "reserved for the future." In the meantime, was it not folly to sit by idly nursing wrongs while other Powers extended their control over large parts of Africa and Asia? "Ought we in the name of an exalted and shortsighted chauvinism," exclaimed Jules Ferry, the protagonist of Republican imperialism, "to force French policy into an impasse and, with our eyes fixed on the blue outline of the Vosges mountains, allow everything to be done, to be undertaken, to be resolved—without us, around us, against us?" This was the reasoning produced by the psychological reaction to defeat and reinforced by a revival of France's traditional belief in mercantilist economics that led her, a country with a declining population, to embark, with direct encouragement from Bismarck, on an active policy of colonial expansion in North and Central Africa, in Madagascar and in Indo-China.

Bismarck's sympathetic interest in French imperialism was an experiment on his side, in the possibilities of Franco-German reconciliation. That France should remain ostracized in Europe was his settled policy, but clearly it was not in the interests of Germany that she should be driven to despair. An outlet for her energies, preoccupation in colonial fields in which Germany had no interest, except for bargaining purposes, had everything to recommend it. The fact that, incidentally, French expansion in North Africa, and particularly in Tunis, would bring her into conflict with Italy, enhanced the attractions of this policy, even if it were not its primary purpose. To the French Ambassador, in January 1879, the Chancellor gave effusive encouragement. "Now indeed, I believe," observed Bismarck,

that the Tunisian pear is ripe and that the time has come for you to pluck it. The effrontery of the Bey has been like the August sun for this African fruit, which might very well have been spoilt or stolen by somebody else if you had let it remain too long on the bough. I don't know what you intend to do or whether it tempts you, but I take the opportunity of repeating . . . my desire to give you proofs of my good will on questions which concern you and in which there are no German interests in opposition to yours.

That Italy had already received German encouragement to seize Tunis must have heightened the Chancellor's satisfaction with French reactions. For his advice was heeded, and by the end of 1881 this former province of the Turkish Empire was securely French and Italy estranged.

Not only France and Italy but also England had traditional interests in North Africa. If it was the anxiety of the Third Republic to restore French self-respect after 1870; of a united Italy to raise herself to the level of a first-class Power by the acquisition of colonies on the southern shore of the Mediterranean; it was England's concern for imperial communications that led her with some reluctance to intervene in Egypt and so come into conflict with France. The Suez Canal of which control had been dramatically acquired by Disraeli was, as Bismarck admitted, "of vital importance" to her Empire being "like the spinal cord which connects the backbone with the brain." It was that fact that left England no freedom of choice. After "Dual Control" had been established in Egypt in the interests of British and French bond-holders in 1876, Lord Salisbury summed up the alternatives before his country. "You may," he said, "renounce, or monopolize or share. Renouncing would have been to place France across our road to India. Monopolizing would have been very near the risk of war. So we resolved to share." But it was not to prove as simple as that. Egyptian nationalist sentiment found a leader in Colonel Arabi Pasha, against whom no resolute action could be taken without provoking a popular outcry in France. Gambetta urged that the greatest sacrifices should be made to continue co-operation with England, but the Chamber was not prepared to heed his advice. So when nationalist riots broke out in Alexandria in June 1882, France withdrew and England acted alone. The forts at Alexandria were bombarded; and General Wolseley gained a decisive and final victory over Arabi Pasha at Tel el Kebir in September. British rule in the name of the Khedive was now assured, and in 1883 Sir Evelyn Baring was appointed British agent and Consul-General in Cairo. No easy task awaited him, for the revolt of the Dervishes in the Sudan, their annihilation of the Khedive's forces under Hicks Pasha, led to the decision to evacuate the whole of the Sudan south of the Wady Halfa. Despite the misgivings of Baring, General Gordon was sent out from London as Governor-General with secret orders to carry out this evacuation, whose sorry sequel is a page in the history of England rather than of Europe.

England's task in Egypt was undertaken with German goodwill, which soon evaporated. Where Bismarck had once acknowledged comparative German indifference in the affairs of Egypt, he felt by the end of 1883 that the time had come when a less passive attitude would better serve his ends. "We are uncommonly grateful to Prince Bismarck," Lord Granville had said to Count Herbert Bismarck in January 1883, "for the friendly attitude of German policy this summer was of great service to us. Our being left with a free hand in Egypt we owe, when all is said, to Germany's goodwill. We are all aware that at a particular moment Prince Bismarck could have upset the coach if he had chosen to, and we realize with much thankfulness that he refrained from doing so." The price however had still to be paid, and in Egypt pressure was easy to apply. For the Gladstone Government, reluctant to contemplate annexation on principle, were left with no practicable alternative to acting as the nominal mandatory of the Powers. That left Britain in a weak and vulnerable position, for, of the Powers, France burned with resentment at her exclusion from Egypt, and Russia, without any direct interest in the Nile Valley, was hostile to the consolidation of Britain's position in the Eastern Mediterranean. This was a situation from which Bismarck was not slow to profit. The situation in Egypt made England, as Baring frankly recognized, dependent on German goodwill.

It seems clear now that Bismarck's colonial policy was more the incidental offshoot of tactical moves in Europe than a departure undertaken on its own merits. The price that Bismarck was most concerned to exact from England in return for German goodwill in Egypt, was some form of guarantee in Europe which would reinsure Germany in the West against French aggression. When it was made plain that this was a price that England was not prepared to pay he decided to explore again the possibility of friendship with

France, founded on Franco-German hostility to England in the colonial field. That he was also influenced by internal political considerations is hardly to be denied. A forward colonial policy was well calculated to enhance the Chancellor's popularity at home. . . .

From 1883 to 1885 the new policy was put into practice. The weak but well-meaning Foreign Secretary, Lord Granville, noticed with dismay the abrupt change in the temper of Anglo-German relations. An atmosphere of friendly co-operation was transformed by a recital of German grievances in many parts of the world, which lost nothing in the telling by the Chancellor's arrogant son, Count Herbert Bismarck. Of all the disputes which followed, the most protracted was concerned with the fate of Angra Pequeña on the west coast of Africa some 200 miles north of the frontier of the Cape Province. There a German trader, named Luderitz, established himself and asked for protection. Could the British Government give protection? inquired Herbert Bismarck, for "if not, the German Government will do their best to extend to it the same measure of protection which they could give to their subjects in remote parts of the world—but without having the least desire to establish any footing in South Africa. . . ." To a German settlement in South-West Africa, London might be comparatively indifferent, but the Cape was resolutely opposed. And in the event, what began as an inquiry about protection at Angra Pequeña developed, against their wishes, into German South-West Africa. The reasons are to be found in the weakness of the British position in Egypt, which made dependence on German goodwill inevitable, and strained relations with Russia which made the more desirable friendly co-operation with the Triple Alliance.

By the end of 1885 Bismarck's new policy had laid the foundation of the German Colonial Empire, for by then she had secured her position in the Cameroons and in New Guinea as well as in South-West Africa together with a foothold in East Africa. Where the British Colonial Empire had been founded largely by the private enterprise of the chartered companies, Germany's was created through the impetus of a deliberate policy of state. If that policy met a weak and dilatory response in London, that was due to misunderstanding of its aim and not to unfriendliness. For it was generally accepted that it was right and just that Germany should have her "place in the Sun." Owing to earlier indifference and her late start, her African territories compared unfavourably with those of France or of the Belgians in the Congo Basin, or of the British. But, judged by her subsequent policy, her interest in colonial expansion remained very secondary to her interests in Europe. By 1914 the total number of German colonial settlers was no more than 23,000.

While the number of European emigrants is in itself no criterion of the quality of colonial government, these trifling numbers are at least an indication that colonies did not serve as an outlet for surplus population in Germany.

While Germany was acquiring a Colonial Empire in Africa and the Pacific, France, assured of German goodwill, extended her empire chiefly in North and West Africa but also by the acquisition of Madagascar, a convenient stepping-stone to Indo-China, between 1883 and 1885, and after a protracted struggle in Tonkin and Annam. It was the losses and set-backs in Tonkin that brought about the fall of the second Ferry Ministry, and with it the end of an active imperialist policy leaning on German goodwill. . . . Bismarck's colonial policy, in so far as it was an experiment in Franco-German reconciliation, had failed.

The years 1885–89 witnessed the height of the scramble for Africa. But unlike the preceding years they were marked by a revival of Anglo-German co-operation under the aegis of Bismarck and Salisbury. If Bismarck, in laying the foundations of a German Colonial Empire, had not effected a reconciliation with France, he had at least succeeded in his other objectives. France and Italy were estranged over Tunis and Italy was compelled to seek alliance with the Central Powers: England and France were divided by Egypt; and England, partly because of her concern for the security of the Nile Valley, which was the cardinal consideration in determining her colonial policy in Africa, and partly because of the advance of Russia to the Afghan frontier, was also impelled towards more friendly relations with the Central Powers. . . .

If German support for French imperial ambitions was an experiment which was tried, failed and abandoned, there was a remarkable consistency about Germany's attitude to Russian expansion in Asia. It was something to be encouraged. About that there were no doubts. It had almost everything to recommend it. It would distract Russia's attention from Europe, thereby lessening the risk of an Austro-Russian conflict in the Balkans; it would keep Russian forces harmlessly occupied; it would, above all, keep alive Anglo-Russian tension by playing on English fears of a Russian invasion of India. "Germany," Bismarck advised his Emperor,

has no interest in preventing Russia if she looks for the occupation which is necessary for her army in Asia rather than in Europe. If the Russian Army is unoccupied it becomes a danger to the internal security of the Empire and the dynasty, and if occupation fails in Asia it must necessarily be sought on the Western front. . . . It is therefore an aim of German policy to-day to bring about hostile rather than too intimate relations between Russia and England. . . .

In more flamboyant language and by more direct methods the Kaiser Wilhelm II pursued in this respect at least, the same policies as the Chancellor he had deposed from office. "Clearly," he wrote to the Tsar Nicholas II in April 1895, "it is the great task of the future for Russia to cultivate the Asian continent and to defend Europa from the inroads of the great Yellow Race. In this you will always find me ready to help you as best I can. You have well understood the call of providence. . . ." But though German policy was consistent, Russia, unlike France, was not a defeated country and her expansion in Central Asia owed little or nothing to German encouragement or German goodwill. Like the British in India, the frontiers of the Russian Empire in Central Asia moved steadily forward because the vacuum in power that existed in the Trans-Caspian regions left her with little alternative. In 1868 Russia had occupied Samarkand and in the next two decades her influence steadily extended eastwards. Southern Turkestan was under her control by 1881 and early in 1884 first Merv was occupied and then Sarakhs on the Persian-Afghan frontier. Russian power henceforward loomed mysterious and menacing close to the frontiers of India.

In 1889, at the time of transition between the old order of the wild Tartar Khanates and the newer rule of Russia, George Curzon visited Central Asia, conscious that this was the moment when the era of "The Thousand and One Nights" with its strange mixture of savagery and splendour, of coma and excitement, was fast fading, before "the rude shock and unfeeling Philistinism of nineteenth-century civilization," though still in the cities of Alp Arslan, and Timur and Abdullah Khan were to be seen a stage "upon which is yet being enacted that expiring drama of realistic romance." But the future Viceroy of India, who in his own day was to be so profoundly concerned with the building up of the Indian Empire into a continental power capable of withstanding a Russian attack from the north, frankly recognized that Russian rule was firmly and fairly established, and loyally accepted by the conquered races. This he attributed to many factors—the ferocious severity of the original blow; the powerlessness of resistance against the tight military grip of Russia, above all the certainty "which a long course of Russian conduct has reasonably inspired that she will never retreat." The last was the fundamental factor. Tsarist or Communist, the Russian Empire does not retreat in Asia. An apologetic advance in the Gladstonian manner coupled with assurances of an early retreat is a practice it has never adopted. When the British Empire in India passed away, the Central Asian Republics of the Soviet Union were only at the dawn of their material development. It is that which in the long run will make Russian expansion in Asia of at least equal significance to the contemporary colonization of Africa by the powers of Western Europe.

If the more enduring achievements of Russian Imperialism are to be found in Central Asia, that has never been the limit of its ambitions. It had also a traditional interest in the Far East. But there it was not a case of bringing "civilization" to nomadic ill-disciplined herdsmen, but of exacting concessions from the disintegrating Chinese Empire. As early as 1885 Russia planned the building of the trans-Siberian railway, and by 1895 the line was completed from the Urals as far as Lake Baikal. Its construction was the condition of effective Russian intervention in the Far East. Alone of the Great Powers, Russia had direct entry into Asia by land, and was therefore in a position to act independently of England's sea power in a way that was possible to none of her rivals. It was a recognition of her advantages that fostered in Russia the dream of an expanding empire in the Far East. Its fascination diverted Russian energies from Europe from 1895 to 1905, much to the dismay of her French allies, and only defeat by Japan, of whose rising power little account had at first been taken, turned her eyes once again to the Balkans.

The Sino-Japanese War of 1894–95 over the fate of Korea, a tributary state of China from which Japan had extracted unilateral concessions, afforded the pretext for European intervention in the Far East on a large scale. Indifferent to appeals for aid from China during the war Russia intervened when Japan had secured by the Treaty of Shimonoseki, in April 1895, the Liaotung Peninsula with Port Arthur at its extremity. To back her intervention she enlisted the support of her ally France and of a Germany concerned to deflect Russian ambitions to the Far East. The Triple Intervention, from which England wisely remained aloof, acting on the principle that "no Power be allowed to increase its territorial possessions at China's expense," compelled Japan to evacuate Port Arthur. The way now seemed open for the fulfilment of Russian designs in the Far East with Russia assuming the rôle of "protector" of the Chinese Empire.

Russia was the foremost but not the only European Power interested in the Far East. The letter in which the Kaiser had assured the Tsar of his support in missionary enterprises against the Yellow Races had concluded with a candid hope of reward in the form of a coaling station in an area which did not conflict with Russian claims. This elicited no cordial response but none the less, in 1897, the Germans seized Kiao-Chow with many expressions of gratitude for Russian support which had not in fact been forthcoming. But Russia, unprepared for war or for indulgence in futile complaint, made an effective countermove by wintering her fleet in Port Arthur, and in March 1898 peremptorily demanding its lease from China. For Japan this was the last straw and so far as Germany was concerned there was no question where the balance of advantage lay. Port Arthur was of far greater value than Kiao-Chow. But even with its lease to Russia the story did not end, for Britain, possibly to the satisfaction of China, and certainly not prepared to be left out in the cold, negotiated the lease of Wei-Hai-Wei. For a moment it seemed as though the last years of the century would see the partition of China among the Great Powers.

In 1900 the victim of Western "protection" revolted with outbursts of violence known as the Boxer Rebellion. Soon suppressed it afforded another opportunity for the display of German initiative in the Far East. The murder of German missionaries, the threat to the European legations at Pekin, excited the Kaiser's obsessed imagination and nothing less would suffice than the organization of an international force under German command. To the parting marines on parade their Kaiser cried,

You must know, my men, that you are about to meet a crafty, well armed, cruel foe! Meet him and beat him! Give no quarter! Take no prisoners! Kill him when he falls into your hands! Even as a thousand years ago, the Huns under their King Attila made such a name for themselves as still resounds in terror through legend and fable, so may the name of German resound through Chinese history a thousand years from now. . . .

That Allied troops had taken Pekin before ever the expedition intended to rescue it had sailed, was a trifle disconcerting, but the expeditionary force was not recalled and with little positive purpose remained in China till 1901 exacting indemnities and concessions. The story is one which, like the speech of the Kaiser, reflects ill on Germany and no small discredit on the Western Powers whose preoccupations with an unending struggle for supremacy made them forget all tolerable codes of international behaviour. The "Hun" speech was a portent and a warning of a declining international morality for which Germany bears a primary, but by no means exclusive, responsibility. It boded ill on the short run for China and it boded ill, too, on the long run for Europe.

It was Lord Salisbury who remarked that Gladstone's impassioned fight for Irish Home Rule had aroused the slumbering genius of Imperialism. It is doubtful, however, if the blatant and boastful temper of the *fin de siècle* deserves so kindly a description. One of its most notable consequences was to estrange Britain from Europe at a moment when her isolation placed her in a position whose perils were better understood in retrospect than at the time.

It was in January 1895 that President Kruger, as the guest of the German

Club in Pretoria on the Kaiser's birthday, spoke of Germany as "a grown-up power that would stop England from kicking the child Republic." On instructions from London the British Ambassador protested against the German encouragement of Boer hostility to Britain, of which Kruger's speech was regarded as a provocative expression. The Kaiser later maintained that the Ambassador had gone so far as to mention the "astounding word, 'war.' " "For a few square miles full of niggers and palm trees England had threatened her one true friend, the German Emperor, grandson of Her Majesty the Queen of Great Britain and Ireland, with war!" According to his own highly coloured narrative the Kaiser retorted with the "clear warning" that England could only escape from her existing isolation "by a frank and outspoken attitude either for or against the Triple Alliance." As things were England's attitude, her policy "of selfishness and bullying" were forcing Germany to make "common cause with France and Russia, each of whom had about a million men ready to pour in over my frontier. . . ." Into this atmosphere of artificial tension came with explosive effect the news of the Jameson Raid. Ill-judged, ill-considered, wholly indefensible, even in its limited Anglo-South African context, it played straight into the hands of the most dangerous forces at work in Germany. The Kaiser responded with a telegram to President Kruger, dated 3rd January 1896.

I express my sincere congratulations that, supported by your people, without appealing for the help of friendly Powers, you have succeeded by your own energetic action against armed bands which invaded your country as disturbers of the peace, and have thus been enabled to restore peace and safeguard the independence of the country against attacks from the outside.

If the telegram was designed to embody every phrase best calculated to inflame sentiment in a country whose first reaction to the news of the Raid was one of profound misgiving, it could not have been better drafted. At once opinion hardened against the Boer Republics. President Kruger was no longer felt to be the much wronged defender of his people's rights, but a collaborator with the Kaiser challenging British rule in South Africa. Self-respect was restored and internal divisions papered over.

To send a telegram was one thing; to intervene effectively in South Africa was another. Germany had no fleet. What course was open to her? Holstein supplied the answer. The Triple Alliance and the Dual Alliance should forget their rivalry and co-operate against Britain. There was a wide field for common action and many colonial ambitions that could be achieved in concert. . . . This superficially was a tempting prospect for one and all. But behind it there were subtle reservations, soon suspected. The ultimate German intention was not the final estrangement of Britain but a practical demonstration of the dangers of isolation and of the need to co-operate with the Triple Alliance. . . .

Holstein's project of European Alliance was stillborn, and it is interesting to notice that when the South African War broke out in 1899, Germany's policy was very different. In 1900 it was Russia who proposed mediation and Germany who declined it, the Kaiser improving the occasion by informing the Queen and the Prince of Wales of his refusal. The Prince paid ironic tribute to this gesture thanking the Kaiser in March 1900—"You have no idea, my dear William, how all of us in England appreciate the loyal friendship you manifest towards us on every occasion." But if the political response was more judicious the lesson deduced in Berlin from the Raid and the South African War was always the same—sea power is the condition of world power. That was the most significant legacy of the Jameson Raid and the South African War to Europe.

In the last decade of the nineteenth century England suffered from the unpopularity that overtakes the Imperialist who outdistances his rivals while explaining conscientiously that new territories are being acquired only with profound reluctance under the inexorable pressure of events. It was not friendliness towards England; it was well-founded mistrust of Germany that induced both France and Russia to disregard Germany's suggestions for a Continental league in 1896, and two years later England and France reached the brink of war on an incident which went far to decide the balance of colonial power in North Africa.

It was in the summer of 1898 that Captain Marchand with his small, devoted band, after a long and perilous march of some 2,800 miles from the Congo, reached Fashoda on the Upper Nile to lay claim to territory which was part of the Sudan, and therefore in the British view under Egyptian sovereignty. In March 1895 Sir Edward Grey had stated categorically that the advance of a French expedition from the other side of Africa into the Nile Valley "would be an unfriendly act and would be so viewed by England." But despite this solemn warning the French Government persisted in an action involving great international risks, whose only practical end was to stake out a claim for bargaining purposes. .   .

In the Sudan the British Government had no intention of making concessions. Salisbury was unyielding in his claim "that all the territories which were subject to the Khalifa passed to the British and Egyptian Governments by right of conquest." But for the prolongation of the crisis public opinion was at least as much responsible as the actual conflict of interest between Governments though it has to be recorded that at least two members of Salisbury's Cabinet, Chamberlain and Hicks-Beach used language which made compromise for the French doubly difficult. Fashoda was, in any case, an incident of a kind well calculated to provoke chauvinistic passions of the worst kind.

Delcassé, who replaced Hanotaux as Foreign Minister, must be given the principal credit for the avoidance of irrevocable measures and for a settlement, not reached till March 1899, which made the watershed of the Nile and the Congo the dividing line between British and French spheres of influence, Britain agreeing not to seek territory or influence westwards and France abandoning her claims eastwards. In the sequel the convention provided a sound foundation for co-operation.

The exercise of restraint in the Fashoda crisis was a profound disappointment to the Kaiser who was on a cruise in the Eastern Mediterranean when the tension reached its climax. "I have received news from London and Paris," he telegraphed to the Tsar on 28th October 1898, "that both countries are mobilizing their fleets. Paris seems to be preparing for a *coup d'état*. In case a collision between the two countries should occur your position *vis-à-vis* to them would be of the greatest value to me. How do you look at the situation?" The Tsar, or his advisers, looked at it with a more sensible detachment and the Tsar replied that "he had no knowledge of an impending conflict between France and England," adding with pleasant irony that he thought in this case one "might await events before taking any decision, the more so, as it is always awkward to interfere, without being asked, with others' business."

Paradoxically enough it may be that Fashoda had a beneficial effect on Anglo-French relations in a wider field. To England it underlined, on reflection, the dangers of being simultaneously on bad terms with the Powers of the Triple and of the Dual Alliance; to France, and above all to Delcassé, it emphasized the need for a deliberate policy, pursued if need be by the sacrifice of interests in Egypt very close to the French heart, if her position in Europe were to be re-established. The Alliance with Russia was in itself not enough, especially in the light of Russian preoccupation in Asia. But it needed both courage and foresight to draw such conclusions while passions were inflamed. . . .

Though on more than one occasion colonial rivalries brought the Great Powers within sight of war, it is not for that reason to be concluded that colonial rivalry was a fundamental cause of war. On the contrary the colonial policies of the Continental states were formulated in the light of the European balance of power and designed to serve European ends. When they no longer served those ends the colonial scene slips unobtrusively into the background. From 1900 onwards there were no important colonial disputes between Germany and England because of the preoccupation of the Powers in the Far East between 1900–04; and after 1904 because the Anglo-French Entente had removed the possibility of attaining the political ends which German colonial policy in the 'eighties had been designed to promote. But if in general the colonial policies of the Powers were subordinate to their European interests, that is not to say that colonial rivalry had little effect on the course of European history, but merely that its consequences were indirect. Of them, two were of outstanding importance. The first was the conviction created in Germany that a powerful navy was an indispensable means to world power; the second was the decline in international morality fostered by the corroding impact of an unscrupulous scramble for, and subsequent exploitation of, overseas territories.

Chapter VIII

THE DIRECTIONS OF NINETEENTH-
CENTURY SCIENCE

☙

1. THE MECHANICAL IDEAL AND THE SCOPE OF SCIENCE

THE ECONOMIC organization of society . . . in the so-called Industrial Revolution has been the source out of which some of the most important of our scientific conceptions and hypotheses have arisen. The conception of energy is illustrative of this. This conception was definitely revolutionary in modern science because it brought together fields which could not be stated in terms of a mechanical science. Newton's statement was taken from the heavens and, of course, was a generalization of Galileo's law of the falling body fused with the observations of Kepler and others. Newton gave a statement of the solar system in terms of attraction, that is, of the movement of masses with reference to each other; and he gave the laws for this solar system. Then this system was carried to earth again and was made the basis for the study of the phenomena that take place about us. It was very fruitful in a field in which you could locate actual masses, but people tried to carry over the conception into fields in which they could not actually locate the different masses on account of the minuteness of the bodies. What they wanted to do was to apply the simple law of Newton's statement to other physical processes.

For example, take such a process as heat, that is, of molecular bodies moving at great velocities with reference to one another. They are beyond the range of our observation. You cannot take that problem and carry it over into the phenomena, because you cannot get a statement of the positions of the bodies that will enable you to work the law out. There were various uniformities which science could locate. Again, take the phenomenon of elec-

---

This chapter consists of material by two different authors. Section 1 is from *Movements of Thought in the Nineteenth Century* (pp. 243–63; Chicago, University of Chicago Press, 1936), by George H. Mead. Section 2 is from "Evolution, Social" (*Encyclopaedia of the Social Sciences,* Vol. V, pp. 657–61; New York, The Macmillan Co., 1931), by Alexander Goldenweiser.

tricity. Here also are uniformities which could be determined. How were these different phenomena to be brought into relationship with each other? They could not be stated simply in terms of the movement of masses with reference to each other as Newton could state the movement of planetary bodies, and yet they must be made into a necessary idea. That is, you can say how much work will be done, how much work is involved in doing this or that thing, and yet not know how the atoms or particular masses are moving with reference to others. All we can determine is just how much work is done in one situation and how much is done in another. Then we have a basis for determining proportionate amounts of energy. We can look at the whole process from the standpoint of energies, from the standpoint of the amount of work done, and not try to determine just what the positions of all the physical particles are in their movements in relation to one another. Such an undertaking goes beyond our vision. But you can still say that energy is expended; you can still say how much work is involved in bringing about a certain situation, and how much can be developed.

The economist turns to the scientist and wants a theory for his new servant, the steam engine. He says, "I want to know how much work it can do." So the scientist takes the unit of work and discovers the amount of energy. That is, he finds that the machine can be depended upon for a certain number of units of work done. Thus, in the physical world you can say that energy is a bookkeeping conception. It takes electricity and light, coal, expansive steam, and the revolving dynamo, and sets up a certain unit by means of which it is able to put them all into the same class, just as the economist takes all sorts of different objects—the machinery, the soil, the plant, the workers—and sets them all together, states them in terms of the amount of labor necessary to get a given commodity. Work or energy, then, is a bookkeeping conception taken over from the economic doctrine, just as I have said the conception of the survival of the fittest in the competition for existence is taken over by Darwin from the economic situation presented by Ricardo and Malthus and generalized in the form of the hypothesis of evolution. It is very interesting to see the sources from which importantly constructive ideas have arisen, to see what an organic thing society is; how ideas that you find in one phase of it appear in some different form in another phase, but come back to common sources. . . .

. . . I have already indicated the independent position of science in the modern world. In a certain sense the Renaissance scientist took up the study of matter and motion as a field which led outside the immediate social interests and ecclesiastic interests of the community. From the point of view of the church God had created the world out of nothing to serve as the field in which would be enacted the drama of man's fall and salvation. Science could make its investigation without coming into conflict with the doctrine of the church. It was to be assumed that an infinitely wise God would work by means of uniform laws; that he would have the ability and the interest of a supreme mathematician. Thus science might find the way in which God operates in the world without finding out his purposes. When, however, the science which dealt with matter, the science of Galileo, and especially his dynamics, which said that matter is nothing but inertia—mass as revealed in inertia—when this science went on into the fields of biology, for example, the going became more difficult. It was difficult because biology is a science which is infinitely more complex than mechanics. If biology is to be reduced to mechanics, it is necessary to carry one's view into very complex situations. Still it is possible to conceive of plants, of animals, and of a physiological mind as mechanical. . . . From the time of the Renaissance on, the Western world was controlling nature and using its forces by very competent investigation of its laws and a complete willingness to obey those laws in carrying out its own purposes, so that a nature that seemed to be outside the ends and the purposes of the creator of the world became more and more important to society. A science which seemed to have abandoned and to have carefully kept itself from theological inquiry in regard to the meaning of the world was coming in by the back door, and, by studying the mechanical order of things, was getting more control of nature and bringing about tremendous changes and becoming more and more important in man's mind. It continually rendered this type of explanation more and more attractive—an explanation from the statement of the efficient cause, from cause and effect and the uniform laws of nature, as over against an explanation from the point of view of final cause, of end, of purpose. Which form of explanation shall we take? Why is the world here? Why are we here? Why should we suffer, be restricted here and there? What is the end that explains all? That earlier, teleological form of explanation was set over against another form which undertakes to show how things have happened, and why, because certain things have happened in a given way, other things must necessarily follow. That is a science of physical necessity, but one which did not carry with it necessity in so far as the conduct of man was concerned. I have said that one gets control over nature by obeying it. You find out how things must happen, and then you can use things that happen in a necessary way to bring about your results. This very separation of mass, of the mechanical process from other processes, psychological and social among others, left people, in some sense, free to utilize these very social purposes.

What I want to bring out is that, while there had been a sort of theological inquiry that is still perhaps present in man's mind as to whether men are free or not, and questions of freedom of the will may still be discussed under sophomoric conditions, the necessity which science presents had not, as yet, carried with it control over human initiative. The more necessary the statement of natural sciences can be made, the greater freedom man has in reconstructing, in bringing about changes in, his environment.

This paradox is of very great importance in our understanding of the position of science in the Western world. Of course, if, with Laplace, you say that everything that takes place is simply a shift of physical particles moving in accordance with absolute law, then you can conceivably have an equation in which you have only to introduce the variables, including time, and you can determine the position of the moon with reference to the earth and sun, and so determine eclipses. You can conceivably get equations which can determine the whole solar and stellar system. Increase its generality, and all you have to do is to introduce the variable time and you can tell just where every physical particle will be at any possible moment in the future as well as in the past. Seemingly, the whole world would be absolutely fixed and determined. That is a conceivable statement of this mechanical science. But what I am pointing out is that the science which gave this sort of a view of the world is the science which was enabling human initiative to reconstruct its world entirely and, through the reconstruction of his environment, enabling man to make an entirely different society. You get this paradox: a statement of the mechanical nature of everything, one which seems to include man also, which, at the same time, gives man greater control over his environment, greater freedom of action, and allows him to set up social objectives.

Man is a physical and biological organism. What he is is the sum of all the physical particles that go to make him up. According to the statement we are now considering, if you can determine where those particles are, you can determine just what he will say and think. Such a doctrine gives you absolute necessity in everything; and yet, in working out as complete a mechanical statement as is possible, you get one which gives man a more complete freedom than he ever had in the past. . . .

The Newtonian doctrine presented a picture of an orderly, mechanical universe, one governed by mechanical laws, a universe of masses in motion. The laws of these motions in their simplest forms could be given. The changes that took place, if in a sufficiently simple situation, could also be traced out. The method of analysis which grew out of the work of Leibnitz and Newton —that of an infinitesimal calculus—sought always to take as simple a situation as possible; and, if a sufficiently simple situation could be found, it was discovered that the laws of change could be determined. The picture, then, which was presented of the physical universe was of one which was in motion, and in motion in accordance with simple laws, and that which moved was mass. There were, of course, many features of the physical universe which could not be brought under terms of mass; but it was assumed, or at least hoped, that something of this kind could be worked out, that such a mechanical statement of things could be made universal. The picture which Laplace presented was of an equation which could determine where all the physical particles of the universe would be at any one moment if you simply introduced the variable of time. Such a picture was what men had before them. So far as they could get into the intricate movement of things, the molecular movements of things, the laws seemed to hold. It was, then, to be assumed that such physical laws as these operated throughout nature, and that the whole of nature could be regarded in terms simply of masses in motion and could be brought under as rigorous laws as those which science had already discovered.

There was, however, the biological field which seemed to offer resistance to the entrance of physical law. The importance of the Darwinian hypothesis was that it seemed to open the door to a natural law in the development of physical forms. If such a hypothesis could be accepted, the changes that took place in animate nature would be due to causes operating from behind, causes which were a posteriori. That is, you would not have to assume a certain nature in plant or animal which determined its growth, but that causes were operating, or rather had been operating, which brought about results here as in inorganic nature. Of course, men had discovered many parts of the process of life which could be stated in physical and mechanical terms. Certain of the so-called "organic products" had been produced artificially in the laboratory. It was perfectly conceivable that changes which took place in living forms were simply physical and mechanical changes, that men and animals and plants were, as Descartes had guessed, nothing but machines so far as the life-processes were concerned.

Now Darwin's hypothesis came in to indicate how particular forms might arise. All it asked for was indefinite variation on the part of young forms, that every young form should vary in some respect from the parent form. Then it asked that there should be competition for life which should be sufficiently strenuous that only the form best adapted to survive would survive. What Darwin pointed out was what had been suggested in Malthus' doctrine, namely, that there were always more young forms arising in nature than could possibly survive. There must then be competition between these forms, and those among them which were less fitted to survive under the conditions in which they found themselves would inevitably disappear. Given this indefinite variation, one could fairly assume that when the difference in the form answered to changes in the environment a new form would arise which, under this competition, would maintain itself while all other forms would disappear. In this way Darwin undertook to explain the appearance of species. Back of it, as I have pointed out, was the recognition of a more or less identical life-process in all forms. The biological form of the plant or animal was the adjustment of this life-process to a particular environment. Suppose, now, that this environment changes; there must be a corresponding change on the part of the animal form if it is to survive. If we grant these indefinite variations, we may assume that through them some forms will be better able to adjust themselves to new conditions, and so new forms may arise.

Here, you see, you have simply variations from behind, indefinite variations due to the very processes of reproduction. Given the changes which are taking place in the environment as a result of geologic and climatic influences, it is possible to account for the development of plant and animal forms in mechanical terms. One could, in this way, get a picture of a mechanical universe which was governed by absolute laws which determined where all physical particles would be and therefore what all the physical things would be and everything that they would be doing, and, finally, every change that took place. It was a picture of such a complete universe as this, with its fixed laws, that is, in a certain sense, a counterpart of the picture of a fixed order of society which grew out of the Manchester doctrine and was formulated by Karl Marx as the basis for his socialist doctrine. Both of them belonged to their period. . . .

The mechanical doctrine which was dominant in the scientific world of the nineteenth century was that of Newton, with its conception of a mechanical process which could be determined by laws of nature which presumably were inevitable and invariable. It took account only of the position of physical particles in their relationship to each other as a whole. It did not deal with the values which objects directly have in our experience—those of sensation, for example, color, sound, taste, and odor. But even as important, and perhaps more important, it did not deal with the characters which belong to living organisms. It simply stated the relative position of all physical particles in their relationship to each other. In this doctrine there was no reason for cutting out certain groups of these particles and dealing with them as separate objects and finding in them a content, a meaning which belonged to them themselves such as is found in all living forms. What this science did do, however, and it is well always to keep this in mind, was to state certain fixed conditions under which these phenomena could appear. Take the phenomenon of life, for example. The physical and chemical sciences could state what the conditions are under which life as we feel it, see it, know it about us, can arise. In so far, of course, it gives us control over the process of life. It is a statement of a mechanical, as over against a teleological, view of the world. It reduces the world simply to a congeries of physical particles, atoms, and electrons; it takes all the meaning out of it. That would be an unjust account of reality, for the development of science has always gone hand in hand with the determination of the conditions under which other characters could appear. We never could have had the advances which we have had in hygiene and medicine but for the mechanical statements which are given in physics and chemistry. We never could have got as close as we have to the life-process as a whole if it had not been for this physical and mechanical statement. From the time of Bacon on, the slogan of science has been, "Knowledge is power." That is, what we learn about nature enables us to control nature. Or, to use another of those expressions that belong to that period, "We can control nature only by obeying nature." Thus, while the mechanical science seems to have presented a world the meaning of which was all emptied out, with nothing but physical particles and their movements remaining, it has actually enabled us to get far greater control than we ever had before over the conditions under which men live as biological, psychological, and social creatures. Thus, it helped to make the ends of social activity much clearer. It is that point to which I wish to draw your attention especially, a point which we must continually keep in mind. Really the mechanical science of this period has not mechanized human conduct. Rather, it has given freedom. Humanity was never before so free in dealing with its own environment as it has been since the triumphs of mechanical science. The ability to look at the world in terms of congeries of physical particles actually has enabled men to determine their environment.

A simple review of the conditions with reference to health, to disease, shows what has been accomplished in these directions by means of scientific method. As I have already said, the food environment is one of the greatest factors in changes which have taken place in the evolution of living forms. Man has reached the point where he can conceivably control his food environment. He is, of course, the only living form that has reached that stage. Curiously enough, we find small beginnings of it in the society of the ants—the beginnings of cultivation, the planting of mushrooms and other plants in their galleries, the importing and conserving of certain insects which supply them with glucose. This seems like the beginnings of human agriculture. But human society has actually, or may actually, determine what vegetation may grow about it. We cannot change the climate, but we can move about. We can get the products that come from the various climates. We are in a position such as no animal form has been, namely, that of controlling specifically the environment in which we live. From the point of view of a Darwinian evolution the various forms have arisen very largely through the changes that have taken place in the environment, climatic and biologic changes, the conflicts that have arisen among vegetable forms; and all these changes have given rise to new species. There we have the species more or less under the control of the environment. But when we reach the human form, we have one which determines what the environment shall be. It cannot, of course, plant wheat in the Sahara Desert; but it can determine what quantity of wheat shall be produced and where it can be grown most successfully. It can measurably control the flow of its streams. It can, to an amazing degree, determine what are the conditions under which life shall take place. There we reach a certain culmination in the evolutionary process. Other forms are more or less under the control of their environments. But the human form turns about and gets control over its environment.

What has given it that control in the great degree in which it has been accomplished in these last three centuries has been the scientific method, which has found its greatest expression in the so-called "mechanical science." It is the scientific method by which the human form has turned around upon its environment and got control over it, and thus, as I have said, presented a new set of ends which control human conduct, ends which are more universal than those which have previously guided the conduct of the individual and of mankind as a whole—the ends, for example, and the policy of the government, of a group of governments, conceivably of the whole human race. The human race can determine where it will live, what plants and trees shall grow there. It can determine its own population. It can set up a definite ideal as to what human stock shall be bred, what the production shall be. It can definitely set about making its own habitat and living in that habitat in accordance with ends which it can itself work out. That has been the result of the application of scientific method. It does, in a very marked degree, you see, alter the outlook of society. It has tended to make a universal science.

2. SOCIAL SCIENCE AND EVOLUTIONARY METHOD

In the nineteenth century the immediate precursor of modern evolutionism was Auguste Comte, whose *Cours de philosophie positive* [1] (1830–42) fore-shadowed the ideology of the classical evolutionists in several important particulars. Building upon Pascal's analogy between the life of an individual and that of the race, Comte for the first time adopted the use of the comparative method on a large scale, confident that the early states of civilized groups may all be observed among primitive peoples distributed in different parts of the globe. . . . Herbert Spencer was undoubtedly influenced by Comte, but the more significant predecessors of Spencerian evolutionism were Karl Ernst von Baer, the embryologist, Charles Lyell, the geologist, and Thomas Robert Malthus, the political economist. . . . Malthus had formulated in the first edition of his *Essay on Population* (1798) the principle that while the food supply increases in an arithmetical ratio population increases in a geometrical one, resulting in inevitable pressure on the food supply. From this theory Spencer derived the concept of survival of the fittest. Spencer's dependence on Darwin in the broader field of evolution should not be exaggerated. . . . [His] ideas were already developed in definitive form, except in regard to the theory of natural selection, when he became acquainted with Darwin's work. Before Spencer could pursue the main argument of the *Principles of Sociology* (1876–96) or E. B. Tylor that of his *Primitive Culture* (1871) they had to meet the theory of degeneration propounded by the theologians to the effect that primitive cultures represented degenerated remains of once higher civilizations. Spencer countered with the observation that these hypothetical higher civilizations, if granted, must have once developed from more primitive conditions and that the argument of the theologians instead of meeting the problem was merely deferring its solution. . . . In the general exposition of his thesis Spencer held that evolutionary change applies to culture as an integrated whole, but he also traced separately the evolution of the different aspects of culture, such as religious, industrial, military and professional institutions. He omitted discussion of material culture and technology . . . but other evolutionists have filled this gap. The effect of his exposition of the theory of social evolution was magnetic. After brief resistance social theory began to reflect its influence everywhere, especially in Russia, France, England and the United States.

In the search for origins interest had long been centered on the primitive or

[1] [*System of Positive Philosophy.*]

preliterary period in man's development, where chronology was vague and relatively few facts were accurately known. It is in this field that the evolutionists made their contributions. In the domain of social organization the theory of Henry Maine was overthrown by J. J. Bachofen, Swiss classicist, John Ferguson McLennan, Scotch jurist, and Lewis H. Morgan, American anthropologist. Maine had taught the priority of the patriarchal individual family. The evolutionists held that the earliest form of social structure, following upon the primal "undivided horde," was based upon the clan, a unilateral hereditary unit with maternal descent. It was their belief that in the course of historic development this was followed by the gens, a unilateral hereditary unit with paternal descent, and that at the dawn of the historic period the gens ceded its place to the bilateral individual family with patriarchal features. Morgan's argument in support of this scheme was based on a vast array of data collected by him and others in many parts of the world, consisting of relationship systems and associated terminologies which were interpreted as indicating corresponding forms of social organization and especially of marriage. Marriage was represented as having had its beginning in a state of promiscuity—no sexual regulations whatsoever—which reigned in the original horde. After two forms of group marriage, in which certain classes of men and women were regarded as actual or potential husbands and wives, individual marriage emerged. . . .

In religion Spencer and Tylor established the doctrine of animism as a "belief in spiritual beings" (Tylor's minimum definition of religion) derived in the main from dream experiences. Spencer stressed in addition the genetic priority of the human spirit or ghost. He regarded fear as the emotional root of religion, inventing in this connection his famous aphorism: all religion comes from the fear of the dead, all society from fear of the living. In discussing worship he placed ancestor worship at the bottom of the genetic scale. J. G. Frazer taught the priority of magic to religion; F. B. Jevons identified totemism with plant and animal worship and then derived the cultivation of plants and domestication of animals from totemism. . . . In art A. C. Haddon argued that realism, based on the representation of natural creatures and objects, came first; that this was gradually conventionalized, assuming more and more geometrical features, and that finally the original realistic connotations became attached to these geometrical features in the form of symbols.

Similar schemes prevailed with reference to economic conditions and property. Economists like Karl Bücher and popularizers like C. Letourneau taught the doctrine of three stages of economy: hunting, pastoral life and agriculture.

Other forms of the three stages were read into the archaeological record: the ages of stone, bronze and iron. Communal property ownership was regarded as the universal primitive form from which individual ownership became differentiated in later periods. Periods and stages were constructed by writers like J. Kohler and A. Post with reference to legal forms and concepts.

In dealing with these diverse topics the evolutionists assumed a general psychic unity of mankind. . . . The psyche of man, reacting to physical environments similar in their general features, expressed itself in a cultural development which was uniform, gradual and in the opinion of most evolutionists progressive. Uniformity here meant that culture everywhere evolved in essentially similar ways and passed through analogous or identical stages —the so-called parallelism in development. By "gradual" the evolutionists meant that cultural changes were slight and cumulative like the imperceptible gradations of the Darwinian biologists. The cultural changes were held to be progressive in so far as they led to higher forms, a belief which introduced an optimistic note into evolutionist thought for which Spencer was largely responsible.

The mode of procedure adopted by the evolutionists came to be known as the comparative method. An inspection of evolutionary treatises . . . reveals bibliographies of extraordinary length reflecting the evolutionist's practise of scanning innumerable sources for illustrations of stages and substages. The evolutionists admitted that errors and inaccuracies were inevitable in view of the defective nature of much of this source material, but they expressed the complacent faith that the errors would cancel out and that thus the very mass of the data assured the fundamental correctness of the resulting picture.

Associated with the comparative method was the use of the concept of survival, a term introduced by Tylor. The evolutionists believed that as culture changes separate cultural elements are not always wholly obliterated but that some survive in a transformed or attenuated form, such as the games of children, which originally functioned as magical rites, or the complex of ideas and practises associated with the mother's brother which, the evolutionists held, belonged to the stage of maternal descent but were frequently encountered in the succeeding stage of father right. Survivals were utilized by the evolutionists as a proof of their contentions about stages in culture.

The determinism implied in evolutionist thought brought to the fore the problem of origins, particularly of first origins. If development was fixed, origins were not casual, and first origins gained prestige as nuclei pregnant with all that was to follow. The evolutionists became tireless origin hunters. Numerous origins of religion, totemism, the stage, of particular technical devices, the dance, forms of address and etiquette, were invented and discussed with enthusiasm. The idea of evolution brought animation and imagination to the field of social thought. Many welcomed a philosophy of history which stood for broad perspectives, logical coherence and finality; others eagerly reaped the rich harvest of new facts, interesting and exciting in themselves, and accepted without too much probing the curious answers to many particular puzzles, such as the origin of Christmas, marriage or the art of making fire. The alliance of social thought with the older more firmly rooted science of biology brought a sense of security and enhanced prestige.

The triumphal phase of evolutionism was, however, of short duration. With the accumulation of adequate anthropological material the concept of uniformity and of stages was shaken and then collapsed altogether. In social organization, for example, it was shown by Starcke, Westermarck, and anthropologists in the United States that the individual family was the one ubiquitous social unit, the most primitive as well as the most persistent. Telling arguments were advanced to the effect that neither the clan nor the gens had rightful claims to universality, that gentes were but seldom preceded by clans and that the notion of a primal matriarchate, in particular, had no factual basis, inasmuch as the socio-political preeminence of women was exceedingly rare in primitive societies still surviving and no convincing arguments in favor of its previous existence had been advanced by the evolutionists. Eduard Hahn and his followers attacked the dogma of the three stages in economics and succeeded in showing that wherever man was a hunter women gathered wild plants; that a pastoral stage did not necessarily follow hunting for there were agricultural tribes in North America and elsewhere who had never known domestication; that the agricultural stage, finally, required an analytical restatement, since two forms of agriculture were to be distinguished which were very different in their cultural status. These were primitive agriculture without domestication, with the hoe as its only tool and mostly practised by women; and historic agriculture with domestication and the use of the plow, practised by the male, whose labors as tiller of the soil were shared by the domesticated cattle and later the horse. The belief in the universality of primitive communisms was forced to give way before the proofs that certain types of personal property were everywhere individually owned and that among some hunting peoples there existed private territorial ownership. In religion animism and magic have been found to be equally primitive, while ancestor worship is recognized as a feature of more advanced rather than most primitive conditions and totemism has been redefined on the basis of fuller data. In art it has been shown that in a number of instances geometrical art does not arise from realistic art but has independent primitive origins.

Other attacks came from among the evolutionists themselves. . . . Anthropologists . . . were able to show that relatively sudden as well as vast changes, for example in religion, were by no means unknown even in primitive society and that similar revolutions were at least probable in early industry. This theory of cataclysm in social evolution can in no way be derived from the parallel shift in biological theory, which came a generation later.

The evolutionist conception of progress prevailed for a long time, but with accumulation of evidence it was recognized that regression was as common in history as progress and that culture, moreover, seldom advanced in all its parts. The rise of Greek civilization, which culminated in the Periclean age and during which architecture, drama, philosophy, the writing of history and the theory of politics advanced simultaneously, was declared to be unique; partial or one-sided progress was found to be the rule. The notion of progress, furthermore, implied judgments as to what constituted improvements, and no such judgments could be made without standards, which are notoriously subjective. The idea of progress was thus relegated from the domain of fact to that of opinion. . . .

Anthropologists also criticized the evolutionists for treating separate tribes or tribal groups as if their culture had developed in a geographical void. Aware of the inner forces which were shaping culture, the evolutionists neglected the outer forces engendered in intertribal contact. When later anthropologists took cognizance of historico-geographical settings of culture and studied intensively particular tribes, tribal groups and culture areas in relation to their neighbors, unforeseen complexities emerged. The part played by borrowed elements in the building of culture was recognized and evolutionary ideology inevitably appeared as an unjustifiable simplification. When the evolutionists had encountered cultural similarities in different tribes they had unhesitatingly referred these to parallel developments from similar or identical origins. But if diffusion was actual, cultural similarities might also be due to a remote common origin or to direct borrowing among the tribes. . . .

The practise of interpreting cultural similarities as parallel developments was also put in question by the doctrine of convergence. . . . Cultural similarities were shown to have developed or converged in two or more places out of conditions or features originally dissimilar or less similar. Parallelism was no longer the only alternative explanation to diffusion wherever cultural similarities were to be accounted for. . . .

Of all social scientists the historians proved most nearly immune to evolutionism, for they knew the facts. They were accustomed to deal with series of successive events, and as their experience did not tally with evolutionism, they proceeded for the most part to ignore it. Had the evolutionists been historians rather than amateur anthropologists, the classical theory of social evolution would probably not have progressed beyond its early phases.

Chapter IX

SOCIETY AND SCIENCE

༃

I. THE SCIENCE OF MAN AND ITS IMPLICATIONS

OUR MODERN scientific method abstracts from the things which had been philosophically, metaphysically defined, and occupies itself with what is happening. It has brought on what we now call the "event" as the object of observation. We do not observe, as Aristotle observed, to see through the process to what the nature of the object itself is. We observe to see what changes take place, what motions are going on, and at what velocities. That is the character of the observation; and that is also true, of course, in the biological world as far as it has its modern expression in evolution. Observation can be directed toward that which is taking place and can, to that extent, be abstracted from the nature of the thing itself. That is, it can ignore metaphysics. Aristotelian science was bound up with its metaphysics. Our biology, until evolution set it free, was bound up with metaphysics. It could explain species only in terms of creation. But an evolution which explains the development of form is free from such a metaphysical statement. Well then, the point that I am making is that modern science is interested in what happens as distinct from the thing which was supposed to be responsible for the nature of the happening. And when it comes to the statement of the thing, it defines it in terms of the process going on. It is free from metaphysics.

Now, the reflection of this in philosophy appears in positivism. Positivism is the statement of reality in terms of so-called "phenomena." These are the things that happen, that which is going on. Positivism abstracts the process, the event, from the nature of the things that are involved in what is going on. That such a process of knowledge should be possible is, of course, due to the experimental method. This method presents a test by means of which you can consider by themselves what the philosopher calls "phenomena" and still

This chapter consists of material by two different authors. Section 1 is from *Movements of Thought in the Nineteenth Century* (pp. 451–66; Chicago, University of Chicago Press, 1936), by George H. Mead. Section 2, designed especially for the present volume, was written for its first edition by Richard Hofstadter.

standardize your knowledge. These are the two characters of scientific method which put it in such an independent place as over against philosophy: it can abstract from the nature of what is involved in the process of the world; it can in that way free itself from metaphysics in so far as it studies phenomena. The philosopher has no method by means of which he can contest its claims. The experimental method set the scientist free from the philosopher.

The attempt to carry this method into philosophy is found in positivism, which undertakes to deal with phenomena. They are called "phenomena" in the philosophic sense; "facts" in the scientific sense. A fact is something that happens, takes place. There is no problem of a certain "nature" in what is taking place. Put it in philosophical terms, and it is something happening that has a relation to a noumenon that lies back of it. Positivism deals with what is there, what is positive and directly experienced, whose processes the mind can follow. It was Comte who undertook to carry over this method into philosophy. He was by no means free from metaphysical taint, but he is the one who gave the first definite philosophical statement to the more descriptive aspect of science. He was the first one to make the attempt to build up philosophy along the lines of the scientific method.

It follows, of course, that such a method is hypothetical. What one does is to follow a curve, so to speak. On the basis of observation, one assumes or makes the hypothesis that the curve is of a certain character. If it is of that character, then a body moving in such a path would have to be at such and such a point at such and such a time, and one could observe and make sure that the body was at that point in its process. The hypothesis is justified, in so far as that movement of the body is concerned; but there may be something in it that the scientist has not been able to determine. In that case it may later be necessary to reconstruct the hypothesis. That is, the scientific method is essentially hypothetical. It is a method of extrapolation, a way of determining what the result may be and justifying one's theory by means of that result. Of course, one can never make a complete statement of all that is involved in anything that happens. In some sense everything is involved in everything that happens. Consequently, the theory must be hypothetical. The experimental method, as applied by science, always implies that a theory is hypothetical.

What positivism undertook to do was to deal with that which falls within the field of philosophic thought as we deal with scientific data, in terms of scientific method. There we deal with the event as it appears. The event as it appears for the scientist, the observer, is the sensation in consciousness. The scientist takes the event as something by itself. Then he finds out what other events are connected with it, finds what uniformity may be discovered, and forms a hypothesis of the way in which these events will be associated with each other. He tests this hypothesis by future events and establishes a theory, but a theory which still remains hypothetical in character. The assumption here is that knowledge is to be obtained only through the observation of events and the testing of hypotheses as they appear in experience, and that the immediate object of knowledge is the event and the thing. Here we have a philosophy which is positivistic in character. If we cannot treat entities in terms of metaphysical things, we can deal with them at least as far as our experience is concerned. The matter that lies back of the qualities of the chair is something that does not enter into experience. It is not positive knowledge. This is a statement which is of the same general character as that of Hume. As far as his account of what we have in our cognitive experience is concerned, Hume comes back to impressions and ideas and the analysis of them. In thinking of the substance of things, he says we have uniformities which reveal themselves in our experience in terms of habit; and that is what Hume was interested in—the relation of events in experience to the so-called "laws of nature."

In the case of positivism, of the form in which it was espoused by Comte, the interest does not lie primarily in reducing nature and its uniformities to associated ideas. What Comte was interested in was the relation between the events as they take place. He did not bring up the question as to where those events take place, whether in the mind or in the world, whether there is something that answers to them as they take place in the mind. He said here are the events; we call some subjective, some objective. Let us find the uniformity of their happening, not only for an observational science but also for philosophy. Comte was particularly interested in the appearance of this method and its relationship to the formal metaphysical content which should lie behind it. . . .

The type of problem which comes with the work of Galileo, as expressing the experimental method, is essentially one which comes from the method of research science, not from the science of the Encyclopedists, not from the type that we sometimes call "systematic." There are certain fields into which this new method has entered comparatively late. Biology, to go back for a generation or a little more perhaps, took into itself everything that men knew; and anything that they did not know, at the time, could be added to it. There were certain groupings of plants—the genera, the families, and their species and subspecies. There was a principle of organization, a principle which was worked out in the eighteenth century by Linnaeus. Into this system could be introduced any new species that might be found, but the system itself did not carry with it any proof.

That is not a research science. Research science has come into biology only with evolution, for the conception of evolution deals with species not as ultimate metaphysical entities but as something that arises out of conditions. Experience, instead of being of such and such a metaphysical entity, becomes a problem. That is, of course, presented to us in Darwin's great work. What is the origin of species? This question indicates a new line of approach. The earlier concept was that characters and species were given in the creation of the plant or animal. God gave to the plants and animals a certain nature for their preservation. The whole life-history of plants and animals shows the development of this nature. The cataloguing system enables us to give them their characters and place them in a complete science. A scientific problem is itself not a statement that here is the oak, the ox, the tiger. It is rather the question: "Why is the oak there; why is it oak instead of another tree; what is the meaning of this species?"

In what I have been saying, you have a very vivid illustration of the passage from the metaphysical over to what Comte would call the "positivistic state." There are, said Comte, these three stages of development, the theological, the metaphysical, the positivistic. And he said this is true not only of communities but of individuals. A child lives in a world of magical things and persons. He loves things that meet his wishes, and he hates things that hurt him. And then comes the later period when he gives up these magical implications and takes to hard and fixed definitions of things. The objects about him have certain natures. They are not to be looked at from the point of view of a fairy tale. It is a common-sense attitude if you like, but an attitude which in itself is metaphysical in that each thing has a certain nature that distinguishes it from other things. Because of its nature, it has certain qualities; and the child utilizes these qualities. It is the common-sense attitude which all persons of adult years reflect in regard to the objects about them. The natural definition of a chair is that it is something having certain necessary qualities—it has hardness, a certain form, and other qualities—inhering in a certain nature. That metaphysical statement is nothing but the abstract formulation of our attitude toward all things as they exist about us. Then we advance to the positivistic, the scientific, stage as Comte stated it. Such a statement as that which had been given of the nature of the chair is recognized as utterly incomplete. What is there that gives to wood its particular strength? For example, how does it compare with iron or steel? We depart from the metaphysical attitude when we ask: "What happens when we do this, that, and the other thing to the object?" We try to find certain uniformities by means of which we can determine what will happen. We have passed out of a world of fixed things as such and come back to data which we can get in experience. We have to distinguish between what the scientist refers to as "hard facts" and the objects about us. Persons are said to "come up against hard facts." Their theory comes in conflict with a fact. But the fact against which the theory comes in conflict is a happening of some sort; it is a happening which is not the happening that we anticipated from a certain theory. Given a certain theory, we expect certain happenings; and then something else happens. It is the contradiction in experience that is the hard fact of science.

That is the phase that we need to keep in mind in getting the scientific method as it appears in such a sytem as that of Comte. What one is dealing with is a set of events that take place in experience. In those events you find uniformities; they never get a final statement, however. Given the statement, we have a theory; we are then able to determine what the results will be on the basis of that theory. If something else happens, then the theory must be reconstructed. The world is a world of events, of things that are going on. The scientist's attitude is the expression of the positivistic statement that succeeds the medieval statement. This exemplifies the three-stage theory of Comte. As communities and as individuals we pass through three stages —the theological, the metaphysical, and the scientific. From the point of view of philosophy, the importance of the view lies, you see, in the statement of the object of knowledge. Is one considering substance or is one considering events that are taking place, what philosophers would call "phenomena"? Is knowledge occupied with these or with something that these reveal? Is our observation a finding, an isolation, of a certain nature or form that lies back of it all? Or is it occupied with the phenomena themselves? It is a question as to what the function of knowledge is. . . .

The step which positivism represents is that of stating a problem so that it is put in the form of a method rather than of a result. Is the method of science the method of philosophy? Can one make the method of science the method of philosophy? One great, somewhat grandiose effort to solve this problem was made by the Romantic idealists. Hegel, who was most complete in his statement, undertook to show that the method of science and the method of human thought in all its endeavor and the method of the universe were all the same, the method which he represented by his dialectic process. His philosophy was in one sense a philosophy of evolution; but the same process, the same method, the same logic, lay back of physical nature, back of moral effort, back of human history, back of all that science presents.

It was, as I said in other connections, a grandiose undertaking which was a failure. Particularly, it was unable to present the scientific procedure within each field. It could not successfully state the method of research science. This is the problem, then, that is presented in positivism. For positivism metaphysics is past; it is gone. Just as metaphysics was supposed to have wiped out theology, so the positivists were presenting a method which could be immediately applied, and through which we could get rid of metaphysics.

Comte had as vivid an interest in the relation of his philosophy to society and its values as any others of the period. He looked for the forms of a society of the human race whose values should determine the conduct of the individual. But, as far as the process of knowing social values was concerned, it would be the same as in the physical and the biological sciences. He assumed that there could be a study of society which could be undertaken in the same way as the study of the physical sciences. That was the most striking character of his doctrine in its immediate impact. The church had a metaphysical doctrine behind it. And this is no less true in this period of what we may call "political science," the theory of law, of ethics, of education. That is, each of them had essential doctrines. The sovereignty of the state, in the attitude of an English community, is to be found in the individuals that form the republic. Sovereignty was a dogma. It was that in the state which exercised absolute power. And the state had to be conceived of in terms of such metaphysical entity as that. Similarly, the family was a certain definite entity, and the school was a certain definite entity. One argued from the nature of the sovereign, of the family, of the school, what the position of the individual under it must be. In each case the attitude was essentially metaphysical. What Comte presented was the demand for the use of positivistic method in the study of society. He presented sociology as a new field. What I want to emphasize is that we do not think of it as another science. We have economics, education, political science; and here comes sociology, another science covering the same field and yet claiming to be different. It has been, in very recent times, a great question as to whether there was any such thing as sociology. And I have seen theses presented in this university for the degree of Doctor of Philosophy in the field of sociology upon the problem of whether or not there is any such thing as sociology. What is characteristic of Comte's position is his demand that society and social events should be approached in the same fashion that the study of plants and animals and moving bodies are approached. He was breaking away from the metaphysical attitude and presenting another science, that of society. As he conceived of society, it inevitably includes the whole human race; and he thought there could be one science of it. Sociology, then, was the attempt to apply the method of positivism, the method of science, to the field of society, an attempt to displace what was, at that time, an essentially metaphysical approach, one which started off with the definition of the state, with a study of the processes of social changes going on in various institutions. Comte undertook to approach human affairs in the way of the scientist who simply analyzes things into their ultimate elements in a positivistic fashion and then from that finds the laws of their behavior. But there lay in the back of Comte's mind pictures of a medieval period, only he would have substituted society for the pope. He was not freed from that. This other side of Comte's doctrine is one that harks back to the medieval period.

I pointed out that early in the century, during the period of De Bonald and De Maistre, reactionary philosophers sought to go back to the church as the source of all authority, as that which must give an interpretation of life. Their statement, however, was different from the medieval statement. They were particularly impressed with the society of Europe in the twelfth and thirteenth centuries, the period which is best represented by Dante. It was a period in which the world realized itself as a single community, in which everything could be explained by the doctrine of the church. There was no difficulty in the explanation, because this world was so created that man can be moral; and, if he can be moral, it must also be possible for him to be immoral. It is a world in which sin has a legitimate place; and if man sins, the punishment of sin follows. The world at that period was entirely comprehensible from the point of view of the church theology. It included everyone. Anything that happened that was undesirable could be explained by the fact that God was using it to bring about the great good, including the good of man. The Western world was conceived of as a single society. It took in nearly the whole of the human race. It was organized through the church. The church took over the statement that St. Paul gives, you remember, of the church as the body of which Christ was the head. In his concept of a unified society everyone has his place and everything can be explained from the point of view of the theory of the church. It was to that conception of a society which was a world society, an organic society, and a society which answered to the immediate impulse of the individual that these philosophers, De Bonald and De Maistre, went back.

Comte was never influenced by this account. His positions freed him from the dogma of the church, but he still looked to such a picture of the whole society of man as representing the idea that should be realized. The curious thing from our standpoint is that he should have copied to such an extent the characters of the church. His idea, too, was that society should be an organic whole. It must then have some organized value. What Comte presents, instead of welfare by the church, is the welfare of the community as a whole. This community as a whole comes to take the place of the glory of God, which, as spoken of by the church, is the end of all existence. For the positivist it is not the glory of God but the good of mankind that is the supreme value. That is the supreme value in terms of which everything should be stated. This point of view is stated in less emotional form in the utilitarianism in England during the same period. Bentham and the Mills are, in a sense, companion figures to Comte. Their idea of the ideal society is one which achieves the greatest good of the greatest number. This welfare of the community transcends the good of any particular individual. This is something all should see, and man's attitude toward it should be a religious attitude. This should be recognized as the supreme value that determines all others. And Comte recognized that an emotional attitude was essential.

John Stuart Mill said that everyone finds himself and his conduct constantly influenced by others. Each can retain his own pleasure by recognizing others in the pursuit of their pleasure. The individual feels continually the presence of the community about him forcing him to recognize the interest of others. It seems a skeptical account which Mill gives the origin of virtue. Comte would put up the good of the community itself through an emotional expression which should be essentially religious in its character. That is, men should actually worship the Supreme Being in the form of society. Society as an organized whole, as that which is responsible for the individual, should be worshiped; and on this basis Comte undertook to set up a positivistic religion. Now, this religion of positivism had some vogue among the followers of Comte. There was a devoted group of this sort to be found in England. It never attained any size. A wag, referring to a dissension among them, said of the sessions, "They came to church in one cab and left in two." It never became a widespread religious movement, but the undertaking to set up such a religion which should find the highest value in society and fuse that into a unity which could be worshiped was characteristic of Comte. He thought and looked for a society that could be organized in the same fashion as medieval society had been by the church. And he attempted to work out in some detail how this sort of ordering of society would take place. He did not try to substitute the value of society itself for the Deity, but tried to take over the religious attitude toward the Deity into the religious attitude of members of the community toward society itself.

This phase of Comte's sociology was not a lasting one. What was of importance was his emphasis on the dependence of the individual on society, his sense of the organic character of society as responsible for the nature of the individual. This is what Comte put into a scientific form. It had already found its theological statement, as I have said, in Paul's account of the relation of men in the church to parts of the body and to the church as the whole. That is, he conceived of the individual as determined by society as an organism, just as there are different organs which must be conceived of as dependent on the organism as a whole. You cannot take the eye as a separate reality by itself. It has meaning only in its relationship to the whole organism of which it is a part. So you must understand an individual in a society. Instead of thinking of society made up of different entities, Comte thought of it in terms of a union of all which was an expression of a certain social nature which determined the character of the individual. There are two characteristics of Comte: first, his recognition that society as such is a subject for study; and second, his conviction that we must advance from the study of society to the individual rather than from the individual to society.

2. THE SOCIAL IMPACT OF DARWINISM

During the Middle Ages when most intellectual activity was religious in nature, social and philosophic thought was necessarily based upon Christian theology. During the Renaissance, and especially after the eighteenth-century Enlightenment, thought became more and more secular. Social thinkers, however, did not change their habit of looking beyond the sphere of society itself for their guiding principles. In place of religion, natural science became the external basis of method and authority. During the eighteenth century and the early decades of the nineteenth, the system of Newton was the source of dominant modes of thought. Under the reign of "natural law" man as well as the universe was interpreted in concepts derived from physics and mathematics. The Newtonian epoch bequeathed to the Darwinian epoch an image of "Nature" as a conclusive area of authority, and after Darwin published *The Origin of Species* in 1859, patterns of social thinking were re-formed around the concepts of evolutionary biology. Eighteenth-century thought had been dominated by the machine; latter nineteenth-century thought was dominated by the living organism. The eighteenth-century philosophical mind had been concerned with a system of order; the nineteenth-century mind was concerned with a pattern of growth. The liberal philosophers of the Enlightenment had expected progress to come through the power of reason to reorganize society. Most thinkers of the nineteenth century expected that progress would come of itself through gradual change at a geologically slow tempo; and many of them also believed that it would come through a process of struggle resulting in elimination of unfit individuals, classes, races, or nations.

In an age which takes evolution so much for granted it is hard to realize what a tremendous impact Darwin's theory of natural selection had upon his contemporaries. Within a dozen years after *The Origin of Species,* the idea of evolution had been adapted to almost every field of social and philosophical inquiry. It is important, however, to remember that Darwin's work was not so much the primary source of evolutionary thinking as its great climactic achievement. Other men, notably Hegel, Marx, Comte, and Spencer had already begun the task of applying evolutionary and developmental concepts to history and to human institutions; still others, like Taine and Buckle, shared with Spencer the use of the idea of environmental influences as a leading principle. Ideas of persistent change, development through stages, and conflict as a source of growth or progress were already familiar in social philosophy, as were ideas of competitive struggle and the fight for survival in political economy. The general idea of organic change, as well as the particular biological concept of natural selection and the struggle for existence, was in the air; there is less question how vital thinkers and scholars came to be affected by it as how they could have avoided it.

Even as a contribution to biology Darwinism was no sudden production of a single genius. A long tradition of speculative evolutionism preceded Darwin, reaching back to some of the philosophers of ancient Greece and coming down to such eighteenth and early nineteenth-century men as Buffon, Goethe, Cuvier, and Geoffroy St. Hilaire. In 1802 the Chevalier de Lamarck had worked out a theory of animal evolution generally similar to natural selection. Lamarck had believed, however, as Darwin did not, that the adaptation of organisms to environment was *purposive;* he also thought that the transmission to offspring of certain traits acquired by parents during their lives was an essential part of evolutionary change. Darwin was content to assume that the adaptation of animals was *accidental* rather than the result of effort, and he did not rely upon the notion of the inheritance of acquired characteristics; but in other respects the resemblance between Lamarck's ideas and Darwin's was considerable.

Among other prophets of evolution was Darwin's grandfather, Erasmus Darwin, who had written in 1794 a philosophical essay, *Zoonomia,* in which he suggested that all warm-blooded animals might have arisen from "one living filament." The great chronological vistas of the geological past had been revealed by the work of such modern geologists as Sir Charles Lyell, whose *Principles of Geology* (1830) helped to clear the ground for the evolutionary hypothesis. The achievement of Karl Ernst von Baer in embryology was also suggestive; he had called attention to the similarity of embryonic development in lower and higher animals, and had set forth the principle that "the more dissimilar two animal forms are, the further we have to go back in evolutional history to find an agreement." Darwin learned, as the historical sketch of evolutionary thought in the second and subsequent editions of *The Origin of Species* shows, that his particular evolutionary theory, natural selection, had been very "distinctly recognised" in 1813 by an American, Dr. W. C. Wells and expounded in 1831 by Patrick Matthew in a work on trees which, said Darwin, gave "precisely the same view on the origin of species as that . . . propounded by Mr. Wallace and myself." Natural selection was almost anticipated by Herbert Spencer in 1852. Alfred Russel Wallace came simultaneously to Darwin's conclusions, and the two men concurrently published the first statements of the theory of natural selection in 1858.

Before Darwin and Wallace, a great many men had believed that an evolutionary process must be inferred to account for the various forms of plant and animal life. What was needed was a plausible explanation of *how* new species might originate, and a really formidable display of evidence for the evolutionary hypothesis itself. Darwin filled both needs in *The Origin of Species;* the first with his exposition of the theory of natural selection, the second with an overpowering array of evidence for evolution from geology, from the geographical distribution of plant and animal forms, and from morphology and embryology.

Darwin's position as official naturalist of the *Beagle* on its expedition to South America and the Pacific in 1831–36 had started him reflecting on the distribution of plants and animals over the earth and the means by which they could have been modified. He was also much interested in the breeding of domestic animals and plants; indeed, Darwinism might have been impossible without the late eighteenth and early nineteenth-century revolution in agricultural methods. Darwin saw in selection "the keystone to man's success," but it puzzled him how there could be a process of selection in nature, unguided by the hand of man. It was at this point, in October, 1838, as he later recalled, that "I happened to read for amusement 'Malthus on Population,' and being well prepared to appreciate the struggle for existence which everywhere goes on from long-continued observation of the habits of animals and plants, it at once struck me that under these circumstances favorable variations would tend to be preserved and unfavorable ones to be destroyed.

The result of this would be the formation of new species." The concept ripened in Darwin's mind for almost twenty years before he published the work whose full title foreshadows so much of the world's intellectual development for fifty years afterwards—*On the Origin of Species by Means of Natural Selection; or, The Preservation of Favored Races in the Struggle for Life.* Twelve years later Darwin published a study of human origins, *The Descent of Man.*

The structure of Darwin's theory of natural selection is simple. The *ratio of increase* among plants and animals is so high that the forms of life are constantly pressing upon limited means of subsistence: "more individuals are produced than can possibly survive." Within each species there is always some spontaneous *variation;* the forms are not absolutely identical. Those plants or animals whose variations are useful in adapting to the environment are more likely to survive, and to transmit the favorable variations to subsequent generations through *inheritance.* The *gradual accumulation of minute variations over a very long period of time* will cause a progressive divergence from the original form, resulting in the extinction of less improved forms and the *emergence of new species.*

This chapter is primarily concerned with the impact of Darwinism on areas of thought other than natural science itself, but it is well to remember that the primary significance of natural selection is in its contribution to biology. It is not necessary here to give a detailed account of developments in biology since Darwin, but it may be desirable to point out that the structure of natural selection has not been left intact. Darwin, it will be noted, was content to assume variations as an observable fact; he did not know what caused variation and had no way of accounting for it. Subsequent biological research has centered more and more upon the facts of variation and inheritance, and biology has shown an increasing tendency to go into the laboratory, to substitute experimentation for observation, classification, and speculation, which were the dominant methods of Darwin's time. The application of mathematical thought to the facts of inheritance, a work which was begun profitably by the monk Gregor Mendel in the 1860s but which went unnoticed for a generation, is outstanding here. But the greatest single modification of natural selection is associated with the name of Hugo de Vries. De Vries found minute variations accumulating over a long period of time inadequate to account for the emergence of new species. Slight variations of this kind are not hereditary and are not significant enough to be of use. But there are actually very drastic variations in forms, when it seems, as De Vries put it,

as though nature has exploded; these sharp deviations, or mutants, De Vries concluded in 1901, are the variations of real significance to evolution.

To the popular mind the most startling implication of Darwin's work lay in its challenge to "special creation," to the Biblical account of man, and to standard "evidences of Christianity." In time, liberal theologians and religious scientists were able to quiet the public with plausible reconciliations of evolution and religion; the complex Darwinian view of nature, they argued, provided the world with a grander conception of the Creator than had ever been entertained before. To serious workers in biology and the sciences of man, however, Darwinism gave fruitful leading ideas and a new stimulus to work. As Thomas Henry Huxley later recalled: "We wanted not to pin our faith to . . . speculation, but to get hold of clear and definite conceptions, which could be brought face to face with facts and have their validity tested. The *Origin* provided us with the working hypothesis we sought."

Darwinism supplied the vital link between man and the rest of nature. It spurred a new quest for the origins of things, a new emphasis on the genetic method and on laborious classification and comparison. It stimulated research in heredity, the hunt for fossils, the measurement of traits, the construction of patterns of evolutionary development. In many areas in which men had previously speculated they now experimented and measured, because they had meaningful concepts by which experimentation and measurement might be guided. In 1909, Ernst Haeckel, a naïve German prophet of *Darwinismus* exulted: "We are now fairly agreed on a monistic conception of nature that regards the whole universe, including man, as a wonderful unity, governed by unalterable and eternal laws."

But in order to understand the full impact of Darwin's work on scientific and philosophical thought, it is necessary to recall the earlier tradition that he was subverting. Previous speculation had looked upon anything that was fixed, final, permanent, as somehow superior to that which changed and passed away. Nature had been considered as a progressive realization of purpose. The end of each form was resident in it from the very beginning, and nothing could be got out of it that did not somehow already exist in the form of an archetypal plan or design. For example, an acorn, when it is planted, grows into an oak. The process is repeated again and again, but the end product, the mature tree, is a thing which somehow always existed in potentiality in the acorn. What was significant was not the origin of both oaks and acorns, but rather the repetitive realization of the final term, the providential destiny of the acorn to become an oak. This was the view of Aristotle and of the scholastics. The forms of life might be arranged in a hierarchy, with man at the pinnacle, but no one would imagine that this represented a chronological, evolutionary sequence; it was rather a sequence of significance or of moral order.

The long advance of science represented by the names of Copernicus, Galileo, Kepler, and Newton had somewhat shaken this view, but had presented no fundamental challenge to it. The emphasis in Newtonian mechanics had been not on change but on motion—on physical processes which continually repeated themselves, in roughly the same way as acorns repeatedly grew into oaks. Copernicus and Galileo had said only that the earth moves. When Darwin showed that species themselves "move," he completed the destruction of the old view. Motion had already been made central in philosophical thought; here was a more sweeping concept: changes in systems of motion, the origination of the things that moved. The old worship of the fixed and permanent gave way to a new investigation of change. The old preoccupation with destiny or final purpose gave way to an equally intense preoccupation with origins.

Darwin's legacy to other thinkers may be considered in two parts: first, his method, and second, his vision of nature. The *method* he had used was to arrange and compare a series of forms, to infer from his data a series of sequences, and to advance a naturalistic causal explanation of these sequences in terms of variation, adaptation, and inheritance. The *vision of life and of nature* that he had set forth was one of a universal battlefield ("the war of nature . . . famine and death"), in which sheer adaptability was at a premium, and in which the higher forms of life were produced at the cost of crushing endless numbers of living individuals over a long and very gradual developmental sequence. "There is grandeur in this view of life," he wrote in the closing lines of *The Origin of Species,* and many agreed. In seventeenth-century England, Thomas Hobbes had also thought that the natural condition of man was universal warfare, but he had so shrunk from this conception that he urged men to accept almost any kind of political state, no matter how tyrannical, that could reduce this chaos to order. After Darwin, the order was in the chaos; there was a tendency to accept the state of natural warfare as an ultimately beneficent thing, as the only source of progress.

Neither a philosopher nor a sociologist, Darwin modestly refrained from trying to serve as arbiter over the use of his concepts in fields other than biology. The philosopher, the systematizer, the sociologist, the propagandist of evolution in other fields was Herbert Spencer. Spencer cannot be called a Darwinian at all, not only because his views had taken form before Darwin's work was published but also because his version of evolution drew heavily upon Lamarck's idea of the inheritance of acquired characteristics. And yet in assessing the spread of the evolutionary idea, it is Spencer who must receive most consideration. Spencer was the man whose works everyone was expected to know, and even those who profoundly disagreed with him often formed their ideas around their deviations from him.

Although in his own day Spencer was a tremendous influence, a far greater one in the United States than in his native England, by the time of his death in 1903 he had gone so completely out of vogue that the twentieth century has underrated him almost as much as his contemporaries overrated him. As a spokesman of science he had to compete, in England, with such luminaries as Darwin himself, Huxley, Tyndall, Galton, and above all with the well-established Utilitarian tradition and the influence of John Stuart Mill. He was too much the amateur in science to impress the scientists, too much the amateur in philosophy to leave an indelible mark on its technical development. It was his custom to carry with him a pair of ear muffs to don when conversation bored him, and so retire to his own speculations. This is symbolic of the insularity that he somehow managed to preserve. Although he read widely for facts, he refused to finish the works of thinkers with whom he disagreed. He was constantly rediscovering familiar ideas as though they were original with himself. He presumed to write a work called *The Principles of Biology* although it is doubtful that he ever entered a laboratory, and he wrote extensively about primitive peoples that no one on earth could have persuaded him to live among and study at first hand. A hypochondriac and a dyspeptic bachelor, he wrote with confidence about the survival of the fittest; he attacked public charities, but became for a while thoroughly dependent upon private subsidies for the completion of his ambitious work—which, with no sense of the irony in the name, he called the *Synthetic Philosophy*. In the main an unattractive personality, he nevertheless exemplified a magnificent dedication to an intellectual enterprise. His contribution to the development of sociology as a discipline—best represented, perhaps, by his excellent work, *The Study of Sociology*—is far from negligible. An almost malign talent for self-contradiction pursued him, however. *The Study of Sociology* laboriously refuted every argument against the possibility of a science of society—and then insisted that the single lesson of this new science was that man could not control his social environment but must let it alone.

A child of nonconformist parents living in a country with an Established

Church, Spencer early contracted a deep suspicion of all state authority. This bias was strengthened by the ardent *laissez-faire* ideas he absorbed while subeditor of the *Economist,* a leading journal of English liberal economics. In the 1850s when he loosed his mind upon scientific and philosophical speculations, five sources gave him his leading notions. From the work of Lyell in geology he took the conception of gradual development over long periods of time. From Lamarck he took the conception of biological evolution, and the idea of the inheritance of acquired characteristics. From von Baer's embryological principle that development or growth is a process of individuation he drew the universal conclusion that the law of development in every sphere of existence is from the homogeneous to the heterogeneous. From thermodynamics (Spencer had also been an engineer) he took the principle of the conservation of energy, a keystone in his system. From reading Malthus he, too, was led to think of the consequences of the pressure of population for the theory of development. In 1852 he coined the phrase "survival of the fittest," and outlined a theory of human progress based upon the survival of the well-adapted. Only his failure to extend the principle to the rest of the animal and vegetable world prevented him from taking an equal place with Darwin and Wallace as a pioneer in the theory of natural selection.

Spencer undertook to unite in one philosophical system both the ideas of evolution and the principle ideas of thermodynamics. The principle of the conservation of energy (which Spencer called "the persistence of force"), a product of physical research in the early decades of the century, was the starting point of his deductive system. Putting the persistence of force together with von Baer's "law," Spencer concluded that since force must act with differential effects upon everything in the universe, everything must have a tendency to differentiate. The fundamental law of the universe, then, is the "instability of the homogeneous." Spencer defined evolution—in words that rumbled impressively through the minds of countless readers—as "an integration of matter and concomitant dissipation of motion; during which the matter passes from an indefinite, incoherent homogeneity to a definite, coherent, heterogeneity; and during which the retained motion undergoes a parallel transformation." The development of the earth from a nebulous mass, the evolution of complex animals from simple ones, the development of the embryo, the history of the human mentality, the progress of human societies, the development of the arts—all these things could be subsumed under this grand generalization.

Evolution would reach its terminus in a state of equilibrium, Spencer believed, since it cannot go on forever in the direction of increasing heterogeneity.

Dissolution, disintegration follow the stage of "equilibration"; an organism dies and decays. But it is not necessary that a society decay; on the contrary, society will pass into a state of permanent equilibrium and complete ethical adjustment. For human society "evolution can end only in the establishment of the greatest perfection and the most complete happiness."

Group struggle, Spencer believed, had formerly been indispensable to social evolution, since it stimulated the earliest forms of social cooperation and made possible the consolidation of small social groups into large ones. "Not simply do we see," he wrote in Principles of Sociology, "that in the competition among individuals of the same kind, survival of the fittest has from the beginning furthered the production of a higher type; but we see that to the unceasing warfare between species is mainly due both growth and organization. Without universal conflict there would have been no development of the active powers." The universal antagonism under which man had lived had caused untold suffering, but without it "the world would still have been inhabited only by men of feeble types sheltering in caves and living on wild food." Under modern capitalism, however, the military state has been replaced by an industrial form of society, the regime of status by a regime of contract. Since industrialism is predominantly peaceful and cooperative, requiring for its progress security of life and property, it conduces to the selection of a pacific human type. The discipline of group conflict has served its purpose. "From war has been gained all that it had to give."

Spencer did not believe that the value of strife in the economic field had undergone similar atrophy. Here competition remained the dynamism of progress. While the industrial order introduced cooperation, it was of a limited sort, and must remain voluntary. As Gladstonian liberalism advanced in England, Spencer grew increasingly stubborn in his opposition to state action. Socialism, he argued, would be more akin to the military than the industrial state. In a book of essays, *The Man versus the State,* he referred to socialism as "the coming slavery," and ridiculed "the current assumption . . . that there should be no suffering, and that society is to blame for that which exists." The truth was that individuals, through their misconduct, were responsible for their own suffering; the way to discourage misconduct was to allow the suffering to have its chastening effect. In this respect, the Spencerean outlook embraced an atomistic individualism: society was more a loose aggregate of individuals than an organization; the quality of a society was determined by the average moral quality of the individuals that composed it; the way to improve the society was not to improve or heighten its organization, but simply to improve the quality of its constituent parts; that

could be done only by letting the poorest ones die out while the better survived and passed their qualities on to subsequent generations. Let the process
alone long enough, and perfection would ultimately result.

Side by side with this individualism, Spencer advanced the theory that a
society is like an organism—for a society, he said, "grows and is not made."
Readers of Spencer were thus confronted with the idea of an organism whose
parts are in competition with each other and which permit each other to
wither and die, an organism which must not allow itself to be centrally controlled or directed. That this organismic theory seemed logically to require a
centralized state (a central brain) and could easily be used to justify socialism
did not escape Huxley, who criticized Spencer in a cogent and widely read
essay; nor has it escaped Spencer's critics ever since.

Spencer's use of evolution and the struggle for existence to justify a harsh
and fundamentally amoral theory of individualism was not a personal idio-
syncrasy, but rather a symptom of the way in which men were using the Darwinian vision of nature. Darwinism was popularized in a period when industrialism was demanding a fearful human price. Its evils had not yet been
much mitigated by "welfare capitalism," by trade unionism, or by effectual
movements of humanitarianism and reform. A fierce struggle, if not for
existence at least for supremacy, was actually being waged. In a certain sense
Darwinism was a projection of the most brutal realities of Western capitalism
into the scheme of nature. It was not an accident that Darwin, Wallace, and
Spencer all took the gloomy reflections of Malthus as a starting point for their
evolutionary theories. Darwin spoke of natural selection as "the doctrine of
Malthus applied with manifold force to the whole animal and vegetable
kingdoms." It is significant, too, that political economy was the social science
whose practitioners seemed to feel that they had least to take from Darwinism; they might well have argued that Darwinism had taken its cue from
economics and that they had long possessed its central truths. Classical liberalism in political economy had already been operating with a doctrine of natural law and a theory of competition and survival. Industry was a struggle of
individuals and enterprises for survival; the most efficient competitors won;
the least efficient died out, and it was well that they did so, for the quest for
success was the motive power of progress, failure the necessary penalty for
incapacity or lack of exertion. "It is a good thing," the French economist
Dunoyer had said long before Darwin, in his *De la liberté du travail* [1] (1845),
"to have a number of inferior places in a society to which families that conduct

---

[1] *On the Freedom of Labor.*

themselves badly are liable to fall, from which they can rise only by dint of good behavior. Want is just such a hell." As early as 1850, Spencer, in his *Social Statics,* an ethical application of *laissez-faire* theory, had argued that the poor were unfit to survive and should be eliminated. "The whole effort of nature is to get rid of such, to clear the world of them, and make room for better." Defects in either mental or physical constitution should properly be penalized by extinction. "If they are not sufficiently complete to live, they die, and it is best they should die." Accordingly, Spencer opposed all devices which would help to prop up weakness and enable it to survive—including such things as free education, poor laws, and state support of public health. "Every restriction of competition is an evil," declared John Stuart Mill, and "every extension of it is always an ultimate good." And after Mill, Francis A. Walker, an influential American economist, declared in 1890: "I must deem any man very shallow in his observation of the facts of life who fails to discern in competition the force to which it is mainly due that mankind have risen from stage to stage in intellectual, moral, and physical power."

Darwinism was used, then, to confirm with the authority of natural science a competitive vision of life that in political economy had already taken firm hold on the industrial mind. The struggle for existence was natural and inevitable; to try to avoid it was useless, indeed harmful, since the struggle was the source of human progress. Reformers' efforts to use the state to interfere with the effect of the struggle on the weak were therefore misguided. To criticize the victorious competitors was to dissent from the processes of nature.

This was a doctrine which the beneficiaries of the system could embrace with enthusiasm. Competition, said Andrew Carnegie, may be hard for the individual but it is "best for the race, because it insures the survival of the fittest in every department." "The growth of a large business is merely a survival of the fittest," said John D. Rockefeller Jr., in a Sunday School lecture. And these pronouncements were echoed by professional economists. "The millionaires," declared William Graham Sumner, "are a product of natural selection, acting on the whole body of men to pick out those who can meet the requirement of certain work to be done." In another essay he declared: "If we do not like the survival of the fittest, we have only one possible alternative, and that is the survival of the unfittest. The former is the law of civilization; the latter is the law of anti-civilization."

Another welcome conservative argument was based upon the idea of gradual change. It was impossible, declared Spencer, Sumner, and their followers, to undertake any reconstruction of society. Society was a sort of superorganism of the most enormous complexity, and the teaching of social science must be that men could not master the intricacies of this organism sufficiently to doctor it by themselves but must rely upon the slow curative powers of nature for amelioration. Sumner wrote, "The great stream of time and earthly things will sweep on just the same in spite of us. . . . That is why it is the greatest folly of which a man can be capable to sit down with a slate and pencil to plan out a new social world." Here the argument on behalf of tradition, gradual change, and the "wisdom of the species" which Burke had used at the end of the eighteenth century was supplemented with a biological sanction. Since Condorcet, the belief in progress had been a doctrine more favored by radicals than conservatives, but men like Spencer successfully appropriated it to the uses of political conservatism. Spencer encouraged the widespread assumption that evolution necessarily meant progress—but to him and his followers it meant progress by the methods of biology and in the tempo of geology. When Henry George heard E. L. Youmans, a leading American evolutionist, declaim against the vices of New York City and asked Youmans what he proposed to do about it, this admirer of Spencer answered: "You and I can do nothing at all. . . . We can only wait for evolution. Perhaps in four or five thousand years evolution may have carried men beyond this state of things."

Darwinism seemed also to strike at the ideal of equality. As Ernst Haeckel wrote, the principle of selection was "as far as possible from democratic; on the contrary, it is aristocratic in the strictest sense of the word." In natural selection the *variations* of organisms were at a premium; without variation there could be nothing to select from and hence no progress. This suggested that all talk of social equality was futile and retrogressive; it is the existence of superior variations and the transmission of these to future generations that makes for progress.

Human genetics received a great impetus from natural selection, and its implications, as it developed in England under the leadership of Darwin's cousin, Sir Francis Galton, also tended to reinforce the defense of the competitive order and to deny the need for social reform. The way to improve the breed, said Galton, who coined the word "eugenics," was to prevent the propagation of the unfit and encourage the fit. It was Galton's belief that "the men who achieve eminence, and those who are naturally capable are, to a large extent identical." In his *Hereditary Genius* (1869) he argued that an able man could not be repressed by environmental discouragement nor a mediocrity raised by social advantages. Those who enjoyed eminence did so because of their intrinsic superiority, those who failed to rise failed because they were unable. Plainly if these conclusions were true, efforts to improve

the condition of the masses through educational and other institutional devices were futile, and should be abandoned in favor of a stockbreeding view
of human life.

Nations, like individuals, were now more than ever graded in an order
of superiority. The Frenchman G. Vacher Lapouge and the German Alfred
O. Ammon tried to use selectionist ideas in social theory. They found that
dolichocephalic "Aryan" "racial" types were the superiors among mankind,
but both believed that the processes of social selection were breeding the inferior types in greater number. Gustav LeBon, a French physician turned
social psychologist, likewise graded the races in a hierarchy, as did Clémence
Royer, Darwin's French translator. LeBon gave his approval to the political
traditions of the Anglo-Saxon and Teutonic peoples as superior.

While in England and America particularly, Darwinism was fused with
economic liberalism to form a doctrine of ruthless competition and *laissez-
faire*, it was put to use in all countries to justify nationalism, imperialism,
racialism, and militarism. Where Darwinians who advocated economic individualism emphasized the struggle between individuals, the militarists,
racists, and nationalists emphasized the struggle between races or groups.
The year of *The Origin of Species* was the year of the Italian war of national
liberation; *The Descent of Man* appeared the year after the Prussian armies
crushed the French. As nationalism in Europe passed from an urge for cultural liberation to a system of mutual fear, hatred, and frustration, as the
imperial colonization of the world once again accelerated, the Darwinian
vision of the battlefield of nature became increasingly plausible and increasingly germane. Army officers, thrust into the realm of politics as lobbyists for
greater striking power, could refurbish their arguments with Darwinian
metaphors. A new literature of group struggle arose. Before Darwin, men
had, of course, believed in racial or national superiority; but now they were
tempted to make a principle of it.

Perhaps the first of the imperial Darwinists was Walter Bagehot, who discussed the pattern of national progress in his *Physics and Politics* (1872) and
observed that "those nations which are strongest tend to prevail, and in certain marked peculiarities the strongest are the best." The historian J. A.
Froude saw the victory of Protestant England over Catholic Spain and the
domination of England over Ireland as exemplifications of the principle, and
concluded that "the superior part has a natural right to govern, the inferior
part has a right to be governed." Nicholas Danilevski, a Russian Pan-Slavist
who later wrote a critical book on Darwinism, found that each group of people
—or race—is like a species, and it seems hardly necessary to add that he found

the Slavs a superior "race." Social Darwinian interpretations became prominent after the Franco-Prussian War among both victor and vanquished. Even Ernest Renan referred to war in 1871 as "one of the conditions of progress, the cut of the whip which prevents a country from going to sleep." Ludwig Gumplowicz, a Polish professor of law, began to elaborate a sociological theory based upon a series of unremitting struggles between racial groups, national states, and social classes. Gustav Ratzenhofer, an Austrian field marshal, elaborated a theory of society based upon self-assertion, the mutual hostility of all men. This hostility, he argued, could be submerged only in war or great projects of cooperative labor. Culture and commerce weakened a social structure, but struggle and war would consolidate it. "War," wrote the victorious Marshal von Moltke, "is an element of the order of the world established by God. . . . Without war the world would stagnate and lose itself in materialism."

In the United States, John Fiske, James K. Hosmer, Albert J. Beveridge, and Josiah Strong predicted the world-wide supremacy of the Anglo-Saxon peoples, John W. Burgess declared that the Teutonic nations were best fitted to exercise the political leadership of the world, Brooks Adams warned that the nations were engaged in "a war to the death," and Theodore Roosevelt predicted that if the American people ceased to live the strenuous life and lost "the great fighting masterful virtues," then "the bolder and stronger peoples will pass us by, and win for themselves the domination of the world." In England, Karl Pearson, who succeeded Galton in the leadership of the eugenics movement, urged that it was to the interest of a vigorous race to be "kept up to a high pitch of external efficiency by contest, chiefly by way of war with inferior races, and with equal races by the struggle for trade routes and for the sources of raw material and of food supply. This is the natural history view of mankind." There was only one way in which a high state of civilization had been produced, "namely the struggle of race with race, and the survival of the physically and mentally fitter race." In Germany, General von Bernhardi, who wrote a classic militarist document, *Germany and the Next War* (1911), argued that since "war depends on biological laws . . . every attempt to exclude it from international relations must be demonstrably untenable."

These quotations illustrate a militant temper that was widespread, *though far from universal,* among Western intellectuals in the latter half of the nineteenth century. Darwinism became a mainstay of the philosophers of material power, whose exponents felt that they had Darwin to thank for liberating their minds from old superstitions and moral sanctions and setting them free to soar in the clear air of realism. Still later generations, finding in the power philosophies of the period only a prelude to war and authoritarianism and in the extreme individualist philosophy only an apology for a ruthless and archaic competitive order, have condemned the entire influence of "naturalism" in social thinking. There are two schools of thought concerning the grounds upon which this condemnation is to rest. The first insists that to base a superior system of ethics upon *any* naturalist philosophy is impossible and concludes that it is necessary to turn from nature to other, supernatural sanctions. The second argues that it was not naturalism in itself but merely a naïve and rather mechanical application of biological concepts to the social and moral realm that was at fault; this school argues that human misbehavior did not begin in 1859, and calls not for an abandonment of science but greater precision in science.

Was Darwin personally responsible for the misuse of his ideas? Certainly there were passages in his works that gave encouragement to the apostles of force. In a sequence of *The Descent of Man* that was devoted to the workings of natural selection among civilized nations, he remarked that civilized men "do our utmost to check the process of elimination; we build asylums for the imbecile, the maimed, and the sick; we institute poor-laws; and our medical men exert their utmost skill to save the life of every one to the last moment. . . . Thus the weak members of civilised society propagate their kind. No one who has attended to the breeding of domestic animals will doubt that this must be highly injurious to the race of man."

Those who looked in other parts of *The Descent of Man* could find an altogether different emphasis. Darwin believed that man had always been a social animal, that even at a very remote period he had practiced division of labor and the exchange of goods. Further, his dominion among the animals was due not to physical force, but to "his intellectual faculties, his social habits." So far as the group was concerned, there was value in sympathy: "Selfish and contentious people will not cohere, and without coherence nothing can be effected." "Those communities which included the greatest number of the most sympathetic members would flourish best, and rear the greatest number of offspring." The struggle between races, Darwin once wrote to Wallace, depended "entirely upon intellectual and moral qualities," rather than physical qualities. Among civilized nations, he asserted in *The Descent of Man,* the continuation of progress does not hang primarily upon natural selection, "for such nations do not supplant and exterminate one another as do savage tribes." The preeminence of the civilized over the barbarous nations rests upon technical achievements which are the products of intellect. He suggested that the decline of the Greek states was probably due in part to "a want of coherence among the many small states." There is evidence in a letter to Lyell that he believed institutional practices more important than biological factors in maintaining a high state of civilization. On Lamarckian assumptions, in which a cumulative development of higher qualities seemed inevitable, he explained, a high state of civilization, once achieved, could not be lost; but under his own view that progress depends "upon the conditions," the decline of such a great society as that of the Greeks was intelligible. "For in a state of anarchy, or despotism, or bad government, or after an irruption of barbarians, force, strength, or ferocity, and not intellect, would be apt to gain the day." Darwin spent much time trying to establish a foundation in biological utility for the "moral sense," and it probably disconcerted him to find that he had opened an intellectual Pandora's box. In one of his letters to Lyell he expressed surprise that an English newspaper had accused him of proving that might is right, "and therefore that Napoleon is right, and every cheating tradesman is also right."

Perhaps the fairest summation would say that Darwin was ambiguous as to the social implications of his ideas. There is a passage in *The Origin of Species* in which he gives a series of meanings of the term "struggle for existence," including in it the "reaction of protection and preservation." This passage contains the sentence: "In these several senses, *which pass into each other,* I use for convenience sake the general term of 'Struggle for Existence.'" Again: "I use this term in a large and metaphorical sense including dependence of one being on another. . . ." Darwin was a careful and masterful collector of data, and he had a great insight with which to organize it, but philosophical precision was not one of his strong points, and one can only agree with his confession that he was "a very poor explainer."

Darwinism, in sum, offered texts for those who wished to justify force, militarism, self-assertion, and ruthless individualism; it also provided texts for the advocates of social solidarity, and the proponents of systems of collective morality. Intrinsically it seems to have been a neutral instrument capable of being adapted by opposing sides to almost every question. At the outset, to be sure, it was used most effectually by apostles of group struggle and rugged individualism. This was probably due much less to the nature of Darwin's ideas than to the nature of the society by which they were interpreted. The fact that Darwinism was treated differently by the thinkers of different nations is suggestive here. The reception of Darwinism in America also shows clearly how dominant social trends influenced interpretations. In the great period of industrial expansion from 1865 to approximately the end of the century, the competitive individualism of Spencer and William Graham Sumner was the dominant note. At the close of this period, however, and increasingly as the Progressive era of humanitarianism, state intervention, and reform got under way, this type of individualism fell under criticism; by the early years of the twentieth century Lester Ward, who had been sharply criticizing individualist Darwinism to an almost negligible audience during the 1870s and 1880s, became the acknowledged master of American sociology. Spencer suddenly went into eclipse. However, the close of the century witnessed a renewed interest in overseas expansion and a resurgence of American imperialism, with the result that the era which saw Darwinian individualism decline also saw a remarkable efflorescence of racialism, militarism, and struggle-for-lifeism, as exemplified in the influence of Theodore Roosevelt, Mahan, Brooks Adams, Jack London, and others.

For only a short time was the field preempted by the apostles of individualism or violence. Before long a number of significant writers arose who used naturalistic and Darwinian premises to come to very different conclusions. Preeminent among these was Thomas Henry Huxley, an early crusader for evolution whose word carried great weight. As early as 1888 in an essay, "The Struggle for Existence in Human Society," Huxley argued that society, although a part of nature, is distinctive in that it has "a definite moral object." The course shaped by ethical man is different from that adopted by man as a part of the animal kingdom. The "primitive savage" fights out the struggle for existence to its bitter end, but the ethical man "devotes his best energies to the object of setting limits to the struggle." In his famous lecture, "Evolution and Ethics" (1893), Huxley protested against what he considered the central fallacy of the so-called ethics of evolution, the notion that because struggle for existence has been the mode of change and of advancing organization among plants and animals it must necessarily govern the progress of man in society. This fallacy, he thought, had arisen from the ambiguity of that fatal phrase, "survival of the fittest." " 'Fittest' has a connotation of 'best'; and about 'best' there hangs a moral flavour. In cosmic nature, however, what is 'fittest' depends upon the conditions." The conditions do not always call forth forms that can be described as superior by ethical criteria. Huxley suggested by analogy that if the earth should cool again, the survival of the fittest might bring about in the vegetable kingdom a population of stunted organisms, until the "fittest" might be nothing but lichens and even simpler types. These would be best adapted to the environment, but in no other sense would they be more fit or superior to the other plant organisms with which man is familiar.

Man in society, Huxley admitted, is subject to the evolutionary or "cosmic" process. But the less rudimentary, the more advanced, man's civilization becomes, the less is this true. "Social progress means a checking of the cosmic process at every step and the substitution for it of another, which may be called the ethical process; the end of which is not the survival of those who may happen to be the fittest, in respect of the whole of the conditions which obtain, but of those who are ethically the best." The ethical process demands self-restraint and mutual help, and its influence is not so much directed to the survival of the fittest as to "the fitting of as many as possible to survive. It repudiates the gladiatorial theory of existence."

In a companion essay, written the following year, Huxley explained more clearly how the life of man in society could be at once a part of and yet distinct from the cosmic process by which the rest of nature is governed. Here he used the analogy of a garden. The gardener creates an artificially favorable environment for his plants; instead of leaving them to adjust to the environment, he adjusts the environment to them. He restricts the multiplication of organisms, alleviates the pressure of individuals upon the means of subsistence, and sets up a process antithetical to the struggle for existence—and yet the possibility of progress remains. Such is the horticultural process. It uses the forces and resources of nature, but in a special way. So it should be, Huxley argued, with the ethical process. Social progress should replace the state of nature with the state of art, just as the gardener does. The ethical process, indeed, is in opposition to the principle of the cosmic process, and tends to the suppression of the qualities of ferocity and self-assertion best fitted for success in the struggle for existence.

Other writers agreed with Huxley that Darwinism was being misused. In the United States, Lester Ward, the founder of American sociology, attacked Darwinian individualism in a series of cogent books and essays dedicated to the thesis of the superiority of the artificial over the natural and the purposive over the non-purposive. The biologist David Starr Jordan argued impressively that modern war was an immensely dysgenic factor in human development and therefore subject to condemnation by biology. The pragmatic school in philosophy showed the inadequacy of Herbert Spencer's passive conception of human reactions as mere adaptations, and argued that human will and purpose took an active part in molding the environment. In Russia, Jacques Novicov dedicated his sociological career to the refutation of antisocial Darwinism, and Prince Peter Kropotkin wrote an influential book, *Mutual Aid,* to show that the primary lesson of nature for man is not to compete but to cooperate. In France such advocates of solidarism as Fouilée and Léon Bourgeois emphasized man's mutual interdependence in society and found reasons to support moderate state intervention on behalf of "the weak." Everywhere the "social Darwinism" of the rugged individualists and the rugged militarists fell under criticism by reformers, humanitarians, pacifists, socialists, and Christian moralists. At the very least, the naturalistic critics of a false naturalism and the Darwinian critics of competitive self-assertion and group violence were able to show that Darwinism could be used to support more than one set of conclusions.

The essential arguments of the critics of social Darwinism can be summarized briefly. Most adaptations of Darwinism to ethical and social thinking had been based upon the assumption that evolution was equal to progress and that the "fittest" were equal to the morally best, the socially most useful, or the strongest in sheer physique. But it was easy to see the force of Huxley's argument that the biological concept of adaptation meant simply adjustment to *any* kind of environment, without presumption that the demands of the environment could be judged good by any reasonable criterion. Critics also attacked the apotheosis of "Nature" which was so common a feature of the social-Darwinian mind. Natural processes, they showed, were too prodigal with resources and with suffering to serve as an economical model for man. Moreover, to regard "Nature" as being in some foredestined and providential way a necessarily beneficent force was not a rational or scientific view at all, but rather a mystical one. Man's distinction was not in accepting but in adapting and surmounting the processes ruling in the rest of nature. The earlier Darwinians had been mistaken—and this was, perhaps, their central error—in looking upon man's adaptive mechanisms as purely *passive* reactions to the environment. Spencer, for example, had defined life as "the adjustment of internal relations to external relations." But it had been the whole course of man's development to turn actively upon nature and adjust external relations to internal needs—in short, to adapt the environment to himself.

The simple adaptation of biological concepts was found as misleading in anthropology, sociology, and history as in ethics and psychology. The social-Darwinians had been intoxicated by their sudden warrant for placing man in the scheme of nature. Having been assured that he was an animal, they had become so obsessed with his animality that they had neglected or misinterpreted his institutions and cultural achievements. Anthropologists, under the leadership of Spencer and Sir Edward Tylor, had constructed schemes of evolutionary development through which, it was assumed, all peoples must necessarily go. Later anthropologists, studying primitive peoples more precisely, found that these courses of development were constructed upon a false schematism, and that there was no universal pattern of social evolution. Historians, among whom E. A. Freeman was notable, had traced the evolution of constitutions and political institutions, comparing, classifying, and labeling them as botanists did with their specimens. Others discovered that this was but one way, and not the most fruitful, of studying history, and began to interpret human culture as an interacting whole, not as a congeries of "institutions" with some sort of independent pattern of life history of their own. Under the Darwinian influence sociologists had represented social processes by metaphor and analogy in biological terms. They presently began to feel that their object should be not analogy but analysis of social processes. They had been explaining principles of social life with concepts derived from another field fundamentally alien to it. In 1909 when they took stock of a half-century of Darwinian thought, the decline of the older evolutionary sociology was a matter of common observation.

As social and philosophic thinkers moved away from the nineteenth-century framework, they showed an increasing tendency to find the biological and selectionist approach to human affairs not merely wrong but startlingly irrelevant to their main problems. Social scientists now based their work on the conception of man as a cultural creature, not a mere animal. Psychology replaced biology as the science which absorbed their attention; but they were no longer inclined to put sociology in so passive a relation to psychology as they once had put it to biology. Instead of deducing the principles and methods of social science from psychology, they infused the concepts of psychology itself with their awareness of man's social character. Man, defined in the eighteenth century as a tool-making animal, then later as a primate with an opposable thumb, was now conceived as a symbol-making, communicative creature. As one writer expressed the twentieth-century perspective, the old practise of following the methods of physical science had driven psychology into physiology, histology, and genetics and had carried it "further and further away from those problems which we ought to be approaching." The generative ideas of physics and chemistry, of medicine and biology, had not given any vivifying concept to social science. The central theme in modern inquiry, whether in logic, psychiatry, religion, or social investigation, is "the *human response* as a constructive, not a passive thing" (Susanne K. Langer).

Any science which is in a state of rapid development is likely to command a great deal of attention. Much important work had gone on in biology during the period of Newtonian mechanics, but it was Newtonian mechanics that became the fountainhead of philosophical systems because it had large organizing ideas to offer. During the Darwinian period important progress in mechanics did not by any means cease, and yet the speculative mind was captured by biology. Great work in both mechanical and biological science has also been done in the twentieth century, but few thinkers are now attracted to creating world views based upon the simple extension of mechanical or biological principles to the whole realm of knowledge. No single area of knowledge holds the same central position in twentieth-century thought that physics did in the eighteenth or biology in the nineteenth. Philosophers have become increasingly skeptical of attempts to interpret the universe in any monistic schematism, and are more receptive to the idea that different areas of knowledge must be approached with different intellectual instruments. As the conviction grows that man has gained a wonderful control of almost every aspect of nature except his own conduct, the focus of attention has been fixed more steadily upon psychology and the social sciences. It is significant that one of the greatest triumphs of modern physics, the release of atomic energy, is not likely to cause anyone to interpret the world in terms of the atom but has rather set the physicists themselves to pondering their social role and their political influence. While eighteenth and nineteenth-century thought were centered about the universe and "Nature," in the twentieth century man has once again taken the center of the stage which he had occupied before the Copernican revolution.

Chapter X

CAPITALISM AFTER 1850

꩜

1. LATER CAPITALIST. THEORY AND PRACTICE

THE GOLDEN AGE of capitalism occurred during the middle decades of the nineteenth century. Between 1846 and 1873 the self-regulating market idealized by Adam Smith and David Ricardo came nearer to being realized than ever before or since. After a historic struggle, medieval and mercantilist fetters had been cast aside, and the limitations imposed on the market by modern welfare states had hardly begun. Chartist agitation had died down in England, and on the Continent the Revolution of 1848, which had momentarily threatened, at least in France, to develop into a proletarian hurricane, had softened into a gentle zephyr pushing the sails of economic liberalism. Trade unionism was still in its infancy, and in England it was about to take the form of a movement amenable to capitalism and organized for the principal purpose of diverting a larger share of the system's fruits to the wage-earning class. Socialism was the theory of only a few intellectuals and educated workingmen. The working classes of England had weathered the worst storms of the Industrial Revolution, and real wages were rising. The Industrial Revolutions of the United States and Germany, which took place in the second half of the nineteenth century, were to be less painful for the laboring classes than had been the earlier industrialization of England. From the vantage point of 1850 the future of the capitalist order appeared bright and long. Economics, the "dismal science" of Malthus and Ricardo, took on a more optimistic note in the writings of John Stuart Mill, the leading political economist of the third quarter of the nineteenth century. The dominant conviction among most thinking people was that at last there had been achieved a natural economic order inherently

---

This chapter consists of material by two different authors. Section 1, written especially for the present volume, is by Dudley Dillard. Section 2 is from *Introduction to Economic History 1750–1950* (pp. 91–105; London, Macmillan & Co. Ltd., 1952), by G. D. H. Cole.

superior to any of its predecessors and to any alternative that might be proposed in the future. Capitalism was champion without a challenger.

THE FREE MARKET AND CLASSICAL THEORY

Free markets were the key institution of classical capitalism. The market system may be divided into a market for products and individual markets for the factors of production—land, labor and capital. Capital is mobilized in what is usually called the "money market." A unique feature of nineteenth-century capitalism, especially in Great Britain, was the practice of treating land, labor and money, as well as products, as commodities, that is, as objects produced for the purpose of being sold in a market. The enclosure movement, the new poor law and the gold standard had achieved commodity status for land, labor and money, respectively, by 1850.

Land became a marketable commodity during early capitalism. Before the soil could be commercialized as part of the market process, feudal tenure rights and obligations had to be replaced by private contract and private property in land. In England with the culmination of the enclosure movement in the first half of the nineteenth century, the economic mobilization of land as a commodity to be rented or bought and sold was fully developed.

Labor required a longer time than land to acquire full commodity status. A new English poor law of 1834, sometimes called the Malthusian poor law, accepted Malthus's position that paternalistic relief merely increases the misery of the poor. In keeping with the spirit of the age, the new poor law rested on the premise that human labor, like other commodities, should be subject to the free play of the forces of supply and demand. This view is expressed in the following statement by one of the English poor law commissioners: ". . . there must be alterations of prosperity and adversity, of activity and stagnation, of the demand for labor exceeding the supply, and of the supply exceeding the demand; and such changes will have the effect of occasionally throwing able-bodied persons out of employment" (Sir George Nicholls, *History of the Poor Laws,* new ed., 1890, II, 427).

The poor law of 1834 was consistent with the fundamental legal and economic relations which bring wage earners and employers together under a free market system. Workers are legally free under capitalism to refuse to work for employers just as employers are free not to employ workers. However, both are under a certain compulsion to co-operate—the worker in order to live and the capitalist in order to profit from his surplus property. If workers are able to live without working by receiving comfortable relief, the market forces are impeded. The purpose behind the poor law of 1834 was to make poor relief so undesirable that no one would choose it in preference to selling his services to private employers in the labor market.

The labor market cannot function in the absence of a class of workers with less property than is required to employ fully their own labor. Where the process of separating workers from the land and other means of production was delayed, the maturing of capitalism was also delayed. Thus in England the enclosure movement created large numbers of propertyless, able-bodied men at an early date, in contrast to France, where the peasant was given unconditional title to his land on the eve of modern industrialism (1793). Capital means surplus property, or a monetary command over surplus property, which the owner cannot fully employ with his own labor. Therefore the worker relies upon the property of others for employment of his labor, and the capitalist relies upon the labor of others for the employment of his capital. The mechanism for their getting together is the labor market, which presumably neutralizes the latent antagonisms between employers and employees. Competition among employers for workers and competition among workers for employment provide a self-regulating mechanism for determining wage rates.

A commodity theory of money developed alongside the commodity theories of land and labor. Metallic monetary standards were widely adopted in the course of the nineteenth century. Again the high point of achievement was in England, where the gold standard act of 1816 and the bank charter act of 1844 attempted to stabilize the value of money in terms of gold as a commodity. The issue of unsupported paper currency was rigidly limited. The gold standard was supposed to regulate automatically the domestic as well as the international value of a nation's currency. All this was consistent with the *laissez-faire* mistrust of the wisdom of politicians in economic affairs. "Monetary policy"—political intervention to regulate the value of money— in the mercantilist or modern sense could not exist so long as the international gold standard was adhered to rigidly. Not until after the First World War, when attempts to restore the automatic gold standard proved disastrously unsuccessful, was the belief in a self-regulating monetary system abandoned. During the Great Depression of the 1930's the classical gold standard became in effect a relic for museums and historians.

Free competition and self-regulation found concrete expression not only in the markets for land, labor and money, but also in the product markets. In this latter connection the repeal of the corn laws in England (1846) was only the most dramatic illustration. A trend toward lower tariffs became general throughout Europe around the middle of the century. England repealed its mercantilistic navigation laws in 1849. Such events helped to prepare the ground for a great experiment in free market economy.

One important question remains to be analyzed. How was the automatic self-regulation of the several markets supposed to reconcile the free pursuit of private gain with the maximum welfare of society?

Admittedly the immediate and necessarily dominant motive of capitalist enterprise is profit. Many ultimate or ulterior motives may account for the participation of individuals in business as entrepreneurs and capitalists: desire to do good, love of playing games for high stakes, urge to fame, pride of possession, desire for power, or a mere urge to activity. Regardless of the ultimate motives, however, a business enterprise cannot survive unless attention is given to profit-making. Significantly, double-entry bookkeeping, which provides the chief measure of business success, is designed to show the net gain or loss sustained by a business during an accounting period. Since the prime objective is to ascertain changes in net worth or net wealth measured in terms of money, making goods is incidental to making money. Although conditions within the business firm are planned and recorded in detail, there exists under capitalism no conscious plan or system of accounting for the economy as a whole. In more recent times, mostly since the Great Depression of the 1930's, there has arisen a system of national-income accounting. Only in so-called planned economies, however, does national-income accounting replace business bookkeeping as the basis for conscious economic calculation in the employment and allocation of resources. If national income and social welfare are maximized under business enterprise, this outcome is accidental in the sense that it is not a consequence of any conscious purpose guided by accounting on an economy-wide basis.

Although business enterprise is preoccupied with private gain, the political economists who theorized about it were concerned with the welfare of society at large. The degradation of political economy into a justification for selfish interests was deeply resented by leading classical economists from Adam Smith to John Stuart Mill. They saw in the profit motive not an end in itself but a vehicle for serving society. They reconciled private profit with public welfare in terms of the free play of self-regulating market forces. Adam Smith's *Wealth of Nations* still stands, perhaps, as the classic exposition of this point. Men seek large personal gain but competition among numerous small rivals denies them their full objective. Profits in some sectors of the economy may become temporarily large, but the entry of new competitors will take away the excess gains. It should be noted that the leading classical economists after Smith, including Ricardo, James Mill, M'Culloch and John

Stuart Mill, were all staunch utilitarians who viewed "the greatest good of the greatest number," or some similar statement of this principle, as the criterion of the validity of economic institutions. Although the effect of utilitarian thinking applied to economic relations may have been to justify profit-seeking, this can hardly be said to have been the dominant purpose of the classical economists.

Despite the fact that the great economists were utilitarians, the principle of utility was not incorporated into economic analysis in a systematic way until late in the third quarter of the nineteenth century. In part this new development was a reaction against socialist thinkers like Marx, who had used classical economics, especially Ricardo's labor theory of value, to criticize capitalism. The new economics of marginal utility also sprang from a more intense concern with the free market as the instrument for maximizing social welfare. Stanley Jevons (1835–82) tried to show that the structure of prices in a free market exactly reflects the subjective preferences ("utilities") of individual buyers and sellers. Market prices in the long run yield a maximum of satisfaction or "utility" for both parties. Free competition thus affords a mechanism for maximizing utility. This bit of analysis added intellectual force to the general contention of classical and neo-classical economics that the free market is the only condition consistent with the greatest good of the greatest number.

Classical capitalism was a unique historical phenomenon. Its logic as worked out by classical and neo-classical economists was a thing of intellectual beauty. The tragedy of classical capitalism was that it took so long to build and was so quickly demolished. In a sense it never quite existed. Yet in the few decades referred to above as the golden age of capitalism, there was an historical approximation to it.

The rest of this chapter shows how the ideal free market of classical economics, which reached the high point of its development in the third quarter of the nineteenth century, began to decline thereafter. The main factors which will be analyzed in this connection are the technology of mass production, the transportation revolution, the return to protection, economic imperialism, monopolistic combinations among businessmen, and labor unions among wage earners. The technology of mass production, in conjunction with the transport revolution, created intolerable market conditions for European farmers and industrialists, who sought refuge in a retreat from free markets, in a return to protective tariffs and in the establishment of monopolistic combinations. The wage-earning class, which had never fully accepted the benevolent theory of free markets, organized to remove competition from the labor market.

THE TECHNOLOGY OF MASS PRODUCTION

Although market capitalism remained dominant between 1850 and 1914, the most significant aspect of the economic history of this period from a present-day vantage point is the development of forces tending to undermine the free market economy. Not only did businessmen form monopolistic combinations, workingmen form labor unions, and farmers and industrialists demand protection from foreign competition, but the automatic gold standard finally gave way to a system of managed currency.

Among the factors contributing to the decline of the free market, the most powerful was probably the application of science to industry, agriculture, transportation and communication. Scientific methods and attitudes were translated into a new technology which multiplied the output of goods and services to such an extent that the capacity to produce threatened to outrun the capacity to consume under existing property relations. Escape from the relentless competition of free markets became the dominant motive of all producers' groups.

The new technology in its economic aspect operated in two main directions to create the Age of Mass Production. (1) Improvements in methods of transportation and communication increased the extent of the market and made possible a greater division of labor. (2) Technological advance contributed to mass production by increasing the size of the most efficient producing plants.

Machine Tools, Precision Manufacture and Interchangeable Parts. The basic elements in the technology of mass production were machine tools (machines for making machines), precision instruments, interchangeability of parts, automatic machines and assembly line production. Precision manufacturing is a relatively late development in the history of mechanical inventions. One of the pioneers in its development was the American inventor, Eli Whitney (1765–1825), who produced muskets for the United States government by first making a separate machine tool for each part. After "tooling up" Whitney produced on a mass scale by making thousands of identical parts of each type required for the musket. He then assembled the finished product from the supply of identical parts. Unlike firearms made by gunsmiths, Whitney's muskets could be assembled without special fitting of one part to another because each individual part was made with sufficient precision to be used interchangeably. The great disadvantage of this method was that no final product could be produced until the entire tooling up process was completed, and this preparation required several years of Whitney's time. However, once all the machine tools were ready, muskets could be turned out very rapidly at a relatively low cost per musket, providing a large number was produced. It was not an operation which could be employed profitably for a small order or a small market or by a producer with small capital.

Another major advantage of Whitney's method was that it enabled him to employ as operatives relatively unskilled workers in place of craftsmen previously employed in making muskets. Although Whitney did not use a continuous assembly line, this principle followed logically from any large-scale operation. The assembly line was first used effectively in the meat-packing industry in the United States, where slaughtered animals were cut up by butchers wielding cleavers and knives as the carcass moved along a continuous belt. In the production of automobiles the assembly-line method of fitting together precision-made parts in a continuous flow is perhaps the highest achievement of mass production.

Machine tools are highly specialized. In order to produce machine tools effectively there had first to be developed a small number of general machine tools to perform the basic operations needed to produce the specialized machine tools. These general-utility machine tools included the automatic lathe, metal planers, metal grinders and metal borers. During the second half of the nineteenth century there also came into use instruments of precise measurement such as gauge blocks, calipers and micrometers. Each advance to greater precision meant more efficient machines and lower costs of production, although only if operations were carried out on a massive scale.

Cheap Steel. Cheap steel was another factor of fundamental importance in the development of mass production. Shortly after 1850 three inventions revolutionized the technology of manufacturing steel. These new techniques, all of which were developed within less than a quarter-century, were the Bessemer converter (1856), the Siemens-Martin open hearth (1865) and the Thomas-Gilchrist basic process (1878).

Sir Henry Bessemer was typical of the new type of inventor-scientist through whom the impact of science was transmitted to industrial technology. In 1856 Bessemer read to a scientific gathering a paper entitled "The Manufacture of Iron Without Fuel." He proposed to by-pass certain intermediate processes in making pure iron and steel. Although Bessemer did not succeed in carrying into practice his original proposal, his scientific training enabled him to develop an ingenious closed converter which reduced the cost of producing steel to about one-seventh its former level.

A major weakness of Bessemer steel was its uneven quality. This difficulty was overcome by the open-hearth process, which was first developed in the 1860's by William Siemens, a British subject of German origin, and the Martin brothers, metallurgists of France. Siemens, like Bessemer, was a professional inventor and a master of applied science. In place of the closed Bessemer converter, the Siemens-Martin process used a large, shallow pan in which the molten metal was processed slowly and remained under precise control at all times. It permitted large-scale production of uniformly high-quality steel. The open-hearth process came into commercial use after 1865 and gradually surpassed the Bessemer process in total output.

Both the Bessemer and Siemens-Martin processes were unsatisfactory in one important respect. Neither could make use of iron ore containing phosphorus, the type most prevalent in Europe. In 1878 the world greeted enthusiastically the announcement of a new process by which steel could be made from phosphoric ore. This new Thomas-Gilchrist method involved lining a Bessemer converter or an open hearth with a basic substance which would combine chemically with phosphorus. One of the inventors, Percy Gilchrist, was a chemist, and his cousin, Gilchrist Thomas, was thoroughly trained in metallurgy. Thus all of the great inventions in steel were by men who understood science and its application to technology.

The fall in price and increase in output of steel resulting from the new processes set in motion other technological changes of such far-reaching consequences as to justify calling the new era the Age of Steel. Steel was now cheap and abundant enough to be used in ways not economically feasible hitherto. For the first time steel became an important building material. Gigantic edifices like the Eiffel Tower of Paris and the skyscrapers of New York stand as monuments to the Age of Steel.

ECONOMIC CONSEQUENCES OF MASS PRODUCTION

Transport Revolution and World Markets. Transportation soon felt the revolutionizing effects of cheap steel, and this in turn set in motion other momentous changes in economic life. Although the railway age had begun before the age of cheap steel, railways now entered a new phase. Steel rails replaced iron rails, the "steel horse" replaced the "iron horse," and steel cars replaced wooden cars. During the 1850's and the 1860's the demand for rails constituted a substantial part of the total demand for iron. Steel rails replaced iron rails within a fairly short period, between 1873 and 1877. Although steel was more expensive rail for rail, it was more durable and could sustain much heavier loads, which made possible the use of the larger and more powerful steel locomotives. Cars and cargoes became much heavier. Costs fell and so did rates.

In ocean transportation cheap steel was no less revolutionary. The modern era of steel ships followed that of wooden ships so closely that there was a period of only about thirty years in which the use of iron predominated. Iron ships had been built before 1855, but they were not common until after that date. Bessemer steel was used in building a number of ships in the years 1863–65, but objections from insurance companies like Lloyds and from the British Admiralty to its uneven and uncertain quality halted steel shipbuilding for a decade. Then, in about 1876, steel assumed the lead in new ship construction, and after the mid-'eighties, when the Thomas-Gilchrist method began furnishing steel quite inexpensively, the relatively brief age of iron ships came to an end.

British ships and American railroads, both made of steel and powered by steam, created world markets for a number of basic commodities in the last quarter of the nineteenth century. The transport revolution thus greatly enhanced the international division of labor. A typical British textile worker ate bread made with wheat from the American Middle West and processed cotton raised in the American South. In 1850 only one loaf of bread in four consumed in Great Britain was made from imported grain, as contrasted with two of every three in 1885. Frozen meat transported in refrigerated ships was first imported into France from Argentina in 1877, and into Great Britain from Australia in 1880. The refrigerated railway car supplemented refrigerated ships. England, which in an earlier age had been one of the great exporters of raw wool, began to import large quantities from Australia and other overseas areas. Completion of the first transcontinental railroads in the United States and the opening of the Suez Canal, both events occurring in 1869, created world markets for other basic commodities. Western Europe became more than ever an exporter of manufactured products and an importer of food and raw materials. As a corollary, other parts of the world became more than ever importers of European manufactured goods and exporters of foodstuffs and raw materials. This was the grand design of the European economy between 1870 and 1914. Neither before nor since has there been such a great degree of concentration of industrial activity. Europe's share of total world manufacturing fell from 68 per cent in 1870 to 42 per cent in 1925–29, and to 25 per cent in 1948.

Return to Protectionism. Free trade attained its height during the third

quarter of the nineteenth century. After Great Britain adopted free trade
in 1846, France moved in the same direction under Louis Napoleon with
the signing of the Cobden Free Trade Treaty with Great Britain in 1860.
Prussia, and later Germany, under Bismarck veered toward free trade. These
steps removed artificial barriers to the international division of labor much as
transportation facilities removed natural barriers. The free trade movement,
however, like other concomitants of the free markets, was short-lived.

Paradoxically, the transport revolution both expanded and restricted the
market. By lowering the cost of distance it removed natural trade barriers,
but it also set in motion social forces which eventually created new artificial
barriers. The momentum arising from the removal, for a time, of both kinds
of barriers, combined with mass production methods in industry and the
mechanization of agriculture in the New World, carried free trade further
than those subjected to the ruthless price cutting of the free market were
willing in the long run to tolerate. Even in Great Britain there was a strong
revival of protectionist philosophy under the leadership of Joseph Chamberlain during the last two decades of the nineteenth century. This movement
was not translated into policy, and British agriculture remained on the sacri-
ficial block. In other countries, however, the pressures for protectionism were
not successfully resisted. Bismarck succumbed to the combined appeal of
German farmers, who clamored for protection against cheap grain brought
in from eastern Europe on the new railways, and German industrialists, who
clamored for protection against British imports. In France, high protective
tariffs were placed on agricultural and industrial products, beginning in
1881. In other countries, including Austria, Spain, Italy, Belgium and Russia,
there was a similar return to protection. The decline of free market capitalism
in international trade was a well-established fact by 1914. Free trade proved
to be a utopian experiment except for Great Britain, which enjoyed by virtue
of its early lead special advantages over the late comers to world trade on a
large scale.

Economic Imperialism. The rapid growth of industrial capitalism was intimately related to that of economic imperialism after 1875. The accumulation of capital on an ever larger scale tended to lower the rate of return from
domestic investment and made foreign investment more attractive. Prior to
1860 the British had been without major competition in the export of capital.
British funds flowed to all parts of the world, and especially into transportation and industry in politically stable, independent countries like the nations
of Europe and the United States. In this manner the British, perhaps ironically,
helped to develop the economic potential of future rivals. As French and

German capitalism matured, these countries produced their own surplus of capital for export and confronted the British with international rivalry in overseas investment.

Instead of entering overseas territories on a competitive basis, Europeans sought to carve out economic empires in which they would enjoy exclusive privileges for investment and exploitation. Special concessions were obtained in backward areas for mines, oil wells, railroads, plantations and the like. Such investments in capital-starved countries were potentially very profitable but highly risky because of the political instability of weak local governments. Political control by investors or their national government was an effective means for insuring the security of investments. Non-economic motives also contributed to political domination of colonial areas by European nations.

A common device for combining capitalist enterprise with political aggrandizement was the chartered joint-stock company. For example, the British South Africa Company was formed in 1889 with a London charter which authorized the Company to do practically anything: make treaties, promulgate laws, maintain a police force, make land grants, engage in mining, establish banks, acquire new concessions, build roads, railroads, harbors, and engage in any type of business. The South Africa Company became the means by which Cecil Rhodes multiplied his millions and by which the British government ultimately took possession of most of southern Africa.

Of the many other economic empires set up in Africa, the Congo Free State, the private venture of Leopold, King of the Belgians, became the most notorious. Its ruthless exploitation and brutal treatment of native labor scandalized a complacent Europe. Although an extreme case, the Congo experience is perhaps indicative of the failure of the advanced economies of Europe to develop successfully the backward areas of the world through the medium of profit-seeking enterprises.

Spread of the Joint-Stock Company. In the heyday of the competitive market economy the most common forms of business enterprise were the partnership and single proprietorship. Adam Smith believed that the corporation or joint-stock company had legitimate uses in only three fields: banking, insurance and public utilities. As late as 1848 another of the great classical economists, John Stuart Mill, took an equally dim view of the future of the corporation. Subsequent events proved Smith and Mill to be poor prophets. The rise of mass production based on interchangeable parts, machine tools, large-scale economy and production for mass markets under conditions of cheap transportation offered great potential economies. Changes in the scale of production required new forms of business organization which could mobilize the large amount of capital necessary to build plants and finance sales on an economy-wide or world-wide basis. Corporate or joint-stock companies, which previously had been confined largely to specifically chartered foreign trading companies enjoying monopolistic grants, came into common use and in time dominated the industrial field.

Liberalization of the conditions under which joint-stock companies could be chartered was an essential condition for their general use in industrial and commercial ventures. The British Bubble Act (1720), which had severely restricted the incorporation of joint-stock companies, was not repealed until 1825. In the 1830's there began a series of parliamentary acts which liberalized conditions for chartering such companies. Whereas previously the right to organize a company had been a special privilege granted only to a few, it now became possible for any group which met certain minimum conditions to receive a charter by application to administrative authorities. Among the important legal changes was the privilege of limited liability of incorporated joint-stock companies formed under administrative procedures. Limited liability means that the potential losses of shareholders are limited to the amount of their investment in the company. In the absence of limited liability the entire personal fortune of a shareholder may be taken to pay claims which the company cannot meet. British joint-stock companies are required to give publicity to their limited liability by placing "Ltd." after the name of the company. Other European countries followed the British in liberalizing legal procedures for the formation of joint-stock companies.

During the past century the joint-stock method of organizing business enterprise has revolutionized the basic capitalist institution of private ownership in the means of production. The functional theory of private property handed down from John Locke taught that one acquired property in a means of production like land by mixing his labor with the land. Property rights were based upon active, functional participation in the creation and management of the object owned. Under this personal form of private property, ownership and control were inseparable. In the giant, quasi-public joint-stock company or corporation, ownership and control have been separated more and more. Just as the factory separated the worker from ownership of the instruments of production, so the modern corporation has separated its owners from control of their property. Ownership becomes passive. The more widely scattered the passive owners, the more easily can effective control be maintained by a minority interest, and in extreme cases a small group of self-perpetuating managers can dictate the use of vast amounts of property to which they have little or no legal title.

On the other hand, by spreading ownership among large numbers of small shareholders there is a broad participation in ownership of productive property and the income which accrues from it. Through organized security markets small investors can use their savings to purchase part ownership in business enterprises. Millions of "little people" who could not hope to go into business for themselves are able to become small capitalists and feel they have some stake in the system.

Whether the giant corporation has done more to promote economic democracy or its opposite is a question that is difficult to evaluate. Functional rather than passive ownership would appear to be essential to the democratic argument. This condition might be realized if workers owned significant amounts of stock in the enterprise which employed them, especially if arrangements were made for worker representatives to share in control of the company. Employees are often encouraged to purchase stock in the company which employs them, but worker participation in policy-making has been actively opposed. Representatives of management characteristically maintain that participation by worker groups is contrary to the principles of business enterprise, and frequently worker groups are not interested in sharing the burdens of management.

In the total picture of modern corporate development the most striking feature is disfranchisement of shareholders through separation of ownership from control. The great mass of shareholders are owners in name only and, in economic fact, mere suppliers of capital. They have no guaranteed return, as in the case of bondholders; the payments to common stockholders often depend entirely on the caprice of an autonomous, non-owning, self-perpetuating management.

The most significant conclusion for contemporary civilization is that a profound change has taken place in property relations. Owners are often not managers, and managers are often not owners. Corporate property is joint property. In its more advanced stage it represents an extreme form of multiple ownership which is difficult to reconcile with an equally extreme theory of economic individualism which carries over from the age of Locke. Despite the fact that the conditions of Locke's times disappeared before the twentieth century, Lockian theories remained vigorous as a rationale of the new system.

Another tendency in business organization arising in connection with the growth of mass production was a division of labor between technologists on the one hand and businessmen on the other. During the period of the Industrial Revolution men like Richard Arkwright, while perhaps not always genuine inventors in their own right, had a basic understanding of the relatively simple technology of the plants they owned and operated. When industry came to be based upon the technology of chemistry and physics, the gap between the technological knowledge required for the conduct of industry and that which could be assimilated by businessmen became much greater than in the earlier era. Of necessity the conduct of business enterprise continued to be governed primarily by monetary considerations, so that the entrepreneur, confronted with becoming either an expert in finance or an expert in engineering, was compelled by logic to choose the former.

These two tendencies, namely, the separation of ownership from management, and the division between engineers and businessmen, represent the essence of what is frequently spoken of as the transition from industrial capitalism to financial capitalism. Finance capitalism means the control of industry by men whose interests are primarily in selling, accounting and similar money affairs and whose knowledge of technology is relatively limited in relation to the total body of knowledge employed in the scientific and technological aspects of production. Thorstein Veblen has referred to this development as a change from captain of industry to captain of solvency.

Growth of the Money Market. One of the truly striking developments of the nineteenth century was the money market, especially the London money market. Money markets had existed since the beginnings of modern capitalism, but it was not until the nineteenth century that they became an indispensable part of private capitalism. In earlier times government securities and the shares of a few great trading companies like the Dutch and British East India Companies constituted the bulk of securities traded in the exchanges. The founding of the Bank of England in 1694 was occasioned by the desire of the government for a long-term loan. In the nineteenth century the railways, and later industrial joint-stock companies, mobilized money capital for their giant enterprises through investment bankers who operated in the money markets of the world. Railway promoters from all corners of the world came to London to raise capital for their joint-stock companies. This was usually achieved by selling their securities to investment bankers, who in turn sold them to the investing public. As Walter Bagehot says in his classic *Lombard Street,* the London money market was a great "floating loan-fund which can be lent to anyone or for any purpose." To a much greater extent than on the Continent, Englishmen kept their money in banks, where it became "borrowable" money.

The London money market was different from others in that it was especially oriented toward international rather than domestic financial needs. Britain attained a dominant position in world commerce before the industrial joint-stock company became important. To a certain degree domestic enterprise in Britain suffered because it played second fiddle to international demands. This was the inevitable result of a money market organized on a world-wide basis. The mobility of money-capital was much greater than that of labor, and also greater than that of physical commodities. What really distinguished the London money market from others was its higher stage of development. Paris, Berlin, Rome, Vienna, New York and other markets were like satellites revolving around London. In every case money markets served both domestic and international functions. There was, however, a sense in which London served world needs for the simple reason that money was cheaper and easier to get in the "main office" than anywhere else.

With increased demands on the money market, banking institutions became differentiated. The main division was between the functions of investment and commercial banking. Investment banking was concerned primarily with long-term lending as represented by stocks and bonds, the funds from the sale of which were used by business enterprises for financing fixed plant and equipment. Commercial banking, on the other hand, functioned primarily to provide short-term loans for particular business transactions. In Britain the two functions tended to center in separate banks, whereas on the Continent investment and commercial functions were characteristically carried on by the same bank. The main reasons for this difference were the higher development of the London money market, especially in the international field, and the late emergence of industrialism on the Continent with the consequent need for raising large amounts of new capital, given the absence of old industrial firms with prior accumulations of capital out of earnings. The greatest intermingling of commercial and investment banking was in Germany, where the Industrial Revolution came late but at a dizzy pace. Great banking houses in Germany were closely allied to nearly all large industrial enterprises. Directors of the great banking houses sat on the boards of German industrial firms. This close marriage of industry and finance in German capitalism helps to explain the development of cartels in German industry. Enterprises that were allied with a common banking firm found it relatively easy to arrive at agreements with respect to business policies.

The relation between the alliance of industry and finance and the combination movement in industry becomes clearer when account is taken of the universal tendency in all major European nations toward concentration in commercial and investment banking. In the case of England the first joint-stock banks, other than the Bank of England, were chartered after 1825. Many joint-stock banks were chartered, but most of these failed or were swallowed up by other banks, and in the twentieth century the "Big Five" joint-stock banks (Barclays, Lloyds, Midland, National Provincial and Westminister) dominate British commercial banking. Each of these banks has many branches. In France there was a similar concentration in four great banking firms (*Crédit Lyonnais, Comptoir Nationale d'Escompte, Société Générale, Crédit Industriel et Commercial*) with many branch banks scattered throughout France. In the case of Germany there was an even greater concentration of banking than in England or France. The famous Big Four "D" banks (*Deutsche, Dresdner, Diskonto-Gesellschaft* and *Darmstadter*) were reduced through mergers to two in 1931.

Private banks—that is, banks which were not organized as joint-stock companies—like the House of Rothschild and Baring Brothers, dominated international banking during most of the nineteenth century, although they were losing ground in its closing decades. These private banking houses came into existence primarily to finance government loans in war and peace. The Rothschild brothers, for example, first came into prominence during the Napoleonic wars, in which they sided with Britain and her allies against France. In the century of peace after 1815 international bankers played a leading role in the diplomacy as well as in the finance of nationalistic European nations. They functioned as forces for peace not because they were idealistic pacifists but because their ability to gain would have been gravely endangered by war among the great powers. They were an integrating and unifying force among national political units operating in an international economy which possessed no international political authority. Their power lay in their supranational character.

Large-scale banking, which came into existence primarily to meet the needs of large-scale business, became in turn an active force promoting large-scale business enterprise. Because it was more profitable to deal in the securities of larger and better known enterprises, there was a tendency for investment bankers to promote the sales of these securities in preference to those of smaller and less well-known companies. Hence small business did not have equal advantage in the money market. During periods of business boom it was especially profitable for investment banking houses to float securities merely for the purpose of enriching the promoters. The larger volume of shares fed speculation in the stock exchanges and extended the scope of commercial crises. This subordination of industry to finance is another aspect of the transition from industrial to financial capitalism.

Crises and Business Cycles. Overproduction relative to effective demand became a more regular characteristic of capitalistic organization in the 1850–

1914 period. Much of the new productive potential was lost through unemployment, which was on a scale greatly exceeding that of the period before 1850. Despite the fact that markets expanded more rapidly than ever before, the economic problem changed from one of producing enough to meet demand to the problem of finding enough demand to keep men and machines at work. Poverty remained in the midst of potential plenty.

A fairly rhythmic pattern of expansion and contraction, punctuated by periodic crises, had become apparent in the half century following the end of the Napoleonic Wars. Crises occurred approximately every ten years—in 1815, 1825, 1836, 1847, 1857 and 1866 in England—and in about the same sequence in all capitalist countries. In the age of mass production after 1870 depressions became longer and more severe. The depression that began in 1873 continued unbroken for six years and was the longest on record. After a slow revival and moderate prosperity another severe depression occurred between 1883 and 1886. Still another bad depression struck in 1890, reached its nadir in 1893 and lasted until 1895. The long-term trend of prices turned upward in 1897, and business cycles were more frequent but the depressions were shorter and less severe than in the 'seventies, 'eighties and 'nineties.

Overproduction had been the subject of a famous controversy between Malthus and Ricardo during the post-Napoleonic disturbances. Malthus took an unorthodox position in arguing that an excessive rate of saving would cause prolonged unemployment and depression. Malthus's suggestion that industrial capitalism is inherently unstable was rejected by Ricardo, who argued that thrift could never interfere with the progress of wealth. Ricardo's view was accepted by the later classical and neo-classical economists. According to this orthodox view, production automatically creates an equivalent volume of effective demand. Since supply thus creates its own demand, there can be no general overproduction, no general deficiency of demand. Underconsumption was ridiculed as a naive logical fallacy. Thus the view that large-scale unemployment of an enduring or chronic type is impossible became an essential part of the theory of the self-regulating market and provided one of the chief theoretical arguments for *laissez-faire*. Such explanations as the orthodox economists gave for unemployment and depression usually ran in terms of monetary and credit aberrations, monopoly, trade union activity or governmental interference with free markets. Only since the Great Depression of the 1930's have economists begun to accept as a permissible proposition of economic analysis the notion that demand may be chronically inadequate for full employment and production. Acceptance of this proposition means that the tendency toward unemployment is inherent in the capitalist process, and this in turn carries with it theoretical grounds for rejecting *laissez-faire*.

GROWTH OF ORGANIZED BUSINESS

Large-Scale Enterprise and Destructive Enterprise. Mass production, cheap transportation, rapid communication, world markets, joint-stock companies and the money market contributed to the development of big business after 1870. The mid-nineteenth century ideal of the self-regulating competitive market presupposed many small firms freely entering and leaving an industry. In the past, capitalist markets had always expanded more rapidly than productive capacity, but now the capacity to produce grew more rapidly than markets. The techniques of mass production required large amounts of investment in fixed plant and equipment before any finished output could be produced. Therefore, firms with large investment sought to expand production so as to spread their fixed (or "overhead") costs over as many units as possible. This brought on the market a flood of goods which could be sold, if at all, only at lower prices—a tendency which contributed to the long period of falling prices from 1873 to 1896. Destructive competition of this sort could not persist in the long run because enterprises which did not get back their investment had not the means to replace plant and equipment after it was worn out.

Since business enterprise cannot survive in the long run by selling at prices which do not cover the total cost of production, the inclination was to abandon competition in favor of monopolistic agreements conforming to the philosophy of "live and let live." Large-scale production thus destroyed the basis of workable price competition and at the same time destroyed the foundation upon which rested the ideal of the self-regulating market.

Tendency toward Monopoly. Competition is profit-destroying and monopoly is profit-preserving. Consequently profit-motivated economic units attempt to establish monopolies whenever possible. There is nothing abnormal or unnatural about monopolies under private business enterprise; on the contrary, monopoly is to be expected in the absence of unusual conditions which prevent it. To some degree these unusual conditions existed in the time of Adam Smith and for a century or so thereafter. The presupposition underlying Smith's "natural" economic order is that effective competition among many small enterprises will reconcile the apparent contradiction between the private pursuit of personal profit and the social goal of maximum general welfare. It was in terms of this presupposition that Smith identified "natural" price with "competitive" price. Smith believed that monopolies were the creatures of government policy, and he also believed that in the absence of special privileges like exclusive charters to joint-stock companies and guilds and other protective legislation monopolies could not persist. The reasonableness of Smith's supposition is suggested by the growth of effective competition following the repeal of mercantilist legislation. The golden age of capitalism occurred during the decades after these artificial forms of monopoly were abolished and before small-scale production gave way to mass production.

In more recent times, and especially since the 1870's, there has been a general tendency in all capitalist countries for business enterprises to form monopolistic combinations. In this context the term combination means a transfer of some or all decision-making power from several hitherto competing enterprises to a group authority. Business combinations take many forms but all have as a common objective the increase or preservation of profits of the participating members. There were very few, if any, complete monopolies, but all combinations were monopolistic in the sense that they reduced the number of autonomous firms and lessened the degree of competition. Competition is defined as a market condition in which there are many small sellers of a uniform product. Each firm is so small in relation to the total size of the market that it cannot appreciably influence the price at which it sells. Competitive price is determined impersonally by the market. A monopolistic firm, on the other hand, has the power to influence and even to determine the price at which it sells its product.

Business combinations sought to increase profits in two ways: either by increasing prices or by lowering costs. Increases in prices tend to reduce the amount of product sold. A monopolist is always faced with weighing the advantages of increases in prices against the disadvantages of smaller (physical) sales.

Although there was a tendency everywhere for business combinations to develop, the extent and form of the combination movement as well as the attitude of public authorities and businessmen toward combinations, differed widely in the several countries of Europe. British and German attitudes provide a sharp contrast. In Britain by virtue of the long period of capitalist evolution and general acceptance of the free market as a rational guide to economic behavior, attitudes were hostile toward monopolies generally and cartels in particular. Under British common law, agreements in restraint of trade were illegal in the sense that anyone who was injured by an agreement could sue in the courts with a reasonable expectation of receiving favorable treatment if he could prove damages. Furthermore any contract for the purpose of establishing an agreement in restraint of trade was unenforceable in courts of law. Parties to such contracts were said to come into the court with "unclean hands."

In Germany, on the other hand, where industrial capitalism rose immediately out of a mixed medieval and mercantilist environment and where there was not the long tradition of a market-determined allocation of resources, business combinations, including cartels, were accepted as desirable and even necessary in the social interest. For example, cartels were viewed as a curb on overproduction crises. The guild attitude of mutual protection to producers and consumers through a monopoly regulated in the public interest led logically to an acceptance of capitalist monopolies subject to governmental control. The medieval notion of the social responsibility of business to the community was carried over from the early nineteenth century guild system to the late nineteenth century capitalist system.

In both Britain and Germany the optimum social performance of private industry was the ultimate objective of national economic policy. In Britain social performance was assumed to be maximized by the free play of market forces, whereas in Germany no such tradition existed. These contrasting views are reflected in the respective attitudes toward mercantilism. After Adam Smith nearly all British opinion was hostile to mercantilism, but in Germany mercantilism was sympathetically interpreted by such an outstanding latter-day social theorist as Gustav Schmoller (1838–1917).

Before proceeding to a discussion of some of the most important types of business combinations it may be well to distinguish three general forms: (1) combinations by agreement among several autonomous firms, usually for a limited time; (2) combinations through financial control, usually involving the manipulation of the voting shares of several operating joint-stock companies by a separate financial concern; (3) direct mergers and amalgamations of the assets of several previously independent firms. Combination by agreement is the loosest form and is typified by the cartel. Sometimes combinations by agreement in the form of cartels were accompanied by a formal selling agency known as a syndicate. Combinations through financial concerns like the holding company and the trust leave less freedom of action to the individual members of the combine than does the looser cartel. The trust was extensively employed in the United States after combinations by agreement in the form of pools proved unsatisfactory because of their legal weakness under Anglo-Saxon common law. Direct merger of assets is the tightest form of business combination. It was widely used in Great Britain and also in the United States after anti-trust legislation outlawed the trust and cast a shadow of legal doubt over the holding company.

The remainder of this section on monopoly and competition is devoted to a discussion of the combination movements in Germany and Great Britain. These were the two leading capitalist nations in Europe after 1870 and their combination movements illustrate significant differences as well as similarities in the growth of organized business in the age of mass production.

Business Combinations in Germany. Among European nations, monopolies and combinations were most widespread in Germany. Combinations of the cartel type had been a feature of Germany as far back as the age of the Fuggers in the fifteenth and sixteenth centuries, but the failure of German capitalism to keep pace with that of countries along the Atlantic seacoast tended to render insignificant the German monopoly problem as a factor in capitalist development. With Germany's economic renaissance in the nineteenth century private monopoly again sprang into prominence. Underlying tendencies arising from mass production, destructive competition and legal sanctions were abetted by the formation of the Empire in 1871, the onset of the Long Depression in 1873 and the return to protection in 1879. Although the mere number of cartel agreements is not necessarily an accurate index of the growth of monopoly and combinations in Germany, the figures do suggest the rapidity of that movement. There were fourteen cartel agreements in 1879, thirty-five in 1885 and approximately four hundred in 1900.

1. German coal cartel. The most remarkable of all European cartel-syndicates has been the one that grew up among the coal producers of the Ruhr valley, probably the most concentrated industrial area in the world. In the Ruhr, coal is the basis of industrial life. Coal producers began to experiment with loose agreements during the 1870's and during the severe depression of 1893 formed the famous cartel and syndicate, officially known as the Rhenish-Westphalian Coal Syndicate. Conditions which stimulated the producers to form a monopolistic union were fierce competition, overcapacity in relation to the market, price cutting and generally unprofitable operations, especially during depressions.

The avowed objectives of the Rhenish-Westphalian Coal Syndicate were to (1) end price competition; (2) establish profitable prices; (3) regulate production; and (4) minimize fluctuations in output. The first three of these aims were achieved with remarkable success. Prices were fixed at levels profitable to members of the cartel by limiting the output of coal for the group as a whole. In areas where no competition existed, the syndicate would charge high prices, and, where competition did exist, the coal syndicate lowered its prices in order to meet the competition of outside groups. The price of coal in Mannheim, which was near the Saar coal mining district, was lower than in Hanover, which was nearer the Ruhr but farther from any other coal producing area. Price discrimination of this sort was common practice among cartels.

Each member of the syndicate was assigned a quota in the total output. Because the quotas were transferable, larger firms bought out smaller ones within the cartel in order to increase their share in the total output. Higher cost mines were bought up and withdrawn from production. The syndicate also attempted to eliminate potential competition by buying up unworked areas. In this way high prices had less tendency to bring new capacity outside the cartel into the market. The German government sanctioned the coal cartel and on occasions when there was a possibility that the agreement might lapse, the government threatened to force the participating firms to continue the cartel.

The fourth objective—to minimize fluctuations in output—was more difficult to achieve within the framework of any single industry because the demand for coal fluctuated with the general level of economic activity. However, it was and probably remains a common contention among German economists and businessmen that cartels are a force for over-all economic stability.

The Ruhr coal cartel was well administered, the provisions were strictly enforced, and from the producers' point of view it was a remarkably successful organization. Strict enforcement of the provisions avoided suspicion on the part of participating members and prevented the kind of trouble which frequently led to a breakdown of pooling agreements in the United States and Great Britain, where the common law made enforcement of similar agreements impossible. The Rhenish-Westphalian Coal Syndicate is another illustration of a successful attempt on the part of businessmen to establish a monopoly in order to avoid the fluctuations in prices and other insecurities that arise in a freely competitive market, especially as it operates under conditions of large-scale production.

2. German Steelworks Union. Second only to the Ruhr coal cartel was the German Steelworks Union (*Stahlwerksverband*) formed in 1904. The general purpose of the steel cartel was similar to that of the coal syndicate, namely, to maintain profits by keeping up prices through limitation of output in the domestic market. Cartel control is easier in the case of minerals like coal and other raw materials, which are easily standardized, than for manufactured products like steel. However, steel industries in all countries have tended toward monopolistic combinations because of certain economic characteristics, especially in the basic steel products for which standardization is more easily

established. Standardization is important because the product which is to be controlled must be carefully defined. Cartels in ladies' hats are most uncommon.

Of all modern industries, except perhaps railways, steel involves the greatest capital investment for efficient production. Because of its relatively late start the German steel industry employed the newest and most efficient methods of production, which meant enormously expensive plant, heavy fixed costs and a large spread between total costs and the direct costs involved in the output of specific units (prime costs). Consequently it was an industry in which destructive price competition always presented a potential threat to the large amounts of invested capital. Given these basic economic characteristics, the incentive to cartellize was especially strong. Other conditions favorable to cartellization were the small number of basic steel producers, a high protective tariff on steel and a close tie up between steel enterprises and the great German banks. The latter had been indispensable in raising the large amounts of money capital required to finance great steel plants.

The *Stahlwerksverband* was a union of a number of existing cartels among steel firms; it was a combination of combinations similar to the United States Steel Corporation, which was formed only three years earlier in 1901. All the organizing genius characteristic of German leaders was necessary to operate successfully the vast cartel of cartels in German steel. A high protective tariff on iron and steel imports was responsible for certain special characteristics in the German steel industry. Although tariffs are not essential for cartels, as seen in the case of coal, on which Germany had no tariff, protective tariffs are a powerful factor in the establishment and enforcement of cartel discipline. Tariffs are walls that shield domestic producers from outside competition. No quotas were placed on the amount of steel that could be exported. This led to the practice of dumping steel in excess of domestic quotas on foreign markets. The export price was characteristically less than the price charged to domestic buyers. International price discrimination of this type was inherent in mass production. It is an outcome of the economics of overhead costs as it operated in international trade. It was profitable to sell at lower prices in foreign markets as long as these prices were sufficient to cover the additional or direct costs of producing and transporting the additional units of steel. The tariff made it impossible to undermine the high cartel-enforced domestic price by buying up German steel in foreign markets to export back into Germany for sale at low prices.

The general practice of price discrimination tended to cause vertical integration, that is, a combination of plants at successive stages of production.

German steel producers operating only a single stage, say the manufacture of tinplate, were severely handicapped in trying to compete with integrated firms. The former had to buy in the open market at the cartel-established prices, while to the integrated firms the cost of steel for tinplate was the actual cost of producing it themselves.

Foreign dumping, which was by no means confined to German cartels, is another phase of cutthroat competition, the domestic aspect of which has already been observed as one of the fundamental consequences of mass production. Control of international price cutting required international cartels of the type formed in Europe in 1926, when the steel producers of Germany, France, Belgium and Luxemburg came together into the European Steel Cartel. An international cartel was possible only after strong domestic cartels had already been established. The existence of a strong steel cartel in France was an exception to the general condition in that country, where the combination movement was relatively weak because of the less developed state of mass production and the traditional French emphasis on quality production.

3. Mixed cartels. High prices and limited quotas on coal and steel led in Germany to the formation of mixed coal and steel firms at the expense of pure coal mines and pure steel mills. Because steel production requires large quantities of coal, many steel companies own coal mines. Coal mined by steel companies for their own use became exempt from the quotas established by the Rhenish-Westphalian Coal Syndicate. Since the actual cost of mining coal was significantly less than the market price, pure steel mills, which bought coal in the market, were at a disadvantage compared with mixed companies. There was an incentive for pure steel mills to acquire their own coal mines. Furthermore, there was an incentive for coal mining companies to align themselves with steel mills in order to gain exemption from the quota on part of their coal production. This meant that a steel company owning coal mines or a coal company owning steel mills enjoyed advantages over pure coal mines and pure steel mills. The growth of large mixed companies simultaneously increasing their quotas in both the coal syndicate and the steel union brought closer ties between the two giant industrial combinations and an increasing concentration of economic power in German heavy industry.

Business Combinations in Great Britain. British hostility toward business combinations in restraint of trade extends back to the age of mercantilism, when there was strong public reaction against widespread grants of monopoly by the Crown and Parliament. "Patents of Monopoly" granted by the Stuart kings were a leading issue in the English Revolution of the seventeenth century. The Stuarts granted monopolies in domestic trade in return for revenues which were used to by-pass Parliament in the historic struggle for control of the purse strings of government.

With the coming of *laissez-faire,* monopolies based on government grants were abolished. A few monopolies which did not rely upon government sanction persisted into the nineteenth century. The most famous was the Newcastle Vend, a cartel arrangement based on control of ocean transport of coal from Newcastle to London. The Newcastle Vend existed, with a few interruptions, from 1585 until 1844, when the coming of the railways provided an inexpensive alternative for transporting coal to the London market. After 1873 attempts were made to re-establish group control, but without success. The number of coal producing areas and the number of coal mining firms were too numerous and the individualistic tradition was too strong to make a coal cartel of the Ruhr type feasible in Britain. Joint action in coal mining with government sanction was attempted during and after the First World War, but the results were not significant. Not until nationalization in 1946 did combinations in coal mining make notable progress, and this was achieved within an entirely different framework than that which characterized the capitalistic form of enterprise under discussion here.

In the British steel industry, combinations were more successful than in coal, although there was nothing comparable to the German Steelworks Union. The new steel processes of the second half of the nineteenth century increased the size and reduced the number of producers to a degree that made combination feasible. Some heavy steel products like ship and boiler plate were effectively monopolized. However, free trade was a major obstacle to the control of steel prices and output. Foreign steel could be shipped into Great Britain duty free until 1932. The supply of steel on the domestic market was at the mercy of conditions beyond the control of British producers. Actually conditions for monopoly in steel were not too unfavorable in the decade preceding the First World War. This was a period of general economic expansion, especially in Germany, where the armament drive left little steel for export to Britain. A loose group authority for disciplining the market was provided by the British Steel Association.

Amalgamation, which along with association ranks as the most important form of British combination, is an actual merging of the assets of several previously competing firms into a single business enterprise under one management, with one balance sheet and one profit-and-loss statement. Amalgamations occurred early among British railways, which were consolidated into four main companies. British joint-stock banks began to amalgamate in the nineteenth century and by the eve of the First World War the Big Five commercial banks had traveled most of the road toward the domination they finally achieved after the war.

One of the most successful British amalgamations occurred in cotton sewing thread. J. and P. Coats merged with four of its rivals in 1896 to form a virtual monopoly of the domestic market and expanded its foreign activities until it dominated cotton sewing thread markets throughout the civilized world. Factories were built inside tariff walls in the United States, Canada, Russia, Germany, Austria and Hungary. The success of this remarkable firm was primarily a function of its efficiency, especially in marketing. Because of the immense value of its trademark and the inelastic demand (that is, a sales volume insensitive to price changes) for thread of high quality, Coats was able to prevent rivals from undercutting on prices by refusing to sell to dealers who sold other brands at lower prices. Annual profits of 20 per cent and more were earned regularly by Coats.

Perhaps the greatest of all British combinations was formed in the soap industry by means of both amalgamation and association. W. H. Lever began a successful soap business in the late 1880's, when vegetable oils were just beginning to be used for making soap. By the end of the century Lever Brothers were operating copra mills in Australia, cotton seed mills in the United States and soap works in Germany and Switzerland. In 1906 Lever attempted a cartel type of agreement with ten other British soap firms, but the arrangement was abandoned after three weeks in favor of a giant amalgamation. In 1914 a soap manufacturers' association under the domination of Lever Brothers was established.

Summary View of Combinations and Monopoly. The foregoing discussion of combinations and monopoly, which has been largely confined to Germany and Great Britain prior to the First World War, may now be summarized. The conclusions stated below would seem to apply with still greater force to the period since 1914. It should be repeated that market capitalism remained dominant between 1850 and 1914. Stress throughout has been upon certain emergent forces that were causing the disintegration of the self-regulating market and not upon the ultimate achievement of this result.

1. The age of mass production witnessed great concentration of economic power in all capitalist nations. The institutional embodiment of this concentration has been primarily the joint-stock company, aided and abetted by devices such as cartels, holding companies, amalgamations and associations.

2. The main purpose of business combination has been to increase the

profitability of participating firms. The method is to restrict output in order to maintain or to raise prices. The general effect has been to replace the free market with a controlled market.

3. Concentration in industry has been facilitated by concentration in banking, especially investment banking. In Germany, and to a lesser extent on the Continent generally, the intermingling of investment banking and commercial banking has gone hand in hand with a close alliance between industry and banking.

4. Free trade has been an important obstacle to the monopolistic control of domestic markets. This accounts in part for the weaker development of combinations in Great Britain as compared with Germany. However, monopolies have developed in Great Britain despite its national policy of free trade.

5. In its positive aspect the combination movement may be viewed as an attempt to achieve a higher institutional synthesis corresponding to the requirements of a highly complex, integrated technology. Cartels, holding companies and trade associations are indirect means of transferring authority from an intra-enterprise to an inter-enterprise basis, and amalgamations are a direct means of doing the same thing. Although business firms may have been striving to maintain and to improve their profit-making position and may have been motivated only to a minor extent by search for a higher form of socio-economic organization, a significant result has been the creation of co-ordinated planning of a type which is necessary for the efficient operation of large-scale technology. Science lay at the roots of this co-operative effort. The experience suggests that attempts to restore the self-regulating market by atomizing large-scale organization are foredoomed to failure by the exigencies of science in the service of industry.

6. Co-ordination on the technological level is a necessary but not a sufficient condition for the efficient performance of the economy as a whole. Price maintenance and output restriction associated with business combination are in fact the exact opposite of what is desirable for social efficiency and general welfare. In this respect the combination movement offered no satisfactory substitute for the free market which it tended to displace. It stopped short of economy-wide co-ordination based on social accounting. On the economic level, as distinguished from the technological level, business combinations were restrictionist in the sense that they tended to increase the discrepancy between actual and potential production.

GROWTH OF ORGANIZED LABOR

Trade union movements, like business combinations, were a reaction against the destructive forces of the free market. The organization of wage earners into trade unions has always been motivated by a desire to remove competition from the labor market. England's Industrial Revolution demonstrated the degrading effect of a free market in labor upon the wage-earning class. Protection of workers first took the form of paternalistic legislation under the sponsorship of aristocratic Tory statesmen who put across the factory legislation of the first half of the nineteenth century in the face of opposition by factory owners. In the second half of the century the working class took protection into its own hands by organizing into trade unions, beginning with the more highly skilled workers and moving downward into the less skilled strata. Since full removal of competition from the labor movement could be achieved only by elimination of capitalism, the labor movements in European countries sooner or later became anti-capitalistic. Among well-disciplined labor groups the dominant philosophy was socialistic. In southern European countries, like Italy and Spain, syndicalism was strong. In France union groups were also inclined toward syndicalism, with little faith in parliamentary means, but a strong and fairly cohesive socialist group operating on the political level was developed by 1905. The following discussion shows how the two most important labor movements in Europe, those of Great Britain and Germany, started from different cultural backgrounds and with different philosophical foundations, but arrived at approximately the same position on the eve of the First World War.

British Labor Movement. 1. Craft Unions for Skilled Workers. After the failure of Robert Owen's Grand National Consolidated Trades Union in 1834 and the collapse of the Chartist movement in 1848, the British working class launched a small but cohesive labor movement in 1851, when several unions in the metal trades formed a federation called the Amalgamated Society of Engineers. These unions were organized on craft lines and their membership consisted mainly of better-paid skilled workmen. These aristocrats of the working class formed a homogeneous group under able leadership with limited goals. They consciously avoided the mistakes of Owen's "one big union" with its heterogeneous membership and revolutionary goals that had aroused the fears and hostility of employers, government and the middle class. The craft unions stood on solid ground. They accepted the capitalist order and devoted their energies primarily to getting higher wages and better working conditions for themselves. Skilled labor was a scarce commodity for which a high price could be demanded if the workers acted in union rather than as individuals.

One important function of the craft union was to provide sickness, unemployment and disability benefits for its members. Since they were able to provide a reasonable measure of security for themselves through their union organization, these skilled workers felt little concern for social security through government. They were more concerned with the safety of the large sums of money which accumulated in their treasuries. Parliament enacted legislation which seemed to protect union funds against embezzlement by union officials and, more important, against claims that might be made against unions in the pursuit of legitimate activities such as strikes.

Apart from the extension of suffrage to urban male wage earners under the reform bill of 1867, the most important gain of the working class in the third quarter of the nineteenth century was the passage of legislation strengthening the legal position of trade unions. Parliamentary legislation in 1871 and 1875 gave full legal status to trade unions. The right to strike was guaranteed by the provision that no act done by a combination of workers was punishable unless the same act by an individual was a criminal offense. Peaceful picketing was expressly legalized. The weapons required for successful collective bargaining were now established by statutory law.

2. Industrial Unionism and Political Representation. The British labor movement entered a new phase of development during the 1880's and 1890's. The old unionism with its conservative outlook, its narrow membership among skilled workers and its essentially *laissez-faire* point of view failed to meet the needs of the growing masses of unskilled, semi-skilled and white collar workers. Even the workers in the metal trades, who had made up the bulk of membership in the aristocratic Amalgamated Society of Engineers, found themselves affected by the new methods of automatic machinery, assembly-line production and other mass production techniques. Furthermore the old unions had been weakened by the Long Depression of the 1870's. As unemployment spread, leaders of the old unions contented themselves with paying unemployment benefits and maintaining wage rates for their employed members. Among the groups which were most important in the growth of the new unionism were the dock workers, gas workers, transport workers, woolen textile workers, miners and white collar workers.

Leaders of the new unionism took a broader view of the labor movement than had those of the old. To the new leaders unionism meant more than benefit payments for old age and unemployment. They saw in the trade union an instrument for molding a better form of society. Whereas the old unions preferred to provide their own social insurance, the lower-paid, less skilled workers in the new unions looked to government for protection against the hazards of industrial society. Since these workers lacked economic bargaining power, they sought to achieve their goals through direct political action. Their philosophy was basically equalitarian; ultimately it became socialistic along the lines of the Fabians, a society of middle class intellectuals who developed the "gradualist" philosophy for the British social movement. The Fabians played a prominent role in the labor movement and in the Labour Party. Although the ultimate aims of the new unionism were socialistic, the immediate goal was to improve the position of the entire working class under capitalism.

The crucial years of the transition from the old to the new unionism were from 1888 to 1893. The most important single event in this transition was probably the famous Dockers' Strike of 1889. Without previous formal organization a great army of unskilled dock workers won a notable triumph in a strike that lasted four weeks. By their model conduct the strikers gained widespread public sympathy and financial support. Success in the Dockers' Strike sparked a trade union boom that increased total union membership from about three-quarters of a million to more than one-and-a-half million in 1892. This doubling of trade union membership was accompanied by substantial increases in wages.

The link between the unions and political action was provided by the Trades Union Congress, the central organization in which representatives from nearly all British trade unions came together in an annual "Parliament of Labour." After gaining control of the Trades Union Congress, the new labor leaders attempted to use it to promote favorable government legislation. Labor representation in Parliament now became a leading objective in the British labor movement. The Independent Labour Party, under the leadership of Kier Hardie, was organized in 1893 with the blessing if not the official backing of the Trades Union Congress. In the constitution of the Independent Labour Party the stated objective was "to secure the collective ownership of all means of production, distribution and exchange." Despite this avowed socialist goal, the term "socialist" was explicitly rejected in choosing a name for the new party. This arose not from a desire to conceal the ultimate ends, but from a greater preoccupation with immediate gains to the laboring classes. "Gradualism" became the keynote of the socialist labor movement in Great Britain.

An official link was forged between the unions and political action in 1900, when the Trades Union Congress established the Labour Representation

Committee, with Ramsay MacDonald as its first secretary. The step from the Labour Representation Committee to the full-fledged Labour Party of 1906 was stimulated by the Taff Vale court decision of 1901. The Taff Vale Railway Company of Wales brought a civil suit against the railway union for damages resulting from loss of business during the strike. There was no legal question of physical damage to the property of the railway company or of any other form of criminal action on the part of the workers or the union. Nevertheless, a court decision, which was upheld in the House of Lords, awarded to the Taff Vale Company 23,000 pounds in damages against the union to be paid from the union treasury. The Taff Vale decision was a crippling blow at the whole labor movement. Gains which appeared to have been won in the 1870's now seemed lost. Each time a union engaged in an organized strike its funds, including those held for old age and other security benefits, were endangered. Therefore the Taff Vale decision virtually ruled out the right to strike as a weapon in labor disputes. Trade unionists had assumed that under the legislation of the 1870's a labor union, as an unincorporated association of individuals, although subject to all the laws of criminal action and destruction of property, could not be sued for damages caused by organized union support of strike actions on the part of the union and its members. However, the law of 1875 applied to criminal liability and this was a civil suit.

Alarm spread among the trade unions. The Labour Representation Committee pushed its activities and gained widespread support from the ranks of all unions. The older, more conservative unions feared they might lose their large security benefit funds. Between 1901 and 1906 the size of the vote for labor candidates grew rapidly. In the election of 1906, forty-four working class representatives and a dozen "Lib-Labs" (Liberal-Labor candidates) won seats in Parliament. The Liberal Government of 1906 worked closely with labor's representatives. One of the first acts of the new Government was to pass the famous Trade Disputes Act of 1906, which removed the danger of another Taff Vale decision. This act provided that courts should not hear any action brought against trade unions for the recovery of damages resulting from the action of a union or its members. By this remarkable law trade union funds became exempt from liability for civil damages.

By the end of 1913 membership in British trade unions had grown to four millions. By 1920 it was in excess of eight millions. In the general election of 1923 the Labour Party returned 191 Members of Parliament and in 1929 the number jumped to 287. On the eve of the Great Depression, Labour had displaced the Liberals as one of the two great political parties.

In the general election at the close of the Second World War the Labour Party won a thumping victory with nearly twelve million popular votes and an overwhelming majority of the seats in the House of Commons. In less than half a century an entirely new political party had arisen out of the trade union movement to first place in a great democracy. The Labour Party immediately began to put into law its long-standing program to socialize the means of production in basic industries (coal, transportation, communication, the Bank of England, public utilities, iron and steel) as part of a planned economy which would realize its long sought goal: to remove labor from the private capitalist market.

German Labor Movement. On the eve of the First World War the German labor movement stood in about the same position as the British labor movement. In both countries there was a close alliance between organized labor and political parties having socialist goals to be attained by gradual, democratic methods. There were, however, important differences in the course of development by which the labor movements in the two countries reached these comparable positions. In Germany the socialist movement fostered the labor unions, whereas in Britain the socialist movement grew out of the labor unions. German socialist political leaders used unions as "a political school for socialism."

The obvious reason for this difference was the same as in the case of the combination movement, namely, the different development of capitalism in the two countries. Industrial capitalism emerged later in Germany and with much less time elapsing from the end of craft guilds and feudal institutions. German craft guilds were still functioning in the third quarter of the nineteenth century, on the eve of the German industrial revolution. Consequently the spirit and structure of early German trade unions, as well as the whole complex of German life within which this labor movement took place, was in contrast to England.

Ferdinand Lassalle was not essentially a believer in labor unions as a method of social reform, but his leadership in establishing a German workers' party in 1863 did much to stimulate the labor movement. About ten years after Lassalle's death his workers' party merged with a Marxist party to form the German Social Democratic Party. Although the Social Democrats were socialists and accepted the general principles of Marxian socialism, the platform which they adopted in 1875 was severely criticized by Marx in his *Critique of the Gotha Programme.*

The political orientation of German unionism proved to be a handicap under the ultra-conservative regime of Chancellor Bismarck. When the Social Democratic Party began to receive a large popular vote, Bismarck put through anti-socialist laws banning all socialist parties and all trade unions sympathetic to socialism. Since most of the German unions were political in nature, the anti-socialist laws virtually banned labor unions. Only small, non-political unions were permitted to exist during the period of the anti-socialist laws (1878–90).

With the end of the anti-socialist laws in 1890 there was a great upsurge of union and socialist activity in Germany. The free trade unions—those associated with the Social Democratic Party—were tied together by the General Commission of German Trade Unions, an organization analogous to the British Trades Union Congress. There was essential harmony between the political party and the unions. Labor leaders, however, strove to improve the standing of the unions. By 1906 the unions had attained co-equal status with the Social Democratic Party.

Amalgamation of smaller unions led to concentration of membership in a few giant industrial unions. On the eve of the First World War, about 20 per cent of the two-and-a-half million members in German trade unions were in the metal workers' union, and two-thirds of the total membership was contained in the five largest unions (metal, building, transportation, woodworkers and general factory workers). Mass unionism contributed to the political power of the labor unions operating through the Social Democratic Party.

One result of the adoption of Marxist principles in the political labor movement was the alienation of certain groups of German workers. Many Catholics would not join an organization with philosophical doctrines critical of their religious beliefs. Another group, the highly skilled workers in craft unions, formed the Hirsch-Dunker Unions. This latter group, which was of the type that had been dominant in Britain for nearly forty years, always remained a small minority element in the total German labor movement. Mass production, industrial unionism and political action along socialist lines left little room for the growth of aristocratic unions in Germany.

Although the official doctrines of the German Social Democratic Party were Marxist, the actual practices of the affiliated labor unions involved more compromise with the existing capitalist order than is consistent with strict Marxist doctrine. The trade unionists of Germany, like those of Great Britain, were interested in getting higher wages and better working conditions immediately, leaving to the future the attainment of ultimate socialist goals. Eduard Bernstein's "revisionist" Marxism was in line with the philosophy of the trade unions and even with the actual behavior of the Social Democratic Party, which officially remained orthodox Marxist. Revisionism was the German counterpart of English Fabianism. Hence the German social movement and the British social movement had reached approximately the same position with respect to social philosophy and political power by 1913. Both were socialist in their ultimate aims but were also much preoccupied with improving day-to-day working conditions through political action stemming from the power of organized industrial unionism. In both countries the working-class political parties were still a minority, but growing in strength. Likewise, both of these parties were to assume larger political responsibility after the First World War.

SOCIAL INSURANCE AND THE RIGHT TO WORK

Labor unions substituted collective bargaining for individual bargaining, but they did not eliminate the insecurity of unemployment, the risks of accident and sickness and the infirmity of old age. Only a small percentage of workers belonged to trade unions which provided security benefits, and such benefits were generally inadequate. Fundamentally the insecurity of wage and salary earners under capitalism stemmed from their complete detachment, except through the market, from any means of production, that is, it stemmed from their economic dependence on the sale of their labor in the market. Slaves and serfs enjoyed more economic security, though less freedom, than wage earners under capitalism. Factory workers who became unemployed, incapacitated, ill or too old had no place to turn except to the degrading poor house. They had no land on which to grow their own potatoes; they probably owned no home; and their wage-earning children were not able to support them. Under the factory system the family ceased to function as an economic unit. In theory, perhaps, workers were supposed to save enough while employed to take care of contingencies arising from lack of employment. For the multitude this was hardly feasible in the face of low wages, lengthening periods of unemployment, the high incidence of accidents under mechanized industry and the increased difficulty of finding employment after middle age. To provide security on an individual basis against these multiplying hazards was impossible for any but the most able, frugal and fortunate worker. Compulsory social insurance on a national scale was the method adopted to meet this situation.

Germany was the first nation to provide a comprehensive system of social security against the hazards of industrial capitalism. Social insurance laws were put into effect by Bismarck in an attempt to appease the German workers, who resented his anti-socialist laws. The Sickness Insurance Act of 1883 provided compulsory health insurance for industrial workers, with contributions paid by both employers and employees. The compulsory provision of this law distinguished it from earlier voluntary schemes of health insurance. The Accident Insurance Act of 1884 provided compensation to workers who were incapacitated by injuries. By defining "accident" broadly the law rendered employers responsible for all injuries incurred by workers during employment and removed the necessity of litigation to prove employer responsibility. The Old Age and Invalidity Act of 1888 provided for contributions from both employer and worker. Benefit payments for old age began at seventy. Protection against premature incapacity to work was also provided under this law. Social security measures of the type instituted by Bismarck subsequently spread to nearly all modern nations. One important type of social security which Bismarck did not attempt was unemployment insurance. It was left to the British to pioneer in this field in the years just prior to the First World War.

At first the Social Democrats did not take kindly to Bismarck's paternalism, but the social insurance measures were so popular with the rank and file of industrial workers that union and socialist leaders eventually reconciled social security under capitalism with their "gradualist" philosophy.

While nearly all elements in the British labor movement accepted social insurance as an important forward step for the working class, the more militant and the more socialist-minded members viewed social insurance as nothing more than a palliative. In the period just before the First World War, when unemployment insurance measures were before Parliament, the Labour Party's own approach to unemployment was a Right to Work Bill. The "right to work" issue had appeared sporadically throughout modern history. It occupied a prominent role in the French Revolution of 1848, in which Louis Blanc and his followers championed a constitutional guarantee of the right to work. The basic idea behind this right is that it is the duty of society, acting through its representative, the government, to find employment for all able-bodied workers and, failing that, to provide adequate maintenance. The right to work, if achieved, would have removed, or gone far toward removing, the commodity status of labor. It is a doctrine which denies the purely private nature of the means of production and is thus in conflict with a fundamental principle of capitalist society.

SUMMARY AND EPILOGUE

European capitalism achieved its highest state of development in the years from 1850 to 1914. During the early part of this period the trend was toward free, competitive markets of the type which the classical economists identified with the ideal form of economic society. In the latter part of the period the trend was away from free markets. Although all levels of the institutional complex moved at different rates and reached turning points at different times, the onset of the Long Depression in 1873 marks a convenient dividing line between competitive and monopolistic capitalism in Europe.

A remarkable coalescence of technological and economic forces interacting upon one another set in motion cumulative changes with revolutionary consequences. Cheap steel, precision manufacture, interchangeable parts and the assembly line created a technology of mass production. Cheap transportation and rapid communication—also arising from technological changes—created world-wide markets, which in turn encouraged further development of mass production. The phenomenal growth of the money market was a response to the spread of the joint-stock company, which was required to finance the massive needs of large-scale production. Once available, the enlarged money market facilitated the formation of joint-stock companies and increased the utilization of mass production techniques. Meanwhile, large, quasi-public joint-stock companies were altering the economic, if not the legal, meaning of the most fundamental institution of capitalism, private ownership in the means of production. Strides in mass production were not equaled by mass consumption. Potential overproduction accentuated economic fluctuations, especially the depression phase, while exerting pressure to expand into underdeveloped areas where the rivalry among European nations in the export of capital contained the seeds of economic imperialism.

Mass production and cheap transportation created conditions that evoked attempts by different groups to escape the uncomfortable, unpredictable and sometimes destructive effects of free competition. Continental farmers and businessmen demanded protective tariffs when confronted with a flood of cheap foreign products. Industrialists formed business combinations which would enable them to maintain prices and limit output to profitable levels. Wage earners formed trade unions in order to remove competition from the labor market, and they formed political parties by which they hoped ultimately to reconstruct economic society along non-capitalistic lines. Social insurance was legislated in order to protect wage and salary earners whose divorce from ownership of the means of production left them at the mercy of the capricious labor market. The over-all picture of European economic development between 1850 and 1914 suggests the self-destructive tendencies of the self-regulating market system.

From the vantage point of the second half of the twentieth century the trends which have been described as characteristic of western Europe between 1873 and 1914 appear as the dynamic forces that were to reshape the entire economic environment in the ensuing decades. After 1914 the four great events in world history all tended to accentuate the retreat from the self-regulating market: the First World War, the Russian Revolution, the Great Depression and the Second World War with its disturbing after-math. All the "New Deals" that emerged under the impact of these events carried out programs that departed sharply from the ideal of the free market: Russian Communism, Italian Fascism, German Nazism, the American New Deal and the British Welfare State. In the political ebb and flow of democracies like Great Britain and the United States the return to power of more con-servative governments appeared to represent a slowing down in the move-ment away from the free market rather than a reversal of the long-term trend.

Attempts to revive market capitalism in western Europe were made after the First and after the Second World Wars. In the 1920's statesmen who sought to return to "normalcy," to restore the prewar gold standard and to re-establish free markets were rewarded with a crushing depression in the 1930's. Among the great powers, only the one which had departed entirely from market capitalism, the Soviet Union, failed to experience mass unemployment and a catastrophic fall in production. The Great Depression was without parallel in its economic magnitude and its political and social consequences. Recovery from the Depression was, for the most part, achieved only by feverish prepara-tion for war and by war itself.

Attempts to revive market capitalism were less vigorous after the Second World War than after the First. The chief stimulus came from outside Eu-rope in the form of dollar-backed exhortations from the United States. Some minor successes were achieved, but the trend away from market capitalism continued largely unabated.

2. ECONOMIC IMPERIALISM

. . . The half century before 1914 witnessed, besides the vast growth of the United States and the rapid industrial development of Great Britain and Ger-many, a swift extension of modern commercial and industrial methods to new countries. Japan, long almost isolated from world trade, not only opened its ports to foreign commerce but proceeded with extraordinary thoroughness and speed to equip itself with the productive techniques of the Western world. British capital covered India with a network of railways and began to develop Indian productive resources for the supply of Western needs—especially tea. The European occupation of Africa, previously confined to a few areas within easy reach of the coast, broadened out until practically the whole continent had been annexed by one or other of the European Powers. Russia, the granary of Europe, borrowed capital extensively from richer countries to build railways to link up its vast territories in Europe and Asia, and attempted, behind a very high tariff, to create modern industries of its own, largely under imported foreign management. New commodities, such as rubber and oil, immensely increased the economic importance of Malaya, the Dutch East Indies, Persia, Burma and Mexico. Commerce ceased to be confined to the old trade routes, and ocean-going ships carried everywhere the mingled blessings and curses of modern civilisation. A fever of railway-building seized on the world and provided vast openings for the investment of capital in the less developed countries. Trade, which in the earlier part of the nineteenth century had been mainly an exchange of goods for goods, often on most unequal terms, came to depend to a growing extent on the investment of capital abroad by citizens of the older countries. With this investment of capital came a startling revival of empire-building and a renewed tendency towards political interference by the more advanced nations in the affairs of the less developed. When a trader sells a man a shirt, that is an end of the transaction; but when a great industrial concern or a group of financiers builds, or finances the building of, a railway in a backward country, payment can be made only by instalments spread over a long period. In such circumstances the providers of the physical capital, or of the money spent on buying it, continue to take a lively interest in what is done with it. The capitalists of the investing countries come to have a stake in the debtor countries and to regard the existence of orderly and debt-honouring governments in these countries as one of the rights of property; and they are apt to call upon their own Governments for help if these rights are challenged, or if disturbed political conditions in the backward country upset their hopes of gain. Moreover, the Governments of the advanced countries themselves set to work to extend their colonial empires in search both of markets for their products and of assured sources for the supply of foodstuffs and raw materials for their use—or even mainly for the sake of preventing their rivals from occupying territories which they may want to control and develop at some future date.

The recrudescence of imperialism in the latter part of the nineteenth century was no merely causeless change of political attitude. It was based on a profound alteration in the economic relationships between the countries of the world. Richard Cobden and John Bright and most of their contemporaries in Great Britain had believed that it was only a matter of time for the white colonies to proclaim their independence and become sovereign States, as the

United States had done in the previous century. Nor did they object to this; for they were convinced that trade would develop all the faster and more advantageously if no attempt were made to influence it by political pressure. In the native areas included within the British Empire, with the exception of India, the early Victorians took little interest; and on India many of them looked askance, as involving expensive responsibilities that were not worth while. Those who did value the Indian empire regarded it chiefly as a field for the expansion of the market for Lancashire cotton goods. The early Victorian capitalists looked at the world with the eyes of traders in finished consumable commodities, and their creed of *laissez-faire* followed logically from their economic ambitions.

But other countries, as they adopted the new industrialism, found themselves less fortunately placed than Great Britain. Their captains of industry found it hard to compete with the British in the open markets of the world, and they had no comparable colonial empires of their own. Just as they protected their own industries against British imports, so they set out to make such colonies as they had as far as possible closed markets for their own goods—and to get more colonies, in order to secure more protected markets and preferential fields for capital investment. British capitalism, confident in its industrial superiority and in its ability to lend capital more readily and on a larger scale than its rivals, felt for a long time no need to close its colonial territories to foreign products, even where it was in a position to impose its own terms; but the newer colonial empires of France and Germany grew up to a far greater extent as closed markets for the goods and capital of the metropolitan countries.

This does not mean that Great Britain was unaffected by the growth of imperialism. On the contrary, the British also set out to annex fresh territory and to build in every part of the Empire railways and other public undertakings which supplied profitable outlets both for British capital and for the products of the British industries making capital goods; nor did British economic activity stop short at the boundaries of the Empire. The Argentine was opened up mainly with British capital and British machinery, and there was active British investment in China, as well as in India, and even in colonies belonging to other Powers, such as the Dutch East Indies.

This expansion of industrialism over almost the whole world is connected intimately with the growth of the metal trades, as closely as the earlier phases of the Industrial Revolution had been with the rise of the Lancashire cotton industry. In the second quarter of the nineteenth century coal, iron and engineering had laid the foundations of the new system of transport. Great

Britain owed a great deal of its advantage at this stage to the abundance of
its coal and to its possession of good supplies of iron-ore in close proximity to
the coalfields. This second phase of the Industrial Revolution consolidated
British economic supremacy. British engineering skill had built the main-line
railways mainly between 1826 and the later 'forties, and thereafter the British
engineers and contractors set out to use their acquired skill and experience
in the profitable task of railway-building for the rest of the world. Great railway contractors such as Thomas Brassey, finding orders no longer plentiful
at home, began to look further afield; but undeveloped countries could not
afford to supply the capital for expensive railway projects, however great the
prospects of economic expansion by their means might be. British capitalists,
enriched by the profits of earlier ventures, could afford to lend the money as
well as supply the skill. British capital, British technicians and British skilled
labour undertook the task of equipping a large part of Western Europe, and
later India and the Argentine, China and Africa, and many other parts of
the world, with the new means of transport.

Railway construction occupies indeed a position of extraordinary significance in the evolution of modern capitalism. On the one hand it has been the
means by which the hinterland of vast continents has been opened up to trade
and settlement, and, jointly with the steamship, the instrument whereby the
raw materials and the producing capacity of the New World, of Africa, and
of the East have been made available for European use; and on the other hand
it has largely influenced and determined both the structure of capitalist business and the growth of overseas investment as a means of hastening the spread
of power production over a larger and larger part of the world.

The railway played an even more important part than the steamship in
the promotion of international trade, for the steamship for the most part only
enabled goods to be carried faster and in greater quantities along the familiar
routes of commerce, whereas the railway multiplied many times over the
area of the world open to commercial exploitation and settlement. Industrialism, before the coming of the railroads, could be hardly more than a fringe
of smoke round the seaboards of even the most advanced countries. The railways industrialised, or at any rate commercialised, the interior as well. Above
all else, they were the making of the United States as an advanced industrial
nation. . . .

No less significant was the effect of railway development in internationalis-
ing the supply of capital. British overseas investment had indeed begun before the coming of the railways; there had been large private investments in
the West Indian plantations and in North America during the eighteenth cen-

tury. Moreover, after the Napoleonic wars there had been a boom in overseas issues, especially loans and investments in the South American States which had just thrown off the Spanish dominion and were looked to as expanding markets for British goods. But before the epoch of overseas railway construction there was not a great deal of investment of capital abroad except in Government loans or in purely private ventures such as the plantations of the West Indies. It was mainly through the building of railways overseas that British investors first learned to trust their money in foreign industrial ventures; and, in this respect too, what began with railways soon spread to other industries. The export of capital took a great and increasing place in the economic development of the modern world, and in this sphere, as in home investment, railway enterprise was the principal pioneer.

In this great movement of overseas investment Great Britain, as the only country with any large mass of surplus capital to invest, led the way. The rapid growth of British capacity to export goods provided the necessary resources, but exports could not develop to the full in a world much poorer than Britain unless British capitalists were prepared to lend to other countries the means of buying what they had to sell and were content to receive a deferred return as interest on their lendings. As we have seen, this overseas lending was largely confined in its early stages to public loans or to plantations; but after the coming of the railways it expanded into private industrial projects on a steadily increasing scale. In 1850 British capitalists had already perhaps £230 millions invested abroad, mainly in Government stocks, with a sprinkling of commercial and mining investment. . . . It has been estimated that in 1914 British investors had at least £4000 millions invested abroad, and of this sum more than £1500 millions was in railway securities and £1000 millions in Government loans.

No other country had in 1914 even half so large a total overseas investment as Great Britain. France is estimated to have had about £1800 millions; Germany about £1200 millions; and the United States about £540 millions. The foreign investments of the United States were mainly in South and Central America; the French and German mainly in Europe and in their own colonies; but in all cases the total included a large mass of investments in railway securities, besides the proceeds of Government loans which had been devoted to the building of State-owned railway systems. France, outside its own colonies, had specialised chiefly in public loans and in the financing of the economic development of Russia; while Germany had distributed its investments about equally between Europe and the rest of the world, with a preponderance of fixed-interest-bearing securities. Only British investment was very widely spread over all countries and every type of bond and share, both public and private.

Undoubtedly this heavy investment of capital overseas greatly speeded up the economic growth of the more backward countries and stimulated in the more developed countries the expansion of the industries producing capital goods. It was indeed largely a result of the concentration of income in the hands of the richer sections of the community, for this both increased savings and limited the home market for consumers' goods, and thus provided an incentive to the active capitalists and financiers to be always on the look-out for fresh markets and fields for investment abroad in order to absorb the growing productivity of capitalist industry and the larger and larger masses of capital looking for profitable outlets. If wages had risen faster in the older countries, the aggregate increase of wealth in the world as a whole might possibly have been slower and the industrialisation of the less advanced areas would probably have been delayed, but there would have been a better diffusion of wealth in the developed countries. There would also have been less international rivalry, less imperialism and subjection of the weaker peoples, and less sowing of the seeds of war.

Yet, obviously, it is in itself a good thing for the richer and better-equipped countries to help on the development of the less advanced. Obviously, it would have been in every way better if this could have been done without either subjecting the borrowers to the political control of the lenders or involving the lending countries in quarrelling with one another about their rights to help in the expansion of the new industrialism. But, as the world was, the less advanced countries became, not so much willing borrowers from the more advanced, as recipients of loans and investments which were thrust upon them even against their wills and were applied to such purposes as suited the needs of the lending rather than of the debtor countries. Investment developed as a means of finding markets and raw materials and foodstuffs needed by the advanced countries, and was uninfluenced by considerations of the well-being of the peoples among whom it was made. Of course, it often raised the national incomes of the borrowing countries; but that was incidental only, and against this has to be set its effect in breaking up the old ways of living without providing any substitute pattern of culture adjusted to local needs. Moreover, the advanced countries were continually squabbling for the rights of their national capitalists to exploit the backward countries' resources. The enterprises set up in the less developed countries were often not only financed by alien capital and managed by alien technicians and supervisors but also conducted under alien control by companies registered and administered in the lending country. The white workers received salaries out of all relation to native incomes; and usually no attempt was made to train native workers for the more skilled tasks. The profits of the enterprises were remitted home to the alien owners; and the countries in which the enterprises were carried on, unless they were recognised as fully civilised nations, had to submit to alien policing and often even to annexation, either open or disguised under the form of a protectorate or a mandate. The native inhabitants became in effect sources of man-power for the less skilled tasks under alien capitalists; and in many areas steps were taken to force reluctant tribesmen to supply labour to man the white man's mines and plantations. In other areas, such as Malaya, mass importation of workers from other backward countries changed the make-up of the local populations and created vast insoluble political problems of mixed societies. In some cases, a large part of the tax revenue of the backward countries came to be earmarked as security for the payment of interest on the alien capital. The capitalist world, in the latter part of the nineteenth century, became far less tolerant of uncivilised peoples and even of peoples backward in relation to Western standards of economic progress. While Europe was asserting within its own borders the rights of nationality and self-determination, it was also denying the right of non-European peoples to abstain from using to the full, according to Western notions, the potential wealth of their lands and their labour power, and was claiming the right to enforce the development of any territory inhabited by less civilised peoples, as part of the civilising mission of the white races.

Of course, from the standpoint of the capitalists in the advanced countries, with their faith in the virtues of large-scale production, there were reasonable arguments in support of this attitude. Modern capitalist industrialism could develop only if it could find both expanding markets for its products and larger and larger supplies of foodstuffs and raw materials which it could receive in exchange for them. It needed not only the produce of the prairie lands of America and the ranches of Australia, where there were relatively few natives to be dispossessed, but also that of tropical Africa, rubber and tin from Malaya and the Dutch East Indies, and a host of other commodities from countries already thickly populated by native inhabitants who would not and could not produce enough to meet the needs of the advanced countries except under the stimulus of white intervention. Why, asked the European capitalist, should these native populations be allowed to ignore the vast economic opportunities of the regions in which they dwelt? Their own standards of wealth and civilisation could rise only if they were taught how to use the resources lying ready to their hands; and only the white man could teach them. That was the white man's mission—a mission, as he saw it, of civilisation for the world as well as of enrichment for himself, a mission necessary in the interests of the progress of industrialism—which was assumed to be good. National self-determination, according to this view, could hold good only for peoples who had their eyes sufficiently open to the economic main chance. A sentimental regard for the cultural traditions and ways of living of the more primitive peoples must not be allowed to stay the civilising march of the capitalist industrial system.

But, unhappily, the white men did not march on their civilising mission either as a united army or with any notion of human equality or brotherhood in their minds. Even those who "got on well with the natives" commonly had a contempt for them and regarded their institutions without respect. Moreover, the white men disputed and even fought one another for the right to exploit the less developed regions of the earth. The partition of Africa was accomplished without actual war between the great Powers, which divided up practically the whole continent, but not without recurrent threats of war. In 1918 the colonial empire of Germany was parcelled out among the victors, and though the form of annexation was hidden under the cloak of the mandatory system and each annexing Power pledged itself to administer its mandated territories in the interests of their inhabitants, in effect most of the mandated areas were virtually added to the empires of the victorious Allies. One thing, indeed, was secured—the open door in these areas for the commerce of all nations—but with that exception the mandatory system differed little from positive annexation. Only after the rise of the Soviet Union and the development of native nationalism, which was greatly stimulated by the Second World War, did the older notions of imperialism go out of fashion; and even then they died hard, especially in the French colonies, but also in Malaya and in East and Central Africa.

The root of the problem lay in the need of the developed countries for ever-expanding markets and sources of supply to keep their industries at work and their peoples fed. It is not in the nature of modern industrialism to stand still. It must either grow or decay, and under the conditions of the nineteenth century it had, in order to grow, to find markets for its products largely outside its own borders—except where, as in the United States, its home population was being reinforced by a stream of immigrants. Especially in Great Britain and Germany, industrialism grew up, not as a balanced system of production and consumption, but as a development of specialised production of certain classes of machine-made goods made largely out of imported raw materials— and under conditions which necessitated the importation of large quantities of foodstuffs as well. Any system of this sort must sell abroad in order to buy, and can raise the standard of living at home only by selling more and more of its products abroad. It must, moreover, if it is to have more to sell, assure itself of a constantly growing supply of necessary materials. This was much less true of France than of either Great Britain or Germany, and it has been still less true of the United States, with its vaster territory and its more balanced economic development of industry and agriculture. But it was broadly true of all the great empire-building countries. The inevitable result appeared in the growth of Economic Imperialism and in the rivalries of the great Powers for the effective possession of sources of supply as well as of expanding markets. The struggle for oil furnishes an outstanding example.

In sum, the latter half of the nineteenth century was marked by the development of a new kind of Economic Imperialism. Between 1884 and 1900 the territory of the British Empire was increased by more than 3.7 million square miles, containing more than 57 million people. France annexed 3½ million square miles, with more than 36 million inhabitants; and Germany, much less favourably placed, built up, chiefly in Africa, a colonial empire of over a million square miles, with nearly 17 million inhabitants. The United States took over Puerto Rico, the Philippines, Hawaii and Alaska. Italy followed France and Great Britain into Northern Africa. Russia and Great Britain squabbled over Persia and intrigued in Afghanistan and the States of Central Asia. France, Spain and Germany fell out in Morocco. Belgium, under Leopold, attempted to develop the Congo on lines which shocked the conscience even of an imperialist world. In 1914 it was very nearly true that there was no territory left on the face of the earth which had not been appropriated or at least dominated by one or another of the "civilised Powers." The great exception was China, which had proved too tough a nut for even modern capitalism to crack: and China, because it could not be partitioned, had found itself at the mercy of the intrigues and rivalries of the great Powers. All the world over, Economic Imperialism had become a dominant force in world politics, and behind it loomed the ever-growing threat of war. . . . There were strong reasons why the capitalist system of the later nineteenth century turned away from the pacific courses of Cobdenism to policies resting on domestic Protection and the attempt to monopolise colonial markets, materials and fields of investment; but these economic forces did not operate in isolation from the political forces, which cannot be correctly represented as simply derivative or secondary. Imperialism is a very much older thing than capitalism, and although in the nineteenth century it took on new forms, deeply affected by changes in what Marx called "the powers of production," the old lusts for power, the old militaristic impulses affecting whole nations and particularly their ruling classes, did not cease to operate: they were merely reinforced when monopolist capitalism became the ally or the auxiliary of militant expansionism, as it did in Japan as well as in Germany. Even in Great Britain it was certainly not from economic motives only that Disraeli caused Queen Victoria to be proclaimed Empress of India. Nor was the new imperialism at all welcome to important sections of the British capitalist classes. The new imperialism was not identical with the old, but it is fully as important to recognise its continuity as to draw attention to the way in which it was affected by the growth in the scale of economic enterprise and by the drive to find markets and materials and scope for the investment of surplus capital outside the older countries.

Chapter XI

SOCIAL AND MORAL PERSPECTIVES OF
THE RECENT PAST

ॐ

T HE BASIC TRANSFORMATIONS in economic and political institutions and practices following 1850 have been accompanied by basic transformations in the ideas by which men interpret and attempt to control their social life. It has become increasingly difficult to understand the growth of monopolies, trusts, labor unions, and other forms of collective action, the revival of economic policies and rivalries, the spread of imperialism, and the like, in terms of laissez-faire economics, individualistic ethics, and older theories of democratic politics. Active democratic citizenship, which implies public spirit and community interests, has been made steadily more difficult by increasing specialization, the growing complexity, bigness, and impersonality of events, and the growing number of conflicting pressures and interests, within nations and between them. Not only has the ideal of a spirited and informed public tended to fade; but the independent business man, the free laborer, the individual owner of private property, the unrestricted consumer, the independent voter—"the individual" whom John Stuart Mill celebrated and justified, has seemed to many to be on the verge of disappearing altogether.

Within this context, the tremendous changes in social theory and practice during the century since 1850 have by and large taken the direction either of direct attack upon, or thoroughgoing revision of, the traditional ideals of the independent individual, and of the civil liberties and social freedom. There is still a further reason why changes should have taken this direction. Traditionally, property rights and "the freedom of contract," interpreted in laissez-faire terms, had been placed among the inalienable civil liberties, and indeed had often been made the basic liberties on which all the others—e.g., freedom of the press—were held to depend. Whether or not it is possible to limit freedom

---

This chapter, designed especially for the present volume, has been revised from its form in the first edition and is by Charles Frankel.

of contract and still maintain civil liberties is one of the major social issues with which our own generation is concerned. Whatever the relationship may be, however, terms like "laissez-faire" and "free competition" have come to seem increasingly misleading, with the growth of massive economic groupings like the industrial monopoly, the financial cartel, and the labor union. And since the civil liberties had in the past been associated with the struggle for, and the philosophical justification of, freedom of contract, many of those who have pointed out the weaknesses of an economy founded on freedom of contract have also extended their criticism to the other liberties as well. As we shall see, some programs of social reform, in their desire to attain economic security, have thought it necessary—or at least not worth hesitating over—to suspend, "temporarily" or otherwise, the civil liberties. Other programs, like that of the present British Labor Party, which are rooted in a liberal tradition, have recognized the integral relationship between economic security and the continued maintenance and extension of the civil liberties, and have attempted to save these ideals by reformulating them in the light of this recognition.

It has now come to seem to many that, if the civil liberties are endangered by economic insecurity and unregulated economic power, it is also true that economic and social security—security in one's job, or security from arbitrary arrest—are dependent on the civil liberties. In any case, the century since 1850 has seen a fundamental reconsideration of the relationship of the economic ideals of the Enlightenment to its cultural and political ideals. There has been either a general rejection of the ideals, economic, political, and cultural, which the Enlightenment fostered or a thoroughgoing reformulation of them in the light of changed conditions. We shall see that both the socialist and the liberal movements of the last century have tended to split internally over the question of the relationship of the civil liberties to property rights.

FABIANISM, REVISIONISM, COMMUNISM, SYNDICALISM [1]

The growth of industrial society has forced revisions of socialist theory and practice that are as extensive and thoroughgoing as those that have taken place in connection with liberalism. Indeed, the tendency of liberalism to break up in a number of conflicting directions is paralleled by a similar tendency within socialism. In this section we shall discuss the following varieties of post-Marxian socialism: Fabian socialism (named after Fabius, the Roman general, who exhausted Hannibal by postponing the final conflict); Revision-

---

[1] An analysis of Fascism, and the problem of dictatorship in general, will be found in chapter xiv.

ist socialism; revolutionary socialism, or Communism; and Syndicalism.

Fabian Socialism. The Fabian socialists are on the rather indefinite border-line that separates positive liberalism from socialism. The Fabians, prominent among whom have been Sidney and Beatrice Webb, Bernard Shaw, and R. H. Tawney, consider themselves to be in a direct line of succession to John Stuart Mill, who did so much to redirect traditional liberalism. The Fabian program, with its evolutionary faith in a gradual transition of capitalism into socialism, is a characteristic product of British political experience, with its compound (as Walter Bagehot suggested) of "custom" and "discussion." Friedrich Engels, anything but a sympathizer with British liberalism, praised the flexible British parliamentary system on account of its capacity for making criticism effective in social progress. For example, the account of evil factory conditions which Karl Marx included in *Capital* was largely based on evidence turned up by Parliamentary investigation. As another example, the parliamentary debates and maneuvers of 1867 resulted in the passage of a Reform Bill more radical than any originally envisaged by either the Liberals or the Conservatives. Perhaps above anything else the Fabians base their program upon their faith in a progressively more democratic system, which is on the one hand more flexible than the American, and on the other hand less subject to the repression and censorship that characterizes continental policy.

The Fabians trace their ancestry back to Owen and especially to the Utilitarians, rather than to Marx. They regard their socialism as watered by the two streams of Utopianism and Philosophic Radicalism.

In the present Socialist movement these two streams are united: advocates of social reconstruction have learnt the lesson of Democracy, and know that it is through the slow and gradual turning of the popular mind to new principles that social reorganization bit by bit comes. . . . Radicals, on the other hand, are perforce realizing that mere political levelling is insufficient to save a State from anarchy and despair. Both sections have been driven to recognize that the root of the difficulty is economic; and there is every day a wider consensus that the inevitable outcome of Democracy is the control by the people themselves, not only of their own political organization, but, through that, also of the main instruments of wealth production; the gradual substitution of organized cooperation for the anarchy of the competitive struggle; and the consequent recovery, in the only possible way, of what John Stuart Mill calls "the enormous share which the possessors of the instruments of industry are able to take from the produce." The economic side of the democratic ideal is, in fact, Socialism itself. (Sidney Webb, in *Fabian Essays in Socialism*.)

In their economic theory (most characteristically expounded by Bernard Shaw) the Fabians do not employ the labor theory of value, but maintain the view of orthodox economists like W. Stanley Jevons and Alfred Marshall that value is a function of utility rather than of labor.

The Fabians differ in another fundamental respect from the Marxists. They do not believe that the class struggle is either the inherent dynamic or the most effective instrument of social change. In the same way that their condemnation of a system of production for profit is the product of their utilitarian concern with production for use, their theory of the continuous development of capitalism into socialism is the outgrowth of the traditional liberal faith in intelligent inquiry and free discussion, and of their belief that education is at once a more economical and a more dependable way of effecting socialism. Instead of regarding socialism as the outcome of the resolution of inherent class antagonisms, they regard the cooperative commonwealth as the natural culmination of the continuous extension of democracy that characterizes much of the contemporary scene. The Fabians interpreted parliamentary factory acts and income taxes, for example, as steps on the path toward increasingly more equitable distribution of wealth.

Sidney Webb is perhaps the most representative spokesman of the Fabian philosophy of social change:

The record of the century in English social history begins with the trial and hopeless failure of an almost complete industrial individualism, in which, however, unrestrained private ownership of land or capital was accompanied by subjection to a political oligarchy. So little element of permanence was there in this individualistic order that, with the progress of political emancipation, private ownership of the means of production has been, in one direction or another, successively regulated, limited, and superseded, until it may now fairly be claimed that the socialist philosophy of today is but the conscious and explicit assertion of principles of social organization which have been already in great part unconsciously adopted. The economic history of the century is an almost continuous record of the progress of Socialism. . . . No philosopher now looks for anything but the gradual evolution of the new order from the old, without break or continuity or abrupt change of the entire social tissue at any point during the process. (*Fabian Essays in Socialism.*)

It is out of such an analysis of the British political and industrial scene that the Fabian tactic emerged. Especially in its earlier phases, this tactic was essentially one of "permeation"—the infiltration of socialist ideas into those sections of the community which hold a decisive influence in the molding of public opinion and in the direction of public policy—the professions, the political parties, and, most important of all, the civil service. Fabian socialism is prepared to work within the existing political framework (which it believes to be eminently suitable for the attainment of its objectives) and to accept leaders from whatever quarter they offer themselves. The evident presupposition in such a program is that methods of intellectual persuasion are in the long run more dependable than appeals to class commitments.

The entrance into the Fabian movement of Beatrice Potter (later Mrs. Sidney Webb) was the occasion, however, of the development within Fabian circles of a greater emphasis upon the importance of working-class organization. Since World War I the Fabians have increasingly addressed themselves to members of the working-class. The Fabians were instrumental in the formation of the Independent Labor Party and in the later formation of the united British Labor Party, of which this earlier group was the nucleus. Indeed, the Fabian policies have now been almost entirely appropriated by the Labor Party. From a movement whose major appeal was "intellectual" Fabian Socialism has developed into an important element in a movement which, in the eyes of many, offers the most viable democratic alternative to Communism in present-day Europe.

Revisionist Socialism. On the Continent, similar attempts were made to reformulate socialist policy in the light of the extension of social democracy, and the increased participation of organized labor groups in the direction of national policies. In contrast with the Fabian approach from within liberalism, these attempts were somewhat complicated by the endeavor to remain within the Marxist tradition. In Germany the leading protagonist of "Revisionist", or "Evolutionary" socialism was Eduard Bernstein. After 1890 the German Social Democratic Party returned to the legal status from which it had been removed by Bismarck, who had fought the socialists at every step either by forcing them underground or by stealing their thunder.

With this restoration of legality the Social Democrats came to play an increasingly active part in the going concerns of German national life. In addition, the edges of the class conflict tended to be blurred in many quarters where the growth of social democracy and the benefits of the growing industries of the nineties had made the class structure more fluid.

Bernstein's evolutionary socialism was the attempt to close the widening gap between the revolutionary formulas of the *Communist Manifesto* and the existing situation: he pointed to the already existing opportunities for individual proletarians to climb out of their class and for working class groups to collaborate actively with bourgeois governments. The main burden of Bernstein's criticism of Marx was his denial of the validity of Marx's prediction of capitalist "accumulation" and the tendency toward the extreme polarization of society into bourgeois and proletariat. He pointed to the fact that the increasing centralization of industry was being complemented by a continuously widening basis of ownership and rise in the standard of living. Since the natural development of the economic system could not be the sufficient condition of the development of revolutionary sentiment, Bernstein proposed to make more elastic the materialist conception of history according to which philosophy is ideology and merely reflects underlying economic conditions. He argued that Socialist theory needed the critical spirit of Kant, and demanded that socialists take more account of the independent ideal factors operative in social progress. Without such an accounting, he maintained, the cause of socialism would be hopelessly weakened. Thus Bernstein departed from the orthodox Marxian tactic of class struggle and favored a program of "collaboration" with all "progressive forces." Distrustful of the capacity of the state to take over large-scale enterprise in any wholesale manner, Bernstein proposed that socialists rest their cause on the gradual, day-to-day struggle for reforms, and the evolutionary development of cooperative schemes of production and distribution. Bernstein never gave up his commitment to the ultimate aim of socialism, but he was frankly suspicious of the importance of that aim in effecting the primary business at hand—the immediate equalization of economic opportunities. And he looked to the final realization of socialism as simply the natural culmination of the gradual growth of industrial democracy.

Bernstein's program was rejected by the majority group in the Social Democratic Party, led by Karl Kautsky. Nevertheless, Bernstein's philosophy was the single most influential theoretical force whenever the Social Democrats took an active part in the national government, and it was a compound of his revisionism and trade unionism that was employed when the Social Democrats were the bulwark of the Weimar Republic. In the final analysis, indeed, Kautsky turned out to be hardly more revolutionary than Bernstein. And in World War I, the Social Democrats of Germany supported the national government with an evolutionary argument—namely, that the German government, though capitalist, was progressive (in contrast with Russia, for example).

The division between Kautsky and Bernstein was paralleled by similar theoretical and practical differences within the socialist movements of other countries. In France, Jules Guesde followed the same policy as that of the majority group within the German party, and refused to acknowledge that the socialist role was other than that of unrelenting criticism of bourgeois society and uncompromising struggle for socialism. So pronounced was his antipathy to the policy of "class collaboration" that he (along with most socialists) refused to take sides in the Dreyfus Affair, which he considered the private fight of the bourgeois. His leading opponent was Jean Jaurès, the most celebrated figure in the French socialist movement before World War I. Not only did Jaurès defend Dreyfus but he permitted a follower of his, Alexandre Millerand, to become a member of the "Cabinet of Republican Defense" under Waldeck-Rousseau. The "Millerand Affair" precipitated a crisis, and at the instance of Guesde, the International Socialist Congress declared itself against the entrance of socialists into bourgeois ministries and thus set itself in principle against the policy of class collaboration. Although Jaurès abided by this decision, the split within socialist theory could not be avoided, and evolutionary socialism became an increasingly attractive program to socialists who were drawn within the framework of parliamentary politics.

This was true also in the United States, where socialist parties began to take their place on the ballots and in general to function as a minority party in democratic politics. The Social Democratic Party was changed in 1901 to the Socialist Party of America. This change in name was the expression of an attempt to link the socialist movement to the international working class. Under the leadership of Eugene V. Debs, and later of Norman Thomas, the Socialist Party attempted to make its program more straight-forwardly socialist and its philosophy more thoroughly Marxist. Proclaiming an allegiance to the ultimate aim of the cooperative commonwealth, the Socialists adopted a program of immediate reforms, patterned after the Erfurt Program of the German Social Democrats and including demands for government ownership of public utilities.

Despite Debs's attempt to infuse the Socialist Party with some of the spirit of class struggle, however, it remained largely reformist. In part this was an accommodation to the attempt of the Socialists to gain a footing within the existing trade-union movement, which was represented principally by the non-political American Federation of Labor committed to Samuel Gompers' program of supporting any friend of labor. For this reason, the A.F. of L. was hostile to a Socialist Party, and the party made little progress in labor union circles. On the whole the Socialist Party in the United States has served as a kind of transmission belt for programs of immediate reform, and has been effective less in promoting the interests of a specific class than in focusing general intellectual and humanitarian protest against the most insistent evils of industrial capitalism. And the most recent pronouncements by Norman Thomas have to a considerable extent renounced Marxism as a theory, and have emphasized the dangers to freedom incident to centralized government control of the economy.

Communism. From the time of the formation of the First International in

1864, the history of the international socialist movement had been a stormy one. At the organizational convention held in London and attended by representatives of practically all shades of working-class opinion, the moderate elements withdrew when Marx, the moving spirit behind the International, presented a constitution committing the organization to revolutionary socialism. Nor did internal dissension cease with the exit of the moderates. For some years bickering went on between the adherents of Marx and the anarchist followers of Michael Bakunin. The anarchists were finally expelled at the instigation of Marx, but the First International was seriously weakened by the struggle, and it went out of existence shortly after the failure of the Paris Commune had indicated to radicals that revolutions on the old model of direct action were no longer practical.

The Second International, which was founded in 1889, reflected a new political climate. It was made up of the socialist parties of the various nations, now committed to political action. Trusting that the enfranchisement of the working class in England, the adoption of universal manhood suffrage in Germany, and the establishment of the Third Republic in France had created a new and favorable situation for socialist dissenters, the Second International excluded all those who favored violence.

In a modern democratic state the conquest of the public power by the proletariat cannot be the result of an uprising; it must be the result of long and assiduous labor of proletarian organization in both political and economic fields, of the physical and moral regeneration of the working class, and of the gradual conquest of municipal and legislative assemblies.

The model party within the Second International was the German Social Democratic Party. In 1891, after the repeal of the German anti-socialist laws, the party met at Erfurt and drew up a program which served as the most influential source for the subsequent formulation of socialist programs throughout the world. The Erfurt program contained the demand for the abolition of private property. In addition, however, it included demands for universal suffrage, proportional representation, the substitution of a popular militia for the standing army, freedom of speech and assembly, civil equality of men and women, separation of church and state, free secular education, heavy income and inheritance taxes, a universal eight-hour workday, and factory reforms. Led by Bebel and Kautsky, the German Social Democrats retained an "orthodox" Marxist point of view, and they showed the way for the orthodox Marxism of Guesde in France and for the Social Democratic Federation in Great Britain, headed by Henry M. Hyndman.

In terms of the ballot, the socialist parties became increasingly powerful during the period of the expansion of industrial society. Nevertheless, the Second International was always on a tenuous basis. Throughout its career it was internally split by the disagreements between orthodox and "revolutionary" Marxists on the one hand, and "reformist" and "gradualist" groups on the other. The division between Bernstein and Kautsky and between Jaurès and Guesde was paralleled in Italy, in Great Britain, and in the United States. And in the final analysis, the Second International as a whole lost its revolutionary standing when it lost its international perspective. Although in 1907 it passed an anti-war resolution, the commitments to their respective nations of the various socialist parties turned out to be stronger when World War I came than commitments to the international working class. The German Social Democrats backed the Kaiser against Russian "barbarism"; the French followed suit by supporting their own government in the fight against Prussian "autocracy." Guesde, the life-long enemy of the policy of "class collaboration," who had had Alexandre Millerand and the "Independent Socialists" expelled from the party, became a member of the cabinet in charge of the direction of the war. Only in America (among the great powers) did the Socialist Party retain an anti-war position; and unlike European socialist parties, the American party possessed a relatively insignificant vote and played no effective role in the two party system guiding American politics.

Revolutionary socialism was apparently submerged with the breakdown of the Second International and the tendency of its various parties to become national as well as socialist. It was against this background of failure and dissension within the Second International that a new and amplified version of revolutionary Marxism arose. The master theoretician as well as the unquestioned leader of this movement was Nikolai Lenin. Cognizant of the increased measure of opportunity for sections of the working class and of the mounting nationalism governing the programs of socialist leaders, but at the same time assured that an imperialistic and progressively reactionary capitalism could not be met with simply reformist measures, Lenin turned to the formulation of tactics that would maintain the revolutionary character of socialism. The theoretical foundation of this program was developed in Lenin's analysis of the imperialistic state of capitalism (in *Imperialism*) and of the relationship of working-class movements to the national state (in *The State and Revolution*). While Lenin always professed complete allegiance to the Marxist philosophy, these books constituted an amplification of the Marxist principles in the light of new experience and represented an independent contribution on the part of Lenin to socialist thought.

In the first of these books Lenin argued that capitalism had entered upon a period that was essentially one of contraction, marked by "the substitution of capitalist monopolies for capitalist free competition." This period of contraction was inevitably attended, according to Lenin, by the struggle among the great powers for division of still unexploited areas. Imperialism marked the end of capitalism as a genuinely progressive force in which freedom of competition pushed constantly toward the general expansion of productive powers; instead, monopolistic financial oligarchies operated to restrict the production of wealth, and to export surplus capital for profitable imperialist investment. In such a system the proletariat has "nothing to lose but its chains."

Lenin recognized that sections of the proletariat had managed to benefit from imperialism and as a matter of fact explained the "betrayal of socialism" —that is, the betrayal of revolutionary socialism—on the grounds that individual proletarians might mistakenly credit to themselves a vested interest in the maintenance of the system from which they profited. But the policy of class collaboration could be only a delusion when one of those classes—the international bourgeoisie—was becoming increasingly like a stagnant *rentier* class, and would be pushed to constantly more reactionary measures in order to maintain its fetters on the expansion of productive powers. The only possibility for such a progressive extension of the sources of wealth, Lenin maintained, rested upon the overthrow of a class that was no longer productive and had become parasitic. And the only class in contemporary society equipped to carry the revolution off was the industrial proletariat.

The immediate point of Lenin's analysis of imperialism as "capital in transition, dying capitalism" was to demonstrate that while Marx was right in advocating working-class support for the liberal national revolutions of 1848 and for the programs of social legislation promulgated by other classes, such a policy was unrealistic after 1871. It was through this consideration of the economics of imperialism that Lenin opposed the tendency toward policies of class collaboration in general, and rejected the support granted by socialist parties to the belligerent governments in World War I.

Lenin's *State and Revolution* was the theoretical framework in which he placed his criticism of the policies of working-class leaders who took places in bourgeois governments, or who looked to the daily progress of reform to culminate in socialism. A great deal of this work is taken up with an interpretation of Engels's phrase, "the withering away of the state," which had been interpreted by some evolutionary socialists to be an argument in favor of their program of gradual reform. Lenin made it quite clear that this phrase could only refer to the proletarian state and not to the bourgeois state, which was essentially and inescapably an instrument for maintaining the economic domination of the ruling class. Consequently, he argued, only the revolutionary overthrow of the entire machinery of the bourgeois state and the seizure of power by the "dictatorship of the proletariat" could effectively abolish the system of exploitation founded upon the profit system. Anything short of such a revolutionary program, any attempt to work within parliamentary forms, was for Lenin doomed to failure because it accepted an institution which was irrevocably the product of the class antagonisms of bourgeois society.

In a sense, Lenin's theoretical considerations were all directed toward maintaining the revolutionary character of socialists and toward combatting the tendency to forsake the path of relentless class struggle. At the same time, Lenin recognized as clearly as any revisionist that the working class had not developed a socialist mentality with the development of capitalism. This was not taken by him, however, as a refutation of Marx's teaching of the historical tendency of capitalist accumulation (and capitalist decline), but a proof that the working class of itself could develop only a trade-union ideology concerned with the immediacies of the class struggle. Such a situation, for Lenin, constituted a challenge to a genuinely revolutionary class-conscious party to instruct and lead the proletariat to the required measures. The most distinctive part of Lenin's ideology is his emphasis, in the essay *What Is to Be Done?* upon the role of a disciplined and organized party in bringing to an intellectual head the undefined and inchoate discontents arising out of the daily friction between classes. The working-class can have only one party of leaders, and without such a vanguard it cannot be "class-conscious." Without a Communist Party the proletarian revolution against imperialist and monopoly capitalism is unthinkable.

The importance of the Communist Party in carrying on and in leading the unrelenting class struggle, and the peculiar interpretation of its nature and structure, are present in Lenin's thought as a constantly guiding factor long before he worked out in detail the analysis of imperialism and of the State in terms of which the role of the Party is intelligible. The special characteristics which Lenin attaches to that Party can be understood against the background of his characteristic attitude toward the class struggle. Lenin always regarded the struggle for the classless society as a plain and unvarnished form of warfare, though it be not always fought with military weapons. The Communist Party supplies the officers—"the vanguard"—of the embattled proletarian legions. The organization of the party is that of an army, and the special virtues of the good Communist are those of the soldier. The "people's front" was a front line of battle. Thus, a sense of discipline in both thought and action comes above all else, and any deviation or intellectual reservation is (at best) equivalent to lending aid and comfort to the enemy and (at worst) equivalent to desertion in action. "To belittle socialist ideology *in any way,* to *deviate from it in the slightest degree,* means strengthening bourgeois ideology." (*What Is to Be Done?* The italics are Lenin's.) The tendency of revolutionary Marxists to make all dissenters members of the enemy camp is, among other things, the product of Lenin's insistence upon the transcendent need for unity in the battle for proletarian power.

The Communist Party is thus "the lever of political organization, with the help of which the more progressive part of the working class directs on the right path the whole mass of the proletariat and the semi-proletariat." It is in terms of this formulation of the role of the Communist Party that Lenin's theory of "the dictatorship of the proletariat," "the organization of the vanguard as the ruling class for the purpose of crushing the oppressor" is developed. Through "the dictatorship of the proletariat" the conquest of the bourgeois state is effected; in this transitional stage the State is used for what it is, an instrument for the domination of one class by another. In this case, however, it is used for "the expropriation of the expropriators," in preparation for the final establishment of the classless society in which the standard "from each according to his abilities, to each according to his needs" will be the rule.

Syndicalism. A pluralist version of revolutionary socialism was syndicalism. The greatest single source of syndicalist thought, in addition to Marxism, was anarchism. The defeat of the revolutionary movements of 1848 had put an end for a time to anarchist propaganda. When it was revived, "Russian godfathers stood around the cradle of modern anarchism," for the two leading figures of the new anarchism were the Russians Michael Bakunin and Prince Peter Kropotkin. The renewal of anarchist activity may conveniently be dated from 1864, the year when the International Workingmen's Association was formed in London. This group was originally composed of French mutualists and followers of Robert Owen, but soon included German, Italian, Spanish, and Swiss workers, and Marxian socialists as well as anarchists. While the International was at first committed to the anarchist policy of exclusive economic struggle, with no participation in political activity, the anarchists were later expelled at the Hague Congress of the International in 1872. The latter then formed a number of Latin federations of workers, and ultimately an Anarchist International.

Bakunin and Kropotkin, both of whom were expelled from the Marxian International, not only contributed to anarchist literature but also took the risks involved in practical propaganda. Thus, Bakunin was thrice condemned to death, both men spent years in prison, and both were exiles from their native land—in consequence of their anarchist activity. Bakunin's adventurous life prevented him from giving systematic form to his views. Like the earlier anarchist writers—he was heavily indebted to Proudhon—he was revolted by the economic injustices of his day, and attributed the evils he saw to the tyranny of religion and government. "Church and State are my two *bêtes noires,*" he once declared. In religion especially he saw the great enemy, since it enslaves the minds of men and is the source of the state's power. His riposte to Voltaire's "If God did not exist it would be necessary to invent him" was "If God did exist it would be necessary to abolish him"; for according to him, "the existence of God implies the abdication of human reason and justice, it is the negation of human liberty and ends not only in theoretical but in practical slavery." Unlike the earlier anarchists, however, Bakunin adopted a collectivist anarchism as his ideal—he had a deep conviction that man's native impulse toward solidarity with his fellow creatures would flourish if religious superstition and governmental coercion were abolished. On the other hand, he had no confidence in political action. "We reject all legislation, all authority, and all privileged, licensed, official, and legal influence, even though arising from universal suffrage, convinced that it can turn only to the advantage of a dominant minority of exploiters against the interests of the immense majority in subjection to them."

Bakunin's ideal society was a loose federation of communes each with the maximum possible autonomy. The members of each commune were to own in common the capital goods required for production, and they were to decide among themselves all issues relevant to the compensation of labor. Bakunin was influenced by the communistic elements in Marxian socialism, although he gave no detailed account of his future ideal society. But he rejected every form of parliamentary action to effect the desired social reforms, and advocated the use of direct economic action and, if necessary, terror—"propaganda by deed" and "insurrectionism." He also insisted—although it was in flat contradiction to his conspiratorial pronouncements and activities—that the revolution would have to be a spontaneous uprising of the masses, and could not be a rigidly disciplined movement led by a small handful of men. As he once declared, "The wish to force the proletariat to adopt a uniform line of conduct or a political program is an absurd and reactionary claim."

Though Bakunin's ideas acquired great influence, especially in the Latin countries, it is Kropotkin who became the theorist *par excellence* of modern anarchism. He dismissed the older anarchism, whether individualistic or collectivistic, as antiquated, and attempted to show that communistic anarchism is the form of society most compatible with the findings of evolutionary science. Thus, in his *Mutual Aid a Factor in Evolution* and elsewhere, he presented evidence to show that mutual aid or spontaneous solidarity is a potent factor in evolution, and that history reveals a tendency both towards "integrating labor with the production of all riches in common" and towards "the fullest freedom of the individual in the prosecution of all aims." The anarchist ideal, accordingly, is simply the next phase of evolution. In this ideal society the instruments of production "will become the common property of society and be managed in common by the producers of wealth," while at the same time the functions of government will be reduced to *nil;* in such a society "the individual recovers his full liberty of initiative and action for satisfying, by means of free groups and federations—freely constituted—all the infinitely varied needs of the human being."

Anarchist society, on Kropotkin's view, will be based on the village community as the nucleus, and will guarantee adequate food, clothing, and shelter to all its members. Moreover, since there will be no parasitic class, and since things will be managed with an eye primarily on human welfare, all the labor necessary for securing a high standard of living will involve no more than five working hours a day. Kropotkin loved to cite the spontaneous emergence in contemporary society, without benefit of governmental control, of associations, such as the Red Cross, inspired by the impulse of mutual aid. He saw in them the anticipations of "a state of society where the liberty of the individual will be limited by no laws, no bonds—by nothing but his own social habits and the necessity, which everyone feels, of finding co-operation, support, and sympathy among his neighbors." Accordingly, he was not a terrorist, and believed communistic anarchism could be established by simply "going to the people"—though at the same time he disapproved of Tolstoy's philosophy of non-resistance.

Kropotkin, like Bakunin, had a large personal following, and his ideas found a wide audience through his charmingly written books. However, anarchism has not developed into a large-scale mass movement such as accompanied the propagation of Marxian socialism. This is perhaps understandable in the light of anarchist abstention from political organization. Moreover, anarchists do not usually support their vision of the future state by an impressive philosophy of history which could generate confidence in the ultimate victory of the ideal.

Syndicalism was the compound of this anarchism with the socialist philosophy of Karl Marx. It registered the extreme distrust on the part of many workers (especially the unskilled workers of southern Europe) of parliamentary institutions and of the State. Like Lenin, the syndicalists regarded it as illusory at best to play the "progressive" and attempt to bring about reforms within the framework of the State—one that was inescapably bourgeois. Unlike Lenin, however, they carried this distrust over into an attack upon the theory and practice of state socialism. The "dictatorship of the proletariat" was for the syndicalists the conquest of power by autonomous industrial unions, the "cells" of the future social organism.

The characteristic tactic of the syndicalists was "direct action" rather than the political action which was turning so many socialist leaders into "worthy progressives" and ineffectual leaders of the proletariat. Such direct action was organized about industrial unions, and its principal and indeed only weapon was the "general strike"—a stoppage of work by all workers in the industry. Such strikes were envisaged by the syndicalists as serving the principal function of giving the worker a vivid sense of class warfare and a consciousness of solidarity within his own class, and were simply preparatory to the universal strike of all labor that would usher in socialism and the dictatorship of the proletariat. Every strike was useful in that it fed the revolutionary flame, and prepared a situation propitious for the leadership of the group of complete revolutionaries, the class-conscious "minority of a minority." (To some extent the syndicalist emphasis upon an intensified class struggle was due to the belief that socialists would always lack a numerical majority.)

Syndicalism gained widespread currency especially in southern Europe (where parliamentary institutions were not firmly geared) and in the I.W.W. (Industrial Workers of the World), which gained some power on the west coast in the United States. Syndicalism had its greatest practical success in France, where its philosophy captured the C.G.T. (*Confédération Générale du Travail*), which was formed in 1895. The C.G.T. was made up of nearly all the French labor unions, and was committed to the following objective: "To unite the workingmen in the economic field with the bonds of class solidarity to struggle for their integral emancipation." In Italy and Spain, likewise, syndicalism was the dominant revolutionary force until some years after World War I.

The ultimate aims of the syndicalists were always vague and attracted less devotion than their philosophy of immediate action. With Georges Sorel, who gave to revolutionary syndicalism its most influential formulation, this preoccupation with direct action and the general strike was given philosophic elaboration. In the case of Sorel it is even doubtful whether he thinks the consummation of syndicalist endeavors might not constitute a defeat of the main purpose of the movement—the awakening of the moral virtues of militance and heroism through unrelenting class warfare.

As we have already seen, anarchist philosophies tended to be practically ineffectual because of a failure to fortify their faith in the victory of their cause by developing an appropriate philosophy of history. Sorel adopted what he took to be the kernel of Marxism—the determinist philosophy of history which guaranteed the ultimate victory of socialism through the dialectic of the class struggle. However, in opposition to Marx, Sorel did not regard this determinist philosophy as in any sense a scientifically grounded prediction. Instead it was a "myth"—an act of intuition "capable of evoking as an undivided whole the mass of sentiments which corresponds to the different manifestations of the war undertaken by socialism against modern society." The justification of such a confidence that the victory of the cause is guaranteed is that it creates the social mentality appropriate for regaining moral qualities. Indeed, Sorel's primary emphasis is upon bringing forth immediate "moral" actions, and his emphasis upon proletarian violence "enlightened by the general strike" is due to the fact that this "very fine and heroic thing" restores to all classes (and not merely to the proletariat) something of their former energy, and so serves "the immemorial interests of civilization."

Sorel's philosophy turns to political use, and undoubtedly distorts, the varied attacks upon philosophic rationalism involved in the philosophies of Friedrich Nietzsche, Artur Schopenhauer, and Henri Bergson. In particular, he is influenced by Bergson, who endeavored to make intellectual analysis subservient to the "élan vital" or "life-force," that process of constant change which can only be grasped by "intuition." Sorel comprehends all of socialism in the ongoing activity of the general strike, and subordinates the revolution itself to the cultivation of a heroic morality.

More than anything else, such a philosophy is expressive of an attempt to restore moral devotion and moral fervor in a protest against the mechanical quality of industrial society. In effect, the protest was like that essayed by the anarchists, but Sorel translated it into terms germane to an era of collective action. Indeed, his most signal contribution to political thought is his recognition of the new dimension that social action takes on when it is pursued in terms of mass action.

Sorel's pervasive moralism tended to remove him from the rank and file of syndicalist endeavor, which was always rooted in immediate economic discontents. In the long run his philosophy of the "myth" was more influential in nationalist and Fascist circles than among syndicalists. A similar attempt to apply philosophic irrationalism to political questions is seen in the work of Vilfredo Pareto, with its insistence on the social influence of the myth, and the never ending historical process of displacement whereby young and virile ruling classes take the place of the decadent and effete. More than anything else, the tradition of philosophic irrationalism was marked by its contempt for bourgeois virtues and ideals. As Professor Sabine remarks, "There is not a little grim humor in its capture by a bourgeois nationalist counter-revolution." Sorel was a strong influence on Fascist propagandists like Mussolini and Goebbels.

MODERN LIBERALISM, GUILD SOCIALISM

For those who have continued to believe in the possibility of a social order based on freedom, almost the whole intellectual structure of social theory has had to be criticized and revised in terms of the newly emerged economic structure. The general philosophic task has been to explain how liberty can be established in the world of big business by using the methods of collective action. Liberty and equality could no longer be regarded as starting points of social analysis, as if they existed "by nature"; they could at best be conceived as possible ideals to be achieved by programs of legislation and organization. Such a program for positive social reform in the interests of freedom became in the latter part of the nineteenth century the preoccupation of a generation of idealist philosophers who rejected the theories of individualistic liberalism in order to formulate new theories of collective freedom. But before examining this new liberalism, we must note the persistence of the old.

Individualistic Liberalism. There are still individualists who are more convinced today than ever that liberty is threatened by any collective trend in industrial society. Among social scientists an "evolutionary" school of sociology continued to assert itself, particularly in America, where disciples of Herbert Spencer and Auguste Comte found receptive ears long after their theories had been discarded in Europe. Most notable of these die-hard American sociologists was William Graham Sumner, who throughout the period from 1870–1910 maintained his faith in free trade, unrestricted competition, and the laws of supply and demand and evolutionary struggle. He made a plea for "the forgotten man" (the phrase was his), who was being buried under a growing burden of taxes, tariffs, high prices, union wage scales, and governmental "services," and condemned both plutocracy and imperialism as twin forms of the use of capital for building up non-productive political power.

"Individualism" of this older variety also persists among captains of in-

dustry and political leaders. Various "liberty leagues" or groups of rugged
disbelievers in governmental compulsion have found relatively recently a
spokesman in Herbert Hoover. Hoover admits that "we have long since abandoned the laissez-faire of the 18th century—the notion that it is 'every man
for himself and the devil take the hindmost' . . . we have gone a long way
toward the abandonment of the 'capitalism' of Adam Smith"; nevertheless,
his philosophy, like that of John Bright and other nineteenth century liberals,
begins with the idea that prosperity depends on increased production, and increased production almost exclusively on "free enterprise." Hoover conceives
a society like that of independent farmers or engineers, each in possession of
private property: "To all practical souls there is little use in quarreling over
the share of each of us until we have something to divide. So long as we maintain our individualism we will have increasing quantities to share and we
shall have time and leisure and taxes with which to fight out proper sharing
of the 'surplus.' " Given such individuals, Hoover is willing to trust "the
emery wheel of competition." This seems to be in general the philosophy of
the first Henry Ford and of other industrialists both here and abroad whose
"emery wheel" has itself been abraded by the double grindstone of finance
capital on the one side and government on the other.

Many industrialists, however, have adopted a compromise. One of the
first and most outspoken of this type was Andrew Carnegie. His *Gospel of
Wealth* became a bible for many philanthropic capitalists. He welcomed big
business, labor unions (especially "company unions"), and inheritance taxes;
but he opposed government ownership, political regulation, and imperialism.
He regarded the accumulation of wealth as a public trust and preached the
doctrine that it is the rich man's duty to administer the distribution of his
wealth in his own lifetime. Accordingly he devoted most of his own fortune
to providing public libraries, hospitals, and parks, to bringing about international peace [2] and the end of imperialism. It was characteristic of his philosophy that he put churches last on his list of approved philanthropies on
the ground that they are "sectarian," not "public." He defended business concentrations on the ground that they prevented competition from being
"ruinous." A similar argument has been put forth by the German economist
and liberal, Adolf Weber, in defense of international cartels:

Cartels will be seen to be nothing else than organizations which transform
ruinous and inappropriate competition into regulated competition. This is not a
repudiation, but an affirmation of the competitive system. Competition is the proper

[2] He even made explicit provisions for the use of the funds of his Peace Endowment after its
object had been attained.

regulating principle of the existing economic order. It compels the producer to grant the consumer a share in improvements in production, but ruinous competition is not necessary to achieve this object. By its nature this cut-throat competition is not a regulatory but an anarchical principle. If the tendency towards an excessive increase in supply be so controlled by common action as to correspond with the real state of economic forces, this is to be welcomed on public as well as private grounds. . . .

Cartels do not spell the end of competition. Even the monopolist stands not outside but within the competitive system. He has to consider the degree and duration of effective demand. He has to bear in mind that a whole series of needs must be met from the given revenue. If prices rise above a certain limit, the inevitable result is a more or less severe contraction of the market. In addition, there is the competition of substitute products, both at home and abroad, and not least the latent competition hidden within an apparently united group of sellers. . . .

Like consumers' associations and labour unions, they are merely another and more convenient form under which competitive struggles may be carried on. (*In Defence of Capitalism.*)

More recently, writers like Friedrich Hayek have seen a "road to serfdom" in the rise of large-scale governmental planning. The revival of such older versions of economic liberalism has served an extremely useful purpose, at the very least as a valuable corrective to the notion that the only alternative to the excesses of monopoly and unbridled competition is total planning under centralized governmental auspices. Nevertheless, it should be noted that, outside the arenas of political speech-making and journalistic propaganda, there are relatively few theorists or practical politicians who now stand for absolutely uncontrolled competition, or are opposed to such measures as unemployment insurance or social security. Hayek himself, for example, is prepared to accept a degree of political activity in the economic sphere which would have been regarded as totally unwarranted intervention by most of his intellectual forbears. On the whole, the scars left by the Great Depression of the thirties have made a permanent change in the spectrum of social outlooks which can now be reasonably entertained, and there is relatively little question that, whatever the merits of absolute "free competition" as a purely theoretical argument in economics, such a program could not now be instituted without the widespread use of repressive techniques.

Positive Liberalism. In sharp contrasts to defenses, like those of Hoover and Carnegie, of the concentration of wealth and power in the hands of private individuals or corporations is the theory of the new liberalism, which seeks to restore freedom of competition and to decentralize wealth and power by means of government regulation. Theodore Roosevelt's "big stick," swung over the heads of trusts, was the symbol of revolt among "progressives," who thought that "trust-busting" would bring a Square Deal. Woodrow Wilson's New Freedom and certain aspects of Franklin D. Roosevelt's New Deal were a continuation and development of this revolt in the interests of creating democratic conditions in business and industry.

The philosophy behind this program Wilson expressed as follows:

One of the interesting things that Mr. Jefferson said in those early days of simplicity which marked the beginnings of our government was that the best government consisted in as little governing as possible. And there is still a sense in which that is true. It is still intolerable for the government to interfere with our individual activities except where it is necessary to interfere with them in order to free them. But I feel confident that if Jefferson were living in our day he would see what we see: that the individual is caught in a great confused nexus of all sorts of complicated circumstances, and that to let him alone is to leave him helpless as against the obstacles with which he has to contend; and that, therefore, law in our day must come to the assistance of the individual. It must come to his assistance to see that he gets fair play; that is all, but that is much; without the watchful interference, the resolute interference, of the government, there can be no fair play between individuals and such powerful institutions as the trusts. Freedom to-day is something more than being let alone. The program of a government of freedom must in these days be positive, not negative merely.

The Square Deal and the New Freedom found expression not only in certain directions of New Deal policy but, before the New Deal, in the program of the La Follettes in Wisconsin. On the whole, this variety of liberalism has articulated the discontents of the farmer and of the small businessman and has won their support in its struggle against the increasing concentration of ownership and control of the basic industries in the hands of finance capitalists.

In Great Britain this type of liberalism came earlier. A. V. Dicey, one of the first historians and liberals to see the theoretical implications of the revolt against individualism, points out that during the seventies English legislation broke with the tradition of allowing business enterprise to regulate itself, and took up the policy of government regulation and control on behalf of general welfare that reached its culmination with the liberal program of Lloyd George.

Essentially this new philosophy of government was a reaction to the traditional atomism which insisted that the individual existed "in nature" independent of government and endowed with certain inherent liberties, respect for which defined the limits of governmental activity. On the contrary, the ideal of individuality or "self-realization" was now taken as a moral objective to be attained. Sensitive to the currents of a growing collectivism, there arose

a number of philosophers who maintained that the self-realization of the individual—that is, the achievement of individuality—was the product, and not
the origin, of general social and cultural conditions. In the words of one of
them, "The individual is not a datum but a problem. The aim of politics is to
find and realize the individual." (B. Bosanquet, *The Philosophical Theory
of the State.*)

The philosophy which attempted a revision of traditional liberal aims in
the light of this new insight was that of the English philosophic "idealists,"
led by Thomas Hill Green, who brought to bear upon the utilitarian formulation of liberalism the idea of "moral freedom" as expounded by Rousseau
and Kant—an influence which had already been not without importance in
the redirection of British thought attempted by Coleridge and Carlyle.
Broadly, the English idealists attempted to introduce the philosophy of Greek
citizenship and to conceive of the state as a partnership in the virtues.

In a paper called "Liberal Legislation and Freedom of Contract," Green
attempted to disengage what he considered the lasting values in liberalism
from the passing forms it had taken in the days of Bentham, when an antiquated aristocracy was the primary obstacle to reform, a situation now long
outgrown. Green distinguished between the traditional notion of freedom
as the absence of restraint and what he called "positive" freedom:

We shall probably all agree that freedom, rightly understood, is the greatest of all
blessings; that its attainment is the true end of all our effort as citizens. But when
we then speak of freedom, we should consider carefully what we mean by it. We
do not mean merely freedom from restraint or compulsion. We do not mean merely
freedom to do as we like. We do not mean a freedom that can be enjoyed by one
man or one set of men at the cost of a loss of freedom to others. When we speak of
freedom as something to be so highly prized, we mean a positive power or capacity
of doing or enjoying something worth doing or enjoying, and that, too, something
that we do or enjoy in common with others.

According to Green, the self-realization of the individual is the process by
which the objects of impulsive and disorganized desires are progressively
made to contribute to an integrated striving after a fuller realization of human
perfection or of "the ideal self." The ultimate value which Green attaches to
individuality is quite different from the utilitarian distinction between the
individual on the one hand and society on the other. It is rather a reinterpre-
tation of the Kantian emphasis upon the subordination of desires to the individual's sense of duty and "the common good," which causes the individual
to consider the consequences if everybody should act as he acts. A concrete
and much more conservative formulation of what was for Green a rather ab-

stract ideal of self-realization appeared in a notable essay by another idealist and contemporary of Green at Oxford, F. H. Bradley, entitled "My Station and Its Duties." He argued that everyone has a "station" in life which imposes specific duties on him, and that he can enjoy freedom only in so far as he willingly performs these obligations. Such "stations" exist, he pointed out, in any society and are not limited to antiquated feudal duties or to class distinctions.

Green criticizes the philosophy traditional since the time of Locke which attaches natural rights to a pre-social or pre-political stage and insists rather that rights are functions of social recognition and that citizenship, or membership in a community, evokes moral qualities which would not otherwise be developed. It is in keeping with this new analysis that Green (like Rousseau) attacked the conception, common to liberal thinkers before him, of the state as purely coercive and restrictive. In opposition to that view he claimed that even coercion may be an instrument of freedom, disciplining the will; and that government therefore has more to do than merely keeping the peace. Will is the basis of the state, though government necessarily uses force. Green was still sympathetic to the individualistic conception of will, and thought that the government could not promote "self-realization" directly (since it used coercion); its function was at best "the hindering of hindrances" to the good life.

The application of this variety of liberalism to the State is represented in England chiefly by one of T. H. Green's students, Bernard Bosanquet. To a far greater extent than Green, Bosanquet made of the State the ultimately unifying factor without which no other kind of association could find any justification. He took this theory largely from Hegel and the German idealists. For Bosanquet's *Philosophical Theory of the State* the State is the peculiar institution in which the "whole man" achieves full self-realization as *man;* other institutions realize only particular and specialized capacities of man. For example, Bosanquet quotes with approval the following remark of Mary P. Follett (whose book, *The New State,* was claimed both by the idealists and by those who opposed them) : "The State cannot be composed of groups because no group nor any number of groups can contain the whole of me and the ideal State demands the whole. . . . My group uses me, and the whole of me is still left to give to the whole. . . . Vocational representation does not deal with men, it deals with masons and doctors. The whole of every man must go into his citizenship."

Bosanquet's theory was an attempt to carry on the idealist effort of making political activity distinctly moral. In the last analysis, however, it is seriously open to question whether Bosanquet does not finish in a position that is practically (whatever the theory of the case may be) identical with the doctrine that all morality is subordinate to the power of the State. The State, just because it is the very highest receptacle of all the virtues, is not subject to any higher moral law. The State can make demands upon the individual at the expense of his duties to "groups"—for example, to his family, to his church, or to his profession. Thus Bosanquet's emphasis upon the absolute claims of the State as against the "ordinary trivial moods" of the individual may be interpreted as giving the government a moral *carte blanche*. This sort of "metaphysical theory of the State" was attacked by one of the leading sociologists and liberals of early twentieth-century Britain, L. T. Hobhouse.

Bosanquet did not, however, identify the "real will" of the State with the commands of the government. His chief aim was to enhance the notion of citizenship and to awaken a moral motive for political reform and public spirit. His doctrine is intended in theory to provide a basis for a common purpose among citizens to which the government should be responsible.

Pluralism. It was as a protest against such a glorification of the State as this that a political theory known as "pluralism" gained strength among liberals. On the whole the contributions of the pluralists to politics have been more critical than constructive. The essential critical point of the pluralists is that the State, whatever it may claim in theory, does not *in fact* involve the activity of the whole man. In the face of fanatical nationalism, state socialism, and the "tyranny of the majority," pluralism is a revival of a concern for liberty. It is not the "Liberty" of the French Revolution, but specific liberties (like those of free inquiry, free worship, and individuality) which are to be protected against the idea of State sovereignty, the idea that "there are, there can be, no rights except the right of the State, and there is, and there can be no other authority than the authority of the Republic." (J. N. Figgis, *Churches in the Modern State.*)

The sources of pluralistic theory are various. Like the idealists, the pluralists emphasized the role of voluntary associations as the basis of political life in contrast to the utilitarian emphasis upon the role of force; many of them go further than the idealists in asserting the "real personality" of groups. Otto von Gierke's notable study of medieval law and corporations was also a contributing factor. It was used primarily by labor leaders who sought legal recognition for labor unions. F. W. Maitland, a distinguished British legal historian, wrote the introduction to the English translation of a part of this work and pointed out its usefulness for corporation law. Catholic theorists, in the effort to protect the Church against the overweening secular state, pointed to the "absolutisms" of secular liberalism. In the Catholic "distributism" of Hilaire Belloc there is the attempt to work out a set of checks to the authority of the centralized state.

In England, J. N. Figgis with his *Churches in the Modern State* (1913) applied von Gierke's theories to church-state relations. Applying the idealist theory of self-realization to groups, Figgis makes the goal of political activity the "self-development" that comes with associated living. He insisted that society is made up of groups which have a "real personality" or corporate existence:

What we actually see in the world is not on the one hand the State, and on the other a mass of correlated individuals; but a vast complex of gathered unions, in which alone we find individuals, families, clubs, trades unions, colleges, professions, and so forth; and further, that there are exercised functions within these groups which are of the nature of government, including its three aspects, legislative, executive, and judicial; though, of course, only with reference to their own members. So far as the people who actually belong to it are concerned, such a body is every whit as communal in its character as a municipal corporation or a provincial parliament.

Figgis's notion of the real personality of groups is, if anything, more metaphysical than the idealistic notion of the State, but it gave philosophical content to the current legal "fiction" of corporate personality. His theory was weakest, however, in not considering the all-important question as to the real personality of the State, and the effect on *its* freedom if it allowed all other "real personalities" to find unhampered self-development.

More influential in British politics than Figgis and the churchmen were a group of Guild Socialists and Labor Party leaders,—notably Cole, Laski, Tawney, and Russell. Their approach is found also in many American philosophers, notably John Dewey.

Harold Laski's pluralism, a view which gave way in the later Laski to a rather doctrinaire Marxism, is the attempt to preserve traditional liberal values such as individual responsibility, freedom of thought, and democratic government, and at the same time to meet the need for socialism. The maintenance of freedom in a context of an ever increasingly collectivized world depends for Laski on our ability "to disperse the sovereign power because it is realized that where administrative organization is made responsive to the actual associations of men, there is a greater chance not merely of efficiency but of freedom also." (*The Foundations of Sovereignty*.)

Social services are to be judged, according to Laski, in terms of their functioning in the life of each individual. Perhaps Laski's primary drive was that of a moralist, concerned to establish individuals responsibly in groups of such a kind and size that it would be possible for them to be effective citizens and to exert power intelligently. Laski's version of pluralism emphasized the ultimate value of the individual, and the necessity of establishing a *de facto* situation in which his will would really be exercised in group activities, because he really has the power to make a choice among competing groups:

You must place your individual at the centre of things. You must regard him as linked to a variety of associations to which his personality attracts him. You must on this view admit that the State is only one of the associations to which he happens to belong, and give it exactly that preeminence—and no more—to which on the particular occasion of conflict, its possibly superior moral claim will entitle it. In my view it does not attempt to take that preeminence by force; it wins it by consent. . . . Surely, too, that State will be the stronger which thus binds to itself its members by the strength of a moral purpose validated. (*The Problem of Sovereignty*.)

As a leader of the Labor Party, Laski later championed party politics as the essential form of political pluralism and political freedom.

Experimentalism. An influential form of liberalism in America has been exemplified by John Dewey. Dewey saw the peculiar problem that confronts liberalism as the conflict between institutions and habits of behavior that originated in a pre-technological age and the new forces set into motion by science and technology. In order to bring political and social institutions into keeping with technological developments, individual men and groups must assimilate the methods of experimental intelligence to everyday practice in the field of moral and social relations. The value of free inquiry, as interpreted by Dewey, lies in making the scientific *method* (not generalizations taken over from physical science) socially basic, in creating institutions of cooperative research and invention. The experimental method seemed to Dewey to represent the model institution in which freedom and social authority were reconciled. As Dewey saw it, in science each individual is obliged to judge the evidence himself but no inquiry is ever independent of a social fund of facts, of a body of common, public criteria, and of a cooperating community.

Dewey relied more on such organized inquiry than on the methods which are involved in representative government and the compromises of political parties. The practicing morality of the scientist engaged in an organized and cooperative inquiry, for example, has little or nothing in common with conventional democratic discussion and debate. Dewey probably over-emphasized the analogy between democratic politics and scientific methods. Nevertheless, his insistence upon scientific experimentalism as a method for the control of social affairs offered a standard of criticism by which totalitarian techniques, including those of self-proclaimed "scientific" experts, could be adjudged for what they are, and by which the failures of democracy, as well as its advantages over other systems, might be exhibited. And at least implicitly it offered a positive conception of liberal morality when applied to politics. A liberal method would subordinate party politics and patronage to the values of publicity, cooperation and impartiality; this method would be an "approximation to the use of scientific method in investigation and of the engineering mind in the invention and projection of far reaching social plans. . . ."

In this connection, Dewey implemented his liberalism with a pluralistic point of view which was close to that of Laski in many respects. The increasing complexities of modern industry are progressively displacing personal controls, according to Dewey, and seemed to him to demand everywhere more varied and more intimate personal associations. Society was for Dewey simply a blanket term for all the ways in which individuals do actually work and play together, and the state was "just an instrumentality for promoting and protecting other and more voluntary associations." The practice of scientific method in relation to political affairs accordingly depends upon the decentralization of political authorities in order that the qualities of individual initiative and responsibility may be stimulated and in order that social planning may be more concretely experimental. Liberalism for Dewey was more empirical than it was for Green, and more pluralistic than it was for Bosanquet. His ultimate emphasis was on "taking the method of science home into our own controlling attitudes and dispositions, employing the new techniques of directing our thoughts and efforts to a planned control of social forces."

Liberalism since 1870 has tended to disintegrate and to become either radical and socialist on the one hand or conservative and individualist on the other. Some liberals, like Laski and Dewey, have come frankly to favor some form of socialistic ownership of property, though not necessarily government ownership; others, however, have defended private competitive capitalism as "the field of liberty." To be sure, liberals, both conservative and radical, have continued to proclaim their allegiance to freedom, and have indeed maintained that their conservatism or their radicalism is the only way of saving liberty in the face of group pressure from labor on the one hand and from expanding nationalisms and monopolies on the other. The major emphasis of liberal theorists like Dewey and Laski, at the present moment, is not only that freedom is possible under planning, but that freedom actually depends on planning.

Guild Socialism. Looking back in the direction of Thomas Carlyle and John Ruskin, one can discern a continuous course of dissent with individualistic and impersonal industrialism and a nostalgic regard for the functional organization of medieval society in terms of the manor and the guild. Carlyle's "gospel of work," in addition to its Calvinism, is the attempt to infuse industry with the sense of an ideal dimension. In Ruskin, who found it impossible to remain exclusively an art critic within a society in which he felt art to be frivolous and an anomaly, we find a representative kind of dissent arising out of the peculiar concerns and the special preoccupations of the artist and craftsman. The most immediate forerunner of guild socialism was William Morris, who followed Ruskin's emphasis upon the political economy of art. Morris thought the special function of art within industrial society to be that of an exemplar of work that was intrinsically rewarding.

The guild socialist movement had its inception in just such concerns as these. It was at first largely a protest, and an attempt to revive the medieval guild, in reaction against the stale and uninteresting features of industrial production and the lifeless and impersonal character of industrial products. The guild movement became more unmistakably socialist with the influence of S. G. Hobson, who, in collaboration with A. R. Orage, wrote a number of books in which the prospects of the guild movement were made to depend upon the possibility of fostering labor control over industry so as to awaken an enlivened sense of proprietary interest. With Hobson, guild socialism was more than a way of restoring the goods of craftsmanship; it was also the specific medium for protecting democratic values against the centralization of industry, whether capitalistically or socialistically organized: "Guild Socialism . . . is democracy applied to industry. Herein it differs fundamentally from State Socialism, which leaves to the bureaucrat the task of organizing the industrial army without regard to the democratic principle." (*National Guilds.*)

Hobson was also influenced by Ruskin, Carlyle, and Morris, but as a onetime orthodox socialist he brought to guild socialism the Marxist emphasis upon the importance of working-class organization within trades unions, and the Marxist emphasis upon the primary importance of abolishing the wage system. He argued for the dispersion of responsibility among the separate industries, and for autonomous government of these industries by the appropriate trades unions. He retained as an element of guild socialist theory, however, the belief that the traditional sovereign State is a useful focus for nationalistic solidarity.

Differences within the guild socialist camp became sharpened with the formation of the National Guilds League in 1915, a propagandist body which attracted such prominent figures as H. H. Brailsford, R. H. Tawney, J. L. Hammond, and Bertrand Russell. Most prominent among the dissenters from Hobson's formulation, and most prominent of the expounders of guild socialism is G. D. H. Cole. Cole gave guild socialist theory a more pronounced pluralist character. Holding that Robert Owen, with his distrust of the State and his trust in self-governing communities, was one of the precursors of the guild movement, Cole believes that economic power must precede political power. Believing with the Marxists that the state as it exists is simply an instrument for capital, Cole argues that the system of workers' self-government can begin within the framework of capitalism through the up-building of the trades unions. His primary disagreement with Hobson and with orthodox Marxists is over the question of socialist administration. Fearing the sovereign State, Cole advocates a pluralistic society in which the administration of socialized industries and services should be entrusted not to government bureaus but rather to self-governing guilds or corporations consisting of all the hand and brain workers employed in each industry. In so far as there is a *State* it is to be simply a kind of "national commune"—a coordinating body built on the voluntary cooperation of the various functional units requiring coordination. Cole does not make quite clear, however, in just what way the coordinating body is to achieve the authority needed for socialist cooperative planning in the event that the voluntary accord of the various guilds is not achieved.

With all his Marxism, Cole retains a large measure of the characteristic regard of the Guildsmen for the medieval ideal of labor. His protests against capitalist industrialism are those of a moralist, and share with the Catholic Albert de Mun the same preconception—namely, that labor is not a commodity. His emphasis upon the functional reorganization of society is in large part a reaction against the liberal theory of a society founded upon abstract rights. Rights and obligations are the products of functional relationships.

The essence of functional democracy is that a man should count as many times over as there are functions in which he is interested. To count once is to count about nothing in particular: what men want is to count on the particular issues in which they are interested. Instead of "one man, one vote," we must say, "One man as many votes as interests, but only one vote in relation to each interest." (*Social Theory.*)

An interesting implication of such "functional" democracy is that political parties, as non-functional organizations, would be outmoded.

Guild socialism stands in the same relation to Fabian socialism as does the pluralism of Laski to the positive liberalism of Green and Bosanquet, and as does the syndicalism of Georges Sorel to revolutionary Marxism. Its distinctive feature is that it is as much a protest against the concentration and centralization of wealth and administrative agencies as it is against the "surplus value" from which the capitalist takes his profit. While the immediate instrument of social change must be the socialization of the means of production, the appropriation of these means by the working class, the primary objective is to restore the democratic process of personal participation in social endeavors through the decentralization of ownership and administration. The peculiar problem that confronts the guild socialists arises out of the fact that such decentralization must be complemented by some kind of overall organization, seemingly required by the intricately interrelated and interdependent structure of contemporary industrialism. Cole's solution of this problem is, on the whole, somewhat vague: "Some form of inclusive association of which every member of the community is a member is indeed clearly necessary; but it may well be that there will be more than one such inclusive association in the community, and that the functions which we have reserved as possible functions of inclusive associations will have to be divided among several such bodies." (*Social Theory.*)

The most direct connection of guild socialism with actual economic and political practice came in 1920 when Hobson induced the builders' union of London and Manchester to take charge of the government housing program. This movement blossomed out, and a National Guild Council was formed in 1922 that was made up of a rather large number of trades unions associated with the movement. The builders' unions were the center of this organization, however, and when the government withdrew its capital and credit the movement collapsed.

Guild socialism as such has had difficulty in winning a large body of adherents. Nevertheless, the movement has not been without influence, especially in Fabian circles. In their *Constitution for the Socialist Commonwealth of Great Britain* (1920) the Webbs show the influence of the Guildsmen. The experience of the Soviet Union has disheartened many socialists with State Socialism, and has won an increased measure of recognition for guild socialism from those concerned with ways of maintaining and extending liberties within a socialist economy.

CHRISTIAN SOCIAL PROGRAMS

Modernism and Neo-orthodoxy. In addition to the political problems created for the Christian churches by liberalism and nationalism, there arose the theological problem of facing evolutionary science and secular theories of history and morals. The churches could not surrender to the ideas of "natural religion" without sacrificing most of their traditional claims; at the same time they could not ignore the discoveries of geology and biology, which made literal belief in many of the traditions and doctrines of Christianity impossible for the educated. The concepts of creation, revelation, and redemption became crucial themes for theologians, who saw the implications of evolutionary science for religion.

Accepting the results of the previous generation of critical historians of the Bible and the life of Jesus, a generation of evolutionary theologians attempted to formulate a modernistic theory of the church and salvation. In Germany, Albrecht Ritschl and his two distinguished followers, Adolf von Harnack and Ernst Troeltsch, interpreted the history of the church as a progressive revelation of religious truth. Ritschl looked for the truths of religion neither in the eternal moral law (as the scholars of the Enlightenment had done) nor in the testimony of individual religious experience (as Schleiermacher, Coleridge, and the believers in "natural supernaturalism" had done), but in the progressive and cumulative revelation of God as exhibited by the historic experience of the "religious community" or church. The judgment and redemption of the world by God is not simply the course of secular history, as Hegel and the secular evolutionists contended, but is the growth of the church as a distinct process of social judgment over and above secular society. The church is God's judgment seat and through the church other human institutions are gradually being "redeemed" and brought nearer to the "Kingdom of God." More recent German theologians have applied this theory of social judgment to revolutionary crises as well as to evolutionary processes. Karl Barth, Emil Brunner, and others have developed what they call a "crisis theology" that assigns to the church and to the "Word of God" a distinctive function in "historical dialectic" or social struggles. The chief outcome of this modern German theology has been to assign a distinctive, "divine" task to the church as an institution of judgment and redemption for secular society.

In England, Cardinal Newman attempted a similar reconciliation between evolution and dogma in his famous *Essay on the Development of Christian Doctrine* (1845) in which he argued that the history of the Church reveals an organic growth of doctrine and that similarly Christian dogma should be expected to "develop" in the future. Applying this idea, a school of Anglican and Catholic theologians known as "modernists" grew rapidly both in England and on the Continent. Among its leaders were the English Jesuit, George

Tyrell, the French historians, Louis Duchesne and Alfred Loisy, and the German historian, Johann von Döllinger, who later organized the Old Catholic Church. In America, one of modernism's leading spokesmen was Augustus Orestes Brownson.

Pope Pius IX had alienated many of the modernists by his ratification in 1869 of the dogma of papal infallibility. His successor, Pius X, in 1907 took a determined stand against modernist tendencies in his encyclical *Pascendi gregis* and excommunicated the leaders of the movement. At the same time he continued the positive policy of his predecessor, Leo XIII, in recommending the study of Thomist philosophy and presenting the discoveries of modern science in terms of Thomist doctrine. Under cover of this neo-scholasticism, as it is often called, a considerable amount of modern science is being gradually incorporated into a philosophical language and system that antedates modern science.

Church and State. Out of the Enlightenment and its liberalism emerged the ideal of a complete separation of church and state. Classic expressions of this ideal are contained in the Virginia Declaration of Rights (1776), the Virginia Bill for Establishing Religious Freedom (1786), and the First Amendment to the Constitution of the United States (1791)—all of them inspired by Thomas Jefferson—and in the famous formula of Cavour, "a free church in a free state." But this ideal proved difficult of realization and has been put into practice by few states. Apart from those groups outside the Christian churches entirely, the "free churches" which advocate complete separation are the extreme Protestant dissenters or separatists, Quakers, Baptists, Methodists, and a few minor evangelical sects, whose conception of the salvation of the soul has been so individualistic as to make it easy for them to separate religion and politics completely. The majority of Christians, however, have held other conceptions of the relation between temporal and spiritual interests. The Roman Catholic Church, the Lutheran and Calvinistic churches, the Anglicans and the Greek Orthodox all agree in theory that the state should be to the church what the body is to the soul; to separate them completely would destroy both instead of freeing either. But in practice they adopt varying policies. The Roman church asserts its sovereignty above all other states (for the Roman church is also a state), and hopes that eventually all temporal powers will acknowledge its spiritual authority in the sense that they recognize the church's teaching in matters of morals and faith. Pope Pius IX defined the Papal position on the relation between church and state in his *Syllabus of Errors* (1864), in which he denounced, among many others, the following "errors":

15. Every man is free to embrace and profess the religion he shall believe true, guided by the light of reason.

16. Men may in any religion find the way of eternal salvation, and obtain eternal salvation.

18. Protestantism is nothing more than another form of the same true Christian religion, in which it is possible to be equally pleasing to God as in the Catholic Church.

20. The ecclesiastical power must not exercise its authority without the permission and assent of the civil government.

24. The Church has not the power of availing herself of force, or any direct or indirect temporal power.

42. In the case of conflicting laws between two powers, the civil law ought to prevail.

44. The civil authority may interfere in matters relating to religion, morality, and spiritual government.

47. The most approved theory of civil society requires that popular schools open to the children of all classes, and, generally, all public institutes intended for instruction in letters and philosophy, and for conducting the education of the young, should be freed from all ecclesiastical authority, government, and interference, and should be completely subject to the civil and political power, in conformity with the will of rulers and the prevalent opinions of the age.

48. This system of instructing youth, which consists in separating it from the Catholic faith and from the power of the Church, and in teaching exclusively, or at least primarily, the knowledge of natural things and the earthly ends of social life alone, may be approved by Catholics.

55. The Church ought to be separated from the State, and the State from the Church.

80. The Roman Pontiff can and ought to reconcile himself to, and agree with, progress, liberalism, and civilization, as lately introduced.

This condemnation of the separation of church and state in theory has not prevented a growing independence of both in fact.

The established churches (state churches) acknowledge a double allegiance: on the one hand to the universal church of Christ, on the other to the spiritual interests of a particular nation. The theories of Hobbes and Thomas Arnold, and the practice of the French Revolution and Napoleon, definitely subordinated the church to the state spiritually as well as temporally; and according to those atheistic communists who believe that religion is merely an opiate, the state owes it to its citizens to tell the "materialist" truth about the churches. One major theme in the history of the nineteenth century is the protracted struggle between these conflicting ideals and interests.

The Churches and Industrial Society. A previous chapter has called attention to the interest shown by churchmen of different denominations in dealing with the problems arising out of the industrial revolution, specifically, to the early forms of Christian socialism. Though Christian socialists have remained a small minority in the churches, they have called attention to the opportunities of the churches for promoting social reconstruction as an extension of their humanitarian mission. The "social gospel," understood as a tendency in the churches to regard concern for problems of social justice and world order as central to the Christian life, is now a commonplace of Christian preaching.

In England, the growth of the labor movement induced Anglicans, for the most part followers of Frederick Denison Maurice, to found in 1877 the Guild of St. Matthew to promote social reform. Later the Christian Social Union and the Church Socialist League were formed. Under the leadership of Bishop Gore the program of this League was officially adopted by the Church of England in 1908. In 1923, however, the term "socialist" was dropped and the League of the Kingdom of God was formed: this league sponsored an elaborate Conference on Christian Politics, Economics, and Citizenship (1924), which made specific proposals for reform. In 1940 this group of left-wing Anglicans, under the leadership of William Temple, Archbishop of York, supported the British Labor Party in its plea for a peaceful revolution. Temple was one of the chief proponents of the argument that (1) the soul of the individual is formed by social conditions; (2) the Church is concerned with the salvation of the individual soul and with whatever affects the possibility of that salvation; (3) therefore, the Church must be concerned with social conditions. This view made possible the justification of social action to those many Protestants whose conception of Christian salvation was exclusively individualistic.

Among the Protestant pioneers of the social gospel in America were F. G. Peabody, Washington Gladden, Josiah Strong, and Walter Rauschenbusch. They carried on the interest stimulated by Edward Bellamy's Social Nationalism in the nineties and by the Christian Economists. More recently the Federal Council of the Churches of Christ has become a national headquarters for social work among the Protestant churches, and its "social creed," formulated in 1912 and revised in 1932, has been widely accepted.

The "social gospel" concern for the institutions of society has been a dominant force in the programs of the various world conferences of Protestant groups, held in many cities of the world during the past twenty-five years as one phase of the growing "ecumenical" movement. The most important of the sponsoring organizations is the World Council of Churches. The Oxford Conference of 1937, on Church, Community, and State, in charting a program for social Protestantism emphasized the need for consideration

of both remote, religious goals and proximate, social goals. To mediate between the remote and the proximate, the Conference set up a series of guiding
principles which they called "middle axioms"; these principles look both
ways—both towards the Divine ideal and towards human needs. Principles
were formulated with respect to economic problems, world peace and order,
race relations, and democratic political institutions. The program of the
Oxford Conference, though it is somewhat general, due to the necessity for
representing the views of Protestant groups from many countries, indicates
that Ecumenical Protestantism is developing a dynamic social program.

On the Continent, German Catholic leaders built up strong labor organizations. Notable among these leaders was the Bishop of Mainz, Baron Wilhelm
von Ketteler, who took a prominent part in the *Kulturkampf*. The growth of
revolutionary and anticlerical Marxism, however, gradually forced the Catholics to repudiate "Christian socialism" and to elaborate a social philosophy
as a rival to that of the Marxian socialists. The foundations of this philosophy
were laid in Leo XIII's encyclical on the Condition of Labor, entitled *Rerum
Novarum* (1891). Stimulated by this papal encouragement, Catholic reform
parties grew rapidly. One of the most successful was the French *action libérale,*
founded in 1901 by the Count de Mun, who since 1871 had been active in
organizing Catholic laborers and in pleading for social reform in the Chamber
of Deputies. One of the most recent and explicit programs of the Catholic
Church is to be found in the encyclical of Pius XI on Reconstructing the Social Order entitled *Quadragesimo anno* (1931), in which he reviewed and expanded the program of Leo XIII's *Rerum novarum*. As a result of the principles enunciated in these encyclicals, it has been possible for Catholics to
support some advanced social legislation so long as they did not attack the
institution of private property.

Chapter XII

EARLY TWENTIETH-CENTURY CURRENTS
OF THOUGHT

꒜

PHILOSOPHIC REACTIONS TO MECHANISM AND NATURALISM

W HAT WAS THE picture which [nineteenth-century] science purported
to give? The idea of evolution, its most novel and revolutionary
concept, has come to stand as a symbol of the scientific faith. But
it was really not so important in forcing that faith as the patient working out
of mechanistic explanation; the latter seemed less of a shock because it had
been in the world since Descartes. Science was advancing and filling in the
details of the Cartesian picture; by the 1860's the results were so impressive
they could no longer be disregarded. The fundamental dogmas of the scientific faith now served to organize a vast body of facts that could not be gain-
said. In the nineteenth century they took the form of sweeping generalizations: the conservation of energy, the laws of thermo-dynamics, natural selection, the mechanistic theory of life, above all an unyielding mechanical
determinism. The laboratory had not yet unearthed so many facts that no
generalization could embrace them all; the recent breakdown of traditional
physical theory had not yet occurred. The idea that all such general statements are leading principles of scientific investigation, instruments to guide
inquiry rather than laws governing the universe, had as yet little support. The
Newtonian framework was not yet burst asunder; the most speculative assumptions, either abandoned or modified to-day, were seized upon to complete a "scientific world-view." With this framework, with these dogmas and
assumptions, shaken believers felt they must come to terms.

This "scientific world-view" of the turn of the century was of course a
faith, a negative faith, not to say an obsession. The dark picture fascinated our
fathers. They loved to paint the alien elements as black as possible, even as
they shuddered in delicious horror before it. It struck terror because they had

This chapter is from *The Making of the Modern Mind* (pp. 580–87, 466–78, 481–83, 512–19,
611–15, revised ed.; Boston, Houghton Mifflin Co., 1940), by John Herman Randall, Jr.

just left the warm affection of the Christian tradition and the optimism of the Romantic faiths. Many believed it because it was so dreadful; they prided themselves on their courage in facing facts. More fled from it as from a nightmare, and used it as a springboard for a faith *quand même*. It surely needed little of the will to believe to maintain that it could not be the whole story: it was so obviously a work of sheer faith, an imaginative rendering of men's gloomiest forebodings. That "alien world" has vanished to-day; the speculative assumptions of nineteenth-century physics on which it was based have given way to others more astounding if less hostile to man's interests. Our newer naturalisms have annulled that divorce of man from nature.

One such picture of the mechanistic and evolutionary world of the last generation [given in *The Garden of Epicurus*], from the master pen of Anatole France, . . . serves as a striking contrast to the world of the Middle Ages. Another is from the hand of that conservative sceptic, Lord Balfour:

Man, so far as natural science by itself is able to teach, is no longer the final cause of the universe, the Heaven-descended heir of all the ages. His very existence is an accident, his story a brief and transitory episode in the life of one of the meanest of the planets. Of the combination of causes which first converted a dead organic compound into the living progenitors of humanity, science, indeed, as yet knows nothing. It is enough that from such beginnings famine, disease, and mutual slaughter, fit nurses of the future lords of creation, have gradually evolved, after infinite travail, a race with conscience enough to feel that it is vile, and intelligence enough to know that it is insignificant. We survey the past, and see that its history is of blood and tears, of helpless blundering, of wild revolt, of stupid acquiescence, of empty aspirations. We sound the future, and learn that after a period, long compared with the individual life, but short indeed compared with the divisions of time open to our investigation, the energies of our system will decay, the glory of the sun will be dimmed, and the earth, tideless and inert, will no longer tolerate the race which for a moment has disturbed its solitude. Man will go down into the pit, and all his thoughts will perish. The uneasy consciousness, which in this obscure corner has for a brief space broken the contented silence of the universe, will be at rest. Matter will know itself no longer. "Imperishable monuments" and "immortal deeds," death itself, and love stronger than death, will be as though they had never been. Nor will anything that *is* be better or be worse for all that the labor, genius, devotion, and suffering of man have striven through countless ages to effect.

Lord Balfour does not believe that this is the final story; but Bertrand Russell does:

That Man is the product of causes which had no prevision of the end they were achieving; that his origin, his growth, his hopes and fears, his loves and his beliefs, are but the outcome of accidental collocations of atoms; that no fire, no heroism, no intensity of thought and feeling, can preserve an individual life beyond the grave;

that all the labor of the ages, all the devotion, all the inspiration, all the noonday brightness of human genius, are destined to extinction in the vast death of the solar system, and that the whole temple of Man's achievement must inevitably be buried beneath the debris of a universe in ruins—all these things, if not quite beyond dispute, are yet so nearly certain, that no philosophy which rejects them can hope to stand. Only within the scaffolding of these truths, only on the firm foundation of unyielding despair, can the soul's habitation henceforth be safely built.

These pictures are, to be sure, but the expression of moods rather than of scientific verities; and all the gloomy predictions of a few decades ago, seeing the ultimate extinction of our sun as the inevitable deduction from the second law of thermodynamics, have been sadly shaken, both by the discovery of radio-activity, and by the reflection that a universe which has existed from all eternity should have run down ere this if that was destined to be its final goal. But without reflecting on this ultimate cosmic death, the picture science presents of man and his destiny is sufficiently different from that of his earlier hopes to give ground for pause. Turn to the astronomer, and he answers:

The Universe itself may be only another single unit, among a multitude of other universes; and if at this point we cease to speculate, it is not because there is no further scope for speculation, but because we have already far outstripped the last shred of solid evidence that our instruments can provide for us. Complete and absolute darkness reigns beyond. If we learn nothing else for certain, we learn at least this: that the farther we travel, the more obscure and insignificant does Man appear. And three points also emerge. Firstly, the uniformity of natural "law" remains as absolute in these regions of infinite greatness as in our own world of human dimensions. Secondly, no sign of purpose can be detected in any part of the vast Universe disclosed by our most powerful telescopes. Thirdly, this great new sphere of experience affords not the smallest trace of evidence for the existence of any spiritual entity. We find nothing but unimaginable tracts of space and time, in which move bodies by fixed laws towards ends which are wholly fortuitous, and have not the smallest relation to the advantage or requirements of Man. (Hugh Eliot.)

Turn to the psychologist or biologist, and he answers that man is a complex physico-chemical organism, the lineal descendant of some bit of primordial slime; all his hopes and aspirations, all his loves and fears, all his self-sacrifice and knowledge, are the result of the peculiar laws governing the chemical reactions that ultimately go to produce his behavior. Turn to the physicist, he who investigates these fundamental units out of which man and his universe are composed in their entirety, and he answers:

Penetration into the secrets of atomic structure has opened up to us a vast new sphere of phenomena whose very existence was previously unsuspected, and which differ *toto cœlo* from all kinds of phenomena with which we were previously acquainted. Yet throughout this new continent of knowledge we find the axioms of materialism as unquestioned as ever. The electrons and the positively charged nuclei of atoms have their unchangeable laws, and illustrate afresh the inviolable relation of cause and effect. Nor, as we approach the very foundations of existence, do we see any more signs than elsewhere of a *purpose* at the basis of the universe. Harmony and order, certainly; that arises from the universality of natural law; it is the same kind of harmony and order that prevails in the larger material masses of the Universe. Even if the Universe is running down to a final doom of extinction, there is no suggestion of purpose there. A clock also runs down, but not by previous intention—not for what we understand by a purpose. Finally, in this new field of discovery, there is no place for any kind of spiritual agency. We know at length what is the basis of matter: it is not spirit, it is energy, a factor exclusively objective in character, and residing on the materialistic, not on the spiritualistic plane. . . . Furthermore, one thing is certain. Whatever matter may ultimately be resolved into, it certainly cannot be resolved into spirit. The wildest speculator in science has never suggested *that* possibility. (Hugh Eliot.)

Following, then, the methods and the principles of scientific investigation, the modern philosopher can arrive at nothing in the universe aside from man that appears to have human interests and human aspirations at heart. In all the reaches of our telescopes and our microscopes there is nowhere discoverable the slightest trace of anything like man, any Friend behind phenomena, any God who cares, any principle that guarantees man success in his struggles and endeavors. So far as the eye of science can see, man is alone, absolutely alone, in a universe in which his very appearance is a kind of cosmic accident. How, then, if this be the very truth, has it come about that he has always, to the present day, in some form or other felt himself at home in his universe, felt that he was the child of the watchful forces of nature, the Son of God whom the Father lovingly cared for? To even this question the scientist has a devastating answer. Turn to the anthropologist, and he will calmly reply:

It is very important in this matter to realize that the so-called belief is not really an intellectual judgment so much as a craving of the whole nature. It is only of late years that psychologists have begun to realize the enormous dominion of those forces in man of which he is normally unconscious. We cannot escape as easily as these brave men dreamed from the grip of the blind powers beneath the threshold. Indeed, as I see philosophy after philosophy falling into this unproven belief in the Friend behind phenomena, as I find that I myself cannot, except for a moment and by an effort, refrain from making the same assumption, it seems to me that perhaps here too we are under the spell of a very old ineradicable instinct. We are gregarious animals; our ancestors have been such for countless ages. We cannot help looking out upon the world as gregarious animals do; we see it in terms of humanity and fellowship. Students of animals under domestication have shown us how the habits of a gregarious creature, taken away from his kind, are shaped in a thousand details by reference to the lost pack which is no longer there—the pack which a dog tries to smell his way back to all the time he is out walking, the pack he calls to for help when danger threatens. It is a strange and touching thing, this eternal hunger of the gregarious animal for the herd of friends who are not there. And it may be, it may very possibly be, that, in the matter of this Friend behind phenomena, our own yearning and our own almost ineradicable instinctive conviction, since they are certainly not founded on either reason or observation, are in origin the groping of a lonely-souled gregarious animal to find its herd or its herd-leader in the great space beyond the stars. (Gilbert Murray.)

The Friend is gone, and man is alone in a cold and alien universe.

That is the sting of it, that in the vast driftings of the cosmic weather, though many a jewelled shore appears, and many an enchanted cloud-bank floats away, long lingering ere it be dissolved—even as our world now lingers, for our joy—yet when these transient products are gone, nothing, absolutely *nothing* remains, to represent those particular qualities, those elements of preciousness which they may have enshrined. Dead and gone are they, gone utterly from the very sphere and room of being. Without an echo; without a memory; without an influence on aught that may come after, to make it care for similar ideals. This utter final wreck and tragedy is of the essence of scientific materialism as at present understood. The lower and not the higher forces are the eternal forces, or the last surviving forces within the only cycle of evolution which we can definitely see. (William James.)

No scientist, of course, can claim that he has *proved* that this is the whole story, and that the vast edifice man has built for his spirit, with its foundations of Godhead, its walls of a loving Providence, and its airy pinnacles of human immortality, may not dwell somewhere beyond the reach of his instruments. On the other side of the moon, indeed, there may stand the Heavenly City with its golden gates and pearly walls and alabaster turrets; and there the saints may be gathered in glory, chanting never-ending hymns to the Eternal Father upon his throne. But, so far as the scientist can discern, there is not one shred of evidence that it is aught but a dream-castle in the clouds; and his knowledge of the mythopœic faculty in man is such as to make him strongly suspect that such is indeed the case. If man continues to believe to-day in what his forbears trusted, it is by faith, and by faith alone, that he can justify himself. And by the side of the solid edifice of scientific verity, such faith seems, and cannot but seem, a slender reed upon which to rest such momentous hopes. The more man actually learns of himself and his universe the less prone he is to trust to such an unaided faith. If he have faith, it is a faith *quand même,* a faith that can remove mountains, a faith stronger than knowledge, stronger than reason, strong as life itself.

By the middle of the last century this seemed so clear to men that they were convinced that they must take it as a fundamental, an irreducible datum. Only on such a firm foundation could they build a habitation for the human spirit; only in a world set in such terms could they hope to achieve whatever measure of the good life was destined to fall to their lot. For those not willing to rest in traditional beliefs, for those who felt that human reason and human intelligence must work out its own destiny and salvation, the great problem was presented, what shall man do about it? What possibilities does such a world offer? How may a good life be led in such a world? Three general types of answer may be distinguished; together they make up the body of modern philosophies. When this realization came like a cold shock to men, the first reaction was one of disillusionment and despair. Mindful of their past hopes, they either lamented their lost dreams in lugubrious measures, or took refuge in the ivory tower of art, where for a while at least the soul might dwell amidst beauty; or, refusing to recognize the picture as more than partially and inadequately true, they retreated to a perfection elsewhere, and in some structure of philosophic idealism found consolation for the emptiness of the world of science. Stronger souls, unable still to envisage humanity as utterly alone in the wind-swept wastes of the universe, turned with pathetic eagerness to the one great process and purpose that science seemed to leave in the world. For them, evolution took the place of Providence; and, reflecting that after all man has been the outcome of the cosmic forces, they sought in the very worship and deification of evolution, in the vigorous acceptance of and rejoicing in the ends of nature, a worthy ideal for human life, and a guarantee that, if man but made his own the ends of cosmic power, he could still triumph with the course of nature. A third group, from the generation that had no longer cherished the fond hopes of the past, and hence had never experienced disillusionment, looked about itself upon the world depicted by science, and saw it neither as an alien world, nor as a great process to be glorified as realizing ideals to which man must adhere; but rather as the natural scene of human life and human striving, a dwelling-place in which man can accomplish his human purposes and bend the materials that are given him to his own will. The various reactions to the alien world—complete pessimism, Promethean defiance of nature, retreat to an idealistic faith behind and beyond the world of science;—the evolutionary faiths in the cosmic process, Progress, Creative Evolution, Pragmatism, the revaluation of values; and a Greek or a Baconian naturalism—these are the main philosophies of the modern world, together with such philosophies as have persisted, like Thomism, relatively untouched by the scientific viewpoint. . . .

Explaining complex phenomena by isolating simpler elements and processes whose behavior can be mathematically formulated and predicted, came
to be known in the nineteenth century as the method of "mechanistic" analysis.
Practically, it meant the search for the mechanism involved: by suitable
manipulation and combination new ways of acting could be discovered, and
the amazing technical triumphs of science achieved. Theoretically, it meant
the drive toward formulating the basic natural processes in mathematical
terms so general that the various types of observed phenomena could be exhibited as special cases. This search for elements with a uniform type of behavior is as old as the Greek atomists; its aim and method had apparently
triumphed with the Newtonians. By the end of the nineteenth century the
elementary substance was assumed to be the atom of "matter" with its fixed
mass, and the elementary process, the motion formulated in the equations of
dynamics. Even phenomena like light that did not seem to possess the two
characteristics of matter, inertia and gravitation, were conceived as wave-
motions of an "ether" itself considered as a kind of substance. In view of what
has since happened to the basic concepts of this closely-knit theory, matter,
energy, and ether, it is well to realize that the method of "mechanistic"
analysis is not bound up with the limitations of this older materialistic and
mechanical view. Nineteenth-century science took the motion of matter as the
ultimate process and form of energy. To-day periodic energy has become
more basic than "matter"; hence our science is no longer, strictly speaking,
"materialistic." And the laws of mechanical motion are not so universal as
those of the behavior of a field of radiation, and may indeed be but a special
form of that behavior. Hence our science is no longer, like Newton's, "mechanical." But its basic method has remained that of "mechanistic" analysis.

In one important respect this method and type of explanation have been
broadened. Having found simpler elements and processes, men have gone
on to investigate how they act when combined in a complex system. In the
various analytic sciences from physics to psychology, it has proved necessary
to consider the way in which processes function, not only in isolation, but
also in the relevant context or "field" in which they normally operate. The
structure of this field or system of interacting processes has thus assumed increasing importance; in the more mathematical sciences it is this structure
which the fundamental equations have come to formulate. To the mechanistic
analysis into component processes there has been added the functional analysis

into the specific way they act in the total situation. The sciences no longer tend to "reduce" complex wholes to their atomic constituents, assuming that no modification of behavior takes place in the combination, and thus "explaining away" the systematic factor. They endeavor rather to discover its precise pattern. But on the other hand they are as eager as ever to find the elementary mechanisms that function in those structures. In consequence, the older issue, in sciences like biology, for instance, between a "mechanistic interpretation" and its denial has ceased to have much importance. Elements are elements of systems, and neither factor can be neglected. . . .

In recording the way in which the method of mechanistic analysis has penetrated every barrier set up to keep it out of privileged fields, we must realize that we are tracing the growth of a scientific faith in a certain method rather than of any final scientific knowledge. The body of believers is still far out-numbered by the masses of the infidels, and within the ranks of investigators themselves there are still heretics, as honest and as sincere as the more orthodox majority. But with the liberalization of that method the number of scientific heretics has been rapidly diminishing.

Three main movements are discernible in the nineteenth-century spread of mechanistic analysis: first, the unification of the fields of physics and chemistry through fundamental generalizations; secondly, the introduction of such analysis into the realm of biology, of living beings; and thirdly, the application of the same viewpoint and method to the study of human nature itself. This is not the place to enter into any detailed consideration of the progress of scientific discovery and theory; that fascinating story has been often told. But since it is beyond question the most important intellectual force in the last hundred years, it is worth while to present even a very inadequate summary of its significance. It was science, the mathematico-physical experimental learning of the seventeenth and eighteenth centuries, that really wrought the changes from the intellectual world of the Middle Ages, changes that neither Renaissance nor Reformation had been able to bring about; and increasingly it has been the growth of scientific knowledge that has caused the steady spread of the naturalistic viewpoint in every field. Science remained unperturbed by the romantic reaction; and science has seen that tide reach its height and roll back, though its waves still beat incessantly upon the citadel of knowledge. What the scientists learned from the romanticists, in a broader and more flexible outlook and method, in a wider conception of the extent of human experience, in a conviction of the fundamental importance of studying origins and development, has served only to intrench more strongly the scientific method and the scientific criterion of truth in the minds of all educated men.

Those sciences, like physics and astronomy and chemistry, in which the Newtonian world had been rooted, witnessed a double movement; on the one hand, they became less confident of mathemetical hypotheses unchecked by the most careful experimentation, and engaged in a great coöperative enterprise to bring to light the multitudes of detailed facts about the world; on the other, this very mass of observations led men to the formulation and verification of sweeping generalizations stating in mathematical terms the fundamental relationships between physical phenomena. Physicists, no longer content with the mechanics of gross bodies, carried their analysis further and further. In the kinetic theory of matter they worked out in detail a molecular mechanics that would draw together all the investigations of solids, fluids, and gases, together with the phenomena of heat and sound, and explain all so-called physical properties of bodies in terms of the energy of motion of their component particles. The vast sciences of electricity and magnetism, mere idle curiosities in the previous century, opened up a new world of electromagnetic energy following laws even more basic than those of mechanics; to explain these phenomena it became necesary to distinguish a further component factor within the atom, the electron. Chemists, bringing order into their science by a verifiable atomic theory set in mathematical terms, discovered the Periodic Law of atomic weights, and were led to the same analysis of the atom into electrons and a nucleus of varying complexity which had been necessary in physics. The two sciences merged in their roots into one, the study of the behavior of the factors within the atom and of the compounds it enters into; and to-day matter and motion together are dissolving into a common form of periodic energy, whose laws when completely formulated promise to include all physical and chemical laws as special instances.

In the achievement of such a mathematical synthesis of all physical phenomena, three main stages may be distinguished. The first was the work of the seventeenth century; Galileo and Newton formulated the universal laws of motion and gravitation. The second sprang chiefly from a study of the steam engine and the other heat-producing machines of the early nineteenth century; it is expressed in the great generalization of the Conservation of Energy. This developed from the determination of the mechanical equivalent of heat, undertaken by Rumford and Davy; but the final enunciation is due mainly to Joule in England and Mayer and Helmholtz in Germany. The latter phrased it:

The last decades of scientific development have led us to the recognition of a new universal law of all natural phenomena, which, from its extraordinarily extended range, and from the connection which it constitutes between natural phenomena of all kinds, even of the remotest times and the most distant places, is especially fitted to give us an idea of the character of the natural sciences. This law is the Law of the Conservation of Force; it asserts, that the *quantity of force which can be brought into action in the whole of Nature is unchangeable,* and can neither be increased nor diminished.

This law is often called the First Law of Thermodynamics; the second law, formulated by Kelvin, is that of the Dissipation of Energy, that while the total energy in the universe is constant, the sum of useful energy is diminishing by its ultimate conversion into non-useful or dissipated heat: that is, kinetic energy seems to be undergoing a degradation into purely molecular motion. These great generalizations, it should be noted, like the earlier Newtonian principle of the universal scope of the laws of mechanics, while marvelously valuable in uniting the varied phenomena of nature under a few fundamental laws, are assumptions rather than absolutely verified theories, assumptions necessary to science, but assumptions of the scientific faith none the less.

It still remained to bring the phenomena of light, electricity, and magnetism together, and to link them with the foundations of mechanics and of chemistry. As a result of the work of Thomas Young and Fresnel, it was definitely established that light is a form of wave-motion in some medium. Coulomb and Ampère in France, Ohm in Germany, and Faraday and Kelvin in England, discovered and formulated the laws of electro-statics, electro-magnetism, and of galvanic currents; and Faraday suggested, with brilliant intuition, though he did not work his theory out mathematically, that all these facts could be referred to the effects of motion in what he called an electro-magnetic field, and that this field possessed much in common with the medium, ether, which the wave theory of light made it necessary to assume.

Thus three great generalizations had been achieved by the middle of the century: Newtonian mechanics, the atomic theory in chemistry, and the kinetic theory of matter, light, electricity, and magnetism.

None of these three principles, however, appeared sufficient to cover the whole field. The law of gravitation embraced cosmical and some molar phenomena, but led to vagueness when applied to molecular actions. The atomic theory led to a complete systematization of chemical compounds, but afforded no clue to the mysteries of chemical affinity. And the kinetic or mechanical theories of light, of electricity, and magnetism, led rather to a new dualism, the division of science into sciences of matter and of the ether. The unification of scientific thought which was gained by any of these three views, was thus only partial. A more general term had to be found under which the different terms could be comprised, which would give a still higher generalization, a more complete unification of knowledge. (J. T. Merz.)

This conception was electro-magnetic energy, and its definition and formulation, begun by Clerk Maxwell, Helmholtz, and Hertz, lies at the foundation of all subsequent study of the electron and radio-activity, as well as of the mathematical synthesis of the other three principles.

Maxwell set to work to study the energy of the electro-magnetic field by applying the law of the conservation of energy. Where Faraday had been content with a mechanical analogy for his fruitful conception, Maxwell, a brilliant mathematician, reduced its properties to exact measurement. He succeeded in identifying all the various experimentally ascertained electric and magnetic phenomena, fixing their nature and quantities in conformity with experience, and arriving finally at the conclusion that the velocity of the transmission of electro-magnetic forces must be the same as that of light, light being but a special form of such wave-motion. "We can scarcely avoid the inference that light consists in the transverse undulations of the same medium which is the cause of electric and magnetic phenomena." Hertz verified Maxwell's calculations by detailed experiment, proving the fundamental character of the electro-magnetic field and its energy. The equations expressing these systematic relationships, "Maxwell's equations," have remained the basis of the new mathematical synthesis. Einstein has described their formulation as the most important event in physics since Newton's time. They not only express the radiation of both electro-magnetic and light waves—the two differ only in wave-length—thus bringing both electrical and optical phenomena under the same formulae. They represent the structure of a field of radiation, and enable us to predict the changes in that field. All the newer developments in physical theory converge on the radiation of energy within a field of definite structure as the most fundamental type of process so far discovered in nature; and the field equations express the laws of this basic and universal type of activity.

At the close of the century physical theory seemed to be reaching a stable and perfected form. Whatever was not matter and its energy of motion—of which heat had been proved an instance—was the energy of motion of the "ether." The various forms of energy were mutually convertible without change of quantity. In this closely-related scheme of matter, energy, and ether, there was a place for every known physical phenomenon.

Then in 1895 Röntgen produced X-rays by bombarding a metal target in a vacuum tube with "cathode rays" or streams of electrons; and the next year Becquerel found the same types of emission and radiation in radio-active substances. The study of the radiation of energy, and of the structure of the atom in terms of the particles and waves it can be made to give off or absorb, took an immense spurt. Now energy had always been regarded as continuous, unlike matter with its atomic structure: bodies could absorb or lose it by smooth and gradual change. But in 1900 Max Planck was led to suggest that energy too must be atomic or granular in character, that in radiation it is transmitted in indivisible units or "quanta." Planck's quantum theory has proved of basic importance in the further study of radiation and of atomic structure. Applied to radiation of the frequency of light, it treats a light ray as a stream of quanta of light-energy, or "photons," rather than as a continuous wave-motion; it takes the different wave-lengths of the spectrum as different degrees of energy in the particular photons for each color. This quantum theory of light is a revival in much subtler form of Newton's corpuscular theory. It has been found to explain certain phenomena which the wave-theory does not; but it fails to explain others, like diffraction, or the bending of light rays around small obstacles, which first established the wave-theory a century ago. In certain relations, light behaves like a shower of photons; in others, like a wave. This situation, in which two mutually inconsistent theories are both needed to deal with the different aspects of light, in which, it has been said, we have to use the wave theory on Mondays, Wednesdays, and Fridays, and the corpuscular theory on Tuesdays, Thursdays, and Saturdays, has been a standing challenge to find a comprehensive and unifying hypothesis. The same problem has developed with the quanta or units of matter: electrons behave not only like particles, but also on occasion like waves. This contradiction led de Broglie and Schrödinger to work out a wave or quantum mechanics, which tries to combine both aspects by treating the matter statistically. In this latest development of the quantum theory, the older classical mechanics of particles or masses appears as a special instance of a more general wave mechanics; and the units or quanta of matter—the electrons—are found to exhibit the same laws as the quanta of energy.

This development of the theory of energy has been intimately connected with the work on the theory of atomic structure. For our knowledge of atoms depends upon the different kinds of charged particles and radiation we can find emanating from them. On the basis of these emissions we try to work out mathematically a mechanism that will act in that precise way. We then employ that structure to suggest new experiments; when they fail to turn out as the theory predicts, we try to reconstruct the equations. Since we thus observe atoms primarily as sources of complex radiation—the lines in that atom's spectrum are a cardinal example—any advance in the knowledge of radiation at once suggests new facts about the atom. The most fruitful model so far devised, that of Bohr, was derived by applying the quantum theory to Ruther-ford's suggestion of 1911 that the atom consists of a positively charged nucleus with one or more negatively charged electrons revolving about it, like planets about the sun. In Bohr's hypothesis, the revolving electrons could radiate energy only when they jumped to a new orbit, and the number of possible orbits was limited by the quantum unit of energy. The ninety-two elements in the periodic table differed in possessing from one to ninety-two revolving electrons. For over ten years this hypothesis was remarkably successful in explaining the experimental facts. But Bohr's equations and planetary model proved too crude to account for all the observed facts; above all, its view of the electron as a charged particle could not explain why electrons at times behaved like waves. De Broglie, developing wave mechanics by applying the theory of relativity to the quantum theory, furnished Schrödinger with a more adequate mathematical expression for the events going on within the atom; the Schrödinger atom has superseded Bohr's. It is difficult to state its structure in non-mathematical terms, which may well be an advantage, for mechanical "models" are misleading as well as illuminating. In this view the atom is not a system of revolving particles, but a continuous electrical charge fluctuating in density with a complex frequency—a kind of pulsating sphere of electricity. The electrons emitted are treated as little bunches of waves or vibratory energy rather than as particles.

Thus wave mechanics, taking seriously the equivalence of matter and en-ergy already calculated by Einstein, regards the older particles or material points as narrow parcels of waves, systems of waves so interfering with each other that they cancel each other out everywhere except at the position oc-cupied by the material point. Matter and energy are mutually convertible, and in place of the principles maintaining their separate conservation, there is the broader principle of the conservation of matter-energy.

An unexpected consequence of the quantum theory is that the position and the velocity of an individual electron cannot both be determined at the same time, and hence its behavior cannot be precisely calculated. To ascertain its position, we must direct rays upon it, and thus alter its velocity; to ascertain its velocity makes its position indefinite. The accuracy of the two measure-ments varies inversely, and is limited theoretically as well as practically by the quantum constant. We can no more follow the movement of an individual electron than we could see a colored picture whose dimensions were smaller than the wave length of its color. The impossibility of predicting the behavior of any individual electron was formulated by Heisenberg as the principle of uncertainty or indeterminacy. This principle has been made the starting-point for much dubious speculation about the absence of strict causality and determinism in nature, and has been extended far beyond the atomic field to which it is relevant. But methodologically it means that the physicist can deal only with masses of electrons, and in statistical terms. The equations of quantum physics consequently take the form of probability functions, and state the periodic changes or waves of the probability of certain events. Such statistical rules make prediction and verification possible under all conditions of observation. But they concern an aggregate, not individuals; and they are verified by a series of repeated measurements.

The major phenomenon so far left out of our account of the unification of physical science in terms of the energy of radiation is gravitation. To bring mechanics and radiation together, to unite both gravitation and electricity in a comprehensive "field theory," has been the basic drive of all Einstein's work. In formulating his special theory of relativity in 1905, he set forth a general scheme for the motion of bodies, including those with a velocity approaching that of light, for which classical mechanics breaks down; Newton's laws appear as a special case for the slower velocities. Einstein's "special theory" was limited to events taking place in systems in uniform rectilinear motion, for which the Newtonian law of inertia holds. In 1917 he went on in his general theory of relativity to deal with systems in any kind of motion, and worked out the equations for the gravitational field.

Starting from the negative results of the Michelson-Morley experiment, which attempted to detect changes in the velocity of light due to the earth's absolute motion through the supposed medium of the ether, he laid down two principles: first, the velocity of light is constant, and unaffected by relative motion between the observer and the light's source; secondly and more generally, the laws of physics are not altered by the motion of the system in which the events are occurring; they are the same in all coördinate-systems moving uniformly relative to each other. This principle had been established for mechanics since Galileo; it was now extended to electro-dynamics as well. To be sure, various surprising things would seem to be happening on another system moving with a high velocity with reference to the observer: there would appear to be a contracting of everything in the other system in the direction of its motion, and clocks in it would seem to be running slow. To an observer on the other system, the same things would be apparent in the system of the first observer. But by taking account of the relative motion between the two systems, and applying the proper rules—the Lorentz transformation laws—the familiar physical laws, for example, Maxwell's equations, would be found obtaining in both systems after this translation. That is, the laws of physics would be invariant with respect to the Lorentz transformation. In just the same way the laws of mechanics are found to be the same in the two systems when the apparent motions in the one are suitably translated by the classical transformation rules. A further consequence of the special theory of relativity is that there is no essential distinction between mass and energy. Energy has mass, mass represents energy, the two are convertible, and their equivalence has been precisely calculated.

The general theory of relativity goes on to consider systems in accelerated motion with respect to each other. Such systems are identical in behavior and structure with a gravitational field. Thus the equations for such motion will describe the operation of gravitational forces; they are formulated in the complicated mathematics of the tensor calculus. Gravitation is looked upon, not as an attractive force inherent in masses, but as the property of a field with a definite structure, in which masses tend to move toward the point of least stress. Einstein's problem was to find the coördinate system or type of geometrical "space" which would describe that structure. He worked out a non-Euclidean or "curved" system in which light rays, following the "shortest" path, are bent or deflected when passing near large masses like the sun. It is to be noted that the experimental consequences of the general theory of relativity differ on only a few points from those of classical mechanics, though on these points observation has confirmed it. Its main advantage is the mathematical simplicity and consistency of its fundamental assumptions.

Einstein's equations for the gravitational field are still quite different from Maxwell's equations for the field of electro-magnetics. In that sense, gravitation has not yet been integrated mathematically with the electrical theory of matter and energy. Einstein has several times announced a general unified "field theory," based on a new coördinate system, or type of space, from which he hoped to deduce both the electro-magnetic and the gravitational equations as special instances. But the task has proved more difficult than he anticipated, and the theory of a comprehensive "field physics" has not yet been constructed. That final unification remains to be accomplished.

The significance of these generalizations is obvious. Modern science began with the attempt to analyze all phenomena into the behavior of certain ultimate components uniting to form various combinations. In the Newtonian world, these elements were masses, and their laws were those of motion. To-day, the elements seem to be rather the waves of energy in an electro-magnetic field, and their laws, the laws of the structure and behavior of such a field. The various portions of physical theory are all in a state of rapid flux: quantum theory still holds untold possibilities of further development, the analysis of the structure of the nucleus of the atom is proceeding apace, no atomic model is completely adequate to the facts, the integration of matter and gravitation into a unified field theory belongs to the future. Many inconsistencies are left, between theories, and between theory and experiment. But if the eighteenth-century vision of a universal mathematico-mechanical synthesis was far too crude, and failed to realize the complexity of analysis required to bring all facts within its comprehensive sweep, its fundamental principles of method and attitude, unswervingly maintained, deepened and broadened in recent years, have reaped their reward: our present-day Order of Nature may be far more intricate, but it is also far more comprehensive and far more solidly established than ever before.

It is hardly surprising that this revolution in physical theory and concepts has provoked an immense amount of philosophizing, both about the new pictures of the world suggested, and about the very nature of the scientific enterprise itself. On the one hand, speculative cosmologies have been erected, only to crumble with some new discovery or change in theory. On the other, both philosophers and scientists have undertaken a careful and critical analysis of the function and nature of scientific theory in general, and of the mathematical formulations of physical theory in particular. The older view that Newtonian science was a direct reading of the structure of nature is no longer tenable. Scientific theory and concepts, it is only too apparent, develop and change in time; and he would be hardy to-day who maintained that any of the present ideas express "the way things really are." The primary function of theory and hypothesis, it is now clear, is to organize discoveries already made and suggest new questions to put to nature. Whether and how far the co-ordinating ideas themselves represent anything to be found in nature is a minor matter, on which our philosophies of science differ. That the equations for probability waves are highly abstract is obvious; and most physicists are now content with a set of mathematical formulae that will predict the events in the field of radiation, and have ceased to look for a mechanical model of the atom that can be pictured in the imagination. This growth of a positivistic and functional attitude toward scientific theory is a major feature of our philosophies of science to-day; they are increasingly concerned with what science does and how it does it, with methods and procedures, rather than with its conclusions of the moment. . . .

The last field into which naturalistic explanation on an experimental basis has entered has been that of human behavior, psychology. Men like Hartley in the eighteenth century had made a crude beginning, but the backwardness of biology had prevented much fruitful work. If biology is now regarded as a very complex branch of chemistry, psychology is coming to be treated by most of the experimentalists as a branch of biology or physiology. Experimental psychology as a natural science was developed by physicians who approached the whole matter from the physiological point of view. Wundt in Germany and William James in America were the pioneers. With James, the problem of a biological psychology became the discovery of the physiological changes in the nervous system which would serve as the mechanism of human behavior and of man's mental life. The American "behaviorists," under the leadership of John B. Watson, have pushed this biological approach in its most radical form. They have made of psychology the study of the physiological reactions of the human organism as a whole. Their science tries to analyze human nature, not, with the eighteenth century, into sensations and ideas, but rather into the biological reactions of the nervous system to specific stimuli.

The whole of mental life, even in its highest reaches of reflective thought, the Behaviorists maintain, can be studied and its laws formulated solely in terms of the physiological structure and activity of the body.

Psychology, as the behaviorist views it, is a purely objective, experimental branch of natural science which needs consciousness as little as do the sciences of chemistry and physics. . . . This suggested elimination of states of consciousness as proper objects of investigation in themselves will remove the barrier which exists between psychology and the other sciences. The findings of psychology become the functional correlates of structure and lend themselves to explanation in physico-chemical terms.

To such a science, thought can be accounted for as a series of reactions of the larynx, the organ of speech, which in themselves are dependent on mechanisms in the central nervous system.

It is not different in essence from tennis-playing, swimming, or any other overt activity, except that it is hidden from ordinary observation and is more complex and at the same time more abbreviated so far as its parts are concerned than even the bravest of us could dream of. (John B. Watson.)

On such a view the human being comes into the world a bundle of pre-potent reflexes, ready to be set off by the proper physical stimulus. During the course of a lifetime various stimuli, from without and within, condition these mechanisms and build them into long trains of habits; the entire process is ultimately a physico-chemical modification of the nervous system. Perhaps the most extreme statement of such a chemical explanation of human actions is to be found in Loeb.

The highest manifestation of ethics, namely, the condition that human beings are willing to sacrifice their lives for an idea is comprehensible neither from the utilitarian standpoint nor from that of the categorical imperative. It might be possible that under the influence of certain ideas chemical changes, for instance, internal secretions within the body, are produced which increase the sensitiveness to certain stimuli to such an unusual degree that such people become slaves to certain stimuli just as the copepods (smaller crustaceans) become slaves to the light when carbon dioxide is added to the water. Since Pavlov and his pupils have succeeded in causing the secretion of saliva in the dog by means of optic and acoustic signals, it no longer seems strange to us that what the philosopher terms an "idea" is a process which can cause chemical changes in the body.

Experimental psychology has to-day lost most of this brash self-confidence; the negative dogmas of the early Behaviorists have been forgotten. But their biological attitude, method, and viewpoint have won general acceptance, at least in America. Most scientific psychologists to-day are "behavioristic" in using the methods of experimental science to study publicly observable human behavior. They have gone on from a primary concern with the elementary constituents of activity to the functional problems of their interaction and integration in the complex adjustments of the organism to its environment. Atomic analysis into minute segments of behavior has been unable to get very far without considering the larger patterns in which they coöperate. The same emphasis on the functioning of simpler processes within a complex system or field which we have seen emerging in physics and in biology has expressed itself here in movements like psychoanalysis and Gestalt psychology. The latter group in particular have not been content, like most of the critics of an analytic method in the sciences of life, merely to attack the validity of a purely atomic or reductive analysis into elements. They have brought a mass of experimental evidence to support the view that organisms respond not merely to isolated stimuli but to complex structures or patterns of relation (*Gestalten*) in the field of behavior. Psychology is likewise broadening its methods to include a functional analysis of its field. . . .

The behavioristic school saw as its fundamental problem the discovery of the simple physiological mechanisms out of which is integrated the behavior of the human organism as a whole, and the analysis of the details of the synthesizing process of habit formation. By a careful analysis of the reactions of human infants, Watson has determined the behavior patterns with which man starts life, and has explored the way in which these simple reflex actions are built up into more complicated forms. Basing his work upon the conception of the "conditioned reflex" investigated by Pavlov in Russia—a response acquired by associating a new stimulus with the one accustomed—he has shown how quickly the native reflexes and random movements are built up into learned reactions. Habit upon habit is formed by the conditioning environment, which, operating upon the given physiological patterns, thus literally moulds the integrated behavior of the adult.

While all agreed that these elements of behavior are physiological in nature, and that they are largely only dimly conscious to the individual, controversy has waxed furious over the question whether they are fixed in some simple inherited pattern at birth, so that the basic human traits can fairly be considered constant and unalterable, or whether they are chiefly habits formed by the environment out of a relatively plastic human nature of almost limitless possibilities. Thorndike in his *Original Nature of Man* and especially McDougall in his *Social Psychology* took the former view, and built up an imposing scheme of original tendencies or instincts, from the combination of which behavior atoms mature conduct arises.

Any man possesses at the very start of his life [said Thorndike] numerous well-defined tendencies to future behavior. Between the situations which he will meet and the responses which he will make to them, pre-formed bonds exist. It is already determined by the constitution of the two germs, that under certain circumstances he will see and hear and feel and act in certain ways. . . . The behavior of man in the family, in business, in the state, in religion, and in every other affair of life is rooted in his unlearned, original equipment of instincts and capacities.

For McDougall these instincts were powerful forces resident in man, impelling him to action, the driving springs without which he would be limp and passive.

We may, then, define an instinct as an inherited or innate psychophysical disposition which determines its possessor to perceive, and to pay attention to, objects of a certain class, to experience an emotional excitement of a particular quality upon perceiving such an object, and to act in regard to it in a particular manner, or, at least, to experience an impulse to such action.

He found some eleven major instincts in man, chief of which are the instinct of flight, of repulsion, of curiosity, of pugnacity, of self-abasement, of self-assertion, and the parental instinct. This is, it must be observed, a logical and teleological classification, in which the instincts are defined in terms of the purposes they serve. Many were the social theories founded upon it.

A decade of careful criticism of this simple atomic conception of human nature has led to the general agreement that it is more fruitful to seek definite and specific reactions that can be experimentally isolated, and that in complex human behavior these reflexes are overlaid by habit after habit conditioned by the environment. Such a view does not give the facile "explanations" of action that come from reading it in terms of a few dominant instincts; but the suspicion has arisen that to attribute the cause, for example, of men's congregating in large cities to a "gregarious instinct" is much like the scholastic dormitive powers of opium, a labeling and not an explanation. In pointing out that the elements of behavior are exceedingly numerous and complex, it destroys a simple atomism, but it opens the way for a closer analysis of individual histories and for a genetic treatment of habit formation that will both predict and control.

The practical consequences of this shift from the vague and animistic "instinct" to the precise "conditioned reflex" as the basic unit are to place a more adequate emphasis on the determining factor of the environment, minimized by the McDougall school, and hence to read human nature as a function of the cultural situation into which it is born rather than as a fixed entity inevitably flowering into the given society. It is no accident that the earlier theory of a fixed and simple human nature has been seized upon everywhere by conservatives opposed to social change, while the critics of that theory, like John Dewey, are hopeful of social amelioration through education and institutional reform. This is especially apparent in the problem of how far individual and group differences, which experiment has revealed and measured and which seem definitely to have overthrown the eighteenth-century theory of the equality of man, so basic in traditional social theory, are hereditary and unalterable, and how far they are environmental products and hence subject to control. Conservatives welcome the former view, seeing the existent order as pretty much biologically necessary, while progressives hope to push back the limits of fixed native endowment as far as possible. This tendency is reflected in the conflict between the biological and the cultural determinists in anthropology, politics, and sociology. But obviously the controversy between the inherited and the acquired can only be solved along the lines of Watson's experiments, with a much fuller knowledge of facts than we now possess.

But this attempt at a new atomic conception of human nature, like that of the eighteenth century except that biological processes have replaced passive sensations as the elements, has other problems to face than those of the nature of its elements. How are these fundamental units built up into their complex human manifestations? Is the process simply an additive one, in which the original units are clearly discernible, or does so much modification and assimilation take place that the value of the whole analytical treatment can be doubted? There has lately grown up a feeling of dissatisfaction with the results of this elucidation of behavior atoms, this "muscle-twitch psychology." The most important psychological phenomena are complex and involve a total situation. Can such situations be reproduced under laboratory conditions? The analysis into behavior-segments gets along famously up to the decorticated rat, but with human actions, conditioned by the individual's entire past experience, it has not proved so fruitful. Can human psychology disregard the response of the whole person to a situation?

The Gestalt school of Wertheimer, Koffka and Köhler maintains that response is always to a set of related stimuli, and exhibits non-additive and transposable patterns subject to "wholeness laws" like those of the structure of an electrical field. Others have also tried to apply "organismic" concepts.

Being interested primarily in human conduct [writes J. R. Kantor], we are therefore required to investigate the actions of human individuals as distinct humanistic occurrences of very particular types. In effect this means that we must take account of the numerous human conditions and institutions which give rise to psychological phenomena and which condition their occurrence. Only by taking into consideration the intimate nuances and refinements of human interactions with things and persons can we hope to describe adequately human behavior and avoid worthless artifacts. We deem it to be the essence of valid scientific method thus to study any given fact as it actually transpires and not to reduce it to something else, not even to a simplified part of itself.

Organismic psychology is based upon the premises that we must never admit anything into our scientific thinking but that which can be actually observed. Nor must we assume for our convenience that the part is the whole. . . . Basing our investigations upon this platform we consider the subject-matter of psychology to be the concrete reactions which an organism makes to its stimuli surroundings. Naturally all the varieties of surroundings are considered; so that organismic psychology considers as part of its subject-matter not only the simple behavior to natural stimuli but also the complex adaptations to social and human institutions. . . . The causes of the organism's reactions are not brain or mental conditions, but the needs of the organism as dictated by the surrounding objects and events. . . . For such a view the explanatory features of the science consist for the most part in the detailed study of the reactional biographies of individuals throughout their various contacts with their actual surroundings.

As yet the elements of behavior are probably too little understood to make such an attempt other than vague, but with a genetic understanding of the more complex forms of habit formation it is inevitable that the higher organizations of behavior will come to be more and more central. The task will be infinite, as it involves the whole social setting; but only when it is accomplished will the science of human nature be able to furnish a fruitful basis for the other social sciences.

It was precisely this attempt to deal with personality as a whole, especially in a practical way on its pathological side, that led to the development by psychiatrists of the theory of psychoanalysis. Out of their clinical experience they have erected a whole system of psychology that has little sympathy with the scientific mechanical analysis we have just traced, and arrogates to itself the title of "the new psychology." As formulated by Freud and his followers, psychoanalysis is a mixture of important experimental discoveries, of fruitful new concepts for attacking the behavior of integrated personalities, and of a general speculative background that can only be called romantic and fantastic in the extreme, made to serve an astonishingly successful therapeutic method. Its core is the principle that the great majority of human reactions are produced by impulses or motives that are below the level of consciousness, and that the precise nature of these impulses in any individual must be explained in terms of his past experience. In particular, most of the pathological disturbances of behavior are due to the unsuspected persistence of emotional drives or complexes occasioned by events or desires that were unpleasant or socially disapproved and hence repressed. It is in bringing to light the emotional consequences of such repression of fundamental impulses that psychoanalysis has most enlarged our knowledge of human nature: a lack of adjustment between the various tendencies in an individual may cause all sorts of disturbances when the cause has been long forgotten, if it was ever known. In cataloguing the emotional drives resulting from typical repressions, such as the Œdipus complex, the inferiority complex, etc., the Freudians have furnished a new set of behavior elements that offer control as well as understanding. They have added new facts to the contention of those who would understand behavior in terms of the building up of habits and associations in the individual's experience, and out of their clinical records have illuminated the process of such formations. So far these behavior elements have been more fruitful in the social sciences than the more rudimentary conditioned reflexes of the behaviorists.

But these ideas have been projected against a conception of mind and a set of theories that, logically inconsistent, necessarily hypothetical and unverifiable, often deliberately involved and fantastic, and in conflict with much that is definitely established, is a recrudescence of the older psychology of the romanticists. The faults of the instinct theory are multiplied; not content with recording the presence of types of behavior that are "unreflective, nondiscriminative, immediate and uncontrolled in operation, ineradicable, and affective" (John T. McCurdy), the Freudians go on to explain this as the expression of an assumed "unconscious," thought of now as a definite realm, now as a mysterious and insistent source of psychic energy. In Freud himself this energy or libido is overwhelmingly sexual, though the limits of sex are so broadened as to rob the term of most of its meaning; in others, like Jung, it forces its way through the three channels of the sex instinct, the ego instinct, and the herd instinct. This energy is vaguely thought of as demanding a fixed quantitative expression, failing which it increases, constantly fed from the inherent energy of the instinct or complex, until it bursts through the obstacle or cuts a new channel. It can be drawn off in another direction by "sublimation." In addition to this mystical foundation, Freud's theory contains such sweeping, dogmatic, and wholly hypothetical elements as to have provoked dissent from most of his own followers; and his readiness to apply it in fields like anthropology where he was patently ignorant has not heightened his prestige among the scientifically minded. But it indisputably contains elements of truth that, interpreted in more objective and experimental terms, will do much to clarify the integration of human personality. The mutual assimilation of the behavioristic and the Freudian genetic attitudes is already proceeding apace.

If we ask on just what points the modern experimental science of human nature has modified the views of its eighteenth-century predecessor, we find basic changes of revolutionary importance for the social sciences. First, the picture of man as a purely logical machine, who first thinks of some end which he desires, and then calculates the means by which that end can be attained, has given way to the infinitely more complex creature of impulse and passion and emotional preference who occasionally directs his irrational desires to some intelligent end. Reason is but the umpire among often unruly and conflicting impulses.

The function of consciousness does not seem to be so much creative as selective and inhibitive. I cannot voluntarily create a wish to do something in my mind. I can only eliminate those wishes (or their expression in conduct) that seem to me inexpedient. Energy must then be directed unconsciously rather than consciously. Since instincts are the great directors of energy, it follows that unconscious instinct motivations must control most of the human organism's mental energy, and that the most important of these will be the permanently unconscious motivations. These will regulate the dominant streams of energy of the man's life. (McCurdy.)

It is such a man who must take his place in any modern economic or political theory.

Secondly, though just what their limits are is still uncertain, it is clear that human behavior is largely determined by forces and energies which demand certain definite normal outlets, failing which they will give rise to disastrous conflicts and outbursts. Human nature, plastic as it is, cannot be distorted too far or changed too suddenly without danger. Rousseau's insight was sounder than Helvetius'. The environment must be so made as to give adequate scope to the more important impulses; asceticism, of either medieval or Puritan variety, can succeed only when directed to ends of extraordinary intensity.

Thirdly, men are individuals. They are not alike at birth, but differ widely in their capacities and aptitudes; and each man's character is a personal and unique synthesis, embodying distinctive traits. Social institutions must recognize that they are dealing with men, not man.

Finally, men live and develop in groups, and what they are is largely a product of the traditions and customs of the group. The group is the conditioning environment of all human action, without which all that is characteristically human would be lost. As Dewey puts it, "Anything which may properly be called mind or intelligence is not an original possession, but is a consequence of the manifestation of instincts under the conditions supplied by associated life in the family, the school, the market-place and the forum." Society comes first in point of time, and moulds individuals more or less successfully in its own image.

Dewey summarizes the consequences of the new science of man for all the social studies:

It transfers attention from vague generalities regarding social consciousness and social mind to the specific processes of interaction which take place among human beings, and to the details of group behavior. It emphasizes the importance of knowledge of the primary activities of human nature, and of the modifications and reorganizations they undergo in association with the activities of others. It radically simplifies the whole problem by making it clear that social institutions and arrangements, including the whole apparatus of tradition and transmission, represent simply the acquired transformations of original human endowments.

THE SEARCH FOR VALUES

With Nietzsche, the acceptance of life and evolution means turning their opportunities to use in a great romantic struggle for the better days to come, and in that struggle itself finding the very zest of living. Less impassioned and more reflective, present-day thinkers have come to feel that in the world as science now displays it man can yet achieve through intelligence a worthy individual and collective life. The world of science is not to be wept over, nor rejected, nor blindly glorified. It is to be accepted, with all its compulsions and all its promise, soberly, but with ever-renewed hope, as the natural setting within which human life must be lived if it be lived at all, and as the material out of which man can with sweat and tears construct a human habitation. If man be a very part of nature and the product of its activity, then his life is a natural life, in fruitful as in bitter interaction with nature's sustaining and imperative forces. His vital interests and ideals are as much the natural flowering of the nature that gave them birth as are his criminal follies and his ruthless passions; and he can hope to turn those forces to his own advantage through his nature-sent gift of intelligence. It is equal folly to think man the darling of the gods, and to think him a homeless outcast wandering on the face of an earth that provides nothing to sustain his cherished enterprises. A sound naturalism eliminates the need of such a choice. Nature does permit us to work and struggle; it is not irrelevant to our ideals and values. They are not idle dreams, but are rooted in the very conditions that nature—and human nature—imposes. This is an alternative alike to the complacent confidence of the supernaturalist, with his egoistic assertion of human power, doomed to early disillusionment and defeat; and to the paralysing despair of the "moral atheist," who sees no possible perfectings of things as they are, no values implicit in nature and human nature that human striving can hope to realize.

What are the problems for philosophies which in some sense accept this naturalistic attitude? There is first the development of an adequate philosophy of nature and of natural science, drawing on all we have learned about both in our generation. A nature of which life and human experience are integral parts is far different from the mechanical "alien world" of the nineteenth century: it is a nature which a chastened and revolutionized physics no longer forbids us. That alien world has gone, and the naturalistic philosophies of to-day bear little resemblance to those travesties, founded on a reductive analysis and the mechanical dogmas of an earlier physics, which went by the name a generation ago. And a science which is essentially a human method of inquiry, an institutionalized technique by which a society deals with its problems, is vastly unlike the simple discovery of the laws governing nature —the terms in which men read the scientific enterprise before their new sophistication.

Secondly, there is the problem of developing an adequate philosophy for industrial society; and this means a philosophy of cultural change. For in industrial society, cultural change is the ultimate challenge to philosophic thought, the ultimate context and subject-matter of all our thinking. We sorely need an understanding, an intellectual attitude and technique, to replace the emotional reactions which now prevail. This involves an exploration of the possibilities of industrial civilization—a clarification of the content of the good life in a technological age—and a formulation and criticism of the techniques of social control. Our greatest intellectual need to-day is for a genuinely experimental philosophy as the background and drive, a philosophy that will emphasize investigation and inquiry into the actual materials of our society, both technological and human. What can be done, and by what means? What are the obstacles? Which are too hard to remove, and must be accepted? which are most easily controlled? In particular, such a philosophy would foster an experimental attitude toward the problem of enlisting the coöperative support of men in doing what has to be done; of determining what can be accomplished with men, and how to get them to accomplish it. It would regard this all-important political problem as itself a matter for scientific inquiry and technological invention. It is childish to convert what is an intellectual problem into a mere fight, especially in America, where the very lag behind Europe, as well as the freedom from intolerable pressure, gives an opportunity to learn the bitter lessons of European experience. Such a philosophy would teach the patience of the experimenter, willing to try and try again, not cast down by a few failures, not demanding that every problem be solved overnight. And like all genuine experimentation, such a philosophy would have the courage to act, would have a faith in intelligence, and a willingness to fight, intelligently, if need be, to enable it to function.

The religious problem is still present, but in the changed form of the adjustment of the values of the philosophies of human experience, of the great cultural traditions and the religions that clarified and expressed them, to the critical knowledge of our scientific naturalisms. Romanticism has persisted, even among physicists, because so far those naturalisms have been so meager and bare, have failed to include important elements in experience. Till we have a naturalism as rich as the idealistic philosophies, because it provides a place for their visions, romanticism in some form will keep alive its eternal call back to the wealth and variety of imaginative experience. As a part of this adjustment, we can perhaps look forward to a further *rapprochement* between Western and Oriental thought.

The development of an adequate philosophy of nature and of science is to-day of central concern, for we are in the midst of the most fundamental scientific revolution since the seventeenth century. The concepts and methods involved in the actual procedures of the sciences have been so basically altered, and our psychological and sociological knowledge of the processes and function of science is so extensive, that the very notions of reason and of experience, and of their relations, on which all modern philosophy has been based, are no longer tenable. Present-day naturalistic philosophies seem split on technical questions, ultimately, on which of the sciences are to furnish the basic categories and methods. Those that start from physics and mathematics make the logical structure of scientific knowledge fundamental; those that start from biology, psychology, and the social sciences emphasize the further context of the process of inquiry within which that structure is discriminated.

Yet both sides seem to be drawing closer together: the concepts developed by the philosophers of mathematical physics, like Whitehead, are approaching those of biology and the sciences of man. Face to face with its world of radiant energy, it is physics to-day that is suggesting the novel ideas; but they in turn are finding application to the sciences of life. There is, first, the common adoption of time as a basic category; both are now taking time and temporal process seriously. The biological and social philosophies have worked out temporal concepts which physics is now deriving from its own subject-matter. The older emphases in physics on structure and in biology on activity and process are being merged in a new synthesis of both. There is a tendency to employ a new language—many call it a new logic—the space-time continuum, events, processes, and activities, rather than things or substances; the subject-attribute relation has given place to functional series and correlations.

Secondly, there is a common emphasis on systematic structure, on the organic wholes and patterns within which simpler processes are discriminated. Those elements have been found by analysis, and when found are discovered operating from the start in an interrelated system. This change we have traced in physics, in biology, and in psychology; in each case the concept of a field, organism, or situation has assumed basic importance.

Thirdly, there is an emphasis on knowing and science as itself an activity, a process—ultimately, an institutionalized way of acting. The data of science are no longer passive sensations, but measurements, activities performed, depending on complicated space-time systems of coördinates and schemes of measurement. Science involves creation, the invention and employment of elaborate theoretical constructions. Knowing is no longer taken as an immediate seeing, either intellectual or sensible; it is mediate and instrumental, not inherently, in its values—men still find it good to know—but in its nature and character. This functional conception is supported by psychology, by the history of science, and by all analyses of the techniques of scientific procedure and of the actual formation of scientific hypothesis and theory. . . .

Chapter XIII

EUROPEAN SOCIETY BETWEEN TWO WARS

1. DESCENT INTO THE MAELSTROM

THE FRANCO-GERMAN WAR ushered in one of the most tragic periods of European history. The atmosphere of the next forty years was charged with a sense of impending disaster. All the world seemed to be slowly sucked into the seething whirlpool of national hates and rivalries, and every nation feverishly armed itself in preparation for the coming Armageddon. It is impossible to portray adequately the nervous hysteria of those years, the uneasiness felt by everyone, the fear that gripped all hearts, the terrible sensation that mankind experienced of living, as it were, on the edge of a simmering volcano, which might burst into eruption at any moment. No one knew but what each day might be the last of the Armed Peace, that bitter reply to the roseate hopes of former days of everlasting concord and harmony among the nations. Europe, having won the intellectual and scientific primacy of the world, was bent now on committing suicide.

After 1871 the center of the European stage was occupied by the new German Empire, a young, virile, proud and victorious nation, which had fought three wars in the course of seven years and had won them all, and had finally marched to unity over the prostrate body of her French rival. The mighty statesman who had made Germany a Great Power for the first time since the days of the Hohenstaufen, realized that after her surfeit of glory she needed a period of peace to consolidate her gains and develop her internal resources. It is uncertain how far Bismarck approved the harsh treatment meted out to defeated France, and whether he was entirely responsible for

This chapter consists of material by three different authors. Section 1 is from *The Age of Revolution* (pp. 235–49; New York, Roy Publishers, 1949) by J. J. Saunders. Sections 2 and 4 are from *A History of the Modern World* (pp. 720–36, 774–81; New York, Alfred A. Knopf, Inc., 1952), by R. R. Palmer. Section 3 is from *The Political Collapse of Europe* (pp. 96–137; New York, Alfred A. Knopf, Inc., 1952), by Hajo Holborn.

the "war scare" of 1875, which was provoked by the unexpectedly rapid recovery of France and by the belief of the German military leaders that their irritatingly vigorous rival should be suppressed once for all and given no chance of securing her revenge. But there is no doubt that for the rest of his career Bismarck pursued a consistent policy of peace and strove to secure his ends by diplomacy rather than by the force of arms.

It was obvious that the first aim of Germany must be to keep France isolated. The latter, with her stationary population of forty millions, could never hope to win a straight fight against a powerful military empire with a population steadily approaching sixty millions. As long as France could be prevented from obtaining allies, Germany was safe. Hence Bismarck labored to secure the friendship of all the Powers France was likely to turn to, namely, Russia, Austria, Italy and England. Of these, Austria was willing to accept Germany's co-operation in order to gain support for her schemes of expansion in the Balkans, where she had found an outlet for her energies since 1866, and Italy was naturally grateful to the nation which had helped her to complete her unification. Russia was uncertain, for between the Teuton and the Slav there was little love lost, but the autocratic Tsardom was unlikely to feel much sympathy for Republican France with its known sympathy for the oppressed Poles, and Bismarck had high hopes of winning her over completely to Germany. No understanding could be reached with England, because she refused to guarantee the German retention of Alsace-Lorraine, but in view of her traditional isolationism, Bismarck had little fear of any close relationship developing between her and France.

The greatest danger lay in the Balkan situation, which was to become for the next forty years the acutest problem in European politics and which has been well described as "the Achilles' heel of Bismarck's diplomacy." Nowhere had the nationalist movement met with a quicker response than among the Christian races of the decaying Turkish Empire. The emancipation of the Greeks and Serbs had fired all the other subject peoples with the hope of independence, and foreshadowed the total dissolution of the Ottoman State in Europe. Russian hopes of hastening the process had been temporarily frustrated by the issue of the Crimean War, but the recognition of Rumanian independence in 1861 and the continued oppression of the Macedonian Christians produced renewed unrest which burst forth in the Bulgarian rising in 1875. In this imbroglio Austria and Russia were intensely interested. Austria feared lest the creation of a strong Rumania and a Bulgaro-Serb State would attract the numerous Slav population within her own empire. If the Southern Slavs freed themselves from Turkish control, she would much rather entice them within her sphere of influence rather than let them grow into vigorous independent states. If Austria secured Rumania and Serbia, Russia would step in and try to dominate Bulgaria. This Austro-Russian rivalry in the Balkans was galling to Bismarck, who wanted these two Great Powers as allies of Germany. It was his cue to act as mediator between them and to preserve peace in the Balkans at all costs.

The Bulgarian revolt in 1875 produced a first-class European crisis. Pan-Slavism had made tremendous headway among the Christians in the peninsula and was powerfully encouraged by Russia, who since the days of Peter the Great had constituted herself the champion of Orthodox Christendom against Islam and who used the Slav movement as a convenient stalking-horse for her imperial ambitions and designs on Constantinople. Austria dreaded the spread of Pan-Slavism, for the creation of the Dual Monarchy in 1867 had given the Magyars political equality with the Austro-Germans and had effectively ruined whatever hopes the Slavs within the Habsburg Empire had entertained of becoming a third partner. If a greater Slav kingdom were created south of the Danube, Austria's Slav subjects would probably attempt to break away and join their kinsmen. When therefore after the "Bulgarian atrocities" had provided an excuse for intervention Russia began to bully the Turks and declared war on them in 1877, Austria backed the Sultan and thus found herself in agreement with England, who feared that a Russian occupation of Constantinople would bring the trade-routes of the Levant and perhaps the Suez Canal itself under the control of the Colossus of the North. The Russians, after taking Plevna, were compelled through financial difficulties to call a halt before venturing to attack Constantinople, but they forced the Sultan to sign the treaty of San Stefano, providing for the creation of a "Big Bulgaria" stretching from the Danube to the Adriatic.

San Stefano was by no means a bad solution of the problem. It would have focused the Slav movement in one big State and perhaps avoided the wretched jealousies and rivalries which made their appearance when the peninsula was subsequently split up into half-a-dozen small States. But England and Austria were both afraid of the extension of Russia's power, and Bismarck, who preferred Austrian to Russian friendship, had perforce to join in the demand for revision which Disraeli put forward at the Berlin Congress in 1878. "Big Bulgaria" was dropped; two little states were substituted for it, one still under Turkish rule though with a Christian governor, and the greater part of Macedonia was left in the Sultan's hands. Austria was granted a "protectorate" over the two provinces of Bosnia and Herzogovina and was thus enabled to ward off the danger of a great Slav kingdom arising on her borders. Russia left the Congress bitterly chagrined and humiliated, and especially furious at what she regarded as Germany's ingratitude for her neutrality in 1870.

Still Bismarck was determined not to break with Russia. He distrusted her, but he was fearful of driving her into the arms of France, since such an alliance would place Germany in peril of having to fight a war on two fronts. He therefore negotiated in 1881 the Dreikaiserbund, or League of the Three Emperors, a strange ghost of the old Holy Alliance of Metternich's day, each party promising neutrality in case of one being involved in war with a fourth party. The next year the seizure of Tunis by France brought into the Triple Alliance an Italy infuriated at this cool annexation of what she had always regarded as her special share of North Africa. Germany could now congratulate herself on the formation of a strong anti-French bloc involving all the great European Powers except England. The Dreikaiserbund seemed to be fulfilling its purpose in restraining both Austria and Russia in the Balkans in 1885–87, when the latter intervened in Bulgaria to eject a prince who had proved himself unresponsive to Russian influences, and Bismarck was thus able to bid defiance to the Boulangist movement in France.

Yet Germany's position at the close of the Bismarckian era was not entirely invulnerable. The great Chancellor was somewhat in the position of a political Atlas, balancing the whole diplomatic world upon his shoulders, and it was not surprising that he sometimes staggered under the burden. The passionate nationalism which was spreading all over the world and affecting even the smallest peoples, was too powerful a force to be held in check by diplomatic jugglery. A clash between Pan-Germanism and Pan-Slavism could not be avoided. Russia declined to renew the Dreikaiserbund in 1887, so Bismarck had to keep her allied to Germany by means of the Reinsurance Treaty, containing the usual promise of neutrality in the event of war with a third party. The Italian alliance was of little value to Germany, for an undercurrent of hostility was bound to remain between Rome and Vienna so long as Italia Irredenta remained in Habsburg hands. And France, though Bismarck tried to distract her mind from "la revanche" by encouraging her colonial expansion in Africa and Indo-China, never reconciled herself to the loss of Alsace-Lorraine. Austria was the only ally upon which fidelity Germany could rely, and her racially-divided Empire was brought nearer to dissolution as nationalism, and especially Pan-Slavism, grew stronger.

The dismissal of Bismarck followed closely upon the accession of the young Emperor William II in 1888. That clever and forceful, but volatile and impulsive, sovereign was destined to be the foremost man in Europe for the next thirty years. He was not a great statesman, but flashy and theatrical, vain and rash, overconscious of his position as head of a young and powerful Empire, and perhaps psychologically impelled to self-assertion as a kind of counter-balance to the physical defect of a withered arm. He had an autocratic temperament, like all the Hohenzollerns, but was totally devoid of that depth and fixity of purpose which had characterized nearly all his ancestors. There was not enough room in Germany for both him and Bismarck, so in 1890 he dropped the pilot, because, as the fallen statesman remarked, the Emperor intended to be his own Chancellor. All Europe soon became familiar with the rather swaggering, fiercely-moustached figure of Germany's new ruler, who had conceived it his duty to make the voice of the Teuton heard in every quarter of the globe.

From the moment of Bismarck's fall, German foreign policy began to degenerate. The real heir of the Bismarckian tradition in foreign affairs was Holstein, who directed policy from the Wilhelmstrasse from 1890 till his resignation in 1905. The successors of Bismarck in the Chancellorship were shadowy figures with little knowledge of diplomacy, which they readily surrendered into Holstein's hands. The latter pulled the strings from behind the scenes; he never emerged into the glare of publicity, and even his relations with the Emperor were conducted through the intermediary of Philipp von Eulenberg, William II's personal confidant. For all his brilliant qualities, Holstein was totally lacking in Bismarck's realistic insight. Where the master had known when to be conciliatory and when to strike hard, the pupil was merely clumsy and provocative and dragged his country through numerous "incidents" and "crises" from which she emerged with diminished prestige. Germany under Holstein was just aggressive enough to irritate everyone else without terrifying them. In Colonial policy the same fault appeared. Holstein had not the foresight and ability to pursue a systematic policy, but contented himself with interfering all over the world and picking up odd bits here and there—a procedure which engendered the uneasy suspicion abroad that Germany was committed to deep-laid schemes of universal expansion.

The first blunder committed by Holstein was the dropping of the Reinsurance Treaty in 1890, on the ground that it encouraged Russia's forward policy in the Balkans. The result was to throw Russia and France together, the very thing Bismarck had striven all his life to avoid, for it meant the beginning of the "encirclement" of Germany. The Tsar was not particularly fond of Republican France with its unstable ministries and parliamentary scandals, and the French Socialists protested volubly against an alliance with the great Eastern despotism with its police spies, prison camps, Cossack knouts and Jewish pogroms, but fear of the German-Austrian-Italian bloc was so strong that the two Powers overcame their mutual dislike and signed a formal military convention in 1894. They agreed to help each other if either were attacked by Germany or Austria. The advantage of an agreement with France was clearly demonstrated when in 1905–06 the revolutionary movement in Russia was suppressed largely by means of substantial loans from Paris.

In these circumstances, it would have been only common-sense to cultivate friendly relations with England. While Bismarck was in power, no ruffle disturbed the harmony of Anglo-German intercourse. The partition of Africa in the eighties had been carried out with surprisingly little friction, and in 1890 England handed over Heligoland to Germany in exchange for Zanzibar. Holstein, however, was not disposed to regard friendship with England as a matter of great importance to Germany. England was unlikely to intervene in any Continental war, owing to the strength of isolationist sentiment among her people, and she was not on good terms with either of Germany's potential enemies. Pendjeh and Fashoda were not easily forgotten. Moreover, Holstein had got it into his head that England was bitterly jealous of Germany's colonial expansion and was putting obstacles in her path: hence he treated her brusquely.

The old friendly relations between the two Powers rapidly weakened as the quarrel between England and the Dutch Boers in South Africa moved to its climax. Popular sympathy in Europe and especially in Germany, was whole-heartedly on the side of the Boers, who were regarded as a heroic little nation of sturdy independent farmers struggling to maintain their freedom against the encroachments of greedy millionaires who were backed by the might of a grasping British Imperialism puffed up with all Kipling's contempt for "lesser breeds." The Boers came of Teutonic stock, and to the Pan-Germans their cause was sacred. German public opinion solidly approved the famous telegram the Kaiser sent to Kruger in 1896 congratulating him on the repulse of the Jameson Raid. But it aroused furious resentment in England, and was in fact a most injudicious move, since Germany without a fleet could afford no material help to the Boers when war broke out in 1899. Realization of Germany's weakness on the sea was the reason for the intensive naval policy inaugurated by von Tirpitz in 1898. Even then the cause of Anglo-German friendship was not wholly lost. Chamberlain, who disliked the Dual Alliance and was somewhat alarmed at the universal hostility shown to England during the Boer War, twice (in 1898 and again in 1901) suggested an agreement with Germany, each time to be repulsed by Holstein, who thought England was hardpushed and wanted help, and refused to be satisfied with anything less than a definite military alliance.

Meanwhile the international situation grew more and more complicated. The world's vacant spaces were filling up, and the German people were dissatisfied with their meager acquisitions of territory overseas. While Britain, France and Russia possessed enormous empires, Germany, who had come late into the field, had only been able to pick up some islands in the Pacific and a few barren, unhealthy and expensive tracts in tropical Africa. China and the Far East were closed to European intervention after the Boxer Rebellion and the Japanese victory over Russia. The United States stood squarely by the Monroe Doctrine and refused to tolerate the slightest European penetration of Latin America. Portugal, probably encouraged by her British ally, declined to sell any of her colonies to Germany. Only two fields of expansion were therefore left: Turkey and Morocco. Germany had already commenced to cultivate the friendship of the Sultan and to reduce the influence which England had so long exercised at Constantinople, when William II during his tour of the Near East in 1898 declared himself the protector of the Moslem world. Shortly afterwards Germany obtained the concession for the Berlin-Bagdad railway, which would open up the vast undeveloped tracts of Asia Minor and the oil regions of Mosul. This was perhaps the greatest success of Holstein's diplomacy.

The repudiation of Chamberlain's second offer to Berlin, followed by the revelation of the German plans for a "big navy," impelled England to abandon the isolationist attitude she had maintained for so many years. Germany claimed with some justice that she must have a fleet to protect her scattered colonies, but England could not view without anxiety the creation of a formidable naval force in the North Sea. It was imperative to seek help on the Continent. Thus in 1904 Edward VII and Lansdowne negotiated the Entente with France, who was especially grateful for British support as her Russian ally was engaged in a desperate struggle with the Japanese at the other end of the world. The French agreed to recognize England's occupation of Egypt and the Sudan in return for an assurance that they would be allowed "a free hand" in Morocco, where intervention was becoming necessary to round off their North African possessions. Germany was at last awakened to the dangers confronting her, but her reactions produced the worst possible consequences to herself. The Kaiser, during one of his periodical cruises in the Baltic, inveigled the Tsar into signing the Treaty of

Björko, providing for a Russo-German alliance against England which France was to be forced into. Nicholas's ministers promptly repudiated it. In 1905 William II, against his better judgment, was persuaded to visit Tangier and to deliver a speech there assuring the Sultan of Morocco that Germany would support his independence—a direct threat to France. The crisis which followed was settled by a conference at Algeciras, in which Germany came out second best and received only lukewarm support from her allies. France was badly scared, and made use of the Entente to sound England as to what attitude the latter would adopt in case of a new Franco-German war. The upshot was a series of secret military conversations between French and British officers in Flanders, during which joint plans were drawn up for the repulse of a German attack which it was presumed would come through Belgium, in view of the huge fortifications France had constructed along the line of the Vosges. By agreeing to these conversations, Grey (who had become British Foreign Secretary in 1905) was really making inevitable the entry of Britain into any war in which the Dual Alliance was engaged, yet he persisted to the end in believing that "her hands were free."

The Algeciras Conference revealed to all the world the isolation of Germany. England and France had stood strongly together. Russia had backed up her ally. Italy had betrayed a friendship for France most disconcerting to Bülow and Holstein, who did not know that she had been "squared" by the recognition of her claims on Tripoli. Austria, the only ally upon which Germany could now count, had failed to give her much encouragement. And although Bülow and the Kaiser summoned up sufficient courage to give Holstein his quietus in 1905, there was no marked improvement in German foreign policy. Scared at Germany's isolation in Europe, Bülow found himself tied more closely than ever to Austria, which grew increasingly aggressive when Aehrenthal became Foreign Minister in 1906. That reckless statesman argued that, with Russia reeling under the shock of the Japanese war and internal revolution and with Germany only too ready to support Austria for fear of losing her last remaining friend, here was a splendid chance to force the issue in the Balkans. In the summer of 1908 the Young Turk revolution broke out in Constantinople, and a liberal constitution was extorted from the terrified Abdul Hamid. A few weeks later a private agreement was made between Aehrenthal and the Russian Foreign Minister Isvolsky: on the ground that a reinvigorated Turkey might endanger the interests of the two Powers, Austria was to annex Bosnia and Herzogovina and Russia was to open the Straits to the passage of her ships. To these changes the assent of the other signatories of the Berlin Treaty of 1878 would be necessary: but while Isvolsky was still sounding the Western Powers, Aehrenthal suddenly proclaimed the annexation on his own responsibility, on the excuse that the Young Turks were plotting to restore Turkish sovereignty over the provinces. Isvolsky was furious; Serbia, who hoped that one day Bosnia and Herzogovina would form part of a Great Serbia, saw her ambitions ruined and her hatred of Austria was intensified, but Russia, to whom she appealed for help, was too weak and exhausted to fight, and as Germany (whom the annexation had taken by surprise) backed Austria, Aehrenthal's coup was successful. But 1908 led straight to 1914; Serb agitation against the Dual Monarchy increased in fury and violence, Austria was encouraged in her "forward" policy, Russia was determined not to suffer a second humiliation but to draw closer to France and England, and Isvolsky, transferred from St. Petersburg to the embassy at Paris, worked grimly for revenge. The Triple Entente, assured of Italy's friendship, faced the Triple Alliance, of which only Germany and Austria counted. Meanwhile, the Kaiser had done his best to antagonize England further by the blazing indiscretion of the *Daily Telegraph* interview, and when Bülow, having smoothed this over as best as possible, hinted to Tirpitz that the pursuance of an aggressive naval policy was intensifying English hostility, he was curtly informed that it was too late and that the full program must be carried through. Disappointed and disillusioned, Bülow resigned the Chancellorship in 1909.

His successor was Bethmann Hollweg, an honest official who saw the storm-clouds gathering but could make no impression on the military and naval chiefs who now had the full ear of the Kaiser. The headlong rush to catastrophe continued. The second German intervention in Morocco (1911), when the *Panther* made its famous spring on Agadir, was a clumsy and provocative move; it indeed secured for Germany compensation in the Congo, but it strengthened the Entente and enabled the British Government to overcome opposition to its naval expansion program. At the same time the two Western Powers encouraged Italy to make war on Turkey and seize Tripoli, in the hope of still further loosening the ties which bound her to the Triple Alliance. The war, which resulted in the defeat of Turkey, encouraged the Balkan Powers to join forces and sweep the common enemy out of Macedonia while he still had his hands full with Italy. The first Balkan War of 1912 ended in the total collapse of the Turks, who were rolled back to the gates of Constantinople. Then Austria stepped in and refused to allow Serbia to expand to the Adriatic; the allies quarreled among themselves over the disposition of Macedonia, and the Second Balkan War broke out in 1913 between Bulgaria and her neighbors, ending in the former's humiliating defeat. When things had been straightened out, Turkey recovered some of her territory, Bulgaria lost some of hers, and Serbia emerged about three times her former size. Austria was irritated at Serbia's expansion, but this time Germany restrained her from acting rashly, while Britain and France held back Russia, who was also threatening to intervene. The net result was a blow to the Central Powers, whose Turkish ally had been defeated and partitioned.

The stage was now set for the final scene. All the statesmen of Europe were convinced that the conflagration was not far off. Every attempt to stop the mad race in armaments had failed. The Peace Conference called at The Hague by the Tsar in 1899 separated without any agreement being reached. A second Conference in 1907 only resulted in the establishment of the Permanent Court of International Justice, which no one appealed to in 1914. The attempt of England to secure some limit to naval competition was interpreted by Tirpitz as being due to fear of losing her supremacy at sea. The Kaiser, whose fleet was his favorite hobby and who watched over it with fostering care, warmly supported the fiery chief of the German Admiralty, and Bethmann's feeble protests and Metternich's despatches from London were brushed aside. The Liberal Government in England, anxious to spend money on social reforms rather than on dreadnoughts, strove to reach an agreement with Germany. Some settlement of the Bagdad Railway question was arrived at and several outstanding colonial points were amicably arranged, but on naval matters Tirpitz and the Kaiser were intransigent. They regarded the slightest yielding as derogatory to Germany's dignity, and pointed out that not even France and Russia made any attempt to limit German land armaments. A last desperate effort was made by Lord Haldane on his visit to Berlin in 1912, but in vain, and the upshot was the secret agreement by which England undertook to police the North Sea and defend the Channel coasts and France transferred the bulk of her fleet to the Mediterranean. Everyone, believing in the inevitability of war, was preparing for "Der Tag." Austria was planning a "final reckoning" with Serbia, Russia was plotting to seize the Straits, German generals were calculating when the favorable moment might arrive at which to strike at France through Belgium, France was hopeful of recovering Alsace-Lorraine if she could be sure of England, and even in England responsible persons were publicly talking of "Copenhagening," *i.e.,* seizing or destroying the German Fleet without a declaration of war. No wonder that Colonel House, writing to Wilson from Berlin in the spring of 1914, described the situation as "militarism run stark mad." The guns were almost ready to go off by themselves. It was in this unbearably tense atmosphere that an unbalanced young Serb student fired a couple of revolver shots in a small

Bosnian town that echoed round the world and cost the lives of ten million men.

The assassination of the Archduke Francis Ferdinand and his wife was an odious crime, and Austria was well within her rights in demanding the suppression of the Pan-Slav agitation which had made it possible. But Berchtold, who had succeeded Aehrenthal as Foreign Minister in 1912, and his colleagues were resolved to use the murder as an excuse for making war on Serbia and reducing her to impotence. They realized that the very existence of the Monarchy was at stake and were in a desperate mood. War was resolved upon even if it brought in Russia, to whom Serbia would naturally appeal for support, because they knew they could count on Germany, the Kaiser, who had been deeply moved by his friend's murder, having unfortunately given *carte blanche* to Austria on July 5th. The ultimatum of July 23rd was deliberately framed so as to render acceptance impossible and hostilities inevitable. The German "blank check" to Austria may be condemned as rash and foolish, but Berlin undoubtedly believed at first that the Austro-Serbian issue could be localized because Russia was too weak to fight and would climb down as she had done in 1908. But Great Powers cannot afford to suffer repeated humiliations. As the Kaiser encouraged Austria, so Poincaré in St. Petersburg encouraged Russia, and the two Eastern Powers were virtually set at each other's throats. Grey's efforts in England were rendered fruitless. A proposal for direct conversations between Austria and Russia came to nothing, an Italian suggestion that the Powers should advise Serbia to submit to the demands of Vienna passed unheeded, and the plan of a European Conference was rejected by Germany, who had unpleasant memories of Algeciras. When after a sharp warning from Grey on July 28th, Germany began to understand that a general war was threatened, and that Russia would probably fight after all, attempts were made to put the brake on Austria. It was too late: war was declared on Serbia on the same day. This moved Russia to decide on partial mobilization, *i.e.,* mobilization against Austria but not against Germany. Once the army machine was set in motion, however, the generals began to take command and the civil authority was reduced to nullity. In St. Petersburg the military chiefs declared that partial mobilization was no good: if it had to be followed by general mobilization, the utmost confusion would be created and their plans would be completely deranged. On July 30th the Tsar was forced by their protests to declare general mobilization. But this directly threatened Germany, and the next day an ultimatum from Berlin demanded its withdrawal. German declarations of war upon Russia and upon her French ally followed as a matter of course. The British Cabinet, uncertain to the last of public support, promised, in accordance with the secret naval agreement of 1912, to defend the French Channel coasts against attack by the German fleet, but when the Germans invaded Belgium on August 3rd it found a pretext for intervention which Parliament and the nation would accept. On August 4th Britain declared war on Germany, nominally to defend the neutrality of Belgium, but actually because her moral obligations to France were so strong that an evasion of her responsibilities would have left her friendless and isolated and exposed to the contempt of the world. The long-dreaded and long-awaited Armageddon had come at last. The lights of peace, of security, and perhaps even of happiness, went out all over Europe.

2. THE RUSSIAN REVOLUTION

War again put the tsarist regime to a test that it could not meet. In this war, more "total" than any had ever been, willing cooperation between government and people was indispensable to success. This essential prerequisite the tsarist empire did not have. National minorities, Poles, Jews, Ukrainians, Caucasians, and others, were disaffected. As for the socialists, who in every other European parliament voted for the war credits, the dozen otherwise disunited socialists in the Duma refused to do so, and were promptly jailed. The ordinary workingman and peasant marched off with the army, but without the sense of personal conviction felt by common people in Germany and the West. More decisive was the attitude of the middle class. Because they patriotically wished Russia to win, the glaring mismanagement of the government was the more intolerable to them. The disasters with which the war opened in 1914, at Tannenberg and the Masurian Lakes, were followed by the advance of the Central Powers into Russia in 1915, at the cost of two million Russian soldiers.

Middle-class people, as in all countries, offered their assistance to government agencies. The provincial zemstvos formed a union of all zemstvos in the empire to facilitate the mobilization of agriculture and industry. Business groups at Petrograd (St. Petersburg lost its Germanic name at this time), formed a Commercial and Industrial Committee to get the factories into maximum production. The government distrusted these signs of public activity arising outside official circles. On the other hand, organized in this way, middle-class people became conscious of their own strength and more critical of the bureaucracy. Some officials in the war ministry itself were known to be at heart pro-German, reactionaries who feared the liberalism of England and France, with which Russia was allied.

Life at court was bizarre even for Russia. The tsarina Alexandra, by origin a German woman, looked upon all Russians outside her own circle with contempt, incited her husband to play the proud and pitiless autocrat, and took advice from a self-appointed holy man, the bearded and weird Rasputin. She was convinced that Rasputin possessed supernatural and prophetic powers, because he had apparently cured her young son, the tsarevich, of hemophilia. Rasputin, by his influence over her, had a voice in appointments to high office. All who wished an audience with the imperial pair had to go through him. Patriotic and enlightened persons of all classes vainly protested. In these circumstances, and given the military defeats, the union of zemstvos and other such war-born bodies complained not merely of faults of administration but of fundamental conditions in the state. The government responded by holding them at arm's length. The tsarist regime, caught in a total war, was afraid of the help offered by its own people.

During the war the Duma was prorogued. It was known that reactionaries —inspired by the tsarina, Rasputin, and other sinister forces—expected that a victory in the war would make it possible to kill liberalism and constitutionalism in Russia. The war thus revived all the basic political issues that had lain latent since the Revolution of 1905. The union of zemstvos demanded the assembly of the Duma. The Duma met in November 1916, and, conservative though it had always been, expressed loud indignation at the way affairs were conducted. In December Rasputin was assassinated. The tsar began to consider repression, and again adjourned the Duma. Machine guns were issued to the police. Members of the Duma, and of the new extra-governmental bodies, concluded that the situation could be saved only by force. It is when moderate persons, normally concerned with their own business, come to such conclusions that revolution becomes a political possibility. The shift of moderates and liberals, their need of a coup d'état to save themselves from reactionaries, likewise raised the long failing prospects of the minority of professional revolutionaries.

Again it was the workers of Petrograd who precipitated the crisis. Food had become scarce, as in all the belligerent countries. But the tsarist administration was too clumsy and too demoralized by graft to institute the controls that had become usual elsewhere, such as maximum prices and ration cards. It was the poorest who felt the food shortage most keenly. On March 8, 1917, food riots broke out, which soon developed, doubtless with the help of revolutionary intellectuals, into political insurrections. Crowds shouted, "Down with the tsar!" Troops within the city refused to fire on the insurgents; mutiny and insubordination spread from unit to unit. Within a few days, on the model of 1905, a Soviet of Workers' and Soldiers' Deputies had been organized in Petrograd.

Middle-class leaders, with the government now helpless, demanded dismissal of the ministry and formation of a new one commanding the confidence of a majority of the Duma. The Duma set up an executive committee to take charge until the situation clarified. There were now two new authorities in the city: one, the Duma committee, essentially moderate, constitutionalist, and relatively legal; the other, the Petrograd Soviet, representing revolutionary forces arising by spontaneous upsurge from below. The Petrograd Soviet (or workers' "council") was to play in 1917 a role like that of the Paris Commune of 1792, constantly pushing the supposedly higher and more nation-wide authority to the left. The Soviet became the public auditorium and administrative center of the working-class upheaval. Since it was generally socialist in its outlook, all the factions of doctrinaire socialists— Social Revolutionaries, Mensheviks, Bolsheviks—tried to win it over and utilize it for their own ends.

The Petrograd Soviet and the Duma committee, by an agreement of March 14, set up a Provisional Government under Prince Lvov. The Duma liberals, as a concession to the Soviet, admitted one socialist to the new government, Alexander Kerensky, a Social Revolutionary, and they furthermore consented to demand the abdication of Nicholas II. The tsar was then at the front. He tried to return to his palace near Petrograd, but the imperial train was stopped and turned back by troops. The army, fatefully, was taking the side of the revolution. The very generals in the field, unable to vouch for the loyalty of their men, advised abdication. Nicholas consented; his brother the grand duke declined to succeed him; and on March 17, 1917, Russia became a republic.

The Provisional Government, following the best precedents of European revolutions, called for elections to a Constituent Assembly, which was to meet late in the year and lay permanent foundations for the new regime. It tried also to continue the war against Germany, with the ill success that has been seen. Pending final decision by the Constituent Assembly, the Provisional Government promised wholesale redistribution of land to the peasants, who, driven by the old land hunger, were already overrunning the rural districts, burning and looting. At the front the armies melted away; many high officers refused to serve the republic, and masses of peasant soldiers simply turned their backs and went home, unwilling to be absent while farmlands were being handed out. The Petrograd Soviet, opposing the Provisional Government, called for speedy termination of the war, and, fearing reactionary officers, issued on March 14 its Order No. 1, entrusting command within the army to committees elected by both officers and men. Discipline collapsed.

The revolution was thus already well advanced when Lenin and the other Bolsheviks arrived in Petrograd in the middle of April. They immediately took sides with the Soviet against the Provisional Government. A Bolshevik-led uprising in July was put down, and Lenin for a time had to flee to Finland, but as a bid for popular support the Provisional Government put the socialist Kerensky at its head, in place of Prince Lvov. Kerensky's middle position was next threatened from the right. A general at the front, Kornilov, led a force of cavalry to Petrograd to restore order. Many liberals and Constitutional Democrats wished him success. Kornilov was defeated, Bolsheviks temporarily rallying with other socialists, and insurrectionary soldiers in the city offering armed resistance. Radicals denounced liberals as accomplices in Kornilov's counter-revolution; and with the liberals thus discredited, Kerensky formed a government composed entirely of non-Bolshevik socialists. Meanwhile the food shortage was worse than ever, with transport disarranged and the farm population in turmoil, so that workers in the city listened more willingly to the most extreme speakers.

The Bolsheviks adapted their program to what the most aroused elements in a revolutionary people seemed to want. Lenin concentrated on four points: first, immediate peace with the Central Powers; second, redistribution of land to the peasants; third, transfer of factories, mines and other industrial plants from the capitalists to committees of workers in each plant; and, fourth, recognition of the soviets as the supreme power instead of the Provisional Government. Lenin, though a rigid dogmatist on abstract questions, was a flexible and bold tactician; and his program in 1917 was dictated more by the immediate situation in Russia than by considerations of theoretical Marxism. What was needed was to win over soldiers, peasants, and workers by promising them peace, land and factories. With this program, and by infiltration and parliamentary stratagems, and by their accuracy as political prophets—predicting the Kornilov counter-revolution and "unmasking" the trend of middle-way liberals to support it—the Bolsheviks won a majority in the Petrograd Soviet and in similar soviets that sprang up in other parts of the country.

Lenin thereupon raised the cry, "All power to the Soviets!" to crush Kerensky and forestall the coming Constituent Assembly. Kerensky, to broaden the base on which he stood, and unable to wait for the Constituent Assembly, convoked a kind of pre-parliament representing all parties, labor unions, and zemstvos. Lenin and the Bolsheviks boycotted this pre-parliament. Instead they called an all-Russian congress of soviets.

Lenin now judged that the hour had come for the seizure of power. The Bolsheviks themselves were divided, but Lenin was backed by Trotsky, Stalin, and a majority of the party central committee. Troops garrisoned in Petrograd voted to support the soviets, which the Bolsheviks now controlled. On the night of November 6–7, 1917, the Bolsheviks took over telephone exchanges, railway stations, and electric lighting plants in the city. A warship turned its guns on the Winter Palace, where Kerensky's government sat. The latter could find no armed defenders except cadets from the military schools. The hastily assembled congress of soviets pronounced the Provisional Government defunct, and named in its place a "council of people's commissars," of which Lenin became the head. Kerensky fled, eventually reaching New York, where he lived for many years.

Thus was accomplished the Bolshevik or November Revolution.[1] But the long awaited Constituent Assembly remained to be dealt with. It met in January 1918. Thirty-six million persons had voted for it. Of these, 9,000,000 had voted for Bolshevik deputies, showing that the Bolshevik program, launched less than a year before by a small band of émigrés, had a widespread mass appeal. But almost 21,000,000 had voted for Kerensky's party, the agrarian-populist, native Russian, peasant-oriented Social Revolutionaries. However, said Lenin, "to hand over power to the Constituent Assembly would again be compromising with the malignant bourgeoisie." The Assembly was broken up on the second day of its sessions; armed sailors despatched by the people's commissars simply surrounded it. "The dissolution of the Constituent Assembly by the Soviet Government," as Lenin observed to Trotsky, "means a complete and frank liquidation of the idea of democracy by the idea of dictatorship." The dictatorship of the proletariat was now established. Two months later, in March 1918, the Bolsheviks renamed themselves the Communist Party.

In these same months the Communists, or Bolsheviks, made the peace of Brest-Litovsk with Germany, surrendering to Germany control over the Baltic provinces, Poland and the Ukraine. The conquests of two centuries were thus abandoned; not since the days of Peter the Great had the Russian frontier been so far from central Europe. To Lenin it made no difference.

---

[1] Also known as the October Revolution, since according to the Julian calendar, used in Russia until 1918, the events described took place in October.

He was convinced that the events that he had just mastered in Russia were the prelude to a general upheaval; that the war, still raging in the west, would bring all Europe to the inevitable proletarian or Marxist revolution; that Imperial Germany was therefore doomed, and that Poles, Ukrainians, and others would soon emerge, like the Germans themselves, as free socialist peoples. In any case, it was largely by promising peace that Lenin had won enough backing to overthrow Kerensky, who on this deep popular demand had delayed too long, waiting for England and France to release Russia from its treaty obligations as an Ally. But real peace did not come, for the country sank immediately into civil war.

Not only old tsarist reactionaries, and not only liberals, bourgeois, zemstvo men, and Constitutional Democrats, but all types of anti-Leninist socialists as well, Mensheviks and Social Revolutionaries, scattered in all directions to organize resistance against the regime of soviets and people's commissars. They found followers among the peasants and obtained aid from the western Allies.

As for the new regime, the oldest of its institutions was the Party, founded as a wing of the Social Democrats in 1903, the next oldest were the soviets, dating from 1905 and 1917, and then came the council of people's commissars set up on the day of the coup d'état. The first institution founded under the new order was a political police, an Extraordinary All-Russian Commission of Struggle against Counter-revolution, Speculation and Sabotage, commonly known from its Russian initials as the Cheka, and in later years, without basic change of methods or purpose, under the successive names of the OGPU, the NKVD and the MVD. It was established on December 7, 1917. In January 1918 the Red Army was founded, with Leon Trotsky as war commissar and virtually its creator.

In social policy the Bolsheviks at first adopted no long-range plans, contenting themselves with a mixture of principle and expediency known as "war communism." To crush the bourgeoisie, they soon nationalized some nine hundred of the largest industrial enterprises. The pressing problem was to find food, which had ceased to move through any normal channels. The peasants, very much as in the French Revolution under similar conditions—worthless money, insecure property titles, unruly hired men, armed marauding, and a doubtful future—were producing less food than usual, consuming it themselves, or hoarding it on their own farms. The response of the government and city workers was also much as in 1793. The new government levied requisitions, required the peasants to make stated "deliveries," and invited labor unions to send armed detachments into the country to procure food by force. Since it was naturally the big farmers who had the surplus, these came into disrepute as starvers of the people. Class war broke out, rabid, ferocious, and elemental, between farmers who feared that their very subsistence as well as their property would be taken away, and city people, often supported by hungry agricultural laborers, who were driven to desperation by famine. Many peasants, especially the larger farmers, therefore rallied to anti-Bolshevik political leaders.

Centers of resistance developed on every side. In the Don valley a small force assembled under Kornilov and Denikin, with many army officers, gentry landowners, and expropriated business people taking part in it. The Social Revolutionaries gathered followers on the middle Volga. At Omsk a disaffected group proclaimed the independence of Siberia. As a military organization the most significant was a force of some 45,000 Czechs, who had deserted or been captured from the Austro-Hungarian armies, and had been organized as a Czech Legion to fight on the side of Russia and the Allies. After the November revolution and the peace of Brest-Litovsk, these Czechs decided to leave Russia by way of the Trans-Siberian railroad, return to Europe by sea, and resume fighting on the Western front. When Bolshevik officials undertook to disarm them they allied with the Social Revolutionaries on the Volga.

The Allied governments believed that Bolshevism was a temporary madness that with a little effort could be stopped. They wished also to bring Russia back into the war against Germany. So long as the war in Europe lasted, they could not reach Russia by the Black or Baltic sea. A small Allied force took Murmansk and Archangel in the North. But for Allied military intervention the best opening was in the Far East, through Vladivostok. The Japanese, who had declined military aid to their Allies in any other theater, received this proposal with enthusiasm, seeing in the ruin of the Russian Empire a rare opportunity to develop their sphere of influence in East Asia. It was agreed that an Interallied military force should land at Vladivostok, cross Siberia, join with the Czechs, break up Bolshevism and fall upon the Germans in eastern Europe. For this ambitious scheme Britain and France could supply no soldiers, engaged as they were on the western front; the force turned out to be American and Japanese, or rather almost purely Japanese, since Japan contributed 72,000 men, and the United States only 8,000. They landed at Vladivostok in August 1918.

The civil war lasted until 1920, or even later in some places. It became a confused mêlée in which the Bolsheviks struggled against dissident Russians; fought in the Ukraine first against the Germans and then against the French, who occupied Odessa as soon as the war ended in Europe; reconquered the Ukraine, Armenia, Georgia, and Azerbaijan, which had declared their independence; put to flight a hundred thousand "Whites" under Wrangel in the South; fought off Admiral Kolchak, who, with a White army in Siberia, proclaimed himself ruler of all Russia; and in 1920, carried on a war with the new republic of Poland, which was scarcely organized when it set out to recover the huge Ukrainian and White Russian territories that had been Polish before 1773. British, French, and American troops remained at Archangel until the end of 1919, the Japanese at Valdivostok until the end of 1922. But the anti-Bolshevik forces could never unite. The anti-Communist Russians represented every hue of the political spectrum from unregenerate tsarists to left-wing Social Revolutionaries. The Allies could not agree; the French sent troops to the Ukraine and gave aid to the Poles, but the British and Americans wanted to be rid of all military entanglements as soon as the armistice with Germany was signed. Leon Trotsky, on the other hand, forged in the crucible of the civil wars the hard and solid metal of the Red Army, recruiting it, organizing it, restoring its discipline, equipping it as best he could, assigning political commissars to watch it, and assuring that trustworthy officers occupied its high command. By 1922 the Bolshevist-Communists had established themselves up to the frontiers of the former tsarist empire in every direction, except on the European side. There the band of states in the *cordon sanitaire* remained independent; and Poland, as a result of the war of 1920, retained a frontier farther east than the Allies themselves had intended.

It was during these civil wars that the Red Terror broke out in Russia. Like the famous Terror in France in 1793, it was in part a response to civil and foreign war, if indeed, the term "war" can be applied to the half-hearted military intervention of the Allies against Bolshevism. Before the Bolshevik Terror the old Jacobin Terror paled. They differed as the cruelty and violence endemic in the old Russia differed from the more humane or law-abiding habits of western Europe. Thousands were shot merely as hostages (a practice unknown to Europe for some centuries); and other thousands without even the summary formalities of revolutionary tribunals. The Cheka was the most formidable political police that had yet appeared. Formerly the individual had had a chance; the heretic who conformed had usually been spared by the Inquisition; the ex-nobleman who accepted his new citizenship had survived the Terror of 1793, which had sentenced only 1,400 nobles to death. The Bolshevik Terror was aimed at the physical extermination of persons of bourgeois class, including intelligentsia who lacked enthusiasm for the Communist regime. Do not, said a chief of the Cheka, look for proofs of activity against the Soviet state: "The first questions you should put to the accused person are, To what class does he belong, what is his origin, what was his education, and what is his profession? These should determine the fate of the accused. This is the essence of the Red Terror." Or as Zinoviev, a leading Bolshevik, put it: "The bourgeoisie kill separate individuals, but we kill whole classes." In 1918 a young woman named Fanny Kaplan shot at Lenin. She deposed that she had favored the Constituent Assembly, that her parents had emigrated to America in 1911, that she had six working-class brothers and sisters; and that she had intended to kill Lenin. She was of course executed, and a massacre of bourgeois and intellectuals followed in Petrograd. When the sailors at Kronstadt, who were among the first adherents won by the Bolsheviks, rose in 1921, objecting to domination of the soviets by the Party (threatening a kind of leftist renewal of the revolution, like the Hébertists who had opposed Robespierre) they were branded as petty-bourgeois and shot down by the thousands. The Terror decimated the revolutionists themselves quite as much as the bourgeoisie.

The Terror succeeded in its purpose. Together with the victories of the Red Army, it established the new regime. Those "bourgeois" who survived took on the protective coloration of "toilers." No bourgeois as such ever again presumed to take part in the politics of Russia. Mensheviks and other socialists fleeing to Europe told appalling stories of the human toll taken by Lenin. Horrified European socialists repudiated communism as an atrocious, Byzantine, Asiatic perversion of Marxism. But, at whatever cost, Lenin and his followers were now able to start building the socialist society as they understood it.

With the suppression of movements for independence in the Ukraine, Transcaucasia and the Far East, with the end of foreign intervention by which these independence movements had been aided, and with the termination of the war with Poland, it became possible in 1922 to establish the Union of Soviet Socialist Republics. Its first members were four in number: the Russian Soviet Federated Socialist Republic, the Ukrainian Soviet Socialist Republic, the White Russian Soviet Socialist Republic and the Transcaucasian Soviet Socialist Republic. In the new Union, which geographically replaced the old Russian Empire, the name Russia was not officially used. The guiding conception was a blend of the national and the international: to recognize nationality by granting autonomy to national groups, while holding these groups together in a higher union, and making it possible for new groups to enter regardless of historic frontiers. In 1922 the expectation of world revolution was still alive. The constitution, in its preamble, pronounced the founding of the U.S.S.R. to be "a decisive step by way of uniting the workers of all countries into one World Soviet Socialist Republic." It made the union, in principle, fluid and expansible, declared that any member republic might secede (none ever has) and that newly formed soviet socialist republics might join. When, in connection with the Second World War, the U.S.S.R. took back territories detached from tsarist Russia after the First World War—Bessarabia from Rumania, Karelia from Finland, parts of White Russia and the Ukraine from Poland, and Estonia, Latvia, and Lithuania after two decades of independence—these territories were sovietized and added to the Union as republics on a footing of legal equality with the old ones.

The federal principle in the U.S.S.R. was designed to answer the problem of nationalism. The tzardom, in its last decades, had tried to deal with this problem by systematic Russification. The nationalities had resisted, and nationalist discontent had been one of the forces fatally weakening the empire. Nationalism, or the demand that national groups should have their own political sovereignty, had not only broken up the Austro-Hungarian empire but "Balkanized" central and eastern Europe. In 1922 the U.S.S.R., occupying a sixth of the world's land area, was adjoined on the west by a Europe which in one twenty-seventh of the world's land surface contained twenty-seven independent states.

A hundred languages were spoken in the Soviet Union, and fifty distinct nationalities were recognized within its borders. Many of these were extremely small, splinter groups or isolated communities left by the ebb and flow of mankind in inner Asia over thousands of years. Many were very primitive, without political consciousness. All recognized nationalities received a cultural autonomy, or the right to use their own language, have their own schools, wear their own dress, and follow their own folkways without interference. Indeed, the Soviet authorities favored the growth of cultural nationalism. Some fifty languages were reduced to writing for the first time, and the new regime encouraged the singing of national songs, performance of dances, and collection of folklore. Administratively the nationalities were put on various levels, with varying degrees of separate identity according to their size, degree of civilization, or importance. Some constituted only regional areas; others became "autonomous republics" within one of the federated soviet republics; others, the most important, were component republics of the Union. An example of the second category was Birobijan in the Far East, administratively an autonomous Jewish republic within the R.S.F.S.R. Politically, by the new Soviet constitution of 1936, an upper house of the

U.S.S.R. legislative body was created, called a Soviet (or council) of Nationalities, to which each Union republic sent twenty-five delegates, each "autonomous" republic eleven, and each regional area five. Armenia with a million people thus had as many delegates to this council as Russia proper, with its hundred million. In practice, the Russian S.S.R., with over half the population and three quarters of the territory of the Union, predominated over the others. When to the Russian were added the Ukrainian (or Little Russian) and White Russian republics, whose people were not very different from the Great Russians, the overwhelmingly Russian and Slavic character of the Union became more marked.

The federal structure, while not disturbing the essential unity of the whole, assured by the great Slavic preponderance, gave a dignity, self-respect and sense of equal co-operation to the numerous minorities, all of which, before the annexations of 1940, were in any case less civilized than the Russians. While separatism did not wholly die down (remaining especially alive in the Ukraine) on the whole the U.S.S.R. was free from internal nationalistic agitation. It is generally agreed (more so than on any other aspect of the controversial Soviet Union) that the U.S.S.R. found a constructive solution to its nationalities question, and is the best example afforded by the twentieth century of a multinational state.

Government in the Union, and in each component republic, followed a pattern worked out during the Revolution. Its chief feature was a system of parallelism. On the one hand was the State, on the other, paralleling the State but technically not part of it, was the Party.

On the side of the State the distinctive institution was the council or soviet. Here elections took place, and authority proceeded from the bottom upward to the top. All "toilers" had the right to vote. Surviving bourgeois, private traders, "persons using the labor of others to make a profit," as well as priests, were excluded from the suffrage until 1936. In each village and town the voters chose a local soviet; the local soviet elected delegates to a provincial soviet, which in turn sent delegates to a soviet of the republic (Russian or other); soviets of the component republics sent delegates to a Union-wide Congress of Soviets, the supreme law-enacting body of the country. Soviets at all levels chose executive officials; the Congress of Soviets chose the Council of People's Commissars, or ministry. In the constitution of 1936 a more direct democratic procedure was introduced, for the State side of the parallelism. Voters henceforth directly elected members of the higher soviets, a secret ballot was adopted, and no class was any longer denied the vote. A bicameral parliament was created, with an upper chamber, the Soviet of

Nationalities mentioned above, and a lower chamber, a Soviet of the Union, in which there was one representative for every 300,000 persons in the whole country. The Supreme Soviet, with its two chambers, chose a Presidium to function while the chambers were not in session. The Presidium supervised the Council of People's Commissars, which the Supreme Soviet continued to elect. On the State side, as set forth in the constitution, especially the constitution of 1936, the government was highly democratic.

Alongside the State, at all levels and in all localities, was the Party. Only one party was allowed, namely the Communist, though non-party members might be elected to the soviets or to other official positions. In the Party, authority began at the top and proceeded downwards. At its apex stood the Central Committee, whose members varied in number from time to time, but were usually about twenty. The Central Committee did its work through a party secretary, an Orgburo, and a Politburo, subcommittees handling respectively matters of party organization and party policy. The Central Committee itself, or an inside group within it, and especially the secretary, determined the membership of the Committee and of its sub-committees. It likewise assigned, transferred, and gave orders to party members through the successive lower levels of its organization. Although party congresses met every year or two, they generally simply registered decisions already made by the Central Committee. Actually, it was the Politburo that dominated the Central Committee. Power and authority flowed downward and outward, as in an army, or as in a highly centralized government agency or large private corporation in the West, except that the Party was not subject to any outside control. Discipline was likewise enforced in ways not used in liberal countries, the fearsome machinery of the Cheka (OGPU, NKVD, MVD) being available for use in extreme cases against Party members as well as those outside.

The number of Party members, men and women, rose to about two million by 1930 and three million by 1940, normally comprising two or three per cent of the adult population. The Leninist ideal of a small, compact, and manageable party, made up of faithful and zealous workers who willingly carried out orders, the ideal on which the Bolsheviks had separated from the Mensheviks in 1903, continued to characterize the Communist Party in the Soviet Union. Old Bolsheviks, those who had been members in the lean years before 1917, long continued to occupy the seats in the Politburo and other important party positions. The problem, once it was clear that the Revolution had come to stay, was to prevent an inrush of careerists, persons who simply wished to belong to the new governing elite, old Mensheviks, Social Revolutionaries, or even former bourgeois now flying Communist colors. A party of two million members, though small in contrast to the population of the U.S.S.R., still represented an enormous growth for the party itself, in which for each old member (who had joined before 1917) there were hundreds of new ones. To preserve Party unity under the new conditions strict uniformity was enforced. Members made an intensive study of the principles of Marx-Leninism, embraced dialectical materialism as a philosophy and even a kind of religion, learned how to take orders without question or compunction, and to give authoritative leadership, assistance, or explanations of policy to the mass of non-party members among whom they worked. The bottom of the party structure consisted in small nuclei or cells. In each factory, in each mine, in each office, in each class at the universities and technical schools, in each labor union, in each at least of the larger villages, one, two, or a dozen of the local people (factory workers, miners, office workers, students, etc., as the case might be) belonged to the Party, and imparted Party views and Party momentum to the whole.

The function of the Party, in Marxist terms, was to carry out the dictatorship of the proletariat. It was to lead the people as a whole to the realization of socialism, and, in day-to-day affairs, to coordinate the ponderous mechanism of government and make it work. Party members were present at all levels. The same men sat, in the Party, in the Politburo of the Central Committee, and, in the State, in the Council of People's Commissars. At the next lower level, in the soviets of the Union and of the component republics, Party members were numerous. Lower down, Party members became more rare. In a small rural soviet there might be no one belonging to the Party at all; the village councilmen would receive instructions, exhortations, or "pep talks" from itinerant Party members. In any event, throughout the whole structure, the Party decided what the State should do.

The role of the Party in the U.S.S.R. has been called, at its best, a "vocation of leadership." Those joined it who were willing to work hard, to devote themselves to Party matters day and night, to absorb and communicate the Party policy (or "line"), to go where they were sent, to attend meetings, speak up, and remain until all others had left for home, to perceive and explain the significance of small passing events for the future of Russia or the world revolution, to master intricate technical details of farming, manufacturing, or the care of machinery, so that others would look to them willingly for advice. The Party was a specially trained elite whose members were in constant touch with each other. It was the thin stream of life blood which, circulating through all the diverse tissues of the U.S.S.R.—the multitudinous republics, soviets, bureaus, army, industrial and other enterprises owned under socialism by the state—kept the whole complex body unified, organic, functioning, and alive.

To the country as a whole the party undoubtedly represented the vocation of leadership. The corollary was that more than ninety-five out of a hundred persons were condemned to be followers, and while it is perhaps true (as apologists for the system have said) that under any system true leadership is exercised by a tiny fraction of people, the difference between Communist and non-Communist in the U.S.S.R. became a clear matter of social status. As the years passed, by the 1930's, many Communists in the U.S.S.R. were less of the type of revolutionary firebrand than of the successful and the efficient man or woman in any social system. They represented the satisfied, not the dis-satisfied. Sometimes they enjoyed material privileges, such as access to the best jobs, better housing, special food coupons, or priorities on trains. They worked faithfully for recognition and promotion in the Party. They developed a bourgeois concern for the advantages of their own children. They became a new vested interest. Within the Party, members had to be not so much leaders as followers. A homogeneous and monolithic organization was desired, presenting a solid front to the far more numerous but unorganized outsiders. Within the Party, from time to time, a great deal of difference of opinion and open discussion was tolerated (indeed, since there was only one Party all political questions were intra-Party disputes), but in the end the entire membership had to conform. The Party favored a certain initiative of action, and a certain fertility of mind in inventing ways to get things done, but it did not favor, and in fact repressed, originality, boldness, or freedom of thought.

In 1920 it was clear that "war communism" had hopelessly antagonized the peasants, who, it was estimated, were cultivating only 62% as much land as in 1914. This fact, together with a severe drought and the breakdown of transportation, produced a great famine. Four or five million people died. The ravages of eight years, of the World War, the Revolution, the civil wars, the Terror, had left the country in ruins, its productive facilities thrown back by decades as compared with the point reached in 1914. The rising of the Kronstadt sailors revealed profound disillusionment in the revolutionary ranks themselves. Lenin concluded that socialization had advanced too fast. Under the slogan, "two steps forward, one step back," he openly advocated a compromise with capitalism. The New Economic Policy, or Nep, adopted in 1921, lasted until 1927. Most of the decade of the 1920's saw a relaxation of tempo for most people in the U.S.S.R.

Under the Nep, while the state controlled the "commanding heights" of the economy, maintaining state ownership of the basic productive industries, it allowed a great deal of private trading for private profit. The basic problem was to restore trade between town and country. The peasant would produce nothing beyond the needs of his own subsistence unless he could exchange his surplus for city-made wares such as clothing or tools. The city people had to be fed from the country if they were to turn out factory products or even continue to live in the city. Under the Nep, peasants were allowed to sell their farm products freely. Middlemen were allowed to buy and sell farm products and manufactured articles at will, to whom they pleased, at market prices, and at a profit to themselves. The Nep therefore favored the big individualist farmer or *kulak*. Indeed, the legislation of Stolypin was still at work; peasant families consolidated millions of acres as private property in 1922, 1923, and 1924. Correspondingly, other peasants became "proletarians," wage-earning hired hands. The Nep also favored the sprouting of a new-rich commercial class, neo-bourgeois who ate expensive dinners in the cafés of Moscow, and whose very existence seemed to explode the dream of a classless society. Under the Nep the worst damages of war and revolution were repaired. But there was no real progress, for in 1928 Russia was producing only about as much grain, raw cotton, cattle, coal, and oil as in 1913, and far less than it presumably would have produced (given the rate of growth before 1913) had there been no revolution.

Lenin died in 1924 prematurely at the age of fifty-four. His embalmed remains were put permanently on view in the Kremlin; Petrograd was renamed Leningrad; a leader cult was built up around his name and image; the Party presented him as a deified equal of Marx himself; and it became necessary for all schools of Communist thought to claim unflinching fidelity to the Leninist tradition. Actually, in his own lifetime, the old Bolsheviks had never regarded Lenin as infallible. They had often differed with him and with each other. After his death his old companions and contemporaries, men in their prime, carrying on the feuding habits of the émigré days, fought with each other for control of the Party in Lenin's name. They disputed over Lenin's intentions. Had he secretly thought of the Nep as a permanent policy? If not, how would he have modified it, and, most especially, how soon? Quietly, behind the scenes, as secretary of the Party, without much attention to broader problems, a hitherto modest member named Joseph Stalin, of whom Lenin had never had an enthusiastic opinion, was drawing all the strings of Party control into his own hands. More openly and vociferously

Leon Trotsky, who as war commissar in the critical years had been only less conspicuous than Lenin himself, raised the basic issues of the whole nature and future of the movement.

Trotsky, in 1925 and 1926, inveighed against the lassitude that had descended upon socialism.[2] The Nep with its tolerance of bourgeois and *kulaks* excited his contempt. He developed his doctrine of "permanent revolution," an incessant drive for proletarian objectives on all fronts in all parts of the world. He stood forth as the exponent of world revolution, which many in the Party were beginning to discard in favor of first building socialism in one country. He denounced the tendency to bureaucratic ossification in the Party, and urged a new movement of the masses to give it life. He called for more forceful development of industry, and for the collectivization of agriculture, which had figured in Communist manifestoes ever since 1848. Above all, he demanded immediate adoption of an over-all Plan, a central control and operation of the whole economic life of the country.

Trotsky failed to carry the Party with him. He was charged with Leftist deviationism, machinations against the Central Committee, and inciting to public discussion of issues outside the Party. Stalin wove his web. At a Party Congress in 1927 854,000 members dutifully voted for Stalin and the Central Committee, and only 4,000 for Trotsky. Trotsky was first exiled to Siberia, then banished from the U.S.S.R.; he lived first in Turkey, then France, then Mexico, writing and propagandizing for the Permanent Revolution, stigmatizing developments in the U.S.S.R. as "Stalinism," a monstrous betrayal of Marx-Leninism, organizing an underground against Stalin as he had done in former days against the tsar. He was murdered in Mexico in 1940 under mysterious circumstances, presumably by Soviet agents or sympathizers.

3. VERSAILLES AND THE TWENTIES

WORLD WAR AND WORLD SETTLEMENTS, 1917-19

. . . The year 1919 was the high watermark of democracy in world history. Not even 1945 can be compared to that year, since in 1945 the democratic nations shared their victory with the Soviet Union and the major spoils of victory went to the latter. In 1919 no autocratic or authoritarian power could obstruct the peace settlement, and peacemaking was the exclusive respon-

---

[2] For communists, though not for socialists, the terms "communism" and "socialism" are almost interchangeable, since Russian Communists regard their own system as true socialism, and all other socialism as opportunistic, reactionary, or false. Communism is also defined, in the U.S.S.R., as a future state of society toward which socialism, *i.e.,* Soviet socialism, is the intermediate stage.

sibility of the democratic nations. Still, "the war to make the world safe for democracy," a phrase first coined by H. G. Wells in August, 1914, to describe the meaning of World War I, brought forth before long the age of the dictators, and "the war to end war" turned out to be the harbinger of even greater disaster.

If we compare the Paris settlement of 1919 to the Vienna settlement of 1815, it is obvious that some of the fundamental elements that made for unity and mutual understanding among the peacemakers of Vienna were lacking in 1919. The wars of 1812–15 had a clear common aim, the defeat of Napoleon's revolutionary attempt at uniting the Continent under his dictatorial power and the restoration of the old European state system. The war of 1914–18 did not have such a single common goal. Of course, the immediate objective of the war, the destruction of Germany's overweening power, was accepted as a general Allied war aim, but no clarity existed among the victorious powers about the type of Europe that they wanted to build or rebuild, supposing, indeed, that they could construct a European political system at all.

World War I had shown that the balance of Europe did not exist any longer; in order to subdue the Central Powers the intervention of the United States and also of the British dominions was required. The United States played a leading, and the British dominions a significant, role in the making of the peace settlement of Paris in 1919. It was natural that they wished to create a world settlement and that they were little concerned about the resurrection of the broken-down European system. The British Government, owing to its own world-wide commitments, easily fell in with this trend. In contrast, Clemenceau, more than any other Allied statesman, thought in terms of the restoration of a European balance of power and made a supreme effort to gain a peace that would place France in an unassailable position of military superiority over Germany. He therefore aimed at the amputation of a maximum of German territories, the blocking of the merger of Austria and Germany, the imposition of heavy reparations, and French control of the left bank of the Rhine.

To the rigid military mind of General Foch this program was the logical expression of French national interest; but Clemenceau himself was too wise to look at politics in such simple logical terms. The last great Jacobin knew the dynamic force of nationalism and realized that a treaty of this description would breed fiery German resentment. It was doubtful, furthermore, whether France by herself could make such a peace settlement effective. France would have succumbed to Germany in the war if it had not been for her Allies, and she had suffered grievous losses that not even victory could recover. Clemenceau was under no illusion that the future security of France did not depend principally on continued co-operation with Britain and the United States.

Although Clemenceau bargained hard to gain the French points, he compromised with Wilson and Lloyd George on the Rhineland issue. France received no German territory outside of Alsace-Lorraine. The Saar district was separated from Germany and France given a preponderant position in its administration, but it was to be under League auspices and a plebiscite was to take place after fifteen years to settle the final status of the region according to the wishes of its inhabitants. No separate Rhenish state was created, and though the Rhineland was demilitarized, its occupation by Allied troops was limited to fifteen years. In exchange for these stipulations made possible by Clemenceau's concessions, France was promised that if during the next fifteen years the Germans were to challenge the arrangements concerning the Rhineland, the United States and Britain would give her military assistance.

The most crucial of all the political problems of Europe was thus settled by arrangements that envisaged the continued participation of a non-European power in the maintenance of the European peace. In the Rhineland this co-operation took the form of a specific guarantee by individual nations. In general the universal League of Nations, composed of members from all continents, was supposed to safeguard the peace of Europe as a part of world peace. No conscious attempt was made to reconstruct a politically self-sufficient European system. Nobody could contend that a Europe similar to that of the nineteenth century could have been revived by the Paris Peace Conference, and the conference dealt almost exclusively with the claims of nations on the one hand and with the building of a world system on the other. The common problems concerned with Europe as a whole found no discussion.

No other political document could have offered as much guidance for the establishment of a peaceful international society as did the American constitution, and it was the greatness of Woodrow Wilson that he projected the American political tradition ably and eloquently into a liberal international faith. The weakness of Wilson's international program lay in the generality of many of its tenets and in the contradictory nature of some of them. The principle of national self-determination, for example, was not universally practicable, and in certain cases it conflicted with other Wilsonian principles, such as the demand of access to the seas for landlocked states. The generality of the Fourteen Points and their lack of absolute logical unity offered the opportunity for perverting Wilson's program at the peace conference by writing many nationalistic war gains into the final settlement. But with more good will Wilson's program could have been adapted to the historic conditions of the hour.

More serious was Wilson's ingrained belief that his abstract ideals could blot out certain realities of political life. Walter Lippmann once pointed out that the Wilsonian principles were formulated on the basis of America's aloofness from world politics as it had existed due to specific and fortunate historical circumstances. "Wilson wished America to take its place in a universal society. But he was willing to participate only if the whole world acted as the United States had acted when it enjoyed isolation during the 19th century." . . .

The history of disarmament at the Paris Peace Conference can serve as a good illustration of the great distance that had to be travelled in order to translate the Wilsonian ideals into practical political arrangements. On the other hand, it offers an example of how eager Wilson was to justify concrete decisions as emanations from absolute principles. There was in Wilson's philosophy, however, a grave misunderstanding of the relation between abstract ideas and power in history. Wilson was deeply convinced that the proclamation of liberal ideals in international life would everywhere rally the common man to their support. In this sense he could say to the American delegation on his way to Paris that only he, and not Lloyd George and Clemenceau, represented the people. But in the formal sense Clemenceau and Lloyd George represented their nations more fully than Woodrow Wilson. He had lost control of Congress in the November elections, and it was unpredictable what opposition his foreign policy might meet at home in the future. In contrast, Lloyd George had called for British elections in December and had gained a strong, if unwieldy, parliamentary majority, while the French Chamber of Deputies had voted 4:1 in favor of Clemenceau after he presented on December 27, 1918, his plans for French policy at the approaching peace conference. Clemenceau was openly hostile to Wilsonian idealism, and the British "khaki elections" were fought by Lloyd George and his liberal and conservative party friends with nationalistic slogans that contradicted the Government's official acceptance of the Wilsonian program. . . .

Still, Wilson's program appealed to the common man, and the popular ovations that he received everywhere he went in Europe were genuine. To almost everybody it seemed that the program offered a way to end the cruel bloodshed and to cure the wounds that four years of war had inflicted on all national societies. It promised gains to all the Allied powers, at the same time promising Germany as well as Austria and Hungary the protection of the principle of nationality. The Wilsonian program had a twofold root and double purpose. It was not only a design of an international peace settlement but also an instrument of political warfare. And as a political weapon it proved a complete success during 1918. It gave hope to the Allied nations in the early months of the year when they reeled under the blows of the German spring offensive in the West, it rallied the separatistic national movements in the Habsburg empire to the support of the Allied cause, and it strengthened the peace sentiment in the enemy countries. American political warfare made a great contribution to the early winning of World War I.

But the immediate impact of American propaganda on Europe was the strengthening of national sentiment. To gain or regain full national independence and the strongest possible military strength to defend it was the dearest objective of every warring European nation. The internationalism of Wilson was shared by the European statesmen only in so far as it did not deny them the full realization of their own nationalistic aims. In Wilson's eyes national self-determination was a means to lay grievances to rest and thus a direct step towards a peaceful international society. To most Europeans the satisfaction of their national dreams was an absolute end, even when their realization violated the national self-determination of others.

Shortsighted as this policy was—and more will be said about it later—the desire of the European states, old and new, to gain national security through a maximum of power, which they measured by area and population, was to some degree understandable. As early as January, 1917, Wilson had proclaimed that there should be no "new balance of power," but instead a "community of power." His concept of a League of Nations, however, though it envisaged the ultimate use of force against an aggressor, rested chiefly on the belief that a united world opinion would act as a deterrent to aggression and that, if this failed, an aggressor could probably be brought to heel by economic boycott and blockade. Collective military action was to be taken, if at all, only after considerable damage had been done. Yet defense against invasion was still a vital problem that the individual states alone or in groups would have to meet. Although Wilson was right when he judged that the balance of power had failed to provide a secure foundation for world peace, the different nations, including the United States and Britain, were far from ready to pool their whole strength in a single "community of power," and the relative balance of power between states remained a matter of vital significance. The League of Nations of 1919 was not what its English name said it was, a closely united group of states ready for immediate concerted action. The French name *Societé des Nations* described the nature of the organization more aptly.

If the League of Nations was to gain true life, its roots had to sink deeply into the soil of national security interests. Such a policy would have required the frank recognition of the balance of power that Wilson rejected. In his opinion the struggle for power had come to an end with the armistice, and the peacemakers should now settle all claims largely on the basis of universally valid principles. Such an attitude was bound to lead to great embarrassment. Inevitably, Wilson had to make continuous concessions to the balance of power. One of the first, made shortly after his arrival in Europe, was his consent to Italy's obtaining the Brenner Pass frontier, in stark contrast to his own Point Nine, which had demanded "a readjustment of the frontiers of Italy . . . along clearly recognizable lines of nationality."

. . . By Wilson's insistence on wrapping up necessary compromises in the language of general principles, his ideals lost much of the radiance that would have made them steady beacons in the evolution of a collective system. Abused ideas have a tremendous aptitude for vengeance. The difficulty during the interwar period of arousing strong popular support for the forceful maintenance of the Paris settlement was largely due to the fact that the intellectual and moral foundation of the peace appeared to be very weak.

This is not to say that all the concessions that the peace conference made to nationalistic demands could be called practical decisions. Actually many of them were patently obnoxious. But the elementary longing of states for security could not be disregarded or met only surreptitiously. Yet it could have been pointed out to them that no European state had ever enjoyed security in isolation and that in spite of all her wars and divisions Europe had managed in the past to restore a communal life after every crisis through which she had gone. The statesmen of the Congress of Vienna had speedily welcomed France back to the European concert without neglecting to take those precautionary measures that kept France from renewing her career of Napoleonic conquest. In the absence of general wars during the later nineteenth century the existence of neutral great powers had exercised a restraining influence upon the victor in a war. But none of these curative forces seemed to have survived the holocaust of World War I in Europe.

Formerly the monarchs and nobility had formed an upper stratum of European society. No doubt, their cupidity had caused many wars, but the similarity of outlook and interest within the group had made bargaining and compromise possible. Woodrow Wilson expected that democracy would be a better maker and guarantor of peace than monarchs and noble elites. Yet this expectation was not fulfilled in 1919.

For one thing, "democratic" foreign policy was in its infancy. Prior to World War I even people in states with a popular constitution paid little attention to the actual conduct of foreign affairs except in periods of tension. Britain had the oldest tradition of parliamentary control, and the British parties, it is true, usually identified themselves with differing foreign policies. In fact British foreign policy often changed with changing parliamentary majorities. Within these limitations, however, the prime minister and foreign secretary had great freedom in the formulation and execution of foreign policy, even to the extent of concluding secret understandings. . . .

Wilson might have been in a better position to modify some of the excesses of nationalism if he could have broadened the scope of the conference debates. Everybody agreed that the political world settlement would require for its support a restoration of world trade and world economy. But the American delegation was not in a position to discuss the revival of a free and stable economy in a comprehensive and systematic fashion.

Four groups of economic problems existed in 1919. There were first the urgent relief needs in the provinces of the Central Powers and the countries that they had occupied during World War I. Second, the world faced the difficulty of rehabilitating Europe's productivity and working out a program of economic development for the new eastern European states. Third, there were the problems arising from the economic transformations that had been brought about by the great expansion during the war of non-European industries and the sudden rise of the United States as the big creditor nation of the world, particularly of Europe. Fourth, there was the difficulty of making a financial settlement between victors and vanquished nations or, more correctly, between the victors and Germany, since the Habsburg empire had disappeared.

The first problems, those of relief, were met. There was some delay due to American insistence on the dissolution of the Allied economic wartime councils after the armistice. Herbert Hoover expressed the American point of view most forcefully when he said that everything should be avoided that would give even the appearance that other powers had a voice in the assignment of American resources. Yet, although most funds and foodstuffs came from the United States, the contribution of the British Commonwealth was by no means negligible, and it was in any case politically unwise to break up the common front, at least prior to the conclusion of peace. New inter-Allied organizations were finally set up in January, 1919, under the Supreme

Economic Council, over which Lord Robert Cecil presided with Herbert Hoover, who was director general of relief. . . .

The difference between relief and rehabilitation is a relative one. No doubt, the Allied relief activities in Europe after 1919 were of crucial significance for the restoration of normal economic production; but European recovery proved a process of many years, since the problems of the second and third groups were never tackled. Wilson was aware that it was necessary to give the political settlement an economic underpinning, but we may question whether he had a clear conception of the way by which this could be done. His Point Three, for instance, demanding the removal of all economic barriers and the establishment of an equality of trade conditions, had been a rather simple expression of his liberal faith. But it had come under strong fire from the United States Senate and was in these debates reinterpreted by the Wilson Administration in such a fashion as to become practically meaningless.

Wilson seemed, indeed, to have resigned himself to a situation that did not allow him to commit the United States to a definite plan for the reconstruction of world economy, much less for special projects of European recovery and development. He did not think it politically possible to discuss even the settlement of the inter-Allied war debts in this light. The British, who had given their allies as many loans as they had received from the United States, early proposed to study the problem of international payments, including inter-Allied debts and German reparations, as one affecting the whole future of world economy. They indicated, too, that they were willing to cancel some of the loans that they had made to their allies in order to help the war effort if their own debts received similar consideration from the United States. But the American delegation at Paris insisted that the American war loans, as enacted by Congress, had been made to individual states on a strict business basis. They could be settled only by negotiations between the United States Government and the individual states. The discussion of inter-Allied debts was thus excluded from the peace conference, and with this decision the opportunity was missed for rebuilding the international economy on a stable foundation.

German reparations consequently was the only major economic problem taken up by the peace conference. In retrospect it is easy to say that nobody, including such critics of the Versailles settlement as John Maynard Keynes or, for that matter, such able financial experts of the German delegation as Carl Melchior, were right in their estimate of the reparations that Germany was able to pay. Everybody overrated Germany's capacity, which was not surprising, since there was no precedent for international payments of comparable magnitude. But if one thing could have been foreseen, it was the close interrelation between any international payments, whether German reparations or inter-Allied debts, and the future development of world economy. If international trade had expanded far beyond the volume of 1913 and if in particular the creditor nations had been willing to receive greatly increased imports from the debtor countries, much larger sums might have been transferred. . . .

The Paris Peace Conference failed to make systematic plans for world recovery that would have solidified their political arrangements. The Paris peace treaties were a diplomatic peace settlement similar to the Vienna settlement, though, of course, the political philosophies of the two differed. Wilson sensed that security of nationality and frontiers was not enough and that economic and social problems as well demanded the attention of modern statesmen. The creation of the International Labor Office was an indication of such awareness. Yet the depth of the revolutionary changes that World War I had caused in the social structure and attitude of nations was hidden from the view of the peacemakers.

Broadly speaking, the wars of earlier times had been wars of armies—armies of restricted, if expanding, numbers limited in their arms and equipment. But World War I had a different character. Formerly the production of arms ceased when war broke out, but after 1916 industrial mobilization became as gigantic as the military levies. The civilians were contributing as much to the war as the soldiers, and the endless casualty lists, invasions, and blockade brought the war home to every person in Europe and Russia. In other words, after 1916 World War I turned into the first modern total war. The impact of this event was greatest in Russia, which tried a total mobilization but broke down under the burden. Germany achieved a rather complete government-directed war economy, the first planned economy in modern history.

Nobody in Paris fully realized the portents of the new age. The peace conferences of Vienna and Paris can be compared in many respects. But they took place at very different moments of history. Vienna was the settlement of twenty-odd years of general war, in which the revolutionary forces had been able to modify, but not to overthrow, the old order of Europe. In contrast, the Paris conference was a first attempt at dealing with a new situation that had begun to unfold during the war itself. It was admitted that the world had become *one* world, and a League of Nations was created. But it was a weak league, and in spite of its unassuming character it had yet to gain universality of membership. The Paris Peace Conference also carried diplomatic activities into the economic and social fields, but it did so in an irregular fashion. . . .

THE EUROPEAN AFTERMATH

The Paris peace treaties were considered to constitute a world settlement; but they never did. The peace conference could do little about the problems of the Far Eastern Pacific except distribute the German colonies located in that area. But of even greater consequence was its failure to deal with Bolshevist Russia. This is not to suggest that a solution of the Russian problem would have been simple or even possible in 1919. The French were stubbornly opposed to any diplomatic contacts with the Bolshevists, whom they judged to be tools of the Germans and traitors of Russian political and financial commitments to the West. Opposed, also, was Winston Churchill, then the British secretary for war. But the West was unable to intervene in the Russian civil war except by giving arms and other implements of war to the White Russian groups fighting in various parts of Russia against the Bolshevists entrenched in Moscow and St. Petersburg. Few Allied soldiers were willing to be sent to Russia, since after the German armistice everybody was convinced that the fighting was over and that Allied war aims had been achieved.

Winston Churchill, in his Boston speech of March 31, 1949, characterized the "failure to strangle Bolshevism at its birth and to bring Russia . . . by one means or another into the general democratic system" as one of the great mistakes of Allied statesmen in 1919. This statement seems historically correct, and Churchill deserves credit for having seen in 1919 the loss and danger to Europe involved in the isolation of a hostile Russia. It still remains doubtful, however, whether the policies in support of the White Russian counter-revolutionaries could ever have been successful, even if they had been conducted by the western European Governments with full unanimity and determination. Churchill himself in retrospect expressed some concern whether the White Russians could ever have won out against the Bolshevists. . . .

The attempt at intervention in Russia after World War I gave the Communist rulers in Moscow the chance to pose as the true defenders of the Russian "motherland." They have derived great strength from this role ever since. It was revealing that the Soviet Government appealed mainly to Russian national sentiment when it officially named the Russo-German war of

1941–45 the "great patriotic war." The Allied interventions in Russia after World War I, undertaken without any realistic plan, greatly helped to make the Bolshevist party appear as the trustee of the historic Russian state.

Lloyd George, like Woodrow Wilson, disliked the military intervention in Russia (they both believed that it would be as self-defeating as foreign intervention in the French Revolution had proved to be more than a century ago) and he wanted to initiate diplomatic negotiations. But in the end nothing decisive was done in 1919. . . . When, however, he resumed his appeal for peaceful relations with the Soviet Union at the Genoa Conference in 1922, it was already too late. Russia and Germany, the two chief opponents of the Paris settlement, had concluded the Treaty of Rapallo, which established, though originally on a tenuous basis, Russo-German co-operation.

The policy of half-hearted intervention was followed by the lukewarm policy of the *cordon sanitaire*. This policy represented the open admission of the inability of the Western powers to influence the course of Russian internal affairs except by increasing the difficulties first of the stabilization and then of the forced expansion of the Russian economy. It must be added, however, that the policy of the *cordon sanitaire* contributed to the defeat of early Soviet attempts to turn the Russian Revolution into a world revolution, although events like the German recovery in the mid-twenties and the anti-Communist turn of the revolution in China were undoubtedly more important.

The failure to integrate Russia in some fashion into a European system created serious uncertainties about the future of the Continent. To be sure, for about a decade or more after the revolution, Russia was too weak to exercise any strong direct influence on Europe beyond the ideological impact of the Third International. But the existence of an independent Communist Russian state that controlled an international political movement made the whole European settlement unsafe. The Communist movement intensified everywhere the social unrest that followed in the wake of the peace settlement of Paris, and the Russian state encouraged every nation willing to resist the peace treaties of 1919.

. . . The new Soviet state grew up in isolation, yet it could not fail to exercise a disruptive influence upon the European order created in Paris, the more so since Moscow ruled not only the Russian empire, now being quickly industrialized and unified in all its parts, but also the international Communist movement.

That the Paris settlement did not become a world settlement was also owing to the withdrawal of the United States from Woodrow Wilson's great design. This withdrawal was not caused by popular dissatisfaction with the treatment meted out by the Paris peace treaties to the vanquished enemies. In so far as the Senate's opposition was more than a display of partisan spirit, it centered around the fear of seeing the United States sucked into an international system whose obligations—if they were clearly understood at all— were dreaded by many Americans. In retrospect it may be asked whether Wilson's adamant insistence on the American ratification of the full Covenant showed good political judgment. Probably even an amended and watered-down Covenant acceptable to the United States Senate would have been preferable to a Covenant rejected by it, since the United States could then have been kept in contact with the unfolding European situation.

But even the rejection of the Covenant by the United States might not have been a major catastrophe if America had backed the Mutual Assistance Pact for the Rhine settlement. . . . From both an American and a universal point of view, it would have been desirable to have the United States join in the establishment of a world organization for the maintenance of peace; but an American guarantee of the crucial western European frontiers could have been equally decisive. In the fierce party struggle between the President and the Senate both possibilities were lost, and the subsequent neglect of international affairs makes one wonder whether or not the American people would in any case have given their support to international commitments for any length of time.

The United States withdrew from world affairs in 1920 as suddenly as it had appeared on the world scene three years before. This retreat was not complete, since the United States continued to care about a settlement of Far Eastern issues and was soon drawn again into some sort of co-operation with the European powers in financial matters. Prior to 1914, the United States had been a debtor nation—that is, foreign investments in America outbalanced American investments abroad. The liquidation of European holdings in America, however, and the big American loans to the European Allies during World War I and in the armistice period made the United States the chief creditor nation, which it has remained ever since. In the period between 1920 and 1933 the country was concerned about its European loans and investments, which greatly increased after 1925, when a seemingly stabilized Europe appeared to offer splendid opportunities for American surplus capital.

Even so, the United States after 1920 felt that it could return to its nineteenth-century insularity. Its isolationism became economic as well as diplomatic. . . . Indeed, all postwar tariffs, of which the American tariffs were only the most outstanding examples, tended to aim at a restoration of the prewar pattern of world economy. But this economy had been irrevocably changed by the World War; Europe could pay her debts to America only if she were allowed to send her products and goods to the United States.

Europe after 1920 was left alone to cope with her political problems. It appeared at once doubtful that she would be able to do so. Quite apart from the great financial and economic questions, which could have been solved only by world-wide arrangements, the whole European scene as envisaged by the peacemakers while they still acted in concert was drastically changed by America's withdrawal. France was immediately affected. She had foregone her demands for a separation of the Rhineland in exchange for an Anglo-American guarantee of the demilitarization of the left bank of the Rhine. The great French concessions at the Peace Conference now seemed to have been made in vain.

France was particularly alarmed by the British refusal to sign the mutual guarantee pact. It was true that the Anglo-French treaty as drafted in Paris depended on the willingness of the United States to subscribe to a parallel treaty. The British decision to drop the treaty was no breach of promise, but it was a grave error of judgment. The Rhine was the natural defense line of Britain as much as of France, as World War I had abundantly shown. If Britain declined to co-operate without reservation in the defense of the Rhine, the French had reasons to distrust the good intentions or the good judgment of British policy. Were the British, once they had achieved the full realization of their war aims—the destruction of Germany as a naval and colonial power—determined to leave the Continent unprotected? France therefore proceeded to build up a system of alliances with the eastern European states. . . .

Actually, France was not in a position to uphold the treaties by her own strength, but in the years immediately following the War she seemed stronger than she really was. The postwar depression, which affected the United States and Britain very severely, hardly touched France, owing to the reconstruction work going on in the war-devastated French provinces. Moreover, although at the end of 1918 the British army and airforce were probably stronger than the French services, British armed strength was dissolved with amazing speed. . . .

The inequality in mobilized military strength added to the air of unreality that surrounded Franco-British relations in the early years after the War. The two powers even indulged in unfriendly squabbles in the Near East. But the French were chiefly worried by the thought that with the return to a small professional army the British would be incapable of assisting them in gaining security—for them the real prize of the War. France wished to see any future war fought east of the French borders and brought to a quick decision there. If Germany could invade France again or if a war should last long enough to enable Germany to mobilize her superior manpower and industrial potential, France would be destroyed again. A simple promise by Britain, as finally offered by Lord Curzon in 1922, that she would consider any German violation of the demilitarization of the Rhineland an act of aggression seemed to Frenchmen an inadequate insurance as long as Britain did not provide military forces ready to act instantaneously with the French army in case of any threat.

Poincaré between 1922 and 1924 attempted to employ the preponderant might of France for the achievement of a European position in which France would no longer have to rely on British support. The occupation of the Ruhr in January, 1923, was undertaken to make Germany pay reparations, or, in the case of German opposition, to secure the productive resources that would recompense France. In spite of German "passive resistance" French policy was successful in finally forcing Germany to come to terms; but France, as a result of her exertions, was financially exhausted and could not impose her own conditions. American and British intervention instituted the Dawes Plan, which for a period of five years removed reparations from the agenda of European diplomacy. More important, France recognized that she could not conduct an independent European policy, but would have to act in close co-operation with Britain, even at the sacrifice of some French advantages and hopes.

It is doubtful that Britain after World War I had a clear conception of the future of Europe. In less than a year after the signing of the Treaty of Versailles she developed, if not a new European policy, at least a new attitude toward European problems. Britain had been severely jolted by her inability, in conjunction with her European allies, to bring the war against the Central Powers to a victorious conclusion. America's intervention had been necessary to decide the war, and the United States proposed to maintain thereafter a navy of a size equal to the British navy. The withdrawal of the United States from European affairs was profoundly alarming to Britain, and the new world situation seemed to make it unwise to assume international obligations as far-reaching as those she had accepted prior to 1914.

The strong support that Britain had received from her dominions during the War had created a warm feeling of unity among the members of the British Commonwealth of Nations, but the British dominions were even more deeply disturbed by America's refusal to join in the guarantee of the Paris settlement than Britain herself. They contributed to the watering down of the Convenant's provisions for automatic sanctions and kept warning Britain against involvement in the problems peculiar to Europe. . . . Actually, the policy of the British dominions went through an evolution toward collectivism in international affairs, largely as a reaction to Japanese and Italian expansionism.

Although the Commonwealth became after World War I sentimentally more important to Britain than the full participation in a European political system, obvious security needs and economic necessity made it impossible for her to withdraw from the European continent. European recovery was an absolute prerequisite for the restoration of a prosperous British economy, which, in turn, hinged on the revival of German productivity. At the same time, under the leadership of the great economic thinker John Maynard Keynes the British underwent a sudden and violent revulsion from the Paris Peace Treaties. Keynes' treatise *The Economic Consequences of the Peace Treaty,* brilliantly penned, produced an instantaneous and profound public reaction as few political pamphlets in history have ever achieved. Most British people soon agreed that the most serious problems "were not political or territorial but financial and economic, and that the perils of the future lay not in frontiers and sovereignties but in food, coal and transport." Yet this judgment was at best a dangerous half-truth; political security and economic prosperity were equally important and interdependent. . . . To the British people, who had achieved all their national war aims at the Paris Peace Conference, political questions may have appeared insignificant; but for France the safety of her eastern frontiers constituted the supreme cause of anxiety and she tended to disregard the economic future of Germany. We have seen already, however, how the consequences of the Ruhr invasion compelled the French to pay heed to the economic realities of Europe; the events of 1923–24 equally forced the British Government to modify its policy. Although the sudden dismay with the peace settlement as far as it applied to the Continent of Europe caused the British nation to assume a very critical attitude towards French policy, the official British opposition to the French defense of the peace treaties could never be of a radical nature. Britain, too, wanted to extract reparations from Germany. Moreover, Britain was in no position to police Europe and had to rely on the French army for the protection of the area of the Continent strategically most vital for British security, the Lowlands and northern France. The British Government found it wise in 1922 to offer to France in the place of the abortive Rhine pact of 1919 a guarantee of her eastern frontiers that Lord Curzon called "the outer frontiers" of

Britain. Britain felt so safe in these years that the British Foreign Secretary could call the proffered guarantee a gracious "gift" to France, although it did not offer any special British contribution to the maintenance of peace. Not even Anglo-French staff conversations comparable to those held before 1914 were contemplated. . . .

In these circumstances the French saw no advantage in the conclusion of the proposed Anglo-French treaty. They felt certain that in case of a German attack against the French frontiers Britain would be forced to come to the assistance of France, since British self-interest, created by geography rather than mere sympathy with France, would compel the British Government to adopt this course of action. Yet without prior agreement on joint military measures to be employed in such an event, both the Rhine and northern France might be overrun before British intervention could take place. The British army estimates of this period never envisaged the possible need for a British expeditionary force to be sent to the Continent. Small wonder the French were at a complete loss to understand why their political reasoning should be deemed overlogical in Britain.

THE SEARCH FOR EUROPEAN SECURITY

While these bilateral negotiations took place, another approach was chosen to explore solutions of the problem of security through the League of Nations. This policy was championed in Britain chiefly by the Liberal and Labor parties, though it had the support of some eminent members of the Conservative party, such as Lord Cecil. In this British school of thought, Wilson's ideas found faithful apostles and followers. They were convinced that bilateral and multilateral alliances would lead only to a new division of the world into armed camps, whereas world peace could be made secure only in a universal system that would establish and extend the rule of law. In order to avoid war it was necessary to eliminate its potential causes, which were found in various facts of international life—the differences between the "haves" and "have-nots," the political inequality of the victorious and vanquished nations of 1919. Above all, they thought, disarmament constituted the sure road to the general pacification of the world.

Frenchmen did not share the British belief in disarmament as a step to security. The League of Geneva was almost exclusively an Anglo-American brainchild. The French plan, defeated at the Paris Conference, and dubbed by Woodrow Wilson "international militarism," aimed at assembling preponderant military power against any nation that would challenge the European order established by the Paris peace treaties. After America's refusal to join, France was even more determined to turn the League into an armed organization for the defense of the *status quo*. . . .

Germany could not hope for more than co-operation with the western European powers, which, at least for economic and financial reasons, was highly desirable; but she could hope for more power in the east. Her strongest resentment against the Versailles Treaty, indeed, arose from its eastern provisions, especially those concerning the Polish corridor and Danzig, but also those affecting Austria. For eastern Europe seemed to offer opportunities for making political gains at not too distant a date. The new states were weak without exception, and in their rear there loomed the Russian colossus; since this colossus was not yet firmly on its feet, Germany could assume leadership in Russo-German co-operation, which had begun with the Rapallo Treaty of 1922.

British policy towards eastern Europe was never certain after World War I. . . . In a conversation with Aristide Briand at Downing Street in December, 1921, Lloyd George said that

the British people were not very much interested in what happened on the eastern frontier of Germany; they would not be ready to be involved in quarrels which might arise regarding Poland or Danzig or Upper Silesia. On the contrary, there was a general reluctance to get mixed up in these questions in any way.

And then, in language closely akin to the tenor of Neville Chamberlain's statement of 1938 on Czechoslovakia as "that far-away country," he added:

The British people felt that the populations of that quarter of Europe were unstable and excitable; they might start fighting at any time and the rights and wrongs of the dispute might be very hard to disentangle. He did not think, therefore, that his country would be disposed to give any guarantees which might involve them in military operations in any eventuality in that part of the world.

These words reflected correctly not only British popular sentiment but also the unwillingness of the British Government of the interwar period to lead public opinion toward a recognition of the crucial role of the eastern states for the future of Europe. This negative attitude prevailed in Britain till 1939 and led, logically enough, to the consideration of Germany as the major bulwark of order west of the Rhine and worthy of receiving a certain freedom of action there. The British bewilderment over the eastern European conditions was a main reason for the reluctance of British diplomacy to participate actively in the protection of the security of the eastern European states.

The historical adviser to the British foreign office, Sir James Headlam-

Morley, in a remarkable and prophetic memorandum warned Sir Austen Chamberlain in February, 1925, that "the danger point in Europe" was not the Rhine but the Vistula, and he went on to inquire:

Has anyone attempted to realize what would happen if there were to be a new partition of Poland, or if the Czechoslovak state were to be so curtailed and dismembered that in fact it disappeared from the map of Europe? The whole of Europe would at once be in chaos. There would no longer be any principle, meaning or sense in the territorial arrangements of the continent. Imagine, for instance, that under some improbable condition, Austria rejoined Germany; that Germany using the discontented minority in Bohemia, demanded a new frontier far from the mountains, including Carlsbad and Pilsen, and that at the same time, in alliance with Germany, the Hungarians recovered the southern slope of the Carpathians. This would be catastrophic, and, even if we neglected to interfere in time to prevent it, we should afterwards be driven to interfere, probably too late.

Headlam-Morley argued that Great Britain could be defended only on the European Continent, irrespective of the fact that she formed at the same time the center of a world-wide empire. England had always been a part of the European political system, and most certainly so in her great days—those of Elizabeth, Cromwell, Chatham, Pitt, Castlereagh, Canning, Palmerston, Salisbury, Lansdowne, and Grey. The British historian was also right in calling it the supreme achievement of statesmanship in the first half of the nineteenth century that France was brought back to the councils of the great European powers, without being allowed to upset the order of Europe established by the Congress of Vienna. He recommended analogous concessions to Germany, particularly by a revision of reparations, but warned the British statesmen not to give Germany the chance to wreck the basic arrangements of the Paris settlement. Such sabotage would be possible, he correctly predicted, if the new eastern European states were left without general protection and if Germany were permitted to co-operate with Russia against them.

But British diplomacy, in line with prevailing public opinion in England, chose a different course. Sir Austen Chamberlain, in spite of his strong personal sympathies for France and his suspicions of Germany, was swayed by the general sentiment that Britain could and should avoid continental entanglements except for limited commitments made for the security of the English Channel. By confining British guarantees at Locarno to western Europe, Britain gave the impression that she was willing to tolerate changes in eastern Europe, in contrast to the declared French policy.

The idea of concluding a Franco-Belgian-German pact reaffirming the Rhine settlement of Versailles and placing this pact under an Anglo-Italian guarantee originated largely in Germany. Germany was anxious to forestall any future repetition of a French invasion of the Ruhr and also to create the basis for the withdrawal of the Allied occupation forces from the Rhineland. It was obvious, however, that the Germany of 1925 could not hope to achieve revisions of the sections of the Peace Treaty of Versailles applying to the Rhine except with regard to the occupation terms, and the German foreign minister Gustav Stresemann found a majority in support of his Locarno policy among the Germans largely because it was hoped that the treaty would open the gates for a revision of the Versailles Treaty in the East. To be sure, Germany had to sign arbitration treaties with Poland and Czechoslovakia, and France strengthened her own political ties with the two states by concluding alliances with them simultaneously with the signing of the Locarno Treaty of Mutual Guarantee [1925]. But the eastern security settlement was not reinforced by a British guarantee. Moreover, Germany, in a special protocol, was assured by the other Locarno powers that her co-operation in the defense of the League Covenant against a Russian infraction would take into account her "military situation" as well as "geographical situation." Germany was thus deliberately given great latitude to determine her relations with Russia without much reference to her League obligations. When in April, 1926, Germany concluded the Treaty of Berlin with the U.S.S.R., providing for neutrality in case of an unprovoked attack by other powers against either signatory, Stresemann could tell the Soviet Government that the question of whether or not the U.S.S.R. would be judged an aggressor by the League of Nations in the event of a conflict with a third state "could only be determined with binding force for Germany with her own consent."

The Locarno treaties and Germany's entrance into the League have often been described as the apogee of the international system of 1919. In reality Locarno did not create a secure foundation of a European peace. It covered up certain deep cracks that had appeared in the building, but failed to repair the structural weaknesses. It would have been desirable, and in any case unobjectionable, to make concessions to Germany between 1924 and 1930 in such matters as the occupation of the Rhineland and reparations. Probably much more should have been done to enable the young German democracy to develop under favorable conditions. But it was absolutely essential for Britain and France to keep control of any changes in Germany's position in Europe. Any revision of the Versailles Treaty should have been sought by procedures of international law and multilateral agreement and by the determined refusal of unilateral *faits accomplis*. It was a tragic fallacy to believe that eastern Europe could be neglected politically and economically without courting the gravest dangers. . . .

The fragile nature of the political conditions of Europe was further endangered by the pious hope that international disarmament by itself constituted a means for the creation of greater security. Large sections of the British people entertained this expectation with an almost religious fervor, and America gave their aspirations strong moral support. But in spite of the idealism of these sentiments, which deserved respect, they were utterly incapable of improving the actual political conditions of Europe. There disarmament could only mean the disarmament of the victors and new strength for Germany. In the absence of ready and fully equipped armed forces elsewhere, the superior industrial and manpower resources of Germany were bound to become even higher trumps than they were before. It would even have been preferable to raise the level of German armaments by international agreement, rather than demand the curtailment of the French army.

In most cases, disarmament was claimed to be the cure of Europe's political ills by the very people who wanted all nations to accept the rule of international law. But they did not admit what is a truism in national life, that unenforceable law becomes a mockery of justice. Who was to protect the eastern states against Germany or against a revived Russia? Who was to defend western Europe, including the Lowlands and Great Britain, against the onrush of a remilitarized Germany, possibly abetted by Russia. Only one lonely European statesman warned the world that the French army was the single stabilizing factor in Europe and that "the sudden weakening of that factor of stability . . . might open floodgates of measureless consequences in Europe at the present time, might break the dyke and 'Let the boundless deep/Down upon far off cities while they dance—/or dream.' "

But the British people were not inclined to listen to Winston Churchill in those years. From 1926 to 1934, first on the Preparatory Commission for the Disarmament Conference, then at the Disarmament Conference itself, which started its sessions in Geneva in 1932, steady pressure was brought on France to decrease her armaments. Even after Hitler's accession to power, Ramsay MacDonald pushed a disarmament plan that would have equalized French and German armed strength. France in British eyes appeared petulant in her insistence upon a system of general security or at least upon international arms inspection as preconditions of a further reduction of armaments. The result of all the disarmament discussions in the interwar period was the further discredit of the peace settlement of 1919 and the psychological preparation of a large segment of world opinion for German rearmament. . . .

By hindsight it is easy to say that the years between 1925 and 1930 were the years in which Europe could have been reconstituted, not as an entirely self-contained political system, but as a strong powerblock in world politics if the beginnings of co-operation between Britain, France, and Germany had been carried to a full understanding on all the major issues of Europe. Such a firm understanding among the three powers could also have led to a common program for the strengthening of the eastern European states. Britain, however, was not willing to consider additional commitments in Europe. Perhaps Germany and France could have acted alone, disregarding the British sensitiveness to separate Franco-German co-operation; but Germany felt that France would never voluntarily make those concessions that Germany considered her due and that France was aiming exclusively at bolstering the *status quo*. Briand's proposal for the formation of a European Federal Union, first broached in 1929, was too vague and did not contain special concessions that might have won over Germany. Britain poured cold water on the plan, while Germany at first took a reserved attitude. Later, in March, 1931, the German Government used the idea of a European federation as a cloak for the Austro-German customs union, judged by France to be a unilateral revision of the Paris settlement rather than a step in the direction of a European federation. By then the chance for real understanding was gone.

The five years after 1925 gave Europe a last Indian summer before the blizzard of the world economic crisis struck in 1931. Nobody foresaw that Europe, politically and economically, lived on borrowed time. Once confidence had been restored, Europe showed her vigor. By 1925 most nations of Europe had achieved their prewar production levels, and in the subsequent five years the expansion of European production proceeded at a faster rate than that of American production during the boom period. Most startling was Germany's progress. In 1919 her industrial production was only one third of what it had been in 1913. By 1922 a considerable recovery had taken place in spite of the instability of the German currency, which was not the result of German reparation payments, as is so often asserted, but of the inability of the German Republic to put its finances in order. The decision to meet the French invasion of the Ruhr by passive resistance and to cover the bill by the printing of money led to the German hyperinflation that was stopped only at the end of 1923, and in that year German industrial production fell again to 40 per cent of the 1913 figure. But in 1924 Germany doubled her output, and by 1927 she had reached her prewar position and resumed her place as the chief industrial country of Europe.

Another aspect of these five years was the ease with which Europe as a whole rebuilt her trading position, even though, while Europe had been at war, the overseas countries, primarily the United States but also other nations such as Japan, had greatly expanded their productive capacity. Higher world production seemed to find a greater world market. It was not recognized that the market conditions were largely the result of the credit expansion caused by American capital looking for profitable investment. The foreign capital issues publicly offered in the United States between 1920 and 1931 amounted to 11.6 billion dollars, of which Europe received 40 per cent, Canada almost 29, and Latin America 22 per cent. In Europe, American capital was augmented by British, Swiss, and Dutch funds. Germany in the six years between 1924 and 1929 received from all these countries more than 4 billion dollars, about half of these funds coming from the United States and constituting a greater grant of foreign funds than the rest of the world received in those years.

The economic expansion of credit thus made it possible to postpone the adjustment to the structural changes of the world economy produced by the war. For the same reason a realistic financial settlement of the World War could be delayed for many years. The Dawes Plan of 1924 had set up a payment schedule of German reparations without, however, revising the original total sum demanded by the Allies in 1921. The stillborn Young Plan of 1929, announced as the final reparation settlement on the eve of the big crash, once again evaded the most fundamental political problems. Germany, beginning in 1926, paid 10,333 million German marks as reparations, which was a little less than two and a half billion dollars. But the transfer of German funds could not have been made if private American loans had not gone to Germany at the same time. The Allies in turn used these sums to service their American loans or war debts. Winston Churchill called this system "insane."

Once the bubble burst and it dawned upon the world that there had been general overproduction and overinvestment, the American Government preferred virtually to stop all intergovernmental debts, reparations, and inter-Allied obligations in order to save the American private loans that more directly affected the American banking situation. President Hoover proposed in 1931 a holiday of reparation and inter-Allied debt payments. In 1932 at the Conference of Lausanne reparations were actually buried. But at that time Germany was already determined not only to demand a radical revision of the Paris settlement in her favor but to force a full reversal of the historic decisions of World War I.

4. THE GREAT DEPRESSION AND THE THIRTIES

The capitalist economic system was a delicate and interlocking mechanism, in which any disturbance was rapidly transmitted with accelerating impact through all the parts. For many basic commodities prices were determined by the free play of supply and demand in a world-wide market. There was much regional division of labor; large areas lived by producing a few specialized articles for sale to the world as a whole. A great deal of production, both local and international, especially in the 1920's, was financed by credit, which is to say by promises of repayment in the future. The system rested upon mutual confidence and mutual exchange—on the belief of the lender, creditor, or investor that he would get his money back, on the belief of the borrower that he could pay his debts, on the ability of farms and factories to market their products at prices high enough to bring a net return, so that farmers and factory people might purchase the output of other factories and farms, and so on round and round in countless circles of mutual interdependence, and throughout the world as a whole.

The five years after 1924 were a period of prosperity, in that there was a good deal of international trade, building and development of new industries. The automobile, for example, still an oddity in 1914, became an article of mass production after the war; and its widespread use increased the demand for oil, steel, rubber, and electrical equipment, caused the building or re-building of tens of thousands of miles of roads, and created whole new secondary occupations for thousands of men as truck-drivers, garage mechanics, or filling-station attendants. Similarly the mass consumption of radios and moving pictures had repercussions in all directions. The ensuing expansion was most phenomenal in the United States, but almost all countries enjoyed it in greater or lesser degree. "Prosperity" became a mystic term, and some thought that it would last indefinitely, that the secret of human plenty had been found, and that progress, science and invention were at last realizing the hopes of ages.

But there were weaknesses in this prosperity, various imperfections in this or that gear or valve of the mechanism, flaws which, under stress, were to bring the whole intricate structure to a halt. The expansion was largely financed by credit, or borrowing. Laboring people received less than a balanced share; wages lagged behind profits and dividends, so that mass purchasing power, even when inflated by installment buying (another form of credit) could not absorb the vast output that it was technically possible to produce. And throughout the world the whole decade of the 1920's was a time of chronic agricultural depression, so that farmers could neither pay their debts nor purchase manufactures to the degree required for the smooth functioning of the system.

During the war wheat fields under cultivation in Europe were reduced by a fifth. The world price of wheat went up, and farmers in the United States, Canada, and elsewhere increased their acreage. Often, to acquire land at high prices, they gave mortgages which in later years they were unable to repay. After the war Europe restored its own wheat production, and Eastern Europe re-entered the world market. Agriculture was increasingly mechanized. Where, in the nineteenth century, one man could cut ten times as much grain with a single horse-drawn reaper as with a scythe, and where, before 1914, he could cut fifty times as much with a combined reaper and binder, he could again increase his output fivefold after the war, by using a tractor-drawn harvester-thresher combine. At the same time dry farming opened up new land, and agronomic science increased the yield per acre. The result of all these numerous developments was a superabundant output of wheat. But the demand for wheat was what economists call "inelastic"; by and large, within the area of the Western World, people already ate as much bread as they wanted, and would buy no more; and the undernourished masses of Asia, which in pure theory could have consumed the excess, could not pay even low costs of production or transportation. The world price of wheat fell incredibly. In 1930 a bushel of wheat, in terms of gold, sold for the lowest price in four hundred years.

Wheat-growers in all continents were faced with ruin. Growers of many other crops faced the same dismal prospect. Cotton and corn, coffee and cocoa all collapsed. Brazilian and African planters were caught by overproduction and falling prices. In Java, where not only had the acreage in sugar been extended, but the unit yield of sugar from the cane had multiplied ten times under scientific cultivation over the past century, the bottom dropped out of prices in the world market. There were indeed other and more profitable forms of agricultural production—for example in oranges and eggs, of which world consumption was steadily growing. But the coffee planter could not shift to eggs, nor the Iowa farmer to oranges. Not to mention the requirements of climate, the ordinary farmer or peasant lacked the capital, the special knowledge, or the access to refrigerated transportation that these newer branches of agriculture demanded. For the one thing that the average farmer or peasant knew how to do—grow wheat and other cereals—the new wonderful world of science and machinery had too little place.

The acute phase of the great depression, which began in 1929, was made much worse by this chronic background of agricultural distress, since there was no reserve of purchasing power on the farms. Contrariwise the farmer's plight became even worse when the city people, struck by depression in industry, cut down their expenditures for food. Agricultural depression, rather than industrial depression, was at the bottom of widespread troubles in the inter-war years throughout Eastern Europe and the colonial world.

The depression, in the strict sense, began as a stock-market and financial crisis. Prices of stocks had been pushed upward by years of continuing expansion and high dividends. At the beginning of 1929 prices on the European stock exchanges began to weaken. But the real crisis, or turning point, came with the crash on the New York Stock Exchange in October 1929. Here values had been driven to fantastic heights by excessive speculation. Not only professional speculators, but quite ordinary people, in the United States, as an easy way to make a good deal of money, bought stock with borrowed funds. Sometimes, trading on "margin," they "owned" five or ten times as much stock as the amount of their own money put into it; the rest they borrowed from brokers, and the brokers borrowed from banks. With money so easy to obtain, people pushed up stock prices by bidding against each other, and enjoyed huge fortunes on paper; but if prices fell, even a little, the hapless owners would be obliged to sell their stock to pay off the money they had borrowed. Hence, the weakening of values on the New York Stock Exchange set off uncontrollable tidal waves of selling, which drove stock prices down irresistibly and disastrously. In a month stock values dropped by forty per cent, and in three years, from 1929 to 1932, the average value of fifty industrial stocks traded on the New York Stock Exchange dropped from 252 to 61. In these same three years five thousand American banks closed their doors.

The crisis passed from finance to industry, and from the United States to the rest of the world. The export of American capital came to an end; Americans not only ceased to invest in Europe, but sold the foreign securities that they had. This pulled the foundations from under the post-war revival of Germany, and hence indirectly of much of Europe. Americans, their incomes falling, ceased to buy foreign goods; from Belgium to Borneo people saw their American markets slip away, and prices tumbled. In 1931 the failure of a leading Vienna bank, the *Creditanstalt,* sent a wave of shivers, bankruptcies, and business calamities over Europe. Everywhere business firms and private people could not collect what was owed them, or even draw on money that they thought they had in the bank. They could not buy, and so the factories could not sell. Factories slowed down or closed entirely. Between 1929 and 1932, the latter year representing the depth of the depression, world production is estimated to have declined by 38 per cent, and the world's international trade fell by two-thirds. In the United States the national income fell from 85 to 37 billion dollars.

Unemployment, a chronic disease ever since the war, now assumed the proportion of pestilence. In 1932 there were 30,000,000 unemployed persons statistically reported in the world; and this figure did not include the further millions who could find work only for a few hours in the week, or the masses in Asia or Africa for whom no statistics were to be had. The worker's wages were gone, the farmer's income now touched bottom; and the decline of mass purchasing power forced more idleness of machinery and more unemployment. Men in the prime of life spent years out of work. Young men could not find jobs or establish themselves in an occupation. Skills and talents of older people grew rusty, young people found no opportunity to learn. Millions were reduced to living, and supporting their families, on the pittances of charity, doles, or relief. Great modern cities saw an outburst of sidewalk-art, in which, at busy street corners, jobless able-bodied men drew pictures on the pavement with colored chalk, in the hope of attracting a few sixpences or dimes. People were crushed in spirit by a feeling of uselessness; months and years of fruitless job-hunting left them demoralized, bored, discouraged, embittered, frustrated, and resentful. Never had there been such waste, not merely of machinery which now stood still, but of the trained and disciplined labor force on which all modern societies were built. And people chronically out of work naturally turned to new and disturbing political ideas.

Optimists at the time, of whom President Hoover in the United States was one, declared that this depression, though a severe one, was basically only another periodic low point in the business cycle, or alternation of expansion and contraction, which had ebbed and flowed in the Western World for over a century. Prosperity, they plaintively said, was "just around the corner." Others felt that the crisis represented the breakdown of the whole system of capitalism and free private enterprise; these people, in many cases, looked for signs of the future in the planned economy then being introduced in Soviet Russia. There was something in both views. After 1932, in part for purely cyclical reasons—because the depression cut down indebtedness, and reduced the costs of doing business—it again became possible to produce and sell. World steel production, for example, which had stood at 121 million tons in 1929, and then collapsed to 50 million in 1932, by 1936 again reached 122 million. (To what degree revival was due to armament building is debated.) On the other hand, the great depression did put an end to the old economic system in the old sense. Even if such a stricken economy had internal powers of full recuperation after a few years, still people would not stand for such terrifying insecurity in their personal lives. The horrors of mass unemployment were long remembered.

All governments took steps to provide work and incomes for their people. All, in one way or another, strove to free themselves from dependency on the uncertainties of the world market. The interlocking world economy collapsed both from the depression itself and from the measures adopted to cure it. The most marked consequence of the depression was a strong movement toward economic nationalism—toward greater self-sufficiency within the sphere which each government could hope to control.

The internationalism of money, the gold standard and the free convertibility of currencies one into the other, were gradually abandoned. Countries specializing in agricultural exports were among the first to be pinched; agricultural prices were so low that even a large quantity of exports failed to produce enough foreign currency to pay for needed imports; hence the exporting country's currency fell in value. The currencies of Argentina, Uruguay, Chile, Australia, and New Zealand all depreciated in 1929 and 1930. Then came the turn of the industrial countries. England, as the depression went on, could not sell enough exports to pay for imports. It had to pay for imports in part by sending gold out of the country; thus the gold reserve supporting the pound sterling declined, and people who had pounds sterling began to convert their pounds into dollars or other currencies for which they thought the gold basis was more secure. This was known, in the poetic language of economics, as the "flight from the pound." In 1931 Great Britain went off the gold standard, which is to say that it devaluated the pound. The Briton or foreigner holding pounds sterling now could not get gold at all; he could use his sterling to buy British goods, or he could convert it to dollars or francs at depreciated rates. A pound was now worth a smaller number of dollars, or, contrariwise, fewer dollars (francs, marks, pesos, etc.) sufficed to buy a pound sterling. Hence other peoples were better able to buy British goods; one purpose of devaluation was in fact to restore Britain's export trade. But after Britain devaluated, some twenty-odd other countries, to protect their own exports and their own industries, did the same. Hence somewhat the same relative position reappeared. Even the United States, which possessed most of the world's gold supply, abjured the gold standard and devaluated the dollar in 1933. The purpose was mainly to help American farmers, for with dollars cheaper in terms of foreign currencies, foreigners could afford to buy more American agricultural products. But it became harder for foreigners to sell to the United States.

Hence the depression, adding its effects to those of the World War and post-war inflation, led to chaos in the international monetary exchanges. Governments manipulated their currencies to uphold their sagging exports. Or they imposed definite exchange controls: they required that foreigners from whom their own people purchased, and to whom they thus gave their own currency, should use this currency to buy from them in return. Trade, which had been multilateral, became increasingly "bilateral." That is, where a Brazilian importer of steel, for example, had formerly bought steel wherever he wished, at such price or of such quality as he preferred, he now had to obtain steel, often regardless of price or precise quality, from a country to which Brazil had sold enough of its own products to make payment possible. Sometimes, notably in the relations between Germany and East European countries in the 1930's, bilateralism degenerated into actual barter. The Germans would exchange a certain number of cameras with Yugoslavia in return for a certain number of pigs. In such cases the very conception of a market disappeared.

Currency control was one means of keeping one's own factories from idleness, by holding or capturing export markets in time of depression. Another way of keeping one's own factories going (or farms, or mines, or quarries) was to shut out competitive imports by the old device of protective tariffs. The United States, hit by depression in 1929, enacted the unprecedentedly high Hawley-Smoot tariff in 1930. Other countries, equally or more distressed, now could sell less to America, and hence buy less American goods. Other countries likewise raised their own tariffs, in the desperate hope of reserving national markets for their own people. Even Great Britain, citadel of free trade in the nineteenth century, turned to protectionism. It likewise revived and adopted Joseph Chamberlain's old idea of an imperial tariff-union, when in 1932, by the Ottawa agreements, Britain and the British Dominions adopted a policy of having lower tariffs against one another than against the world outside. Thus the British manufacturers strove to hold a privileged market in the empire, and the harassed wheat-growers of Canada, or wool-growers of Australia, tried to assure themselves of a reliable outlet in Great Britain.

Even tariffs were not always enough. Quotas or quantitative restrictions were adopted in many states. By this system a government said in effect, not merely that goods brought into the country must pay a high tariff duty, but that above a certain amount no goods could be brought in at all. Increasingly both importers and exporters worked under government licenses, in order that a country's entire foreign trade could be centrally planned and managed. Such methods approached those of the Soviet Union, which asserted a government monopoly of all foreign trade, exported only in order to finance imports, and determined, without the bother of tariffs, the exact quantity of imported commodities that it would take.

Thus the world economy disintegrated into fiercely competing national economic systems. In the oceanic wreckage of the great depression, each state tried to create an island of economic security for its own people. Even before the great depression the new states of Eastern Europe, and such other new states as the Turkish republic, had surrounded themselves with tariffs in order to make themselves more modern, industrial, Western or up-to-date. This process, by depriving the older industrial countries of former markets, had in fact been one cause of depression. Now, with the depression, old and established industrial countries also retreated within their own borders. There were, indeed, attempts to break down the rising barriers, to unfreeze a world economy that was congealing into separate national blocks. An International Monetary and Economic Conference met at London in 1933. It attempted to open the clogged channels of world trade; but it ended in failure because each national delegation was afraid to entrust its people to the ups and downs of a world market. Plans to stabilize the exchange rates of various currencies were especially blocked by the attitude of the United States. Since the vast lending and purchasing power of the United States made it the world's economic center of gravity, the unwillingness of the United States at this time to take part in international economic reconstruction reinforced the trend to economic nationalism everywhere else.

Everywhere the demand was for security. Each state tried to live economically, so far as possible, within itself. Each, increasingly regulating, controlling, guiding, planning or rescuing its own economic system, tried to be as little influenced as possible by the unpredictable behavior of other states, or by the free rise and fall of prices in an uncontrolled world market. On the one hand this trend advanced the principles of the welfare state and social democracy; it protected the individual against the worst evils of unemployment and destitution. But on the other hand the same economic trend became one aspect of the totalitarianism which spread alarmingly in the 1930's.

Chapter XIV

TOTALITARIAN LIFE AND POLITICS

❦

1. THE WAYS OF DICTATORSHIP

IN WHAT RESPECT ALL DICTATORSHIPS ARE ALIKE

DICTATORSHIP . . . severs the state from the community, and never more so than when it proclaims the two to be one. Every other kind of government conforms to a pattern somehow sanctioned within its proper community. Every other kind is constitutional, in the sense that the succession to power is predetermined under a fundamental law which the acceding government does not make or break. Every other kind is in this sense *legitimate*. Dictatorship alone makes its sheer will the sole justification of its authority. At all stages of society men have been concerned with the source of authority, finding it in the community or in the will of God or in sanctified tradition. Dictatorship sweeps aside all such concern. Its own being is the only answer it permits.

Dictatorship ignores the community. The order it sets up is not harnessed to the communal frame of order. It arrogates to itself complete independence from that frame. It has no abiding rules, no fundamental laws. Its own law is always that of the hour. There is no law, or basis of law, beneath it. The will of the dictator is untrammeled by legal processes. No law has any higher status than his mere decree. There is no social ground on which his pronouncement of justice rests. The social firmament is denied and in its place there is only the changeful expression of an arbitrary definition of right. Dictatorship characteristically comes into being when the social order is shaken or broken, in the time of crisis when men forsake their traditions, in the time of desperate conflict when men are willing to sacrifice much if only the strong man restores to them assurance and order. In such times they aban-

---

This chapter consists of material by two different authors. Section 1 is from *The Web of Government* (pp. 225–66, New York, The Macmillan Co., 1947), by Robert M. MacIver. Section 2 is from *A History of the Modern World* (pp. 736–50; New York, Alfred A. Knopf, Inc., 1952), by R. R. Palmer.

don the accepted standards of legality. This antithesis between dictatorship and legality has been recognized since the days of the Greek city-state. An unknown Sophist wrote during the Peloponnesian War that disregard for law is the way of dictatorship.

The coming of dictatorship is usually abrupt. It represents a sharp break from tradition. Consequently it is where the ground is to some extent being prepared for democracy that the conditions most congenial to dictatorship develop. When a people is strongly bound by tradition the crises of the state do not affect the form of government but rather the residence of power. There are *coups d'état,* palace revolutions, changes of dynasty, but the old system lives on. The class structure resists any genuine revolution. Where the class structure is itself challenged the hold of tradition is already weakened. Then democracy becomes possible. But democracy . . . requires a process of maturation. The resistances may be too strong for its peaceful evolution, or the contentions between classes or between ethnic, religious, or other groups may be too irreconcilable for orderly settlement. A crisis occurs. The old legality cannot be restored and the people is unready for the alternative of democracy. That is the type of situation in which dictatorship has its birth.

In this manner dictatorship appeared in Ancient Athens, shortly after a degree of democracy was inaugurated under Solon. In the civic dissension that ensued the first known Athenian "tyrant," Pisistratus, having professed himself an extreme democrat, seized the reins of power. Similar phenomena occurred in a large number of Greek cities, so that the seventh and sixth centuries before Christ became known as "the age of the tyrants." It was after the hereditary kings had been deprived of authority, when unstable oligarchies failed to win the allegiance of this first people ever to break on a grand scale with the tradition of class rule. So, in Corinth and Syracuse and Argos and in the cities of Asia Minor and of Sicily, the "tyrants" arose, forceful men who sometimes ruled well and sometimes ill, who sometimes brought order and sometimes only new troubles, but who alike resorted to unconstitutional means to gain or to maintain their power. In Rome likewise, in the later days of the Republic, the framework of an outmoded city-state democracy was too narrow to restrain the strife between opposing factions, led by men who, as generals and as proconsuls over large territories, were habituated to imperial authority. So the soldier Marius, son of a day-laborer, followed Caius Gracchus and attempted to overthrow the constitution. He in turn was followed by Sulla and Pompey and Caesar, until Augustus came and brought the Republic to its close.

Before we leave Rome we should observe that while the name "dictator" originated there the institution to which the name was given falls outside the category of dictatorship in its modern usage. The Roman dictatorship was a constitutional device under which the constitution was suspended during a grave crisis of the state. The Roman city-state government was ill adapted to cope with any sudden emergency, such as an invasion or a conspiracy. It was a peculiarly elaborate magistracy, with its two co-equal consuls, its plethora of other officials, its senate, and its three kinds of public assembly. From very early times the constitution made provision by which the government could suspend the authority of the magistrates and nominate a single person, usually a general, to take control of affairs during a crisis. The dictator was the trustee of the state and when his mission was ended had to give account of his trusteeship. There were many such dictators in the earlier period, and none held power for more than six months. Cincinnatus returning to his plow became the exemplar of the office. After the wars with Hannibal the institution fell into abeyance, though the senate claimed the right to establish a kind of martial law, advising the magistrates under a special formula to "see to it that no harm befell the republic." In B.C. 82 Sulla forced the senate to nominate him dictator, taking the old name, but destroying the old meaning. Constitutionality was at an end.

With the Middle Ages the reign of tradition was restored. The myth of authority took on its most impressive character, responsive to some profound need for a new basis of solidarity. In a new manner it bound up authority with the land, the earth men cultivated, while it invoked the highest heaven to sanction the union of the two. Tradition was so firmly restored that for a whole millennium there was little striving toward democracy and no sign of dictatorship. With the waning of that tradition democracy began to emerge, sporadically in the anti-feudal cities, more consistently in England. During one crisis in England, when a particularly severe break with tradition occurred, there appeared its only dictator, Oliver Cromwell. The breach was repaired at his death and after a period of reaction the democratic processes began again to operate. The next great break with tradition happened in France, where, as previously in England, a monarch was executed and where the demands for a complete and immediate democracy burst with the intensity of forces long pent in. The sequel was the dictatorship of Robespierre, followed by the dictatorship of Napoleon, though the latter sought to invest his regime in constitutional forms.

The nineteenth century became the great age of democratic expansion. Many conditions conspired to weaken the older myth of authority, including the remarkable advance of science and of technology, the spread of economic opportunity to hitherto subject classes, and the fusion and the clash of cultures. The process continued through a time of comparative peace, with few major crises. It was not until the great crises consequent on the First World War brought irreconcilable civil conflicts that dictatorships appeared again in Europe. Prior to this upheaval a series of dictatorships arose in the countries of Latin America. There the situation was very different, though it illustrated equally well the common principle. There too, with the dissolution of the status of colonial dependency, the old union of government and authoritarianism was rifted. The rift unloosed localized demands for democracy in countries socially and culturally unready for it. Dictatorial authority, often masquerading as democracy, took the vacant thrones.

The war-bred crises of Europe precipitated dictatorships in countries that had a brief or relatively brief experience of democracy. On the whole the countries where democracy was most fully developed or longest established resisted the impact, though some, particularly France, felt the pressure of it. The trend to dictatorship was strongly aided by the growth under crisis of the communist movement. The first of the new dictatorships was a communist one, and this unlooked-for fulfillment stimulated the extreme left in other countries, breaking the solidarity of the left against reaction from the right, and increasing the intransigence of the various conflicting groups. In many countries the demand for and the readiness to accept a dictatorship of the right were thereby greatly enhanced. With this aid Mussolini took advantage of democratic turmoil and nationalist dissatisfaction, winning an easy victory for fascism. With the same aid Horthy was able to seize power in Hungary in the first hour of its republicanism, and Franco in revolutionary Spain. With the same aid Germany, after a time of the severest stresses during which it was making experiment with its first really democratic constitution, was turned over to Hitler. Outside of Europe the chief manifestation of the same "law of dictatorship" was offered in China, where the long continuance of civil war and foreign invasion made negligible the chances of the promised democracy.

Germany offers a significant example of how the turnover to dictatorship may take place. Here there had been a fairly strong popular trend toward democracy, but the social structure remained under the control of the ancient myths. The prestige of the Junker class had on the whole survived the threat, the honorific role of the profession of arms quickly regained its social dominance, the traditional concepts of status still permeated social behavior. The cleavage depicted by Veblen, between the industrial masses who followed a rationalist ethic adapted to the conditions of modern technology and the upper stratum which clung to archaic feudal-militarist ideas, still survived. But now the outcome depended on the attitude of the middle classes. They had suffered most severely in the vicissitudes of the period after the First World War, and particularly because of the great inflation. They were at the same time strongly nationalist and deeply sensitive to Germany's humiliation in defeat. The spread of international communism alarmed the majority of them and when the German democratic front was broken by the policy of the Third International, the struggling republic, beset by many difficulties and lacking confident leadership, was endangered. The Hitler movement, expounding a combination of fervent nationalism and a specious small-bourgeois "socialism," found its opportunity. It failed in its first *coup d'état,* but when it built a strong ruthless organization and began to attract many more converts, important large industrialists, apprehensive of communism, threw their weight to its side. Since, moreover, its first and clearest objective was the rebuilding of Germany's military might it won the support of the officer class, and thus of the Junkers who, though not enamored of its methods or of its leadership, believed they could make it the instrument of their own purposes. The situation was thus prepared, and there remained only the question of the technique by which power should be seized. In this respect fortune favored the conspiracy against the republic. Hitler, without seeming affront to democratic processes, was appointed chancellor, and immediately destroyed the whole apparatus which had served him in his ascent to power.

A variation of this condition is found where the old traditions of social class have weakened but a new communist authoritarianism has taken some hold and disrupted or seriously challenged the democratic front. Always there is a state of tension, precipitated by a crisis, in which the immature democracy loses its common ground and falls at the mercy of whatever clique or insurgent group acquires most efficiently the techniques of gaining power. Always there is the strong ruthless leader and the compact inner organization that practises sporadic terrorism before it wins authority, institutionalizing this practice when once the dictator has been set up.

Hence every dictatorship conforms to a distinctive pattern consistent with the unconstitutional manner in which it seizes control and maintains its power. While dictatorship has certain features in common with other types of oligarchy—the elevation of the executive above the legislative and the consequent assimilation of the decree to the law, the insistence on political orthodoxy and the suppression of opinion unfavorable to the regime, and the general exaltation of the state effected through the investment of the ruler with sacrosanct majesty—it differs from them in some crucial respects. Because of its detachment from the community it sets up a graded hierarchy of power that does not correspond, as in other oligarchical systems, to the general hierarchy of social class. The head of the system is often a man of the people, as in Fascist Italy, in Nazi Germany, in Soviet Russia, and frequently in Latin-American dictatorships. Even where he is not so, where he represents a conservative counter-action, as in Spain under Franco, in Portugal under Carmona and Salazar, and in Hungary under Horthy, the ruler's lack of constitutionality compels him to depend on an organization of power that distributes place and prestige in a manner distinctly variant from that which prevailed under the older class structure.

This organization is the "party," the disciplined and highly selective membership of which is clearly demarcated from the rest of the population. Its discipline is maintained by the inner power structure. The typical modern dictatorship maintains a special guard as the core of the party together with a secret police system of some sort. Nazi Germany afforded the most elaborate example, with its black-uniformed Elite Guard (SS), its brownshirt Storm Troopers (SA), and its Secret State Police (Gestapo). Below these were various auxiliary and affiliated organizations, including cadres for the indoctrination of the young—the Hitler Youth, the Students' Association, and so forth. By such means, previously developed in Soviet Russia and in Fascist Italy, a vigilant and unremitting surveillance was maintained over every aspect of social life. The very necessity for such controls makes it impossible for the dictatorial regime to construct any road back to constitutionality. It is a fact of great significance that there remained in Nazi Germany a complete dualism of the all-controlling party and the formal organization of government, each with its separate staff, its separate machinery, and even its separate armed forces. In Soviet Russia a similar dualism is suggested by the contrast between the powerless President of the USSR and the all-powerful Secretary of the Party.

Here once more is revealed the fundamental difference between dictatorship and all other forms of government. It builds its own organizations, but they are not integrated into the associations that everywhere arise in the community. These new organizations, instead of being incorporated with the rest, merely control them from without, distorting them from their congenial modes of expression and of development where they are not suppressed altogether. Dictatorship is a system of governing that remains invincibly external to the social framework. It is a corollary of this fact that dictatorship can invent no constitutional device for the succession to dictatorial power. If it were to achieve any such device it would become legitimate and in so becoming would cease to be dictatorship.

THE LATIN-AMERICAN TYPE

The countries of Latin America, from Mexico to Argentina, afforded throughout the period of their colonial status a particularly tragic illustration of the way in which exploitative imperial government can be an instrument of ruin. Perhaps nowhere has there been a greater continuous spoliation and destruction of human life and of material resources than in these lands, up to the time of their liberation in the earlier part of the nineteenth century. The legacy of this reckless imperialism, under which native populations were everywhere turned into serfs, except for the Indian groups that found protection in unhealthy swamp lands, in the deep forests, and in the reaches of the great mountains, contributed largely to the conditions that explain the Latin-American type of dictatorship.

At the beginning of the nineteenth century these lands were all subject to Spain except for the great Portuguese colony of Brazil. The achievement of independence by the United States had been the first break in the colonial status of the whole American hemisphere, but while the United States provided an impressive precedent and later became the constitutional model for the countries of Latin America, its liberation from Europe had no immediate consequence in this respect south of the Rio Grande. The Latin-American countries were culturally detached from North America and wholly responsive to European influences. The French Revolution had some repercussions but the precipitant of the revolutionary movements was Napoleon's blow to the independence of Spain when he occupied it and set his brother on its throne. There ensued a series of bitter and almost anarchic wars for liberation, at the end of which the former colonial provinces became independent states, under leaders who grandiloquently proclaimed the principles of democracy.

But the achievement of democracy was another matter. On the one hand there was no cultural preparation. The mass of the people was illiterate. All the influences to which it had been subjected for centuries were authoritarian. The Church, which controlled what education there was, inculcated the authoritarian tradition. The new movements, stemming from the insurgent liberalism that arose in Western Europe, and for a time in Spain itself, scarcely touched the local life of countries where communications were primitive and geographical barriers formidable. On the other hand the economic conditions were unfavorable. A particularly backward variety of feudalism prevailed. Industrial development was negligible. The middle class was small, weak, with relatively little opportunity to give effective expression to its anti-feudal sentiments. The great land-owners held all the controls and over against them lay the serf population, living in abject poverty.

Thus the end of colonialism meant the beginning of ruthless struggles between detached ambitious leaders who attracted a personal following, mustered their forces, and made a violent bid for supremacy. Where they succeeded they set up their dictatorships, in the earlier period over provinces, later over whole countries. Their careers were mostly meteoric, like the rule of the ancient "priest of the grove,"

> The priest who slew the slayer
> And shall himself be slain.

Insurrection and civil war became endemic. Some countries suffered less than others. Brazil in particular found a relatively stable form of government as an independent empire ruled by a prince of Portugal, which endured through most of the nineteenth century. But elsewhere stability was conspicuously lacking. There was little, if any, relation between the democratic constitutions and the policies of the strong adventurers who had fought their way to power. They were mostly generals of "revolutionary" armies, men of the landowning class who had no conception of democratic methods and who could scarcely have adopted, under the conditions, such methods even had they so desired. The "cultural lag" between the professed principles of democracy and the authoritarian principles that governed the everyday life of very poor peasant populations was not to be overcome so easily. It could indeed be claimed that the unstable rule of dictators was the necessary apprenticeship for more democratic regimes which countries so backward economically and so unprepared socially had to pass through.

There were, as there still are, great differences between the countries of Latin America in size, in resources, in geographical character, in composition of population, and in degree of advancement. But they had a common culture superimposed on them, a common system of land tenure, a similar experience of slavery and serfdom, and they had a similar release from colonialism—save for the relatively small Guianas. One legacy of Spanish or Portuguese imperialism lay heavily on them all. The conqueror had been an exploiter without becoming himself a colonist. The small minority of ruling whites had been separated by a great gulf from the masses of the native population. The latter lived a highly localized life, fearing and hating government from without. Between the whites and the Indians there were the *mestizos,* the offspring of the two races. The history of Latin America is the history of the expansion and the triumph of the *mestizo*. In nearly all its countries—Uruguay and to some extent Argentina being exceptions—there occurred a remarkable mixture of races into a common stock, absorbing the once dominant whites and presenting a complete contrast to the situation in North America. These likenesses were prepotent over the differences in determining the political history of Latin America. The dictator, the *caudillo,* has featured that history since colonial times.

The *caudillos* were men of various types. In appraising them it must be remembered that the chaotic conditions, at least during the first period of liberation, the lack of unity and the economic and social unpreparedness of the people, seemed to admit no alternatives to dictatorship. Even the great liberator, Simon Bolivar, who was certainly animated by the sense of his mission, could find no way to rule except as dictatorial "president." In Venezuela, Colombia, and Peru he was in no position to emulate the example of his prototype of the North, George Washington. Some *caudillos* were genuine champions of their peoples, like Rivadavia of Argentina, Francia of Paraguay, and, at least in his earlier period, Diaz of Mexico; many followed no line but that dictated by their own ambition. Some were cultured Spaniards, like Rosas of Argentina; some came from the soil, like Jaurez the great Indian leader of Mexico. Some introduced serious reforms; many were regardless of the people's wellbeing. But they all alike ruled unconstitutionally, maintaining their place by placating their followers and by the swift resort to force against the first signs of opposition. The order they established was always precarious. Nevertheless, by and large, it sufficed to permit a considerable degree of social and economic progress throughout these vast areas that had suffered at the least stagnation and more often retardation throughout the long colonial regime.

The sub-structure of Latin-American dictatorship has a typical form. The party of the dictator is not compact and disciplined, as in the modern European systems. It is a "party of interests," with little pretension to ideology, a loose body of followers and office-holders professing a personal allegiance to the head of the government. The ruling elite generally retains a rather feudalistic character. Industry is of little importance, except in a few urban areas, and the mass of the population remains inert to government. Social life is highly localized. The elite itself is associated with a traditional culture that is little vitalized by new movements. The army is not so much a national as a governmental organization, and military control counts out of all proportion to its efficiency or its military function.

This kind of dictatorship is peculiarly denuded of myth. The junta at the top is held together by the perquisites of office and the prestige that goes with the exercise of authority, but it is not organically connected with the rest of the population. It is fond of patriotic proclamations that are full of gesture and rhetoric but have little relation to policy. Its loyalty does not bite deep enough to prevent some new adventurer, within or outside its ranks, from seizing power at the first opportunity. The acceptance of the regime is for the most part due to the remoteness of the people in general from the ways of politics, their habit of subjection to authority encouraged by the authoritarian precepts of the Church, and the grinding discipline of poverty that limits their horizon and denies them the means and aptitudes of social action. The sheer poverty of the people makes it easier for the junta to amass wealth, since it conceals from them all knowledge of the operations of government. The cruder forms of economic exploitation flourish. Government itself becomes the most lucrative form of business enterprise, making highly profitable deals with contractors and entrepreneurs and finding new occasions for enrichment whenever a highway or a railroad or a public building is constructed or whenever private business requires a franchise or a favor.

This is the typical picture, but there are variations and partial exceptions. In the more prosperous of these republics the middle class has been growing, and public opinion has become more articulate, preparing the way for a more democratic or at the least a less narrowly oligarchical system of government. There have been notable advances in Colombia, Guatemala, and Uruguay. There have been important developments in other countries, such as Chile. But for the study of Latin-American dictatorship the most significant situations are those presented respectively by Argentina and by Mexico.

Argentina differs in one primary respect from the other countries of Latin America. It possesses the only great area of rich well-watered agricultural soil south of the Rio Grande. Largely as a consequence of its good fortune in this respect, combined with its more temperate climate, it is occupied, along with its neighbor Uruguay, by a population in which white men of European, and especially Spanish, origin vastly predominate. These differences did little to remove Argentina from the common experience of dictatorship—though there were fewer revolutions than in many Latin-American countries—but they have much to do with its more recent development and with the problem of its further political evolution. The extent and fertility of its prairie soil, the *pampa,* has made it a favorite country for the investment of foreign, especially British, capital. Its feudal-type *estancias* are vast farms or ranches owned by a rather small number of wealthy and powerful men. These constitute, together with a military-political clique, the highly conservative aristocracy which, except for short periods, has made and dominated the government of Argentina.

Over against them stand the growing middle classes. They are anti-feudal and democratically minded. Their chief political triumph was the election of President Irigoyen, who, though himself no model democrat, during his two terms of office gave Argentina its first genuine approach to a democratic government. Since the counter-revolutionary overthrow of Irigoyen in 1930 they have been politically ineffective. The authoritarian tradition is strong, and the control exercised by the conservative elements, military, landowning, and clerical, has not so far been seriously impeded by a constitutional framework that, while thoroughly democratic, is neutralized by all the devices of chicanery, corruption, and violence. One factor limiting the political influence of the industrial groups is that the administrative positions of many concerns financed by foreign capital are largely occupied by foreign appointees of the owning companies. Industry in general has been retarded by policies and regulations, including tariffs, conceived in the interest of the land-owning class. Nevertheless it has been advancing with considerable rapidity and is bound to become steadily more important in the total economy. Trade unionism and other anti-feudal organizations make some headway in spite of governmental hostility. The pressure of liberal public opinion has been increasing. It finds somewhat fitful expression through the party of the *Radicales,* and there is also a socialist party that has some following in the larger cities.

These conditions set the stage for a struggle of parties that is already undermining the older form of dictatorship and is likely in time to bring Argentina into the current of modern politics. Already, although dictators continually succeed one another in the traditional manner of Latin America, dictatorship itself approaches nearer to the fascist form. The task of suppressing or silencing the opposing forces grows more difficult. The advancing economy makes new demands and puts new tasks on government, with which the old-style dictatorship finds it hard to cope. To crush countermovements the junta of the dictator has to set up a more compact organization and to adopt more elaborate methods of military and police control. Censorship must be more rigorous and more vigilant. The whole system is beset by greater dangers. The "party" significantly changed its name to become the "National Democratic Party." It seeks popular support by intensifying its appeal to Argentinian nationalism and to this end sows suspicion, of the "colossus of the North." It has at the same time imperialistic aspirations. But these bids for popular support cannot overcome the cleavage of interests between the dominating *estancieros* and the rising middle classes.

At the other end of Latin America, Mexico, a federal state like all the other large countries of the whole continent, has followed a very different road. In Mexico the process of transformation from the rough-and-ready dictatorship indigenous to Latin America has advanced much further than elsewhere, and yet social and cultural evolution has lagged so far behind revolutionary political changes that the ways of dictatorship still persist. After its liberation from Spanish dominion Mexico had more than its share of the civil wars and disorders experienced throughout Latin America, and in addition it was embroiled in war with the United States and again with European expeditionary armies that prepared the way for the hapless rule of the Emperor Maximilian. Territorial losses, foreign invasions, and the resentment roused against Maximilian intensified the sense of Mexican nationalism; and the popular rising that restored Juarez to power carried with it a demand for agrarian reform and the continuation of Juarez's program for the confiscation of the vast areas owned by the church. This program was defeated by Diaz who during his long tenure of office brought enough stability to permit considerable economic development but at the same time by his reversal of agrarian policies confirmed the abject peonage of the Mexican peasant. The fall of Diaz in 1911 brought new conflicts, but the revolutionary party triumphed and under Carranza and Obregon a series of fundamental changes was inaugurated, far beyond anything that had occurred hitherto in Latin America. The great estates, or *haciendas,* including those owned by the church, were divided among the peasants. Lands and other properties owned by foreigners were taken over by the state, including the rich oil concessions. There were laws encouraging labor unions and promoting universal education. There was a bitter struggle with the church, which was deprived of most of its privileges and even of many of its edifices.

The rigor of this extreme reversal has been modified by conditions that no single revolution, however sweeping, can abolish. Although the revolution introduced the policy of universal schooling education is still backward over large areas. The poverty, insanitation, and subjection to endemic diseases that have plagued Latin America are still prevalent. The mountains and high plateaus that feature the land are arid and bare, having lost their forests through the ravages of men and of governments. The poverty of the peasants and their still rather primitive methods of agriculture, applied to dry sun-baked soil, have militated against their successful cultivation of the land they have come to own. The desert still encroaches and peasants forsake their new possessions, moving to the cities where they offer themselves as unskilled workers—a labor commodity in excessive supply—or migrating, if they get the chance, to the United States. There is improvement over the old peonage but the dreams of the revolution are unfulfilled. For the great peasant majority there is no new philosophy of life to take the place of the authoritarian tradition. At the other end of the scale the ruling group, the *politicos,* easily lose the sense of a mission and become opportunistic. They pay glowing lip-service to the revolution but they become a kind of closed shop, monopolizing government much in the manner of the old dictatorship, keeping their party together by means of the spoils of office and showing themselves not unready to use strong-arm methods against any threats to their tenure.

This state of affairs, somewhat better or somewhat worse with the times, does not constitute a return to the old order. The revolution made an end of the old feudalism, and the creeping counter-revolution has but blunted some effects that might otherwise have followed from this decisive action. The economic condition of Mexico has improved rather slowly, for there are stubborn difficulties to be overcome. The revolution itself had some adverse consequences in frightening away the foreign investment that, under proper safeguards, might have been made serviceable to economic advance. Mexico has been opened to new influences, but the liberation cannot of itself overcome the poverty and the attendant ills that beset its much-enduring people.

Surveying the whole picture of Latin-American government we see again that when the props of constitutional oligarchy are removed and cannot be restored, some kind of dictatorship is the inevitable resort, so long as the socio-economic conditions are unripe for democracy. The dissolution of the colonial system in the earlier part of the nineteenth century left these lands with no native political tradition. They would otherwise have gone through the experience of constitutional oligarchy congenial to their circumstances. Instead, the surge of their liberation from exploitative dominion expressed itself, responsive to the examples set by the United States and by Western Europe, in the proclamation of democratic principles. But the experience of subjection, the lack of unity, the prevalence of religious authoritarianism, the dire poverty, the conjunction of different cultures and different racial groups, and the difficult geographical conditions all conspired to make the immediate realization of democracy impossible. Everywhere the result was the rise of the *caudillos,* the ruthless and adventurous men who could seize the opportunity. Their regime has been, like that of directors everywhere in the past, full of turmoil, and marked by endless revolutions. But they achieved some degree of order, however insecure. In the longer perspective of history they were the necessary bridge between the downfall of colonialism and the attainment of more stable government, rooted more deeply in the consensus of the people.

THE FASCIST AND NAZI TYPES

Whether we regard the dictatorships of the ill-omened "Axis" as two distinct species of modern dictatorship or subsume them as a single species under the more inclusive designation of "fascist," remains a matter of opinion. They exhibited certain notable resemblances. Both originated as lower-middle-class movements, developing into a kind of nationalistic mass insurgence. In this respect they are differentiated from the old-line reactionary governments of men like Rivera and Franco in Spain and also from the exclusive proletarianism of the Soviet dictatorship. Both succeeded in enlisting diverse groups and classes to a program of expansionist aggression, finding common ground in the respective treatment meted out to them in the Treaty of Versailles—though one was chafing in defeat and the other discontented with the rewards of victory. But there were very marked differences between them. The deep-biting dogma of the Nazi creed was of a totally different character from the shifting and opportunistic doctrines of the fascists. The situation of Germany at the end of the First World War was wholly unlike that of Italy. The experience of Germany under Hitler had only a superficial analogy with the experience of Italy under Mussolini. Although the two movements came to power through similar processes, and although the two systems in which they culminated met at the same time the same fate, they are certainly different enough to deserve separate treatment.

We should, however, recognize that the difference expressed itself more in the respective ideologies of the two systems than in their governmental structure. In both instances a disoriented small-bourgeois group, in a time of social upheaval and economic trouble, found a leader who was master of the mass appeal. The preceding war had inculcated habits of blind obedience to the command of the superior but the authority behind the command had been discredited. Men were groping for a new myth of authority. They were susceptible to the gospel of new demagogues. It is an old story that under conditions of grave stress, with the breaking of tradition, the people, and especially the young, lose the finer cohesion that gives play to the personality of each, and are more easily reduced to the mass, the populace, the mob. Then comes the leader, whether he be fanatic or ambitious adventurer, and by his devices and his eloquence advances the process, at length making the mass the instrument of his purposes. Mussolini belonged to the adventurer type, Hitler was the fanatic. Always there are some whose ears are open to the piping of the mass leader, but the more desperate the crisis the more numerous they become. Especially after the experience of disillusionment in war, while they still are habituated to the word of command, they merge in to the Nietzschean "herd beast prepared for obedience."

So it was in Italy, and then in Germany. Communist leaders gained ground; nationalist leaders found their opportunity in anti-communist movements. Each side formed its gangs. There were street fighting, intimidation, organized lawlessness. There were banners and manifestoes. The nationalist movement grew into a "party." It became a wedge driven ever deeper into the weakened political order. Thus fascism arose, with its dedication to "audacious" and terroristic methods. Thus later Hitlerism arose. Each prepared itself for the coming *coup d'état.*

In Italy the tension, though considerable, was not so widespread or so deep-seated as in defeated Germany. There were great differences in economic development, in cultural attitudes, and in popular sentiment between the various regions of Italy. It was in the industrial north that the new bands of anti-communist nationalists appeared and gathered strength. They took for their symbol the fasces of Republican Rome, the bundle of rods bound by a leather thong out of which an ax projected, the insignia of authority carried before the Roman magistrates by their officers, or "lictors." Mussolini, head of the Milan *fascio,* previously a radical journalist, quickly dominated the movement. It was a time when the bold adventurer had unusual opportunity, as D'Annunzio had shown by the seizure of Fiume. Mussolini came forward as the champion of the disgruntled imperialism of Italy. The government in power was unstable and vacillating. Disunity everywhere prevailed. Mussolini had the grand gesture and soon cultivated the grand manner. The industrialists, fearful of communism, gave him support. After some local successes he planned the "march on Rome." The weak government fell. Mussolini became premier.

In one thing he showed consistency throughout his career—his contempt for democracy. Exulting over the "decaying corpse of the Goddess of Liberty," he proceeded to tear down, piece by piece, the parliamentary structure. He nullified and then abolished all political parties except "the" party. He dominated the Chamber of Deputies, resorting in the process to one assassination, that of Matteoti. He changed his office of premier into that of "head of the government." He had a "law" passed to give executive decrees the effect of laws. He made the party the organ of the state, with a hierarchical system of controls from the local party boss to the Grand Council of Fascism. His regime became a personal government of the most extreme type. The members of the party were sworn to boundless obedience to his orders. The various organizations that nurtured or maintained the fascist discipline, the Young Fascists and numerous other categories, were indoctrinated in an exclusive loyalty to his person. He had his personal army, the blackshirt Militia, bound exclusively to his service. The new political structure of fascist dictatorship was built inside the pre-existing system, until all that remained of the old order was a hollow façade. The king still "reigned," the senate still met, but one man, backed by his disciplined cohorts, commanded Italy.

What made this fascist dictatorship so peculiarly personal was the lack of any clear positive philosophy behind its organization. In this respect it was not unlike the Latin-American dictatorships. In this respect it differed notably from the Soviet type, and also from the Nazi type. The party, not merely the inner junta, was held together by interests and not by principles. The Duce preached the subordination of the individual to the state. The state, as embodied in the Duce, was the supreme object of devotion. But what did the state stand for? What did it offer to the individual who was bidden to renounce his individuality in order to serve it? Let us listen to the words of the Duce. The individual was exhorted to rejoice in the glory and the pomp, the power and the triumph, of Imperial Italy. But throughout there was more form than content, more gesture than revelation, in the high-sounding language of the sedulous philosophers of fascism. The individual, were he so minded, might experience some sense of personal amplitude, some enlargement of the ego, in the task of advancing the sacred imperium. But for multitudes, apart from the chances of a little security or a little profit, it remained—

Like a tale of little meaning, tho' the words are strong.

Fascism developed its own style of language. There was much talk of destiny, of the inexorable ineffable will of the state. But the majority of the people continued to speak another language, one that had meaning for them.

Mussolini, the adventurer, the ex-radical and ex-internationalist, the disciple of Machiavelli, could not make his totalitarianism live. He could not cement the people into the unity of a common cause. His vaunted fascist era had no future, his boisterous appeals to the spirit of youth faded as the years went by. A cleavage inevitably appeared within the fascist ideology. The doctrine instilled in the masses laid stress on unconditional obedience, unswerving discipline, the unerring intuition of the leader, the subjection of personal aims in the service of the state. Quite contrary was the ideology of-the elite. This was more the ideology of Sorel than the ideology of Hegel. It was the exuberant belief in dramatic action, in the . . . seizure of the moment, in the men of power who defy tradition and are not bound by history. It was the belief in the elite itself, the makers of history, the molders of the inert masses, feeding them with the myths that are serviceable to the purposes of the elite. The totalitarianism of the Italian fascists was shallow and specious. It did not penetrate the life or the thought of the people.

Furthermore, the principle of totalitarianism was confronted in Italy by a special obstacle to its realization. One organization, also centered in Rome, was too powerful, too well entrenched, too international, to be co-ordinated. This was the Roman Catholic Church. From the first Mussolini recognized the necessity for coming to terms with it and, reversing his previous attitude, he restored religious education in the public schools, associated Catholic chaplains with his youth organizations, and made overtures to the Church leading to a settlement of its long-standing dispute with the Italian state. But the "concordat" under which the respective spheres of the two organizations were defined was an uneasy one. It is true on the one hand that fascism seemed to make its most effective appeal to Catholic areas. The Church and the Fascist State alike laid stress on invincible authority, on hierarchy, on discipline. But the authority claimed by the one clashed with the authority claimed by the other. Hence considerable friction remained underneath the concordat. The conflict centered around the education of youth. The Fascist State claimed the minds as well as the bodies of its subjects. The Church could never admit the former claim. The best Mussolini could obtain was a troubled compromise. Co-ordination was impossible.

The disparity between form and substance, between pretension and realization, pervaded Italian fascism. It ruled with a high hand, suppressed personal liberties everywhere, set up its secret police and its swarming spies, filled its concentration camps, and made its capricious reign of fear the substitute for justice. But it was almost as though an alien power were ruling the country. Many of those who enlisted on its side did so from motives of expediency. The loudly proclaimed mission of the state carried little conviction. The endless indoctrination never penetrated deep but instead began to lose some of its earlier impressiveness. The parades and the ceremonies were stage pieces.

The same disparity showed itself in the structure of corporations that constituted "the corporate state," regarded by its chief author as his great contribution to political architecture. Mussolini took over from his socialist days the notion of "functional" government through occupational syndicates. It was the notion publicized by Georges Sorel, and one of Sorel's disciples, Rossoni, who had been active in the radical I.W.W. unions of the United States, worked out in the first years of fascism a plan for allying with the movement the "patriotic" labor syndicates. With the abolition of the former labor unions this early plan was developed and repeatedly revised, ending in a most elaborate scheme of local and regional syndicates of employers and of workers in all categories, presided over by twenty-two national corporations. Fascist writers, including Mussolini himself who published a book on the subject, gave great acclaim to the new system as a revolutionary development of epochal significance. The syndicates or corporations were represented as the autonomous organs of the modern state. The inclusive organization was the "cornerstone" of fascism, its distinctive and original creation. It contained the solution of all economic problems. It was the great planning agency of government. It was the virile substitute for the parliaments of the obsolete democracies. It was the answer to communism. It was the successor to capitalism.

But the syndicates served no such large ends. They were no more than auxiliary fascist agencies. They had no autonomy. They did not transform the economic system. They did not legislate. The Chamber of Fasces and Corporations, which was at length set up in the last years of fascism, never approached the importance of a parliament. The majority of the workers of the various categories were not enrolled in the respective syndicates. The corporations were instruments of fascist control, responsive to the purposes of the party and completely subservient to the will of the Duce. The whole system was in practice little more than a device for "co-ordinating" economic interests and agencies. It fulfilled this objective quite efficiently.

Through its much-heralded corporations, through its youth organizations, through the schools, through the party, through the army, through the Dopolavoro—the special agency for providing the workers with recreation and "culture," through an endlessly ramifying assortment of institutions and associations, the fascist dictatorship labored to impress its stamp on the community. Like all dictatorships it feared the community. It dared not let the community life find any free expression in any direction. It spread fear, and it lived in fear, fear of the forces that liberate themselves in the thoughts and spontaneous activities of men. It sought to hide this fear behind loud pretensions and grandiose designs. It tried to stimulate an artificial unity through the pursuit of imperialist aims, its major exploit being the conquest of Ethiopia. But dictatorship, in spite of its propagandist skills, never becomes the serene master of the community. Here Italian fascism failed conspicuously.

It set its image on a high pedestal for the worship of the people, but the contrast between the image and the reality could not be concealed.

In this as in various other respects the Nazi model made some improvement on the fascist original. It was no accident that Adolf Hitler was a fanatic, not an adventurer. The German people were not, in the period after the Peace of Versailles, merely restless and discontented, suffering a post-war disillusionment, like the people of Italy. The German people had gone through other and more devastating experiences. The humiliations of defeat had been driven home by the heavy demands of the Treaty of Versailles, causing national prostration and impotent rage. The democratic system established under the Weimar Constitution, the first of its kind in the history of Germany, had severe problems to face. There were powerful threats from the growing communist party; there was the opposition of the conservative right, including the Junkers; there were new nationalist movements making appeal to the bourgeois classes. The last-mentioned section suffered the worst shock of the destructive inflation Germany passed through in 1923. The country might nevertheless have weathered all these storms had the economic policies of Europe, and of the United States, followed a different road in the period between the two world wars. But the dismal political record of this period, in which government exhibited a short-sightedness exceeding the common myopia of international statesmanship, contained among its other exhibits a resort to the extremest forms of economic protectionism. One of its many consequences was an aggravation of social distress in Germany. Unemployment rose to unprecedented figures. The combination of economic distress and nationalist resentment made a fertile soil for the seed of dictatorship. The Nazi movement grew to formidable proportions. Mustering under its banner the disinterested, the disoriented, the aggressive, the indoctrinated young, the men with ideals distorted by failure and defeat, it made its bid for power.

When after various vicissitudes, advances, and retreats—the movement never won a clear majority of the electorate—it achieved its goal, the Nazi dictatorship soon demonstrated that it was a more formidable and more challenging phenomenon than fascism. It immediately destroyed every vestige of constitutionalism. It organized the exclusive hierarchical party. It set up the paraphernalia of dictatorship, the bodyguard of the Führer, the party troops, the secret police, the propagandist control (Goebbels' Ministry of Propaganda and Enlightenment), the concentration camps, the labor camps, the official agencies of indoctrination. But it was more ruthless and thorough than its fascist predecessor.

The depth of the convulsion in Germany is evidenced by many signs. Here was a very different situation from that of Russia, the first and hitherto the most absolute example of modern dictatorship. Here was a country of high industrialization, with a large middle class, with a great cultural development. Yet this country was completely taken over by the Nazis. The forces of opposition were silenced. The Lutheran Church was co-ordinated, with only a sporadic protest. The Roman Catholic Church was rendered impotent. The Junkers, who thought they could control the upstart, were harnessed to his chariot. The right-wing nationalists were dissolved. The older type of militarist leadership, expressed through the Reichswehr [1] and the Stahlhelm,[2] was subordinated. The industrialists and the financiers were made subservient, and a few of them who had hopefully promoted the Nazi movement, like Thyssen, found it expedient to take refuge in flight. While all who showed any spirit of resistance to the aims or methods of the regime—liberals, social democrats, communists, religious objectors—were consigned to the prisons or the concentration camps.

Here was something that struck more deeply than did the flourishes and tyrannies of the Italian fascists. The superficial adulation paid to Mussolini never approached the aura—the *charisma*, as some Germans name it—surrounding the Führer. The massed cohorts of the Piazza Venezia never exhibited the reverential devotion of the Nuremberg party festivals. The nationalist pride of humiliated Germany rose to new fervor. "Heil Hitler" was the only word. When the Führer began to preach the obligation of Germans to produce larger families the birth rate went up. Mussolini had been preaching the same doctrine, but the Italian birth rate—though indeed it was much higher to begin with—made no evident response.

The gospel of this unleashed nationalism was aggressive, vengeful, simple, mystical, barbaric in its overtones. To its service everything was transformed, all literature, all philosophy, all art, all science. The mission of the state was not only over all, it comprised all. The principle, "He that is not for us is against us," was applied in the most extreme form. The state as incorporated in the dictatorship was not only sacred, it was utterly set apart from everything else on earth, and first of all from every other state. It was a wrathful and inexorable deity, demanding endless sacrifice. All that the individual might prize, all the values the group might cherish, counted for nothing be-

[1] [German defensive land and naval forces.]
[2] [German association of ex-servicemen.]

side the all-devouring service of the state. Internationalism was a deadly contagion. And for a symbol of all things detestable to this new God of Wrath the Nazis set up the Jew, the man bereft of a native state. From the first Hitler had fulminated against "the Jewish international world conspiracy." Now he set in motion a persecution of the Jews that finally reached a scale unparalleled in the tragic history of that people.

The original party program of the Nazis, like that of the fascists, contained a mélange of diverse elements. It is easy to forget that their party was officially the "National Socialist German Workers' Party." This was in line with its policy to use the techniques and the appeals of democracy in order to destroy democracy. The various clauses of the party proclamations, such as the opposition to "interest bondage," were devices to enlist various dissatisfied groups. The objective behind it all was the enthronement of a militant nationalism, exclusively directed by a small clique of ruthless men.

Once in power, this group proceeded to develop and inculcate its appropriate ideology. It is a necessity of modern dictatorship to monopolize the expression of opinion. There exists no longer any public opinion, there is only official proclamation of it. The spontaneous processes of opinion were suppressed by two main agencies. One of these was controlled by Goebbels, the other fell under the command of Himmler. Himmler as the head of the secret police punished any deviation from the official line, while Goebbels manufactured the substitute for public opinion, using all the devices of his psychological craft. But Goebbels could not have succeeded without Himmler. The ministry of "propaganda and enlightenment" would have been inefficacious without the concentration camp.

The ideology identified the dictator and the state with a peculiarly Germanic concept, the spirit of the folk (*Volksgeist*). In a cruder form it had already been expressed in *Mein Kampf*.[3] Now it was given a mystical restatement. The chief among its many prophets was Alfred Rosenberg, who in his *Myth of the Twentieth Century* expanded into a turgid rhetorical philosophy the notion of the pure and now at length triumphant German spirit. This spirit was released from its bondage to the impure and race-destroying myths that had dominated modern civilization, the myths of socialism and of individualism, of freemasonry and of humanitarianism, the myth of "raceless" democracy, the myth of Judaism, the myth of modern "bloodless" Christianity with its "Syrian and Etruscan elements." All these shadows on the folk-spirit were now dissipated in the rising effulgence of the heroic German soul. The myth of the twentieth century was in the ascendant.

[3] [*My Struggle*, by Hitler.]

This folk-spirit, incarnated in the state, was a Hegelesque revival of the old tribal God. As presented it was a curious mixture of old traditions and new falsifications, of motifs derived from primitive folklore, from the nine-teenth-century philosophers of Germanism, and from the contemporary re-actionaries who glorified race and soil, such as H. S. Chamberlain and Oswald Spengler. It was a compensatory gospel for a people who had passed through political disaster and economic despair. The new state, the "Third Reich," deprived them of all liberties but it made them the chosen people, the chil-dren of destiny, the inheritors of the earth. The deep "trauma" they had suffered—to use a term from the psychoanalysts—made a sufficient number of them emotionally ready to hail the leader, who stridently proclaimed this gospel.

The Third Reich was conceived and begotten in crisis and its being was adapted only to crisis. It could not live in a peaceful world. By the necessity of its nature it must maintain the tensions of which it was the expression. It had to be for ever the father of the violence of which it was also the child. From the first it was geared to war. Its protestations of peaceful purpose were calculated deception. The period in which it built up its armed forces was characterized by the bankruptcy of statesmanship in the Western democratic countries. They were obsessed by the same fear of communism that had already served the Nazis so well, although the Soviet government, in marked contrast to the Hitler regime, showed then no signs of military aggressive-ness, being wholly absorbed in its domestic plans. At the same time they pursued increasingly severe policies of economic protectionism that impover-ished the larger countries and reduced the smaller ones, especially the new creations of the Versailles settlement, to a ruinous condition. These policies played into the hands of the Nazi dictatorship. From re-armament it advanced to conquest. By threat of war it achieved far more than it could have hoped. But it could not stop there. When the war came, over Poland, it won great victories against the unprepared democracies and seized vast territories. But it could not stop there. Its demon drove it on to war with Soviet Russia as well. Thus it at length fulfilled its destiny, dragging down in its fall the neighbor dictatorships that were enlisted under its banner.

THE SOVIET DICTATORSHIP

The Soviet dictatorship is so novel, so distinctive, so revolutionary, that it constitutes a type by itself. It differs from the rest in another respect, in a certain ambiguity that has led different authorities to give the most conflicting reports concerning its character and its institutions. To some it is the fulfillment of the age-old yearnings of mankind for a better world, and all they write about it conveys the impression that it is built as near perfection as mortal man could possibly attain under the conditions and in the short space of time since it was first set up. To others it is the most ominous of portents, a world-filling threat to the slowly won liberties of man, to the creative struggle in which his vision has been extended to ever new horizons, and to the initiative and enterprise of individuals and groups by means of which they have fought their way upward and brought advancement to their societies. Each side adduces the evidences that support its case.

Formally the Soviet system is a union of sixteen federated republics. Formally the federation assures an unusual autonomy, extending even to foreign relationships, to its member states. There is no experience on the basis of which we can tell what in practice is meant by the diplomatic and military autonomy assigned to the constituents in a recent re-statement of the constitution. The federation admits, however, another kind of autonomy that is easier to assess. Russia is composed of a large number of ethnic or nationality groups. Each national group within the total structure is given the right to retain its own language, its own schools, its own cultural institutions. In areas such as the Caucasus, with its various localized cultures, a system of regional autonomy has been proclaimed, so that ethnic or tribal minorities should not be disadvantaged. In this respect the Soviet philosophy accepts the Marxian thesis that ethnic and racial differences are not intrinsic, that they are environmental variations of no great significance and playing no important part in the major processes of human history.

The Soviet system, the first of the modern dictatorships, was not initially the expression of any mass-generated sentiment. The breakdown of the traditional Russian oligarchy in the stresses of war, the revelation of its incompetence, bureaucratic ineptitude, and general decay, did arouse widespread revulsion through the defeated country. In the ensuing chaos the Czar abdicated, and a provisional government, headed first by Prince Lvov and then by Kerensky, took over. The new government represented the democratic liberalism that had been finding an outlet through the Duma, the representative assembly which had become the focus of the democratic movement. But its policy for the continuance of the war was disliked by the war-weary masses and its unwillingness to take instant action to satisfy the land-hungry peasants destroyed its prestige. The occasion was seized by the small Bolshevik minority, always alert for drastic action and, though its ulterior aims were different, offering without hesitation to make the peasants the owners of the soil. This minority had the further advantage that it was led by a man with a genius for statesmanship—Lenin.

It is one of the great paradoxes of history that the revolution vaticinated by Marx, the revolution that was to overthrow capitalism in favor of a proletarian collectivism, should have been inaugurated in Russia, where there was no swelling proletariat and very little capitalism. Much of what followed in the course of the Soviet dictatorship is illuminated by that paradox. The Bolsheviks started with a complete Marxist creed. When they seized power they proclaimed a new order based on this creed. In the name of this creed they rallied their forces, and in its name they won adherents in many other lands. The creed had several aspects. There was the doctrine of the socialist or communist economy, demanding the collectivization of all productive wealth, the abolition of capitalism, and the [ultimate] establishment of the formula: from each according to his abilities, to each according to his needs. There was the doctrine of equality, denying advantage or privilege to any class, race-group, or interest. There was the doctrine of internationalism, opposing the dominance and the exclusiveness of the nationalist state. There was the doctrine of democracy, making all authority the expression of the people's will. And there was the doctrine of the "withering state," attacking the whole system of power politics and envisaging a future in which the role of the state as power would disappear and the classless society would function in liberty. To these doctrines was attached an elaborate "dialectic" of the inevitable historical processes through which the transformation must take place.

The creed was supreme, indivisible, infallible. It was an admirable creed to inspire groups suffering from economic exploitation or social discrimination, groups burning with discontent against overmastering authority. It gave them a program, a faith, an assurance of ultimate victory. It was a fighting creed, very explicit about the plan of campaign but leaving in a kind of utopian dream the post-revolution world. Such was the creed the Bolsheviks set out to realize in Russia. The Soviet system was the result. As with every other system that is the offspring of a doctrine and a situation the new order took a character very different from the expectations of its friends and of its foes alike. To understand what happened one has to understand not only the principles of Marxism but also the condition of Russia—and even then one must summon hindsight as well as foresight. The history of Soviet Russia is the history of the institutionalization of a creed, of the various crises through which the new institutions passed, and of the successive impacts upon them of external forces and of the forces generated within them.

The definitive act of the Revolution was the incorporation of the vast area of Russia within the framework of a collectivist economy. To establish a democracy at the same time was beyond the power, if not beyond the will, of the founders. For them the economic transformation was the primary change from which would follow all the other changes they desired. The temporary "dictatorship of the proletariat" would take charge of things until the revolutionary process was complete. Thus would come the final inauguration of the realm of freedom, wherein all "master-slave" relations would be extinct, a classless and "stateless" society superseding the whole epoch of class struggle that has existed since the time of primitive man. In accordance with this mythology the Bolshevik Party, headed by Lenin and Trotsky, seized its rare opportunity, nationalized the banks and industrial and trading enterprises, divided the large estates among the peasants, and later proceeded to collectivize agriculture as well. The dictatorship, of course, was never a "dictatorship of the proletariat." It was the dictatorship of Lenin and his group. The Communist Party became the guardian and the instrument of the new order.

The successive storms through which the Revolution passed hardened the policy of the dictatorship and raised ever more challenging questions concerning its relation to its original creed. First it had to maintain and consolidate its power against external war and internal opposition. It survived these perils and ruthlessly "liquidated" anti-revolutionary elements within its borders. Soviet Russia thus became a state among the major states of the world, and for a time modified its collectivist program, permitting small traders to operate and giving the peasants the facility to sell their produce in their own way. With the death of Lenin in 1924 and the accession of Stalin to power signs were appearing of the internecine struggle among leaders that lies in wait for the dictatorial system. The new ruler Stalin, officially the General Secretary of the Party, departed from the line of Lenin in various ways. He set out to build "socialism in a single country," rejecting the internationalist theory of the communist revolution. To this end he engineered vast programs for a planned economy, the collectivization of agriculture, the first Five-Year Plan and its successors. No material enterprise on so heroic a scale had ever been attempted, or accomplished, before. Its immediate human costs were enormous, but it succeeded. No less drastically Stalin set himself to crush all dissidents among the old revolutionaries, all potential rivals, beginning with Trotsky and ending with an extraordinary series of purges and heresy trials that completely eliminated, with many others, the old Bolshevik leaders. Thus the absolutism of the dictatorship was confirmed, and Stalin proceeded to "revise" the Marxist dogma of the "withering" of the state. The revived nationalism of Soviet Russia was given new impetus when Hitler forced Stalin into the Second World War, when after tremendous defeats the Red Armies fought back with even more tremendous victories, and when it fell to Stalin to represent one of the three super-powers in the reorganization of the world. The "Hymn of the Soviet Union," which at the end of 1943 was substituted as the national anthem for the "Internationale," echoes precisely the same sentiment that animates "God Save the King" or "The Star-Spangled Banner."

The outcome of it all has been a remarkable contradiction, at several vital points, between the established myth and the operation of the dictatorship. Under other systems the central myth of government is often violated in practice, but of these it may on the whole be said that their inconsistencies are the shortcomings men and nations alike reveal with respect to the goals they set themselves. Thus in the United States the myth of the equal rights of men is flouted in the treatment of very considerable groups, and particularly of the Negroes. But here the disparity causes uneasiness, some sense of maladjustment or of failure. It is a declension from a standard that is attained in very large measure for the rest of the community. Again, the myth of the totalitarian state was far from being fully realized in Fascist Italy, but at least it was the consummation toward which the government moved. But the situation that has developed in Soviet Russia is different. For here some of the primary doctrines of the creed are refuted by every activity of government, and moreover the contradiction is stoutly denied. Any declension from the projected ideal is explained on the ground that the process to full communism is still incomplete.

The doctrine of the temporary dictatorship is contradicted by the intensive centralization of economic and cultural activities, and the "stateless" society is relegated to the Greek Kalends. The doctrine of the people's rule is flatly rejected by the rigorous insistence on the party line. The thoroughly democratic constitution of 1936 proclaimed that all political power [was] vested in "the working people of town and country." There is an impressive framework of electoral systems stretching all the way from the local soviets to the Supreme Soviet of the U.S.S.R. There are everywhere People's Courts and People's Commissars. But the voting at elections is practically unanimous, and the one party retains complete control. The doctrine of the abolition of class has been negated by the occupational gradings, but far more thoroughly by the pyramid of power, which rises as steeply as, and perhaps more rigidly than, it did under the Czarist regime. . . . Two types of functionaries regulate the everyday life, first the functionaries of the party, the officials, and next the closely allied managers of industrial and other enterprises. The doctrine of the free press and of cultural liberty is lauded, but the public expression of opinion is everywhere closely censored, and the monopolization of propaganda has been maintained by the characteristic devices of modern dictatorship, including the secret police, the spy, and the labor camp. The government puts the material facilities for press publication at the disposal of the people, but only those who adhere to the party line avail themselves of the privilege. The freedom of religion is guaranteed, but the restored Orthodox Church responds subserviently to the call of the state. Finally, the doctrine of internationalism has suffered eclipse. Born in war, the Soviet state lived continuously under the shadow of war and at length endured the brunt of the greatest war in history. These conditions forged a new nationalism in Russia, and this nationalism was not uncongenial to the mood of the dictatorship.

It is clear there is fundamental conflict here between the ideology and the whole scheme of government. No dictatorship can promote or even tolerate the cultural liberty professed by the Soviet Union. Modern dictatorship is in the first instance a control of the mind by power. To this end it employs all the monopolized agencies of propaganda, making insistent appeal to mass emotions. It is a peculiarity of this appeal that it professes to give the people precisely the thing it takes away from them—cultural liberty. Discerning students of dictatorship pointed out this fact long ago. Thus in the time of Napoleon, Benjamin Constant, who used the term "usurpation" to denote what we name dictatorship, wrote that dictatorship has need of the form of liberty to achieve its ends and therefore offers men a counterfeit of liberty. It even compels people to pretend they are free and bribes writers to convince them. Despotism, says Constant, "allows men the right to be silent" but dictatorship compels them "to lie to their conscience, depriving them of the only consolation remaining to the oppressed." So long as only one "party" is permitted to function in the state, so long as policy is determined by the program of the exclusive party, according to the party line enunciated from the top, there can be no cultural liberty. The numerous electoral exhibits, cited by uncritical partisans as evidences of democracy in being, are merely, with their near-unanimous polls, an additional revelation of its absence.

Moreover, even under the most favorable conditions there would remain the question whether and how so drastic an economic collectivism as that of the Soviet Union could be reconciled with a system of democracy. If that question can be solved at all it has certainly not been solved under the conditions of Soviet Russia. The comprehensive nationalization of the means of production creates peculiar problems in this respect, problems the advocates of this form of economy seem reluctant to admit. When the state takes over all essential economic functions it confers on the political authorities new duties and new powers of the greatest moment. The decisions it must make are not of the kind on which public opinion can well be brought to bear. They are executive rather than legislative decisions. They involve many technical considerations requiring highly expert knowledge. The greater issues of a vast economic enterprise can hardly be determined by majority vote of the electorate, any more than a factory can be run on similar principles. Hence the power vested in government is enormously extended, without any corresponding extension of the checks on government. This power reaches so far into the everyday affairs of every man that those who wield it have levers whereby to control every aspect of life. To expect them to refrain from so doing is contrary to our knowledge of the psychology of power—unless some as yet undeveloped safeguards can be applied.

Within a completely collectivized economy two primary forms of social power, which under other systems remain partly detached and partly opposed, merge into a single focus. Under feudalism economic power is broadly coincident with political power, but the urban economy and the trading economy remain unintegrated with it and in any event there is a total absence of centralization. Under socio-capitalism the power of private or corporate control over wealth can never be wholly unified. There is always some conflict of economic interests. Even though there are great mergers of capital there will be some opposition between industrial and financial groups, between one kind of big business and another, between big business and small business, between the importer and the domestic producer, between the labor union and the employers' organization, between agricultural blocs and industrial blocs. Under such conditions economic power can never be identified with political power. There will be various adjustments and deals between the two, but government can never be all-powerful nor can wealth. There will always be conflict somewhere between multi-centered economic power and uni-centered political power. Interest groups will continue to use their power directly against one another. But under complete collectivism there is the greatest possible concentration of power, since power is both unified and centralized. . . .

In his work on *Representative Government* John Stuart Mill maintained that "human beings are only secure from evil at the hands of others in proportion as they have the power of being, and are, self-protecting." Complete collectivism, as we now know it, takes away from men and groups an important means of self-protection. Where there is distributed and non-political control over the means of livelihood, while it may mean that some groups exploit others, it does provide a basis of resistance against power. Where there is no area for private enterprise every man is directly or indirectly an employee of the government. His security, his advancement, even his economic existence, depend on some political authority. They are most likely to be endangered should he overtly disapprove of the policies of the powers that be. He needs permission to quit his job or to look for another. If he offends one authority he offends all. He is thus at the mercy of government in a way that is alien to the spirit of democracy. We should not forget that in the evolution of modern democracy, first in England and later in America, the resistance of the men of means, as tax-payers no less than as opponents of absolutism, to the arbitrary demands of government was of crucial importance. In the Soviet state this ground of resistance is taken away. The same necessity weighs on everyone, from the lowest to the all-but-highest. It is even more compelling on the higher-ups, since any independence on their part can be construed as treason. Under such conditions a strong orthodoxy is inculcated, even were it not involved in the initial establishment of the regime.

In another milieu than that of Soviet Russia the transition from revolutionary zeal for new human liberties to the autarchy of the socialist state might have been tempered or even diverted. But in Russia both internal conditions and external pressures made any democratic evolution impossible. The dictatorship held starkly to its power and still affirmed its ideology. The materialistic premise of this ideology, that the "material"—in other words, the economic—order is the supreme determinant of human history and human destiny, was itself fatally inadequate. It assumed, among other things, that if wealth were socialized the human spirit would at last find free expression. Among other things it failed to recognize that wealth can indeed be socialized—but not power. Wealth can be converted into the common possession of the community, but power is always exercised by a man or a group of men. Political power can be controlled only by being made responsible.

Even apart from the aggravation created by the collectivist economy Russia could not at the time of the Revolution have established a democratic order. At that time this vast country was overwhelmingly peopled by unpolitical peasants, inured to absolute authority, even though they were disaffected by the disasters it had brought upon them. Over such a land only an autocratic government could in the chaos of the war have maintained itself. Moreover, the Soviet government was confronted by the hostility of the whole outside world, of its enemies and of its former allies alike, and had to prepare not only against internal revolt but also against the new war loosed against it by the capitalist states. Later, it became evident that a re-arming Germany was looking for conquest toward the East. The threat of war never ceased until at last Russia was engulfed in the Second World War.

Consequently the achievements of Soviet Russia inevitably lay along another road, not in the fulfillment of democratic aspirations. These achievements were indeed remarkable. The transformation of a predominantly feudalist system into a collectivistic one ruled by totally different principles was an extraordinary feat, whatever opinions we may hold regarding either the objective itself or the methods employed—including the ruthless liquidation of the more prosperous farmers or *kulaks* in the process of establishing the collective farms (*Kolkhozes*). About certain other achievements there need be no controversy. Never has an industrial development been accomplished so rapidly on so grand a scale. The technological lag of Russia behind the major industrial countries was virtually eliminated within a generation. The illiteracy of the Russian peasant was overcome under a system of universal education which, though rigidly doctrinaire, at least provided for backward multitudes the first facilities of knowledge.

In these respects the Russian Revolution is a more enduring thing than its system of dictatorship and its Marxist orthodoxy. It is not unreasonable to conjecture that this revolution will go the way of other epoch-making revolutions. It has already gone some distance in that direction. The ideal it sought will not be attained in the manner visioned by its prophets. Their vision was too limited by the faults and by the virtues of their time and of their situation. The failure of actuality to correspond to the myth will give dominant groups at length the opportunity to pursue other goals. The social forces it suppresses, the impulses in men its established forms refuse to acknowledge, will find outlet. Periods of reaction and of counter-action will cause confusion within it. Its leaders will pass, new myths will be insurgent, and its first orthodoxy will become obsolete. But the history not only of Russia but of the world will be different because of it. Its inherent mission, not that of its founders, will be accomplished.

2. THE SOVIET UNION

THE FIVE-YEAR PLANS

Hardly had the Party expelled Trotsky when it appropriated certain fragments of his program. In 1928 it launched the First Five-Year Plan, aimed at rapid industrialization and the collectivization of agriculture. "Planning," or the central planning of a country's whole economic life by government officials, was to become the distinctive feature of Soviet economics, and the one which was to have the greatest influence in the rest of the world.

In retrospect, it seems strange that the Communists waited ten years before adopting a Plan. The truth seems to be that the Bolsheviks had only confused ideas of what to do after their seizure of power. Marxism for the most part gave only general hints. Marxism was primarily an analysis of existing or bourgeois society. It was also a theory of class war. But to portray any details of a future society, or specify what should be done after the class war had been won by the proletariat, was according to Marx and Engels sheer utopian fantasy. The bourgeoisie, to be sure, would be destroyed; there would be "social ownership of the means of production," and no "exploitation of man by man"; everyone would work, and there would be neither leisure class nor unemployment. This was not much to go on in the operation of a modern industrial system.

One great constructive idea had been mapped out, most clearly by Engels. *Within* each private enterprise, Engels had observed, harmony and order reigned; it was only *between* private enterprises that capitalism was chaotic. In the individual factory, he noted, the various departments did not compete with each other; the shipping department did not purchase from the production department at prices fluctuating according to daily changes in supply and demand; the output of all departments was planned and coordinated by management. In a larger way, the great capitalist mergers and trusts, controlling many factories, prevented blind competition between them, assigned specific quotas to each, anticipated, coordinated, and stabilized the work of each plant and each person by an over-all policy. With the growth of large corporate enterprise, observed Engels, the area of economic life under free competition was constantly reduced, and the area brought under rational planning was constantly enlarged. The obvious next step, according to Engels and other socialists, was to treat *all* the economic life of a country as a single factory with many departments, or a single enormous monopoly with many members, under one unified, vigorous and far-seeing management.

During the War the governments of belligerent countries had in fact adopted such centralized controls. They had done so not because they were socialistic, but because in time of war people were willing to give up their usual liberties and willing to do as they were told by the government, and because all else was subordinated to a single overwhelming and undisputed social purpose—victory. The "planned society" therefore made its first actual (though incomplete) appearance in the First World War. It was partly from socialist doctrine as exemplified by Engels, and partly from experience of the War as exemplified especially by the "war socialism" of Germany, that the Party in Russia gradually developed the idea of a Plan. The war experience was especially valuable for the lessons it gave on technical questions of economic planning, such as what kind of bureaus to set up, what kind of forecasts to make, and what kind of statistics to collect.

In the U.S.S.R. it was decided to plan for five years into the future, beginning with 1928. The aim of the plan was to strengthen and enrich the country, to lay the groundwork for a true workers' society, and overcome the Russian reputation for backwardness. As Stalin said in a speech in 1929:

We are advancing full steam ahead along the path of industrialization to Socialism, leaving behind the age-long Russian "backwardness." We are becoming a country of metal, a country of automobiles, a country of tractors. And when we have put the U.S.S.R. in a motor car and the *muzhik* in a tractor . . . we shall see which countries may then be "classified" as backward and which as advanced.

The First Five-Year Plan was declared fulfilled in 1932, and a Second Five-Year Plan was launched, lasting until 1937. The Third was interrupted by war, the Fourth (1946–50) was devoted to post-war recovery.

The First Five-Year Plan (like its successors) was administered by a supreme agency called the Gosplan. Within the frame of general policy set by the Party, the Gosplan determined how much of every article the country should produce, how much of the national effort should go into the formation of capital and how much into producing articles for daily consumption, what wages all classes of workers should receive, and at what prices all goods should be exchanged. At the bottom level, in the individual factory, the local management drew up its "requirements," or estimates of what it would need, in raw material, machinery, trained workers, plant facilities and fuel, if it was to deliver the planned quantity of its product at a stated date. These estimates were passed up the planning ladder (or, thousands of such estimates up thousands of ladders) until they reached the Gosplan, which, balancing them against each other and against other needs as seen at the top, determined how much steel, coal, etc., should be produced, and in what qualities and grades; how many workers should be trained in technical schools, and in what particular skills; how many machines should be manufactured, and how many spare parts; how many new freight cars should be constructed, and which lines of railway track needed repair, and how, where, when, and to whom the steel, coal, technicians, machines, and rolling stock should be made available. The Plan, in short, undertook to control, by conscious management, the flow of resources and manpower which under free capitalism was regulated by shifts in demand and supply, through changes in prices, wage levels, profits, interest rates, or rent.

The system was exceedingly intricate. It was not easy to have the right number of ball bearings, for example, arrive at the right place at the right time, in exact correspondence to the amounts of other materials or to the number of workers waiting to use them. Sometimes there was overproduction, sometimes underproduction. The Plan was often amended as it was applied in action. Countless reports, check-ups, and exchanges of information were necessary. A huge class of white-collar office workers came into existence to handle the paper-work. But the Plan achieved its aim.

The primary objective of the First Five-Year Plan was to build up the heavy industry, or capital wealth, of the U.S.S.R. The aim was to industrialize without the use of foreign loans.[4] Russia in 1928 was still chiefly an agricultural country. The world offered hardly any case of a country shifting from agriculture to industry without borrowing capital from abroad. Great Britain, the original home of the Industrial Revolution, was the best example, although even there, in the eighteenth century, a great deal of capital invested in England was owned by the Dutch. An agricultural country could industrialize from its own resources only by drawing upon agriculture itself. An Agricultural Revolution had been prerequisite to an Industrial Revolution in England. By enclosure of land, the squeezing out of small independent farmers and the introduction of scientific cultivation, under the auspices of a growing class of wealthy landowners, England had both increased its production of food and released many of the rural population to find employment in industry. The First Five-Year Plan called for a similar agricultural revolution in Russia, without benefit to landlords and under the auspices of the state.

The Plan provided for the collectivization of agriculture. It set up collective farms, averaging a few thousand acres apiece, which were considered to be the property not of the state but of the peasants collectively who resided on them. Individual peasants were to pool their privately owned fields and livestock in these collectives. Those peasants who possessed fields or stock in considerable amount, the prosperous peasants or *kulaks,* resisted surrendering them to the new collectives. The *kulaks* were therefore liquidated as a class. Zealous detachments of Communists from the cities often used more violence than the Plan envisaged; poor peasants turned upon rich ones; hundreds of

---

[4] The Bolsheviks had repudiated the entire debt of the tsarist empire. Their credit in capitalist countries was therefore not good, so that, in addition to fearing dependence upon foreign lenders, they were in any case unable to borrow large sums.

thousands of *kulaks* and their families were killed, and many more transported to labor camps in remote parts of the Soviet Union. The trend that had gone on since Stolypin and indeed since the Emancipation, building up a class of property-owning, labor-hiring, and "bourgeois" peasants, was now abruptly reversed. Politically, the obstinate obstruction of individualistic farmers was removed, and the peasantry was converted into a class more nearly resembling the proletariat of Marxian doctrine, a class of people who as individuals owned no capital and employed no labor, and so were better able to feel the advantages of a proletarian state. The year 1929, not 1917, was the great revolutionary year for most people in Russia.

Collectivization was accomplished at the cost of village class war in which the most capable farmers perished, and at the cost also of a wholesale destruction of livestock. The big farmers slaughtered their horses, cattle, pigs, and poultry rather than give them up. Even middling and small farmers did the same, caring nothing about animals that were no longer their own, or naively expecting that under collectivism the state would soon furnish a new supply. The ruinous loss of animals was the worst unforeseen calamity of the First Five-Year Plan. For years, meat, dairy products, leather, animal fats, and horse power were in short supply. Agricultural disorder, together with two summers of bad weather, was followed by temporary but deathly famine in southeast Russia.

By introducing thousand-acre units in place of very small ones, collectivization made it possible to apply capital to the soil. Formerly the average peasant had been far too poor to buy a tractor, and his fields too tiny and dispersed for him to use one, so that only a few rare *kulaks* had employed any machinery. In the course of the First Five-Year Plan hundreds of Machine Tractor Stations were organized throughout the country. Each, in its region, maintained a force of tractors, harvesting combines, expert agronomists, etc., which were despatched from one collective farm to another by local arrangement. The application of capital increased the output per peasant. It was also much easier administratively for higher authorities to get control over the agricultural surplus (products not consumed by the village itself) from a single collective farm than from numerous small and unorganized peasants. Each collective was assigned a quota on which it contracted in advance to make delivery; members of the collective could sell in a free market any products they raised beyond this quota; but meanwhile the government knew the quantity of agricultural produce it could count on, either to feed the cities and other regions that did not produce their own food, or for export in the world market to pay for imports of machinery from the West. For various reasons, both technical and administrative, in the six years from 1927 to 1933 the marketable surplus in grains almost doubled, and more than doubled in cotton, flax and wool. Simultaneously, the villages needed less labor, so that between 1926 and 1939 twenty million people moved from country to city.

Collectivization of agriculture was therefore a great success for the purpose for which it was intended. Unfriendly critics have observed that it threw the peasant back into something like the *mir,* condemning him to the rounds of communal living, robbing him of the chance to make any decisions of his own. By obliging peasants to make "deliveries" below market prices, it even revived some features of the type of serfdom and forced labor that had prevailed a century before over most of Eastern Europe. It is probable, however, that in Russia half or more of the peasantry was glad to retain the communalism of the *mir.* It seems likely, too, that by 1939 a great many of the rural people were better housed and better fed than they had been before the Revolution. *Kulaks* who might have remembered better conditions had not survived.

With the agricultural base thus revolutionized, industrialization went rapidly forward. At first there was considerable dependence on the capitalist countries. Engineers and other technicians from western Europe and the United States took service in the Soviet Union. Much machinery was at first imported. But the world-wide depression that set in about 1931, bringing a catastrophic fall of agricultural prices, meant that foreign-made machines became more costly in terms of the cereals that were the chief Soviet export. The international situation also deteriorated. Both Japan and Germany in the 1930's showed an increasing hostility to the U.S.S.R. The Second Five-Year Plan, launched in 1932, differed from the first in its greater determination to cut down imports and achieve national self-sufficiency, especially in the heavy industry that was basic to war production.

No ten years in the history of any Western country ever showed such a rate of industrial growth as the decade of the first two Plans in the Soviet Union. In Great Britain industrialization had been gradual; in Germany and the United States it had been more rapid, and in each country there had been decades in which output of coal or iron doubled; but in the U.S.S.R., from 1928 to 1938, production of iron and steel expanded four times, and that of coal three and a half times. In 1938 the U.S.S.R. was the world's largest producer of farm tractors and railway locomotives. Four-fifths of all its industrial output came from plants built in the preceding ten years. Two plants alone, at the new cities of Magnitogorsk in the Urals and Stalinsk a thousand miles farther east, produced as much iron and steel as the whole Russian Empire in 1914.

The Plans called for a marked development of industry east of the Urals, and so brought a modernization of life for the first time to inner Asia, in a way comparable only to the movement of machine industry into the once primitive Great Lakes region of the American Middle West. Pittsburghs, Clevelands, and Detroits rose in the old Turkestan and Siberia. Copper mines were opened in the Urals and around Lake Balkash, lead mines in the Far East and in the Altai Mountains. New grain producing regions were developed in Siberia and in the Kazakh S.S.R., whence grain was shipped westward to Russia proper, or southward to the Uzbek S.S.R., which was devoted mainly to cotton. Tashkent, the Uzbek capital, formerly a remote town of bazaars and caravans, grew to be a city of over half a million, a center of cotton culture, copper mining and electrical industries, connected with the North by the newly built Turksib railway. The Kuznetsk basin, two thousand miles inland from every ocean, was found to possess coal deposits of high grade. Kuznetsk coal and the iron ores of the Urals became complementary, though separated by a thousand miles, somewhat like Pennsylvania coal and Minnesota iron in the United States. The opening of all these new areas, requiring the movement of food to Uzbekstan in exchange for cotton, or of Ural iron to the new Kuznetsk cities, demand a revolution in transportation. The railroads in 1938 carried five times as much freight as in 1913.

These astounding developments were enough to change the relative economic strength of the world's peoples with respect to one another. It was significant that inner Asia was for the first time turning industrial. It was significant, too, that although the U.S.S.R. had less foreign trade than had the Russian Empire, it had more trade than the old Russia with its Asian neighbors, with which it formed new and close connections. The Russia that went to war with Germany in 1941 proved to be a different antagonist from the Russia of 1914. Industrialization in the Urals and in Asia enabled the U.S.S.R. (with a good deal of Allied assistance) to survive the German occupation and destruction of the older industrial areas in the Don valley. The new "socialist fatherland" proved able to absorb the shock.

At the same time, the degree of industrialization of the U.S.S.R. should not be exaggerated. It was phenomenal because it started from so little. In efficiency, as shown by output per worker employed, the U.S.S.R. continued to lag behind the West. In intensity of modernization, as shown by output of certain items in proportion to the whole population, it also lagged. Per capita of its huge population, in 1937, the U.S.S.R. produced less coal, electricity, cottons, woollens, leather shoes, or soap than did the United States, Britain, Germany, France, or even Japan, and less iron and steel than any of them except Japan. Production of paper is revealing because paper is used in so many "civilized" activities—in books, newspapers, magazines, correspondence, placards, maps, pictures, charts, business and government records, and household articles and amenities. Where the United States about 1937 produced 103 pounds of paper per person, Germany and Great Britain each 92, France 51, and Japan 17, the U.S.S.R. produced only 11.

Industrialization in Russia, as formerly in other countries, was put through at great sacrifice on the part of the people. It was not merely that *kulaks* lost their lives, or that others, whose numbers have never been known except to Soviet authorities, were found to be enemies of the system and sent off to correctional labor camps. All were required to accept a program of austerity and self-denial, going without the better food, housing, and other consumers' goods that might have been produced, in order that the capital wealth and heavy industry of the country might be built up. As much as a third of the national income was re-invested in industry every year—twice as much as in the England of 1914, though probably not more than in the England of 1840. The Plan required long hours of work, and low wages. People looked to the future, to the time when, the basic industries having been built, better housing, better food, better clothing, and more leisure would follow. Morale was sustained by propaganda. One of the chief functions of Party members was to explain why sacrifices were necessary. In the late 1930's life began to ease; food rationing was abolished in 1935, and a few more products of light industry, such as dishes and fountain pens, began to appear in Soviet retail stores. But the need for war preparations, as the world again approached chaos, again drove back the vision of the Promised Land.

Socialism, as realized in the Plans, did away with some of the evils of unrestrained free enterprise. There was no unemployment. There was no cycle of boom and depression. There was no such misuse of women and children as in the early days of industrialism in the West. There was no absolute want or pauperization, except for political undesirables, and except for temporary conditions of famine. There was a minimum below which no one was supposed to fall. On the other hand, there was no economic equality. Marxism, indeed, had never seen equality of income as a virtue. While there was no handful of very rich people, as in the West (where the income of the rich came from property), the differences in wages and salaries were as great as in Europe or the United States. Managers, engineers, and intellectual workers received the highest pay. People with large incomes, by buying government bonds or accumulating personal possessions, could build up little fortunes for themselves and their children. They could not, however, under socialism, own any industrial capital.

Competition persisted. In 1935 a miner named Stakhanov greatly increased his daily output of coal by devising improvements in his methods of work. He also greatly increased his wages, since Soviet workers were paid at piece rates. His example proved contagious; workers all over the country began to break records of all kinds. The government publicized their achievements, called them Stakhanovites and "labor heroes," and pronounced the movement to be "a new and higher stage of socialist competition." In labor circles in the United States such straining to increase output would be called a speed-up, and piece-work wages had long been anathema to the organized labor of all countries. Nor was management free from competitive pressure. It was quite possible to go bankrupt, for state banks continued to advance funds to industrial enterprises. A factory manager who failed to show a profit upon which the Plan counted, or who failed to meet his quota of output, might lose not only his job but his social status or even his life. Poor management was often construed as sabotage. Poor use of the men and resources allocated to a factory was considered a betrayal of Soviet workers and a waste of the property of the nation. The press, not otherwise free, freely denounced whole industries or individual executives for failures to meet the Plan.

The sense of competition or emulation, the feeling that everybody was busily toiling and struggling to create a socialist fatherland, was perhaps the most distinctive achievement of the new system. Workers had a real belief that the new industrial wonders were their own. The sense of participation, of belonging, which democracy had given to the average man in the West in political matters, was widely felt in the U.S.S.R. in economic matters also. People rejoiced at every new advance as a personal triumph. It became a national pastime to watch the mounting statistics, the fulfilling of quotas or hitting of "targets." Newspaper readers read no comic strips; they read eagerly of the latest doings (or misdoings) on the economic front. Never had there been such unalloyed delight in material and mechanical progress, not even in America in the Gilded Age. No class difference was felt between labor and management. There was apparently little envy, since differences of income, being socialistic, were regarded as necessary and fair. In creating this solidarity, this widely shared willingness to contribute, this trust in one's economic superiors and pride in collective accomplishment, the U.S.S.R. offered one of its most serious challenges to the private enterprise and private capitalism of the West.

How real this feeling was, how much of it was spontaneous, and how much was inculcated by a watchful and dictatorial government, are questions on which there has been much difference of opinion. Solidarity was purchased at the price of totalitarianism. The government supervised everything. There was no room for skepticism, eccentricity of thought, or any basic criticism that weakened the will to achieve. As in tsarist times, no one could leave the country without special permission, which was given far more rarely than before 1914. There was only one Party. There were no free labor unions, no free press, no freedom of association, and at best only an irritable tolerance for religion. Art, literature, and even science became vehicles of political propaganda. Dialectical materialism was the official philosophy. Conformity was the ideal, and the very passion for solidarity made for fear and suspicion of all who might go astray. As for the number of people sacrificed to the Juggernaut, liquidated bourgeois, liquidated *kulaks,* purged Party members, disaffected persons sentenced to long terms in labor camps, not even an approximate estimate can be made, but it certainly reached many millions over the years.

In 1936 socialism was judged to have proved so successful that a new constitution for the U.S.S.R. was proclaimed. It enumerated, as rights of Soviet citizens, not merely the usual civil liberties of Western democracy but the rights to steady employment, rest, leisure, economic security, and a comfortable old age. It reorganized the soviet republics as explained above, and granted a democratic system of voting. The new constitution was favorably commented upon in the West, where it was hoped that the Russian Revolution, like former revolutions, had at last turned into more peaceable and quiet channels. It soon became apparent, however, that the Communist Party remained the sole governing group in the country. And the Party was racked by internal troubles.

It was natural that the complex and multifarious operations of the Five-Year Plans should produce divergences of opinion among the men who carried them out. The Party elders, however, were engaged not merely in discussions of policy but in the older game of the seizure of power. On the Right, led by Bukharin, was a group that believed in more gradual methods of collectivizing the peasants. More important was the element described as Leftist. Its mastermind and rallying point was the exiled Trotsky. Probably there was some kind of secret Trotskyist machine within the U.S.S.R. and within the Party. Possibly, as was later charged, some Trotskyists had intrigued with some Germans to overthrow and replace Stalin; it seems less inherently improbable when we recall that it was the Germans who had shipped Lenin to Russia in 1917. As early as 1933 the Party underwent a drastic purge, in which a third of its members were expelled. In 1934 Serge Kirov, an old friend and revolutionary companion of Stalin since 1909, now a member of the Central Committee and of its Politburo, was assassinated in his office. The Party, horrified, struck back at its unknown enemies by a revival of terror, executing 103 persons before the assassin, who proved to be a Party member, was apprehended.

Then in 1936 sixteen Old Bolsheviks—Zinoviev and others—were brought to trial. They were charged with the murder of Kirov, with plotting the murder of Stalin, and with having organized, in 1932, under Trotsky's inspiration, a secret group to disorganize and terrorize the Central Committee. To the amazement of the world, all the accused made full confession to the charges in open court. All blamed themselves as unworthy and erring reprobates. All were put to death. In 1937, after similar trials, another batch met the same fate; and in 1938 Bukharin and the Rightists, charged with wanting to restore bourgeois capitalism and conspiring with Trotsky to revolutionize the U.S.S.R., were likewise executed. The same confessions and self-accusations followed in almost every case. How these confessions were obtained in open court, from men apparently in full possession of their faculties and bearing no sign of physical harm, has remained one of the great mysteries of modern statecraft. Meanwhile, in 1937 and 1938, severe purges of Trotskyists and others were made in the Party rank-and-file, the administration, the schools, and the army. Marshal Tukhachevski and seven other ranking generals, accused of Trotskyism and of conspiring with the Germans and Japanese, were tried in a secret court martial and put to death. The murder of Trotsky himself in 1940 has been mentioned.

By these famous "purge trials" Party discipline was enforced. It is likely that a real danger of renewed revolution was averted. Had the tsarist government dealt as summarily with Bolsheviks as Bolsheviks dealt with one another there could have been no November Revolution. Stalin rid himself by the trials of all possible rivals for his own position. He disposed of the embarrassment of having men about him who could remember the old days, who could quote Lenin as a former friend, or belittle the reality of 1937 by recalling the dreams of 1917. After 1938 there were virtually no Old Bolsheviks left. Or, to put a different light on the matter, it may be said that a new Party and a new leadership had emerged. The aging but still explosive professional revolutionaries were now dead. A younger group, products of the new order, successful men of affairs, practical, constructive, and impatient of "agitators," were now operating what was now an established system.

THE INTERNATIONAL IMPACT OF COMMUNISM

Marxism had always been international in its outlook. To Marx, and the early Marxists, existing states (like other institutions) owed their character to the class struggle. They were committees of the bourgeoisie to govern the proletariat. National states were regarded as frameworks, destined to be dismantled and pass away in the course of inevitable historic processes. After Marx's death, as Marxist parties grew in numbers, and as the states of western Europe became more democratic, most people who called themselves Marxists actually accepted the national state, seeing in it a means by which the workingman's lot could be gradually improved. This view was part of the movement of "revisionism," or what more rigorous Marxists called "opportunism." . . .

Lenin, until his death in 1924, believed that the Russian Revolution was only a local phase of a world revolution—of *the* revolution of strict Marxian doctrine. Russia, for him, was the theater of currently most active operations in the international class war. Because he expected proletarian upheaval in Germany, Poland, the Danube valley, and the Baltic regions, he accepted without compunction the treaty of Brest-Litovsk. He took no pride in Russia; he was no patriot or "social-chauvinist," to use his own term. In the founding of the U.S.S.R. in 1922 he saw a nucleus around which other and greater soviet republics of any nationality might coalesce. "Soviet republics in countries with a higher degree of civilization," he wrote, "whose proletariat has greater social weight and influence, have every prospect of outstripping Russia as soon as they start upon the road of proletarian dictatorship."

The First World War was in fact followed by revolutions in Germany and eastern Europe. With the German and Austro-Hungarian empires wrecked, socialists and liberals of all descriptions strove to establish new regimes. Among socialists the old differences persisted, between Social Democrats favoring gradual, non-violent and parliamentary methods, and a more extreme (and smaller) group which saw in post-war disintegration a chance to realize the international proletarian revolution. The first group looked upon the Bolshevik revolution with horror. The second looked upon it with admiration. The first group included not only trade union officials and practical socialist politicians, but such pre-war giants of Marxian exegesis as Karl Kautsky and Eduard Bernstein. In the second group were Karl Liebknecht and Rosa Luxemburg, who, organizing the Spartacist [5] movement in Germany, attempted to overthrow the majority-socialist government in Germany, in January 1919, as Lenin had overthrown the Provisional Government in Russia in November 1917. In the second group also was Bela Kun, who had turned Bolshevik during a sojourn in Russia, and who set up and maintained a soviet regime in Hungary for several months in 1919.

Lenin and the Bolsheviks, though absorbed in their own revolution, gave all possible aid to the fringe of Left socialists of Europe. They sent large sums of money to Germany, to Sweden, to Italy. When the Bolshevik Radek was arrested in Berlin he was found to have a plan for proletarian revolution in all Central Europe in his possession. The Party considered sending Russian troops to Hungary to support Bela Kun. But the chief instrument of world revolution, created in March 1919, was the Third or Communist International.

The Second International, which since its foundation in 1889 had met every two or three years until 1914, held its first post-war meeting at Berne in 1919. It represented socialist parties and labor organizations of all countries. The Berne meeting was stormy, for a small minority vehemently demanded "revolution as in Russia, socialization of property as in Russia, application of Marxism as in Russia." Overruled at Berne, they repaired to Moscow, and there founded a new International in conjunction with the Russian Communist Party, and with Lenin and the Russians dominating it completely. It was Lenin's hope, by founding a new International of his own, to discredit moderate socialism and to claim for the Communists the true line of succession from the First International of Karl Marx. The First International, he declared, had laid the foundations for proletarian struggle, the Second had broadened it, the Third "took over the work of the Second International, cut off its opportunistic, social-chauvinist, bourgeois and petty-bourgeois rubbish, and began to carry into effect the dictatorship of the proletariat."

The first congress of the Third International in 1919 was somewhat haphazard, but at the second, in 1920, the extreme Left parties of thirty-seven countries were represented. The Russian party was supposedly only one component. Actually, it supplied most of the personnel and most of the funds; the Bolshevik Zinoviev was its first president, remaining in this office until his disgrace as a Trotskyist in 1927. The Third or Communist international— the Comintern—was in part a spontaneous rallying of Marxists from all countries who accepted the Bolshevik Revolution as the true fruition of Marxism, and so were willing to follow the Russian lead; but, even more, it was the creation and weapon of the Bolsheviks themselves, by which to disgrace and

[5] So named from Spartacus, a Roman slave who led a slave revolt in south Italy in 72 B.C.

isolate the moderate socialists and effectuate world revolution. Of all enemies the Communists hated the socialists most, reserving for them even choicer epithets than they bestowed upon capitalists and imperialists, because Communists and socialists were competing for the same thing, the leadership of the world's working class.

Parties adhering to the Comintern were obliged to drop the old name "socialist" and call themselves Communist. They were obliged to accept strong international centralization. Where the Second International had been a loose federation, and its congresses hardly more than forums, the Third International put strong powers in the hands of its Executive Committee, whose orders the Communist parties of all countries had to obey. Since there was a kind of interlocking directorate by which members of the Central Committee of the Party in Russia sat also as members of the Executive Committee of the Third International, the top Communists in Russia had, in the Comintern, an "apparatus" by which they could produce desired effects in many countries—the use of party-members to penetrate labor unions, foment strikes, propagandize ideas, or interfere in elections. The second congress, in 1920, endorsed a program of Twenty-one Points, written by Lenin. These included the requirements that each national party must call itself Communist, repudiate "reformist" socialism, propagandize labor unions and get Communists into the important union offices, infiltrate the army, impose an iron discipline upon members, require submission of each party worker to his national committee and to the orders of the international Executive, use both legal channels and secret underground methods, and expel promptly any member not hewing to the party line. Making no pretense of respect for parliamentary democracy, the second congress ruled that "the only question can be that of utilizing bourgeois state institutions for their own destruction." As for the labor movement, Lenin wrote that "the struggle against the Gomperses, the Jouhaux, the Hendersons [6] . . . who represent an *absolutely similar* social and political type as our Mensheviks . . . must be waged without mercy to the end." The Comintern was not an assemblage of humanitarians engaged in welfare work; it was a weapon for revolution, organized by revolutionaries who knew what revolution was.

For several years the U.S.S.R., using the Comintern or more conven-

---

[6] Samuel Gompers (1850–1924), began as a cigar maker, president of the American Federation of Labor, 1886–1924; Léon Jouhaux (1879–), began as a factory worker, secretary-general of the French General Confederation of Labor, 1909–47, resigned in 1947 to found a new labor organization in opposition to Communism; Arthur Henderson (1863–1935), began as an iron-moulder's apprentice, chairman of the Parliamentary Labor Party, 1908–10, 1914–17, Member of Parliament, 1903–31, Secretary of State for Foreign Affairs, 1929–31.

tional diplomatic channels, promoted world revolution as best it could. Communists from many countries went to Russia for indoctrination. Native-born or Russian agents proceeded to the Dutch Indies, to China, to Europe, to America. Until 1927 the Chinese revolutionists welcomed assistance from Moscow; the Russian, Borodin, became an adviser in their affairs. In 1924, in England, publication of the "Zinoviev letter," in which, at least allegedly, the Comintern urged British workers to provoke revolution, led to a great electoral victory for the Conservative party. The Bolshevik menace, real and imagined, produced everywhere a strong reaction. It was basic to the rise of fascism. . . .

In 1927, with the suppression of Trotskyism and world-revolutionism in Russia, and with the concentration under Stalin on a program of building socialism in one country, the Comintern entered upon a period of inaction. About 1935, as fascist dictators became more noisily bellicose, the U.S.S.R. turned to a policy of international collective security, and the Comintern instructed all Communist parties, each in its own country, to enter into coalitions with socialists and advanced liberals, in what were called "popular fronts," to combat fascism and reaction. During the Second World War (in 1943), as a gesture of good-will to Great Britain and the United States, the U.S.S.R. abolished the Comintern entirely, but it reappeared in 1947 under a new name, the Communist Information Bureau or Cominform. In the revolutionary unrest that followed the Second World War, as in similar circumstances after the First World War, the Communist offensive was resumed.

Outside Russia (as, indeed, in it) the number of actual "card-carrying" members of Communist parties remained very small. They were a tiny minority from which no people had anything to fear. Even in Russia, only the accumulated effects of war, revolution, and disaster had made possible Lenin's seizure of power. What others had to fear was war and disaster, not Communism as such.

It was not through the Comintern that the U.S.S.R. exerted its greatest influence on the world. It exerted its influence by the massive fact of its very existence. By 1939 it was clear that a new type of economic system had been created. However one judged the U.S.S.R., no one could dismiss its socialism as visionary or impracticable. An alternative to free enterprise and capitalism had been brought into being. Marxism was not merely a theory; there was an actual society, embracing a sixth of the globe, which called itself Marxist. In every country those who were most critical of capitalist institutions compared them unfavorably to those of the Soviet Union. Many believed, or hoped, that something like Soviet results might be obtained without the use of Soviet methods, which were dismissed as typically Russian, a deplorable heritage from Byzantine empire and the tsars. With the appearance of an extreme Communist Left, socialism and socialist ideas seemed in contrast to be middling and respectable. Everywhere in the 1930's the idea of "planning" began to find favor. Everywhere workers obtained more security against the fluctuations of capitalism. The so-called "backward" peoples, especially in Asia, were particularly impressed by the achievement of the U.S.S.R., which had shown how a backward country could develop a scientific industrial civilization without falling under the influence of foreign capital or foreign guidance.

Those who hoped to profit from Soviet experience were not generally communist, and had no intention of following the dictates of Moscow. Wholly accepting neither Russian Communism nor historic Western capitalism, they hoped to combine the best attributes of both. Even to say this much is to suggest the tremendous implications of the Russian Revolution. Before 1917 no one in Europe or Asia had thought that anything was to be learned from Russia. Twenty years later even critics of the U.S.S.R. feared that it might represent the wave of the future. Its sheer power was soon demonstrated in the Second World War. In its power, its prestige, its ideas, its anti-imperialist appeal to many of the earth's peoples, the U.S.S.R. was a force on which all had to reckon; and, while undeniably violent and terroristic, ruthless in its disregard for individual persons and individual liberties, it also raised questions of social justice to which Western countries had to find an answer.

Chapter XV

THE PROBLEM OF WORLD PEACE

❧

1. INTERNATIONAL ORDER AND DISORDER (1919–1939)

THE BACKGROUND OF WORLD WAR I

THE WORLD WAR of 1914–18 was a demonstration of the extent to which Western civilization had become disintegrated. There had been untold wars in European history, but never before had a war between European nations been so largely conceived as a war between national cultures, and never before had the sense of the community of European civilization been so fundamentally denied as during those years. This was the outcome of a long process of gradual weakening of the old bonds of unity which had at other times acted as a counterbalance against the tendencies dividing the European nations.

The earliest of these bonds was Christianity, for it had been the first moulder of European society. As long as it was present in the hearts and heads of men it had kept them from considering their conflicts, however serious these might be, as "total" conflicts, and it had provided a common point of reference and common standards of judgment. Its impact on political life had, however, weakened during the eighteenth and nineteenth centuries as one realm of life after another had become secularized and as the Church itself, partly because of a lack of spiritual vigor, but partly also because it desired to regain its liberty, withdrew more and more from public life. The Churches thus "ceased to give form to life," and religion became a private affair.

The place which Christianity had occupied as a formative element in society was largely taken by that European movement which began in philosophy as the Enlightenment and then expressed itself politically in the various

---

This chapter is from two sources. Section 1 is from *International Conciliation* (Carnegie Endowment for International Peace, 1940), No. 363, by the International Consultative Group of Geneva. Section 2 is from *A History of the Modern World* (pp. 810–821; New York, Alfred A. Knopf, Inc., 1952), by R. R. Palmer.

forms of Liberalism and Democracy. Its main tenets were the dignity and freedom of men and the power of human reason over social and political conditions. While these tenets were partly borrowed from Christianity, they were soon transformed into a new faith—the faith in the essential goodness of man and the rational character of history. This alternative to the Christian faith became so powerful that even the Christian Churches adapted their teaching to a large extent to the new doctrines, and to that extent gave up their own insights into the life of man and of society.

The result of the new doctrines on the life of the nations was two-fold. On the one hand, they succeeded in creating a new equilibrium between society and the individual and elaborated the conception of the State as limited by law in relation to its own citizens and in relation to other States. It is due to the Enlightenment acting upon the personal monarchies of the eighteenth century that a modern system of international law was first elaborated. On the other hand, these doctrines led to a loosening of the bonds by which society had been held together. The new individualism undermined the religious and moral convictions which had given society its cohesion. The results of this process became especially evident where and when the old common religious convictions lost ground.

Another important nineteenth century development was the growth of nationalism as an ideological factor. As the spread of democracy led to participation in national affairs by classes which had hitherto remained passive, the consciousness of nationhood became intensified. This new nationalism took different forms ranging from the nationalism of liberation from foreign domination to the aggressive nationalism which dreams of the world hegemony of one particular nation. In so far as this development was not checked by the concept of international solidarity or of a law binding upon all nations, it became a powerful factor in the breaking up of European unity.

Thus in the early years of this century there was in Western civilization no strong sense of a common heritage or of a common mission. Between the nations of Europe which had adopted the philosophy of Liberalism as their national philosophy and the nations which had not, there was no deep bond which could transcend the political and economic conflicts. The World War was the expression of European disintegration rather than its cause.

THE SPIRIT OF THE POST-WAR SETTLEMENT

The world of 1918 and of the period immediately following was a world in which extravagant idealism and bitter cynicism, high hopes and utter despair, lived side by side. The division between the two moods was not a political-geographical one as between the victorious and the defeated countries. For Germany had at that time not only its embittered nationalists, but also its youth movement and various other movements which believed deeply in social justice and international collaboration. And the Western European nations had not only their League of Nations supporters, but also their headstrong "realists" who believed only in pure power politics.

It is nevertheless true to say that, in view of the predominance of the Anglo-Saxon nations and the added prestige of democracy, the main note of that period was one of an optimistic liberalism based on faith in progress and in the harmonious outcome of the free interplay of political and economic forces. The war was conceived as an interlude and it was believed that the remarkable nineteenth-century advance in political and economic life, under the auspices of Liberalism, could now be resumed. Further education would dispel the forces of reaction and inaugurate an era of peace and prosperity for all.

Unfortunately the actual conduct of political affairs was in flagrant contradiction to the professed ideals. This was most easily perceived by those who suffered from these policies, that is the defeated nations and the working classes. Thus there grew up a deep-rooted suspicion that all political idealism was merely a smoke-screen for imperialistic and capitalistic designs.

The curious blend of utopianism and "realism," characteristic of this period, found expression in the League of Nations; for the League was conceived by some as the embodiment of a great new ideal, by others as a mere tool in the old game of power politics. It was in fact something of both, according to circumstances and occasions. The tragedy of the League, and indeed of the whole postwar settlement, is that it became the plaything of Utopians who made impossible claims for it and surrounded it with a mystic glamor, and of hardheaded "realists" who sabotaged its efficacy. Thus public opinion often swung between moods of optimism and cynicism, and the League was constantly diverted from its true object of making slow but real progress toward the ordering of international life.

The post-war settlement broke down because it reflected rather than transcended the contradictions inherent in Western society. It did not point toward a new integration, but tried to continue an order of life which was itself in process of disintegration. A fundamental change in international relations proved impossible as long as the nations did not accept corresponding changes in the ideological, political, and economic structure of their national life.

ECONOMIC CAUSES OF THE PEACE FAILURE

The role of economic factors in the peace failure of 1919–1939 was not of first importance. Political and psychological considerations played a more active part. But at every point, interpenetrating the whole complex structure of international relationships during these twenty critical years, economic factors are to be found. They did not pass unnoticed. Repeatedly the League of Nations and the International Labor Organization brought the nations of the world together in a long series of attempts to deal with the principal social and economic problems of the time. Questions of monetary stability, freer trade, the control of raw materials, the prevention of industrial depressions, and the improvement of working conditions and the standard of life have been studied and discussed as never before in the history of mankind. As a result much has been done which would otherwise have been neglected. The net outcome, nevertheless, has been negative, in the sense that peace was not preserved; and unquestionably economic unpreparedness was in part responsible. We cannot afford to make the same mistakes twice. The main purpose of this paper is to see what lessons may be learned for the future from the experience gained in the course of the last two decades. With this end in view it is necessary to distinguish some of the principal ways in which economic considerations enter into the peace-war calculus.

Economic Factors Making for War. Considered absolutely, economic factors are no longer direct causes of war. In the far-distant past the possession of certain hunting or grazing lands may well have been a matter of life or death for the competing tribes. Today, with modern methods of production, no country is forced to war by sheer economic need; which is fortunate, since otherwise war would probably be unpreventable. But the fact that, under present-day conditions, the economic causes of war are indirect does not deprive them of importance. Their influence has been felt in three main spheres: social, political, and military.

1. Social discontent as a seed-bed for war. In all probability the principal means by which peace is disturbed and war provoked by economic factors is through their effect on popular feeling. People who are steadily improving their economic position, and realize they have something to lose, do not readily go to war. On the other hand, people who feel they are suffering from economic injustice, people whose economic status is being brought down, people

who have lost their means of livelihood or are deprived of their standby of savings, are ripe to be worked upon by anyone who can point to a plausible enemy. Partly by inadvertence, partly by design, countries have not used their productive capacity effectively to promote human well-being in the last twenty years. Especially have they fallen short wherever international economic cooperation was involved.

2. *Political motives dressed up as economic necessities.* The second major factor in the economic causation of war plays perhaps a larger part in propaganda than in reality. Markets, colonies, protectorates, spheres of influence, control of raw materials, and similar quasi-economic considerations are frequently represented as of vital economic importance to a nation. In certain circumstances they may be. If countries, having secured such controls, follow a dog-in-the-manger policy they can do great damage to the rest of the world. But provided a reasonably liberal policy is pursued, though certain advantages unquestionably accrue to the possessing nation, it is no life or death matter to the others. Food and raw materials in particular have been so freely available over the last ten years that producers have not known what to do with their stocks, and are frequently driven to sell at prices below the costs of production.

Behind this much discussed question the real motives are political rather than economic. The considerations weighing most with the ruling elites of the principal countries are power and prestige. These considerations are of capital importance, since upon them depends the loyalty of the people to the ruling elite. In the game of power politics colonies, control of raw materials, protectorates and the like serve in the nature of a scoring device, indicating who has the upper hand. As a genuine economic causes of way they are of relatively little importance, provided always (and it is an essential provision) the liberal and not the dog-in-the-manger policy is followed. At most their retention or acquisition would represent to the people of the countries concerned some relatively small decrease or increase in the average income: certainly not the difference between starvation and affluence.

3. *Fear of economic weakness in case of war.* The third and most actively potent of the economic factors entering into the peace-war calculus is the fear felt by almost every country that, in the event of hostilities, it might find itself cut off from necessary supplies (food or essential war materials) and so be made to yield by sheer economic pressure. This fear may easily lead to aggression. A country so placed will seize upon a favorable occasion of going to war, in the hope that, by reason of the advantages so gained, it may be in

a better position to resist economically should it at some time be attacked. Similar considerations apply to the acquisition or retention of fueling stations and fortified points on trade routes.

This dread of economic weakness in the event of war sets up a series of vicious circles. Almost invariably one country's security automatically involves another country's danger. Territorial or economic readjustments which constitute an assurance to one side inevitably appear as a threat to the other. So long as such a situation persists, war is likely to remain a standing menace. This in turn means that a large and increasing proportion of the world's capacity to produce will go in armaments. The higher armaments are piled the more liable they are to explode. And the more liable they are to explode the higher they must be piled. The natural desire of every country to make itself secure places the whole world in peril.

These three specific factors entered largely into the post 1919 debacle. Many related influences might be mentioned, some of which in particular circumstances have attained a certain importance. Economic misery among the people, liable to give rise to political disturbance, may lead a government to court war as a means of diverting attention to more exciting themes. Similarly, fear of imminent economic collapse may drive an irresponsible government to risk war. In a rather different direction it is often alleged that industrial and banking groups have promoted war as a means of swelling profits, of enlarging markets, or of getting control of areas containing oil, gold or other valuable materials. This factor seems to have played relatively little part in the present breakdown; but the possessions amassed as an outcome of earlier wars so motivated are unquestionably a factor in the continuance of a war psychology. From yet another angle, vested interests and fear of unemployment exercise in combination a powerful counter-influence to the movement toward a reduction of armaments, or to the conclusion of any far-reaching political or economic settlement. At every stage, indeed, in the building up of a war situation, economic considerations and motives appear. But, singly or collectively, they do not make hostilities inevitable. The great wars of the twentieth century are not between the poor and starving countries of the world but between the richest. There is no longer an economic imperative, driving nations to fight.[1]

Underlying Characteristics of the Economic Situation. In evaluating the

---

[1] Probably the nearest approach to such an imperative was to be found in the case of Japan with its large and rapidly increasing population, all cultivable land in use, no considerable raw material resources, no possibilities of emigration on a sufficient scale, and world markets partially closed against its exports. But even here there was no likelihood of a decline in the standard of living, though some slackening in the very rapid rate of increase in *per capita* income was to be expected.

part played by these various factors in the breakdown of peace it is necessary to take into account certain of the underlying characteristics of the world economic situation in the twentieth century.

1. Technological advance and the standard of life. The first of these is the great dynamic factor of industrialism. Technical methods of producing goods have been revolutionized in the course of the last two hundred years. As a result, the standard of life has been, is being and can be enormously improved. To take a specific instance, the average real income per head in Sweden is now three and a half times what it was some seventy years ago; and that in spite of considerable population increase and reduction in hours of work. Improvement to about this degree is typical of all countries using modern methods of production and is continuing. According to the index calculated by Carl Snyder, world physical production increased at the rate of 3.15 per cent per annum over the period 1865–1914 and 3.9 per cent during 1924–29. This in itself is a force making for peace, provided productive capacity is actually used to raise the standard of life. But it does not necessarily follow that it will be so used. Mass production methods can be made to serve death and destruction much more easily than they can be harnessed to human well-being.

2. "Poverty in plenty." Even where increasing industrial capacity goes principally to raise the standard of life, catastrophic interruptions in the rhythm of progress can have untoward consequences. From the earliest days of the industrial revolution the economic system has been subject to business cycles. For a while goods are produced in increasing quantities; buying remains strong and may even outdistance production; industry is fully employed. Then comes the slump. Buying fails to keep pace with output. Production is cut down; unemployment becomes severe; the demand for goods declines. This process, moreover, once started feeds upon itself. Unemployed men cease to buy as freely as before and production is further reduced. Lower production leads to further unemployment, and so on. After a more or less protracted period of such "poverty in plenty" industry is able to resume something approaching normal output; but only to break down again at a later stage. The world entered upon the post-war period with this central problem of the economic system unsolved and to a large extent unrecognized.

3. Unequal distribution of income within countries and between countries. Partly owing to the recurrent crises and to the scarcity of jobs even in "normal" times, the low ranks of the working population secure only a very small fraction of the total income. Thus, in the United States, the lowest 10 per cent of families receive only one-sixtieth of the total national income, while the

upper 10 percent receive more than one-third. The disparity between countries is equally great. The average real income per occupied person in the United States might very roughly be put at one hundred dollars a month. In India and China the average monthly income per occupied person should be the equivalent of some five or ten dollars at the most. This situation, moreover, tends to perpetuate itself. The countries with low *per capita* incomes have not the means to obtain modern equipment in sufficient quantities and to train the necessary workers. Furthermore, the fact that, generally speaking, population is increasing most rapidly in the poorest countries and least rapidly in the richest countries makes this discrepancy in *per capita* income tend to grow larger rather than less. Gross inequality of income is not perhaps directly productive of war, but it can be highly destructive of peace.

4. The passing of laissez-faire. From about the beginning of the twentieth century the system of private competitive enterprise known as laissez-faire was already showing signs of decrepitude. Monopolies of many kinds, from "all-in" trusts and international cartels to trade unions and price-rings, impaired the ready adjustment to changed circumstances which was the saving feature of the system. The war of 1914–18 not only accelerated this tendency towards monopoly but gave rise to an enormous number of maladjustments with which the rapidly ossifying system was unable to cope. State expenditure on an inordinate scale, huge debts burdens, the progressive industrialization of agricultural countries, the increasing restriction of trade and of migration, and above all, the extraordinary violence of industrial depression were among the many problems which helped to make laissez-faire unworkable. The aim of all countries (with the exception of Soviet Russia) at the conclusion of the struggle was nevertheless to return to pre-war practices, to "normalcy" as it was called. Accordingly, the first post-war decade was spent in laboriously rebuilding the economic system along traditional lines; the second decade in recovering from the collapse of the structure so erected.

Quite apart from the specific merits or demerits of laissez-faire as a method, many people would consider it basically defective on a wider view; believing that to rely upon acquisitive motives for the drive required to run the economic machine necessarily promotes a system of values incompatible with peaceful relationships, whether between classes or between States.

Outstanding Economic Events 1919–39. From this brief account it is evident that the general economic tide on which the peace of 1919 was launched had dangerous shoals beneath the surface. On all of these, in one fashion or other, the world crashed. In addition, it met economic disasters directly or indirectly resultant of the war and the peace settlement.

1. The attempt to extract reparations from Germany and to pay war debts to the United States. The peace settlement left Germany with huge reparation payments to make to the Allied nations, which in turn were in debt for enormous sums to the United States. This attempt to make war into an economic proposition was doomed to failure from the outset. For a time, however, it appeared to work; principally because United States speculators, by investing heavily in Germany, supplied the funds with which Germany paid the Allied nations, and they in turn paid the United States. With the onset of the world depression of 1929–32 investments into Germany ceased, and the United States, the residual creditor country, shut the door against payments by extraordinary tariff increases. This lamentable imbroglio and its ultimate breakdown made for great international tension and ill will.

2. The 1923 inflation in Germany. The printing of paper by the German monetary authorities, to the point where the mark became worthless, did more than any other single thing to wreck the social and economic structure of the country. In particular, it destroyed the savings of the German middle class. This cut away one of the principal foundations of social stability in a country already severely shaken. More even that the war or the peace the inflation destroyed all feeling of confidence and security in the established state of things. National Socialism derived much of its strength from the monetary mismanagement of 1923.

3. Soviet Russia. The emergence of the Communist regime from the crucible of war and and the efforts of the Soviet Government to exploit on a collectivist basis the huge natural resources of the largest land-tract in the world, produced a ferment wherever inequality of income was particularly marked. In many countries this had an undermining effect upon the economic system; in some, notably Italy and Germany, it produced reactions which, while different in appearance from the Soviet system, were sometimes not dissimilar in fact; and generally, throughout the world, it was instrumental in accentuating social and economic discontent.

4. The world depression of 1929–32. The general attempt to return to economic "normalcy" was finally defeated by the greatest depression of all time. No country was prepared for it. Few, if any, knew how to cope with it. If nations could have agreed to concentrate on expanding their own internal markets, unemployment could have been effectively met, and each would have helped to expand, instead of contracting, the external markets of others. But the opposite course was taken. Every country tried to save itself at the expense of the rest of the world.[2] The system of free enterprise ceased to function.

[2] The fact that this was done in the name of a world system—the international gold standard—is an added touch of irony.

Government control, based upon opportunism rather than economic principles, became the rule; to the great damage of international trade, international investment and the world economic relationships generally. The last opportunity, if it was not then already too late, was lost when the nations assembled at the London Monetary and Economic Conference of 1933 failed to find any basis of agreement. In Germany the six millions of unemployed, one worker in every three, recorded at the bottom of the depression led directly to the triumph of National Socialism.

5. *Economic planning for war.* With the breakdown of the economic system in 1929–32 a number of countries went over in varying degrees to some form of "economic planning"—the more or less complete control by the State of the economic machine. This in itself was neither good nor bad. The vital question, which is political rather than economic, was whether this planning was to be for higher living standards or for war. It rapidly became evident that in a number of countries economic planning had military preparedness as its principal aim. Other countries were of necessity drawn in. From that time war on a world scale became probable, perhaps inevitable.

The Need for Adaptation to a Changing World. For these various reasons the economic circumstances of 1919–39 proved destructive of peace. But to represent the record of these years as no more than, or even principally, a series of failures would do violence to the facts. It was far from being that. The advance made in economic knowledge, in international cooperation, and in the adoption of new methods was extraordinary. But it was not sufficient. The reason for this is now beginning to become clear. During the nineteenth century a number of highly dynamic movements were at work. Nationalism, machine technique, and an economic system in which unbridled acquisitiveness was the driving force, together produced an almost explosive mixture. The framework within which they were contained has now burst. As a consequence, the world is faced with the necessity of making a series of fundamental adjustments. Seen from the economic angle the following are among the most important.

1. *The need for machinery of economic adaptation.* Under the system of laissez-faire the economic policy of the State was to be self-effacing. Its supreme duty was not to interfere. With the breakdown of laissez-faire the State, for good or for ill, finds itself compelled to intervene at every turn. But in the great majority of countries no adequate mechanism has been set up to enable it to do this either effectively or with foresight. The whole situation has altered but the machinery of government on the economic side has remained practically unchanged. It is no one's task to look ahead or to see the situation as

a whole. Nor is there any organization designed to make this possible. As a consequence almost invariably governmental economic action is taken too late, is uncoordinated, is not informed by any broad purpose or aim, and is unrelated to the other concerns of the State. Adequate machinery for economic adjustment, national and international, is one of the outstanding requirements, and outstanding deficiencies, of the present age.

2. The need for international safeguarding of social progress. A second major problem of adjustment is at the point where economics and politics meet. Every advanced industrial country can now produce a huge surplus over and above the basic needs of its population. The people of the United States, for instance, could, if driven to it, subsist on about one-third of their present productive capacity, leaving the remaining two-thirds to be devoted to other purposes. The question is, How will this potential surplus be used? The great mass of mankind would unquestionably wish to see it used to increase human well-being. But circumstances may render this impracticable. If the government of any important country chooses to direct its industrial capacity not toward well-being but toward preparation for war, it can pile up an overwhelming striking force. Its neighbors, on pain of submission to military despotism, are bound to do likewise. Their neighbors in turn become alarmed; and so the process continues until it has circled the globe. The decision of any major country to use its productive power primarily for military purposes means that the whole world is forced to go over from planning for plenty to planning for war.

This situation in the acute form in which it now exists is the direct outcome of economic advance. In earlier times there was not the huge surplus in excess of basic needs. Almost all of the productive powers of a country went in keeping its people supplied with the bare means of subsistence. Nor were the instruments of war so sudden, so far-reaching, and so mechanized that mere human courage stood no chance against them. Modern technique had made the world not only an economic but also a military unit. International organization to meet this situation is imperative if countries are to be free to use their industrial capacity to improve the standard of life and well-being of their peoples.

3. The need for a broader conception of economic policy. Underlying the whole catena of adjustment is the need for a change over from extensive to intensive development. The difference between the nineteenth and twentieth centuries is that of a world in which there was still room for expansion and a world which, politically speaking, has "filled up." So long as there was ample elbow-room an acquisitive society could exist in relative quiet, if not in amity.

That time has passed. It is no longer possible to annex new territories or colonial possessions cheaply. Most of the material wealth of the world has been divided up. The resultant situation is one highly inimical to peace. Countries deficient in natural resources are bitterly envious of those having such resources under their control. An outstanding feature of the last thirty years has been the irreconcilable views of the "have" and "have-not" nations. Where this deficiency implies economic weakness in the event of war, the nightmare of every sovereign State, the feeling of divergent interests is enormously accentuated. Furthermore, during recent years the relatively liberal policies previously followed by nations rich in resources have been much curtailed. Wealthy countries have barred their frontiers round with tariffs and prohibitions. The gates have been closed against migration. The open door to colonial markets has been put upon the chain. On top of this, practically every country in the slump of 1929–32 tried to save itself at the expense of others by endeavoring to "export unemployment." Purchases abroad were cut down to the minimum and every effort made, legitimate and otherwise, to dump goods abroad. The net outcome was exaggerated protectionism, an enormous reduction in international trade, practical cessation of international investment, much breaking of contracts and nonpayment of debts, and a great deal of bad blood between countries over the more than questionable methods used. Subsequently, as military preparedness became increasingly the aim of economic planning, all of these tendencies were accentuated. The elevation of autarky to the rank of a sacred principle was only the last link in a long chain of progressive economic relationships.

In all these ways economic events have undermined the attempts to reinforce world solidarity. Yet, while it is sure that the world has "filled up" politically, in another direction it has opened out. Modern machine technique enables any and every country to achieve a high standard of living, provided the necessary industrial equipment is procurable and it is given access to the requisite raw materials and markets. That this is possible technically there can be no question. That it is in the right direction from the standpoint of peaceful relationships there can be little doubt. What is required if the world is to meet the challenge of the present age is that, severally and collectively, the nations shall pass over from a policy of aggressive expansion to one of cooperative development. Changes no less fundamental have occurred in the course of the last two hundred years. Political economy had as its initial aim the maximization of the wealth and power of the king. Later this resolved itself into the maximization of the wealth of the nation. This again evolved into the maximization of the individual economic welfare of the people making up the nation. What is now needed is the maximization of human well-being in its broadest sense, the advancement of social justice both within and between communities.

But it would be altogether illusory to represent this as merely or even primarily a change in economic structure. What is called for is a far-reaching transformation in the dynamic values actuating mankind. Provided this is forthcoming, the setting up of the necessary economic mechanism presents no insuperable difficulty. Without it, mere modifications in structure are likely to have only a limited effect. It would be illusory also to represent such a change, were it brought about, as certain to insure peace. No economic machinery, however successful, can do this. Man does not and cannot live by bread alone; and while economic measures such as these may provide an invaluable foundation, in the last analysis it is in the hearts and minds of men that peace has to be achieved.

POLITICAL CAUSES OF THE PEACE FAILURE

The Peace Settlement. Any attempt to assess the main factors in the history of the years between 1919 and 1939 must start from the Peace Conference of Paris. The international institutions that were created by that Conference introduced entirely new standards into the world of international politics. The Covenant implied a new political morality, the substitution of responsibility for power; it predicated a settlement which all were more concerned to preserve than to destroy. But the same Conference that drafted the Covenant was also the Conference that designed the new settlement. That settlement, which is embodied in the Treaties of Versailles, St. Germain, Trianon, and Neuilly, was not wholly, or indeed mainly, an immoral or vindicative settlement; it was none the less a settlement which not all States were equally interested in maintaining.

It was perhaps inevitable that after a world war in which human passions had been aroused in the service of nationalist ends, statesmen should have been unable to control those passions or deflect them into the service of the international community; it was perhaps inevitable that after four years' strain these statesmen should themselves have been too tired to attempt such a task. It was natural that when so many States, old and new, found themselves facing for the first time problems of the magnitude that appeared in 1919, the interests of Europe as a whole, or of the world as a whole, should have gone by default. But none the less the failure to take a European view, or a world view, must be assessed as the heaviest responsibility of 1919. It was a collective failure.

The Case of Germany. The most startling example of the collective failure was the attitude adopted toward Germany, not only in the clauses of the settlement, but still more in the manner of their presentation. General willingness to cooperate in the future obviously presupposed a minimum of common interest in preserving the settlement. The discrepancy between the principles of the settlement and its details brought both the principles and their advocates into disrepute in many States. Germany, Bulgaria, Hungary, and subsequently Italy, rejected them in varying degrees. In particular, the refusal to negotiate with Germany created an attitude of mind in that country that was never subsequently changed.

Attitude of the United States and Its Effect. But the initial mistakes were not irreparable. The Treaty of Versailles had the tremendous advantage that it contained in itself provisions for its own amendment. The damage done might very easily have been remedied had there been an attempt during subsequent years to make the settlement as attractive to the vanquished as it was to the victors. No such attempt was made.

We are forced to conclude that a major factor explaining this failure was the refusal of the United States to ratify the Treaty of Versailles. The nature of the Treaty itself, the unpleasant impression created in the United States by the Paris negotiations, the provision in the Constitution of the United States that a two-thirds vote in the Senate is necessary for the ratification of treaties, all these, and many other factors played their part in leading the United States to withdraw from Europe. This failure of the United States to ratify was certainly the hardest blow to the new institutions. The intervention of the United States had created a military and political situation that might have been stabilized had that country remained; the situation was hopelessly unstable from the moment she withdrew.

Relations between France and Great Britain. The withdrawal of the United States tended to widen the breach between France and Great Britain that had done so much to vitiate the work of the Peace Conference. On the one hand France sought by all means to preserve the situation that had resulted from the war, and this all the more when the security that she had expected from the Anglo-American guarantee of her territory failed to materialize. Without that guarantee France inevitably saw in the power of Germany a menace to her own independence, and endeavored by all means to circumscribe that power.

On the other hand, Great Britain reverted to her historic policy of preserving a balance of power in Europe. By an extraordinary perverse repetition of the mistake of Metternich in 1815 she continued to see a danger to the security of Europe in France itself. Beset by one of her periodic desires to withdraw from the Continent and fearing that a maintenance of the 1919 situation would give supremacy in Europe to France, she refused to accept security obligations that were the essence of the new system.

The tendency to pull away from Europe, very similar to that shown by the United States, was due only in part to traditional policy. The task of re-adjustment to a position of lesser power is always both painful and difficult. For Great Britain this task was complicated by developments in the British Commonwealth. The grant of self-government to the various Dominions had not been accompanied by any means of coordinating the foreign policies of the various States that owed allegiance to the British Crown. There was at one and the same time a desire in the Dominions not to be bound by any decisions of the Imperial Government, an intense feeling of being outside Europe (similar to that of the United States), and yet a fervent emotional desire to preserve the unity of the Commonwealth. Unity in these circum-stances was best achieved by an all-round agreement to do little or nothing. Traditional reasons, difficulties in the organization of the Commonwealth, problems arising from the changed position of Great Britain in the world, combined to make British policy negative.

Lack of Leadership. But it was positive policy, not negative, that was needed if the new order was to grow. At the outset replacement of anarchy by a system of law in any form of society always works against those members of the society who have been less successful during the period of anarchy. Laws survive if those who have been more successful show themselves prepared both to resist attacks on the system from those whom it benefits least, and to operate the system in such a way that their advantages are shared with the less fortunate. If the League system was to survive, action along three lines was needed. It was necessary that efforts be made by the process of revision or peaceful change to modify the settlement of 1919 so that it would be in the interest of all, rather than in the interest of a group, to preserve. It was im-perative that the specific obligations which the settlement of 1919 imposed upon certain States should be extended so as to limit equally all the members of the League. It was vital that security of each member of the international community be assured by the society, and that the obligations of various members of that community be enforced. Development of this kind is not obtained unless there is courageous and imaginative leadership. Such leader-ship did not appear, and it must be accounted as a collective failure of all the States members that it was not forthcoming.

Failure to "Generalize" the Obligations of 1919. It is evident that although in such matters as reparations and the military occupation of Germany the Paris settlement was modified, no considerable effort was made to revise the more questionable of its territorial provisions. Equally striking was the failure to extend to all States the obligations that the settlement imposed on a few.

Society advances more by the development of obligations than by their limitation. But if society is to advance, these obligations must be borne equally by all members of society; if they fall on a few rather than on all, they will become seeds of discord, rather than of concord. In the end they will be enforced rather than accepted, or denounced if not enforced.

Disarmament, mandates, minorities, the internationalization of rivers, all of these and other provisions of the 1919 treaties contained the germ of fruitful development.

In no case however were those obligations extended to all the States members of the League, and the States subjected to them have therefore sought to end their inequality by freeing themselves from the obligation. In one case, Turkey adopted the unexceptionable procedure of obtaining international consent for the modification of the Straits Regime. Yet even in this case, though in its form it was perfect example of peaceful change, was a retrograde step in that it abolished an obligation rather than extending its application. In other cases the inequalities were ended not through the mechanisms of society, but in defiance of them. In 1934 Poland denounced the obligations of the minority treaties, though at the same time announcing that she intended to continue to observe them; in 1935 Germany denounced the disarmament clauses of Versailles; in 1936 Germany denounced the demilitarizations clauses of Versailles and those concerning the internationalization of rivers; and in 1939 France ignored the obligations of the mandate in transferring Alexandretta to Turkey. In each case the inequality resulting from a specific obligation imposed on one State was ended not by the constructive method of extending its application to all States, but by the destructive method of releasing the individual State affected from its obligation.

Security. If in the end, despite moments when a happier fate seemed in store, the States of the League failed to organize justice, no less striking was their failure to organize security. The inexorably linked questions of security and disarmament were almost inextricably complicated by the Versailles settlement. Because it was a dictated, not a negotiated, peace—and this in its outward form to a still greater extent than in its inward content—it was impossible to discuss general disarmament at Paris. In the years that followed the conflict of aims between Great Britain and France prevented a solution of the problem of equality of rights and equality of security. In the end, the States members of the League failed to implement security when the test came in 1935–36.

Germany and Europe. The major problem around which the conflict of aims between Great Britain and France revolved was that of Germany. From the point of view of the historian, the unification of Germany in 1870 created a problem exactly similar to very many of the problems that Europe had had to face during the preceding three hundred years. In the past that problem had been solved by the formation of an alliance of the other European powers against the largest and most powerful of them.

From the point of view of the diplomat, the new system of international organization was an attempt to provide another answer to this problem. "Collective security" might have replaced the alliance as a method of assuring those States who felt themselves threatened by Germany. The failure to organize the security that the new institutions could have provided led those States that feared Germany to take no steps that, by ending her inequality, would have strengthened her. The absence of such organized security prevented any effective steps being taken to check her when she began to destroy those inequalities in defiance of the international society. Europe was driven back to the alliance system to solve its security problem.

But it was not only the security problem that centered in Germany; it was the State that inevitably stood to lose the least at the inauguration of a system of law and order, because of the lateness of its creation and its consequent limited success in the period of anarchy; it was the State that was affected by almost every one of the specific obligations imposed by the Versailles settlement and that, therefore, was most interested in seeing its equality restored by the extension of those obligations to all States.

A Joint Responsibility. Countries that benefited from the 1919 settlement showed no alacrity in modifying that settlement, either by accepting its obligations for themselves, or in surrendering advantages it gave to them. But countries that sought revision showed no greater appreciation of their membership of an international society. The positive manifestations of their national egoisms were at least as important as the more negative nationalisms of those who were slow to move toward revision. The responsibility of an aggressor cannot be accounted less than the responsibility of the State that refused to aid the victim of aggression. The States that sought modification of the settlement of 1919 showed themselves at least as unappreciative of the interests of the wider community as did those States who profited by the maintenance of that settlement.

NEED OF A NEW SPIRIT

Writing in 1935, Sir Alfred Zimmern said: "The process of dove-tailing or codification or synthesis carried through in the letter of the Covenant assumes a new spirit in the whole field of international politics. It presupposes a transformation of power politics into responsibility politics, or at least a sincere and consistent effort on the part of the Great Powers to begin to face the innumerable tasks of adjustment which such a transformation would carry with it" (Zimmern, *The League of Nations and the Rule of Law*).

Today we know that neither of these presuppositions was to be fulfilled. Instead there was unreadiness on the one hand to accept the obligations, positive and negative, of responsibility politics, and on the other a definite attempt to exalt power politics to the dignity of a religion.

Even though the day of plenty for all has not yet come, it is no longer true that the economic necessities of man must drive him to dispute with his fellows the possession of the earth. That cooperation as distinct from conflict is the ultimate interest of the vast majority would probably be generally accepted. In so far as the State is, or should be, merely the instrument of its citizens, cooperation (responsibility politics as distinct from power politics) must equally be its ultimate interest. The twenty years following 1919 witnessed in all States a sacrifice of those ultimate or long-term interests to sectional short-term policies. What were the causes of this almost universal phenomenon?

It would be idle to deny that a major cause is the power of special interests. The economic nationalism that is a startling manifestation of the particularization of the modern State was "the inevitable nemesis of letting this new ecumenical force of industrialism loose in a world in which parochial States were the reigning political institution" (Toynbee, *A Study of History*, Vol. IV). Inevitably industrialism produces powerful interests which are concerned to prevent a modification of the order that protects them. But, though it would be foolish to deny the existence or the power of such special interests, it is impossible to assess their influence.

More important is the fluidity of the modern world. A century ago it was natural to plan for the future. In their private affairs our ancestors could act on the assumption that their grandchildren would lead a steady life not substantially unlike their own. Statesmen could think of their country's future in the confident expectation that that future would not surprise them. Today we have no such confidence. The disarray that has thereby been introduced into both private and public affairs is there for all to see. In international affairs that very instability not only makes forward-looking policy difficult; it often renders it apparently futile. Why undertake the difficult and laborious task of solving a problem that may have passed away before the remedy has begun to operate?

Failures of Democracy. We cannot acquit democracy itself. It may very well be that the conduct of foreign affairs under a democracy is much less changeable and capricious than under an autocracy. But it is clear that none the less the tendency to postpone action is even more clearly marked in a democracy than in an autocracy. In all States, whatever be their constitution, inertia plays a most powerful part, but in none so much as in a democracy. During the post-war years this tendency to postpone consideration of difficult problems was exaggerated just because those were the post-war years. The mental and spiritual fatigue that followed the war had hardly disappeared when the economic blizzard hit the world. The extension of the incidence of war itself *(la guerre totale)* meant that this fatigue was probably more widespread than after any previous conflict since the Thirty Years' War.

This was the more important since it was during the twenties that the opportunities should have been taken. Though they did not know it the statesmen of that period were working against time. They could not foresee the effects of the inflation in Germany and of the economic crisis of 1931. Inertia and fatigue encouraged them to regard the new institution as a plant and allow it to grow. Had they realized what lay ahead they might have thought of it as a fortress or at least as a breakwater, and have spent those precious ten years in building.

Sovereignty. It is customary in modern discussions of the breakdown of the Geneva institutions to direct major criticism against the doctrine of sovereignty. To do so is, in large measure, to mistake cause for effect. A juridical doctrine is seldom more than a decent theoretical garment to cloak current political thought and action. The doctrine serves to justify the essential amorality of States, and thereby brings us nearer to the core of our problem.

It is a truism that the sovereign State, the unit of modern international society, does not feel the same compulsion to honor its obligation as does the socially minded individual in a civilized community. It is equally evident that though the State is amoral in its relations with other States, it is, in its relations with its own citizens a moral agency. It is the difference in the moral outlooks, the *mores* within the boundaries of sovereign States, that explains the attitude of those sovereign States to the obligations that they have contracted toward each other. There is an observable difference between the State that accepts an obligation, believing that the burden of its fulfilment will be outweighed by the advantages accruing to it from the obligation imposed simultaneously on its cosignatories, and the State that has no intention of attempting to carry out its obligation after it has reaped the advantage accruing therefrom. Equally evident in all States is the difference in their attitude to positive and negative obligations. An obligation not to go to war is accepted more readily, and indeed more honestly, by most States than is a corollary obligation to take positive action against a State that has gone to war. Yet the doctrine of sovereignty knows no difference between obligations; it allows all to be broken with the same impunity.

It was not the doctrine of sovereignty that led to the breakdown of the League; it was the passion for independence felt by all peoples. Submission to a legal system is a limitation of that independence; those States, that because of their power are able to enjoy the greatest measure of independence, resist more strongly restraints upon them. It is not a theoretical sovereignty that matters; it is a simple desire to do as you please and be answerable to no man. We are here faced with a modified form of the central problem of all political thinking, the relation of individuals, or groups of individuals, to the society in which they live and whose existence is necessary for their "good life." At all times the individual seeks that liberty which his fellow-dwellers in society characterize as license; whenever he obtains it the society in which he lives is thereby undermined or destroyed, and with that society disappears the "good life" that it alone made possible.

Parochialism. The resolution of this same problem in the international sphere is infinitely more difficult than it was in the national sphere. The individual member of a national society may have resisted the bonds of the State, and he may have called in religion to aid him in the search of liberty or even of license; he never reached the idolatry of making himself his own God. Yet this is exactly what the modern State has done. It was to no imaginary evil that the late Pope Pius XI addressed himself when he said: "Whoever detaches race, or the nation, or the State, or the form of State, or the Government from the temporal scale of values and raises them to be the supreme model and deifies these with idolatrous worship falsified the divinely created order of things." (Papal Encyclical of March 14, 1937.) This curse of exaggerated nationalism, the substitution of the part for the whole as the object of devotion, is a comparatively recent scourge in modern society. The parochialism that has always existed throughout the fifteen hundred years of the history of that society, has in the last century been transformed into an idolatry by the impact of industrialism and democracy on the political organization of our society. "By thus giving this parochialism an immense accession of strength, the two great new forces in the world have actually been raising up, by their own action, the most formidable obstacles to that unification of the world which it is their nature to bring about" (Toynbee, *A Study of History,* Vol. IV).

Loyalty. It was on this rock of national parochialism that the League foundered. It is only individuals, not governments or States, that can feel loyalties, and although during the twenty years of its existence the new institution did arouse in many people and groups of peoples a loyalty toward it, that new loyalty was never, as it proved (though for a moment it seemed that there might have been a different result), sufficiently strong to over-ride the, by now, deeply rooted loyalty to the State. Self-interest alone could not bind men and *a fortiori* States to an organization that flaunted the modern idolatry.

It may seem surprising that reflections upon the political causes of the breakdown of the peace settlement should end in a key apparently so far removed from politics. Yet it is the "inarticulate major premises" that dominate men's thinking, feeling, and action. To suggest that the breakdown was due primarily to faults of institutions, to mistaken judgments, and even to positive malignity, would be to ignore what is the very stuff of politics.

That so great a spiritual revolution as was needed to insure the success of the League of Nations could come in half a generation was perhaps too much to expect. The greatest of the League's misfortunes was that it should have had to face major trials of strength so soon after its foundation. To go further and attempt to assess whether that spiritual revolution is today nearer realization, and if so what its effect is likely to be on our international political organization in the future, would be to trespass beyond the field of this survey.

THE RENEWED APPEAL TO ARMS

Diplomatic Realignment. Foremost among the factors which made for a second resort to arms in the twentieth century was the breakdown of the League of Nations and its principle of the collective guarantee of peace. The ineffectiveness of the League Covenant was first made clear by the Japanese invasion of Manchuria in 1931. Emboldened by the apathy of the European nations in the face of this aggression, the Italian dictator, Benito Mussolini, determined upon the invasion of Abyssinia, an independent native African kingdom which had been admitted to the League of Nations in 1923. When the League declared that a state of war existed between Abyssinia and Italy in October, 1935, Article 16 of the Covenant, providing for economic sanctions against aggressor nations, was invoked against Italy. Never before had the League resorted to an economic boycott of a warring nation. That the economic weapon was used on this occasion bespoke the anxiety of Britain and France over the threat to their own African Empires. Apart from imperialist motives, the League sanctions were heartily supported by public opinion in Britain, France, and the United States. The opposition of the British and French publics to the peace plans of their governments, embodied in the Hoare-Laval proposals, induced these governments to apply sanctions in the hope that Italy would yield. However, the crucial embargo on oil, a commodity for which Italy depended entirely upon imports, could not be applied, partly because of imports to Italy from countries outside the League, partly because the German occupation of the Rhineland in March, 1936 so alarmed Europe that the question of the oil embargo was quietly forgotten. The remaining sanctions did not prevent Italy from carrying out the conquest of Abyssinia and the completion of that task marked the end of the era of the collective guarantee of peace.

By this time the threat to the peace of Europe inherent in the German Revolution had made itself clear. When Adolf Hitler first became the German Chancellor on January 30, 1933, the world, in the throes of the economic depression, regarded the change in government as another attempt of a poverty-stricken, debt-ridden European government to effect an internal reform. This optimism was quickly dispelled by the speed and decision with which the German Chancellor dealt with Germany's foreign debts and obligations. The Weimar Republic had ceased payment of reparations; Hitler now declared them to be illegal. Just as swiftly, Germany withdrew from the Disarmament Conference after she received no response to her offer to "disband her entire military establishment and destroy the small amount of arms remaining to her, if the neighboring countries will do the same thing with equal thoroughness." (From Speech of Adolf Hitler, May 17, 1933.) On October 14, 1933 Germany formally withdrew from the League of Nations after it became apparent that France and England would use the instrumentalities of the League to prevent revision of the Treaty of Versailles. To the German nation Hitler declared that he proposed to restore Germany's full equality with other European nations, and to abrogate the humiliating clauses of the Treaty of Versailles. In the first of a series of plebiscites, the German nation was asked in November, 1933 to ratify the acts and policies of the Chancellor. In a vote which permitted no opposition party or opposition opinion to influence public sentiment, the electorate approved by a 96.3 per cent majority.

German expansionist ambitions were revealed by the failure of the plot against Austria in 1934. Hitler's avowed aim of incorporating all the German speaking peoples in Europe within one great state had an obvious inference for Austria. This German-speaking nation, established on a republican basis by the Treaty of St. Germain in 1919, had guarantees of independence from the western powers and Italy. Mussolini looked on the maintenance of Austrian independence as a cardinal point in Italian foreign policy, lest he be forced to have a powerful Germany on his own frontier. To this end Italian military support and secret subsidies were given the government of Chancellor Dollfuss, who was himself little else than a dictator. One party rule in Austria had been promoted by the decimation of the socialist party in February of 1934 in a series of assaults that revealed the strength of the government's "private army" known as the *Heimwehr*. Only the followers of Adolf Hitler remained to dispute the authority of the Christian Socialist government of Chancellor Dollfuss and Vice-Chancellor Schuschnigg. Abortive fighting between the Austrians and National Socialists began in the spring and broke out in full fury in July, 1934. The *Heimwehr* quickly restored order after Chancellor Dollfuss was assassinated by Nazis. A menacing military demonstration by Italy in the Brenner Pass made the German government disavow any connection with the revolt. Italy had secured Austrian independence in its first test of strength with the new German dictatorship. Within two years, on July 11, 1936, Germany acknowledged the sovereignty of the Austrian state and disclaimed any interest in its domestic affairs.

Throughout the year 1935 the German problem became more acute. Public opinion in western Europe and America had been aroused against Germany for the persecution of minorities and the establishment of the Nazi dictatorship, with its exaltation of the German race and its attendant disregard for individual liberties. Nevertheless, the year began with the peaceful settlement of the Saar question. This coal producing section of western Germany had been administered by the League of Nations, according to the Treaty of Versailles. For fifteen years the coal mines were to be operated by France as compensation for the destruction wrought by the World War, and at the end of that period there was to be a plebiscite under the direction of the League to decide the political fate of the region. On January 13, 1935 this plebiscite was held, offering the people three alternatives: continuation of League rule, union with France, or union with Germany. To the amazement of the world 90 per cent of the Saar people voted union with Germany. This was the first revelation of the popular strength of the National Socialist revolution.

The annexation of the Saar to Germany proceeded smoothly and the apparent intention of Hitler to use the Saar decision as a stepping stone to improve relations with France prompted diplomatic activity on numerous fronts. England and France pressed for the adoption of an Eastern Locarno pact, similar to the treaties which the western powers had signed in 1925. The German reaction was cool to suggestions that the existing eastern frontier be recognized as permanent, and moreover, there was the ideological antipathy between Germany and Russia. Hitler had justified his assumption of control on the grounds that he had saved Germany, if not western Europe, from Communism. To make a pact that included Soviet Russia among the signatories was at this stage of the German Revolution inconceivable. Moreover, the rumors of a vast secret rearmament in Germany had begun to complicate the relations among the Great Powers.

For more than a year the diplomatic corps of Europe, and in a less specific way the press of the world had been aware of the secret German military preparations. On March 4, 1935 the British government explained the need for rearmament in a White Paper that openly hinted at knowledge of the extent of the German measures. France replied to Germany with the announcement on March 15, 1935 that the service of conscripts would be extended from one to two years. These circumstances and the rapidly growing tension among the western powers brought forth a public declaration of the existence of a German army. In a speech of March 16, 1935 Adolf Hitler proclaimed the restoration of conscription and announced his intention of building a great army for the defense of Germany. The Versailles signatories were condemned for their refusal to carry out a real disarmament. Germany's defenselessness in the face of Czechoslovakia with five times as many troops permitted to it as to Germany, and before the armed might of Poland and Russia, as well as the incredible barrier of the Maginot Line were all cited in justification of the decision to rearm. With that decision the world was launched on an armament race that dwarfed the efforts before 1914.

Europe's reaction to the German rearmament was a vain search for a collective guarantee against aggression. In April, 1935, at Stresa in Italy, England and France under Mussolini's persuasion joined Italy in condemning the abrogation of the armament clauses of the Treaty of Versailles. At the same time these powers renewed their pledge to seek a collective guarantee of European peace under the aegis of the League. The agreement was short-lived for England almost immediately embarked upon the policy that later became known as "Appeasement." By June 18, 1935 England had concluded a naval treaty with Germany that not only broke the Stresa front but gave the sanction of a Versailles signatory to the latest violation of the Treaty. Germany was permitted to build up to 35 per cent of the British fleet in all classes of ships except submarines. Germany demanded parity in these vessels but agreed to a temporary limitation to 45 per cent of the British submarine tonnage. The French were irritated by the English action but assured themselves that the military alliance which had been made with Russia in May, only a month after Stresa, was an adequate guarantee. A subsequent alliance between Russia and Czechoslovakia gave France the further assurance that an eastern military front would be created against the Germans.

Mindful of the military pressure which France could exert through the Maginot Line and the system of eastern alliances, the Germans swept into the demilitarized sections of the Rhineland on March 3, 1936. This zone of fifty kilometers within the German frontier had been created by the Treaty of Versailles. German adherence to the Locarno Pacts of 1925 had approved this zone; the action of Hitler had now destroyed the Locarno agreements. To replace this guarantee of European peace Hitler now proposed a new European peace pact and a conference that would consider disarmament and the outlawry of modern implements of war, including heavy artillery, tanks, gas, and aerial bombs. The German peace plan asked for the formation of a new demilitarized zone embracing French and Belgian, as well as German territory, a twenty year non-aggression pact, an agreement on aerial warfare, and the re-entrance of Germany into the League.

The negotiations among the powers to establish a new Locarno were doomed to an early failure. In France there were some voices raised in behalf of a preventive war with Germany, but the French found little support except in Belgium. Both England and Russia were concerned with other matters, Russia with internal problems, while England was deeply embroiled with Italy over Abyssinia and the Mediterranean. The atmosphere of sanctions and the Abyssinian War was not favorable to talk of peace. A fundamental realignment of the powers was under way. The era in which Germany had played a lone hand and Italy had entered into temporary agreements with England and France was coming to an end. France and England while not yet prepared for a firm stand against the Fascist powers had begun to realize the threat to their European position and their colonial empires. The resumption of Anglo-French staff conversations heralded a diplomatic and military alliance, which was all the more necessary now that French influence in eastern Europe was waning.

German occupation of the Rhineland had widespread repercussions among the smaller nations allied to France. The Balkan and middle European nations no longer felt that France could protect them from a German attack, especially when the Germans announced that they were constructing a system of fortifications of their own. The Little Entente, Yugoslavia, Czechoslovakia, and Rumania, began to act in an independent manner and it seemed likely that Yugoslavia would fall in with the Italo-German combination. Poland, always irked by its position of tutelage to the French, resumed negotiations with neighboring powers and counted for protection on the non-aggression pact made in 1934 with Germany. Belgian irritation at the failure of the French to act when the Germans occupied the Rhineland led to the abandonment of the alliance with France and the resumption of the neutral status of 1914. Within a year and a half, Delbos, the French Foreign Minister, had to confess that, except for Czechoslovakia, France had no friends in middle and eastern Europe. A strong German commercial drive in these regions, reminiscent of the pre-war *Drang nach Osten*,[3] garnered the lion's share of foreign trade and completed the task that military pressure and diplomacy had begun.

A visible sign of the realignment of powers was the formation of the Rome-Berlin Axis in October, 1936. British insistence on the application of economic sanctions to warring Italy had brought the Fascist powers together in a military alliance. It was evident that Italy was willing to abandon the policy of maintaining Austrian independence to get German aid against the French and British. For Germany the alliance was a prelude to the Anti-Comintern Pact with Japan made in November, when it became increasingly clear that the anti-democratic states were closing their ranks. Japan, already deep in the intrigue and politics of China, found the tie with Germany useful in view of the menacing position of Russia. Ostensibly, the Axis and Anti-Comintern powers were combining to fight Communism. German and Italian government propaganda continually stressed this motive in explanation of their policies. For Germany it was a credible analysis and it had the virtue of keeping alive the pro-German sympathies of certain sections of the British public. There were other motives behind the Axis commitments, however, and not the least of these was the identity of German and Italian interests in the Spanish Civil War.

*The Spanish Wa*r. A revolt supported by the nationalist and conservative

3 [*Drive to the East.*]

parties in Spain had broken out against the republican government in July, 1936. By the fall Italy had intervened on a large scale and the transfer of great quantities of war material had enabled General Franco, the Nationalist leader, to invade Spain from Morocco, where the revolt had begun. His steady drive, aided by Italian aviation and mechanical equipment, came to a halt before Madrid in November, where an International Brigade, with the example of Petrograd and the Red Guard before them, made a determined stand. Not until March, 1939 was the city surrendered, and then only because the route to the sea and Catalonia had been cut off. In the military stalemate that ensued after the failure before Madrid, the international character of the civil war became apparent with the arrival of masses of Russian military equipment and numerous technicians for the government, or Loyalist, side. The "war of ideologies," which the Axis powers publicly stressed, had begun.

All the powers were members of the Non-Intervention Commission, which had begun its work in September, 1936 in the hope of preventing the spread of the Spanish civil war to the rest of Europe. Its activity was obviously a facade behind which active intervention on a large or small scale could be carried out. All the attempts of the Commission to regulate or control the foreign troops present in Spain ended in failure. Control over the traffic in munitions ended when the German battleship, *Deutschland,* was bombed by Loyalist planes and the Germans retaliated by shelling a Spanish coastal town. Germany and Italy formally withdrew from the Commission's control plan after this incident, and through the summer of 1937 attacks on neutral shipping by "pirate" submarines gave evidence of the Axis' intention of helping the Nationalists and harrying the western powers.

German and Italian military intervention became more obvious in 1937 and 1938 as the discrepancy in armaments enabled General Franco to renew successfully the campaign which had ended at Madrid. Russian armaments and technicians were sent in a steady stream to the Loyalists, but the quantity never equaled that of the Axis. Both sides found the war a convenient testing ground for military equipment, and the use and design of tanks, planes, and guns suggested methods and types which the powers were not slow to copy. At no time was enough modern material assembled to bring the war to a quick end, and the dragging, painful course of the operations reflected the bitter hates and passions that had brought about the struggle. In the spring of 1938 it became clear that the Nationalists had victory within reach, but the shipment of vast stores of French army material slowed the offensive and prolonged the war for another dreary year. Finally, in the winter and early spring of 1939 an assault by the Nationalists, in which Italian aviation and artillery played a leading part, ended the war by taking Valencia and Barcelona, and the industrial province of Catalonia. Peace was restored to Spain but at a great price. Russia had been worsted in an encounter with the Axis. Franco looked forward to cooperation with Hitler and Mussolini. The Spanish Civil War had revealed with startling clarity the superiority of the Axis powers in modern, mechanized warfare. German tanks and aviation had played a large role in the Nationalist victory, and the western powers began to realize the scope and enterprise of the German rearmament. Italy was less fortunate than Germany. Participation in the Abyssinian and the Spanish wars scattered and destroyed quantities of material that Italy needed for her own defense.

Germany was already preparing for the future. In September of 1936 a Four Year Plan to make Germany independent of foreign imports was begun. Production of *Ersatz* [4] commodities and the stimulation of agriculture and industry received attention abroad, but the establishment of a military economy in time of peace did not immediately arouse comment except among professional economists. The organization of the national economy on a war time basis before the outbreak of hostilities proved one of the greatest innovations in statecraft; an innovation that gave Germany a vast productive advantage over her potential enemies. This was especially marked in the case of France. For several years domestic issues culminating in a series of blunders and incipient Fascist revolts curtailed national production and gave France a handicap in the armament race that was never overcome.

Throughout these fateful years the dictators retained the diplomatic initiative. The Spanish Civil War provided the background of turmoil and potential European war that enabled Hitler to stage his three most effective coups: the annexation of Austria, the Munich agreement, and the bloodless conquest of Czechoslovakia. Without the omnipresent danger of a universal conflagration the daring German diplomacy would have met the firm resistance of the Versailles signatories. But so weary was the world of war, and so desirous of sparing the new generation the horror of another conflict, that statesmen everywhere yielded to the German demands and found consolation in the hope that they had given the world "peace in our time."

Japanese Expansion. This wish expressed the hopes of Europe, but in Asia war was already under way; the summer of 1937 witnessed a large scale invasion of China by the Japanese. After dominating the coastal areas the Japanese penetrated inland over lines of communication several thousand miles in length. Despite defeats at every hand the Chinese held on grimly

---

[4] [*Substitute* (mostly synthetic) commodities.]

and trusted to Russian, British, and American aid to keep their armies and guerrilla bands in the field. The struggle naturally complicated the relations of Japan with Russia, the United States, and Great Britain. The British government, being absorbed with the problems of Europe, was inclined to leave diplomatic remonstrances to the United States. On the other hand, the Sino-Japanese War brought Germany and Italy closer to the Japanese point of view, and their common enmity to the western powers and Russia eventually took the form of a military alliance.

The Austrian Anschluss. In Europe, there was a diplomatic lull during 1937. The German Fuehrer attempted nothing more serious than his routine denunciation of the Soviet Union. But 1938 began inauspiciously with the removal of key personalities from the German Foreign Office and Ministry of War. The implication of these changes did not become clear until Hitler reopened the Austrian question on February 12, by summoning Chancellor Schuschnigg to confer with him. In the face of German military power Schuschnigg yielded and appointed Nationalist Socialists to important positions in the Austrian government. This capitulation was followed almost immediately by a violent speech in which Hitler denounced Britain and the League, and affirmed the Reich's intention to protect German-speaking people everywhere. His words found an echo in the activity of the Austrian National Socialists, now freed of all restraint, who worked and agitated for the annexation of Austria to Germany.

To counter the National Socialists, Chancellor Schuschnigg announced that a plebiscite would be held on March 13 to decide the political fate of Austria. The announcement of a vote which might have revealed an anti-German sentiment aroused enormous ire in Berlin, and led to the demand there for Schuschnigg's immediate resignation. This demand was backed up by the presence of several hundred thousand troops mobilized on the Austrian border. Faced with the imminent danger of invasion and the revolt of a turbulent minority, Schuschnigg resigned his office to Seyss-Inquart, the leading National Socialist in the Austrian government. The new Chancellor thereupon asked for German intervention to protect the nation from disorder; armed with this legal authority the German troops began the occupation of Austria on March 11, 1938. The first conquest of the German army had been completed, and the inevitable German plebiscite on April 10 confirmed Austria's acquiescence.

The powers were alarmed by the German action, but their policies were too confused and contradictory to restrain Hitler. France had been without a government between March 10 and 13, and when Leon Blum managed to form one the annexation had been completed. Britain was critical of the violation of the agreement made between Germany and Austria in 1936, but unofficial opinion insisted that the union was compensation for the harshness of Versailles, and that the realization of her language frontiers was Germany's destiny. Czechoslovakia, of the smaller nations, felt alarmed until the Germans gave assurances that the Arbitration Convention of 1925 would remain in effect and France publicly renewed the pledge of military aid. Mussolini concluded after the *fait accompli* that the Brenner pass was the "natural boundary" between Germany and Italy.

The Partition of Czechoslovakia. During the spring and summer of 1938 the German press, mouthpiece of the government, began a drumfire barrage against Czechoslovakia that was the certain herald of diplomatic, or military, action. Fired by the success of the party in Austria, Konrad Henlein, leader of the Sudeten Germans sympathetic to National Socialism, had begun an agitation for autonomy and larger political liberties within the Czechoslovak state. His movement was supported officially in Berlin as evidenced by the use of the propaganda resources of the German government, as well as by secret concentrations of the German army. The German claim of mistreatment and political discrimination had some justification as impartial British investigators found later, but by and large the Sudeten agitation was a screen behind which Hitler could prepare for the annexation of the German speaking regions to the Reich. Relations between Czechoslovakia and Germany remained tense throughout the summer, but the willingness of the Czechs to negotiate with Henlein gave some assurance of a peaceful settlement. When these negotiations broke down in July the British government offered the services of Lord Runciman as mediator, since it had become apparent that the Czech crisis was the most severe since the rise of Hitler.

If any doubt of the German seriousness remained it was dispelled by the speech of Hitler on September at the Nurnberg Party Congress. Hitler in thundering tones declared the German people would no longer tolerate the oppression of their fellows, and that Germany would find means in the face of what he referred to as a "united front of Bolsheviks and democracies," to restrain the Czechs. Amid this ominous atmosphere, as Czechoslovakia continually refused to cede the Sudentenland to Germany, Neville Chamberlain made his historic flight to confer with Hitler at Berchtesgaden. Their meeting made clear Hitler's intention of obtaining the right of self-determination for the Sudetens, and it was on this basis that the Anglo-French plan of September 21 was developed and forced on the Czechs on the penalty of the French withdrawal from their military alliance. But the second meeting between Hitler and Chamberlain at Godesberg on September 22 revealed that the German Fuehrer had new demands on the Czechs. A period of intense anxiety followed as the world awaited the decision for peace or war. France declared general mobilization and the British fleet was sent to its battle stations. Chamberlain appealed to Mussolini to intervene and apparently his influence caused Hitler to yield, for on September 28 he proposed a four power conference to be held at Munich.

There on September 30 Hitler, Chamberlain, Daladier, and Mussolini reached an agreement on the cession of the German speaking areas which the Czech leaders were peremptorily forced to accept. The occupation of the Sudeten areas, in which the Czechoslovak fortifications and military installations were located, began on October 1 and was complete within ten days. Subsequent treaties gave the Polish-speaking city of Teschen to Poland and part of Slovakia to Hungary. Russia was not consulted in any of these arrangements, but from Geneva the Russian foreign minister indulged in a burst of oratory over Russian concern with treaty obligations. Future peace was believed assured by the bi-lateral pacts made by Germany with England and France. At Munich Chamberlain had concluded a pact with Germany which expressed "the symbolic desire of our two peoples never to go to war with one another again," while on December 6 Germany reached a similar agreement with France which abjured territorial differences and referred all future questions to arbitration. These documents and Hitler's avowed assurance that the Sudetenland was his last territorial claim in Europe seemed to justify the great concessions that had been made.

The Failure of Appeasement. Thus Hitler won his greatest diplomatic victory. Munich had marked the triumph of "Appeasement," but already there were signs that this policy had run its course. Liberal opinion throughout the world condemned the sacrifice of Czechoslovakian territory as a fatal and useless measure. This group felt that Hitler's policy of uniting all the Germans in one state embraced a larger plan for aggrandizement that was just beginning to unfold. But to the war-weary peoples of Europe Munich came as a welcome relief after an awful week of dread in which the spectre of another war had hung over their heads.

At the beginning of 1939 the outlook for peace was favorable but there were many disturbing factors. In the Orient the Sino-Japanese war, still undeclared, blazed with a new fury and the loss of Oriental trade was beginning to be serious for Great Britain. The end of the Spanish Civil War was in sight, but the relation of Franco to the dictators gave the western powers a new problem in diplomacy. After the spectacular triumphs of Germany, Mussolini had adopted a more aggressive tone but for the moment his threats were confined to his speeches. Russia was still an enigma for western Europe but in the event of an armed clash the adherence of the Soviets to the Anglo-French side seemed the most obvious conclusion. All the powers were profoundly disturbed by the armament race which had increased to a new pace despite the assurances of the Munich agreements. In this competition England and France were beginning to feel the advantage of the Germans with their militarized economy. And finally there was the conflict of ideologies. Whether the constitutional governments of England and France could exist in Europe along with totalitarian dictatorships was a question that was poised for the future. Behind England's foreign policy was the assumption that there was safety in balancing the Reich against the Soviets, and the persistence of Hitler's enmity for Russia provided a basis for this belief.

Speculation about the future of Europe was brought to a sudden and sharp halt on March 15 by the descent of the German troops on Bohemia and Moravia. The chancellories of Europe were caught by surprise as Germany occupied these areas left to Czechoslovakia by the Munich agreement. Within two days Germany had declared Slovakia independent but a protectorate of the Reich. The point was not lost on statesmen that these territories were non-German, and that the great principle of the linguistic unity of the German Reich had been discarded. It did not matter that on March 22 Germany annexed from Lithuania the German-speaking city of Memel; the Great German Empire which had been darkly hinted at in National Socialist literature was in formation.

In the face of this threat France and Britain resumed their *Entente cordiale* and commenced building a great coalition against Germany. The policy of Appeasement was abandoned as it became clear that Germany could be tempted to open hostilities with Russia by attempting to gain the Ukraine. At once Britain began negotiations with Poland, where the Corridor threatened to become the next issue in German foreign policy. On March 31 England guaranteed Poland assistance in case of an attack, and this temporary agreement was implemented by a formal understanding made known to the public on April 6. Not since the agreements with Russia in 1907 had the British government engaged in a military pact with an eastern power. It was a change in British policy, and a fateful one, for it brought the British Empire into headlong collision with the growing power of the Reich.

The Invasion of Poland. The British pledge to Poland, which had been ratified by France did not come too soon, for on April 7 the Fascist powers struck again. This time it was Albania that yielded to a swift invasion by

Italy. Again British diplomacy countered the Axis drive by a guarantee of military assistance to Greece and Rumania, and by concluding on May 12 a mutual aid pact with Turkey. The military power to make these pledges effective was assured in part by conscription which was begun in Britain in April, the first draft of man-power in the peace-time history of the British Isles. But the Axis was not inactive for on May 22 Italy and Germany concluded a military alliance that served notice on the western powers that the lines of battle were beginning to form.

Germany's next move was made clear in the April speech of the Fuehrer, in which he denounced the Non-Aggression pact with Poland and demanded the return of Danzig to the Reich as well as the cession of a route of communications through the Corridor. In return Germany offered a 25 year non-aggression pact and full recognition of Polish economic rights in Danzig. That city emerged as the focal point of danger as the local National Socialist leader began to press for the return to Germany. Reich propaganda supported this demand and throughout the summer of 1939 kept up a steady chorus of complaint against Poland, asserting that the German minority in the corridor was persecuted under Polish rule and that unspeakable atrocities had been committed. Poland threatened to become the scene of the final test of power between the axis and the western powers.

With this prospect in view the Anglo-French negotiations begun with Russia in the spring assumed a new importance. The Russian attitude might easily decide the question of peace or war, for if a great coalition could be built up against Germany, Hitler would not dare threaten European peace as he had before Munich in September, 1938. Public opinion in western Europe was confident of at least a commercial agreement with Russia but there had been alarming delays and a pronounced Russian procrastination. Unknown to the average person a German delegation had been negotiating with Russia simultaneously with the British and the French. When the news of the German and Russian intention to sign a commercial treaty broke on August 20 it came therefore like a bombshell. The public in Britain and France, and even the cabinets, were momentarily dazed, but they were somewhat reassured when Molotov announced that the new agreement did not infringe any of Russia's non-aggression pacts. But when the terms of the treaty became known on August 24, it was obvious that Russia and Germany intended extensive economic cooperation, and that Russia would observe a benevolent neutrality in any action Germany might undertake.

The pact with Russia was clearly the greatest stroke of the pre-war diplomatic maneuvers, but the suddenness of Germany's reversal of policy lacked an immediate explanation. The growing ideological similarity of Germany and Russia may have contributed to the abandonment of their traditional enmity, but a great sense of *Realpolitik* among the Soviet leaders enabled them to see that Russian neutrality in the coming struggle in Europe would be the most profitable course. Besides there was the Russian irritation in Britain for failing to include the Soviets in the Munich conference. Other obstacles to an agreement with the western powers included their inability to offer territorial compensation in the Baltic states and Finland, and Poland's obstinate refusal to permit the transit of Russian troops to fight the Germans.

If Hitler counted on the Russian treaty to weaken Paris, London, or Warsaw he was mistaken. The Poles grimly determined to fight if Danzig or the Corridor was seized, and the British supported them in a fruitless series of negotiations with the German Fuehrer. To make clear the legal basis of British aid to Poland these nations had concluded a formal alliance on August 25, but the complete assurance of military aid did not deter Germany from pursuing a policy deemed vital to her national interests. Efforts of neutrals to mediate the crisis, including the generous offers of Italy, Leopold III, President Roosevelt, Pius XII, and the joint offer of Leopold III and Queen Wilhelmina, sovereigns of the traditionally neutral Low Countries, proved unavailing. With the exhaustion of all negotiations and peace efforts the advance of the German armies was decreed, and early on the morning of September 1 the invasion of Poland began. British and French ultimatums followed immediately, and when they went unanswered, a state of war with Germany existed as of September 3. For the second time in a quarter of a century the Great Powers of Western Europe had resorted to war as the only "solution" to their international problems.

2. THE PROSPECTS FOR ONE WORLD

The Second World War left the world in a worse state of shock and disorder than the First. Physical destruction was incomparably greater. The trench warfare of the First World War had thoroughly destroyed limited regions; in the Second World War the ground fighting made a ruin of western Russia, and the air bombing reduced whole cities, especially in Germany, to piles of debris. The so-called "strategic" bombing had blighted the productive industry and the transport facilities of the Continent. Goods even if produced could not be moved; millions of refugees from bombed out cities or from hostile political regimes sought miserably for an asylum; more people died of starvation or cold, in civilized Europe in 1945 and 1946, than at any time in generations or even in centuries.

The Second World War, like the First, was followed by a wave of revolution. There was nothing quite so epochal as the replacement of tsarism by communism in Russia. But where communism in 1918 was chaos, in 1945 it was the way of life of an organized Great Power. There had been communist scares all over Eastern and Central Europe in 1919. In 1946 communism with Soviet backing materialized with more effect. In Italy and France a third of the people voted for candidates of the Communist Party, but this represented a maximum beyond which under existing conditions communism in Western Europe seemed unable to go. In Eastern Europe, most of it occupied by Russian troops, in one country after another, from the three Baltic States in 1940 to Czechoslovakia in 1948, the native agrarian or peasant parties were pushed aside by communists, who, by dictatorial methods, set up "people's republics" closely bound to the Soviet Union.

Other parallels can be found in the sequelae, as doctors would say, of the two wars. There was again a resounding victory of democracy; to what degree it was real or apparent was one of the critical questions. It was an indubitable triumph for democracy to rid the world of the two chief fascist dictators. Fascism even had a purging effect in the democratic countries; after Adolf Hitler, racialistic and vehemently anti-rational or vitalistic philosophies lost repute in America and Western Europe. In Italy, after twenty-one years under Mussolini, democratic processes were resumed. France set up a Fourth Republic, which inherited most of the troubles of the Third. In Britain the war was hardly over when the voters unseated Winston Churchill and put in a Labor government instead. Once the center of high capitalism, Great Britain now became the world's chief exemplar of a parliamentary socialism. In the United States President Truman's Fair Deal carried on the New Deal of Roosevelt. In both Germany and Japan, after the First World War, there had been moderate yet significant democratic tendencies under native auspices. In both countries, after the Second World War, the victorious Allies, especially the Americans, used military occupation as a means of inculcating democracy, defined more in political than in economic terms, and with results that subsequent history had yet to disclose.

The revolt of Asia likewise continued. The old colonial system, battered after the first war, collapsed after the second. The Japanese had fanned Asian hopes of independence from Europeans, who could henceforth rule in Asia only at prohibitive military cost, if indeed at all. India and the Netherlands Indies became independent. Syria and other Arabic states, which had emerged from the first war as European mandated areas, came out of the second war as independent countries. Arabic indignation was aroused by the post-war triumph of Zionism. The homeless survivors of European Jewry, assisted by Jewish organizations in America, sought out Palestine as a place of refuge, where after a short war they founded the republic of Israel. Almost a million Arabs were dispossessed. To all Arabs Zionism looked like a new form of Western invasion of their country. In China, after the war, the communists overthrew the demoralized Nationalists of the Kuomintang, whom the Chinese people showed no inclination to support. The Chinese communists, reviving the doctrine of Sun Yat-sen, denounced capitalism and imperialism as Western impositions. The day of European privilege in China was over. The Chinese communist leaders maintained close relations with Moscow, but it remained a question whether they were not sufficiently nationalistic, and primarily Chinese, to oppose Soviet influence as they had opposed European. In China, in India, in Indonesia, the new regimes faced the desperate problems of over-population and mass poverty. Having blamed their troubles on world capitalism, having made promises and aroused hopes, they had to find rather better answers to these problems than the imperial authorities had ever offered. With less experience in government, they were obliged to deliver more. Otherwise, instability in Asia would hardly cease.

Broadly speaking, the Second World War created no wholly new problems for mankind, but it greatly aggravated certain basic problems that had troubled the world for over a century, making them both more difficult and more urgent. Three can be singled out—the problem of science, the problem of industrialism, and the problem of national sovereignty or independence. They were aspects of the one and only super-problem, the moral question of man's fate: how could the real human person, man, woman or child, the being said by some to be made in the image of God and by others to have a right to be happy, live out his life, or realize his humanity in a world where science, industrialism, and national sovereignty pressed upon him from every side?

The problem of science was dramatized by the atomic bomb. The world shuddered at the instantaneous destruction of Hiroshima. With the war ending on this note, it was realized that a third world war would be unimaginably more awful. The use of guided missiles, radio controls, proximity fuses and probably biological warfare could be foreseen. Man, it was said, now possessed the means to annihilate not only his civilization but the very existence of human life on the planet. This thought, which possibly would not have perturbed St. Augustine, was appalling to a world which had set its highest values in social progress. And in truth, the reflective person wondered more than before how he himself or members of his family might meet their deaths, or what sufferings they might be called upon to endure.

The problem of science was not new. Science, with its partner invention, had for a long time transformed the methods used in both industry and war. Observant people had long known that science could be applied either constructively or destructively, that knowledge was power, that the intelligence was the instrument of the will. It was the magnitude of destructive possibilities that made people formerly indifferent now see and worry over the problem. Scientists themselves rushed forward, after the first atomic explosion, to affirm the need of a moral regeneration. They insisted that science was neutral, that it was free from blame for the horror of Hiroshima, that scientific investigation must remain free, that the trouble lay only in the uses to which scientific knowledge was put. Never since the days of Galileo had scientists been so embarrassed, or so aroused over moral and social issues. Somehow science, or the exaggerated reliance on science, had misfired. The dream of those prophets of a scientific civilization, Bacon and Descartes, the idea that accumulation of scientific knowledge would automatically bring more human welfare, had taken on the ghastly distortions of a nightmare.

One answer was that there must be more social science. With better understanding of society and of human behavior, it seemed, men need not use physical science to kill each other. It was certainly true that the more fully society was understood the better for all concerned. But in social science, too, lay the same kind of danger. From the scientific understanding of human behavior it was a short step to the scientific control of human behavior. We have seen how, in totalitarian states, governments not merely accepted the fact that people were shaped by environment but undertook to monopolize the environment and do the shaping themselves. A society in which science was pursued as one of many interests was one thing. A purely "scientific" society was another. In the latter, people might simply be manipulated by experts. Prophets of a scientific civilization had formerly drawn alluring pictures of a New Atlantis. Now, in the mid-twentieth century, prognosticators were more likely to portray a drab and mechanized world of the future, in which a ruling elite governed by scientific "techniques," using plenty of carbon paper and long-distance telephones, poring over statistical reports, card indexes, photographs and fingerprints, advised by social psychologists, public opinion pollsters, and propaganda technicians, and exercising a new technocratic despotism with the help of the police.

The problem of science in short passed over into the political problem. It was not science, but the practical uses of science, and the question of who should determine its practical uses, that created the difficulty. Scientific understanding of nuclear fission produced the atomic bomb, not because of anything in the nature of science or of nuclear fission, but because of something in the nature of human society and the clash of human wills.

The problem of industrialism was likewise aggravated by the war. Industrialism produced a high degree of division of labor. Specialization reigned among persons within the same small community, and among the great regions of the earth. Each was dependent on continuing interchange with others. Each person, moreover, could perform his task only with the use of a great deal of capital. Railroad workers had to have a railroad; the farmer had to have access to a tractor; even the musician, after composing a symphony, could not hear it played unless someone paid a hundred performers' wages. These modern facts of life led to a great deal of difficulty. There were theoretically two opposite social poles. At one, represented by the U.S.S.R., all capital was owned by the state and supplied to workers as needed, and all interchange was planned out in detail by public authorities in advance. At the other pole, best represented by the United States, capital was owned by private persons, who chose the channels of investment and hence determined the availability of jobs, and interchange took place through the mechanism of the market. Neither system was in practice logically pure, but the difference remained pronounced. The drawback in the Soviet system was its lack of freedom, in the American system its lack of stability or of economic security. Americans spent a good deal more time trying to correct the lack of security than the Soviets did in trying to correct the lack of freedom.

The Second World War ruined the industrial system in one of the world's chief industrial areas. The dense European population could support itself only by an industry and exchange that now broke down. The war damage, chiefly bomb damage, destroyed the capital accumulation of generations— housing, paved streets, utilities plants, foundries, factories—and the ruin of freight-yards, rolling stock, and bridges brought the interchange of commodities to a standstill. Town was cut off from country. City people dispersed to live with their country cousins, or reverted to primitive methods of hunting for food and fuel. In a year or two the worst local devastation was repaired. The basic problem remained. Industrial Europe was unable to exchange with agricultural Eastern Europe or with the world. The Continent as a whole was left in the position in which the First World War left Vienna. Europe was a world metropolis, a kind of huge continental city, now cut off from the trading area with which it had exchanged. It was a former world capital in danger of becoming a slum. It lived by large and uninterrupted imports for which it could no longer afford to pay. It could not pay because in the second war, as in the first, Europeans lost most of their overseas investments, and overseas countries built up their own industries and had less need of those of Europe. Europe's capacity to manufacture for export was also injured by the war. At the same time, as an advanced industrial region, Europe had a politically awakened population. Europeans would not starve or suffer in mute resignation. The European economy, at the very time when its own productivity was badly impaired, had to carry a rising burden of social services and maintain the welfare state.

One of the chief post-war questions was therefore the rescue of Europe, or, in practical politics, who Europe's "rescuer" was to be. There were only two candidates for this honor, the U.S.S.R. and the United States. Europeans did not relish the prospect of being rescued by either. Communism most Europeans regarded as slavery. Dependency even on the benefactions of the United States they feared as a wild gamble; remembering the depression of 1929, and how all Europe had then gone down after the cessation of American loans, they had no desire to be linked to American capitalism. They were obliged, however, to choose. Not all chose in the same way; many countries were divided internally between pro-Soviet and pro-American elements. The former swelled the post-war communist movement. The latter, unfortunately, included some people who, before or during the war, had shown favor for Hitler and Mussolini.

Thus the problem of a ruined industrialism, of a society unable to produce with efficiency, yet obliged to produce enough to satisfy a civilized population, led like the problem of science straight into the thick of political questions. Nor was Europe the only center of trouble. Throughout Asia, especially in India and Java, the conditions of a world-wide industrialism had helped to build up dense populations. The new governments, in the Dominions of India and Pakistan, or in the United States of Indonesia, or in communist China, had to feed and satisfy these great multitudes of people. They believed that only by industrializing could they raise their living standards. They needed machinery, loans, advisers; they looked in part to Europe, and in part to the Soviet Union, and in part to the United States. Imperialism in Asia was dead, but the need of Asians for assistance was still alive, and in the furnishing of assistance there was bound to be a certain competition.

Was the modern world really One World, or was it not? The answer was both yes and no. It was one world in the sense that it required a good deal of mutual exchange, and in the sense that political repercussions traveled over it rapidly. But it was far from homogeneous. Half a dozen great cultures and hundreds of little ones clung to their identity. All admired the steam turbine, and stood in awe of atomic fission, but beyond the material level their schemes of values widely diverged. None wished to be subordinated to another, or to lose its own way of life in the gray vagueness of a uniform world civilization. Here lay the root of the problem of national independence.

In the Second World War, as in the First, the President of the United States took the initiative in planning a post-war international organization to prevent war in the future. A conference of all anti-Axis powers, held at San Francisco in 1945, established the United Nations on the basis of wartime co-operation. The United Nations, like the League of Nations which it superseded, had numerous organs of which two were central: a General Assembly in which all recognized sovereign states, however small, were considered equal; and a Security Council made up of the states regarded as great powers—the United States, Great Britain, France, China, and the Soviet Union—plus six elected members chosen by the Assembly. Each great power enjoyed a veto. The Security Council could act on important matters only if the great powers were unanimous.

Since only a great power could bring about a great war, and since any great power bent on war would obviously veto any measures aimed against it, it was clear that the United Nations could not prevent a great war if one were actually imminent. Hence many people criticized the provision in the United Nations charter for a great-power veto. They declared that it recognized the very national sovereignty which led to international war, and they urged some kind of world state in its place, which should have the authority to put down violence anywhere in the world as the national state put down violence within its own borders. It was certain, however, that the veto was necessary. The U.S.S.R. demanded it most frankly, but no other great power would have consented to enter the United Nations without this safeguard to its own freedom of action. Or, in practice, without the veto, one or more great powers would withdraw, and the U.N. would become a mere alliance against non-members. In the following years even small peoples—notably the Dutch in Indonesia and the Zionists in their new republic of Israel—refused to abide by judgments of the United Nations. It seemed likely that no people possessing a state of its own was yet willing, in a matter considered vital, to forego its independence.

The war in effect left only two great powers still standing in any strength, the United States and the Soviet Union. Since the seventeenth century the world has normally had some half-a-dozen great powers. There being now only two made a great difference. The characteristic of a two-state system, not found in a multiple-state system, is that each super-power knows positively in advance who its only dangerous enemy can be. In such a situation all diplomatic delicacy breaks down. All measures that either power takes for its own security seem to be provocations to the other. Each likewise tends to make allies of the middling and lesser states. And every move by a middling or lesser state, even if entirely spontaneous, since it is bound to favor one of the superpowers in one way or another, is suspected by the other super-power of being instigated by its rival as a hostile act. After the war the United States and the U.S.S.R. fell into this unpleasant dualistic relationship.

At the close of hostilities Russian armies occupied Eastern Europe as far west as the river Elbe. American, British, and French armies held the remainder of Germany, most of Austria and all of Italy. The movement of ground armies during the fighting had determined the spheres of influence after the peace. In addition, the Soviets at the last moment declared war on Japan and moved into Manchuria and Korea; and in the following months they lent aid to separatists in northern Iran, pressed the Turks for joint control of the Turkish Straits, favored the communists in Greece, forced a communist government upon Poland, and called for an active offensive of the communist parties of war-torn Western Europe. It was not possible for anyone (even in Russia) to know what the men in the Kremlin really believed or intended. Probably, as confirmed Marx-Leninists, they considered a clash between the U.S.S.R. and the Western powers to be bound to come at some indefinite future date. Probably they were disturbed by American possession of the atomic bomb. Probably they felt that the fluid post-war situation gave a chance to establish an outer buffer zone favorable to Russia, a program on which they had already embarked in their alliance with Germany in 1939, which had allowed them to absorb eastern Poland and the Baltic States—or to re-absorb them, since these regions had been Russian for over a century before 1918. Probably also they saw in the aftermath of the Second World War, as they had seen in the aftermath of the First World War, an opportunity to advance the international Marxist revolution.

The U.S.S.R. rejected a plan put forward by the United States, and accepted by other powers, to put the manufacture of atomic weapons under international supervision and control. Disarmament in the past had always failed because some disarmed and some did not. The United States proposal therefore carried a condition: that the international control body, to prevent the manufacture of atomic bombs by national governments, should have the right to send inspectors at will into all countries, and to enforce sanctions, regardless of the veto, against any country found guilty of unauthorized uses of atomic power. To the Soviets the idea of having foreigners examine their new society had always been repugnant. They declared that inspection would violate national sovereignty. They questioned the good faith of the American proposal. Preferring to rely on themselves, they proceeded with their own atomic research, as did the United States. The atomic armaments race, universally dreaded, thus began. In 1949 it became apparent that the U.S.S.R. was equipped to conduct atomic warfare.

The Soviet Union, to protect its interests in an international body where the majority was consistently against it, made increasingly frequent use of its veto in the United Nations. Action by the U.N. did result in Soviet withdrawal from Iran, after sundry Soviet objections. But the United States, finding the U.N. unworkable as a check on communist expansion, began to develop a positive national policy of its own. In 1947, by the "Truman doctrine," it supplied military equipment and professional military advisers to Greece and Turkey. It announced a policy of assisting all peoples to prevent forcible capture of their governments by minority parties. The Soviets denounced the American "war-mongers." With the United States arming Greece and Turkey, with American carriers able to sail the length of the Mediterranean or lie off the coast of Murmansk, with American air bases established or easy to establish in the Near and Middle East, with the Americans in occupation of southern Korea and Japan, and virtually annexing Okinawa, and with the bulk of the United States lying across the North Pole from the vital centers of the Soviet Union, and the American capacity for long-range bombardment already sufficiently demonstrated, the Soviets not unnaturally felt encircled. Soviet suspicions dating from Munich, and even from the civil war of 1918–19, were inflamed. Relations between the two super-powers went from bad to worse.

The main object of rivalry was Europe. Europe, the main protagonist of this long history, was now in ruins. But it was not yet negligible; its combined population exceeded that of either the super-powers, and even in ruins it possessed one of the world's leading industrial plants. Europe was divided by its many national frontiers, and by social cleavages between economic classes. Short of catastrophe Europe would not go communist. In France and Italy, to be sure, a third of the people voted the communist ticket, and communists held important positions in labor unions, but the number of those actually desirous of a communist society was not large. Nor was the number large of those who wished to be remodeled according to the economy or culture of the United States. Europe, like the world's other great aggregates, wanted to preserve its identity and at least its spiritual independence. But between the programs of the two super-powers there was this difference: the Soviets had more to gain by chaos in Europe, and the United States had more to gain by its rebuilding. The United States after the war sent billions of dollars' worth of goods to relieve the distress of Europe. Its motives were much discussed and even impugned. In effect, the Americans thus satisfied their humanitarian impulse, found markets for their own industries (at the American taxpayers' expense), and reduced the drift of working-class Europeans into the communist camp.

The key to the rebuilding of Europe was Germany. The Ruhr was still Europe's industrial heartland. The victors at first agreed to occupy Germany jointly. They agreed that Germany should pay reparations, especially to Russia, which had suffered most heavily from German attack. Gradually the American government, to make Europe self-supporting and less dependent on American aid, came to favor the economic reconstruction of Germany. The Russians became apprehensive. The Russians wished to use Germany to rebuild the Soviet Union. The Americans wished to use it to rebuild Europe. They did not wish to pour aid into Germany to have it drained off as reparations to the U.S.S.R. Joint administration of Germany broke down. The Russians reaffirmed their hold on eastern Germany; the Americans, British and French went their own way in the West. Each side competed for the good will of the late enemy. Each accused the other of partitioning the country in violation of their agreements. By the partition, for it was a partition in fact, the West got control of the German industrial heartland, to the great disadvantage of Russia. But the Russians, by controlling the more agricultural eastern Germany, along with all eastern Europe, also held strong cards against the West; for in the long run the economic welfare of Europe required the restoration of interchange between western factories and eastern farms. The Germans, meanwhile, in the division between the victors, saw the chance to reassert their own national identity and restore their own importance.

The American secretary of state, General Marshall, announced in 1947 what came to be called the Marshall Plan. By this plan the huge grants to Europe were continued, but they were no longer regarded as stop-gap relief. American aid was henceforth to be so apportioned among various countries, and so coordinated with each country's policies and with joint policies of European countries acting together, as to enable Europe to stand on its own feet and play its own part in international trade at the end of five years. American officials urged Europeans to reduce their tariff barriers and currency controls against each other. They declared that only by creating a free and Europe-wide internal market could Europeans obtain the advantage of mass production and lower costs such as prevailed in the United States. They favored a European economic and even political union. Great Britain, France, the Netherlands, Belgium, and Luxembourg did in fact in 1948 establish a rather shadowy federation called the Western Union. They began to make common military plans—the unspecified but only enemy being Soviet Russia. By the North Atlantic Pact, in 1949, the United States agreed to supply equipment for European rearmament, and guaranteed Western Europe against invasion.

The U.S.S.R. could not be expected to view with equanimity the creation of a new super-power on its own western border—for a super-power, the equal of any, is what a restored and unified Europe would be. Any power, not merely the Soviet Union, would object to such consolidation among its neighbors. The American desire to unify Europe thus seemed to Russia another hostile act. But the likelihood of any real European unity was far from established. The European governments showed no haste to tear down their tariffs, lose control of their currencies, or expose their industries and the jobs of their workers to the competition of their neighbors. Their combined military planning was unavoidably indefinite. In the event of war, though much would depend on the circumstances in which war might come, Europe would still suffer from uncured social diseases; many of its soldiers would sympathize with the Soviet Union.

So Europe, the homeland of modern and of Western civilization, faced a whole series of impossible dilemmas. It might be torn to pieces by the ideological tug between the Soviet Union and the United States. In war between these two, it might be occupied by the former and bombed into extinction by the latter. If it unified itself, it would antagonize Russia. If it did not unify, it might be left as a backwater, historically outmoded by the growth of super-powers, as the thriving cities of medieval Germany and Renaissance Italy had been historically outmoded by the rise of national states. If a European union left Germany out, it would be helpless; if it included Germany, the Germans might come to dominate the whole. If a European union should one day become an effective political entity and if the newly awakened great Asian aggregates some day became effective political entities also, then there might again be half a dozen "great powers" in the world; and the globe as a whole might recapitulate the modern history of Europe, with world-states contending as the European great powers had contended in their heyday.

Against such frightening eventualities one hope lay in international organization, in the actual or in an improved United Nations. Organization was important, but in the end it was only a mechanism. Just as parliaments did not work in countries where people wished each other's ruin, so international organization did not work where nations feared each other's designs upon their very existence. The world needed smoothly functioning mechanisms, but above all it needed confidence. Confidence was a matter of mind and spirit. Of all things, once lost, it was the hardest to create.

So the cataclysm carried on. But even a cataclysm, as already intimated, is not a time of downfall only. Mountains crumble, but others are thrust up. Lands vanish, but others rise from the sea. So it is with the social cataclysm of our times. Old landmarks are worn down. The British Empire and the gold standard pass away. The ascendancy of Europe, of the West, of the white races nears its close; all these must learn to negotiate with others, not to rule them. Upper and middle-class people lose their former ease of life; but times are better for miners and the few remaining domestic servants. Everywhere there is what those of the old school regard as a new crudeness, a disregard for amenities, from the conduct of diplomacy to the writing of novels; but both diplomacy and fiction grapple boldly with real problems. Never has war been so scientifically destructive, and it is certain that another world war would blight some centers of civilization; but it would be parochial to suppose that no civilization anywhere would survive. Individual lives are fragile. But man as such is a tough animal, and a very widespread one. To close this book on a note of placidity would indeed be foolish, but so would it be to close it on a note of universal doom. It is entirely possible that if everybody in the world could vote on the question, provided only that literally everybody were included, as many or more would say that the land is rising as that it sinks.

ACKNOWLEDGMENTS

GRATEFUL ACKNOWLEDGMENT is made to the following publishers for their kind permission to use copyrighted material appearing under their imprint:

CARNEGIE ENDOWMENT FOR INTERNATIONAL PEACE for permission to reprint from *International Conciliation* by the International Consultative Group of Geneva, 1940.

UNIVERSITY OF CHICAGO PRESS, Chicago, for permission to reprint from *Movements of Thought in the Nineteenth Century* by George H. Mead, 1936.

HARCOURT, BRACE & CO., New York, for permission to reprint from *The History of Western Civilization* by Harry Elmer Barnes, with the collaboration of Henry David, 1935.

HARPER AND BROS., New York, for permission to reprint from *Reaction and Revolution, 1814–1832* by Frederick B. Artz, 1934.

HENRY HOLT & CO., New York, for permission to reprint from *Imperial Russia, 1801–1917* by Michael Karpovich, 1932.

HOUGHTON MIFFLIN CO., Boston, for permission to reprint from *The Making of the Modern Mind* by John Herman Randall, Jr., revised ed., 1940.

ALFRED A. KNOPF, INC., New York, for permission to reprint from *The Political Collapse of Europe* by Hajo Holborn, 1952; *A History of the Modern World* by R. R. Palmer, 1952.

LONGMANS, GREEN & CO., London, for permission to reprint from *The Coming of the First World War* by Nicholas Mansergh, 1949.

THE MACMILLAN CO., New York, for permission to reprint from "Evolution, Social," in the *Encyclopaedia of the Social Sciences,* by Alexander Goldenweiser, 1931; *Some Origins of the Modern Economic World* by E. A. J. Johnson, 1935; *The Web of Government* by Robert M. MacIver, 1947.

MACMILLAN & CO., LTD., London, and ST. MARTIN'S PRESS, New York, for permission to reprint from *Introduction to Economic History, 1750–1950* by G. D. H. Cole, 1952.

w. w. NORTON & CO., New York, for permission to reprint from *The Commerce of Nations* by J. B. Condliffe, 1950.

ROY PUBLISHERS, New York, for permission to reprint from *The Age of Revolution* by J. J. Saunders, 1940.